Florence & Tuscany

Northwestern
Tuscany
(p247)

Florence
(p62)

Eastern
Tuscany
(p294)

Central
Coast &
Elba
(p217)

Siena & Central
Tuscany
(p137)

Southern
Tuscany
(p195)

Nicola W

PLAN YOUR TRIP

Welcome to Tuscany 4
Florence & Tuscany map . . . 6
Tuscany's Top 15 8
Need to Know 16
First Time Tuscany 18
What's New 20
If You Like 22
Month by Month 25
Itineraries 29
Accommodation 36
Getting Around 38
Eat & Drink
Like a Local 41
Activities 48
Family Travel 56
Regions at a Glance 59

ON THE ROAD

FLORENCE 62

SIENA & CENTRAL
TUSCANY 137

Siena 140
Chianti 156
Greve in Chianti 156
Badia a Passignano 158
San Casciano in
Val di Pesa 162
Castellina in Chianti 163
Radda in Chianti 164
Gaiole in Chianti 165
San Gimignano 167
Monteriggioni 174

Volterra 175
Val d'Orcia 179
Montalcino 180
Pienza 184
Montepulciano 187
Chiusi 193

SOUTHERN
TUSCANY 195

Alta Maremma 198
Massa Marittima 198
Monte Amiata 202
Vetulonia 203
Città del Tufo 204
Pitigliano 204

DELICATESSEN, PITIGLIANO
P204

CHIUSI P193

Contents

Sovana 207
Sorano 208
Bassa Maremma 209
Grosseto 212
Parco Regionale della
Maremma 213
Orbetello 215
Monte Argentario 215

**CENTRAL COAST
& ELBA 217**
Livorno 220
Etruscan Coast 227
Castiglioncello 227
Bolgheri 228
San Vincenzo 229

Suvereto 232
Golfo di Baratti 233
Tuscan Archipelago . . . 234
Elba 234
Giglio, Gorgona
& Pianosa 246
Capraia 246

**NORTHWESTERN
TUSCANY 247**
Pisa 250
Lucca 261
Pistoia 270
San Miniato 277
**Apuane Alps &
Garfagnana 279**
Castelnuovo di
Garfagnana 279
Barga 281
Bagni di Lucca 283
Carrara 284
Versilian Coast 286
Pietrasanta 287
Viareggio 289
Lunigiana 292
Pontremoli 292

**EASTERN
TUSCANY 294**
Arezzo 295
Sansepolcro 303
Casentino Valley 307
Poppi 307
Parco Nazionale delle
Foreste Casentinesi 309
Val di Chiana 313
Cortona 313

UNDERSTAND

History 318
**The Tuscan
Way of Life 329**
The Tuscan Table 333
**Tuscany on
Page & Screen 341**
Art & Architecture 344

SURVIVAL GUIDE

Directory A–Z 358
Transport 364
Language 369
Index 377

SPECIAL FEATURES

Lazy Days in Florence . . .112
Wine Tour of Chianti . . . 160
**Medieval
Masterpieces 171**
**Exploring the
Val d'Orcia 182**
**Etruscan Wine &
Oil Road 230**
Lazy Days in Elba 242
Why Pisa Leans 254
Via Francigena 290
**Magnificent
Monasteries 305**
**Go Slow in the
Valle del Casentino . . . 310**
Tuscan Artists 349
Tuscan Architecture . . . 352

STAINED-GLASS WINDOW,
BASILICA DI SANTA MARIA
NOVELLA P88

Welcome to Tuscany

With its lyrical landscapes, world-class art and a superb cucina contadina *(farmer's kitchen), the Tuscan experience is perfectly in symbiosis with the land.*

Perfect Landscapes

Tuscany has a timeless familiarity with its iconic Florentine cathedral dome, gently rolling hills dipped in soft morning mist and sculptural cypress alleys. But then, this *regione* in central Italy is postcard material. Golden wheat fields, silver olive groves and pea-green vineyards marching in sharp terraced rows on hillsides form a graceful prelude to soul-soaring medieval hilltop villages, mountain ranges and fecund forests in the north, and a garland of bijou islands beaded along the coastal south. Get out, explore, hike and ding your bicycle bell, as this rousing landscape demands.

Living History

Ever since the Etruscans dropped by to party and stayed, Tuscany has seduced. The Romans stocked their grain silos here, Christians walked a medieval pilgrimage route, and Napoleon plundered art (and suffered terribly in exile in a neoclassical villa with fig trees and sea view on the island of Elba). Florence's historic churches and monuments were a key stop for British aristocrats on 19th-century Grand Tours – and remain so. And at sundown when the river Arno turns pink, whether you like things old-fashioned and simple or boutique chic, this handsome city obliges.

Sensational Slow Food

No land is more caught up with the fruits of its fertile earth than Tuscany, a gourmet destination where locals spend an inordinate amount of time pondering and feasting on food and wine. Local, seasonal and sustainable is the Holy Trinity and Tuscans share enormous pride in the produce quality. Tuscan travel is grassroots: from wineries to taste blockbuster wines like Brunello di Montalcino and Vino Nobile di Montepulciano; to a family-run *pastificio tradizionale* where artisan pasta is cut by hand; or road trips in quest of the finest *bistecca alla fiorentina* (chargrilled T-bone steak).

An Artistic Powerhouse

Then there's the art. The Etruscans indulged their fondness for a classy send-off with exquisite funerary objects, and the Romans left their usual legacy of monumental sculptures. But it was during the medieval and Renaissance periods that Tuscany struck gold, with painters, sculptors and architects creating world-class masterpieces. Safeguarded today in churches, museums and galleries all over the region, art in Tuscany is unmatched. Edgy street art in Florence and countryside sculpture parks bring the art scene right up to the 21st century.

Why I Love Florence & Tuscany

By Nicola Williams, Writer

Tuscany won me over at a farm in the Garfagnana. We were tucking into dinner when the farmer's wife rushed in mid-*secondi* and urged us to join her in the stable to watch a calf being born. Later, when she joyfully declared, 'We'll call her Kaya after your daughter!', I was speechless. So my nine-year-old now has a cow in Tuscany and I the honour of being privy to yet another intimacy of this wildly diverse, soulful, earth-driven region. This (and its truffles, Florence, *aperitivo* tradition, Renaissance art and Chianti wine) is why I love Tuscany.

For more about our writers, see p384

Above: San Gimignano, Tuscany (p167)

Florence & Tuscany

ADRIATIC SEA

Apuane Alps
Hike wildflower-adorned marble mountains (p279)

Florence
Visit a Renaissance time capsule (p62)

San Miniato
Hunt and eat precious white truffles (p277)

Chianti
Tipple Italy's best-known wine (p156)

Lucca
Pedal or promenade atop medieval walls (p261)

Pisa
Climb the famous leaning tower (p250)

Parco Nazionale delle Foreste Casentinesi, Monte Falterona e Campigna

Monte Falterona (1654m)

Parco Regionale delle Alpi Apuane

Riserva Naturale Vallombrosa

Parco Regionale Migliarino San Rossore Massaciuccoli

LE MARCHE

EMILIA-ROMAGNA

LIGURIA

LIGURIAN SEA

Modena
Bologna
Sansepolcro
Arezzo

Lunigiana
Pontremoli
Castelnuovo di Garfagnana
Barga
Bagni di Lucca
Garfagnana
Carrara
Massa
Pietrasanta
Viareggio
Versilian Riviera
Lucca
Pistoia
Fiesole
Florence
Florence Airport
Pisa
Pisa International Airport
Livorno
San Miniato
San Gimignano
Chianti Fiorentino
Greve in Chianti
Chianti
Chianti Senese
Castellina in Chianti
Gaiole in Chianti
Stia
Poppi

Arno
Arno
Tevere

Gorgona

44°N

25 miles
50 km

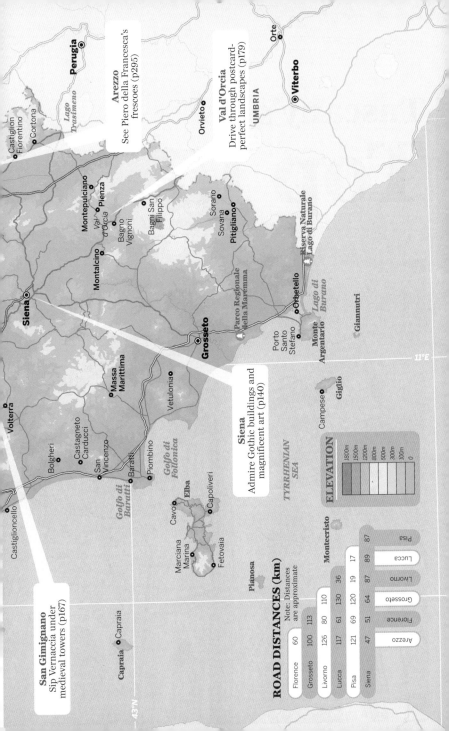

San Gimignano
Sip Vernaccia under medieval towers (p167)

Arezzo
See Piero della Francesca's frescoes (p295)

Val d'Orcia
Drive through postcard-perfect landscapes (p179)

Siena
Admire Gothic buildings and magnificent art (p140)

UMBRIA

Orte
Viterbo

Perugia
Lago Trasimeno
Castiglion Fiorentino
Cortona

Orvieto

Montepulciano
Val d'Orcia • Pienza
Bagno Vignoni
Bagni San Filippo
Sorano
Sovana
Pitigliano

Montalcino

Riserva Naturale
Lago di Burano

Siena

Massa Marittima

Vetulonia

Parco Regionale
della Maremma

Orbetello
Lago di Burano

Volterra

Castiglioncello

Bolgheri
Castagneto Carducci
San Vincenzo
Baratti
Piombino

Golfo di Baratti

Golfo di Follonica

Grosseto

Porto Santo Stefano

Monte Argentario

Giannutri

Capraia • Capraia

Cavo
Marciana Marina
Elba
Capoliveri
Fetovaia

Pianosa

Campese
Gigli o

TYRRHENIAN SEA

Montecristo

ELEVATION

	1800m
	1500m
	1200m
	800m
	500m
	300m
	100m
	0

11°E

43°N

ROAD DISTANCES (km)
Note: Distances are approximate

Florence	60							
Grosseto	100	113						
Livorno	126	80	110					
Lucca	117	61	130	36				
Pisa	121	69	120	19	17			
Siena	47	51	64	87	89	87		
	Arezzo	Florence	Grosseto	Livorno	Lucca	Pisa		

Tuscany's
Top 15

1

The Duomo, Florence

1 The *duomo* (cathedral; p76) isn't just the most spectacular structure in Florence – it's up there with Rome's Colosseum and Pisa's Leaning Tower as one of Italy's most recognisable icons. Its polychrome marble facade is vast, striking and magnificent. But what makes the building so extraordinary is Filippo Brunelleschi's distinctive red-brick dome, one of the greatest architectural achievements of all time. Scale the steep, narrow staircase to the base of the dome and peer down on the toylike cathedral interior far below – then climb some more for a stunning city panorama.

Galleria Degli Uffizi, Florence

2 Few art galleries evoke such an overwhelming sense of awe and wonderment as the world-class Uffizi (p70), at home in a 16th-century Medici *palazzo* in Florence. Vast, labyrinthine, architecturally magnificent and rich in history, the building alone stuns. Add to this an art collection chock-full of Renaissance masterpieces, with works by Giotto, Botticelli, Michelangelo, da Vinci, Raphael, Titian and Caravaggio all jostling for the limelight, and you'll know you've arrived in art-lover heaven. Allow ample time to savour slowly, in several bite-sized visits if need be.

ANAMARIA MEJIA/SHUTTERSTOCK ©

KAHRAMANKAYAS/SHUTTERSTOCK ©

Val d'Orcia

3 Cruise in second gear on quiet, gently rolling roads along this unassuming valley laced with vines, the medieval abbeys of Sant'Antimo and San Galgano, splendidly Renaissance Pienza and the blockbuster wine towns of Montepulciano and Montalcino. Explore abbeys where pilgrims once overnighted en route along the Via Francigena from Canterbury to Rome, indulge in a long, lazy Brunello-fuelled lunch and congratulate yourself on uncovering one of Tuscany's finest road trips – there's good reason why the Val d'Orcia (p179) is a Unesco World Heritage Site.

Piazza del Campo, Siena

4 Horses race around it twice a year, local teens hang out on it, tourists inevitably gasp on seeing it for the first time – Siena's strangely sloping, perfectly paved central piazza (p141) is the city's geographical and historical heart, staked out since the 12th century. Presided over by the graceful Palazzo Pubblico (pictured) and fringed with bustling cafe terraces, Piazza del Campo is the finest spot in Siena to promenade, take photographs and lap up the soul-soaring magic of this unique, gloriously Gothic and architecturally harmonious city.

Chianti

5 This ancient wine region (p156) is the Tuscany you have seen in postcards, where cypress alleys give way to pea-green vineyards and silver olive groves, honey-coloured stone farmhouses and secluded Renaissance villas built for Florentine and Sienese nobility. Luxurious accommodation and the very best of modern Tuscan cuisine provide the right ingredients for an idyllic short escape – peppered with romantic walks and road trips along narrow green lanes to wine cellars for tastings of Italy's best-known wine, the ruby-red, violet-scented Chianti Classico.

Flavours of Tuscany

6 'To cook like your mother is good, to cook like your grandmother is better', says the Tuscan proverb. Indeed, in foodie Tuscany age-old recipes are passed between generations and form the backbone of the local cuisine – a highlight of any Tuscan trip. Devour feisty T-bone steak in a family-run trattoria such as Mario (p118) near Florence's Mercato Centrale (pictured), savour modern Tuscan fare amid a sea of ancient Antinori vines at Rinuccio 1180 in Chianti, shop at local markets bursting with seasonal produce, and wish fellow diners *'Buon appetito!'*

Medieval Festivals

7 Throw yourself into local life with an exuberant and eye-catching festival – a compelling snapshot of Tuscan culture, washed down with much food, wine and merrymaking. Come the warm days of spring and summer, almost every town hosts its own fest: locals don medieval costumes and battle with giant crossbows or lances, often reenacting ancient political rivalries between different *contrade* (neighbourhoods). The prize? Wonderful trophies evocative of medieval pageantry such as the golden arrow and silk banners of Massa Marittima's Balestro del Girifalco (pictured; p199).

Medieval Towers, San Gimignano

8 These towers form one of the world's most enchanting skylines, sheltering everything from family homes to contemporary art galleries, and bringing history alive for every visitor – the medieval towers of San Gimignano (p167) are an iconic Tuscan sight. Few can be scaled these days – Torre Grossa in the Palazzo Comunale is a notable exception – but you can explore in their shadow and reflect on the civic pride and neighbourhood rivalry that prompted their construction and gave this diminutive hilltop town its unique appearance.

INSADCO PHOTOGRAPHY/ALAMY ©

FOOTTOO/SHUTTERSTOCK ©

Hunting for Truffles

9 The most precious product in the Italian pantry, the white truffle is snuffed out by dogs in damp autumnal woods around hilltop town, San Miniato. Much secrecy, mystique and cut-throat rivalry between local *tartufaio* (truffle hunters) surrounds the business – making a bite into a truffle-laced omelette all the more exciting and glam. From October to December, join the excitement of a truffle hunt (p279), or follow your nose to San Miniato on November weekends when the Mostra Mercato Nazionale del Tartufo Bianco (National White Truffle Market) takes over the town.

Relaxing in an Agriturismo

10 Whether you want to wallow in the idyllic beauty of the landscape from an infinity pool on a luxurious Tuscan estate or get your hands dirty in the fields, an *agriturismo* (rural accommodation on a working farm, winery or agricultural domain) is a five-star way of experiencing country life in Tuscany. Home-cooked dinners of seasonal farm produce and mountains of green space are a given. Barbialla Nuova (p278) has just the right mix of adventure (unpaved country roads) and panache (stylish decor and staggering views).

Sacred Art in Arezzo

11 It's a step off the trodden tourist trail, but that only adds to the impossible charm of laid-back Arezzo (p295), a small town in eastern Tuscany that shows Siena a thing or two when it comes to cinematically sloping central squares (pictured). Medieval churches safeguarding precious crucifixes, frescoes and sacred works of art stud Arezzo's shabby-chic streets and, should you be in the market for an artwork of your own, one of Italy's best-known antiques fairs is held here on the first weekend of each month.

Pedalling around Lucca

12 Hire a bike, stock up on gourmet picnic supplies and freewheel along the cobbled streets of lovely Lucca (p261) in northwestern Tuscany, zooming through tree-shaded piazzas and stone-paved alleys concealing medieval churches, a Romanesque cathedral and cinematic 17th-century *palazzi* (mansions). End with a delicious lunch of local produce atop the monumental city walls, slicked with a circular, silky-smooth cycling path (a sweet loaf of *buccellato* from pastry shop Taddeucci is a Lucchese must), or hit the open road to swoon over opulent villas in the countryside.

Exploring the Apuane Alps

13 This rugged mountain range, protected within Parco Regionale delle Alpi Apuane (p279), beckons hikers, bikers and drivers with a peaceful, soul-soothing trail of isolated farmhouses, medieval hermitages and hilltop villages. Its most spectacular sights are the slopes providing a backdrop to the town of Carrara, scarred with marble quarries worked since Roman times. Come here to visit a quarry and sample *lardo di colonnata* (thinner-than-wafer-thin slices of local pig fat), one of Tuscany's greatest gastronomic treats, in the tiny village of Colonnata.
Bagni di Lucca (p284)

Aperitivo

14 *Aperitivo* (predinner drinks accompanied by cocktail snacks) is one of Tuscany's finest food and wine rituals, best partaken of after a *passeggiata* (early-evening stroll) with seemingly half the town along Florence's boutique-beaded Via de' Tornabuoni, Lucca's Via Fillungo or another car-free urban strip. People-watching is an essential part of both elements. In Florence, grab a pew on the pavement terrace of wine bar Le Volpi e l'Uva (p129), with Florentine hipsters sipping garden cocktails in Santarosa Bistrot (p127) or between red-brick walls at Mad Souls & Spirits (p127). Enjoy!

Piazza dei Miracoli, Pisa

15 History resonates when you stand in the middle of this piazza (p252). Showcasing structures built to glorify God and flaunt civic riches (not necessarily in that order), this cluster of Romanesque church buildings possesses an architectural harmony that is remarkably refined and very rare. Hear the acoustics in the baptistry, marvel at Giovanni Pisano's marble pulpit in the *duomo* and confirm that, yes, the famous tower does lean. Living up to its name, this square really is a field full of miracles.

Need to Know

For more information, see Survival Guide (p357)

Currency
Euro (€)

Language
Italian

Visas
Visas are not needed for residents of Schengen countries or for many visitors staying for less than 90 days.

Money
ATMs are widely available. Most hotels and many restaurants accept credit cards.

Mobile Phones
European and Australian phones can use local SIM cards. Set other phones to roaming.

Time
Central European Time (GMT/UTC plus one hour)

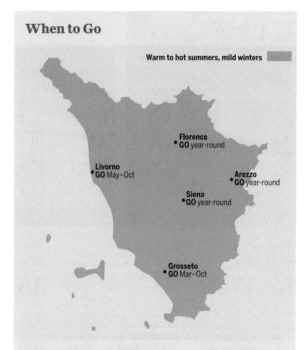

When to Go

Warm to hot summers, mild winters

Florence
• GO year-round

Livorno
• GO May–Oct

Arezzo
• GO year-round

Siena
• GO year-round

Grosseto
• GO Mar–Oct

High Season
(May, Jun, Sep & Oct)

➡ Accommodation prices rise by up to 50%.

➡ Perfect weather for travelling, but it can be crowded.

➡ Major festivals fall June to September.

Shoulder Season (Apr, Jul & Aug)

➡ April weather is pleasant and prices are reasonable.

➡ High summer can be hot inland and too crowded on the coast.

➡ Most attractions stay open until sundown during summer.

Low Season
(Nov–Mar)

➡ Accommodation bargains abound, but many hotels close for the season.

➡ Some tourist-information offices close.

➡ Many restaurants close for annual holidays.

Useful Websites

Visit Tuscany (www.visit tuscany.com) Official site of the Tuscany region.

The Local (www.thelocal.it) Reliable one-stop shop for the day's regional and national Italian news in English.

Il Sole 24 Ore (www.italy24. ilsole24ore.com) Digital, English-language edition of Italian newspaper *Il Sole 24 Ore*.

Important Numbers

Italy country code	☑39
International access code	☑00
Ambulance	☑118
Police	☑113
Emergency from mobile phone	☑112

Exchange Rates

Australia	A$1	€0.61
Canada	C$1	€0.68
Japan	¥100	€0.84
New Zealand	NZ$1	€0.57
UK	UK£1	€1.11
US	US$1	€0.91

For current exchange rates, see www.xe.com.

Daily Costs

Budget:
Less than €90

➡ Dorm bed: €20–45

➡ Sandwich: €5–8

➡ Trattoria dinner: €20

➡ Coffee standing at bar: €1.20

➡ Bicycle rental: €12

Midrange:
€90–200

➡ Midrange-hotel double room: €110–200

➡ Restaurant meal: €30–45

➡ *Aperitivo:* €10

➡ Admission to museums: €5–20

➡ E-bike rental: €39

Top End:
More than €200

➡ Top-end-hotel double room: €200 plus

➡ Upmarket restaurant dinner: €45–70

➡ Coffee sitting on a cafe terrace: €5

➡ Tour guide for two hours: €140

Opening Hours

Opening hours vary throughout the year. We've provided summer (high season) and winter (low season) opening hours where appropriate, but hours may differ in the shoulder seasons.

Banks 8.30am–1.30pm and 3.30pm–4.30pm Monday to Friday

Restaurants 12.30pm–2.30pm and 7.30pm–10pm

Cafes 7.30am–8pm

Bars and pubs 10am–1am

Shops 9am–1pm and 3.30pm–7.30pm (or 4pm–8pm) Monday to Saturday

Arriving in Tuscany

Pisa International Airport (p260) LAM Rossa (red) buses run into central Pisa (€1.20, 10 minutes). PisaMover automated trains run to Pisa's Stazione Pisa Centrale (€5, five minutes); regular trains run to/from Florence's Stazione di Santa Maria Novella (€8.70, 50–80 minutes). Taxis cost €10 to central Pisa.

Florence Airport (p135) Trams run to/from Florence's Stazione di Santa Maria Novella (€1.50 from ticket machines at tram stops or €2.50 on board; 22 minutes) and Volainbus shuttle buses (€6; 20 to 30 minutes) head to the central bus station. Taxis cost a fixed €22 to central Florence (€24 on Sunday and holidays, €25.30 between 10pm and 6am), plus €1 per bag and €1 supplement for a fourth passenger.

Dangers & Annoyances

➡ Watch for pickpockets in heavily touristed zones: Florence's Piazza del Duomo and Ponte Vecchio; Piazza dei Miracoli in Pisa; Siena's Piazza del Duomo.

➡ Keep alert on crowded buses to/from the airports.

➡ In rural Tuscany has horse-flies, mosquitoes and various other pesky insects in the height of summer. Bring repellent and/or cover up.

➡ Street hawkers flogging everything from bottled water, sunglasses and cheap knock-off handbags to phone covers and selfie sticks (banned in most museums) can be extremely annoying in Florence, Pisa and other tourist-busy towns. Don't be intimidated: simply say 'no' politely and move on.

For much more on **getting around**, see 364

First Time Tuscany

For more information, see Survival Guide (p357)

Checklist

→ Check passport validity and visa requirements

→ Arrange travel insurance

→ Confirm airline baggage restrictions

→ Reserve accommodation and high-profile restaurants

→ Buy tickets online for Florence's Uffizi and iconic cathedral dome, and Pisa's Leaning Tower

→ Buy museum passes (eg Firenzecard)

→ Book guided tours (eg to Siena's cathedral dome)

→ Organise international roaming on your phone if needed

What to Pack

→ Sturdy walking shoes

→ Italian phrasebook

→ Travel plug (adapter)

→ Driving map and GPS for the car (or phone app)

→ Sunscreen, sunhat and sunglasses (summer)

→ Umbrella and/or raincoat (except in high summer)

→ Corkscrew – Italian winemakers dislike screw-top bottles

Top Tips for Your Trip

→ Always carry some cash. Unattended petrol (gas) stations don't always accept foreign credit cards, and some restaurants and hotels accept cash only.

→ Don't rely solely on a GPS in rural areas – cross-check routes on a printed road map.

→ Track down free wi-fi access around *palazzi comunali* (town halls) and tourist offices.

→ To cut costs in Florence, visit during National Museum Week (first week of March) or on the first Sunday in October to March, when admission to state museums is free.

→ Beat tourist crowds by meandering away from blockbuster sights, delving into less-explored, local-loved neighbourhoods (such as San Frediano in Florence) instead.

→ Foodies should invest in *Osterie d'Italia,* an annual restaurant guide published by Slow Food Editore as an app (Apple and Android) and book (English or Italian).

→ Selfie sticks are forbidden in most Tuscan museums.

→ Many towns and cities (Florence, Siena and Lucca included) have a ZLT (Zona a Traffico Limitato; Limited Traffic Zone) that is off-limits to motorised traffic, making driving in these cities highly inconvenient. For your own sanity, dump your car in an out-of-town car park and walk.

What to Wear

A sense of style is vital to Tuscans, who take great pride in their dress and appearance. Maintaining *la bella figura* (ie making a good impression) is extremely important. Steer clear of shorts, miniskirts and flip-flops unless you're at the beach; and always dress up – not down – at restaurants, clubs and bars. Smart-casual outfits will cover you in most situations; trainers are definitely frowned upon after dark.

Cover yourself when entering a church (no shorts, short skirts or sleeveless or off-the-shoulder tops). Topless and nude bathing are unacceptable at most beaches.

Sleeping

Book accommodation in advance, particularly in spring, summer and autumn. Check online for cheaper rates.

➡ **Agriturismi** Accommodation on farms, wineries and rural estates: perfect for those with a car and/or families.

➡ **Palazzo hotels** Historic 'palace' hotels, designer in vibe, are the boutique option for those with a midrange to top-end budget.

➡ **B&Bs** Small family-run guesthouses with a handful of rooms, offering bed and breakfast; bathrooms are occasionally shared.

Queues

Standing in queues to get into major sights is a fact of life year-round in tourist-busy Florence and Siena. Plan ahead and book tickets online. In situ, carry an umbrella or parasol to avoid melting in the mid-day sun.

Bargaining

Tuscans don't bargain, so neither should you.

Tipping

➡ **Taxis** Round the fare up to the nearest euro.

➡ **Restaurants** Most visitors leave 10% to 15% if there's no service charge.

➡ **Cafes** Leave a €0.10 coin for a coffee at the counter or 10% of the bill if you sat at a table.

➡ **Hotels** Bellhops expect €1 to €2 per bag.

Language

Many locals in towns and cities speak at least one language other than Italian – usually English or French. But venture into the deep Tuscan countryside and you'll need that Italian phrasebook. Region-wide, many traditional places to eat have no written menu at all, or just a menu penned in spidery handwriting in Italian.

See Language (p369) for more information.

 What's the local speciality?
Qual'è la specialità di questa regione?
kwa·le la spe·cha·lee·ta dee kwes·ta re·jo·ne

A bit like the rivalry between medieval Italian city-states, these days the country's regions compete in speciality foods and wines.

 Which combined tickets do you have?
Quali biglietti cumulativi avete?
kwa·lee bee·lye·tee koo·moo·la·tee·vee a·ve·te

Make the most of your euro by getting combined tickets to various sights; they are available in all major Italian cities.

 Where can I buy discount designer items?
C'è un outlet in zona? che oon owt·let in zo·na

Discount fashion outlets are big business in major cities – get bargain-priced seconds, samples and cast-offs for *la bella figura*.

 I'm here with my husband/boyfriend.
Sono qui con il mio marito/ragazzo.
so·no kwee kon eel *mee·o* ma·ree·to/ra·ga·tso

Solo women travellers may receive unwanted attention in some parts of Italy; if ignoring fails have a polite rejection ready.

 Let's meet at 6pm for pre-dinner drinks.
Ci vediamo alle sei per un aperitivo.
chee ve·dya·mo a·le say per oon a·pe·ree·tee·vo

At dusk, watch the main piazza get crowded with people sipping colourful cocktails and snacking the evening away: join your new friends for this authentic Italian ritual!

Etiquette

➡ **Greetings** Shake hands and say *buongiorno* (good morning) or *buonasera* (good afternoon/evening). If you know someone well, kiss both their cheeks (starting with their left).

➡ **Polite language** Say *mi scusi* to attract attention or say 'I'm sorry'; *grazie (mille)* for 'thank you (very much)'; *per favore* to say 'please'; *prego* for 'you're welcome' or 'please, after you'; and *permesso* if you need to push past someone in a crowd.

➡ **Cafes** Don't linger at the bar; drink your espresso and go.

➡ **In churches** Never intrude on a mass or service.

➡ **Selfie sticks** Officially banned in Florentine museums. Elsewhere don't stick them in front of people's faces or those trying to view art in peace.

What's New

State coffers are diminishing but Tuscany's fabled love of fine food, super wines and world-class art ensures enticing urban openings in Florence, Siena and Pisa. Amid a cinematic rush of vineyards and cypress alleys, rural Tuscany clings to its grassroots heritage, urging travellers to mingle with winegrowers in 21st-century-smart cellars and food courts.

Uffizi Ticketing

Visiting the Uffizi (p70) art gallery in Florence is finally getting easier: expect seasonal prices (dramatically lower in winter); a combination ticket covering the Uffizi, Palazzo Pitti and Giardino di Boboli; a new 'quick' exit; and, by 2020, time-slot coupons to reduce ticket queues.

Hi-Tech Wine Tasting

In the Brunello-rich Val d'Orcia, insanely sleek 'n' stylish, high-tech tasting rooms are sprouting like mushrooms after the rain: Cantina di Montalcino (p181), a cooperative of 100 grape growers, and Ciacci Piccolomini d'Aragona (p181), on a 17th-century estate, are two exquisite examples of smart millennial spaces dedicated to one of Tuscany's most timeless grassroots riches: wine.

Corridoio Vasariano

The suspense is over: the enigmatic passageway (p86) linking three Medici palaces in Florence will reopen to visitors in 2021 after a €10 million makeover.

E-Biking

In Montepulciano, savvy new bike shop Urban Bikery (p365) is pioneering e-bike tourism in the region. Customised off-road electric bikes come equipped with GPS devices programmed with cycling routes, making light work of two-wheeling touring in Tuscany. **E-Bikes Florence** (www.e-bikesflorence.com) likewise rents e-bikes loaded with ingenious GPS maps and self-guided itineraries.

LOCAL KNOWLEDGE

WHAT'S HAPPENING IN FLORENCE & TUSCANY

Nicola Williams, Lonely Planet writer

Cultural excitement is running higher than ever in my favourite Renaissance city on earth, where Florentines appear to be torn between cursing the tourist masses crowding out their historic centre year-round and celebrating the late arrival of their city into the 21st century (think: shiny new tram linking Florence airport with city centre, new Uffizi ticketing, e-bikes, etc). Thankfully there's been no need this summer for city mayor Dario Nardella to spray church steps with water to stop visitors sitting on them to picnic – flyers circulating around town as part of a new #enjoyrespectfirenze media campaign highlighting Florence's sustainable ethics and encouraging responsible tourism seem to be working a treat.

Tuscany marked the 500th anniversary of the death of local lad, Leonardo da Vinci, in 2019, with a year-long bonanza of cultural happenings. And in 2020 it will be 60 years since architect extraordinaire Brunelleschi began work on Florence's iconic cathedral cupola. I, for one, can't wait for the birthday celebrations (which will include the reconstruction of the dome in Lego on Piazza del Duomo) to commence.

Museo Diocesano d'Arte Sacra Volterra

The sacred art showcased in this soulful new museum (p176), powerfully at home in still-functioning Chiesa di San Agostino, promises an enriching museum experience in Volterra.

Craft Beer

Tuscany is not only about exceedingly fine wine; small, experimental, artisanal beer breweries are suddenly popping up like mushrooms after the rain. At the sleek Birrificio San Quirico (p185) in the medieval hilltop town of San Quirico d'Orcia in the Val d'Orcia, different wheat beers are named after local literary and historical folk, past and present. Other interesting addresses to enjoy a unique craft brew:

➡ Archea Brewery (p128), Florence

➡ Art. 17 Birreria (p126), Florence

➡ La Stafetta (p259), Pisa

➡ Vapori di Birra (p185), Sasso Pisano

Mura di Pisa

Both first-time and return visitors to Pisa will be enamoured with the wonderful new perspective of Pisa's iconic Leaning Tower and architecturally magnificent Piazza dei Miracoli from atop the city's medieval walls (p251), finally accessible to visitors year-round.

Inferno & Triumph of Death

After decades of restoration, monumental frescoes depicting Hell in all its Satanic glory by 14th-century painter Buonamico Buffalmacco have returned to their original location inside Pisa's Camposanto (p253) – a haunting new visual feast for medieval art lovers.

White Carrara Downtown

Michelangelo loved the stuff, as do festival devotees who can't get enough of this new 10-day celebration (p285) of Carrara's unique marble culture. Get ready for

FAST FACTS

Food T-bone in a millennial steakhouse

Wine production 263.1 million litres per year

Oldest olive tree 3500 years

Population 3.69 million

population per sq km

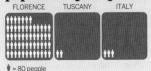

FLORENCE TUSCANY ITALY

👤 ≈ 80 people

hands-on sculpture workshops, spectacular shows staged in marble quarries and other wild cultural happenings.

Officine Bocelli

In keeping with urban Tuscany's love for street food, wine growers in rural La Sterza have followed suit with Officine Bocelli (p283), an experiential food court, wine boutique and bistro – on the family estate of celebrity opera singer Andrea Bocelli to boot.

If You Like...

Food

There are so many ways to enjoy Tuscan food: from dining at one of the region's many fabulous restaurants to trawling local food markets or learning how to do it yourself.

Bistecca alla fiorentina Florence's iconic T-bone steak hails from the Val di Chiana; tuck in at Ristorante Da Muzzicone. (p312)

Antipasto toscano Open your meal with a mixed platter of cured meats, cheeses and pâté-topped toasts; in Florence try a traditional trattoria like Trattoria Le Mossacce or Osteria Il Buongustai. (p117)

White truffles Decadent, unique and utterly memorable: hunt them at Barbialla Nuova. (p278)

Colonnata Discover *lardo* (pig fat) ageing in marble vats of olive oil in this mountain village near Carrara. (p286)

Mercato Centrale Excite taste buds with a foodie stroll around Florence's covered food market; lunch upstairs afterwards. (p118)

Street food Sink your teeth into a tripe *panini* from a traditional Florentine *trippaio* such as L'Antico Trippaio. (p120)

Porcini mushrooms Revel in these precious seasonal fungi, fresh in autumn and paired per-

haps with chestnuts or truffles, at Siena's upmarket Osteria La Taverna di San Giuseppe. (p153)

Seafaring cacciucco Treat taste buds to a sassy taste of the Tuscan coast with a steaming bowl of Livorno's traditional fish stew; local favourite La Barrocciaia is the hotspot to try it. (p225)

Wine

Aperitivi A predinner glass of wine with feisty nibbles is a cornerstone of Florentine culture – indulge at Il Santino. (p127)

Antinori nel Chianti Classico The king of Chianti wine cellars: tasting and dining James Bond style. (p162)

Strada del Vino e dell'Olio Costa degli Etruschi Motor through Etruscan Coast wine country, visiting vineyards, *cantine* (cellars) and local artisan food producers. (p230)

Bolgheri Target the home of the groundbreaking Sassicaia 'Super Tuscan' on the Etruscan Coast. Fave wine bars include Enoteca Tognoni and Enoteca de Centro. (p228)

Montalcino Time your visit with the release of the new vintage of Brunello in February. (p180)

Montepulciano Taste and buy Vino Nobile de Montepulciano in this illustrious winemaking town. (p187)

Castello di Brolio Visit Italy's oldest winery, with museum, garden, tasting cellars and restaurant. (p166)

Renaissance Art

Galleria degli Uffizi It doesn't get any better than this Medici art collection in Florence. (p70)

Museo di San Marco No frescoes better portray the humanist spirit of the Renaissance than Fra' Angelico's in Florence. (p92)

Cattedrale di Santo Stefano Gorge on Fra' Filippo Lippi frescoes in crowd-free Prato. (p288)

Museo Diocesano di Arte Sacra Small but sensational collection of Renaissance art in Cortona. (p313)

Museo Civico Siena's most famous museum is a feast of secular art. (p140)

Piero della Francesca Trail eastern Tuscany's greatest Renaissance painter, beginning with his famous *Legend of the True Cross* in Arezzo. (p295)

Camposanto Enjoy a Renaissance study of Hell with ghoulish frescoes by 14th-century painter Buonamico Buffalmacco, restored and returned to their rightful place inside Pisa's monumental walled cemetery. (p253)

Collegiata Vivid 14th-century frescoes, depicting episodes from the Old and New Testaments, inside San Gimignano's Romanesque cathedral. (p167)

Scenic Drives

Passo del Vestito Twist down this hair-raising mountain pass from Castelnuovo di Garfagnana to Massa on the Versilian coast. (p282)

Colle d'Orano & Fetovaia A twinset of gorgeous golden-sand beaches are linked by a dramatic drive on Elba's western coast. (p241)

Monte Argentario Bring along nerves of steel to motor the narrow Via Panoramica encircling this rugged promontory. (p215)

Val d'Orcia Take your foot off the pedal in this serene World Heritage–listed valley of rolling hills and Romanesque abbeys. (p182)

Chianti Bump along age-old back roads woven through vineyards, olive groves and photogenic avenues of cypress trees. (p156)

Strada del Vino e dell'Olio From hilltop towns to the Etruscan Coast via cypress alleys and *enoteche* (wine bars) – this drive is gourmet. (p230)

Natural Landscapes

Parco Nazionale dell'Arcipelago Toscano Europe's largest marine-protected area has the magical island of Elba at its core. (p235)

Val d'Orcia Picturesque agricultural valley in central Tuscany, and a World Heritage–listed Natural Artistic and Cultural Park to boot. (p179)

Apuane Alps Not snow but marble whitens these dramatic mountain peaks around famous mining town Carrara. (p279)

Garfagnana A trio of remote valleys in northwestern Tuscany forested with chestnut groves and porcini mushrooms. (p279)

Top: Leaning Tower (p252), Pisa

Bottom: Chianti (p156)

Parco Nazionale delle Foreste Casentinesi Discover dense forests, sparkling rivers and medieval monasteries in Tuscany's northeast. (p309)

Parco Regionale della Maremma This spectacular regional park protects pine forests, marshy plains, unspoilt coastline and the Uccellina mountains. (p213)

Riserva Naturale Provinciale Diaccia Botrona Follow tens of thousands of migrating birds to coastal marshlands around Castiglione della Pescaia. (p214)

Contemporary Art

Museo Novecento Modern and contemporary Italian art, brilliantly at home in a 13th-century Florentine *palazzo* (mansion). (p86)

Tuttomondo Who would guess that the last wall mural painted by American pop-artist Keith Haring adorns a Pisan church facade? (p259)

Palazzo Fabroni Get acquainted with Pistoian contemporary artists at this riveting art museum. (p271)

Fattoria di Celle Count four hours to tour this extraordinary al fresco collection of installation art. (p270)

Castello di Ama Ancient winemaking traditions meet cutting-edge contemporary art on this Chianti wine estate. (p165)

Galleria Continua Ogle world-class contemporary art in medieval San Gimignano. (p168)

Il Giardino dei Tarocchi Franco-American artist Niki de Saint

Phalle brings the tarot-card pack to life. (p213)

Borgo Corsignano Sleep in a farmhouse in northeastern Tuscany, its grounds replete with fabulous art. (p308)

Il Giardino di Daniel Spoerri Explore 16 hectares of countryside peppered with contemporary-art installations by 55 international artists. (p202)

Gardens

Giardino Torrigiani Explore Europe's largest privately owned green space within a historic town centre. (p102)

Villa e Giardino Bardini This quintessential Florentine garden boasts an orangery, marble maidens and Tuscany's finest garden restaurant. (p107)

Villa Grabau Skip, giddy as a child, around potted lemon trees and fountains in ornate villa gardens near Lucca. (p266)

Palazzo Pfanner Invite romance to a chamber-music concert in the baroque-styled garden of this Lucchese 17th-century palace. (p263)

Orto de' Pecci Track down peace, tranquillity, an organic farm, a medieval garden and an experimental vineyard in this Sienese oasis. (p145)

Museo di Casa Vasari Few know about the bijou Renaissance rooftop garden atop Giorgio Vasari's childhood home in Arezzo. (p299)

La Foce Enjoy a guided tour of these formal, English-designed gardens in the Val d'Orcia. (p191)

Vignamaggio These magnificent formal gardens featured in Kenneth Branagh's film adaptation of *Much Ado About Nothing;* bookings essential. (p156)

Medieval Towers

Campanile Scale 414 steps to the top of Florence cathedral's bell tower for an uplifting city panorama. (p78)

Torre d'Arnolfo Admire one of Europe's most beautiful cities atop Palazzo Vecchio's 94m-tall crenellated tower. (p80)

Hotel Torre Guelfa Savour *aperitivi* at sundown in the tiny bar atop Florence's tallest privately owned *torre* (tower). (p114)

Leaning Tower The bell tower of Pisa's cathedral leaned from the moment it was unveiled in 1372. (p252)

Torre Guinigi Bask in the shade of oak trees planted at the top of this 14th-century red-brick tower, one of 130 that once dotted medieval Lucca. (p263)

Torre del Mangia Views of Siena's iconic Piazza del Campo from atop this graceful tower are predictably swoon-worthy; count 500 steps up. (p145)

Torre Grossa Gorge on spectacular views of San Gimignano's centuries-old streets and the picture-postcard countryside beyond. (p168)

Torre del Candeliere Quintessentially Tuscan views of a hilltop town and rolling landscape seduce atop Massa Marittima's cute Candlestick Tower. (p198)

Month by Month

TOP EVENTS
Carnevale di Viareggio, February to March

Maggio Musicale Fiorentino, April to June

Giostra del Saracino, June and September

Palio, July and August

Puccini Festival, July to August

January

There's a chill in the air and snow might be covering the gnarled stubby vines in a pretty sprinkling of white. Outside Florence, low season might find you enjoying rural Tuscan sights in relative solitude.

☆ Palio della Vittoria

A fixture since 1441, Anghiari's annual Palio on 20 January is among Tuscany's oldest. Participants run from the historic battlefield outside town up the hill to Piazza Baldaccio Bruni in the town centre.

February

It's only towards the end of this month that locals are coaxed out of their winter hibernation. Weather conditions can be bone-chillingly cold in mountainous areas and windswept hill towns can appear all but deserted.

✷ Festa di Anna Maria Medici

Anna Maria Luisa de' Medici, the last Medici, bequeathed Florence its vast cultural heritage, hence this feast on 18 February marking her death in 1743: there's a costumed parade from Palazzo Vecchio to her tomb in the Cappelle Medicee, and free admission to state museums. (p110)

✷ Carnevale

The seaside resort of Viareggio goes wild during carnevale, an annual festival that kicks off 40 days before Ash Wednesday. The famous month-long street party revolves around fireworks, floats featuring giant satirical effigies of political and other topical personalities, parades and round-the-clock revelry. (p292)

☆ Bright Lights Festival

Digital arts and electronic music are celebrated at this annual festival (www.brightfestival.com) in Florence which sees dozens of international DJs take to the stage for three days at the city's Stazione Leopolda; side events and happenings break out at Florence's Student Hotel. (p114)

✕ Funk e Frattaglie Festival

Confirmation that street food in Tuscany is hot: this two-day festival (www.facebook.com/funkfrattaglie) at Florence's edgy experimental venue Manifattura Tabacchi celebrates traditional Florentine street food – offal in particular – and funky music. Cooking workshops introduce adults and children alike to slow food, regenerative agriculture and eye-opening tech. (p120)

March

Locals start to get into the springtime swing of things in the weeks leading up to Easter. Many regular visitors time their trips for this period to take advantage of low-season prices and uncrowded conditions.

✷ Torciata di San Giuseppe

An evocative torchlit procession down Pitigliano's mysterious, Etruscan-era *vie cave* (sunken roads) ends in a huge bonfire in the town. Held on the eve of the spring equinox (19 March), it's a symbol of purification and winter's end.

✥ Settimana Santa

Easter Week is celebrated in neighbouring Umbria with processions and performances in Assisi. Other Easter celebrations in the region include Florence's dramatic Scoppio del Carro, aka Explosion of the Cart, in front of the *duomo* on Easter Sunday. (p110)

April

Wildflowers carpet the countryside, market stalls burst with new-season produce and classical music is staged in wonderfully atmospheric surrounds. Easter sees the tourist season kicking off in earnest.

☆ Maggio Musicale Fiorentino

Italy's oldest arts festival, a 1933 creation, brings world-class performances of theatre, classical music, jazz and dance to Florence's sparkling opera house and other venues in the city. Concerts continue through April into June. (p110)

May

Medieval pageants take over the streets of towns and cities across the region from late spring to early autumn, highlighting ancient neighbourhood rivalries and the modern-day love of street parties.

✥ Balestro del Girifalco

Cinematic flag-waving opens this Massa Marittima archery festival, held on the fourth Sunday in May and again on 14 August. Archers from the town's three *terzieri* (districts) don medieval garb and, armed with 15th-century crossbows, compete for a symbolic golden arrow and painted silk banner. (p199)

✝ Eroicas Montalcino

Cyclists gather for a weekend in late May to follow one of five biking routes along dusty white, gravel roads in the Val d'Orcia; Montalcino is the festival hub. Race participants ride 'vintage' bikes – no modern racing, mountain or e-bikes allowed. (p168)

June

It's summer and, yes, the living is easy. The start of the month is the perfect time to tour the paradisiacal isle of Elba, and any time is right to gorge on seafood and strawberries.

✥ Luminaria

After dark on 16 June, Pisans honour their city's patron saint, San Ranieri, with thousands upon thousands of candles on windowsills and doorways, and blazing torches along the banks of the Arno, climaxing at 11pm with a spectacular fireworks display.

✥ Festa di San Giovanni

The feast of Florence's patron saint, San Giovanni

(St John), on 24 June is a fantastic opportunity to catch a match of *calcio storico* (historic football) – headbutting, punching, elbowing, choking and all – on Piazza di Santa Croce. The grand finale is fireworks over Piazzale Michelangelo. (p111)

✝ Giostra del Saracino

A grandiose affair deep-rooted in old-fashioned neighbourhood rivalry, this tournament sees the four *quartieri* (quarters) of Arezzo each put forward a team of knights to battle on the beautiful Piazza Grande; jousts are held on a Saturday in June and the first Sunday in September. (p300)

☆ San Gimignano Estate

Battles between fearless knights in shining armour, archery contests, falconry displays, fiery tugs of war and theatre performances evoke all the fun and madness of San Gimignano's medieval heritage during the Ferie delle Messi, usually held the third weekend in June. (p169)

✥ Gioco del Ponte

The atmosphere is electric during Pisa's Gioco del Ponte, when two teams in elaborate 16th-century costume battle to capture the city bridge, Ponte di Mezzo. It's held on the last Sunday in June. (p257)

✥ White Carrara Downtown

Music concerts inside marble quarries (brilliant acoustics), marble-carving workshops, open-air sculpture exhibitions, food and wine tastings, quarry treks on foot and by bike, and art happenings galore fill Carrara with visitors during this one-week festival (www.whitecarrara downtown.it) celebrating the Tuscan town's unique marble heritage and culture.

July

Cyclists and walkers take to the mountains, but everyone else heads to the beach, meaning that accommodation prices in inland cities and towns drop. Summer music and arts festivals abound.

🎊 The Palio

The most spectacular event on the Tuscan calendar, the Palio is held on 2 July and 16 August in Siena. Featuring colourful street pageants, a wild horse race and generous doses of civic pride, it exemplifies the living history that makes Tuscany so brilliantly compelling. (p144)

☆ Cortona Festivals

The hill town of Cortona is alive with music in summer. Late July ushers in the Cortona Mix Festival (www.mixfestival.it), an enticing cocktail of classical music, rock, theatre, literature and film. Watch for the winter edition in February and the jazz edition in late April.

☆ Lucca Summer Festival

This month-long music festival (www.summer-festival.com) lures big-name international pop, rock and blues acts to lovely Lucca, where they serenade crowds under the stars in some of the city's most atmospheric piazzas.

☆ Pistoia Blues

BB King, Miles Davis, David Bowie, Sting and Santana have all taken to the stage at Pistoia's annual blues festival, an electric al fresco fest around since 1980 that packs out central square Piazza del Duomo. (p273)

☆ Medieval Evenings

Oh, how apt it is for Suvereto, one of Tuscany's most beautiful medieval villages on the Etruscan Coast, to host July's Serate Medievali (Medieval Evenings). The festival transforms the serene red-brick cloister of the 13th-century Convento di San Francesco into a bustling medieval marketplace. (p232)

☆ Puccini Festival

Opera buffs from around the world make a pilgrimage to the small town of Torre del Lago for this annual event in July and August (www.puccinifestival.it). Performances are staged in an open-air lakeside theatre next to the great man's house.

August

Locals take their annual holidays and the daily tempo of life in the cities slows to a snail's pace. The weather can be oppressively hot and beaches are inevitably crowded.

🎊 Volterra AD 1398

On the second and third Sundays of August, locals in Volterra roll back the calendar some 600 years, take to the streets in period costume and party like it's 1398. (p177)

🎊 Bravio delle Botti

Thick-armed men from Montepulciano's eight *contrade* (districts) flex their muscles and bust a gut to push 80kg wine barrels uphill in this compelling race, held in the wine-producing town on the last Sunday in August. (p190)

🛍 Antiques Fairs

Head to eastern Tuscany in late August or early September for antiques market Cortonantiquaria (www.cortonantiquaria.it), inside Cortona's beautiful 18th-century Palazzo Vagnotti. Pair it with Tuscany's most famous antiques fair, Fiera Antiquaria di Arezzo, held in Arezzo the first Sunday and preceding Saturday of every month. (p300)

🍷 Montepulciano Calici di Stelle

During this popular evening event in August, wine tastings, live music and traditional flag-throwing and drumming enliven central Piazza Grande in Montepulciano.

September

Gourmets, this is the Tuscan month for you. Autumn ushers in La Vendemmia (the grape harvest) and a bounty of scented porcini mushrooms and creamy chestnuts in the forests.

Settembre diVino – Festa delle Cantine

Wine aficionados, prepare your tasting palate for plenty of dry and lively white Bianco di Pitigliano at the popular wine-cellar fest Settembre diVino – Festa delle Cantine, held the first weekend of September in the spectacular hilltop town of Pitigliano in southern Tuscany.

Palio della Ballestra

Sansepolcro's party-loving locals don medieval costumes and strut around town on the second Sunday of September while hosting a crossbow tournament between local archers and rivals from the nearby Umbrian town of Gubbio. (p306)

Expo del Chianti Classico

There is no finer or more fun opportunity to taste Chianti Classico than at Greve in Chianti's annual Expo del Chianti Classico, held the second weekend in September. Festivities begin the preceding Thursday. Buy a glass and swirl, sniff, sip and spit your way round. (p156)

Festival Barocco di San Gimignano

Lovers of baroque music will be in their element during this classical-music fest that graces the town of San Gimignano with a wonderful series of concerts (www.accademiadeilegi gieri.org) on September weekends. (p169)

Slow Travel Fest

Celebrating the culture of travel on foot and by bicycle, this annual festival features cultural events and plenty of peregrination on the local Monteriggioni stretch of medieval pilgrim route, the Via Francigena. (p175)

October

Those aromatic porcini and sweet chestnuts just keep on giving. Very much between seasons, this is a quiet, and often grey, month to tour Tuscany.

Eroica

On the first Sunday in October vintage cycling enthusiasts gather on vintage (pre-1987) bikes, and dressed in vintage gear – in Chianti and the Crete Senese for this iconic cycling race on gravel roads. Five routes vary in difficulty and length (45km to 209km). (p168)

November

November is when restaurateurs and truffle tragics come from every corner of the globe to sample and purchase Tuscany's bounty of strong-smelling and utterly delicious white truffles.

Mostra Mercato Nazionale del Tartufo Bianco

The old stone streets of San Miniato are filled with one of the world's most distinctive aromas at the National White Truffle Market, held on the last three weekends in November.

Itineraries

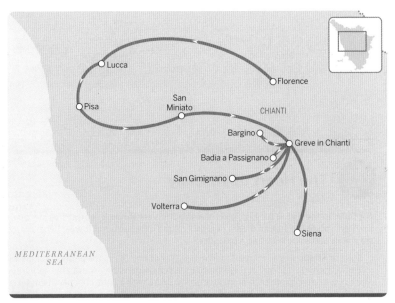

 Only the Best

This road trip takes in a classic Tuscan mix of world-class art, medieval architecture, gorgeous countryside and outstanding food and wine. Devote three days to exploring Renaissance **Florence**. Visit the Uffizi and stroll the Arno riverbanks. Day two, discover opulent Medici chapels, extraordinary frescoes and Michelangelo's *David* in San Marco and San Lorenzo. Last day, lose yourself in the Oltrarno's ancient web of lanes laced with artists' workshops or head into off-the-tourist-radar San Frediano.

Day four, go slow in 16th-century walled **Lucca**. Rent a bicycle to cruise along enchanting cobbled streets and graceful, butter-coloured piazzas. On day five, head to **Pisa** early to climb the Leaning Tower, then hit the eastbound road to Chianti with a lunch break in foodie-town **San Miniato**. Use an *agriturismo* (farm stay) around **Greve in Chianti** or elsewhere in Chianti as a base for three days, and explore the magically preserved medieval town of **San Gimignano**, artistic enclave **Volterra** and Antinori wine cellars in **Bargino** and **Badia a Passignano**. End in Gothic **Siena** for two days of breathlessly beautiful piazzas, churches, museums and restaurants.

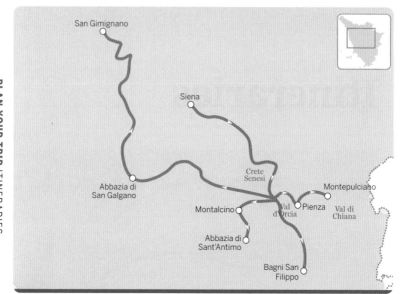

The Heart of Tuscany

For those in the region for a limited time, this itinerary through central Tuscany more than lives up to the Tuscan dream of gently rolling hills, medieval towns, Renaissance splendour and some very fine wine indeed.

Start in **Siena**, historical rival to Florence. A walking tour is the perfect prelude to the splendid Gothic symphony of this iconic Tuscan city. Gravitate towards the *duomo* and Museo Civico to explore each in greater depth. Break with a *caffè* on a pavement terrace on famously sloping Piazza del Campo. Continue your city exploration: Siena's delightfully intact *centro storico* (historic centre) is a Unesco World Heritage Site for good reason.

On day two (or three if Siena begs you to linger), motor southeast through the rounded hills and cypress alleys of Crete Senesi to Unesco-loved **Pienza**, a stroke of Renaissance architectural genius that, with a couple of lovely sleeping and eating options in and around town, is a brilliant base for exploring this tasty neck of the Tuscan woods. Or meander 15km east to blockbuster wine town **Montepulciano** in the gourmet Val di Chiana and use that as a base. Spend the next three days pandering to your culture-hungry soul and appetite for world-class wine and food: in the Val d'Orcia, tour vineyards around **Montalcino**, savour the serene beauty of **Abbazia di Sant'Antimo**, wander through the ruined Cistercian abbey of **San Galgano** and soak in hot cascades at **Bagni San Filippo**. In Montepulciano, sink your teeth into a feisty slab of local Chianina beef, slicked in fragrant olive oil and accompanied by a glass of Brunello di Montalcino or Vino Nobile di Montepulciano (two of Italy's greatest wines).

End your sojourn in this idyllic area by looping back along scenic secondary roads to romantic **San Gimignano**, home to medieval tower houses, a lavishly frescoed *duomo* and cutting-edge contemporary art. Dine on pasta dishes scented with locally grown saffron, drink the town's golden-hued Vernaccia wine and, whatever you do, don't miss out on the superb saffron-and-Vernaccia sorbet by former gelato world champion, Sergio Dondoli.

Top: Piazza del Campo (p141), Siena

Bottom: Sacro Eremo e Monastero di Camaldoli (p312), Tuscany

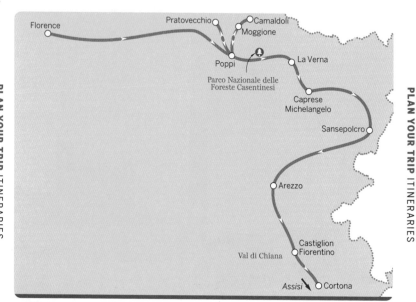

12 DAYS Into the East

The perfect trip for Tuscan connoisseurs, this itinerary varies the pace with a mix of well-known destinations and intriguing alternatives.

Spend three days admiring the Renaissance splendour of **Florence** before motoring east into the little-known Casentino region, home to the idyllically isolated Parco Nazionale delle Foreste Casentinesi. Base yourself around the fortified hill town of **Poppi** for three days and visit isolated, windswept medieval monasteries in **Camaldoli** and **La Verna**, hike trails in the national park, lunch on local *cucina tipica casentinese* (typical Casentino cuisine) in family-run village restaurant Il Cedro in **Moggione**, and dine after dark in **Pratovecchio**.

Next head southeast. Stop in **Caprese Michelangelo** to see where *David*'s creator lived for the first few months of his life. Then continue to **Sansepolcro**, proud possessor of masterpieces by the Renaissance painter Piero della Francesca. Tear yourself away after two nights and continue to the Val di Chiana for a few days of eating, drinking and sightseeing. Allow a full day for provincial capital **Arezzo**, with its marvellous central square and cafe life. Get acquainted with the architect who designed Florence's world-famous Galleria degli Uffizi at the Museo di Casa Vasari, and spend a quiet moment in the town's beautiful churches. Join locals for lunch at Antica Osteria Agania followed by a late-afternoon *passeggiata* (stroll) with locals on shop-lined Corso Italia.

Foodies are obliged to stop in the medieval hilltop town of **Castiglion Fiorentino**. Tuscany's famed Chianina cow hails from this valley and the *bistecca alla fiorentina* (T-bone steak) served at Ristorante Da Muzzicone is the best there is. Devote time also to **Cortona**: walk up steep cobbled streets to its Fortezza Medicea, and admire the collections at the Museo dell'Accademia Etrusca and Museo Diocesano. From Cortona it is an easy day trip to **Assisi**, one of Italy's most famous pilgrimage centres with extraordinary Giotto frescoes.

1 WEEK Pisa & its Provinces

Tick off Pisa's blockbuster icon before indulging in a crowd-free road south to the coast. Start in **Pisa**, allowing time for the Museo Nazionale di San Matteo as well as tourist-packed Piazza dei Miracoli. Scale the famous engineering project gone horribly wrong, aka the Leaning Tower. Come dusk, hit bijou art-town **Pietrasanta** for an excellent dinner and overnight stay. On day two, pay homage to Italy's Vespa scooter at Museo Piaggio in **Pontedera** or skip the scooters to see spaghetti being made in **Lari**. Lunch in the village, then motor to gourmet-town **San Miniato**. Overnight at **Barbialla Nuova** near Montaione and, if the season's right, hunt white truffles.

From here, head to spectacularly sited **Volterra** in the Val di Cecina to visit alabaster ateliers and Etruscan art. On your fourth day, move to the coast, where wine-lovers can meander south to taste Super Tuscan Sassicaias in **Bolgheri**. Drive north along the Etruscan Coast: dip your toes in the sea in the delightfully old-fashioned resort of **Castiglioncello** and end the day on a gourmet high with a seafood feast at La Barrocciaia in port-city **Livorno**.

1 WEEK The Maremma

Outdoors-lovers will adore southern Tuscany: dramatic landscapes etched out of porous volcanic rock, local cowboy culture and a heap of wild activities provide a welcome adrenaline boost.

Start in little-visited but delightful **Massa Marittima** and spend a couple of days visiting its museums and sampling Maremmese food and wine in its rustic cafes. Day three, check out an archaeological dig, Etruscan tombs and an impressive museum at the ancient hilltop settlement of **Vetulonia**, overnight in an *agriturismo*. From here, head down the coast to the wild and wonderful **Parco Regionale della Maremma** to walk, canoe, cycle or horse ride alongside the famous cowboys known as the *butteri*. End your journey inland amid the stunning surrounds of the Città del Tufo where you must visit the towns of **Pitigliano**, **Sovana** and **Sorano**. Sample local Morellino di Scansano wine at Sovana's hybrid cafe-*enoteca* Vino al Vino; explore the amazing Etruscan necropolises at the Parco Archeologico 'Città del Tufo'; and spend a day taking an 8km walk along the enigmatic sunken roads known as *vie cave*.

Off the Beaten Track

THE GARFAGNANA

Assuming nerves and stomach can handle the ride, driving the dozens of narrow spaghetti roads in this overwhelming rural region rewards with dramatic mountain passes, subterranean lakes and mountains of alpine fauna. (p279)

LARI

A pilgrimage to this medieval village between Pisa and Volterra is a must for curious foodies: it is home to the world's smallest pasta factory, aka an artisan workshop run by the Martelli family since 1926. (p278)

LAJATICO

Ringed by a natural amphitheatre of soul-stirring hills, this tiny village raises the curtain on an extraordinary open-air opera concert once a year, and gourmet winetasting and dining on the Bocelli family estate. (p283)

TERME DI SASSETTA

Take a break from tasting super-hot Super Tuscans along Tuscany's Central Coast with a flop in natural hot springs in a remote chestnut wood near Sassetta, central Tuscany. (p234)

RISERVA NATURALE PROVINCIALE DIACCIA BOTRONA

Explore the watery realms of this small nature reserve by boat; bring binoculars to make the most of the extraordinary bird life waiting to be watched in pristine silence. (p214)

0   50 km
0   25 miles

IL CEDRO

Gourmet travel in Tuscany means tracking down far-flung dining legends, unchanged for decades, and cooking up seasonal fruits of the land. Enter Il Cedro in the Parco Nazionale delle Foreste Casentinesi, Monte Falterona e Campigna. (p308)

CAPRESE MICHELANGELO

Dedicated Michelangelo fans won't do better than an off-track drive to the tiny medieval village in eastern Tuscany's Valle del Casentino where *David*'s creator spent his childhood roaming the countryside and painting. (p316)

ABBAZIA DI MONTE OLIVETO MAGGIORE

Seek out solitude and soul-soaring fresco art at this medieval abbey, a forest retreat for Benedictine monks southeast of Siena. Its church, frescoed refectory, library and historic wine cellar are equally uplifting. (p192)

ABBAZIA DI SANT'ANTIMO

Revel in the silence and natural magnificence of this serenely beautiful and isolated Romanesque abbey, a three-hour walk or 11km drive from Montalcino. (p186)

GIARDINO DEI TAROCCHI

Never say Tuscany lacks variety. Franco-American artist Niki de Saint Phalle lived in a sculpture while creating the 22 oversized Gaudí-influenced sculptures that tumble down the hillside at this fantastical sculpture garden in southern Tuscany. (p213)

Adriatic Sea

Parco Nazionale delle Foreste Casentinesi, Monte Falterona e Campigna

Monte Falterona (1654m)

Florence Airport
Fiesole
Florence
Chianti Fiorentino
Greve in Chianti
Chianti
San Gimignano
Chianti Sense
Castellina in Chianti
Gaiole in Chianti
Siena
Stia
IL CEDRO
Poppi
CAPRESE MICHELANGELO
Arno
Arezzo
Cortona
ABBAZIA DI MONTE OLIVETO MAGGIORE
Montepulciano
Val d'Orcia
Montalcino
Pienza
ABBAZIA DI SANT'ANTIMO
Bagno Vignoni
Bagni San Filippo
Monte Amiata
Vetulonia
Grosseto
Sorano
Orvieto
Parco Regionale della Maremma
Sovana
Pitigliano
Porto Santo Stefano
Orbetello
GIARDINO DEI TAROCCHI
UMBRIA
Monte Argentario
Lago di Burano
Riserva Naturale Lago di Burano
Giannutri

Accommodation

Find more accommodation reviews throughout the On the Road chapters (from p61)

PRICE RANGES

The following price ranges refer to a double room with private bathroom in high season; unless otherwise stated, breakfast is included in the price.

€ less than €110

€€ €110–200

€€€ more than €200

Accommodation Types

Agriturismo Working farm or winery with rooms; family-run and often with homely evening dining.

Albergo Hotel: budget or business, luxurious or a characterful midrange choice.

B&B Guesthouse offering bed and breakfast.

Boutique hotel Small, stylish hotel, midrange to top end, with a select, intimate vibe.

Castello Literally a castle but in reality anything from a converted farm outbuilding to a fully fledged castle with crenellated towers.

Locanda Country inn offering B&B in rustic surrounds.

Ostello Hostel offering dorm beds and budget private rooms.

Palazzo hotel Many urban hotels languish in century-old *palazzi* – literally 'palaces' but in reality historic mansions; some have original frescoes and period furnishings, others contemporary interiors.

Pensione Small, family-run guesthouse offering B&B; the owners live on-site.

Rifugio Mountain hut with bunk rooms, open June to September.

Best Places to Stay

Best on a Budget

In city or hilltop town, by the sea or deep in lush green countryside at the end of a bumpy dirt track, atmospheric budget crash pads – camp grounds, hostels, B&Bs, hotels and farmstays – are not hard to find. Low season (October to March) sees hotel rates slashed, as does August in Florence. Avoid tourist magnets like San Gimignano; base yourself in more affordable Siena or low-key Volterra instead.

➡ Hotel Scoti (p114), Florence

➡ Rosselba Le Palme (p239), Elba

➡ Dolce Rosa (p306), Sansepolcro

➡ La Primavera (p177), Volterra

➡ Belvedere di Suvereto (p233), Suvereto

Best for Families

Agriturismi and country resorts are the best option for those travelling with children: they often have self-catering facilities, bags of space, and kid-friendly activities like swimming, tennis, horse riding, mountain biking and farm animals to enjoy. In larger towns and cities, ample hotels offer spacious family rooms sleeping up to four or five.

➡ Hotel Palazzo Guadagni (p116), Florence

➡ Hotel Davanzati (p111), Florence

➡ Al Benefizio (p282), Barga

➡ Borgo Corsignano (p308), Poppi

➡ Montebelli Agriturismo & Country Hotel (p204), Vetulonia

➡ Barbialla Nuova (p278), near San Miniato

Best for Solo Travellers

Be it the exceptionally vast range of fun add-ons accommodation in Tuscany offers – helping with the grape harvest, cooking or yoga classes, biking, sculpture-garden tours and so on – solo travellers are well-entertained. Florence in particular is a brilliant city for meeting people and hooking up with other travellers. Few hotels have *camera singola* (single rooms); solo travellers usually pay a slightly reduced price for a *camera doppia* (double room).

➡ Student Hotel (p114), Florence

➡ Villa I Barronci (p162), Chianti

➡ La Bandita (p180), Val d'Orcia

➡ Locanda dell' Artista (p169), San Gimignano

➡ Sant'Egle (p208), Sorano

Best for Nature Lovers

Be it rustic self-catering farmhouse on truffle-hunting estate, luxurious gourmet retreat amid Chianti vines and olive groves, or island idyll amid aromatic olive and lemon trees, rural Tuscany delivers.

Research location information on your accommodation's website – obscure locations that don't appear on standard road maps are as common as muck and GPS can be unreliable when it comes to navigating unnamed lanes and Tuscan dirt tracks.

➡ Barbialla Nuova (p278), near San Miniato

➡ Borgo del Cabreo (p157), Greve in Chianti

➡ Agriturismo Due Palme (p239), Elba

➡ Foresteria Podere Brizio (p180), near Montalcino

➡ Al Benefizio (p282), Barga

➡ Podere San Lorenzo (p178), Volterra

BOTOND HORVATH/SHUTTERSTOCK ©

Camping.it (www.camping.it) Directory of campgrounds in Tuscany.

Lungarno Collection (www.lungarnocollection.com) Boutique collection of luxurious hotels owned by the Ferragamo fashion empire: penthouse suites in Florence to tropical resorts on the Tuscan coast.

Monastery Stays (www.monasterystays.com) Monastery and convent stays.

Booking

Book all accommodation well ahead, particularly in Florence and Siena and along the coast in summer. During busy periods, some hotels may impose a multinight stay (usually beach hotels over July and August, and in Siena during the Palio). Country hotels, villas and *agriturismi* often close in winter.

Lonely Planet (lonelyplanet.com/italy/tuscany/hotels) Find independent reviews, as well as recommendations on the best places to stay – then book them online.

Hotel Tax

Cities and towns levy a *tassa di soggiorno* (hotel occupancy tax) on top of advertised hotel rates. It is always charged in addition to your hotel bill and must generally be paid in cash. The exact amount (around €1.50 to €5 per guest per night) varies between cities and depends on how many stars a hotel has and the time of year. Under 10s or 12s are not taxed; 11- to 16-year-olds are usually charged 50% of the adult tax.

Getting Around

For more information, see Transport (p364)

Travelling by Car

Urban meanderings aside, this is undoubtedly the best option for discovering the picture-postcard Tuscany – the romantic cypress alleys, the softly rolling mist-kissed hills, the patchwork of vineyards and fruit orchards, and the medieval hilltop villages. Not only is it the quickest (and often only) way to get from A to B via C in this essentially rural region, but it's also the key to accessing some of the most authentic accommodation options, sights and traditional off-the-beaten-track experiences.

Car Hire

Major car-rental companies have desks at Florence and Pisa airports, making car hire upon arrival easy and straightforward. To rent a car you must be a last 25 years old and have a credit card. Make sure you understand precisely what is included in the price: Italian drivers can be unpredictable, streets are narrow and city parking is impossibly tight, meaning it might be worth paying extra to reduce the collision damage waiver excess to zero or at least a couple of hundred euros.

Driving Conditions

Tuscany has an excellent network of roads, ranging from toll-paying *autostrade* (motorways) to bucolic country lanes where two cars can just about squeeze past each another. The FI-PI-LI is a free motorway link between Florence, Pisa and Livorno.

RESOURCES

Automobile Club d'Italia (ACI; www.aci.it) The driver's best resource in Italy. For 24-hour roadside emergency service, dial 803 116. Foreigners do not have to join but instead pay a per-incident fee.

Autostrade per l'Italia (www.autostrade.it) Route planning, weather, webcams and real-time traffic information for motorways (highways) in Tuscany and Italy.

RTL (102.5 FM; http://rtl1025fm.radio.net/) Regular traffic news and updates.

Isoradio (103.3 FM; www.isoradio.rai.it) Traffic reports, weather information and nonstop music in between.

Driving in towns and cities is best avoided. Limited traffic zones (ZTL; Zona a Traffico Limitato) make entry into historic city centres impossible, and parking is expensive and hard to find. Away from urban areas, the pace and mood changes: motorists can take their foot off the pedal and cruise at an enjoyable speed through drop-dead-gorgeous scenery.

Maps

Use a GPS device or smartphone app to map routes and navigate, but equip yourself with a decent road map too: in remote areas like the Val d'Orcia, Apuane Alps and Garfagnana, GPS coordinates can be wrong or direct you onto unpaved back roads. Phone reception can be poor or nonexistent.

No Car?

Bus

A reasonably extensive regional bus network links major towns. To get from Florence to Siena, for example, the *corse rapide* (express) bus service is your best bet. Many other routes can involve long trips, and services are reduced or nonexistent at weekends. Regional companies are loosely affiliated under the Tiemme (www.lfi.it) network.

On public buses in towns and cities, tickets must be time stamped or you risk a €50 on-the-spot fine.

Train

High-speed trains run by **Trenitalia** (p367) link Florence, Arezzo and Cortona, as well as Grosseto, Livorno and Pisa. Slower *regionale* (regional) trains link Florence, Lucca and Pisa. Otherwise, the train network throughout Tuscany is limited.

Time-stamp your ticket before boarding or risk an immediate €50 fine.

Bicycle

Cycling is a national pastime and rewards in the countryside with grand views. Bikes can be taken on trains that have a bike logo, but they need a ticket – the price of a single ticket for *regionale* services and €12 on international services. Bike-hire outlets are common throughout the region and rent GPS-equipped e-bikes as well as traditional road and mountain bikes. Tourist offices in popular cycling areas like Chianti and along the Etruscan Coast have plenty of itinerary information.

PLAN YOUR TRIP GETTING AROUND

DRIVING FAST FACTS

Right or Left? Right

Manual or automatic? Manual

Top speed limit: 130km/h

Legal driving age: 18

Signature car: Fiat 500 (preferably convertible)

Alternative vehicle: A classic-cool Vespa scooter

ROAD DISTANCES (km)

	Florence	Pisa	Lucca	San Miniato
Pisa	69			
Lucca	61	23		
San Miniato	37	47	70	
Siena	51	87	30	77

Don't Miss Drives

Wine Tour of Chianti (p160) Take your foot off the pedal and indulge in four days of slow meandering through Tuscan wine country.

Exploring the Val d'Orcia (p182) One of Tuscany's most beautiful road trips, this extraordinary Unesco World Heritage Site in a valley in central Tuscany demands exploration.

Etruscan Wine & Oil Road (p230) Allow a full day for this coastal cruise along the Etruscan

Coast's Wine and Oil Road; book winery tastings in advance.

Go Slow in the Valle del Casentino (p310) An easy day trip from Florence, this short one-day itinerary delves into the wild and remote Casentino Valley in eastern Tuscany.

Via Francigena (p290) Trace the path of medieval pilgrims – by foot, bicycle or car – in the rural Lunigiana in northwestern Tuscany.

Fresh produce stall, Florence

Plan Your Trip

Eat & Drink Like a Local

For Tuscans, eating and drinking is a fine art to rival their master-piece surroundings. Thanks to an ancient cuisine sourced in the family farmstead from seasonal fruits of the land and sea, Tuscans eat exceedingly well – and around a shared table. Titillate your taste buds with these food-trip essentials.

The Year in Food

Spring (March–May)

Markets burst with violet artichokes, asparagus, fresh garlic and – towards the season's end – cherries, figs and zucchini flowers begging to be stuffed.

Summer (June–August)

There are strawberries and capsicums, and the start of San Gimignano's saffron harvest (July to November). On the coast beat the heat with seafood, and elsewhere with a gelato – chestnut, fig and honey, or saffron-and-pine-nut flavour.

Autumn (September–November)

Olives and grapes are harvested, forest fruits like chestnuts and porcini mushrooms (August to October) are gathered, and game is hunted. Oenophiles head to Greve in Chianti in September for Chianti's biggest wine fair. Mid-October opens Pisa's white-truffle season.

Winter (December–February)

The truffle season, which continues until mid-December, peaks with San Miniato's truffle market. Montalcino wine producers crack open the new vintage at February's Benvenuto Brunello.

Food Experiences

Meals of a Lifetime

Enoteca Pinchiorri, Florence Tuscany's only three-Michelin-star address, stratospheric and smug in a 16th-century Florentine *palazzo* (mansion). (p121)

Peperino, San Miniato Dinner for two at the world's smallest, and possibly most romantic, restaurant. (p279)

Il Leccio, Sant'Angelo in Colle Simple-but-spectacular cuisine sourced from the garden, washed down with extraordinary Brunellos. (p184)

Osteria di Passignano, Chianti Elegant, wine-fuelled dining on an Antinori estate. It doesn't get more Tuscan glam. (p159)

Osteria La Taverna di San Giuseppe Sienese dining centred around three of Tuscany's greatest indulgences: steak, truffles and porcini mushrooms. (p153)

La Pineta, Marina di Bibbona Possibly Tuscany's finest seafood restaurant, with memorable wine pairings to match; practically on the sand on central Tuscany's coast. (p232)

Ristoro di Lamole Contemporary Tuscan with one of Chianti's most spectacular panoramic views. (p164)

Cheap Treats

Pecorino Ewe's-milk cheese perfect in fresh, crunchy *pane* (bread).

Porchetta rolls Warm sliced pork (roasted whole with fennel, garlic and pepper) in a crispy roll.

Torta di ceci Savoury chickpea pancake.

Castagnaccio Hybrid cake-crepe, sweet and made from chestnut flour.

Gelato The best Tuscan ice cream uses seasonal, natural ingredients: figs, chestnuts, pine nuts, honey, saffron, wild strawberries...

Dare to Try

Bistecca alla fiorentina Blue and bloody is the only way to eat Florence's iconic T-bone steak; Trattoria Mario (p118) is the address.

Lampredotto Cow's fourth stomach, chopped, simmered and cooked up at every Florentine *trippaio*.

Trippa alla fiorentina Tripe in tomato sauce; once eaten, never forgotten at **Da Nerbone** (Map p92; Piazza del Mercato Centrale; meals €5-10; ⏱7am-2pm Mon-Sat) in Florence's Mercato Centrale.

Lardo di colonnata Carrara's luscious pig lard, aged in marble vats, keeps cardiologists in the black.

Biroldo Local version of haggis, included in tastings at Osteria Vecchia Mulino (p280) in Castelnuovo di Garfagnana.

Mallegato San Miniato's Slow Food–accredited blood sausage, usually on the menu at the restaurant of butcher Sergio Falaschi (p278).

Mercato Centrale (p118), Florence

Local Specialities

Spicy green olives, extra-virgin olive oils, full-bodied red wines, smoky porcini mushrooms and bags of beans are culinary trademarks across the Tuscan board, but delve deeper to discover geographic differences every gourmet will revel in.

Florence

Tuscany's leading lady is a born-and-bred gourmet. Be it Slow Food or fine dining, a tripe *panino* at a family-run food truck or a brilliantly blue T-bone steak served in a market trattoria unchanged since 1915, Florence meets every gastronomic taste with style and panache. Modern Tuscan cuisine also makes its presence felt here thanks to a bevy of creative young Tuscan chefs.

The day's end ushers in **aperitivi** (predinner drinks), a sacrosanct ritual big and buzzing in Tuscany's largest city: so copious are the complimentary buffets of snacks and nibbles laid out to accompany drinks that savvy young Florentines increasingly forgo dinner for **apericena** (*aperitivi* and dinner rolled into one).

Northwestern Tuscany

Wedged between wind-whipped sea and mountain, this unexpected culinary haven is known for its fresh *pecorino* cheese, *zuppe di cavolo* (cabbage soup) and other humble farm fare. Slow Food town San Miniato, near Pisa, is the source of Tuscany's exceptional white truffles.

In **Castelnuovo di Garfagnana**, fresh porcini, chestnuts and sacks of farm-grown *farro* (spelt) fill autumnal markets. Sweet *castagnaccio* (chestnut cake) is to locals in Garfagnana what *buccellato* (a sugared bread loaf studded with sultanas and aniseed) is to those in Lucca.

Not far from the coast, pig fat is aged in Carrara-marble vats and eaten 12 or 24 months later as wafer-thin, aromatic slices of *lardo di colonnata*.

Central Coast & Elba

Two words: sensational seafood. The grimy port of **Livorno** is the place to feast on superb affordable dining and **cacciucco**, a zesty fish stew swimming with octopus, rockfish and a shoal of other species.

Gelateria Dondoli (p172), San Gimignano

Inland, vineyards around the walled village of **Bolgheri** produce Super Tuscan Sassicaia and other legendary full-bodied reds – a perfect match for *cinghiale* (wild boar). On **Elba**, sweet red Aleatico Passito DOCG is the nectar amid the raft of sun-drenched wines grown on the island; spunky olive oils too.

Siena & Central Tuscany

Siena is the GPS coordinate where Tuscan cuisine originates, say locals, for whom *caffè* (coffee) and a slice of *panforte* (a rich cake of almonds, honey and candied fruit) is a mandatory part of their weekend diet.

Chianti is for serious foodies: cheery, dry, full red wines; butcher legend Dario Cecchini (p165) in Panzano in Chianti; tip-top Chianti Classico DOP olive oils; *finocchiona briciolona* (pork salami made with fennel seeds and Chianti) from Antica Macelleria Falorni (p161) in Greve in Chianti; and some of Tuscany's most exciting modern Tuscan cuisine.

Montalcino is famed for red Brunello wine, the consistently good Rosso di Montalcino and prized extra-virgin olive oils. **Montepulciano,** home of Vino Nobile red and its equally quaffable second-string Rosso di Montepulciano, also produces fine beef and Terre di Siena DOP extra-virgin olive oil.

Cheese aficionados make a beeline for **Pienza**, where some of Italy's finest *pecorino* is crafted, and the **Val di Chiana**, where sheep cheese is wrapped in fern fronds to become *ravaggiolo*. The same gorgeous rolling green valley is also where the world-famous Chianina beef comes from, making it the perfect place to sample *bistecca alla fiorentina,* perhaps after a tasty *primo* (first course) of *pici* (a type of local hand-rolled pasta).

Something of a culinary curiosity, fiery red **San Gimignano** saffron was the first in Europe to get its own DOP (protected origin) stamp of quality. Saffron gelato at San Gimignano's Gelateria Dondoli (p172) is particularly memorable.

Southern Tuscany

When it comes to quality-guaranteed beef, chicken and game, Maremma is a byword. **Pitigliano** is a mecca for the sweet-toothed thanks to handmade biscuits crafted locally, including the traditional Jewish honey-and-walnut pastry *lo sfratto.*

Brunello di Montalcino wine (p181)

Aperitivo (aperitif) is the all-essential postwork, early-evening drink that takes place any time between 5pm and 10pm. The price of your cocktail (around €10 in Florence) includes a copious buffet of nibbles, finger foods, or even salads, pasta and so on.

Cena (dinner) is traditionally lighter than lunch. The legendary Tuscan belt-busting, five-course whammy only happens on Sunday and feast days. Standard restaurant times are 7.30pm to around 10pm (often later in Florence and across the board in summer); locals never eat before 8pm.

Where to Eat

In a **ristorante** (restaurant) expect to find crisp linen, classic furnishings, formal service and refined dishes. A **trattoria** is a restaurant, often family owned, with cheaper prices, more relaxed service and classic regional specialities. Intimate and relaxed, the **osteria** has its origins in a traditional inn serving wine with a little food on the side; these days it's hard to differentiate between an *osteria* and a trattoria. For a cheap feed, cold beer

Then there's Pitigliano's very own DOC Bianco di Pitigliano, a fresh and fruity, Trebbiano-based white wine.

How to Eat & Drink

It pays to know what and how much to eat, and when – adopting the local pace is key to savouring every last exquisite gastronomic moment of the Tuscan day.

When to Eat

Colazione (breakfast) is a quick dash into a bar or cafe for a short, sharp espresso and *cornetto* (croissant) or *brioche* (pastry) standing at the bar.

Pranzo (lunch) is traditionally the main meal of the day, though Tuscans now tend to share the main family meal in the evening. Standard restaurant times are noon or 12.30pm to 2.30pm; locals rarely lunch before 1pm.

Merenda (afternoon snack) is the traditional afternoon snack, much revered by school children, workers and actually pretty much anyone who loves their food. Indulged in around 4pm, it is often bread-based.

TASTY CULINARY READS

Florence: Walking Through Food & Culture (Fabio Picchi; 2018) Compellingly personal and intimate insights into the foodie loves, passions and curiosities of Florentine celebrity chef Fabio Picchi.

Florentine (Emiko Davies; 2019) Beautifully illustrated coffee-table book evoking traditional Florentine life in and out the kitchen, by a Japanese-Australian writer and photographer living in Florence with her Italian husband and children.

Acquacotta (Emiko Davies; 2017) Part–recipe book, part–travel journal by Tuscany's most stylish food writer, exploring the flavours and culinary fashions, past and present, of the Tuscan coast.

The Tuscan Year (Elizabeth Romer; 1984) Unsalted bread, an old-lady dash of *mistra* (sweet aniseed-flavoured liqueur in black coffee), wild hops and tobacco: ancient Tuscan secrets and customs tied to the land and seasons come alive in this part-autobiographical novel about a farming family in rural Tuscany.

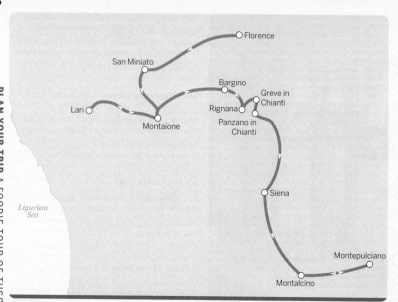

Ligurian Sea

A Foodie Tour of Tuscany

To taste, drink and dine exceedingly well, travel your taste buds through Tuscany's gourmet heart. No city plays the gourmet better than **Florence** (p62): shop for olive oils at La Bottega Della Frutta and Mercato Centrale, then lunch at Trattoria Mario. Later, indulge in a chocolate *degustazione* (tasting) with local foodie Alessandro Frassica at 'Ino. At dusk join Florentine gastronomes for *aperitivo* at All'Antico Vinaio (superb salami-and-cheese platters). Florence's *enoteche* (wine bars), such as Le Volpi e l'Uva, are other superb predinner-drink stops. Complete the evening with the dazzling contemporary Tuscan cuisine of Simone Cipriani at warehouse-turned-lounge Essenziale or a theatrical supper rooted in the traditional Tuscan cuisine of legendary Florentine chef Fabio Picchi at Il Teatro del Sale.

On day two, motor 30km into hilltop **San Miniato** (p277), a Slow Food town with stunning lunch options; nip into Sergio Falaschi's famous butcher shop to eye up the local cured meats. Overnight on white-truffle estate Barbialla Nuova in **Montaione** (p278).

Next morning, drive an hour west to **Lari** (p278) to watch artisan pasta makers at work, or dive into Chianti for a cellar visit and lunch at Antinori nel Chianti Classico in **Bargino** (p162). Dine and overnight at **Rignana** (p159). It's a short drive the next day to **Greve in Chianti** (p156) to visit Enoteca Falorni, Chianti's biggest wine cellar. Buy *finocchiona briciolona* (fennel-seed-studded pork salami) for a picnic lunch at Antica Macelleria Falorni and end the day at Badia a Passignano.

On day five, drive south to **Panzano in Chianti** (p165). Lunch with celebrity butcher Dario, then head to **Siena** (p140), where you could consider an afternoon cooking class at Fonte Giusta Cooking School, shop at Il Magnifico for *panforte* to take home, indulge in world-class gelato at La Vecchia Latteria and dine at La Taverna di San Giuseppe. On your final day, drive to **Montalcino** (p180) for a cellar tour at Poggio Antico, lunch at Il Leccio and a quick trip to the Enoliteca Consortile in wine town **Montepulciano** (p187). End the day on yet another culinary high back in Montalcino at Re di Macchia (p184).

TRUFFLES

They're not a plant, they don't spawn like mushrooms and cultivating them is impossible. Pig-ugly yet precious, these wild knobs of fungus excite and titillate. They're said to have aphrodisiacal qualities, and one whiff of their aroma is enough to convince: the smell of truffles, especially the more pungent white truffle, is seductive.

Truffles grow in symbiosis with oak trees and are *bianco* (white – actually a mouldy old yellowish colour) or *nero* (black – a gorgeous velvety tone). They are sniffed out by dogs from mid-October to late December, in San Giovanni d'Asso near Siena, and San Miniato, between Florence and Pisa. Truffles are typically served raw and thinly shaved over simple, mild-tasting dishes to give the palate full opportunity to revel in the subtle flavour. Some top truffle tastings:

Barbialla Nuova, Montaione (p278) Tuscany's golden ticket for hunting white truffles.

Boutique del Tartufo, Volterra (p179) Truffle shop selling fresh and conserved truffles, made-to-order truffle-infused cheese *panini* (sandwiches), truffle paste etc.

Pepenero, San Miniato (p279) Celebrity-chef Gilberto Rossi gives truffles a creative spin.

Ristorante Da Ventura, Sansepolcro (p307) Nothing beats a simple omelette sprinkled with fresh truffle shavings.

I Sette Consoli, Orvieto (☑0763 34 39 11; www.isetteconsoli.it; Piazza Sant'Angelo 1a; meals €40-45, tasting menu €45; ⊙12.30-3pm & 7.30-10pm, closed Wed & dinner Sun) Special dishes of the day celebrate the truffle season.

L'Osteria di Casa Chianti, Fiano (p163) Speciality truffle dishes.

Osteria La Taverna di San Giuseppe, Siena (p153) The address for truffle dining in Siena.

and a buzzing, convivial vibe, head for a **pizzeria**.

Enoteche (wine bars) are increasingly casual, atmospheric places to dine and taste Tuscan wines by the glass.

Dining on a farm at an **agriturismo** (farm stay) gives you the best of Tuscany – a copious, never-ending feast of homemade cooking using local produce, set against a quintessential Tuscan backdrop of old stone farmhouse, cypress alley and pea-green rolling hills.

At the **gelateria** (ice-cream shop), rain, hail or shine, a queue outside the door marks the best. The astonishing choice of flavours will have you longing for a gelato long after you've left Tuscany.

Menu Decoder

Menù di degustazione Tasting menu.

Coperto Cover charge, around €2 per person, for bread.

Piatto del giorno Dish of the day.

Antipasto A hot or cold appetiser.

Primo First course, usually pasta, rice or *zuppa* (soup).

Secondo Second course, *carne* (meat) or *pesce* (fish).

Contorno Vegetable side dish.

Dolce Dessert, often *torta* (cake) or *cantucci* (dry almond-studded biscuits) dunked into a glass of sweet Vin Santo wine.

Acqua minerale (mineral water) A bottle of *frizzante* (sparkling) or *naturale* (still) with a meal is a Tuscan standard.

Vino della casa (house wine) Wine in restaurants is reasonably priced and good; the cheapest is *vino della casa,* ordered in carafes of 25cL (250mL), 50cL (500mL), 75cL (750mL) or 1L.

Plan Your Trip
Activities

High mountains, gentle hills, pristine shores: Tuscany's natural environments deliver irresistible activities. Hiking, cycling, sailing, kayaking, diving, riding – you can do them all here amid superb scenery. In fact, along with the culture, food and wine, it's these memorable outdoor adventures that make Tuscany a must-come-back-to place.

Top Outdoor Experiences

Best Short Walks
Along *vie cave* (Etruscan sunken roads) below Pitigliano (p205).

From Montalcino to Val d'Orcia's Abbazia di Sant'Antimo (p186).

Best Easy Bike Rides
With elegance atop the city walls of Lucca (p261).

Around vineyards and olive groves in Chianti (p157).

Island touring on Elba (p245).

With a preprogrammed e-bike (p365) in Montepulciano wine country.

Best on the Water
Slicing silent waterways with a canoe in Parco Regionale della Maremma (p213).

Sea kayaking, diving and stand-up paddleboarding (SUP) offshore from Elba (p234).

Urban rafting beneath the iconic Ponte Vecchio on the Arno in Florence (p108).

When to Go

Lapping up sea and mountain air, heady with the scents of wild sage and pine, is an integral part of the Tuscan outdoor experience. Spring and autumn – with their warm, dry days, wildflowers and forest fruits – are the most picturesque times to be outdoors. July (less hot and crowded than August) is the best month for water sports and hiking in the Apuane Alps. Autumn, when the wine and olive harvests start, has a particularly mellow appeal and, with summer's warmth lingering well into October, there's plenty of daylight for morning hikes through mushroom-rich forests and crunchy leaves.

Times to Avoid

Easter The first key period of the Italian holiday year, this two-week slot in late March or April sees too many people jostle for too little trail space.

August Italians take their summer holidays, crowding paths, cycle routes and roads. On lower terrain, August's intense heat can be oppressive.

Winter This often means wet, slippery roads and poor visibility for cyclists.

Where to Go

Chianti (p156) Tuscany's key wine-growing area enables easy walking and cycling between achingly pretty vine and olive groves.

Spiaggia di Sansone (p241), Elba

Apuane Alps & Garfagnana (p279) Ruggedly scenic and remote, with the region's most dramatic mountains, marble quarries and forested valleys: go hiking, caving, mountain biking and horse riding.

Etruscan Coast (p227) Hit the beach in July and August for sand, sea and water-sport action. Cycling is dirt track to silky smooth.

Elba (p217) A summer island idyll with stunning sea kayaking, sailing, diving and snorkelling; there's beautiful hiking between coves through scented *macchia* (herbal scrub) and parasol pines.

Val d'Orcia (p179) Family walking and cycling near Siena.

Parco Regionale della Maremma (p213) Hiking, biking, horse riding and backwater canoeing on Tuscany's southern coast.

Planning & Information

The tourist-board website (www.visittusca ny.com) features background information, interactive maps and inspiring walking,

---

BEST WALKS IF YOU LIKE...

Etruscan ruins Golfo di Baratti (p233), Pitigliano (p205)

Birdwatching Riserva Naturale Provinciale Diaccia Botrona (p214), Oasi WWF Laguna di Orbetello (p215)

Wine Chianti (p156), Montalcino (p180), Montepulciano (p187)

Pilgrim paths Marciana (p240), Abbazia di Sant'Antimo (p186), Monteriggioni (p174)

Sweeping coastal panoramas Monte Capanne (p240), Marciana (p240)

Art and sculpture Il Giardino di Daniel Spoerri (p202), Fattoria di Celle (p270)

Unspoiled coast Parco Regionale della Maremma (p213)

cycling and horse-riding routes. It also covers caving, spas and water sports.

Throughout Tuscany, tourist offices and national-park offices have mountains of activity-related information, including lists of guides as well as accommodation options near trails. It's best to buy maps and guidebooks before leaving home.

Activity specialists:

Toscana Adventure Team (www.tateam.it) Outdoor-adventure specialists organising everything from mountain biking, horse riding and coasteering to heli-biking, abseiling, hiking and caving.

Hedonistic Hiking (☑Australia +61 (0)428 198 918, UK +44 (0)1858 565 148; www.hedonistichiking.com) Multiday treks around Siena and Chianti with luxurious villa accommodation, luggage transfer and gourmet meals.

Discovery Chianti (p157) Organises cycling and hiking tours through Chianti.

Be Tuscan for a Day (p156) Slow trekking, experimental archaeology, vineyard tours and cultural orienteering are among the more unusual activities and grassroots experiences offered by this central Tuscan setup.

Walking & Hiking

Hiking in Tuscany takes you straight to its soul. People have been criss-crossing this region on foot for millennia, and tracing those heritage-rich trails reveals the best of Tuscany today, opening up wine estates, town-crowned hills, mountains, marshes and sandy shores.

The Apuane Alps

On the spine of the Apennines, the challenging Apuane Alps and the stunning Garfagnana valleys (p279) are for serious hikers. Hundreds of trails encompass everything from half-day hikes to long-distance treks. The main town, Castelnuovo di Garfagnana, is the best base camp and the place to pick up information on *rifugi* (mountain huts with dorm-style accommodation). The Parco Regionale delle Alpi Apuane (www.parcapuane.it) has plentiful hiking information.

Grande Escursione Appenninica

This epic 400km trek takes in the Due Santi pass above La Spezia, Sansepolcro in eastern Tuscany and the Tuscan-Emilian Apennines. The route of ridge and valley hiking is split into 23 day-long stages, peaks at 2000m and can normally be tackled between April and October. Cicerone Press (www.cicerone.co.uk) publishes the guidebook *The GEA – The Grande Escursione Appenninica*.

Via Francigena

Devise a holiday with a difference by walking or driving parts of the Via Francigena, one of Europe's most important medieval pilgrimage routes, connecting English cathedral city Canterbury with Rome. In Central Tuscany, the route goes past or through towns including San Gimignano, Monteriggioni, San Quirico d'Orcia and Radicófani.

Touring Club Italiano publishes *Via Francigena Toscana*, an English-language guide and hiking map (1:175,000). You'll find it for sale in tourist offices and bookshops throughout the region. Also check

LEARN A NEW SKILL

Can't face another insanely graceful, vine-stitched hill demanding to be pounded up? Create a whole new spin to your Tuscan perspective with one of these alternative activities.

Beekeeping

Learn how acacia or chestnut nectar is extracted and made into a sweet single-flower honey (or take part in the olive harvest) at Al Benefizio (p282), a rustic *agriturismo* near Barga in northwestern Tuscany.

Photography

Photography tours are just one of the many fun and creative activities cooked up by Be Tuscan for a Day (p156), an innovative project designed to promote experiential travel in central Tuscany. Cultural orienteering, medieval dining and other experiences are on the packed agenda.

Summer Solstice

Joining locals in a solstice festival is just one of the many unique and inspiring activities organised by Sapori e Saperi (p286) in northwest Tuscany. Other fun stuff: watching a shepherd make *pecorino* (sheep's-milk cheese) and ricotta with milk from the flock; foraging for wild herbs; textile tours with local artisans; and taking part in July's *farro* (spelt) harvest.

Vespa Tours

Don your Audrey Hepburn hat and hit the road on the back of a Vespa; Florence Town (p110) is one of several agencies to organise guided trips.

Yoga & Mindfulness

Tuscany is home to the real thing: head to the Dzogchen Community & Cultural Association (p203) in southern Tuscany for Yantra yoga, meditation and traditional dancing with Tibetan monks.

---

www.viafrancigenatoscana.org (in Italian) or www.viefrancigene.org/en. The latter is packed with information and has an interactive map.

Chianti

For some this insanely scenic, wine- and vine-laden region is the big hiking favourite. It'll see you rambling between vineyards, wine cellars and century-old farms, then sitting down at a shared table to dine on homemade pasta and homegrown oil and wine.

One of the most popular walks is between Florence and Siena. Routes head south out of Florence, across Chianti (often via Greve and Rada in Chianti) to Siena. Handily, there are plenty of restaurants, *enoteche* (wine bars) and *agriturismi* (farm-stay accommodation) along the way. Factor in distances of around 80km to 120km between the two cities (five to seven days), depending on your chosen route.

Il Mugello

Starting a few kilometres northeast of Florence, the Mugello region (www.mugellotoscana.it) is ideal for half- and full-day hikes among gentle hills, river valleys and low mountains.

Elba

A prime hiking spot for dramatic scenery, Elba has only one really stiff hike: up Monte Capanne (p240).

Cycling

Whether you're out for a day's gentle pedal around Florence, a sybaritic Chianti weekend winery tour or a serious two-week-long workout, Tuscany has bags of cycling scope.

NATIONAL & REGIONAL PARKS

PARK	WEBSITE	FEATURES	ACTIVITIES	BEST TIME TO VISIT
Parco Nazionale dell'Arcipelago Toscano	www.islepark.it	Europe's largest marine park, covering 180 sq km of land & 600 sq km of sea; typical Mediterranean island flora & fauna	sea kayaking, sailing, diving, snorkelling, water sports, walking, cycling, wine tasting	spring & summer
Parco Nazionale delle Foreste Casentinesi	www.parco forestecasenti nesi.it	Source of the river Arno & Italy's most extensive, best-preserved forest: ancient pines, beech, five maple types & the rare yew; deer, wild boar, mouflon, wolves & 97 nesting bird species	walking, hiking, birdwatching	spring & autumn
Parco Regionale delle Alpi Apuane	www.parc apuane.it	Mountainous regional park cascading to the sea from the Garfagnana; golden eagles, peregrine falcons, buzzards & the rare chough (the park's symbol)	hiking, mountain biking, caving	summer & autumn

Practicalities

Bike types All-terrain bikes, suitable for both paved and country routes, are the most versatile for Tuscan roads.

Equipment You'll need sun, wind and rain protection, plus a helmet. Carry enough liquids if you're heading into the high hills.

Bike transportation If bringing your own bike from home, check with your airline whether there's a fee and how much disassembling it requires. Bikes can be transported by train in Italy, either with you or to arrive within a couple of days (p365).

Bike hire Hire outlets are common in Tuscany. Book through EcoRent (www.ecorent.net) or on arrival in towns including Florence, Pisa, Lucca and Siena. Hotels and *agriturismi* often have bike rental.

Access While most historic town and city centres are closed to cars, cyclists are often free to enter at will – double-check the Zona a Traffico Limitato (ZTL; Limited Traffic Zones) signs locally.

Regions & Routes

Via Francigena (p50) Cyclists are welcome on this medieval pilgrimage trail.

Chianti The picturesque **Strada Chiantigiana** (SS222) waltzes through Chianti en route from Florence to Siena, opening up smooth cycling and short, challenging climbs. If you're fairly fit and have a multigear mountain bike, consider peeling off the SS222 onto Chianti's tranquil back roads (sometimes just gravel tracks), which snake between hamlets and vineyards. Either way, farmstay accommodation abounds.

Etruscan Coast Relatively gentle coastal cycling south from Livorno. Ask at the town's tourist office (p227) for the 20-route *Costa degli Etruschi: Cycling Itineraries* booklet.

Strada del Vino e dell'Olio (www.lastradadelvino. com) A wine- and olive-oil-themed 150km tourist itinerary winding south from Livorno to Piombino

PARK	WEBSITE	FEATURES	ACTIVITIES	BEST TIME TO VISIT
Parco Regionale Migliarino, San Rossore, Massaci-uccoli	www.parcosan rossore.org	Coastal reserve stretching from Viareggio to Livorno; extraordinary birdlife (over 200 species) in its marshes, dunes & wetland	easy walking, cycling, horse riding, bird-watching, canoeing	spring, summer & autumn
Parco Regionale della Maremma	www.parco -maremma.it	Regional park comprising the Uccellina mountains, pine forest, agricultural farmland, marshland & 20km of unspoiled coast-line; oak & cork oak, herb-al *maquis* (scrubland); Maremma cows, horses & wild boar	walking, hiking, cycling, horse riding, canoeing	spring & autumn (mid-Jun–mid-Sep visits largely by guided tour only)

and then across to Elba. The 36km stretch from Bolgheri to Suvereto via the hill towns of Castagneto Carducci and Sassetta is particularly scenic; expect switchbacks galore.

Le Crete & Val d'Orcia Extensive, hilly itineraries where bursts of hill climbing are interspersed with cruises amid golden wheat fields and cypress alleys.

Monte Amiata A 1700m volcanic dome in southern Tuscany whose roads are a test for aspiring hill climbers.

Guided Bike Tours

Florence is a top spot to hook up with a cycling guide and venture into Chianti. On the following guided tours everything is supplied, including bike and helmet. Expect to pedal around 20km a day. Most outlets offer the choice of regular or electric bikes.

Florence By Bike (p136) Tour of northern Chianti (one day) with lunch and wine tasting; rents out bikes and suggests self-guided itineraries too.

I Bike Italy (p157) Two-day tours from Florence to Siena, including accommodation and meals.

We Bike Tuscany (p157) One-day tours for all levels, departing from Florence.

Discovery Chianti (p157) Guided bike tours in Chianti and elsewhere in Tuscany.

Tuscany Ride A Bike (p265) Full-day guided bike tours departing from Lucca in northwestern Tuscany; themed wine, food and beach tours. Bike rental and self-guided itineraries too.

FiesoleBike (p134) Guided, 21km sunset pedal from Fiesole to Florence.

Ballooning

Drifting noiselessly over Tuscany's pea-green vineyards and silvery olive groves is slow, serene and cinematic.

The ballooning season is late spring to early autumn. Takeoff is around 6am; flights last 1¼ hours and cost €250 to €280 per person, often including a 'sparkling wine' breakfast.

Tuscany Ballooning (p162) Near Florence.

Ballooning in Tuscany (☑338 1462994; https://booking.ballooningintuscany.com; adult/child under 12 €280/220; ⊙mid-May–mid-Oct) Take off in Siena or Colle di Val d'Elsa.

Avignonesi Winery (p189) Ballooning and brunch at a Montepulciano winery (€340).

Ballooning over a vineyard, Tuscany

Horse Riding

Sauntering serenely on horseback through chestnut and cork-oak woods, between vines and past fields of bright yellow sunflowers and wild red poppies, is hypnotically calming, aromatic and oh so Tuscan.

Maremma Riding is particularly high profile in this rural slice of southern Tuscany – it's home to the famous *butteri* (Maremmese cowboys); experienced riders can sign up for a day herding cows with them at Tenuta di Alberese (p214). Or opt for two- to four-hour guided horseback tours (suitable for all experience levels); the Parco Regionale della Maremma (p213) can advise. Montebelli Agriturismo & Country Hotel (p204) is one of a handful of hotels in the region to offer horse riding.

Etruscan Coast A horseback itinerary takes riders from Livorno 170km southeast to Sassetta along sun-scorched coastal paths (best in spring and autumn) and shaded cart tracks. It recommends targeted accommodation en route; the tourist office (p227) in Livorno has more info.

Elba The Parco Nazionale dell'Arcipelago Toscano (p235) features old military and forest tracks that double as equestrian pathways; the Portoferraio tourist office (p235) has maps, brochures and trail details.

Water Sports

Tuscany's lesser-known coast squirrels away a horizon of shimmering blue water speckled with islands. Add sea kayaks, sailboats and sandy coves reached only from the sea, and you have the source of great outdoor action.

Diving & Snorkelling

Elba is among Italy's top year-round diving spots. Wreck-diving sites include Pomonte, where the *Elvisco* cargo boat sits on the seabed 12m down, and the German WWII plane *Junker 52*, wrecked at a more challenging 38m near Portoferraio.

Aquatic flora and fauna is protected and dramatic. Several Elba diving schools rent out gear and organise guides and courses. Less intrepid water lovers can snorkel.

BEST BEACHES

Sansone & Sorgente (Elba; p241)
White shingle and turquoise waters
equal snorkelling bliss.

Golfo di Baratti (Etruscan Coast;
p233) Sandy coves fringed by parasol pines.

Innamorata (Elba; p241) A wild sand-
meets-pebble cove backed by euca-
lyptus trees.

Castiglioncello (Etruscan Coast;
p227) A sandy strip on the town's
northern fringe.

You can also dive along the mainland
Etruscan Coast and in Porto Ercole on
Monte Argentario.

Kayaking & Canoeing

Hot summer afternoons are best spent
lapping up the slow rhythm of Tuscan
travel in a sea kayak or canoe – especially
along **Elba's** cove-clad coast. Adventure
specialists **Il Viottolo** (☑329 7367100; www.
ilviottolo.com; Via degli Albarelli 60) in Marina
di Campo offer sea-kayaking treks.

The Parco Regionale della Maremma
(p213) has a fabulous guided canoe trail.

Sailing & Surfing

The coves of the Tuscan archipelagos and
around **Monte Argentario** are superb for
sailing, windsurfing and kitesurfing. Rent
equipment and receive instruction at all
the major resorts. **Viareggio** holds several
annual sailing regattas.

Rafting

A handful of outfits in the spa town of
Bagni di Lucca in northwestern Tuscany
organise white-water rafting expeditions
on the Lima river.

In Florence, Firenze Rafting (p108) offers urban rafting expeditions along the
river Arno, afloat a sturdy inflatable raft
with an aperitif beneath the arches of the
city's iconic Ponte Vecchio. It also organises guided stand-up paddleboard and
rafting expeditions along the river.

Spas

Tuscany is one of Italy's thermal-activity
hotspots, with the province of Siena particularly rich in mineralised waters. Options range from swish indoor spas to
natural woodland pools, and tracking
them down – and trying them out – is a
delight.

Bagni di Lucca Terme (p284) Thermal swims and
massage treatments in a northwestern spa town.

Bagni San Filippo (p190) Free al fresco back-
woods bathing at its best in the Val d'Orcia.

Calidario Terme Etrusche (p229) Spa treatments
and atmospheric outdoor swims on the Etruscan
Coast.

Terme di Sassetta (p234) Elegant spa on a
biodynamic farm, with quintessential 'Tuscan hills'
panorama.

Plan Your Trip
Family Travel

There is far more to Tuscany than churches and museums. The region is a quietly child-friendly destination and, with savvy planning, families can revel in a wonderful choice of creative, educational, culinary and old-fashioned-fun things to see, do and experience.

Keeping Costs Down

Sleeping
Many hotels welcome families with family rooms that sleep four or five comfortably; baby cots are free. Campgrounds near beaches pepper the Etruscan Coast.

Eating Out
Many restaurants offer a *menù bambini* (children's menu), or order a half-portion or a plain plate of pasta with butter or olive oil and Parmesan.

Sightseeing
Kids with EU passports aged under 18 receive free entry into many museums. Otherwise, children aged under 18 years generally pay half the adult admission; under fives are free.

Transport
A seat on a bus costs the same for everyone (toddlers and babies on laps are free). Children under 12 pay half-fare on trains.

Children Will Love...

Museums

➡ **Museo Galileo** (Florence; p85) Astronomical and mathematical treasures, with ample hands-on opportunities.

➡ **Palazzo Vecchio** (Florence; p80) Guided tours for children and families through secret staircases and hidden rooms.

➡ **Museo Piaggio** (Pontedera; p260)**,** Learn about Italy's iconic Vespa scooter.

➡ **La Citadella di Carnevale** (Viareggio; p289) Watch artists craft giant clowns, kings etc for carnival floats; papier-mâché workshops.

Foodie Fun

➡ **Curious Appetite** (Florence; p108) Learn how to make gelato (and eat it).

➡ **Martelli** (Lari; p278) Watch spaghetti being made at this artisanal pasta workshop.

➡ **Antonio Mattei** (Prato; p288) Watch bakers at work in Tuscany's most famous *biscottificio* (biscuit shop).

➡ **Barbialla Nuova** (Montaione; p278) Get hands dirty with a bread- or pizza-making workshop on a Tuscan cattle farm and truffle estate.

➡ **Al Benefizio** (Garfagnana; p282) Learn how honey is made with a skilled beekeeper.

Wildlife Encounters

➡ **Museo di Storia Naturale del Mediterraneo** (Livorno; p223) Meet Annie, the whale skeleton.

➡ **Riserva Naturale Provinciale Diaccia Botrona** (Southern Tuscany; p214) Spot flamingos and herons on a boat tour through the marshes.

➡ **Parco Regionale della Maremma** (Southern Tuscany; p213), Hike, cycle or canoe through this huge coastal park.

➡ **Acquario di Livorno** (Livorno; p220) A thoroughly modern aquarium by the seaside.

Towers to Climb

➡ **Torre del Mangia** (Siena; p145) Steep steps and awesome views at the top.

➡ **Duomo** (Florence; p76) **& Campanile** (Florence; p78) Climb up Giotto's bell tower or into Brunelleschi's dome.

➡ **Leaning Tower** (Pisa; p252) Accessible to children aged eight years and up; otherwise snap photos of your kids propping up the tower.

➡ **Torre Guinigi** (Lucca; p263) Count 230 steps to the top of this 45m-high tower crowned with seven oak trees.

Cool Stuff

➡ **Cave di Marmo Tours** (Carrara; p285) Take a Bond-style 4WD tour of the open-cast quarry or follow miners inside 'marble mountain'.

➡ **Grotta del Vento** (Garfagnana; p282) Explore subterranean abysses, lakes and caverns.

➡ **Cabinovia Monte Capanne** (Elba; p240) Ride a 'bird cage' up Elba's highest peak.

➡ **Pistoia Sotteranea** (Pistoia; p272) Discover subterranean rivers underneath a 13th-century hospital.

Useful Resources

Lonely Planet Kids (www.lonelyplanetkids.com) Loads of activities and great family-travel blog content.

Visit Tuscany (www.visittuscany.com) Tuscany's tourism board website devotes pages to beaches, activities and other family-themed topics.

Region by Region

Florence

Fascinating museums – some interactive, others with creative workshops and tours for children like Palazzo Vecchio (p80), Museo Novecento (p86), and Palazzo Strozzi (p69) – make Florence a favourite for families with school-age kids. For the under fives, gentle riverside ambles, hide-and-seek in city parks such as Giardino di Boboli (p106) or pool-clad Parco delle Cascine (p102), Piazza della Repubblica's vintage carousel, fantastic *gelaterie* (ice-cream shops) and a vast choice of dining options add appeal.

Siena & Central Tuscany

Siena is more fun than any school textbook when it comes to learning about Renaissance architecture and history. Young children can run wild in Piazza del Campo (p141), Fortezza Medicea (p154) or between outdoor art and farm animals in the Orto de' Pecci (p145). For more Siena-specific suggestions, see p154.

Elsewhere in this picture-postcard part of green Tuscany, families can dip into Etruscan history at Volterra's Museo Etrusco Guarnacci (p176); enjoy fun, thought-provoking contemporary art at San Gimignano's Galleria Continua (p168); scale fortress battlements in Montalcino; or hook up with locals through Be Tuscan for a Day (p156) to horse-ride, hike, bike, join a photography tour or cooking class.

Southern Tuscany

Marammese cowboys, archaeological ruins and mysterious sunken roads in the Parco Archeologico 'Città del Tufo' (p204), sandy beaches and snowy mountains: this region might be rural, but it's a cracker when it comes to farm-stay accommodation, outdoor action and quirky sights to pique kids' natural curiosity. Hiking, biking, horse riding and swimming opportunities are plentiful and wonderful in the wild Parco Regionale della Maremma (p213).

Central Coast & Elba

This predominantly coastal region is the ultimate family paradise: a golden shoreline laced with beautiful sandy beaches, swimming and water sports, Livorno's world-class aquarium (p220) and 'Venetian' waterways to explore by boat (p223), and the paradise island of Elba to sail to. Inland, curious young archeologists can uncover gigantic circular burial grounds dug by the Etruscans at the Parco Archeologico di Baratti e Populonia (p233).

Northwestern Tuscany

Main towns Pisa and Lucca demand a family visit with their iconic sites: the Leaning Tower (p252) and Lucca's fairy-tale city walls to cycle. Head to the Apuane Alps and Garfagnana to stay on Tuscan farms, see marble being mined in Carrara, and explore subterranean lakes and caverns.

Eastern Tuscany

The least exciting region perhaps for children, this is a rural retreat with rich wildlife to discover in the Parco Nazionale delle Foreste Casentinesi (p309) and some outstanding, family-friendly country resorts such as Borgo Corsignano (p308) and Fattorie de Celli (p308). Read: complete get away from it all (parents) while the kids kick back in the pool and grounds.

Good to Know

Look out for the 🚼 icon for family-friendly suggestions throughout this guide.

Agriturismi Tuscan accommodation on farms, wineries and agricultural estates is family gold: pick olives, feed black pigs, make bread in a stone oven, learn about saffron cultivation etc.

Sightseeing Most sights offer engaging audio guides for kids (around €5). Museums in Florence run children's tours and workshops.

When to go Time your visit with a kid-cool festival: Siena's Palio (p144), Viareggio's Carnevale (p292), Florence's Scoppio del Carro (p110) or Pisa's Luminaria di San Ranieri (p256).

Prams & strollers Cobbled streets and narrow pavements make towns hard to navigate; bring a back carrier to transport tots.

Dining out Children are warmly welcomed in restaurants, especially in casual *trattorie* and *osterie* – often family-owned with overwhelmingly friendly, indulgent staff.

Car travel Children under 150cm or 36kg must be buckled into an appropriate child seat for their weight and are not allowed in the front.

Kids' Corner

Say What?

Hello.	Buongiorno. *bwon·jor·no*
Goodbye.	Arrivederci. *a·ree·ve·der·chee*
Thank you.	Grazie. m *gra·tsye*
My name is ...	Mi chiamo ... *mee kya·mo...*

Did You Know? ℹ️

- America is named after Amerigo Vespucci, an explorer from Florence.
- Tuscans eat tripe.

Have You Tried?

gelato allo zafferano
saffron ice cream

Regions at a Glance

Florence

Food
Art
Shopping

A Vibrant Culinary Scene

The city's exceptional dining scene ranges from *enoteche* (wine bars) bursting with cured meats and cheeses to no-nonsense trattorias, bustling food markets, modern Tuscan cafes and the only restaurant in Tuscany with three Michelin stars.

Galleries & Museums

The Uffizi is one of the world's most famous art galleries, but it's not the only repository of artistic masterpieces in the city. Churches, chapels and a bevy of lesser-known museums showcase masterpieces galore.

Designers & Artisans

From designer fashion boutiques on chic Via de' Tornabuoni to tiny workshops hidden on backstreets in the traditional artisanal districts of Oltrarno and Santa Croce, the city where Gucci was born is the last word in quality shopping.

p62

Siena & Central Tuscany

Food
Wine
Hill Towns

Sienese Treats

Sample Siena's famous cakes and biscuits, with coffee or dunked in a glass of Vin Santo wine at the end of a meal.

Famous Wines

Tuscan wine hotshots Brunello, Vino Nobile, Chianti Classico and Vernaccia all hail from this rich part of Tuscany, with estates throughout the region opening their atmospheric cellar doors and vine-laced estates to the viticulturally curious for tastings.

Architecture & Views

Explore scenic hill towns such as Montalcino, Montepulciano, Volterra and San Gimignano, where the intact medieval architecture is as impressive as the sweeping panoramic views that reward those who hike to the top.

p137

Southern Tuscany

Food
History
Nature

Local & Seasonal

This is a no-fuss zone when it comes to cuisine. Chefs buy locally, stick to the season and subscribe to the concept of Slow Food. And the results are superb.

Archaeological Sites

The Etruscans certainly left their mark: the countryside of the extraordinary Città del Tufo is littered with their tombs. The Romans didn't shirk their duties here either, as a visit to the archaeological sites of Roselle or Vetulonia confirms.

Untouched Landscapes

Europe's bird species stop here on their migration to North Africa for good reason – huge tracts of pristine landscape boast an impressive range of flora and fauna.

p195

Central Coast & Elba

Food
Beaches
History

Seafood

Livorno does seafood like nowhere else in Tuscany. Feisty locals in this waterside port city are staunchly proud of *cacciucco*, a remarkable seafood stew swimming with at least five types of fish.

Island Paradise

Visit Elba, the palm-tree-clad paradise where Napoleon was banished. This bijou island offers a sensational mix of sunbathing, sea kayaking, snorkelling and swimming.

Etruscan Ruins

Exploring the remains of ancient Etruscan tombs and temples hidden beneath sky-high parasol pines on the Golfo di Baratti's sandy shoreline is an extraordinary experience. Pair it with gentle walking and a picnic lunch for the perfect day.

p217

Northwestern Tuscany

Food
Mountains
Outdoors

Truffles

No single food product is lusted over quite as much as the perfectly perfumed fresh white truffle – hunted in dew-kissed autumn forests around San Miniato and eaten with gusto during truffle season (mid-October to December).

Apuane Alps

Take a drive from the Garfagnana through rugged peaks and richly forested valleys laced with walking trails to witness the majestic marble mountains of the Apuane Alps in their full glory.

Garfagnana

The trio of valleys that forms the Garfagnana region perfectly suits holiday-makers keen on hiking, biking and eating. Trails criss-cross chestnut woods and forests rich in berries and porcini mushrooms.

p247

Eastern Tuscany

Food
Holy Sites
Art

Steak

Come to the Val di Chiana to eat Italy's best *bistecca alla fiorentina*, the succulent, lightly seared piece of locally raised Chianina beef that is Tuscany's signature dish.

Shrines to St Francis

St Francis is closely associated with this part of Tuscany. Born in nearby Assisi, he is said to have received the stigmata at the Santuario della Verna in the wonderfully wild Casentino forest.

Masterpieces

The adage 'quality before quantity' applies here. Follow a trail highlighting the works of Piero della Francesca, but also look out for works by Cimabue, Fra' Angelico, Signorelli, Rosso Fiorentino, the Lorenzettis and the della Robbias.

p294

On the Road

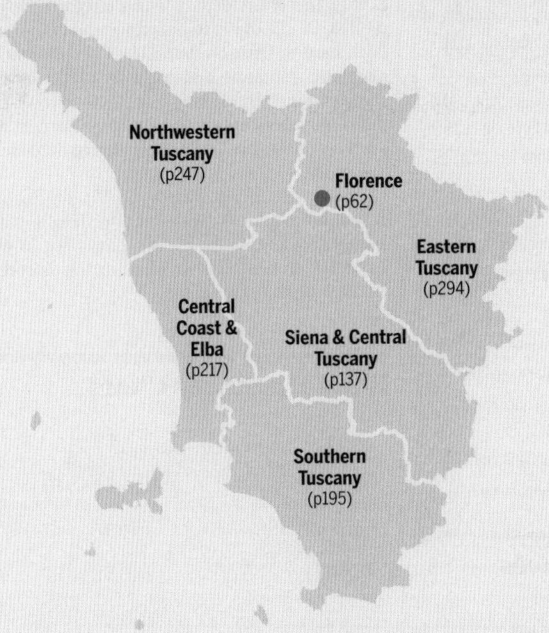

Northwestern
Tuscany
(p247)

Florence
(p62)

Eastern
Tuscany
(p294)

Central
Coast &
Elba
(p217)

Siena & Central
Tuscany
(p137)

Southern
Tuscany
(p195)

Florence

📞 055 / POP 382,250

Includes ➡

History	63
Sights	68
Activities	108
Tours	108
Festivals & Events	110
Sleeping	111
Eating	117
Drinking & Nightlife	123
Entertainment	129
Shopping	129

Best Places to Eat

➡ Essenziale (p122)

➡ Trattoria Mario (p118)

➡ La Leggenda dei Frati (p123)

➡ Il Teatro del Sale (p120)

➡ Il Santo Bevitore (p121)

Best Places to Stay

➡ AdAstra (p116)

➡ SoprArno Suites (p116)

➡ Hotel Scoti (p114)

➡ Academy Hostel (p114)

➡ Student Hotel (p114)

➡ Hotel Davanzati (p111)

Why Go?

Return time and again and you still won't see it all. Stand on a bridge over the Arno river several times in a day and the light, mood and view changes every time. Surprisingly small as it is, this riverside city looms large on the world's 'must-see' list. Cradle of the Renaissance and of tourist masses that flock here to feast on world-class art, Florence (Firenze) is magnetic, romantic and busy. Its urban fabric has hardly changed since the Renaissance, its narrow streets evoke a thousand tales, and its food and wine are so wonderful the tag 'Fiorentina' has become an international label of quality assurance.

Fashion designers parade on Via de' Tornabuoni. Gucci was born here, as was Roberto Cavalli, who, like many a smart Florentine these days, hangs out in wine-rich hills around Florence. After a while in this absorbing city, you might want to do the same.

Road Distances Chart

	Florence	Pisa	Lucca	San Miniato
Pisa	69			
Lucca	61	23		
San Miniato	37	47	70	
Siena	51	87	30	77

History

Florence's history stretches back to the time of the Etruscans, who based themselves in Fiesole. Julius Caesar founded the Roman colony of Florentia around 59 BC, making it a strategic garrison on the narrowest crossing of the Arno in order to control the Via Flaminia that linked Rome to northern Italy and Gaul.

After the collapse of the Roman Empire, Florence fell to invading Goths, followed by Lombards and Franks. The year AD 1000 marked a crucial turning point in the city's fortunes, when Margrave Ugo of Tuscany moved his capital from Lucca to Florence. In 1110 Florence became a free *comune* (city-state) and by 1138 it was ruled by 12 consuls, assisted by the Consiglio di Cento (Council of One Hundred), whose members were drawn mainly from the prosperous merchant class. Agitation between differing factions in the city led to the appointment in 1207 of a foreign head of state called the *podestà*, aloof in principle from the plotting and wheeler-dealing of local cliques and alliances.

Medieval Florence was a wealthy, dynamic *comune,* one of Europe's leading financial, banking and cultural centres, and a major player in the international wool, silk and leather trades. The sizeable population of moneyed merchants and artisans began forming guilds and patronising the growing number of artists, who found lucrative commissions in this burgeoning city.

Struggles between the pro-papal Guelfi (Guelphs) and the pro–Holy Roman Empire Ghibellini (Ghibellines) started in the mid-13th century, with power yo-yoing between the two for almost a century. Into this fractious atmosphere were born revolutionary artist Giotto and outspoken poet Dante Alighieri (a Guelph). After the Guelphs split into two factions, the Neri (Blacks) and Bianchi (Whites), Dante went with the Bianchi – the wrong side – and was expelled from his beloved city in 1302, never to return.

In 1348 the Black Death almost halved he city's population. The history of Medici Florence began in 1434, when Cosimo the Elder (Cosimo de' Medici), a patron of the arts, assumed power. His eye for talent and tact in dealing with artists saw Alberti, Brunelleschi, Luca della Robbia, Fra' Angelico, Donatello and Fra' Filippo Lippi flourish.

Under the rule of Cosimo's popular and cultured grandson, Lorenzo Il Magnifico (1469–92), Florence became the epicentre of the Renaissance ('Rebirth'), with artists such as Michelangelo, Botticelli and Domenico Ghirlandaio at work. Lorenzo's court, filled with Humanists (a school of thought begun in Florence in the late 14th century that affirmed the dignity and potential of humanity and embraced Latin and Greek literary texts), fostered a flowering of art, music and poetry, turning Florence into Italy's cultural capital.

Florence's golden age effectively died with Lorenzo in 1492. Just before his death, the Medici bank had failed and two years later the Medici were driven out of Florence. In a reaction against the splendour and excess of the Medici court, the city fell under the control of Girolamo Savonarola, a Dominican monk who led a stern, puritanical republic. In 1497 the likes of Botticelli gladly consigned their 'immoral' works and finery to the flames of the infamous 'Bonfire of the Vanities'. The following year Savonarola fell from public favour and was burned as a heretic.

The pro-French leanings of the subsequent republican government brought it into conflict with the pope and his Spanish allies. In 1512 a Spanish force defeated Florence and the Medici were reinstated. Their tyrannical rule endeared them to few and when Rome, ruled by the Medici pope Clement VII, fell to the emperor Charles V in 1527, the Florentines took advantage of this low point in the Medici fortunes to kick the family out again. Two years later though, imperial and papal forces besieged Florence, forcing the city to accept Lorenzo's great-grandson, Alessandro de' Medici, a ruthless politician whom Charles made Duke of Florence. Medici rule continued for another 200 years, during which time they gained control of all of Tuscany, though after the reign of Cosimo I (1537–74), Florence drifted into steep decline.

The last male Medici, Gian Gastone, died in 1737, after which his sister, Anna Maria, signed the grand duchy of Tuscany over to the House of Habsburg-Lorraine (at the time effectively under Austrian control). This situation remained unchanged, apart from a brief interruption under Napoleon from 1799 to 1814, until the duchy was incorporated into the Kingdom of Italy in 1860. Florence briefly became the national capital in 1865, but Rome assumed the mantle permanently in 1871.

Florence was badly damaged during WWII by the retreating Germans, who blew up all of its bridges except the Ponte Vecchio. Devastating floods ravaged the city in 1966, causing inestimable damage to its buildings and artworks. Since 1997, amid a fair amount of controversy, the Uffizi Gallery has been engaged in its biggest-ever expansion – a €65-million investment project, dubbed the 'New Uffizi project'. Its end date remains a mystery.

Florence Highlights

❶ Galleria degli Uffizi (p70) Admiring the world's finest collection of Renaissance paintings in this world-class gallery.

❷ Duomo (p76) Climbing inside Brunelleschi's spectacular dome, superstar of the city skyline and crowning glory of Florence's Duomo.

❸ Museo di San Marco (p92) Contemplating the artistic genius of Fra' Angelico with Renaissance frescoes inside this unsung monastery museum.

❹ Piazzale Michelangelo (p104) Hiking uphill to meet *David*'s lookalike and enjoy the most magnificent sunset show and city panorama.

❺ Museo delle Cappelle Medicee (p87) Admiring hauntingly beautiful tomb sculptures by Michelangelo in the burial place of the Medici dynasty.

❻ Cafe Culture (p126) Dipping into Florentine cafe culture at a timeless historic cafe, on-trend coffee roastery or backstreet address in artisanal Oltrarno.

❼ Fiesole (p134) Escaping the city heat for a mooch between olive groves and Roman ruins in this hilltop retreat; cycling home to Florence at sunset with a local guide.

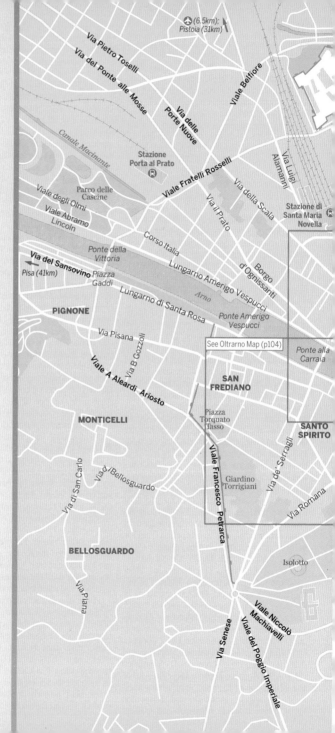

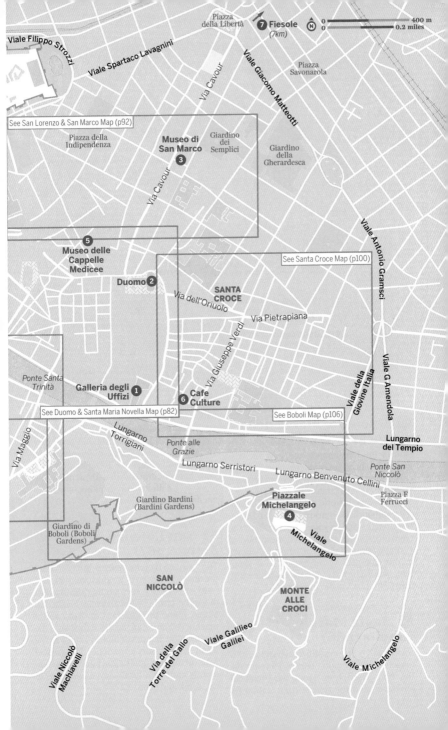

Viale Filippo Strozzi

Viale Spartaco Lavagnini

Piazza della Libertà

7 Fiesole (7km)

N

0   400 m
0   0.2 miles

Via Cavour

Viale Giacomo Matteotti

Piazza Savonarola

See San Lorenzo & San Marco Map (p92)

Piazza della Indipendenza

Museo di San Marco
3

Giardino dei Semplici

Giardino della Gherardesca

Via Cavour

Viale Antonio Gramsci

5
Museo delle Cappelle Medicee

Duomo 2

Via dell'Oriuolo

SANTA CROCE

See Santa Croce Map (p100)

Via Pietrapiana

Via Giuseppe Verdi

Viale della Giovine Italia

Viale G Amendola

Ponte Santa Trinità

Galleria degli Uffizi 1

6 Cafe Culture

See Duomo & Santa Maria Novella Map (p82)

See Boboli Map (p106)

Lungarno del Tempio

Via Maggio

Lungarno Torrigiani

Ponte alle Grazie

Lungarno Serristori

Lungarno Benvenuto Cellini

Ponte San Niccolò

Piazza F Ferrucci

Giardino Bardini (Bardini Gardens)

Piazzale Michelangelo
4

Giardino di Boboli (Boboli Gardens)

Viale Michelangelo

SAN NICCOLÒ

MONTE ALLE CROCI

Viale Niccolò Machiavelli

Via della Torre del Gallo

Viale Galileo Galilei

Viale Michelangelo

❶ Duomo & Piazza della Signoria (p68)

Hub of the Renaissance and now the cosmopolitan heart of modern Florence, the enchanting maze of narrow streets between the *duomo* and Piazza della Signoria packs one almighty historic and cultural punch. A neighbourhood harking back to Dante, the Romans and beyond, this is where the city's blockbuster sights – and most tourists – can be found. Cafe life is naturally vibrant in this chic neck of the woods, as is shopping, which climaxes with the designer strip, uberfashionist Via de' Tornabuoni.

❷ Santa Maria Novella (p86)

Anchored by its magnificent basilica, this ancient and intriguing part of Florence defies easy description. From the rough-cut streets around the central train station it's only a short walk to the busy social scene around increasingly gentrified Piazza di Santa Maria Novella and the hip boutiques on the atmosphere-laden, old-world 'backstreets' west of Via de' Tornabuoni. Shopping here, intermingled with a multitude of attractive dining and drinking options, is among the best in Florence.

❸ San Lorenzo & San Marco (p87)

This part of the city fuses a gutsy market precinct – a covered produce market and noisy street stalls surrounding the Basilica di San Lorenzo – with capacious Piazza San Marco, home to Florence University and a much-loved museum. Between the two is the world's most famous sculpture, *David*. The result is a sensory experience jam-packed with urban grit, uplifting art and some fabulously authentic, locally loved addresses to eat, drink and shop.

taking their neighbourhood's reinvention as hipster central – epicentre of the city's bar and club scene – with remarkable aplomb.

❺ Oltrarno (p103)

Literally the 'other side of the Arno', this achingly hip neighbourhood is traditionally home to Florence's artisans and its old-world, bohemian streets are sprinkled with *botteghe* (workshops), independent boutiques and hybrid forms of both. It embraces the area south of the river and west of Ponte Vecchio; its backbone is Borgo San Jacopo, clad with shops and a twinset of 12th-century towers, Torre dei Marsili and Torre de' Belfredelli. Cuisine – prepared using artisanal ingredients, of course – is a real strength here, with bags of fashionable restaurants and drinks to entice.

❻ Boboli & San Miniato al Monte (p104)

When museum and/or tourist overload strikes – a common occurrence in this culturally resplendent city – consider stretching your legs amid some urban greenery in this soul-soothing eastern neighbourhood on the Oltrarno. Fronted by the grandiose palace of Palazzo Pitti, jam-packed with museums, Boboli's magnificent tier of palaces, villas and gardens climbs uphill to San Miniato, a hilltop area famously crowned by a copy of Michelangelo's *David* and one of the city's oldest and most beautiful churches. Views, predictably, are sweeping and soul-soaring.

❹ Santa Croce (p98)

Despite being only a hop, skip and jump from the city's major museums, most of this ancient part of Florence is far removed from the tourist maelstrom. The streets behind main sight Basilica di Santa Croce are home to plenty of locals, all of whom seem to be

👁 Sights

Florence's wealth of museums and galleries house many of the world's most exquisite examples of Renaissance art, and its architecture is unrivalled. Yet don't feel pressured to see everything: combine your personal pick of sights with ample meandering through the city's warren of narrow streets broken by cafe and *enoteca* (wine bar) stops.

Churches enforce a strict dress code for visitors: no shorts, sleeveless shirts or plunging necklines. Photography with no flash is allowed in museums, but leave the selfie stick at home – they are officially forbidden.

👁 Duomo & Piazza della Signoria

⭐ **Museo di Palazzo Davanzati**   MUSEUM
(Map p82; 📞 055 064 94 60; www.bargello musei.beniculturali.it; Via Porta Rossa 13; adult/reduced €6/3; ⏱ 8.15am-2pm Mon-Fri, 1.15-7pm

Sat & Sun) Home to the wealthy Davanzati merchant family from 1578, this 14th-century *palazzo* (mansion) with a wonderful central loggia gives you a view into precisely how Florentine nobles lived in the 16th century. Spot the carved faces of the original owners on the pillars in the inner courtyard, and don't miss the 1st-floor Sala Madornale (Reception Room) with its painted wooden ceiling, exotic Sala dei Pappagalli (Parrot Room) and Camera dei Pavoni (Peacock Bedroom).

The 2nd and 3rd floors of the palace can only be visited by guided tours that run at 10am, 11am and noon on weekdays and at 3pm, 4pm and 5pm during weekends; reservations (by telephone or online) are obligatory. Note the windows in the beautiful Camera delle Impannate are not made from glass – a luxury only nobles could afford in Renaissance Florence – but from waxed cloth panels tacked to the wooden

THREE PERFECT DAYS IN FLORENCE

Day One

Journey into the Renaissance with mind-blowing 15th- and 16th-century art at the Uffizi (p70), then lunch at 'Ino (p124). Meander south to the river and cross Ponte Vecchio (p103) to the 'other bank of the Arno'. Explore Basilica di Santo Spirito (p104) and magnificent Cappella Brancacci (p103). As the sun starts to sink, hike uphill to Piazzale Michelangelo (p104) for swoon-worthy views of the city, followed by a wine-fuelled *aperitivo* at Le Volpi e l'Uva (p129). After dinner at Essenziale (p122), hit fashionable, bar-busy San Frediano for craft cocktails at Mad Souls & Spirits (p127). While away the wee hours at Rasputin (p128), the city's secret speakeasy.

Day Two

Prepare yourself for a sensational morning of sacred art and architecture on Piazza del Duomo: visit the cathedral (p76) then climb up its campanile (p78) and duck into its baptistry (p78). End on a giddy high with a hike up into the frescoed dome of Brunelleschi's cupola (p77), and complete the story with a tour of the insightful Grande Museo del Duomo (p79). Window shop on Via de' Tornabuoni, with a break for a cheeky truffle *panino* at Procacci (p130). Travel west to the marvellous Basilica di Santa Maria Novella (p88). Enjoy dinner at Il Santo Bevitore (p121), followed by a scenic riverside walk to Santarosa Bistrot (p127) for a night of dancing to spaghetti jazz and quaffing cocktails beneath the stars.

Day Three

Begin the day with a glorious 360-degree admiration of the world's most famous naked man, Michelangelo's original *David*, at the Galleria dell'Accademia (p90). Next up in this fascinating 'hood is the soulfully uplifting Museo di San Marco (p92), after which a warm-from-the-oven chunk of *schiacciata* (Tuscan flatbread) spiked with salt and rosemary perhaps beckons at the Pugi (p119) bakery across the square. Saunter south to Palazzo Vecchio (p80) in time to visit the fortress palace and catch sunset views from the top of its striking Torre d'Arnolfo – a Florentine landmark. If you're dining at Il Teatro del Sale (p120), sit back and enjoy the theatre show. Otherwise explore the happening district of Santa Croce by night.

ⓘ DISCOUNT CARDS

Firenzecard (www.firenzecard.it; €85) Valid for 72 hours and covering admission to 70-plus museums, villas and gardens in Florence, as well as unlimited use of public transport and free wi-fi across the city. To add on unlimited public transport, pay an additional €7 for a Firenzecard+ add-on. The card's biggest advantage is reducing queueing time in high season – museums have a separate queue for card-holders. The downside of the Firenzecard is it only allows one admission per museum, plus you need to visit an awful lot of museums to justify the cost. Buy the card online (collect it on arrival in Florence or download the Firenzecard App and store it digitally) or in Florence at tourist offices or the ticketing desks of the Uffizi (Gate 2), Palazzo Pitti, Palazzo Vecchio, Museo del Bargello, Cappella Brancacci, Museo di Santa Maria Novella, Museo Novecento and Giardini Bardini. If you're an EU citizen, your card also covers family members aged under 18 travelling with you.

Friends of the Uffizi Card If you prefer to split your Uffizi forays into a couple of visits and/or you're not from the EU and are travelling with kids, the annual Friends of the Uffizi Card (adult/reduced/family of four €70/40/100) is a good deal. Valid for a calendar year (expiring 31 December), it covers admission to 22 Florence museums (including Galleria dell'Accademia, Museo del Bargello and Palazzo Pitti) and allows return visits. Have your passport on you as proof of ID to show at each museum with your card. Buy online at www.amicidegliuffizi.it or from the Amici degli Uffizi Welcome Desk next to Gate 2 at the Uffizi.

frame. The kitchen is placed on the top floor, to ensure living rooms remained cool and free of unsavoury cooking odours and possible fires.

Palazzo Strozzi   GALLERY
(Map p82; ☑ 055 264 51 55; www.palazzostrozzi.org; Piazza degli Strozzi; exhibition adult/reduced €12/4; ☺10am-8pm Fri-Wed, to 11pm Thu; ⓐ) This 15th-century Renaissance mansion was built for wealthy merchant Filippo Strozzi, one of the Medici's major political and commercial rivals. Today it hosts exciting art exhibitions spanning all periods and genres – its contemporary art events are particularly sensational. There's always a buzz about the place, with fashionable Florentines milling around the palace's elegant interior courtyard and lingering over drinks at Strozzi Caffè (p124); during major exhibitions, grab a coffee to take away from here to enjoy while waiting in line.

Art workshops, tours and other activities aimed squarely at families make the gallery a firm favourite with everyone. If you plan to visit the Museo dell'Opera del Duomo (p79) the same day, buy a combination ticket (adult/reduced €16/6).

Via de' Tornabuoni   LANDMARK
(Map p82) Renaissance palaces and Italian fashion houses border Via de' Tornabuoni, the city's most expensive shopping strip. Named after a Florentine noble family (which died out in the 17th century), it is referred to as the 'Salotto di Firenze' (Florence's Drawing Room). At its northern end is Palazzo Antinori (Map p82; Piazza degli Antinori 3), owned by the aristocratic Antinori family (known for wine production) since 1506. Opposite, huge stone steps lead up to 17th-century Chiesa dei Santi Michele e Gaetano (Map p82; ☺7.30am-7.30pm Tue-Sat, 8am-8pm Sun, 2-7pm Mon).

Chiesa e Museo di Orsanmichele   CHURCH
(Map p82; Via dell'Arte della Lana; ☺church 10am-4.50pm daily, closed Mon Aug, museum 10am-4.50pm Mon, 10am-12.30pm Sat) **FREE** This unusual and inspirational church, with a Gothic tabernacle by Andrea Orcagna, was created when the arcades of an old grain market (1290) were walled in and two storeys added during the 14th century. Its exterior is decorated with niches and tabernacles bearing statues representing the patron saints of Florence's many guilds, commissioned in the 15th and 16th centuries after the *signoria* (city government) ordered the guilds to finance the church's decoration.

These statues represent the work of some of the greatest Renaissance artists. Only copies adorn the building's exterior today, but all the originals except one are beautifully displayed in the church's little-known, light and airy museum, two floors above the church.

TOP SIGHT
GALLERIA DEGLI UFFIZI

Home to the world's greatest collection of Italian Renaissance art, Florence's premier gallery occupies the vast U-shaped Palazzo degli Uffizi. The world-famous collection, displayed in chronological order, spans the gamut of art history from ancient Greek sculpture to 18th-century Venetian paintings. But its core is the Renaissance collection – a morning can be spent enjoying its unmatched collection of Botticellis alone.

The Nuovo Uffizi

As part of a gargantuan €65-million refurbishment, the Uffizi has been under constant renovation since 1995, with exhibition space doubling and artworks reorganised to fill – at the last count – some 100 rooms across two floors. The contemporary loggia, designed by Japanese architect Arato Isazaki in 1998 for the gallery's exit, appears something of a pipe dream these days: future project work will focus more on areas earmarked for temporary exhibitions and conferences. When planning a visit, check on the museum website which rooms are closed that day.

Tuscan 13th-Century Art

Arriving in the Primo Corridoio (First Corridor) on the 2nd floor, the first room to the left of the staircase (Room 2) is designed like a medieval chapel to reflect its fabulous contents: three large altarpieces from Florentine churches by Tuscan masters Duccio di Buoninsegna, Cimabue and Giotto. They show the transition from Gothic to nascent Renaissance style.

DON'T MISS

➡ Sala del Botticelli (2nd Floor, Rooms 10 to 14)

➡ Leonardo da Vinci (2nd Floor, Room 35)

➡ Michelangelo (2nd Floor, Room 41)

PRACTICALITIES

➡ Uffizi Gallery

➡ Map p82

➡ ☎ 055 29 48 83

➡ www.uffizi.it

➡ Piazzale degli Uffizi 6

➡ adult/reduced Mar-Oct €20/10, Nov-Feb €12/6

➡ ⏱ 8.15am-6.50pm Tue-Sun

Sienese 14th-Century Art

The highlight in Room 3 is Simone Martini's shimmering *Annunciazione* (1333), painted with Lippo Memmi and setting the Madonna in a sea of gold. Also of note is *Madonna con il bambino in trono e angeli* (Madonna with Child and Saints; 1340) by Pietro Lorenzetti, which demonstrates a realism similar to Giotto's; unfortunately, both Pietro and his artistic brother Ambrogio died of the plague in Siena in 1348.

Renaissance Pioneers

Perspective was a hallmark of the early-15th-century Florentine school (Room 8) that launched the Renaissance. One panel from Paolo Uccello's striking *Battle of San Romano* (1436–40), which celebrates Florence's victory over Siena in 1432, shows the artist's efforts to create perspective with amusing effect as he directs the lances, horses and soldiers to a central disappearing point. In the same room, don't miss the exquisite *Madonna con bambino e due angeli* (Madonna and Child with Two Angels; 1460–65) by Fra' Filippo Lippi, a Carmelite monk who had an unfortunate soft spot for earthly pleasures and scandalously married a nun from Prato. This work clearly influenced his pupil, Sandro Botticelli.

Duke & Duchess of Urbino

In the same room (Room 8), revel in the realism of Piero della Francesca's 1465 warts-and-all portraits of the Duke and Duchess of Urbino. The crooked-nosed duke lost his right eye in a jousting accident, hence the focus on his left side only, while the duchess is deathly stone-white to convey the fact that the portrait was painted posthumously.

Botticelli

Learn about the seven cardinal and theological values of 15th-century Florence with the huge painting *The Seven Virtues* by brothers Antonio and Piero del Pollaiolo in Room 9, commissioned for the merchant's tribunal in Piazza della Signoria. The only canvas in the series not to be painted by the Pollaiolos is *Fortitude* (1470), the first documented work by Botticelli.

The spectacular Sala del Botticelli, numbered 10 to 14 but really two light and graceful rooms, is always packed. Of the many Botticelli works displayed in the Uffizi, his iconic *La nascita di Venere* (The Birth of Venus; c 1485), *Primavera* (Spring; c 1482) and *Madonna del Magnificat* (Madonna of the Magnificat; 1483) are the best-known by the Renaissance master known for his ethereal figures. Take time to study the lesser known *Annunciazione* (Annunciation), a 6m-wide fresco painted by Botticelli in 1481 for the San Martino hospital in Florence.

FLORENCE GALLERIA DEGLI UFFIZI

PALAZZO DEGLI UFFIZI

Cosimo I de' Medici commissioned Vasari to build the huge U-shaped Palazzo degli Uffizi in 1560 as a government office building (*uffizi* means 'offices'). Following Vasari's death in 1564, architects Alfonso Parigi and Bernado Buontalenti took over, with Buontalenti modifying the upper floor to house the artworks keenly collected by Cosimo I's son, Francesco I. In 1580 the building was complete. When the last Medici died in 1743, the family's enormous private art collection was bequeathed to Florence on the strict proviso that it never leave the city.

For a fast exit after admiring the 2nd-floor Renaissance stars, take the 'quick exit' route signposted next to the cafe.

THE CLOSED DOOR

Spot the closed door next to Room 25 leading to the Medici's Corridoio Vasariano (p86), a 1km-long covered passageway connecting Palazzo Vecchio (p80) with the Uffizi and Palazzo Pitti (p105). It was designed by Vasari in 1565 to allow the Medicis to wander between palaces in privacy and comfort.

Northern Influences

In the next room (Room 15) don't miss the single work by Botticelli: *Flagellazione di Cristo* (Flagellation of Christ; 1505–10), part of a cycle of paintings illustrating the life of Christ; it was one of Botticelli's last works before his death from illness and old age in 1510.

Room 15 otherwise explores the clear influence northern European artists had on Florentine artists during the Renaissance with works by Flemish painter Hugo van der Goes (1430–82). His monumental *Portinari Altarpiece* (1476–78), a triptych 2.5m tall and 3m wide representing the Adoration of the Shepherds, arrived in Florence in 1483 and was displayed in the church inside Florence's Santa Maria Novella hospital. Van der Goes painted it for Tommasso Portinari, director of the Medici bank in Bruges – admire his portrait and that of his wife and their three children on the side panels.

The Tribune

The Medici clan stashed away their most precious art in this octagonal-shaped treasure trove (Room 18), created by Francesco I between 1581 and 1586. Designed to amaze, it features a small collection of classical statues and paintings on its upholstered silk walls and 6000 crimson-varnished mother-of-pearl shells encrusting the domed ceiling.

Michelangelo & Raphael

Room 34, with sage-green painted walls, displays sculptures from classical antiquity – of great influence on the young Michelangelo – and from the Medici-owned sculpture garden in San Marco where Michelangelo studied classical sculpture as an apprentice from the age of 13.

Michelangelo's dazzling *Doni Tondo,* a depiction of the Holy Family, hangs in Room 41. The composition is unusual and the colours as vibrant as when they were first applied in 1504–06. It was painted for wealthy Florentine merchant Agnolo Doni (who hung it above his bed) and bought by the Medici for Palazzo Pitti in 1594.

The other High Renaissance masterpiece in this room is Raphael's *Madonna col Bambino e San Giovanni* (Madonna with Child and St John; 1505–06), otherwise known as Madonna of the Goldfinch after the red-feathered goldfinch cradled in the chubby hands of a baby John the Baptist. Raphael painted it during his four-year sojourn in Florence and it has been in the Uffizi since 1704.

Medici Portraits

Rooms 64 and 65 showcase Agnolo Bronzino (1503–72), who worked as official portrait artist at the court of Cosimo I from 1539 until 1555 (when he was replaced by Vasari). His 1545 portraits of the Grand Duchess Eleonora of Toleto and her son Giovanni together, and the 18-month-old Giovanni alone holding a goldfinch – symbolising his calling into the church – are considered masterpieces of 16th-century European portraiture. Giovanni was elected a cardinal in 1560 but died of malaria two years later.

Leonardo Da Vinci

Three early Florentine works by Leonardo da Vinci are shown off to perfection in Room 35. His *Annunciazione* (Annunciation; 1472) was deliberately painted to be admired not face on (from where Mary's arm appears too long, her face too light and the angle of buildings not quite right), but rather from the lower right-hand side of the painting. *Adoration of the Magi* (1481–82), originally commissioned for the altar of the monastery of San Donato a Scopeto near Florence and never

Ceiling art

CEILING ART

Take time to study the make-believe grotesque monsters and unexpected burlesques (spot the arrow-shooting satyr outside Room 15) waltzing across the eastern corridor's fabulous frescoed ceiling. Admire more compelling art in Rooms 19 to 23, whose ornate vaulted ceilings were frescoed in the 16th and 17th centuries depicting military objects and allegories, as well as illustrations of historical battles and traditional festivals that took place on Florence's many beautiful and distinctive piazzas.

Head to the Uffizi's rooftop cafe for coffee, fresh air and fabulous views.

finished, is typical of Florentine figurative painting in the 15th century. *Battesimo di Cristo* (Baptism of Christ; 1475) depicts John the Baptist baptising a very naturalistic Christ on the banks of the Jordan.

Caravaggio

Rooms 96 and 97 are filled with paintings by Caravaggio, deemed vulgar at the time for his direct interpretation of reality. The *Head of Medusa* (1598–99), commissioned for a ceremonial shield, is supposedly a self-portrait of the young artist, who later died at the age of 39. The biblical drama of an angel steadying the hand of Abraham as he holds a knife to his son Isaac's throat in Caravaggio's *Sacrifice of Isaac* (1601–02) is glorious in its intensity.

TICKETING TIME-SLOTS

The gallery is road-testing a new time-slot reservation system aimed at reducing queue time. Visitors wanting to buy a same-day ticket can simply print off a voucher with QR code and admission time from a 'digital kiosk' beneath the arches outside the gallery; they then return at the allotted time to purchase their ticket and enter the Uffizi. This time-slot reservation system should be rolled out by 2020.

The Uffizi

JOURNEY INTO THE RENAISSANCE

Navigating the Uffizi's chronologically-ordered art collection is straightforward enough: knowing which of the 1500-odd masterpieces to view before gallery fatigue strikes is not. Swap your bag (travel light) for floor plan and audioguide on the ground floor, then meet 16th-century Tuscany head-on with a walk up the *palazzo's* magnificent bust-lined staircase (skip the lift – the Uffizi is as much about masterly architecture as art).

Allow four hours for this journey into the High Renaissance. At the top of the staircase, on the 2nd floor, show your ticket, turn left and pause to admire the full length of the first corridor sweeping south towards the Arno river. Then duck left into room 2 to witness first steps in Tuscan art – shimmering altarpieces by ❶ **Giotto** et al. Journey through medieval art to room 8 and ❷ **Piero della Francesca's** impossibly famous portrait. After Renaissance heavyweight ❸ **Botticelli** (don't miss his solitary work hidden in Room 15), duck out into the corridor to break beneath playful ❹ **ceiling art**. Stroll past the Tribuna (potential detour) and enjoy the daylight streaming in through the vast windows and panorama of the ❺ **riverside second corridor**. Lap up soul-stirring views of the Arno, crossed by Ponte Vecchio and its echo of four bridges drifting towards the Apuane Alps on the horizon. Then saunter into the third corridor, pausing between rooms 25 and 34 to ponder the entrance to the enigmatic Vasari Corridor. Give a nod to the teenage Michelangelo in the ❻ **San Marco sculpture garden**, enjoy a brilliant encounter with ❼ **Leonardo da Vinci**, and end on a High Renaissance high with ❽ **Michelangelo and Raphael**.

Giotto's Madonna
Room 2
Draw breath at the shy blush and curvaceous breast of Giotto's humanised Madonna and Child (*Maestà di Ognissanti*; 1306–1310) – so feminine compared with those of Duccio and Cimabue painted just 25 years before.

Portraits of the Duke & Duchess of Urbino
Room 8
Revel in realism's voyage with these uncompromising, warts-and-all portraits (1472–75) by Piero della Francesca. No larger than A3 size, they originally slotted into a portable, hinged frame that folded like a book.

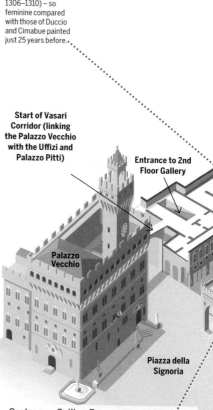

Start of Vasari Corridor (linking the Palazzo Vecchio with the Uffizi and Palazzo Pitti)

Entrance to 2nd Floor Gallery

Palazzo Vecchio

Piazza della Signoria

Grotesque Ceiling Frescoes
First Corridor
Take time to study the make-believe monsters and most unexpected of burlesques (spot the arrow-shooting satyr outside room 15) waltzing across this eastern corridor's fabulous frescoed ceiling (1581).

ALIZADA STUDIOS/SHUTTERSTOCK ©

The Genius of Botticelli
Room 10–14

Botticelli's tondo twinset, *Madonna of the Pomegranate* (c 1487) and *Madonna of the Magnificat* (c 1483) hang in heavy gilt frames. Both are round, a sure sign during the Renaissance that they were commissioned for a private home rather than church.

View of the Arno

Indulge in intoxicating city views from this short glassed-in corridor – an architectural masterpiece. Near the top of the hill, spot one of 73 outer towers built to defend Florence and its 15 city gates below.

Second Corridor

First Corridor

Tribuna

Arno River

5

6

7

Original entrance to Vasari Corridor

2

3

4

1

8

San Marco sculpture garden
Room 34

A 13-year-old Michelangelo studied classical sculpture as an apprentice at Lorenzo de Medici's sculpture school in San Marco. Admire relief-sculpted sarcophagi that had such a massive influence on this artist.

Leonardo da Vinci
Room 41

Futuristic climate-controlling, anti-glare, anti-terrorist glass cases protect three early masterpieces by Leonardo da Vinci, including *Adoration of the Magi*, still unfinished when da Vinci left Florence for Milan in 1482 and a Uffizi treasure since 1670.

Stairs by cafe to 1st Floor Gallery and Ground Floor 'Quick Exit'

Third Corridor

Doni Tondo
Room 41

The creator of *David*, Michelangelo, was essentially a sculptor and no painting expresses this better than *Doni Tondo* (1506–08). Mary's muscular arms against a backdrop of curvaceous nudes are practically 3D in their shapeliness.

Tribuna

No room in the Uffizi is so tiny or so exquisite. It was created in 1851 as a 'treasure chest' for Grand Duke Francesco and in the days of the Grand Tour, the Medici Venus here was a tour highlight.

MATTER OF FACT

The Uffizi collection spans the 13th to 18th centuries, but its 15th- and 16th-century Renaissance works are second to none.

VALUE LUNCHBOX

Try the Uffizi rooftop cafe or – better value – gourmet *panini* at 'Ino (www.ino-firenze.com; Via dei Georgofili 3-7r).

NINOPAVISIC/SHUTTERSTOCK ©

TOP SIGHT
DUOMO

Properly titled **Cattedrale di Santa Maria del Fiore** (Cathedral of St Mary of the Flower), but known as the *duomo* (cathedral), this is Florence's iconic landmark. Designed by Sienese architect Arnolfo di Cambio, construction began in 1296 and took almost 150 years. The result – with Brunelleschi's distinctive red-tiled cupola, graceful *campanile* (bell tower) and pink, white and green marble facade – is breathtaking.

Facade

The neo-Gothic facade was designed in the 19th century by architect Emilio de Fabris to replace the uncompleted original. The oldest and most clearly Gothic part of the structure is its south flank, pierced by the Porta dei Canonici (Canons' Door), a mid-14th-century High Gothic creation (you enter here to climb to the dome).

Interior

After taking in the incredibly richly adorned facade as best as one can, the spartan nature of the *duomo's* vast interior – 155m long and 90m wide – comes as something of a visual relief. Most of its artistic treasures have been removed and those that remain are unexpectedly secular, reflecting the fact that the *duomo* was built with public funds as a *chiesa di stato* (state church).

Down the left aisle two immense frescoes of equestrian statues portray two *condottieri* (mercenaries) – on the left Niccolò da Tolentino by Andrea del Castagno (1456), and

DON'T MISS

➡ Climbing inside Brunelleschi's cupola

➡ City view from atop the *campanile*

➡ Sala del Paradiso, Museo dell'Opera del Duomo

➡ Michelangelo's *La Pietà*

PRACTICALITIES

➡ Cattedrale di Santa Maria del Fiore

➡ Map p82

➡ ☏ 055 230 28 85

➡ www.museumflorence.com

➡ Piazza del Duomo

➡ ⊙ 10am-5pm Mon-Wed & Fri, to 4.30pm Thu & Sat, 1.30-4.45pm Sun

on the right Sir John Hawkwood (who fought in the service of Florence in the 14th century) by Paolo Uccello (1436). In the same aisle, *La Commedia illumina Firenze* (1465) by Domenico di Michelino depicts poet Dante Alighieri surrounded by the three afterlife worlds he describes in the *Divine Comedy*: purgatory is behind him, his right hand points towards hell, and the city of Florence is paradise.

Mass Sacristy

Between the left (north) arm of the transept and the apse is the Sagrestia delle Messe (Mass Sacristy), accessible only by guided tour. All four walls are panelled in a marvel of inlaid wood carved by Benedetto and Giuliano da Maiano between 1436 and 1468. The fine bronze doors were executed by Luca della Robbia – his only known work in the material. Above the doorway is his glazed terracotta *Resurrezione* (Resurrection).

Crypt of Santa Reparata

Excavated remains of the very first church that stood on this site, the 5th-century Chiesa di Santa Reparata, can be admired in the *duomo*'s Cripta Santa Reparata (Map p82; ⊘10am-5pm Mon-Wed & Fri, to 4.30pm Thu & Sat) – access it from the staircase, not far from the main entrance, in the south aisle. Down below, secreted among the ancient stones, are the cathedral gift shop, remains of Roman dwellings, marble floor mosaics (for early Christians the peacock was a symbol of eternal life) and the tomb of 15th-century architect Filippo Brunelleschi.

Cupola

When Michelangelo went to work on St Peter's in Rome, he reportedly said, 'I go to build a greater dome, but not a fairer one', referring to the huge but graceful terracotta-brick dome (Brunelleschi's Dome; Map p82; ⊘8.30am-7pm Mon-Fri, to 5pm Sat, 1-4pm Sun) atop Florence's *duomo*. It was constructed between 1420 and 1436 to a design by Filippo Brunelleschi and is a highlight of any visit to Florence. Its sheer scale alone is breathtaking: 45m wide and 90m high (116m with the crowning lantern).

One of the finest masterpieces of the Renaissance, the cupola is a feat of engineering and one that cannot be fully appreciated without climbing its 463 interior stone steps. Taking his inspiration from Rome's Pantheon, Brunelleschi arrived at an innovative engineering solution – a distinctive octagonal shape of inner and outer concentric domes rests on the drum of the cathedral rather than the roof itself, allowing artisans to build from the ground up without needing a wooden support frame. Over four million bricks

TICKETS

One ticket covers all the sights and is valid for 72 hours (one visit per sight; adult/reduced €18/3); purchase at www.museumflorence.com or at the Duomo ticket office (Piazza San Giovanni 7; ⊘8.15am-6.45pm), opposite the baptistry entrance.

Dress code is strict: no shorts, miniskirts or sleeveless tops.

A MATHEMATICAL WHIZZ

Architect, mathematician, engineer and sculptor, Filippo Brunelleschi (1377–1446) spent an incredible 27 years working on the dome of Florence's *duomo*. Starting work in 1419, his mathematical brain and talent for devising innovative engineering solutions enabled him to do what many Florentines had thought impossible: deliver the largest dome to be built in Italy since antiquity.

were used in the construction, all of them laid in consecutive rings in horizontal courses using a vertical herringbone pattern.

The Climb

The climb up the spiral staircase is relatively steep, and should not be attempted if you are claustrophobic. Make sure to pause when you reach the balustrade at the base of the dome, which gives an aerial view of the octagonal coro (choir) of the cathedral below and the seven round stained-glass windows (by Donatello, Andrea del Castagno, Paolo Uccello and Lorenzo Ghiberti) that pierce the octagonal drum.

As you climb, snapshots of Florence can be spied through small windows. The final leg – a straight, somewhat hazardous flight up the curve of the inner dome – rewards with an unforgettable 360-degree panorama of one of Europe's most beautiful cities.

The Last Judgement

Don't forget to look upwards as you mount the stairs. Giorgio Vasari and Federico Zuccari's late-16th-century *Giudizio universale* (1572–79) fresco decorating the 4500-sq-metre surface of the cupola's inner dome is one of the world's largest paintings. Look for a spent Mother Nature with wrinkled breasts and the four seasons asleep at her feet. Less savoury are the poor souls in hell being sodomised with a pitch fork.

Bell Tower

Set next to the *duomo* is its slender campanile (Bell Tower; Map p82; ⊙ 8.15am-7pm), a striking work of Florentine Gothic architecture designed by Giotto, the artistic genius often described as the founding artist of the Renaissance. The steep 414-step climb up the square, 85m-tall tower offers the reward of a view that is nearly as impressive as that from the dome.

The first tier of bas-reliefs around the base of its elaborate Gothic facade are copies of those carved by Pisano depicting the creation of humanity and the *attività umane* (arts and industries). Those on the second tier depict the planets, the cardinal virtues, the arts and the seven sacraments. The sculpted prophets and sibyls in the upper-storey niches are copies of works by Donatello and others.

Baptistry

Across from the *duomo's* main entrance is the 11th-century Battistero di San Giovanni (Baptistry; Map p82; ⊙ 8.15-10.15am & 11.15am-7.30pm Mon-Fri, 8.15am-6.30pm Sat, 8.15am-1.30pm Sun), an octagonal, striped structure of white-and-green marble. Dante is among the famous people to have been dunked in its baptismal font – still used every third Sunday of the month to baptise babies born within the surrounding San Lorenzo parish.

The Romanesque structure is most celebrated, however, for its three sets of doors illustrating the story of humanity and the Redemption. The gilded bronze doors by Lorenzo Ghiberti's at the eastern entrance, the *Porta del Paradiso* (Gate of Paradise), are copies – the originals are in the Museo dell'Opera del Duomo (p79). Andrea Pisano executed the southern doors (1330), illustrating the life of St John the Baptist, and Lorenzo Ghiberti won a public competition in 1401 to design the northern doors, likewise replaced by copies today.

The baptistry's interior gleams with Byzantine-style mosaics. Covering the dome in five horizontal tiers, they include scenes from the lives of St John the Baptist, Christ and Joseph on one side, and a representation of the Last Judgement on the other. A choir of angels surveys proceedings from the innermost tier.

Detail of Ghiberti's *Porta del Paradiso*

Museo dell'Opera del Duomo

This awe-inspiring museum (Cathedral Museum; Map p100; Piazza del Duomo 9; ⊙9am-7pm) tells the magnificent story of how the *duomo* was built through art and short films. Its spectacular main hall, Sala del Paradiso, is dominated by a life-size reconstruction of the original facade of the *duomo*, decorated with some 40 14th- and early-15th-century statues carved for the facade by 14th-century masters (including a rather spooky, glass-eyed Madonna by Arnolfo di Cambio, dating from 1300–05). Building work began in 1296 but it was never finished and in 1587 the facade was eventually dismantled. This is also where you will find Ghiberti's original 15th-century masterpiece, *Porta del Paradiso* (Doors of Paradise; 1425–52) – gloriously golden, 16m-tall gilded bronze doors designed for the eastern entrance to the Baptistry – as well as those he sculpted for the northern entrance (1403–24). In late 2019 the final set of doors (1330–36), designed for the southern door by Andrea Pisano, arrived in the museum after five painstakingly long years of restoration.

Michelangelo's achingly beautiful *Pietà,* sculpted when he was almost 80 and intended for his own tomb, is displayed in the Tribuna di Michelangelo. Dissatisfied with the marble quality and his own work, Michelangelo broke up the unfinished sculpture, destroying the arm and left leg of the figure of Christ. Donatello's mid-15th-century, wooden sculpture of a gaunt, desperately desolate Mary Magdalene is the star of Room 8.

DUOMO CLOCK

Upon entering the *duomo*, look up to see its clock with a fantastic, 4.6m-wide frescoed face resembling a flower. One of Europe's first monumental – and unconventional – clocks, it notably turns in an anticlockwise direction, counts in 24 hours starting at the bottom and begins the first hour of the day at sunset (rather than midnight). The clock was painted by eclectic Florentine painter Paolo Uccello (1397–1495) between 1440 and 1443. To this day, it is lovingly tended by two caretakers who enter the tiny door on ground level below the clock, climb the steep narrow staircase hidden between the *duomo's* thick interior and exterior walls, and adjust the clock mechanism to take into account the changing hour of sunset.

Visit early in the morning to escape the crowds and avoid queuing in the hot sun.

CUPOLA RESERVATIONS

Reservations are obligatory for the *duomo's* cupola; book a time slot online or at a self-service Ticketpoint machine inside the Piazza di San Giovanni ticket office.

TOP SIGHT
PALAZZO VECCHIO

Dominating Florence's most glorious square, this fortress palace was the hub of political life in medieval Florence. Built for the *signoria* (city government) between 1298 and 1314, the 'Old Palace' hosted nine *priori* (consuls) – guild members picked out of a hat every two months. Cosimo I lived here in palatial ducal apartments from 1540 until 1549, and views from its iconic crenellated tower are mesmerising.

Salone dei Cinquecento

Cosimo I commissioned Vasari to renovate the interior of Palazzo Vecchio in 1540, living here for nine years before moving across the river to Palazzo Pitti. What impresses is the 53m-long, 22m-wide Salone dei Cinquecento (pictured) with dramatic battle scenes painted by Vasari and his apprentices. Cosimo commissioned Vasari to raise the original ceiling 7m in height and had himself portrayed as a god in the centre of the panelled ceiling. It took Vasari and his school, in consultation with Michelangelo, just two years (1563–65) to construct the ceiling and paint the 34 gold-leafed panels.

Quartiere di Leo X

On the same floor lie the private apartments of Cardinal Giovanni de' Medici (1475–1521), pious son of Lorenzo Il Magnifico who became a cardinal when he was just 13 years old and went on to became pope in 1513 – Giovanni took the name Leo X. In the Sala di Leo X find a visual celebration of his life and, in the stairwell, a wonderful wall fresco featuring Palazzo Vecchio in 1558.

DON'T MISS

➡ Vasari battle scenes in the Salone dei Cinquecento

➡ Cosimo's Studiolo on a 'Secret Passages' tour

➡ City panorama from atop Torre d'Arnolfo

PRACTICALITIES

➡ Map p82

➡ ☎ 055 276 85 58

➡ www.musefirenze.it

➡ Piazza della Signoria

➡ adult/reduced museum or tower €12.50/10, museum & tower €17.50/15, museum & tour €16/13.50, tour €4, combination ticket €19.50/17.50

➡ ⊙ museum 9am-11pm Fri-Wed, to 2pm Thu Apr-Sep, shorter hours rest of year, tower 9am-9pm Fri-Wed, to 2pm Thu Apr-Sep, shorter hours rest of year

Studiolo

Cosimo I commissioned Vasari and a team of Florentine Mannerist artists to decorate this sumptuous study for his introverted, alchemy-mad son Francesco I; spot him disguised as a scientist experimenting with gunpowder in one of the 34 wall paintings. The lower paintings conceal 20 cabinets in which the young prince hid his treasures. Visit on a 'Secret Passages' tour.

Private Apartments

Upstairs, on the 2nd floor, the private apartments of Eleonora and her ladies-in-waiting are an unabashed celebration of Medici glory. Eleonora's private chapel, decorated with exquisite frescoes by Agnolo Bronzino (1503–72) in intervals between 1540 and 1565, is one of the finest examples of Florentine Mannerism. Sadly Eleonora died of malaria in 1562, unable to appreciate the splendid masterpiece complete. Ridolfo del Ghirlandaio was inspired by designs from Nero's Domus Aurea in Rome in creating the ceiling in the Camera Verde (Green Room), while Donatello's original *Judith and Holofernes* graces the Sala dei Gigli, named after its frieze of fleur-de-lis, representing the Florentine Republic.

Backstage at the Palace

Imaginative guided tours take you into parts of Palazzo Vecchio otherwise inaccessible. You need a valid museum ticket in addition to the guided-tour ticket.

The 'Secret Passages' tour (adult/reduced €5/2.50, 1¼ hours) leads small groups along the secret staircase built between the palace's superthick walls in 1342 as an escape route for French Duke of Athens, Walter de Brienne, who seized the palace and nominated himself Lord of Florence, only to be sent packing back to France by the Florentines a year later. It follows this staircase to the Tesoretto (Treasury) of Cosimo I and Francesco I's sumptuous Studiolo. The tour ends in the palace roof above the Salone dei Cinquecento – admire the huge wooden trusses supporting Vasari's ornate ceiling.

The 'Secrets of Inferno' tour (adult/child €5/2.50, 1¼ hours), open to visitors aged 10 and older, follows in the footsteps of Robert Langdon from Dan Brown's bestseller *Inferno* novel. The 'Invitation to the Court' tour (adult/child €5/2.50, 1¼ hours), for ages eight years and upwards, ushers in actors dressed in Renaissance costume. Other children's tours end with 16th-century dressing-up sessions and there are also storytelling sessions (adult/child €5/2.50, 1¼ hours). Reserve in advance with Mus.e (p108) by telephone, email, or at the Palazzo Vecchio ticket desk.

THE MAP ROOM

For a fascinating snapshot of how the world was viewed during the Renaissance, absorb Cosimo I's collection of maps displayed in the Sala delle Carte Geografiche (Map Room). His 16th-century maps chart everywhere in the known world at the time, from the polar regions to the Caribbean.

Vasari's battle scenes in the Salone del Cinquecentto glorify Florentine victories by Cosimo I over arch-rivals Pisa and Siena: unlike the Sienese, the Pisans are depicted bare of armour; play 'Spot the Leaning Tower'.

TOP TIPS

➡ Take a 418-step hike up the palace's striking **Torre d'Arnolfo** – the 360-degree city panorama between the tower's corbelled ramparts is worth it. No children under six years.

➡ Visit on a dry sunny day (the tower is closed when raining).

➡ Rent a tablet with multimedia guide (€5/4 per person for one/two people) at the ticket desk or download the Palazzo Vecchio app (€2).

Duomo & Santa Maria Novella

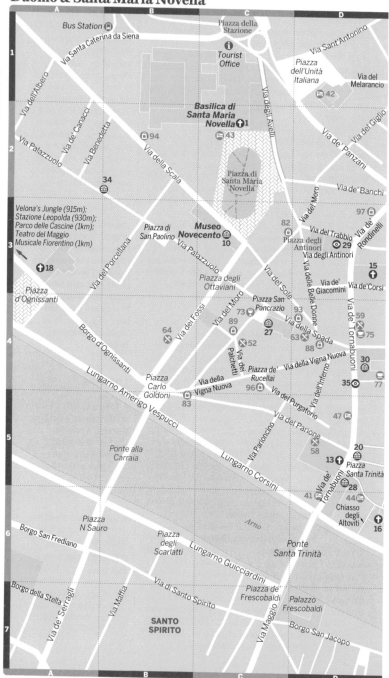

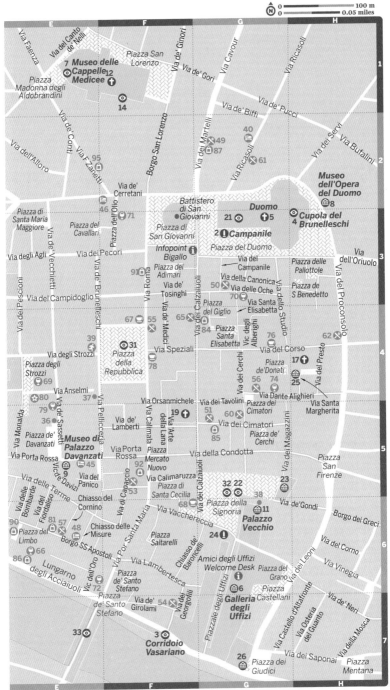

Duomo & Santa Maria Novella

◎ **Top Sights**
1 Basilica di Santa Maria Novella............C2
2 Campanile...G3
3 Corridoio Vasariano F7
4 Cupola del Brunelleschi.........................H3
5 Duomo..G3
6 Galleria degli Uffizi.................................G6
7 Museo delle Cappelle Medicee E1
8 Museo dell'Opera del Duomo................H2
9 Museo di Palazzo Davanzati..................E5
10 Museo Novecento....................................C3
11 Palazzo Vecchio......................................G6

◎ **Sights**
12 Basilica di San Lorenzo..........................F1
13 Basilica di Santa Trinità D5
14 Biblioteca Medicea Laurenziana...........F1
15 Chiesa dei Santi Michele e Gaetano.....D3
16 Chiesa dei Santissimi Apostoli.............D6
17 Chiesa di Santa Margherita...................H4
18 Chiesa d'Ognissanti...............................A3
19 Chiesa e Museo di Orsanmichele F5
20 Collezione Roberto Casamonti.............D5
21 Cripta Santa Reparata G3
22 Fontana di Nettuno.................................G5
23 Gucci Garden...G5
24 Loggia dei Lanzi......................................G6
25 Museo Casa di Dante H4
26 Museo Galileo...G7
27 Museo Marino Marini..............................C4
28 Museo Salvatore Ferragamo..................D5
29 Palazzo Antinori......................................D3
30 Palazzo Strozzi..D4
31 Piazza della Repubblica.........................F4
32 Piazza della Signoria G5
33 Ponte Vecchio...E7
34 Street Levels Gallery B2
35 Via de' Tornabuoni.................................D4

⊕ **Activities, Courses & Tours**
36 ArtViva...E5
37 Florence Town...E4
38 Mus.e...G6
39 Relax Firenze...E4

⊟ **Sleeping**
40 Academy Hostel.......................................G2
41 Antica Torre di Via de' Tornabuoni 1....D6
42 Grand Hotel Baglioni...............................D1
43 Grand Hotel Minerva...............................C2
44 Hotel Cestelli...D6
45 Hotel Davanzati..E5
   Hotel Pendini................................(see 39)
46 Hotel Perseo..F2
47 Hotel Scoti...D5
48 Hotel Torre Guelfa E6

⊗ **Eating**
   Da Vinattieri...................................(see 17)

49 FAC...G2
   Floret...(see 91)
50 Grom...G3
   Gucci Osteria da Massimo
      Bottura..(see 23)
51 I Due Fratellini...G5
52 Il Latini...C4
53 Il Trippaio del Porcellino........................F5
54 'Ino..F7
55 Irene F4
56 L'Antico Trippaio.....................................G4
57 Mangiafoco...E6
58 Mariano..D5
59 Obicà..D4
60 Osteria Il Buongustai...............................G5
61 Regina Bistecca.......................................G2
62 Trattoria Le Mossacce............................H4
63 Trattoria Marione....................................D4
64 UqBar...B4
65 Venchi..F4

⊙ **Drinking & Nightlife**
66 Amblé...E6
67 Caffè Gilli...F4
68 Caffè Rivoire..F6
69 Colle Bereto..E4
70 Coquinarius..G3
71 Fiaschetteria Nuvoli................................F3
72 La Terrazza Lounge Bar..........................E6
73 Manifattura...C4
74 Mayday Club..G4
75 Procacci...D4
76 Shake Café...G4
77 Strozzi Caffè..D4
78 Tosca & Nino..F4
79 YAB...E5

⊕ **Entertainment**
80 Odeon Cinehall E4

⊟ **Shopping**
81 Angela Caputi..E6
82 Aprosio & Co..C3
83 Benheart..B5
84 Benheart..G4
85 Benheart..G5
86 Boutique Nadine......................................E6
87 Eataly G2
88 Grevi...D4
89 La Bottega della Frutta...........................C4
90 La Bottega dell'Olio.................................E6
91 Luisa Via Roma..F3
92 Mercato Nuovo..F5
93 Mio Concept...D4
94 Officina Profumo-Farmaceutica di
      Santa Maria Novella....................B2
95 Penko...E2
96 Pineider..C4
97 Richard Ginori...D3

Piazza della Signoria   PIAZZA

(Map p82) The hub of local life since the 13th century, Florentines flock here to meet friends and chat over early-evening *aperitivi* (predinner drinks) at historic cafes. Presiding over everything is Palazzo Vecchio (p80), Florence's city hall, and the 14th-century Loggia dei Lanzi (Map p82) FREE, an open-air gallery showcasing Renaissance sculptures, including Giambologna's *Rape of the Sabine Women* (c 1583), Benvenuto Cellini's bronze *Perseus* (1554) and Agnolo Gaddi's *Seven Virtues* (1384–89).

In centuries past, townsfolk congregated on the piazza whenever the city entered one of its innumerable political crises. The people would be called for a *parlamento* (people's plebiscite) to rubber-stamp decisions that frequently meant ruin for some ruling families and victory for others. Scenes of great pomp and circumstance alternated with those of terrible suffering: it was here that vehemently pious preacher-leader Savonarola set fire to the city's art – books, paintings, musical instruments, mirrors, fine clothes and so on – during his famous 'Bonfire of the Vanities' in 1497, and where he was hung in chains and burnt as a heretic, along with two other supporters, a year later.

The same spot where both fires burned is marked by a bronze plaque embedded in the ground. Nearby, Ammannati's Fontana di Nettuno (Map p82), with pin-headed bronze satyrs and divinities frolicking at its edges, dazzles again thanks to a €1.5-million restoration in 2017–19 funded by Florentine fashion house Salvatore Ferragamo. It was originally unveiled in 1565 to celebrate the wedding of Francesco I de' Medici and the Grand Duchess Giovanna d'Austria.

Equally impressive are the equestrian statue of Cosimo I by Giambologna in the centre of the piazza, the much-photographed copy of Michelangelo's *David* guarding the western entrance to the Palazzo Vecchio since 1910 (the original stood here until 1873), and two copies of important Donatello works: *Marzocco,* the heraldic Florentine lion – for the original, visit the Museo del Bargello (p98) – and *Giuditta e Oloferne* (Judith and Holofernes; c 1455; original inside Palazzo Vecchio).

The Loggia dei Lanzi at the piazza's southern end owes its name to the Lanzichenecchi (Swiss bodyguards) of Cosimo I, who were stationed here.

Gucci Garden   MUSEUM

(Map p82; ☑ 055 7592 7010; www.gucci.com; Piazza della Signoria 10; adult/reduced €8/5; ☺10am-8pm) Elegantly housed in 14th-century Palazzo della Mercanzia, Gucci Garden is an all-out whimsical ode to the Florentine fashion giant. The practically psychedelic, boudoir-styled boutique on the ground floor is designed as much for experiential browsing as high-end shopping, while gallery rooms on the 1st and 2nd floors illustrate the Gucci story. Born in 1921, the brand's history is shown with clothing, accessories, video installations and a highly popular 'selfie' wall emblazoned with the famous double-G monogram, glossy red lips, stilettos and other 'walk the talk' emojis.

Museo Galileo   MUSEUM

(Map p82; ☑ 055 26 53 11; www.museogalileo.it; Piazza dei Giudici 1; adult/reduced €10/6; ☺9.30am-6pm Wed-Mon, to 1pm Tue) On the Arno river next to the Uffizi in 12th-century Palazzo Castellani – look for the sundial telling the time on the pavement outside – is this state-of-the-art science museum, named after the great Pisa-born scientist Galileo Galilei, who was invited by the Medici court to Florence in 1610. Don't miss two of his fingers and a tooth displayed here.

Collezione Roberto Casamonti   GALLERY

(Map p82; ☑ 055 60 20 30; www.collezionerobertocasamonti.com; Piazza Santa Trinità 1; adult/reduced €10/8; ☺by advance reservation 11.30am-7pm Wed-Sun) Paintings and sculptures by 20th-century artists provide a colourful contrast to 16th-century Palazzo Bartolini Salimbeni which this gallery inhabits so graciously. Showcase for the private collection of Florentine art dealer Roberto Casamonti, the gallery hosts two exhibitions a year: 20th-century works up to the 1960s, and the 1970s to present-day. Visits must be reserved at least 24 hours in advance.

Piazza della Repubblica   PIAZZA

(Map p82) The site of a Roman forum and heart of medieval Florence, this busy civic space was created in the 1880s as part of a controversial plan of 'civic improvements' involving the demolition of the old market, Jewish ghetto and slums, and the relocation of nearly 6000 residents. Vasari's lovely Loggia del Pesce (Fish Market) was saved and re-erected on Via Pietrapiana.

THE EXTRAORDINARY VASARI CORRIDOR

Bathed in mystery, this must be the world's most infamous and enigmatic corridor. Look above the jewellery shops on the eastern side of Ponte Vecchio to see Florence's Corridoio Vasariano (Vasari Corridor; Map p82; guided visit by reservation Mar-Oct €45, Nov-Feb €20), an elevated covered passageway joining the Palazzo Vecchio on Piazza della Signoria with the Uffizi and Palazzo Pitti across the river. Around 1km long, it was designed by Vasari for Cosimo I in 1565 to allow the Medicis to wander between the two palaces in privacy and comfort. From the 17th century, the Medicis strung it with self-portraits – of Andrea del Sarto (the oldest), Rubens, Rembrandt and Canova among others.

The original promenade incorporated tiny windows (facing the river) and circular apertures with iron gratings (facing the street) to protect those who used the corridor from outside attacks. But when Hitler visited Florence in 1941, his chum and fellow dictator Benito Mussolini had big new windows punched into the corridor walls on Ponte Vecchio so that his guest could enjoy an expansive view down the Arno from the famous Florentine bridge.

On the Oltrarno, the corridor passes by Chiesa di Santa Felicità (Map p106; Piazza di Santa Felicità; ⊙9.30am-noon & 3.30-5.30pm Mon-Sat), thereby providing the Medici with a private balcony in the church where they could attend Mass without mingling with the commoners. Stand in front of the Romanesque church on Piazza di Santa Felicità and admire the trio of arches of the Vasari Corridor that runs right above the portico outside the otherwise unnotable church facade. Inside, walk towards the altar and look backwards to see the Medici balcony up high (and imagine the corridor snaking behind it). Oh, and before leaving the church, don't miss Ghirlandaio's *Meeting of St Anne and St Joachim* hung at the end of its right transept.

Closed since 2017, the corridor is expected to open again in 2021 once the €10-million renovation work is complete. Restored to its original state, visitors will follow in Medici footsteps past a line-up of antique statues, 16th-century frescoes once adorning the corridor's external walls, and memorials to Florence bombings in 1944 and 1993. Guided visits organised by Firenze Musei (☑055 239 60 51; www.firenzemusei.it; Via dei Calzaiuoli, Chiesa e Museo di Orsanmichele; ⊙9am-4.30pm Mon-Sat) will be by reservation only.

Museo Salvatore Ferragamo MUSEUM
(Map p82; ☑055 356 28 46; www.ferragamo.com/museo; Via de' Tornabuoni 2; adult/reduced €8/5; ⊙10am-7.30pm mid-May–mid-Mar) The splendid 13th-century Palazzo Spini-Feroni has been home to the Ferragamo fashion empire since 1938. Anyone with even the faintest tendency towards shoe addiction or an interest in the socio-historical context of fashion will enjoy the themed exhibitions held in the small basement museum. One permanent room displays a selection of original Ferragamo shoes from the 1920s and 1930s.

⊙ Santa Maria Novella

The main sights in this district are clustered on Piazza di Santa Maria Novella, fronted by the shimmering green-and-white facade of Santa Maria Novella's venerable basilica. Heading south towards the river, don't miss some of the city's finest frescoes in Basilica di Santa Trinità; Chiesa d'Ognissanti, a must for Botticelli fans; and the small but fascinating Museo Marino Marini.

★ **Museo Novecento** MUSEUM
(Museum of the 20th Century; Map p82; ☑055 28 61 32; www.museonovecento.it; Piazza di Santa Maria Novella 10; adult/reduced €9.50/4.50; ⊙11am-8pm Sat-Wed, to 2pm Thu, to 11pm Fri summer, 11am-7pm Fri-Wed, to 2pm Thu winter) Don't allow the Renaissance to distract you from Florence's fantastic modern art museum, at home in a 13th-century pilgrim shelter, hospital and school. A well-articulated itinerary guides visitors through modern Italian painting and sculpture from the early 20th century to the late 1980s. Installation art makes effective use of the outside space on the 1st-floor loggia. Fashion and theatre also get a nod, and the itinerary ends with a 20-minute cinematic montage of the best films set in Florence.

Museo Marino Marini GALLERY
(Map p82; ☑055 21 94 32; www.museomarinomarini.it; Piazza San Pancrazio 1; chapel adult/reduced €6/4; ⊙10am-7pm Sat-Mon, by online reservation only Tue-Fri) Deconsecrated in the 19th century, Chiesa di San Pancrazio is home to this small art museum displaying sculptures

by Pistoia-born sculptor Marino Marini (1901–80) intertwined with various contemporary art exhibits (free admission). But the highlight is Cappella Rucellai with a tiny scale copy of Christ's Holy Sepulchre in Jerusalem – a Renaissance gem by Leon Battista Alberti. The chapel was built between 1458 and 1467 for the tomb of wealthy Florentine banker and wool merchant Giovanni Rucellai.

Basilica di Santa Trinità
CHURCH

(Map p82; Piazza Santa Trinità; ⊙ 7am-noon & 4-7pm) FREE Built in Gothic style and later given a mannerist facade, this 14th-century church shelters some of the city's finest frescoes. Right of the main altar, paintings (1483–85) by Ghirlandaio depict the life of St Francis of Assisi through portraits of illustrious Florentines of the time in Cappella Sassetti, (pop €0.50 in the slot to illuminate the frescoes). In Cappella Bartholini Salimbeni, the gated side chapel, Lorenzo Monaco's *Annunciation* (1422) sits above the altar and wall frescoes illustrate the life of the Virgin Mary.

Look out for the crest of the Bartholini Salimbeni family on the floor of the chapel – it features poppies and the motto *'Per Non Dormire'* (For Those Who Don't Sleep), a reference to the fact that the family fortune resulted from the acquisition of an important cargo of wool from Northern Europe. The deal was sealed unbeknown to their business rivals, who had been doped with opium-laced wine at a lavish party the night before the cargo was due to arrive in Florence.

Street Levels Gallery
GALLERY

(Map p82; ☑ 339 2203607; https://street-level-gallery.business.site; Via Palazzuolo 74r; ⊙ 3-7pm Tue-Sat) Take a break from Renaissance art with this pioneering urban street-art gallery. Exhibitions showcase the work of local street artists, including street-sign hacker Clet (p111), the stencil art of Hogre, and Exit Enter, whose work is easily recognisable by the red balloons holding up the matchstick figures he draws. A highlight is the enigmatic Blub, whose caricatures of historical figures wearing goggles and diving masks adorn many a city wall – his art is known as *L'Arte Sa Nuotare* (Art Knows how to Swim).

Chiesa d'Ognissanti
CHURCH

(Map p82; ☑ 055 239 87 00; Borgo d'Ognissanti 42; ⊙ 9.30am-12.30pm & 4-6pm Mon-Sat, 9-10am & 4-5.30pm Sun) FREE Stroll along Borgo d'Ognissanti from Piazza Carlo Goldoni towards ancient city gate Porta al Prato, past antiques shops and designer boutiques, to reach this 13th-century church, built as part of a Benedictine monastery. Its highlight is Domenico Ghirlandaio's fresco of the Madonna della Misericordia protecting members of the Vespucci family, the church's main patrons. Amerigo Vespucci, the Florentine navigator who gave his name to the American continent, is supposed to be the young boy whose head peeks between the Madonna and the old man.

Also here are a *Crucifixion* by Taddeo Gaddi in the sacristy, and between the third and fourth altars, Ghirlandaio's *St Jerome* (1480) and the pensive *St Augustine* (1480) by Botticelli, who is buried in the church. The early-Renaissance artist had requested to be buried at the feet of Simonetta Vespucci, the married woman whom he was said to be in love with and who served as a model for one of his greatest masterpieces, *Primavera* (Spring). Look for the simple round tombstone marked 'Sandro Filipepe' in the south transept. Botticelli grew up in a house on the same street.

◉ San Lorenzo & San Marco

San Lorenzo is Medici territory – come here to see their palace, church, library and mausoleum, all decorated with extraordinary works of art. San Marco meanwhile offers far more than the city's most famous resident, one Signore *David*; the frescoes in the Museo di San Marco are nothing short of superb.

★ Museo delle Cappelle Medicee
MAUSOLEUM

(Medici Chapels; Map p82; ☑ 055 238 86 02; www.bargellomusei.beniculturali.it/musei/2/medicee; Piazza Madonna degli Aldobrandini 6; adult/reduced €8/4; ⊙ 8.15am-2pm, closed 2nd & 4th Sun, 1st, 3rd & 5th Mon of month) Nowhere is Medici conceit expressed so explicitly as in the Medici Chapels. Adorned with granite, marble, semiprecious stones and some of Michelangelo's most beautiful sculptures, it is the burial place of 49 dynasty members. Francesco I lies in the dark, imposing Cappella dei Principi (Chapel of Princes) alongside Ferdinando I and II and Cosimo I, II and III. Lorenzo Il Magnifico is buried in the graceful Sagrestia Nuova (New Sacristy), which was Michelangelo's first architectural work.

It is also in the sacristy that you can swoon over three of Michelangelo's most haunting sculptures: *Dawn and Dusk* on the sarcophagus of Lorenzo, Duke of Urbino; *Night and*

TOP SIGHT
BASILICA DI SANTA MARIA NOVELLA

This monastery, fronted by its basilica's mesmerising green-and-white marble facade, hides serene cloisters and stunning frescoed chapels. The basilica safeguards several artistic masterpieces, including breathtaking Domenico Ghirlandaio frescoes and a luminous painted Crucifix by Giotto (c 1290).

Holy Trinity

Upon entering the church, admire Masaccio's superb fresco *Trinità* (Holy Trinity; 1424–25), one of the first artworks to use the then newly discovered techniques of perspective and proportion.

Cappella Maggiore

Admire the main altar, Altare Maggiore (1858–61), inside Capella Maggiore. This tiny chapel is adorned in vibrant frescoes painted by Ghirlandaio between 1485 and 1490. Relating the lives of the Virgin Mary, the frescoes are also celebrated for their realistic depiction of Florentine life during the Renaissance. Spot portraits of Ghirlandaio's contemporaries and members of the Tornabuoni family (who commissioned the frescoes).

DON'T MISS

➡ Cappella Maggiore

➡ Chiostro Verde

➡ Cappellone degli Spagnoli

➡ Cappella del Papa

PRACTICALITIES

➡ Map p82

➡ ☎ 055 21 92 57; www.smn.it

➡ Piazza di Santa Maria Novella 18

➡ adult/reduced €7.50/5

➡ ⏰ 9am-7pm Mon-Thu, 11am-7pm Fri, 9am-6.30pm Sat, noon-6.30pm Sun Jul & Aug, shorter hours rest of year

Cappella Strozzi di Mantova

To the far left of the altar, up a short flight of stairs, is this wonderful chapel covered in soul-stirring 14th-century frescoes by Niccolò di Tommaso and Nardo di Cione. The fine altarpiece (1354–57) here was painted by the latter's brother, Andrea, best known as Andrea Orcagna.

Chiostro Verde

From the church, duck through a side door into the peaceful Green Cloister (1332–62), part of the sizeable monastery constructed for Dominican friars after their arrival in the city in 1219. The cloister is named after the green-earth base used for the frescoes on three of its four walls. On the west side of the Chiostro Verde, another passage leads to the 14th-century Cappella degli Ubriachi and the large Refettorio (Refectory; 1353–54) showcasing a 1583 *Last Supper* by Alessandro Allori and various ecclesiastical relics.

Cappellone degli Spagnoli

A door off the cloister's northern side leads into this chapel, named in 1566 when it was given to the Spanish colony in Florence (Spagnoli means Spanish). Its dazzling frescoes (c 1365–67; pictured) by Andrea di Bonaiuto depict the *Resurrection, Ascension* and *Pentecost* (in the vault); on the altar wall are scenes of the *Via Dolorosa, Crucifixion* and *Descent into Limbo*.

TOP SIGHT
GALLERIA DELL'ACCADEMIA

A lengthy queue marks the door to this gallery, purpose-built to house one of the Renaissance's greatest masterpieces, Michelangelo's *David* (pictured). Fortunately, the world's most famous statue is worth the wait. Also here are Michelangelo's unfinished *Prigioni* sculpture and paintings by Andrea Orcagna, Taddeo Gaddi, Domenico Ghirlandaio, Filippino Lippi and Sandro Botticelli.

Michelangelo's David

Carved from a single block of marble already worked on by two sculptors, Michelangelo's most famous work was challenging to complete. Yet the subtle detail of the enormous work of art – the veins in his sinewy arms, the leg muscles, the change in expression as you move around the statue – is indeed impressive. Thankfully for Michelangelo, when the statue of the nude boy-warrior – depicted for the first time as a man rather than young boy – appeared on Piazza della Signoria in 1504, Florentines immediately adopted *David* as an emblem of power, liberty and civic pride.

DON'T MISS

➡ Michelangelo's *David*

➡ The Slaves

➡ Botticelli's *Madonna del mare*

PRACTICALITIES

➡ Map p92

➡ ☎ 055 238 86 09

➡ www.galleriaaccademia firenze.beniculturali.it

➡ Via Ricasoli 60

➡ adult/reduced €12/6

➡ ⊙ 8.15am-6.50pm Tue-Sun

The Slaves

Another soul-soaring work by Michelangelo, *Prigioni* (1521–30) evokes four 'prisoners' or 'slaves' so powerfully that the figures really do seem to be writhing and struggling to free themselves from the ice-cold marble. The work was intended for the tomb of Pope Julius II in Rome, which was never completed.

Coronation of the Virgin

This remarkable piece of embroidery – an altar frontal 4m long and over 1m wide – portrays the *Coronazione della Vergine* (Coronation of the Virgin; 1336) in exquisite detail using polychrome silks and gold and silver thread. Completed by master embroiderer Jacopo Cambi, it originally covered the high altar of the Basilica di Santa Maria Novella.

Botticelli's Madonna

Madonna del mare (Madonna of the Sea; 1477), a portrait of the Virgin and child by Sandro Botticelli, exudes a mesmerising serenity. Compare it with works in the gallery by Botticelli's master and mentor, Fra' Filippo Lippi (c 1457–1504), to whom some critics attribute it.

FLORENCE SIGHTS

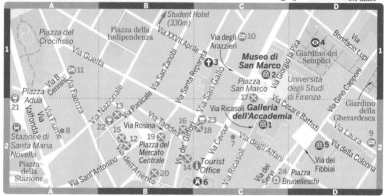

San Lorenzo & San Marco

San Lorenzo & San Marco

◉ Top Sights
1 Galleria dell'Accademia C2
2 Museo di San Marco...........................C1

◉ Sights
3 Cenacolo di Sant'Apollonia C1
4 Giardino dei Semplici D1
5 Museo degli Innocenti.........................D2
6 Palazzo Medici-Riccardi......................C2

◉ Activities, Courses & Tours
7 Caf Tour & Travel...............................C2
8 City Sightseeing Firenze A2

◉ Sleeping
9 Hotel Morandi alla Crocetta D2
10 Hotel Orto de' Medici..........................C1
11 Ostello Archi Rossi.............................A1

◉ Eating
12 Da Nerbone B2
13 De Plek B2
14 La Ménagère B2
15 Mercato Centrale B2
16 My Sugar B2
17 Pugi C1
18 SimBIOsi...C2
19 Trattoria Mario....................................B2
20 Trattoria Sergio Gozzi.........................B2

◉ Drinking & Nightlife
Caffè del Verone .... (see 5)
21 Fabbricato Viaggiatori A2
22 PanicAle B2
23 SimBIOsi Caffè C2

◉ Shopping
24 Street Doing..C2

Day on the sarcophagus of Lorenzo's son Giuliano (note the unfinished face of 'Day' and the youth of the sleeping woman drenched in light aka 'Night'); and *Madonna and Child,* which adorns Lorenzo's tomb. Since early 2019 clever new lighting recreates the soft, indirect sunlight Michelangelo originally intended to illuminate his work.

★ **Museo di San Marco** MUSEUM
(Map p92; ☑ 055 238 86 08; Piazza San Marco 3; adult/reduced €8/2; ⓘ 8.15am-1.50pm Mon-Fri, to 4.50pm Sat & Sun, closed 1st, 3rd & 5th Sun, 2nd & 4th Mon of month) At the heart of Florence's university area sits Chiesa di San Marco and an adjoining 15th-century Dominican monastery where both gifted painter Fra' Angelico (c 1395–1455) and the

sharp-tongued Savonarola piously served God. Today the monastery, aka one of Florence's most spiritually uplifting museums, showcases the work of Fra' Angelico. After centuries of being known as 'Il Beato Angelico' (literally 'The Blessed Angelic One') or simply 'Il Beato' (The Blessed), the Renaissance's most blessed religious painter was made a saint by Pope John Paul II in 1984.

Enter via Michelozzo's Chiostro di Sant' Antonio (St Antoninus Cloister; 1440). Turn immediately right to enter the Sala dell'Ospizio dei Pellegrini (Pilgrims' Hospital Hall) where Fra' Angelico's attention to perspective and the realistic portrayal of nature come to life in a number of major paintings, including the *Deposition from the Cross* (1432).

ESCAPE THE CROWDS

The days when there was an actual low season in Florence appear to be over. Crowds of visitors fill the narrow stone-paved streets in the *centro storico* (historic centre) year-round, making it that much harder to savour the Renaissance beauty in peace.

But nothing's impossible. Florence's blockbuster sights, *duomo* and Uffizi included, are concentrated in the historic centre, so plan sightseeing in less-crowded neighbourhoods such as San Marco (home to *David* at the Galleria dell'Accademia, p90, and the wonderfully emotive, unsung Museo degli Innocenti) and the Oltrarno (with the enormous Palazzo Pitti; p105).

Allow ample time for hapless meandering in neighbourhoods traditionally off the tourist radar: San Frediano has no big sights but is rich in 'lapping up local vibe' opportunities. Ditch the most-direct, invariably busiest route for atmospheric backstreets and alleys (of which historic Florence has plenty).

There's no need to ignore Florence's celebrity museums and monuments: avoid the mainstream crowd by arriving early (there's good reason why admission to Palazzo Pitti is 50% off before 9.25 am) or booking a more enriching guided tour. Not only will you learn far more about the sight than visiting alone, but tours often allow you to access parts of a building otherwise closed to the public (the backstage tours offered at the Duomo complex, p76, are a fantastic example of this).

Plan a day trip out of town. Fiesole (p134) in the Florentine hills is the easiest spot to escape for peace, quiet and lunch with a spectacular view, but avoid weekends when Florentines head this way. Motoring out of the city through vineyards and olive groves in a vintage Fiat 500 with the 500 Touring Club (p110) or in a vintage sidecar with De Gustibus (p110) is another option.

Be prepared to walk that extra mile. Staying a stone's throw away from the centre is an easy way to escape the crowds at the end of the day and always rewards – with soothing green views of Europe's oldest walled garden (AdAstra; p116), a chic rooftop pool (Student Hotel; p114) or a sweeping romantic city panorama (Torre di Bellosguardo; p115) perhaps.

Giovanni Antonio Sogliani's fresco *The Miraculous Supper of St Dominic* (1536) dominates the former monks' **Refettorio** (Refectory) in the cloister. Fra' Angelico's huge *Crucifixion and Saints* fresco (1441–42), featuring all the patron saints of the convent and city, plus the Medici family who commissioned the fresco, decorates the former **Capitolo** (Chapterhouse). But it is the 44 monastic **cells** on the 1st floor that are the most haunting: at the top of the stairs, Fra' Angelico's most famous work, *Annunciation* (c 1440), commands all eyes.

A stroll around each of the cells reveals snippets of many more religious reliefs by the Tuscan-born friar, who decorated the cells between 1440 and 1441 with deeply devotional frescoes to guide the meditation of his fellow friars. Most were completed by Fra' Angelico himself, with others by aides under his supervision, including Benozzo Gozzoli. Among several masterpieces is the magnificent *Adoration of the Magi* in the cell used by Cosimo the Elder as a meditation retreat (Nos 38 to 39); only 10 people can visit at a time. The frescoes in the cell of San Antonino Arcivescovo (neighbouring Fra' Angelico's *Annunciation*) are gruesome: they show Jesus pushing open the door of his sepulchre, squashing a nasty-looking devil in the process.

Contrasting with the pure beauty of these frescoes are the plain rooms (Cell VI) that Savonarola called home from 1489. Rising to the position of prior at the Dominican convent, it was from here that the fanatical monk railed against luxury, greed and corruption of the clergy. Kept as a kind of shrine to the turbulent priest, the three small rooms house a portrait, a few personal items, fragments of the black cape and white tunic Savonarola wore, his rosary beads and the linen banner he carried in processions, and a grand marble monument erected by admirers in 1873.

Museo degli Innocenti   MUSEUM
(Map p92; ☑ 055 203 73 08; www.museodegl innocenti.it; Piazza della Santissima Annunziata 13; adult/reduced €7/5; ⊙10am-7pm) Shortly after

its founding in 1421, Brunelleschi designed the loggia for Florence's Ospedale degli Innocenti, a foundling hospital and Europe's first orphanage, built by the wealthy silk-weavers' guild to care for unwanted children. Inside, a highly emotive, state-of-the-art museum explores its history, climaxing with a sensational collection of frescoes and artworks that once decorated the hospital and a stunning rooftop-cafe terrace (fab city views). Brunelleschi's use of rounded arches and Roman capitals marks it as arguably the first building of the Renaissance.

Andrea della Robbia (1435–1525) added the facade's distinctive terracotta medallions of infants in swaddling clothes.

In 1445 the first unwanted baby (female, as was commonly the case at the time) was found abandoned on the hospital's doorstep; by the end of the 15th century it was home to over 1000 children. In the 16th century, such was the demand that the hospital replaced the *pila* (a concave stone on which infants were left) with a revolving door in which newborns could be left in relative warmth. On display are the various sentimental objects that often appeared with a foundling – coins, rosary beads, a crucifix, ribbons, one half of a broken medal allowing parents to later identify their child. From 1667 the hospital also accepted young mothers as wet nurses, and by the mid-19th-century the orphanage was accepting 2000 unwanted children a year.

No museum visit is complete without a drink in the rooftop cafe, Caffè del Verone (p125), at home in the foundling hospital's *verone* (drying room) where linen was stretched and hung to dry in the 15th century.

Biblioteca Medicea Laurenziana   LIBRARY

(Medici Library; Map p82; ☎ 055 293 79 11; www.bml.firenze.sbn.it; Piazza San Lorenzo 9; €3, incl Basilica di San Lorenzo €8.50; ⊗9.30am-1.30pm Mon-Fri) Beyond the Basilica di San Lorenzo ticket office lie peaceful cloisters framing a garden with orange trees. Stairs lead up the loggia to the Biblioteca Medicea Laurenziana, commissioned by Giulio de' Medici (Pope Clement VII) in 1524 to house the extensive Medici library (started by Cosimo the Elder and greatly added to by Lorenzo Il Magnifico). The extraordinary staircase in the vestibule, intended as a 'dark prelude' to the magnificent Sala di Lettura (Reading Room), was designed by Michelangelo.

Palazzo Medici-Riccardi   PALACE

(Map p92; ☎ 055 276 03 40; www.palazzo-medici.it; Via Cavour 3; adult/reduced €7/4; ⊗8.30am-7pm Thu-Tue) Cosimo the Elder entrusted Michelozzo with the design of the family's town house in 1444. The result was this palace, a blueprint that influenced the construction of Florentine family residences such as Palazzo Pitti and Palazzo Strozzi. The upstairs chapel, Cappella dei Magi, is covered in wonderfully detailed frescoes (c 1459–63) by Benozzo Gozzoli, a pupil of Fra' Angelico, and is one of the supreme achievements of Renaissance painting.

Gozzoli's ostensible theme of *Procession of the Magi to Bethlehem* is but a slender pretext for portraying members of the Medici clan in their best light; spot Lorenzo Il Magnifico and Cosimo the Elder in the crowd. The chapel was reconfigured to accommodate a baroque staircase, hence the oddly split fresco. The mid-15th-century altarpiece of the *Adoration of the Child* is a copy of the original (initially here) by Fra' Filippo Lippi. Only 10 visitors are allowed in at a time; in high season reserve in advance at the ticket desk.

The Medici lived at Palazzo Medici until 1540, while the Riccardi family moved in a century later. They remodelled the palace and built the 1st-floor Sala Luca Giordano, a sumptuous masterpiece of baroque art. Giordano adorned the ceiling with his complex *Allegory of Divine Wisdom* (1685), a rather overblown example of late baroque dripping with gold leaf and bursting with colour.

Take time to mooch around the palace's peaceful courtyard garden, created in the 15th century as a green sanctuary for the Medici, with its exquisite boxwood hedges, fragrant plants and elegant sculptures, including Donatello's bronze *Judith and Holofernes* (1455–60), subsequently moved to Palazzo Vecchio. A couple of lesser-known sculptures remain today, atmospherically wedged between potted lemon trees.

Basilica di San Lorenzo   BASILICA

(Map p82; ☎ 055 21 40 42; www.operamedicealaurenziana.org; Piazza San Lorenzo; €6, with Biblioteca Medicea Laurenziana €8.50; ⊗10am-5.30pm Mon-Sat) Considered one of Florence's most harmonious examples of Renaissance architecture, this unfinished basilica was the Medici parish church and mausoleum. It was designed by Brunelleschi in 1425 for Cosimo the Elder and built over a 4th-century church. In the solemn interior,

ℹ MUSEUM TICKETS

In July, August and other busy periods such as Easter, unbelievably long queues are a fact of life at Florence's key museums – if you haven't prebooked your ticket, you could well end up standing in line for four hours or so.

For €3 per ticket (€4 for the Uffizi and Galleria dell'Accademia), tickets to nine *musei statali* (state museums) can be reserved, including the Uffizi, Galleria dell'Accademia, Palazzo Pitti, Museo del Bargello and the Medicean chapels (Cappelle Medicee). In reality, the only museums where prebooking is vital are the Uffizi and the Accademia – to organise your ticket, book online through Firenze Musei (Florence Museums; www.firenzemusei.it), with ticketing desks at Door 2 of the Uffizi (Piazzale degli Uffizi; ⊗ 8.15am-6.05pm Tue-Sun), Palazzo Pitti (🗐 055 29 48 83; Piazza dei Pitti; ⊗ 8.15am-6.05pm Tue-Sun) and inside the Via del Cimatori entrance of Chiesa e Museo di Orsanmichele (p69).

At the Uffizi, signs point prebooked ticket holders to Door 3 opposite the main gallery where tickets can be collected; once you've got the ticket you go to Door 1 of the museum (for prebooked tickets only) and queue again to enter the gallery. It's annoying, but you'll still save hours of queuing time overall. Many hotels in Florence also prebook museum tickets for guests.

Admission to all state museums, including the Uffizi and Galleria dell'Accademia, is free on the first Sunday of each month between October and March, for six days in the first week of March during Italy's National Museum Week, and on 18 February, the day Anna Maria Louisa de' Medici (1667–1743) died. The last of the Medici family, it was she who bequeathed the city its vast cultural heritage.

Visitors aged under 18 and over 65 get into Florence's state museums for free, while EU citizens aged 18 to 25 pay just €2. Have your ID with you at all times. Note that museum ticket offices usually shut 30 minutes before closing time.

---

look for Brunelleschi's austerely beautiful Sagrestia Vecchia (Old Sacristy) with its sculptural decoration by Donatello. Michelangelo was commissioned to design the facade in 1518, but his design in white Carrara marble was never executed, hence the building's rough, unfinished appearance.

Inside, columns of *pietra serena* (soft grey stone) crowned with Corinthian capitals separate the nave from the two aisles. The gilded funerary monument of Donatello – who was still sculpting the two bronze pulpits (1460–67) adorned with panels of the Crucifixion when he died – lies in the Cappella Martelli (Martelli Chapel) featuring Fra' Filippo Lippi's exquisitely restored *Annunciation* (c 1440).

Donatello's actual grave lies in the basilica crypt, today part of the Museo del Tesoro di San Lorenzo (San Lorenzo Treasury Museum); the crypt entrance is in the courtyard beyond the ticket office. The museum displays chalices, altarpieces, dazzling altar cloths, processional crucifixes, episcopal brooches and other precious sacred treasures once displayed in the church. Across from the plain marble tombstone of Donatello is the tomb of Cosimo the Elder, buried inside the quadrangular pilaster in the crypt supporting the basilica presbytery – his funerary monument sits directly above, in front of the high altar in the basilica.

Cenacolo di Sant'Apollonia CONVENT

(Map p92; 🗐 055 238 86 07; www.polomusealetoscana.beniculturali.it; Via XXVII Aprile 1; ⊗ 8.15am-1.50pm daily, closed 1st, 3rd & 5th Sat & Sun of month) FREE Once part of a sprawling Benedictine monastery, this *cenacolo* (refectory) harbours arguably the city's most remarkable *Last Supper* scene. Painted by Andrea del Castagno in the 1440s, it is one of the first works of its kind to effectively apply Renaissance perspective. It possesses a haunting power with its vivid colours - especially the almost abstract squares of marble painted above the apostles' heads - as well as the dark, menacing figure of Judas.

In season, look for occasional additional guided tours of the convent on Wednesday afternoon between 3pm and 5pm; contact nearby Museo di San Marco (p92) for information and reservations.

Synagogue & Jewish Museum of Florence SYNAGOGUE

(Sinagoga e Museo Ebraico di Firenze; Map p100; 🗐 055 234 66 54; Via Luigi Carlo Farini 6; adult/reduced €6.50/5; ⊗ 9.30am-6.30pm Sun-Thu, to

SERGIO TB/SHUTTERSTOCK©

1. Palazzo Vecchio (p80), Florence
A Renaissance palace containing several museums.

2. Mercato Centrale (p118)
Florence's food market maze.

3. Basilica di Santa Maria Novella (p88), Florence
This monastery is home to beautiful frescoes.

4. Ponte Vecchio (p103), Florence
An iconic bridge dating from 1345 that houses many jewellery shops.

5pm Fri summer, 10am-5.30pm Sun-Thu, to 3pm Fri winter) Built between 1874 and 1882, just after the Jewish community in Italy had gained full emancipation after centuries of persecution, this vast Moorish-styled synagogue is a beautiful, polychrome hodgepodge of Islamic, Jewish and Christian religious architecture that recalls the Aya Sophia in Istanbul. A small museum on the 2nd floor documents the history of Jewish Florence.

◉ Santa Croce

Presided over by the massive Franciscan basilica of the same name on the neighbourhood's main square, this area has a slightly rough veneer to it. The basilica aside, the other major sight is the Museo del Bargello, with its sensational collection of Tuscan sculpture from the Renaissance period. Michelangelo's family lived in Santa Croce at what is now the Museo Casa Buonarroti house-museum.

★ Museo del Bargello   MUSEUM

(Map p100; ☑ 055 238 86 06; www.bargello musei.beniculturali.it; Via del Proconsolo 4; adult/reduced €8/4; ⊗ 8.15am-2pm, closed 2nd & 4th Sun, 1st, 3rd & 5th Mon of month) It was behind the stark walls of Palazzo del Bargello, Florence's earliest public building, that the *podestà* (governing magistrate) meted out justice from the 13th century until 1502. Today the building safeguards Italy's most comprehensive collection of Tuscan Renaissance sculpture, with some of Michelangelo's best early works and several by Donatello. Michelangelo was just 21 when a cardinal commissioned him to create the drunken grape-adorned *Bacchus* (1496–97). Unfortunately the cardinal didn't like the result and sold it.

Other Michelangelo works are in the ground-floor Sala di Michelangelo e della Scultura del Cinque Cento (first door on the right after entering the interior courtyard). Look out for the marble bust of *Brutus* (c 1539), the *David/Apollo* from 1530–32 and the large, uncompleted roundel of the *Madonna and Child with the Infant St John* (aka the Tondo Pitti; 1505). After Michelangelo left Florence for the final time in 1534, sculpture was dominated by Baccio Bandinelli (his 1551 *Adam and Eve,* created for the *duomo,* is also displayed here) and Benvenuto Cellini (look for his playful 1548–50 marble *Ganymede* in the same room).

Back in the interior courtyard, an open staircase leads up to the elegant, sculpture-laced loggia (1370) and, to the right, the Salone di Donatello. Here, in the majestic Sala del Consiglio where the city council met, works by Donatello and other early-15th-century sculptors can be admired. Originally on the facade of Chiesa di Orsanmichele and now within a tabernacle at the hall's far end, Donatello's wonderful *St George* (1416–17) brought a new sense of perspective and movement to Italian sculpture. Also look for the bronze bas-reliefs created for the baptistry doors competition by Brunelleschi and Ghiberti.

Yet it is Donatello's two versions of *David,* a favourite subject for sculptors, that really fascinate: Donatello fashioned his slender, youthful dressed image in marble in 1408 and his fabled bronze between 1439 and 1443. The latter is extraordinary – the more so when you consider it was the first free-standing naked statue to be sculpted since classical times.

Criminals received their last rites before execution in the palace's 1st-floor Cappella del Podestà, also known as the Mary Magdalene Chapel, where Hell and Heaven are frescoed on the walls, as are stories from the lives of Mary of Egypt, Mary Magdalene and John the Baptist. These remnants of frescoes by Giotto were not discovered until 1840, when the chapel was turned into a storeroom and prison.

The 2nd floor moves into the 16th century with a superb collection of terracotta pieces by the prolific della Robbia family, including some of their best-known works, such as Andrea's *Ritratto idealizia di fanciullo* (Bust of a Boy; c 1475) and Giovanni's *Pietà* (1514). Instantly recognisable, Giovanni's works are more elaborate and flamboyant than either father Luca's or cousin Andrea's, using a richer palette of colours.

★ Basilica di Santa Croce   BASILICA

(Map p100; ☑ 055 246 61 05; www.santacroce opera.it; Piazza di Santa Croce 16; adult/reduced €8/6; ⊗ 9.30am-5.30pm Mon-Sat, from 2pm Sun) The austere interior of this Franciscan basilica is a shock after the magnificent neo-Gothic facade enlivened by varying shades of coloured marble. Most visitors come to see the tombs of Michelangelo, Galileo and Ghiberti, but frescoes by Giotto in the chapels to the right of the altar are the real highlights. The basilica was designed by Arnolfo di Cambio between 1294 and 1385 and owes

WHO'S THAT GUY?

Name *David*

Occupation World's most famous sculpture.

Vital statistics Height: 516cm tall; weight: 19 tonnes of mediocre-quality pearly white marble from the Fantiscritti quarries in Carrara.

Spirit Young biblical hero in meditative pose who, with the help of God, defeats an enemy more powerful than himself. Scarcely visible sling emphasises victory of innocence and intellect over brute force.

Commissioned In 1501 by the Opera del Duomo for the cathedral, but subsequently placed in front of the Palazzo Vecchio on Piazza della Signoria, where it stayed until 1873.

Famous journeys It took 40 men four days to transport the statue on rails from Michelangelo's workshop behind the cathedral to Piazza della Signoria in 1504. Its journey from here, through the streets of Florence, to its current purpose-built tribune in the Galleria dell'Accademia in 1873, took seven long days.

Outstanding features (a) His expression, which, from the left profile, appears serene, Zen and boylike, and from the right, concentrated, manly and highly charged in anticipation of the gargantuan Goliath he is about to slay; (b) the sense of counterbalanced weight rippling through his body, from the tension in his right hip on which he leans to his taut left arm.

Why the small penis? In classical art a large or even average-sized packet was not deemed elegant, hence the daintier size.

And the big head and hands? *David* was designed to stand up high on a cathedral buttress in the apse, from where his head and hands would have appeared in perfect proportion.

Beauty treatments Body scrub with hydrochloric acid (1843); clay and cellulose pulp 'mud pack', bath in distilled water (2004).

Occupational hazards Over the centuries he's been struck by lightning, attacked by rioters and had his toes bashed with a hammer. The two pale white lines visible on his lower left arm is where his arm got broken during the 1527 revolt when the Medici were kicked out of Florence. Giorgio Vasari, then a child, picked up the pieces and 16 years later had them sent to Cosimo I who restored the statue, so the story goes.

its name to a splinter of the Holy Cross donated by King Louis IX of France in 1258.

Some of its frescoed chapels are much better preserved than others – Giotto's murals featuring John the Baptist in the Cappella Peruzzi (1310–20) are in particularly poor condition. Those painted between 1320 and 1328 in the neighbouring Cappella Bardi, depicting scenes from the life of St Francis, have fared better. Giotto's assistant and most loyal pupil, Taddeo Gaddi, frescoed the nearby Cappella Baroncelli (1328–38) with scenes from the life of the Virgin.

Taddeo's son Agnolo painted the Cappella Castellani (1385), with frescoes depicting the life of St Nicholas, and was also responsible for the frescoes above the altar.

From the transept chapels a doorway designed by Michelozzo leads into a corridor, off which is the Sagrestia (Sacristy), an enchanting 14th-century room with Taddeo

Gaddi's fresco of the Crucifixion. On the left as you enter, look for the late-15th-century glazed terracotta bust of Christ by Andrea della Robbia, all too often overshadowed by the large painted wooden cross (c 1288) by Cimabue suspended from the wooden ceiling. One of many priceless artworks to be damaged in the 1966 floods that inundated Santa Croce in more than 4m of water, the crucifix took 10 years to restore and has since become a symbol of the catastrophe that struck the city and its subsequent comeback.

Through the next room, the church bookshop, you can access the Scuola del Cuoio (Map p100; 055 24 45 33; www.scuoladelcuoio.com; Via di San Giuseppe 5r; 10am-6pm), a leather school where you can see bags being fashioned and buy the finished products.

At the end of the corridor is a Medici chapel with a fine two-tone altarpiece in

Santa Croce

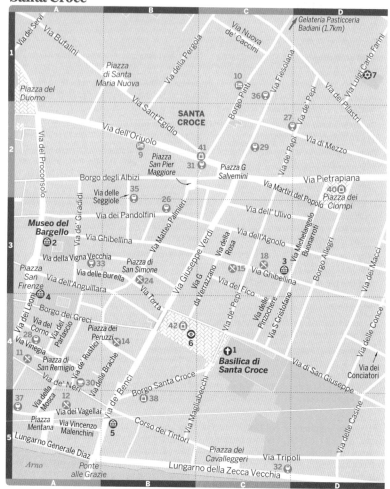

glazed terracotta by Andrea della Robbia. This was the original burial place of Galileo, from his death in 1642 until 1737 when arrangements were finally made for his reburial in the nave of the basilica. A small room to the left of the altar contains a bust of the scientist and a plaque marking the spot where his first tomb was.

Post-chapel, backtrack to the church and follow the 'Uscita' (exit) sign, opposite the main entrance, to access the basilica's two serene cloisters designed by Brunelleschi just before his death in 1446. His unfinished Cappella de' Pazzi, on the left at the end of the first cloister, is notable for its harmo-

nious lines and restrained terracotta medallions of the Apostles by Luca della Robbia, and is a masterpiece of Renaissance architecture. It was built for, but never used by, the wealthy banking family destroyed in the 1478 Pazzi Conspiracy – when papal sympathisers sought to overthrow Lorenzo Il Magnifico and the Medici dynasty.

Continue to the second cloister where a glass door leads into a gallery showcasing various artworks, climaxing with the cavernous Cenacolo where 150 Franciscan monks shared meals together in the 15th century, warehouse goods were stored in the 20th century and floodwaters hit a high of

5m in 1966. While Taddeo Gaddi's dazzling *The Last Supper* (1334–56) fresco fills the entire far wall, it is Georgio Vasari's magnificent *The Last Supper* (1546) that steals the show. Submerged in floodwater for at least 12 hours, the severely damaged oil painting was only returned to Santa Croce in 2016, following 50 years of restoration.

Santa Croce

Top Sights

1 Basilica di Santa Croce C4
2 Museo del Bargello A3

Sights

3 Fondazione Casa Buonarroti C3
4 Fondazione Zeffirelli A4
5 Museo Horne B5
6 Piazza di Santa Croce B4
7 Synagogue & Jewish Museum of Florence D1

Activities, Courses & Tours

8 Tuscany Bike Tours E4

Sleeping

9 Hotel Dalí B2
10 Hotel Monna Lisa C1

Eating

11 All'Antico Vinaio A4
12 Brac A5
13 Ciblèo E2
14 Club Culinario Toscano B4
15 Enoteca Pinchiorri C3
16 Il Pizzaiuolo E2
17 Il Teatro del Sale E3
18 Le Vespe Café C3
19 Santarpia F3
20 Semel E3
21 Terrazza Menoni E3
22 Trattoria Cibrèo E2
23 Trippaio Sergio Pollini E2
24 Vivoli B3

Drinking & Nightlife

25 Art. 17 Birreria E2
26 Babylon Club B3
27 Bitter Bar C2
28 Blob Club A4
29 Buca 10 .... C2
30 Ditta Artigianale A4
31 Eby's C2
32 Empireo C5
33 Full Up A3
34 Le Murate F4
35 Locale B2
36 Rex Café C1
37 Vanilla Club A5

Shopping

38 Aquaflor B5
39 C.BIO E2
40 Mercato dei Fiori D2
41 Sbigoli Terrecotte C2
42 Scuola del Cuoio B4

Fondazione Zeffirelli MUSEUM

(Map p100; ☎055 265 84 35; www.fondazionefrancozeffirelli.com; Piazza San Firenze 5; adult/reduced €10/7; ⊙10am-6pm Tue-Sun) Opera buffs will adore this museum celebrating more than seven decades of work by the late, internationally renowned, Florence-born film director Franco Zeffirelli (1923–2019). Housed in the San Firenze Complex, a magnificent late-Baroque *palazzo* which previously served as the city's tribunal and courthouse (until it moved out of the historic centre to Novoli), the exhibition begins in 1953 and spans 20 'chapters' or rooms. Admire scene sketches, costumes, posters, flyers, set-design models, original drawings and behind-the-scenes photographs. The exquisite, ground-floor music room hosts occasional chamber-music concerts and film screenings.

Fondazione Casa Buonarroti   MUSEUM
(Map p100; ☑ 055 24 17 52; www.casabuonarroti. it; Via Ghibellina 70; adult/reduced €8/5; ⊙ 10am-5pm Wed-Mon summer, to 4.30pm winter) FREE Though Michelangelo never lived in Casa Buonarroti, his heirs devoted some of the artist's hard-earned wealth to the construction of this 17th-century *palazzo* to honour his memory. The little museum contains frescoes of the artist's life and two of his most important early works – the serene, bas-relief *Madonna of the Stairs* and the unfinished *Battle of the Centaurs*.

Piazza di Santa Croce   PIAZZA
(Map p100) This square was cleared in the Middle Ages to allow the faithful to gather when the church itself was full. In Savonarola's day, heretics were executed here. Such an open space inevitably found other uses, and from the 14th century it was often the colourful scene of jousts, festivals and *calcio storico* (historic football) matches. The city's 2nd-century amphitheatre took up the area facing the square's western end: Piazza dei Peruzzi, Via de' Bentaccordi and Via Torta mark the oval outline of its course.

Still played in this square in the third week of June (p111) each year, *calcio storico*

LOCAL KNOWLEDGE

URBAN GREEN: PARKS & GARDENS

Blockbuster garden twinset of Giardino di Boboli (p106) and Giardino Bardini (p107) aside, urban Florence squirrels away a clutch of historic parks and gardens – a breath of fresh air, quite literally, on a hot summer's day when their pristine lawns and beautifully varied flora provide a refreshing green escape from the city-centre crowds.

Giardino Torrigiani (Map p104; ☑ 055 22 45 27; www.giardinotorrigiani.it; Via de' Serragli 144; 1½hr guided tours by donation; ⊙ advance reservation via email) Astonishing. Behind the unassuming facades of Via de' Serragli lies a vast, secret garden – Europe's largest privately owned green space within a historic centre, owned by the Torrigiani Malaspina and Torrigiani di Santa Cristina families. It's possible to visit this well-kept and loved leafy retreat in the engaging company of the charismatic Marquis Vanni Torrigiani Malaspina and his wife, Susanna. Tours (in English or Italian) are intimate and offer a rare glimpse into a very different and privileged Florentine world.

Giardino dei Semplici (Orto Botanico; Map p92; Via Pier Antonio Micheli 3; adult/reduced €6/3; ⊙ 10am-7pm Thu-Tue summer, to 4pm Sat & Sun winter) Founded in 1545 to furnish medicine to the Medici, Florence's botanical gardens – managed today by the university – are a wonderfully peaceful retreat in a stretch of the city with little green space. Its greenhouse is fragrant with citrus blossoms, and medicinal plants, Tuscan spices, 220 tree types and wildflowers from the Apennines pepper its 2.3 hectares. Don't miss the magnificent yew tree, planted in 1720, and an ornamental cork oak from 1805. Several themed footpaths wend their way through the gardens.

Parco delle Cascine (Viale degli Olmi) Florence's largest park is dotted with playgrounds and is a great place to let the little 'uns loose. Families take over at weekends and the park is a colourful scene with rollerbladers, kite-flyers, joggers and kids on bikes. In summer you can also use Le Pavoniere swimming pool.

The Medici dukes made this a private hunting reserve, but Peter Leopold opened it to the public in 1776, with boulevards, fountains and bird sanctuaries (now the swimming pool). In the late 19th century, horse racing began here. Queen Victoria was a fan of Florence and would toddle along to the Cascine during her stays.

At the extreme west end of the park is a monument to Rajaram Cuttiputti, an Indian maharajah who, while holidaying in Florence in 1870, came down with gastroenteritis and died. His retinue was surprisingly granted permission to cremate him by the river. Four years later a statue and memorial were designed by British artisans.

is like a combination of football and rugby with few rules (headbutting, punching, elbowing and choking are allowed, but sucker-punching and kicks to the head are forbidden).

Museo Horne   MUSEUM
(Map p100; ☑ 055 24 46 61; www.museohorne.it; Via de' Benci 6; adult/reduced €7/5; ◷ 10am-2pm Thu-Tue) One of the many eccentric Brits who made Florence home in the early 20th century, Herbert Percy Horne bought and renovated this Renaissance *palazzo,* then installed his eclectic collection of 14th- and 15th-century Italian art, ceramics, furniture and other oddments. There are a few works by masters such as Giotto and Fra' Filippo Lippi. More interesting is the furniture, some of which is exquisite.

◉ Oltrarno

The Oltrarno's main sights lie snug on Piazza Santo Spirito and nearby Piazza del Carmine. When you reach museum overload and need to stretch your legs and see some sky, meander east towards neighbouring Boboli where the tiers of parks and gardens behind Palazzo Pitti entice.

Ponte Vecchio   BRIDGE
(Map p82) Dating from 1345, iconic Ponte Vecchio was the only Florentine bridge to survive destruction at the hands of retreating German forces in 1944. Above jewellery shops on the eastern side, the Corridoio Vasariano (p86) is a 16th-century passageway between the Uffizi and Palazzo Pitti that runs around, rather than through, the medieval Torre dei Mannelli at the bridge's southern end.

The first documentation of a stone bridge here, at the narrowest crossing point along the entire length of the Arno, dates from 972.

Floods in 1177 and 1333 destroyed the bridge, and in 1966 it came close to being destroyed again. Many of the jewellers with shops on the bridge were convinced the floodwaters would sweep away their livelihoods; fortunately the bridge held.

They're still here. Indeed, the bridge has twinkled with the glittering wares of jewellers, their trade often passed down from generation to generation, ever since the 16th century, when Ferdinando I de' Medici ordered them here to replace the often malodorous presence of the town butchers, who used to toss unwanted leftovers into the river.

Cappella Brancacci   CHAPEL
(Map p104; ☑ 055 238 21 95; www.museicivici fiorentini.comune.fi.it; Piazza del Carmine 14; adult/reduced Wed-Fri €8/6, Sat-Mon €10/7; ◷ 10am-5pm Wed-Sat & Mon, 1-5pm Sun) Fire in the 18th century practically destroyed 13th-century Basilica di Santa Maria del Carmine (Map p104; Piazza del Carmine; ◷ 6.15am-noon & 5-6.45pm Mon-Sat, 9.15am-1pm & 5-7pm Sun), but it spared its magnificent chapel frescoes – a treasure of paintings by Masolino da Panicale, Masaccio and Filippino Lippi commissioned by rich merchant Felice Brancacci upon his return from Egypt in 1423. The chapel entrance is right of the main church entrance. Only 30 people can visit at a time, limited to 30 minutes in high season; pricier weekend tickets include admission to the Fondazione Salvatore Romano (p103).

Masaccio's fresco cycle illustrating the life of St Peter is considered among his greatest works, representing a definitive break with Gothic art and a plunge into new worlds of expression in the early stages of the Renaissance. *The Expulsion of Adam and Eve from Paradise* and *The Tribute Money,* both on the left side of the chapel, are his best-known works. Masaccio painted these frescoes in his early 20s, taking over from Masolino, and interrupted the task to go to Rome, where he died, aged only 27. The cycle was completed some 60 years later by Filippino Lippi. Masaccio himself features in his *St Peter Enthroned;* he's the one standing beside the Apostle, staring out at the viewer. The figures around him have been identified as Brunelleschi, Masolino and Alberti. Filippino Lippi also painted himself into the scene of *St Peter's Crucifixion,* along with his teacher, Botticelli.

Fondazione Salvatore Romano   MUSEUM
(Cenacolo di Santo Spirito; Map p104; ☑ 055 28 70 43; www.museicivicifiorentini.comune.fi.it; Piazza Santo Spirito 29; adult/reduced €10/7; ◷ 10am-4pm Sat-Mon) For a change of pace from the Renaissance, head to this Gothic-style former refectory safeguarding an imposing wall fresco by Andrea Orcagna depicting the *Last Supper and the Crucifixion* (c 1370), one of the largest 14th-century paintings to survive. The museum itself displays a collection of rare 11th-century Romanesque sculpture, paintings and antique furniture donated to the city by art collector and antiquarian Salvatore Romano (1875–1955). Tickets are sold at Cappella Brancacci (p103); one ticket covers admission to both sights.

FLORENCE SIGHTS

Oltrarno

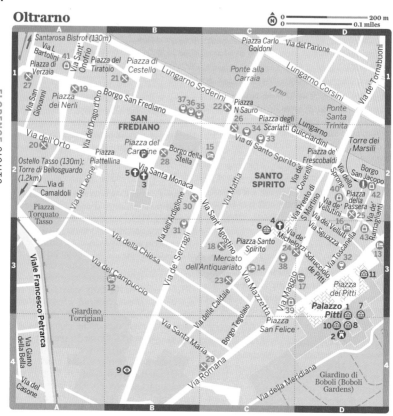

Basilica di Santo Spirito   CHURCH

(Map p104; www.basilicasantospirito.it; Piazza Santo Spirito; ☺8.30am-1pm & 3-6pm Mon, Tue & Thu-Sat, 11.30am-1.30pm & 3-6pm Sun) The facade of this Brunelleschi church, smart on Florence's most shabby-chic piazza, makes a striking backdrop to open-air concerts in summer. Inside, the basilica's length is lined with 38 semicircular chapels (covered with a plain wall in the 1960s), and a colonnade of grey *pietra forte* Corinthian columns injects monumental grandeur. Artworks to look for include Domenico di Zanobi's *Madonna of the Relief* (1485) in the Cappella Velutti, in which the Madonna wards off a little red devil with a club.

Filippino Lippi's poorly lit *Madonna with Child and Saints* (1493–94) is in the Cappella Nerli in the right transept.

The main altar, beneath the central dome, is a voluptuous baroque flourish, rather out of place in Brunelleschi's characteristically spare interior.

Don't miss the door next to Cappella Segni in the left aisle leading to the sacristy, where you'll find a poignant wooden crucifix attributed by some experts to Michelangelo. Michelangelo used to visit the hospital inside the neighbouring monastery at night to study the anatomy of corpses yet to be buried, hence his donation of the exquisitely sculptured Christ, or so the story goes.

⊙ Boboli & San Miniato al Monte

The neighbourhood's sights are split between Piazza dei Pitti – dominated by the vast Palazzo Pitti with its cache of museums – and Piazzale Michelangelo up the hill in San Miniato.

Piazzale Michelangelo   VIEWPOINT

(Map p106; ▣13) Turn your back on the bevy of ticky-tacky souvenir stalls flogging *David* statues and boxer shorts and take in the

Oltrarno

◎ **Top Sights**
1 Palazzo Pitti.............................D3

◎ **Sights**
2 Appartamenti Reali....................D4
3 Basilica di Santa Maria del
   Carmine..................................B2
4 Basilica di Santo Spirito.............C3
5 Cappella Brancacci....................B2
6 Fondazione Salvatore Romano...........C3
7 Galleria d'Arte Moderna...............D3
8 Galleria Palatina.....................D4
9 Giardino Torrigiani...................B4
10 Museo della Moda e del
   Costume..................................D4
11 Tesoro dei Granduchi..................D3

⬤ **Sleeping**
12 AdAstra..................................B3
13 Hotel La Scaletta.....................D3
14 Hotel Palazzo Guadagni...............C3
15 Oltrarno Splendid C2
16 Palazzo Belfiore......................D3
17 SoprArno Suites.......................D3

⬤ **Eating**
18 #Raw C3
19 Berberè A1

20 Burro e Acciughe.......................A2
21 Essenziale..............................B1
22 Gelateria La Carraia..................C1
23 Gurdulù.................................C3
24 Gustapizza.............................D3
25 Il Magazzino..........................D2
26 Il Santo Bevitore......................C2
27 iO Osteria Personale..................A1
28 L'OV....................................B2
29 Osteria dell'Enoteca..................C4
30 S.Forno.................................B2

◎ **Drinking & Nightlife**
31 Archea Brewery.........................B3
32 Enoteca Pitti Gola e Cantina.........D3
33 Gosh....................................C2
34 Il Santino.............................C2
35 La Cité.................................B1
36 Love Craft.............................B1
37 Mad Souls & Spirits...................B1
38 Rasputin................................C3

⬤ **Shopping**
39 Avavav..................................C3
40 Bjørk...................................D2
41 Laboratorio Jane Harman..............A1
42 Obsequium..............................D2
43 Scicc'Art..............................D3

spectacular city panorama from this vast square, pierced by one of Florence's two *David* copies. Sunset here is particularly dramatic. It's a 10-minute uphill walk along the serpentine road, paths and steps that scale the hillside from the Arno and Piazza Giuseppe Poggi; from Piazza San Niccolò walk uphill and bear left up the long flight of steps signposted Viale Michelangelo. Or take bus 13 from Stazione di Santa Maria Novella.

★ **Palazzo Pitti**   MUSEUM
(Map p104; ☑ 055 29 48 83; www.uffizi.it/en/pitti-palace; Piazza dei Pitti; adult/reduced Mar-Oct €16/8, Nov-Feb €10/5, combined ticket with Uffizi incl Giardino di Boboli Mar-Oct €38/21, Nov-Feb €18/11; ⊙ 8.15am-6.50pm Tue-Sun) Commissioned by banker Luca Pitti in 1458, this Renaissance palace was later bought by the Medici family. Over the centuries, it was a residence of the city's rulers until the Savoys donated it to the state in 1919. Nowadays it houses an impressive collection of silver and jewellery, a couple of art museums and a series of rooms recreating life in the palace during House of Savoy times. Stop by at sunset when its entire facade is coloured a vibrant pink.

➡ *Ground Floor*
Exquisite amber carvings, ivory miniatures, glittering tiaras and headpieces, silver pillboxes and various other gems and jewels are displayed in the **Tesoro dei Granduchi**, a series of elaborately frescoed audience chambers, also known as Museo degli Argenti (Silver Museum). Notable (but not always open) is the **Sala di Giovanni da San Giovanni**, which sports lavish head-to-toe frescoes (1635–42) celebrating the life of Lorenzo Il Magnifico – spot Michelangelo giving Lorenzo a statue. 'Talk little, be brief and witty' is the curt motto above the painted staircase in the next room, the public audience chamber, where the grand duke received visitors in the presence of his court.

➡ *1st Floor*
Raphaels and Rubens vie for centre stage in the enviable collection of 16th- to 18th-century art amassed by the Medici and Lorraine dukes in the **Galleria Palatina**, reached by several flights of stairs from the palace's central courtyard (bear right from the main entrance). This gallery has retained the original display arrangement of paintings (squeezed in, often on top of each other), so it can be visually overwhelming – go slowly and focus on the works one by one.

Boboli

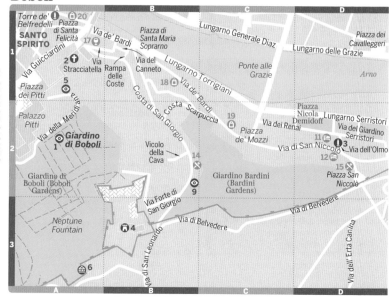

Highlights in the Sala di Prometeo include Fra' Filippo Lippi's *Madonna and Child and the Birth of Virgin Mary* (1452) and Botticelli's *Portrait of a Woman* (c 1475–90), thought to be a portrait of Simonetta Vespucci, lover of Giuliano de' Medici, and one of the gallery's oldest portraits. Admire Raphael's *Madonna of the Window* (1513–14) in the Sala di Ulisse; and Caravaggio's brutally realistic *Sleeping Cupid* (1608) in the Sala dell'Educazione di Giove. Don't miss the Sala di Saturno, full of magnificent works by Raphael, including the *Madonna of the Chair* (1513–14), *Madonna and Child* (c 1505–06) and *Madonna and Child enthroned with Saints* (1507–08). Next door, in the Sala di Giove, the same artist's *Lady with a Veil* (aka La Velata; c 1516) holds court alongside Giorgione's *Three Ages of Man* (c 1500).

Past the Sala di Venere are the Appartamenti Reali (Royal Apartments), a series of rooms presented as they were c 1880–91 during House of Savoy times.

➜ *2nd Floor*

The Galleria d'Arte Moderna curates 18th- and 19th-century works. Paintings of the Florentine Macchiaioli school (the local equivalent of Impressionism) dominates the collection.

Crowning the palace is the Museo della Moda e del Costume (Fashion & Costume Museum), host to some colourful temporary exhibitions with a fashion focus.

Cent-saver alert: buy your Palazzo Pitti ticket before 8.59am and actually enter the palace before 9.25am to get a 50% reduction on the ticket price.

★ Giardino di Boboli   GARDENS
(Map p106; ☑ 055 29 48 83; www.uffizi.it/en/boboli-garden; Piazza dei Pitti; adult/reduced incl Giardino Bardini & Museo delle Porcellane Mar-Oct €10/2, Nov-Feb €6/2, combined ticket with Uffizi incl Palazzo Pitti Mar-Oct €38/21, Nov-Feb €18/11; ⊙8.15am-6.50pm summer, reduced hours winter, closed 1st & last Mon of month) Behind Palazzo Pitti, the fountain- and sculpture-adorned Boboli Gardens – slowly but surely being restored to their former pristine glory thanks to a €2 million investment by Florence's homegrown fashion house Gucci – were laid out in the mid-16th century to a design by architect Niccolò Pericoli. At the upper, southern limit, beyond the box-hedged rose garden and Museo delle Porcellane, beautiful views over the Florentine countryside unfold.

Within the lower reaches of the gardens, don't miss the fantastical shell- and gem-encrusted Grotta del Buontalenti.

FLORENCE SIGHTS

Boboli

⊙ Top Sights
1 Giardino di Boboli A2

⊙ Sights
2 Chiesa di Santa Felicità A1
3 Clet...D2
4 Forte di Belvedere.............................B3
5 Grotta del Buontalenti.......................A1
6 Museo delle Porcellane A3
7 Piazzale Michelangelo F3
8 Torre San Niccolò E2
9 Villa e Giardino Bardini B2

⊙ Activities, Courses & Tours
10 Urban Beach E2

⊙ Sleeping
11 Hotel Silla D2
12 Palazzo San Niccolò D2

⊙ Eating
13 Easy Living...E2
14 La Leggenda dei Frati B2
15 ZEB...D2

⊙ Drinking & Nightlife
16 Flò F3
17 Le Volpi e l'Uva A1

⊙ Shopping
18 Il Torchio..B1
19 Lorenzo Villoresi C2
20 Uashmama A1

Villa e Giardino Bardini   GARDENS

(Map p106; ☑ 055 2006 6233; www.villabardini.it; Costa San Giorgio 2, Via de' Bardi 1r; adult/reduced villa €10/5, gardens €6/3, gardens with Giardino di Boboli ticket free; ⊙ villa 10am-7pm Tue-Sun, gardens 8.15am-7.30pm summer, shorter hours winter, closed 1st & last Mon of month) This 17th-century villa and garden was named after 19th-century antiquarian art collector Stefano Bardini (1836–1922), who bought it in 1913 and restored its ornamental medieval garden. It has all the features of a quintessential Tuscan garden, including artificial grottoes, orangery, marble statues and fountains. Inside the villa, the small Museo Pietro Annigoni displays works by Italian painter Pietro Annigoni (1910–88). End with city views from the romantic roof terrace.

April and May, with the garden's flower beds of azaleas, peonies and wisteria in bloom, are lovely months to visit, as is June with its flowering irises. Its Michelin-starred garden restaurant, La Leggenda dei Frati (p123), with stone loggia overlooking the Florentine skyline, is one of the most romantic spots in the city to dine.

Forte di Belvedere   FORTRESS

(Map p106; Via di San Leonardo 1; ⊙ hours vary) FREE Forte di Belvedere is a rambling fort designed by Bernardo Buontalenti for Grand Duke Ferdinando I at the end of the 16th century. From the massive bulwark, soldiers kept watch on four fronts – as much for internal security as to protect the Palazzo Pitti against foreign attack. Today the fort hosts summertime art exhibitions, which are well worth a peek if only to revel in the sweeping city panorama that can be had from the fort. Outside of exhibition times, the fort is closed.

To get here from Piazza de' Mozzi, turn east down Via dei Renai, past leafy Piazza Nicola Demidoff, dedicated to the 19th-century Russian philanthropist who lived nearby in Via di San Niccolò. At the end of Via dei Renai, turn right onto Via di San Niccolò; walk east to emerge at the tower marking Torre San Niccolò (p108), all that is left of the city walls. To get an idea of what the walls were once like, walk south from Chiesa di San Niccolò Oltrarno through Porta San Miniato. The wall extends a short way to the east and for a stretch further west, up a steep hill that leads you to the fortress.

FLORENCE ACTIVITIES

Torre San Niccolò
GATE

(Map p106; ☑ 055 276 85 58, 055 276 82 24; www.musefirenze.it; Piazza Giuseppe Poggi; guided visit every 30min €4; ☺5-8pm late Jun-late Sep) Built in 1324, the best preserved of the city's medieval gates stands sentinel on the banks of the Arno. In summer, with a guide you can scale the steep stairs inside the tower to enjoy blockbuster river and city views. Visits organised by Mus.e are limited to 15 people at a time (no children under eight years) and advance reservations are essential; book online, by email or by phone. Tours are cancelled when it rains.

Basilica di San Miniato al Monte
CHURCH

(☑ 055 234 27 31; www.sanminiatoalmonte.it; Via Monte alle Croci; ☺9.30am-1pm & 3-7.30pm summer, to 7pm winter) FREE Five minutes' walk uphill from Piazzale Michelangelo is this wonderful Romanesque church, dedicated to St Minius, an early-Christian martyr in Florence said to have flown to this spot after his death down in the town (or, if you want to believe an alternative version, walked up the hill with his head tucked underneath his arm). The church dates from the early 11th century, although its typical Tuscan multicoloured marble facade was tacked on a couple of centuries later.

Inside its unlit interior, 13th- to 15th-century frescoes adorn the south wall and intricate inlaid marble designs line the nave, leading to a fine Romanesque crypt. The sacristy in the southeast corner features frescoes by Spinello Arentino depicting the life of St Benedict. Slap bang in the middle of the nave is the bijou Capella del Crocefisso, to which Michelozzo, Agnolo Gaddi and Luca della Robbia all contributed.

Don't miss an atmospheric stroll in relative solitude in the Cimitero Monumentale delle Porte Sante behind the church. Something of a mini-town for the dead in its own right, this sea of monumental graves was laid out in the 18th century. Among the many celebrated Florentines buried here are Carlo Lorenzini (1826–90), author of *Pinocchio*, and philosopher and writer Giovanni Papini (1881–1956).

Activities

Urban and art rich to the core, Florence is hardly a hardcore activity centre: cooking, paddling along the Arno or indulging in a morning jog along its grassy riverbanks, up narrow stone-walled lanes to San Miniato al Monte or in Parco delle Cascine is about as active as most Florentines get.

Firenze Rafting
RAFTING

(☑ 349 0921540; www.firenzerafting.it; €25; ☺Mar-Nov) View Ponte Vecchio, the Uffizi and other Florence landmarks from a different perspective – afloat a sturdy inflatable raft on the Arno. Trips, departing from the riverbanks across the Torre San Niccolò in the Oltrarno, last two hours and include an aperitif beneath the arches of Ponte Vecchio.

Urban Beach
BEACH

(Map p106; ☑ 055 234 11 12; www.easylivingfirenze.it; Piazza Giuseppe Poggi; ☺May-Sep) Be it relaxing beneath a parasol on a sun-lounger, playing beach volleyball or joining a sunset yoga class, Florence's sandy riverside beach is the place to be in summer. Run by the creative folks behind the neighbouring Easy Living (p122) kiosk, Urban Beach rocks with a buoyant crowd quaffing cocktails at the bar and snacking on salads and *panini* using organic products.

Relax Firenze
HEALTH & FITNESS

(Map p82; ☑ 055 28 46 83; www.relaxfirenze.com; Via degli Strozzi 2; ☺9am-8pm Mon-Fri, 10.30am-7pm Sat) This small-but-lovely spa overlooks Piazza della Repubblica. The soothing massages (€70/100 for 60/90 minutes), yoga and tai chi classes (€20) – not to mention the invigorating Himalayan salt room (€25 for 40 minutes) and other wellness treatments – offered are, quite frankly, heaven on earth after a long day spent pounding the city's crowded cobbled streets. Advance reservations are essential.

Tours

Mus.e
TOURS

(Map p82; ☑ 055 276 82 24, 055 276 85 58; www.musefirenze.it; info@muse.comune.fi.it; tours & activities €4; reservations 9.30am-1pm & 2.30-5pm Mon-Sat, 9.30am-12.30pm Sun) Imaginative guided tours, including family-themed tours, in a handful of city museums, including Palazzo Vecchio (p80), Museo Novecento (p86), Basilica di Santa Maria Novella (p88) and Cappella Brancacci (p103). Reserve tours in advance by email or phone, or at its ticket desk inside Palazzo Vecchio.

Curious Appetite
TOURS

(☑ 391 4005956; www.curiousappetitetravel.com; 3hr group tour per person €85) Personalised bespoke and small-group culinary tours and tastings led by Italian-American Coral Sisk and her team of knowledgeable guides, most of whom are trained sommeliers too. Tours

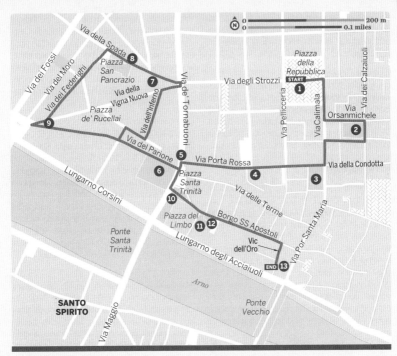

City Walk
Quintessential Florence

START PIAZZA DELLA REPUBBLICA
END LA TERAZZA LOUNGE BAR
LENGTH 2.5KM; TWO HOURS

Start with coffee on ❶ **Piazza della Repub-blica** (p85), then walk one block south along Via Calimala and turn left onto Via Orsan-michele to ❷ **Chiesa e Museo di Orsan-michele** (p69), a unique church with ornate facade statuary and a museum inside. Back-track to Via Calimala and continue walking south until you see the loggia of ❸ **Mercato Nuovo** (p130), a market selling cheap leather on Florence's 16th-century market place. Florentines know it as 'Il Porcellino' (The Piglet) after the bronze statue of a wild boar on its southern side. Rub its snout to ensure your return to Florence.

Walk past the market and along Via Porta Rossa to ❹ **Palazzo Davanzati** (p68) with its magnificent studded doors and fascinat-ing museum. Continue to ❺ **Via de' Torna-buoni** (p69) with its luxury fashion designers. Swoon over frescoed chapels in ❻ **Basilica**

di Santa Trinità (p87), then lose yourself in tiny boutiques on Via del Parione, Via della Vigna Nuova and Via della Spada: milliner ❼ **Grevi** (p131), ❽ **Mio Concept** (p131) packed with Tuscan-made homewares and fashion accessories, and leather designer ❾ **Benheart** (p130) are grassroot favourites.

Backtrack to Via de' Tornabuoni and turn right, past 13th-century ❿ **Palazzo Spini-Feroni** (p86), home of Salvatore Ferragamo's flagship store and shoe museum, to Borgo Santissimi Apostoli. A short way ahead on Piazza del Limbo is the Romanesque ⓫ **Chiesa dei Santissimi Apostoli** (Map p82; ☏ 055 29 06 42; www.santiapostoli.com; Piazza del Limbo 1; ⊙ 7.30am-noon & 4-7pm Tue-Sun), in a square once used as a cemetery for unbaptised babies.

Shop for Tuscan olive oil in ⓬ **La Bottega dell'Olio** (p131), then continue east to the Hotel Continentale with its rooftop terrace ⓭ **La Terrazza Lounge Bar** (p123) – the perfect spot for an uplifting sundowner with a Ponte Vecchio view.

are themed: at the market, *aperitivi,* Italian food and wine pairings, 'dinner crawl', gelato etc. Cocktail lessons too with a Florentine mixologist.

Explore Florence
TOURS

(www.exploreflorence.net) Delve into Florence's heart and soul through art, architecture, culture and contemporary lifestyle with highly recommended California-raised, Florence-adopted tour guide, art historian and passionate 'slow travel' advocate Alexandra Lawrence. Small-group and custom-made bespoke tours.

Caf Tour & Travel
CULTURAL

(Map p92; ☑ 055 21 06 12, 055 28 32 00; www. caftours.com; Via degli Alfani 151r; ⊘8am-8pm Mon-Sat, to 5pm Sun) This travel agency takes bookings for dozens of tours and activity workshops (cookery, gelato, pizza) in and around Florence, on foot, by minivan and bus. Guided half-day visits of the Uffizi (€49), Galleria dell'Accademia (€39) and *duomo* complex (€42) include museum tickets and avoid queueing. Tours too by electric bike, Vespa, Segway and in the backseat of an iconic Fiat 500.

De Gustibus
TOURS

(☑ 055 384 23 94, 340 5796207; www.de-gustibus. it) This umbrella association for local farms in the surrounding Florentine countryside organises extremely tasty tours to small family-run organic farms. Tours are invariably themed – wine, truffles, olive oil – and can be by car, Vespa scooter, vintage sidecar, bicycle or on foot. Check its website or Facebook page for details of upcoming tours.

500 Touring Club
DRIVING

(☑ 346 8262324; www.500touringclub.com; Via Gherardo Silvani 149a) Hook up with Florence's 500 Touring Club for a guided tour in a vintage motor – with you behind the wheel! Every car has a name in this outfit's fleet of gorgeous vintage Fiat 500s from the 1960s. Motoring tours are guided (hop in your car and follow the leader) and themed – families love the picnic trip, couples the wine tasting.

Florence Town
WALKING

(Map p82; ☑ 055 28 11 03; www.florencetown.com; Piazza della Repubblica 1; ⊘7.30am-8pm summer, 8.30am-6.30pm winter) Organised themed tours (walking, cycling), activities and workshops in and around Florence. They include memorable 1½-hour boat tours at sunset with *aperitivo* aboard a traditional *barchetto* (Florentine-style gondola; €59) and one-day guided countryside hikes with wine-tasting and lunch (€99). Reserve at the kiosk beneath the arches, next to the Apple store overlooking the southwestern corner of Piazza della Repubblica.

City Sightseeing Firenze
BUS

(Map p92; ☑ 389 2467905, 055 29 04 51; www. firenze.city-sightseeing.it; Piazza della Stazione 1; 1/2/3 days adult €24/28/33, reduced €12/14/17) Explore Florence by open-top bus, hopping on and off at stops around the city along two different routes: lines A and B go up to Piazzale Michelangelo, and Line B also ticks off neighbouring Fiesole. Buy tickets online, directly from the driver or at the small office by the Via Fiume 8-10r stop. Find route maps online.

Tuscany Bike Tours
CYCLING

(Map p100; ☑ 339 1163495, 055 386 02 53; www. tuscany-biketours.com; Via Ghibellina 34r) Cycling tours in and around Florence, including a 2½-hour city bike tour with gelato break (adult/reduced €39/35) and a full-day bike ride into the Chianti hills (adult/ reduced €85/75). For the less energetic, consider a Chianti day trip by Audrey Hepburn–style scooter (adult/reduced/ passenger €130/120/95, including lunch, castle visit and wine or olive-oil tasting) or Fiat 500 (driver/passenger €150/90, including lunch). Bike hire too.

Festivals & Events

Festa di Anna Maria Medici
CULTURAL

(⊘18 Feb) Florence's Feast of Anna Maria Medici marks the death in 1743 of the last Medici, Anna Maria Luisa de' Medici, with a costumed parade from Palazzo Vecchio to her tomb in the Cappelle Medicee.

Scoppio del Carro
FIREWORKS

(⊘Mar/Apr) A cart of fireworks is exploded in front of the cathedral on Piazza del Duomo at 11am on Easter Sunday.

Maggio Musicale Fiorentino
PERFORMING ARTS

(www.maggiofiorentino.com; ⊘Apr-Jun) Italy's oldest arts festival features world-class performances of theatre, classical music, jazz, opera and dance. Events are staged at the Teatro del Maggio Musicale Fiorentino (p129) and other key venues across the city.

LOCAL KNOWLEDGE

STREET ART: CLET & CO

Should you notice something gone awry with street signs in Oltrarno – on a No Entry sign, a tiny black figure stealthily sneaking away with the white bar for example – you can be sure it is the work of French-born Clet Abraham, one of Florence's most popular street artists. In his Oltrarno studio (Map p106; ☑ 339 2203607, 347 3387760; Via dell'Olmo 8r; ☺ hours vary) you can buy stickers, postcards, T-shirts and tote bags featuring his hacked traffic signs and, if you're lucky, catch a glimpse of the rebellious artist at work.

If you fall completely and utterly head over heels in love with Clet's work, you can either order a reproduction street sign directly from his workshop (from €500) or purchase an original (numbered and signed, from €2500) limited edition from Mio Concept (p131) – Clet produces only 13 of each design. Examples of his earlier work is occasionally displayed at Street Levels Gallery (p87).

Festa di San Giovanni RELIGIOUS
(☺ 24 Jun) Florence celebrates its patron saint, John, with a *calcio storico* match on Piazza di Santa Croce and fireworks over Piazzale Michelangelo.

🛏 Sleeping

Florence is unexpectedly small, rendering almost anywhere in the city centre convenient. Advance reservations are essential between Easter and September, while winter ushers in some great deals for visitors – room rates are practically halved. Many top-end boutique options hide in courtyards or behind the inconspicuous door of a *residenza d'epoca* (historical residence) – not listed as hotel or graced with any stars, making such addresses all the more atmospheric and oh-so-Florentine.

🛏 Duomo & Piazza della Signoria

Hotel Cestelli HOTEL €
(Map p82; ☑ 055 21 42 13; www.hotelcestelli.com; Borgo SS Apostoli 25; d €100, s/d without bathroom €60/80; ☺ closed 2 weeks Jan & 10 days Aug; ☂) Housed in a 12th-century *palazzo* a stiletto-strut from fashionable Via de' Tornabuoni, this intimate eight-room hotel is a gem. Rooms reveal an understated style, tastefully combining polished antiques with spangly chandeliers, vintage art and silk screens. Owners Alessio and Asumi are a mine of local information and are happy to share their knowledge. No breakfast. Ask about low-season discounts for longer stays.

★ **Hotel Davanzati** HOTEL €€
(Map p82; ☑ 055 28 66 66; www.hoteldavanzati.it; Via Porta Rossa 5; s/d €202/252; ✳ @ ☂) Twenty-six steps lead up to this family-run

hotel. A labyrinth of enchanting rooms, frescoes and modern comforts, it oozes charm – as do Florentine brothers Tommaso and Riccardo, and father Fabrizio, who run the show. Rooms come with a mini iPad (meaning free wi-fi around town), direct messaging with the hotel, handy digital city guide and complimentary access to a nearby gym.

Hotel Pendini HISTORIC HOTEL €€
(Map p82; ☑ 055 2 11 17; www.hotelpendini.it; Via degli Strozzi 2; d €120-205; ✳ @ ☂) Very much part of city history, the Pendini opened in 1879 as an upmarket *pensione* – hence the giant 'Pensione Pendini' lettering dominating its privileged facade on Piazza della Repubblica. Its 44 comfortable rooms are up-to-the-minute, with polished parquet floors, antique furnishings, and beautiful floral fabrics and wallpapers. Historic B&W photographs adorn the corridors and classical music plays in the enchanting, vintage-styled lounge.

Hotel Perseo HOTEL €€
(Map p82; ☑ 055 21 25 04; www.hotelperseo.it; Via de' Cerretani 1; s €160, d €181-195, tr €230-256, q €256-299; ✳ @ ☂) Perseo is a perfect family choice with its 25 rooms, comfy lounge, Scandinavian-styled breakfast room and friendly hosts, New Zealander Louise and Italian husband Giacinto. Rooms come with kettle, tea and coffee, and fridge; those on the 5th floor (there's a lift as far as the 4th floor) smooch with the rooftops and gorgeous *duomo* views. Book online for the cheapest rates.

Romantics won't be able to resist the stylish 'penthouse' suite (€270 to €350), split across four levels and spilling out onto a rooftop terrace with a rare 360-degree panorama and brazen full-frontal view of the *duomo*.

LAZY DAYS IN FLORENCE

Florence is not just about gorging on art masterpieces, scaling the duomo (cathedral) and packing in too many museums. To get under the skin of Florentine culture and understand what makes this Renaissance city tick, take time out to laze with locals.

SERIOUS COFFEE

Weekending Florentines spend hours hanging out with friends, people watching or discussing latte art over a picture-perfect al fresco cappuccino. Historic cafes like **Caffè Rivoire** (p130) are timeless. Or mingle with younger Florentines over a single-origin espresso or mug of V60 brew prepared by skilful baristas at new-generation cafe and speciality coffee roaster **Ditta Artigianale** (p126). **Santarosa Bistrot** (p127), wedged between river and ancient city wall, is the garden choice for a serious coffee al fresco.

A VERY LONG LUNCH

Food is of extreme importance to most Florentines, hence the lazy lunch. Join bon vivants on the chic Piazza della Repubblica terrace of bistro **Irene** (p118) or indulge at Michelin-starred **La Leggenda dei Frati** (p123), romantically at home in the Giardini Bardini. Alternatively, grab your picnic rug, buy a gourmet burger at food truck **La Toraia** (p120) or feisty tripe sandwich at **Easy Living** (p122), and flop on the grassy banks of the Arno for a leisurely lunch riverside.

A GARDEN STROLL

Florentines have been flocking to the **Boboli** (p106) and **Bardini** (p107) gardens since the 16th century. But for a quieter change of scene, retreat to **Giardino dei Semplici** (p102), the city's peaceful botanical gardens in San Marco, where fragrant citrus blooms mingle with ancient medicinal plants and Tuscan wildflowers.

1. Palazzo Pitti (p105) and Giardino di Boboli (p106)
2. Galleria degli Uffizi's (p70) rooftop cafe and Palazzo Vecchio (p80)

TTPHOTO/SHUTTERSTOCK ©

Hotel Torre Guelfa

HISTORIC HOTEL €€€

(Map p82; ☑055 239 63 38; www.hoteltor reguelfa.com; Borgo SS Apostoli 8; d/tr/q from €200/215/225; P✳@🖥) If you want to kip in a real-McCoy Florentine *palazzo* without breaking the bank, this 31-room hotel with fortress-style facade is the address. Scale its 13th-century, 50m-tall tower – Florence's tallest privately owned *torre* – for a sundowner overlooking Florence and you'll be blown away. Rates are practically halved in the low season.

🛏 Santa Maria Novella

The city's smartest shopping strip bejewels the eastern fringe of this neighbourhood and, as such, is home to a couple of beautiful places to stay – both budget and top end. There are plenty of cheap, unexceptional hotels around the train station.

★ Student Hotel

HOSTEL €

(☑055 062 18 55; www.thestudenthotel.com; Viale Spartaco Lavagnini 70; s/d from €92/109; ✳@🖥) Designed for anyone with a fun 'student-for-life' spirit, this hostel-hotel hybrid embodies 21st-century living – in a historic *palazzo* from 1864. Sharp interior design throws in a shiny grand piano for guests to tinkle on, co-working spaces, break-out zones and bags of communal space. Rooms, shared kitchens, and the 360-degree city views from the rooftop pool, gym and sky bar are positively hedonistic.

★ Hotel Scoti

PENSION €€

(Map p82; ☑055 29 21 28; www.hotelscoti.com; Via de' Tornabuoni 7; d/tr €140/165; 🖥) Wedged between designer boutiques on Florence's smartest shopping strip, this hidden *pensione* is a fabulous mix of old-fashioned charm and value for money. Its traditionally styled rooms are spread across the 2nd floor of a 16th-century *palazzo;* some have lovely rooftop views. Guests can borrow hairdryers, bottle openers, etc and the frescoed lounge (1780) is stunning. Optional breakfast €5 extra.

Antica Torre di Via de' Tornabuoni 1

BOUTIQUE HOTEL €€€

(Map p82; ☑055 265 81 61; www.tornabuoni1.com; Via de' Tornabuoni 1; d €355; ✳🖥) Footsteps from the Arno, inside beautiful 13th- to 19th-century Palazzo Gianfigliazzi, is this understated luxury hotel. Rooms are spacious and contemporary, but it's the stunning 6th-floor rooftop terrace that steals

the show: lounge in the winter garden here, bask on the sun terrace, drink at the bar and swoon over Florence graciously laid out at your feet.

Velona's Jungle

GUESTHOUSE €€€

(☑055 274 15 36; www.velonasjungle.com; Via Montebello 86; d from €298; 🖥) A 15-minute stroll from the *duomo* brings you to this designer address, an exquisitely curated 'jungle' of colour and exuberant eye-catching detail arranged around a family collection of vintage objets d'art. Four luxurious suites pamper to every need, breakfast (until noon) is vegan and organic, and host Veronica ensures each guest feels very looked after.

🛏 San Lorenzo & San Marco

San Lorenzo, slightly rough around the edges by both the market and on its western fringe (a five-minute walk from Stazione di Santa Maria Novella), is home to plenty of unremarkable two- and three-star hotels and two of the city's best hostels. For more-elegant midrange digs head to San Marco.

★ Academy Hostel

HOSTEL €

(Map p82; ☑055 239 86 65; www.academy hostel.eu; Via Ricasoli 9; dm €30-45, d €70-90; ✳@🖥) This classy hostel – definitely not a party hostel – sits on the 1st floor of Baron Ricasoli's 17th-century *palazzo*. The inviting lobby, with books to browse, was once a theatre and is a comfy spot to chill on the sofa over TV or a DVD. Dorms sport four, five or six beds, high moulded ceilings and brightly coloured lockers.

Ostello Archi Rossi

HOSTEL €

(Map p92; ☑055 29 08 04; www.hostelarchi rossi.com; Via Faenza 94r; dm €15-32, d €45-80; ☺closed Dec; @🖥) Guests' paintings and artwork brighten this busy hostel near Stazione di Santa Maria Novella, with friendly brothers Marco and Leonardo behind reception and bright white dorms sleeping three to nine. There are washing machines and microwaves for guests to use and the cosy basement lounge is a welcome chill-out zone. No curfew but guests must ring the bell after 2am.

Hotel Monna Lisa

HOTEL €€

(Map p100; ☑055 247 97 51; www.monnalisa.it; Borgo Pinti 27; d €140-200; P🖥; 🖥) At home in a Renaissance *palazzo* endowed with beautiful paintings and sculptures, Monna Lisa is one chic place. Its 45 rooms are old-world and four-star, but what really stuns are the

OUT-OF-TOWN ROMANCE

Should you want to get away from it all, amid cypress alleys and old-world Tuscan romance in the Florentine hills...

Ostello Villa Camerata (☑ 055 532 61 94; www.ostellofirenze.it; Viale Augusto Righi 2-4; dm €18-20; P @ ⑤) In a golden 15th-century villa framed by extensive grounds, not far from hilltop Fiesole, HI-affiliated Villa Camerata is among Italy's most beautiful hostels.

Il Salviatino (☑ 055 904 11 11; www.salviatino.com; Via del Salviatino 21, Fiesole; d from €600; P ✳ @ ⑤ ▣) Hidden among cypress trees 3.5km east of Florence, Italian literati gathered here in the 17th century, and today Europe's moneyed hipsters spoil themselves in the spa, cascading infinity pool and manicured Italian gardens.

Torre di Bellosguardo (☑ 055 229 81 45; www.torrebellosguardo.com; Via Roti Michelozzi 2; d €300; P ✳ @ ⑤ ▣) Time travel to old-world Tuscany at this romantic villa upon a hill on the city fringe. Built as a hunting lodge in 1200, the historical residence later became the hub of Florentine noble life with its intellectual salons and beautiful gardens. Period furnishings dress its 16 elegant rooms and the views of Florence from the pool are just divine, darling.

communal spaces – the glorious loggia with painted ceiling; the period lounges; and the peaceful garden with gravel paths, jasmine and lime trees.

Hotel Morandi
alla Crocetta   BOUTIQUE HOTEL €€
(Map p92; ☑ 055 234 47 48; www.hotelmorandi.it; Via Laura 50; s/d €120/170; P ✳ ⑤) This medieval convent-turned-hotel away from the madding crowd in San Marco is a stunner. Rooms are refined and traditional in look – think antique furnishings, wood beams and oil paintings – with a quiet, old-world ambience. Pick of the bunch is frescoed room No. 29, the former chapel.

★**Hotel Orto de' Medici**   HOTEL €€€
(Map p92; ☑ 055 48 34 27; www.ortodeimedici.it; Via San Gallo 30; d from €220; ✳ @ ⑤) This four-star hotel in San Marco redefines elegance with its majestic ceilings, chic oyster-grey colour scheme and contemporary furnishings, set off to perfection by the historic *palazzo* in which it languishes. Hunt down the odd remaining 19th-century fresco, and don't miss the garden with lemon trees in terracotta pots and rambling ivy. To splurge, go for a room with its own flowery terrace.

🛏 Santa Croce

★**Hotel Dalí**   HOTEL €
(Map p100; ☑ 055 234 07 06; www.hoteldali.com; Via dell'Oriuolo 17; d €95, s/d without bathroom €40/70; P ⑤) A warm welcome from hosts Marco and Samanta awaits at this lovely small hotel. A stone's throw from the *duomo*, it has 10 sunny rooms, some overlooking a leafy inner courtyard, decorated in a low-key modern way and equipped with kettles, coffee and tea. No breakfast, but – miraculous for central Florence – free parking in the rear courtyard.

Villa Landucci   B&B €€
(☑ 055 66 05 95; www.villalanducci.it; Via Luca Landucci 7; s/d €130/140; P ⑤) Five elegant and refreshingly spacious rooms are named after Tuscan wines at this gourmet-themed B&B, a short walk away from Santa Croce. The best in the house, 'Bolgheri' and 'Chianti', open onto the well-tended garden with veggie patch, magnolia tree, age-old palm and kids' play area. Breakfast is predominantly organic and there is free parking (a rarity in Florence).

🛏 Oltrarno

While not right in the heart of the action, Oltrarno is a peaceful place to stay. Its bespoke portfolio includes a couple of hostels and some stunning boutique hotels and guesthouses, at home in historic *palazzi*.

Ostello Tasso   HOSTEL €
(☑ 055 060 20 87; www.ostellotassofirenze.it; Via Villani 15; dm €38-40, s €55-58, d €130-150, without bathroom s €45-48, d €95-98; @ ⑤) Hostel in style at this chic crash pad, a two-minute walk from Piazza Tasso. Coloured bed linen and floor rugs give three- to six-bed dorms a boutique charm, the courtyard garden is a dream and DJs spin tunes in the hip lounge bar (open to nonguests too). The hostel's monthly open-mic evening is a honeypot for local artists and performers.

Oltrarno Splendid
B&B €€

(Map p104; ☑055 464 85 55; www.oltrarnos plendid.com; Via dei Serragli 7; d €160-240; @ 🖤) Original frescoes and Toile de Jouy wall fabrics, decorative fireplaces and a wonderful collection of vintage curios create an enriching sense of home at this exquisite guesthouse – the latest on-trend creation by calligrapher Betty Soldi and partner Matteo. All 14 rooms enjoy romantic rooftop views of Florence, and the welcome from maître d' Alberto could not be warmer or more charming.

Palazzo Belfiore
APARTMENT €€

(Map p104; ☑055 26 44 15; www.palazzobelf iore.it; Via dei Velluti 8; d €200-215, q €290-310, extra bed €25; 🖤) The smartly painted taupe door with shiny black doorknob reflects the contemporary twist on the historic at this stylish residence, at home in a Renaissance *palazzo* on the Oltrarno. Its seven apartments with fully equipped kitchens sleep two to six and are spacious and swish, and owner Federico goes out of his way to ensure guests feel right at home.

★AdAstra
B&B €€€

(Map p104; ☑055 075 06 02; www.adastra florence.com; Via del Campuccio 53; d €280-350; ☺reception 8.30am-7.30pm; P 🖤 @ 🖤) There is no other address quite like it in Florence. Seductively at home in a 16th-century *palazzo* overlooking Europe's largest private walled garden, this uberchic guesthouse rocks. A creation of the talented British-Italian duo behind SoprArno Suites, AdAstra sports 14 beautiful rooms adorned with Betty Soldi's calligraphy, Matteo's vintage collectibles, claw-foot bathtubs and the odd 19th-century fresco or wooden herringbone floor.

★SoprArno Suites
GUESTHOUSE €€€

(Map p104; ☑055 046 87 18; www.soprarno suites.com; Via Maggio 35; d €280-342; 🖤) This boutique gem, tucked in a quaint Oltrarno courtyard, creates an intimate home-from-home vibe while making each guest feel special. Thirteen designer rooms are exquisitely dressed in vintage objets d'art and collectibles – the passion of Florentine owner Matteo and his talented Florence-born, British-raised wife, Betty Soldi (a calligrapher and graphic designer).

Hotel Palazzo Guadagni
HOTEL €€€

(Map p104; ☑055 265 83 76; www.palazzo guadagni.com; Piazza Santo Spirito 9; d/tr/q €250/270/310; 🖤 🖤) This romantic mid-range hotel overlooking Florence's liveliest summertime square is legendary – Zeffirelli shot scenes from *Tea with Mussolini* here. Housed in an artfully revamped Renaissance palace, it has 15 spacious rooms with old-world high ceilings and the occasional fresco or fireplace (decorative today). In summer bartenders serve cocktails on the impossibly romantic loggia terrace with wicker chairs and predictably dreamy views.

🛏 Boboli & San Miniato al Monte

Accommodation options are scant in this hilly and more 'rural' part of the city; if you don't find what you are looking for, head west to the Oltrarno's Santo Spirito and San Frediano districts.

★Palazzo San Niccolò
APARTMENT €€

(Map p106; ☑055 24 45 09; www.palazzo sanniccolo.it; Via di San Niccolò 79; d €160-245, q €200-270, extra bed €25; 🖤 🖤) Country-style contemporary decor marries with lovingly restored vintage inside this 14th-century *palazzo,* named after the 'hood in which it slumbers and squirrelling away a handful of luxurious, serviced apartments. Complimentary tea and coffee is available in the lounge; longer stays enjoy clean laundry and housekeeping every three days; there is a communal washing machine and – best of all – a serene secret garden.

Hotel Silla
HOTEL €€

(Map p106; ☑055 234 28 88; www.hotelsilla.it; Via dei Renai 5; d/tr/q €170/215/242; P 🖤 🖤) With its elegant courtyard entrance and peachy shabby-chic facade, this San Niccolò *palazzo* – home to the Russian Demidoff family in the 15th century – is a delightful pied-à-terre one step away from the crowds. Its 36 rooms are dressed in a classic Florentine style and the hotel terrace, with sweeping Arno and city views, was clearly designed with al fresco lounging in mind.

Hotel La Scaletta
HOTEL €€

(Map p104; ☑055 28 30 28; www.hotellascal etta.it; Via Guicciardini 13; d/tr/q €175/258/305; 🖤) High ceilings, original fireplaces and spacious rooms are trademarks of this vintage-chic hotel, in a 15th-century *palazzo* near Palazzo Pitti. The priciest rooms peep down on Giardino di Boboli, and savouring a summertime breakfast or early-evening drink on the dreamy roof terrace is absolutely fabulous.

BACKSTREET FLORENCE: DANTE

Italy's most divine poet was born in 1265 in a wee house down a narrow lane in the backstreets of Florence. Tragic romance made him tick and there's no better place to unravel the medieval life and times of Dante than the Museo Casa di Dante (Map p82; ☑055 21 94 16; www.museocasadidante.it; Via Santa Margherita 1; adult/reduced €4/2; ☺10am-6pm summer, 10am-5pm Mon-Fri, to 6pm Sat & Sun winter).

When Dante was just 12 he was promised in marriage to Gemma Donati. But it was another Florentine gal, Beatrice Portinari (1266–90), who was his muse, his inspiration and the love of his life (despite only ever meeting her twice): in La Divina Commedia (The Divine Comedy) Dante broke with tradition by using the familiar Italian, not formal Latin, to describe travelling through the circles of hell in search of his beloved Beatrice.

Beatrice, who wed a banker and died a couple of years later aged just 24, is buried in 11th-century Chiesa di Santa Margherita (Map p82; Via Santa Margherita 4; ☺hours vary), in an alley near Dante's house; note the wicker basket in front of her grave filled with scraps of paper on which prayers and dedications evoking unrequited love have been penned. This chapel was also where the poet married Gemma in 1295. Dimly lit, it remains much as it was in medieval Florence. No wonder novelist Dan Brown chose it to set a scene in his most recent Dante-themed thriller, Inferno (2013), that takes place in Florence.

Crown the old-world experience with a centuries-old tripe panino (sandwich) from hole-in-the-wall Da Vinattieri (p120), eaten squatting on a simple wooden stool in this alley in backstreet Florence.

✖ Eating

Quality ingredients and simple execution are the hallmarks of Florentine cuisine, climaxing with the bistecca alla fiorentina, a huge slab of prime T-bone steak rubbed with tangy Tuscan olive oil, seared on the chargrill, garnished with salt and pepper and served beautifully al sangue (bloody). Be it dining in a traditional trattoria or contemporary, designer-chic space, quality is guaranteed.

✖ Duomo & Piazza della Signoria

★ Osteria Il Buongustai   OSTERIA €
(Map p82; ☑055 29 13 04; www.facebook.com/ibuongustaifirenze; Via dei Cerchi 15r; meals €15-20; ☺9.30am-3.30pm Mon-Sat) Run with breathtaking speed and grace by Laura and Lucia, 'The Gourmand' is unmissable. Lunchtimes heave with locals and savvy students who flock here to fill up on tasty Tuscan home cooking at a snip of other restaurant prices. The place is brilliantly no frills – watch women in hair caps at work in the kitchen, share a table and pay in cash. No credit cards.

Trattoria Le Mossacce   TRATTORIA €
(Map p82; ☑055 29 43 61; www.trattoria lemossacce.it; Via del Proconsolo 55r; meals €20; ☺noon-2.30pm & 7-9.30pm Mon-Fri) Strung

with legs of ham and garlic garlands, this old-world trattoria lives up to its vintage promise of a warm benvenuto (welcome) and fabulous home cooking every Tuscan nonna would approve of. A family address, it has been the pride and joy of the Fantoni-Mannucci family for the last 50-odd years and their bistecca alla fiorentina is among the best in town.

Mangiafoco   TUSCAN €€
(Map p82; ☑055 265 81 70; www.mangia foco.com; Borgo SS Apostoli 26r; meals €40; ☺noon-midnight) Aromatic truffles get full-page billing at this small and cosy osteria (casual tavern) with buttercup-yellow walls, cushioned seating and an exceptional wine list. Whether you are a hardcore truffle fiend or a truffle virgin, there is something for you here: steak topped with freshly shaved truffles in season, truffle tagliatelle (ribbon pasta) or a simple plate of mixed cheeses with sweet truffle honey.

Obicà   ITALIAN €€
(Map p82; ☑055 277 35 26; www.obica.com; Via de' Tornabuoni 16; meals €30-50; ☺noon-4pm & 6.30-11.30pm Mon-Fri, noon-11pm Sat & Sun) Given its exclusive location in Palazzo Tornabuoni, this designer address is naturally ubertrendy – even the table mats are upcycled from organic products. Taste 10 different types of mozzarella cheese in the cathedral-like interior or snuggle beneath heaters over pizza and salads on sofas in the enchanting

star-topped courtyard. At *aperitivo* hour, nibble on *taglierini* (tasting boards loaded with cheeses, salami and deep-fried veg).

★ **Irene** BISTRO €€€
(Map p82; 📞 055 273 58 91; www.roccoforte hotels.com; Piazza della Repubblica 7; meals €60; ⊗ 7.30am-10.30pm) Named after the accomplished Italian grandmother of Sir Rocco Forte of the eponymous luxury hotel group, Irene (part of neighbouring Hotel Savoy) is a dazzling contemporary bistro with a pavement terrace (heated in winter) overlooking iconic Piazza della Repubblica. Interior design is retro-chic 1950s and celebrity chef Fulvio Pierangelini cooks up playful, utterly fabulous bistro cuisine.

Gucci Osteria da Massimo Bottura OSTERIA €€€
(Map p82; 📞 055 7592 7038; www.gucci.com/int/en/store/osteria-bottura; Piazza della Signoria 10; meals €50; ⊗ 12.30-3pm & 7-10pm; 📞) Inside the oh-so-glamorous Gucci Garden, amid pea-green walls on the ground floor of Palazzo della Mercanzia, three-Michelin-star chef Massimo Bottura oversees a menu that mixes iconic Italian dishes like tortellini in Parmesan sauce with innovative twists on international favourites, such as hotdog made with Tuscan Chianina beef. Tasting menus €70 and €90. Diners get free admission to the fashion house's museum (p85).

✕ Santa Maria Novella

UqBar CAFE €
(Todo Modo; Map p82; 📞 055 239 91 10; www.todo modo.org; Via dei Fossi 15r; meals €15-25; ⊗ 10am-8pm Tue-Sun, closed Sun May-Sep; 📞) Grab a vintage pew between book- and bottle-lined shelves inside the city's most dynamic independent bookshop, select a glass of well-chosen wine, and tuck into a tasty 'slow food' lunch that changes daily. Outside of lunch hours (12.30pm to 3.30pm), enjoy fresh coffee and homemade cakes in the company of a good book. *Aperitivo*, from 6pm, is the other hot date.

Trattoria Marione TRATTORIA €€
(Map p82; 📞 055 21 47 56; Via della Spada 27; meals €30; ⊗ noon-5pm & 7-11pm) For the quintessential 'Italian dining' experience, Marione is gold. It's busy, it's noisy, it's 99.9% local and the cuisine is right out of *nonna*'s Tuscan kitchen. No one appears to speak English so go for Italian – the tasty excellent-value traditional fare is worth it. If you don't get a com-

plimentary *limoncello* (lemon liqueur) with the bill, you clearly failed the language test.

Il Latini TRATTORIA €€
(Map p82; 📞 055 21 09 16; www.illatini.com; Via dei Palchetti 6r; meals €30; ⊗ 12.30-2.30pm & 7.30-10.30pm Tue-Sun summer, 7.30-10.30pm Wed-Fri, 12.30-2.30pm & 7.30-10.30pm Sat & Sun winter) A veteran guidebook favourite built around traditional *crostini, pappa al pomodoro* (tomato and bread soup), Tuscan salami, fine pasta, Florentine tripe and roasted meats served at shared tables. In high season there are two dinner seatings (7.30pm and 9pm), with service ranging from charming to not so charming. Reservations mandatory.

✕ San Lorenzo & San Marco

★ **Trattoria Mario** TUSCAN €
(Map p92; 📞 055 21 85 50; www.trattoria-mario. com; Via Rosina 2; meals €25; ⊗ noon-3.30pm Mon-Sat, closed 3 weeks Aug; ⊕) Arrive by noon to ensure a spot at this noisy, busy, brilliant trattoria – a legend that retains its soul (and allure with locals) despite being in every guidebook. Charming Fabio, whose grandfather opened the place in 1953, is front of house while big brother Romeo and nephew Francesco cook with speed in the kitchen. No advance reservations; cash only.

Mercato Centrale FOOD HALL €
(Map p92; 📞 055 239 97 98; www.mercato centrale.it; Piazza del Mercato Centrale 4; dishes €5-15; ⊗ market 7am-3pm Mon-Fri, to 5pm Sat, food hall 8am-midnight; 📞) Wander the maze of stalls crammed with fresh produce at Florence's oldest and largest food market, on the ground floor of an iron-and-glass structure designed by architect Giuseppe Mengoni in 1874. Head to the 1st floor's buzzing, thoroughly contemporary food hall with dedicated cookery school and artisan stalls cooking steaks, burgers, tripe *panini,* vegetarian dishes, pizza, gelato, pastries and pasta.

Trattoria Sergio Gozzi TRATTORIA €
(Map p92; 📞 055 28 19 41; Piazza San Lorenzo 8r; meals €25; ⊗ 10am-4pm Mon-Sat) Keep things simple with a traditional Tuscan lunch at this two-room trattoria, tucked between cheap leather shops near Mercato Centrale. Dining is at marble-topped tables in a spartan vintage interior clearly unchanged since 1915 when it opened. Expect all the classics: plenty of pasta, roast meats, tripe and *bollito misto* (boiled beef, chicken and tongue) included.

Pugi BAKERY €
(Map p92; ☑ 055 28 09 81; www.focacceria-pu
gi.it; Piazza San Marco 9b; per kg €15-25;
⏱ 7.45am-8pm Mon-Sat, closed 2 weeks mid-Aug)
The inevitable line outside the door says
it all. This bakery is a Florentine favourite
for pizza slices and chunks of *schiacciata*
(Tuscan flatbread) baked up plain, spiked
with salt and rosemary, or topped or stuffed
with whatever delicious edible goodies are
in season.

De Plek CAFE €
(Map p92; ☑ 348 5903187; www.facebook.com/
deplekfirenze; Via Panicale 7r; meals €25, brunch
€10-12; ⏱ 11am-midnight Mon-Fri, 5pm-midnight
Sat) With a Dutch name that translates as
'The Place' (one of the four owners is a cool
Amsterdammer), contemporary De Plek is
the place in San Lorenzo for serious coffee,
healthy shakes, amazing homemade mint-
and-basil-laced lemonade, Italian craft beer
and creative zero-kilometre cuisine. Its €10
lunch deal is excellent value and weekends
rock with a fashionable brunch crowd.

★ **La Ménagère** INTERNATIONAL €€
(Map p92; ☑ 055 075 06 00; www.lamenagere.
it; Via de' Ginori 8r; meals €15-70; ⏱ 7am-2am;
🛜) Be it breakfast, lunch, dinner, coffee or
cocktails, this industrial-styled space lures
Florence's hip brigade. The concept store is
a fashionable one-stop shop for chic china
and tableware, designer kitchen gear and
fresh flowers. For daytime dining, pick from
retro sofas in the boutique, banquette seating or bar stools in the bistro or a table between flower pots in the conservatory-style
restaurant.

FAC ITALIAN €€
(Fast and Casual; Map p82; ☑ 055 015 36 10; www.
fastandcasual.com; Via de' Martelli 22; meals €30;
⏱ noon-10pm) Celebrated Florentine chef Simone Cipriani from Essenziale (p122) cooks
up affordable, 'fast and casual' dining inside
food emporium Eataly (p132). Head up to
the 1st floor to savour Italian-inspired street
food to share – pulled-beef taco with cabbage and coriander, polenta with squid-ink
ragout, meatballs in tomato sauce – around
shared picnic tables, or snag a table in the
laid-back trattoria.

Regina Bistecca STEAK €€€
(Map p82; ☑ 055 269 37 72; www.reginabistec-
ca.com; Via Ricasoli 14r; menus €25-59, meals
€40-50; ⏱ 12.30-3pm & 7-10.30pm Tue-Sun; 🛜)
Plump for a high stool and beautifully mixed

Negroni in the wood-panelled American bar,
lined with bookshelves and vintage prints
in homage to the space's former life as an
antiquarian bookshop (since 1875). Or relax
in the effortless elegance of the colonnaded,
white-table-clothed restaurant where exquisitely cooked, charcoal-grilled steak reigns
supreme.

✖ Santa Croce

★ **Terrazza Menoni** STREET FOOD €
(Map p100; ☑ 055 248 07 78; www.terrazzame
noni.it; Piazza Ghiberti 11; meals €15-20; ⏱ noon-
2.30pm Mon-Sat) Luca Menoni's meat stall
inside the Sant'Ambrogio covered market
has been a favourite with locals since 1921
(his father first ran the business) and now
the Florentine artisan has struck gold with
a sassy self-service, zero-kilometre *risto macelleria* (butcher's eatery) above his market
stall. Everything is homemade and ingredients are sourced fresh from the morning
market.

★ **All'Antico Vinaio** OSTERIA €
(Map p100; ☑ 349 3719947, 055 238 27 23; www.
allanticovinaio.com; Via de' Neri 65r; tasting platters
€10-30; ⏱ 10am-4pm & 6-11pm Tue-Sat, noon-
3.30pm Sun) The crowd spills out the door of
this noisy Florentine thoroughbred, pride
and joy of the Mazzanti family since 1991.
Push your way to the tables at the back to

STREET ETIQUETTE

In a bid to keep things clean and pretty
in Renaissance Florence, the city mayor
passed a law in September 2018 banning
al fresco eating at certain times on specific streets and squares in the historic
centre – on Via de'Neri, Via della Ninna,
Piazzale degli Uffizi and Piazza del Grano
from noon to 3pm and 6pm to 10pm.
The mayor also introduced stiff fines of
up to €500 for those who dared disobey.
In reality, however, street eating remains
very much alive and well in town, with
huge crowds happily gathering outside
popular eateries at lunchtime to chow
tripe-stuffed *panini* and other Florentine
street-food delights on the hop. To avoid
the wrath of both the city mayor and
city-proud Florentines, avoid littering and
head for the riverbanks or a city park to
dine al fresco.

LOCAL KNOWLEDGE

TRIPE: FAST-FOOD FAVOURITE

When Florentines fancy a fast munch-on-the-move, they flit by a *trippaio* – a cart on wheels or mobile stand – for a tripe *panino*. Think cow's stomach chopped up, boiled, sliced, seasoned and bunged between bread.

Those great bastions of good old-fashioned Florentine tradition still going strong include Il Trippaio del Porcellino (Map p82; 335 8070240; Piazza del Mercato Nuovo 1; tripe €4.50; 9am-6.30pm Mon-Sat) on the southwest corner of Mercato Nuovo; L'Antico Trippaio (Map p82; 339 7425692; Piazza dei Cimatori; dishes & panini €5; 9.30am-8pm); Trippaio Sergio Pollini (Map p100; Piazza Sant'Ambrogio; tripe €3.50; 9.30am-3.30pm Mon-Sat) in Santa Croce; and hole-in-the-wall Da Vinattieri (Map p82; www.facebook.com/davinattieri; Via Santa Margherita 4; panini €4.50; 11.30am-7pm) tucked down an alley next to Dante's Chiesa di Santa Margherita. Pay €4.50 to €5 for a *panino* with tripe doused in *salsa verde* (pea-green sauce of smashed parsley, garlic, capers and anchovies) or garnished with salt, pepper and ground chilli. Alternatively, opt for a meaty-sized bowl of *lampredotto* (cow's fourth stomach that is chopped and simmered for hours).

Tripe aficionados seeking a more refined dining experience sitting down should join Florentines venerating the offal side of their city's traditional cuisine at traditional *osteria* Il Magazzino (Map p104; 055 21 59 69; Piazza della Passera 2/3; meals €40; noon-3pm & 7.30-11pm); its *trippa alla fiorentina* (tripe simmered with tomatoes and herbs) is legendary. To watch tripe cooked up in front of your very eyes by some of the city's top chefs, try to be in town for February's Funk e Frattaglie Festival (p25), an alternative celebration of traditional offal and funk music.

taste cheese and salami in situ (reservations recommended). Or join the queue at the deli counter for a well-stuffed focaccia wrapped in waxed paper to take away – the quality is outstanding. Pour yourself a glass of wine while you wait.

La Toraia
STREET FOOD €

(www.latoraia.com; Lungarno del Tempio 3450; meals €5-10; noon-midnight mid-Apr–mid-Oct) 'Bringing the countryside to the city' is the driver behind this cherry-red artisan food truck whose name translates as 'breeding shed'. Parked riverside, a 15-minute stroll east of Piazza di Santa Croce, the truck cooks up sweet 140g burgers, crafted from tender Chianina meat sourced at the family farm in Val di Chiana and topped with melted *pecorino* (sheep's-milk cheese).

Brac
VEGETARIAN €

(Map p100; 055 094 48 77; www.libreriabrac. net; Via dei Vagellai 18r; meals €20; noon-midnight, closed 2 weeks mid-Aug;) This hipster cafe-bookshop – a hybrid dining-*aperitivo* address – cooks up inventive, home-style and strictly vegetarian and/or vegan cuisine. Its decor is recycled vintage with the occasional kid's drawing thrown in for that intimate homey touch; the vibe is artsy. Lunchtime ushers in a fantastic-value

piatto unico (€15) comprising your choice of three dishes served on a single plate.

Le Vespe Café
CAFE €

(Map p100; 055 388 00 62; www.levespecafe. com; Via Ghibellina 76r; meals €10-15; 9am-3pm Mon-Fri, from 10am Sat & Sun;) A particular favourite with Florence's vegetarian and vegan crowd, this retro-fashioned cafe in Santa Croce is a hipster spot to hang out over freshly squeezed juices and cleansing green smoothies, ginger-spiced spinach bread and fabulous weekend brunches. The pocket-sized street terrace gets crammed and a constant queue marks the entrance.

★ Il Teatro del Sale
TUSCAN €€

(Map p100; 055 200 14 92; www.teatrodelsale. com; Via dei Macci 111r; brunch/dinner €20/30; noon-2.30pm & 7-11pm Tue-Fri, noon-3pm & 7-11pm Sat, noon-3pm Sun, closed Aug) Florentine chef Fabio Picchi is one of Florence's living treasures who steals the Sant'Ambrogio show with this eccentric, good-value, members-only club (everyone welcome, membership €7) inside an old theatre. He cooks up brunch and dinner, culminating at 9.30pm in a live performance of drama, music or comedy arranged by his wife, artistic director and comic actress Maria Cassi.

Club Culinario Toscano
ITALIAN €€

(da Osvaldo; Map p100; ☑055 21 79 19, 347 8562670; www.clubosvaldo.com; Piazza dei Peruzzi 3r; meals €20-30; ☺noon-3pm & 7pm-midnight) When an eatery is synonymous with a 'culinary club' you know it's gonna be good. Wholesome, hand-made *tortelli* (large ravioli-like pasta cushions) stuffed with a wonderful variety of seasonal fillings and topped with a meaty *ragù* form the backbone of the menu at this highly recommended address, known for its hearty regional Italian fare packed with locally sourced produce.

Ciblèo
FUSION €€€

(Map p100; ☑055 247 78 81; www.cibreo.com; Via del Verrocchio 2r; fixed menu €50; ☺7-10.30pm Tue-Sat, closed Aug) Iconic Florentine chef Fabio Picchi draws on his past experience working in Japan to give Tuscan staples an oriental twist – chopsticks provided – at this intimate fusion eatery, across the street from Sant'Ambrogio's covered food market. Snag one of eight stools at the bar or a table (reservations recommended), sip sake, and revel in a glorious seasonal symphony of Asian-Tuscan small plates.

Enoteca Pinchiorri
TUSCAN €€€

(Map p100; ☑055 2 63 11; www.enotecapinchiorri.com; Via Ghibellina 87r; 7-/8-course menu €250/275; ☺7.30-10pm Tue-Sat, closed Aug) Niçoise chef Annie Féolde applies French techniques to her refined Tuscan cuisine and does it so well that this is the only restaurant in Tuscany to brandish three shiny Michelin stars. Imagine pigeon roasted in a cocoa-bean crust, with a salted-peanut emulsion and black-truffle sauce. The setting is a 16th-century *palazzo* hotel and the wine list is out of this world.

✕ Oltrarno

★ #Raw
VEGAN €

(Map p104; ☑055 21 93 79; www.hashtagraw.it; Via Sant'Agostino 11r; meals €8-15; ☺10am-6pm Tue-Fri, 11am-8pm Sat & Sun; ☎🖉) Should you desire a turmeric, ginger or aloe vera shot or a gently warmed, raw vegan burger served on a stylish slate-and-wood platter, innovative Raw hits the spot. Everything served here is freshly made and raw – to sensational effect. Herbs are grown in the biodynamic greenhouse of charismatic and hugely knowledgeable chef Caroline, a Swedish architect before moving to Florence.

★ Il Santo Bevitore
TUSCAN €€

(Map p104; ☑055 21 12 64; www.ilsantobevitore.com; Via di Santo Spirito 64-66r; meals €40; ☺12.30-2.30pm & 7.30-11.30pm, closed Sun lunch & Aug) Reserve or arrive right on 7.30pm to snag the last table at this ever-popular address, an ode to stylish dining where gastronomes eat by candlelight in a vaulted, whitewashed, bottle-lined interior. The menu is a creative reinvention of seasonal classics: pumpkin gnocchi with hazelnuts, coffee and green-veined *blu di Capra* (goat's-milk cheese), *tagliatelle* with hare *ragù*, garlic cream and sweet Carmignano figs...

Gurdulù
RISTORANTE €€

(Map p104; ☑055 28 22 23; www.gurdulu.com; Via delle Caldaie 12r; meals €40, tasting menu €55; ☺7.30-11pm Tue-Sat, 12.30-2.30pm & 7.30-11pm Sun; 🖥) Gourmet Gurdulù seduces fashionable Florentines with razor-sharp interior design, magnificent craft cocktails and seasonal market cuisine from young local chef Gabriele Andreoni. A hybrid drink-dine, this address is as much about noshing gourmet *aperitivi* snacks over expertly mixed cocktails (€12) or an expertly curated Tuscan wine flight (€25 for four wines) as it is about dining exceedingly well.

iO Osteria Personale
TUSCAN €€

(Map p104; ☑055 933 13 41; www.io-osteriapersonale.it; Borgo San Frediano 167r; 4-/5-/6-course tasting menus €40/49/57; ☺7.30-10pm Mon-Sat) Persuade everyone at your table to order the tasting menu to avoid the torture of picking just one dish – everything on the menu at this fabulously contemporary and creative *osteria* is to die for. Pontedera-born chef Nicolò Baretti uses only seasonal products, natural ingredients and traditional flavours – to sensational effect.

ⓘ OLTRARNO DINING

New places to eat are forever popping up in this increasingly gentrified neighbourhood on the 'other side' of the Arno, which is home to some outstanding restaurants. Vegetarian, organic and raw cuisine are also at their Florentine best here. Several gourmet choices frame Piazza della Passera, an impossibly enchanting square with no passing traffic

FAVE GELATO STOPS

Gelateria Pasticceria Badiani (☑ 055 57 86 82; www.buontalenti.it; Viale dei Mille 20r; ☺ 7am-1am summer, to midnight Sun-Thu, to 1am Fri & Sat winter) Out of the town centre, but well worth the walk.

My Sugar (Map p92; ☑ 393 0696042; Via de' Ginori 49r; cones €2.50-4.50, tubs €2.50-5; ☺ 1-11pm summer, to 8.30pm winter, closed Jan & Feb) Sensational artisanal gelateria near Piazza San Marco.

Grom (Map p82; ☑ 055 21 61 58; www.grom.it; Via del Campanile 2; cones & tubs €2.60-5.50; ☺ 10am-midnight Sun-Fri, to 1am Sat summer, 10.30am-10.30pm winter) Top-notch gelato, including outstanding chocolate, near the *duomo*.

Vivoli (Map p100; ☑ 055 29 23 34; www.vivoli.it; Via dell'Isola delle Stinche 7; tubs €2-10; ☺ 7.30am-midnight Tue-Sat, from 9am Sun, to 9pm winter) Vintage favourite for coffee and cakes as well as gelato.

Gelateria La Carraia (Map p104; ☑ 055 28 06 95; www.lacarraiagroup.eu; Piazza Nazario Sauro 25r; cones & tubs €1.50-6; ☺ 11am-midnight) Florentine favourite across the river.

Venchi (Map p82; ☑ 055 26 43 39; www.venchi.com; Via dei Calzaiuoli 65; 2-/3-/4-scoops €3.20/4/5; ☺ 10am-11pm Sun-Thu, to midnight Fri & Sat) Who can resist an entire wall flowing with melted chocolate?

Burro e Acciughe
TUSCAN €€

(Butter & Anchovies; Map p104; ☑ 055 045 72 86; www.facebook.com/burroeacciughe; Via dell'Orto 35; meals €35; ☺ 7-11.45pm Tue-Fri, noon-2pm & 7pm-midnight Sat & Sun) Carefully sourced, quality ingredients drive this tiny trattoria that woos punters with a short but stylish choice of raw (tartare and carpaccio) and cooked fish dishes. The gnocchi topped with octopus *ragù* is out of this world, as is the *baccalà* (salted cod) with creamed leeks, turnip and deep-fried polenta wedges. Excellent wine list too.

L'OV
VEGETARIAN €€

(Osteria Vegetariana; Map p104; ☑ 055 205 23 88; www.osteriavegetariana.it; Piazza del Carmine 4r; meals €30; ☺ noon-2.45pm & 7-11pm; ☑) The team behind gluten-free favourite **Quinoa** (www.ristorantequinoa.it) is the creative energy behind this appealing San Frediano address, a hit with vegetarians, vegans and coeliacs alike. The menu features no specific courses – rather a tantalising melody of seasonal dishes bursting with local produce: broccoli and bean burgers, violet artichokes with mint and *pecorino*, and so forth.

★ Essenziale
TUSCAN €€€

(Map p104; ☑ 333 7491973 055 247 69 56; www.essenziale.me; Piazza di Cestello 3r; 6-/8-course tasting menu €65/80; ☺ 7-10pm Tue-Sat; ☎) There's no finer showcase for modern Tuscan cuisine than this loft-style restaurant in a 19th-century warehouse. Preparing dishes at the kitchen bar in rolled-up shirt sleeves

and navy butcher's apron is dazzling young chef Simone Cipriani. Order one of his tasting menus to sample the full range of his inventive, thoroughly modern cuisine inspired by classic Tuscan dishes.

✕ Boboli & San Miniato al Monte

There might not be a wide range of eating options in this green part of Florence, but dining is at least gourmet, memorable and – when the weather allows – riverside.

Easy Living
STREET FOOD €

(Map p106; ☑ 055 234 11 12; www.easylivingfirenze.it; Piazza Giuseppe Poggi; snacks €3.50-4.50; ☺ 9am-7pm Mon-Sat winter, longer hours summer) Born out of a project to class up the Arno's riverbanks, this riverside kiosk – a romantic, wrought-iron structure in San Niccolò that wouldn't look out of place in Paris – is a local institution with young Florentines seeking al fresco snacks. As much summertime bar as street-food outlet, it's a chilled spot for homemade burgers, hot dogs, steaming bowls of tripe and *panini*.

ZEB
TUSCAN €€

(Map p106; ☑ 055 234 28 64; www.zebgastronomia.com; Via San Miniato 2r; meals €35; ☺ 12.30-3pm & 7.30-10.30pm Thu-Tue, closed Mon-Wed winter) Local gastronomes adore this modern, minimalist address with five-star wine list at the foot of the hill leading up to Piazzale Michelangelo, in village-like San Niccolò.

Post-panorama, sit around the deli-style counter and indulge in a delicious choice of cold cuts and creative Tuscan dishes prepared by passionate chef Alberto Navari and his *mamma* Giuseppina.

 La Leggenda dei Frati TUSCAN €€€
(Map p106; 055 068 05 45; www.laleggendadeifrati.it; Villa Bardini, Costa di San Giorgio 6a; menus €105 & €130, meals €90; 12.30-2pm & 7.30-10pm Tue-Sun;) Summertime's hottest address. At home in the grounds of historic Villa Bardini (p107), Michelin-starred Legend of Friars enjoys the most romantic terrace with a view in Florence. Veggies are plucked fresh from the vegetable patch, tucked between waterfalls and ornamental beds in Giardino Bardini, and contemporary art jazzes up the classically chic interior. Cuisine is Tuscan, gastronomic and well worth the vital advance reservation.

Drinking & Nightlife

Florence's drinking scene covers all bases. Be it historical cafes, contemporary cafes with barista-curated specialist coffee, traditional *enoteche* (which invariably make great eating addresses too), trendy bars with lavish *aperitivo* buffets, secret speakeasies or edgy cocktail or craft-beer bars, drinking is fun and varied. Nightlife, less extravagant, revolves around a handful of dance clubs.

Duomo & Piazza della Signoria

La Terrazza Lounge Bar BAR
(Map p82; 055 2726 5987, 342 1234710; www.lungarnocollection.com; Vicolo dell'Oro 6r; 3.30-10.30pm Apr-Sep) This rooftop bar with a wood-decked terrace accessible from the 5th floor of the Hotel Continentale is as chic as one would expect of a fashion-house hotel. Its *aperitivo* buffet is a modest affair (simple nuts and juicy olives), but who cares with that gorgeous panorama of Florence. Dress the part, or feel out of place. Count around €20 for a cocktail.

Amblé BAR
(Map p82; 055 26 85 28; www.amble.it; Piazzetta dei Del Bene 7a; 10am-midnight Tue-Sat, from noon Sun) 'Fresh food and old furniture' is the catchy strapline of this cafe-bar hidden in an alleyway near Ponte Vecchio. Vintage furniture – all for sale – creates a shabby-chic vibe and the tiny terrace feels delightfully far from the madding crowd on summer evenings. From the river, follow Vicolo dell'Oro to Hotel Continentale, then turn left along the alley running parallel to the river.

Mayday Club COCKTAIL BAR
(Map p82; 055 238 12 90; www.maydayclub.it; Via Dante Alighieri 16; cocktails €8-10; 8pm-2am Tue-Sat) Strike up a conversation with passionate mixologist Marco Arduino at Mayday. Within seconds you'll be hooked on his mixers and astonishing infusions, all handmade using wholly Tuscan ingredients. Think artichoke- and thistle-infused vermouth, pancetta whisky and porcini liqueur. Marco's cocktail list is equally impressive – or tell him your favourite flavours and let yourself be surprised.

Beer lovers will enjoy the pale ales, bitters and other artisanal brews from Bagno a Ripoli's Birrificio Fiorentino microbrewery, 9km east of Florence. Two-hour mixology and infusion workshops too.

Tosca & Nino CAFE
(Map p82; 055 493 34 68; www.toscanino.com; Piazza della Repubblica 1, La Rinascente; meals €25-35; 9am-midnight Mon-Sat, from 10.30am Sun) 'Tasting Tuscany' is the driver behind the rooftop hybrid crowning central department store La Rinascente on people-busy Piazza della Repubblica. As much quality eatery as a fashionable place to drink: nip up here between boutiques to gloat with the birds over coffee, cocktails or wine on its rooftop terrace. Views of the *duomo* and Florentine hills beyond are predictably dreamy.

Coquinarius WINE BAR
(Map p82; 055 230 21 53; www.coquinarius.com; Via delle Oche 11r; 12.30-3pm & 6.30-10.30pm Wed-Mon) With its old stone vaults, scrubbed wooden tables and modern air, this *enoteca* run by the dynamic Nicolas is spacious and stylish. The wine list features bags of Tuscan greats and unknowns, and outstanding crostini and *carpacci* (cold sliced meats) ensure you don't leave hungry.

Colle Bereto LOUNGE
(Map p82; 055 28 31 56; www.cafecollebereto.com; Piazza degli Strozzi 5r; 8am-5am;) The local fashion scene's bar of choice that never tires, this American lounge-bar is where the bold and the beautiful come to see or be seen for breakfast, lunch, dinner or at *aperitivo* hour. Summertime ushers in al fresco hobnobbing on the square behind Palazzo Strozzi.

TOP FIVE: SANDWICH SHOPS

Count on paying €5 to €8 for a lavishly filled *panino*.

S.Forno (Map p104; ☑055 239 85 80; www.facebook.com/sfornofirenze; Via Santa Monaco 3r; ☺7.30am-7.30pm Mon-Fri, from 8am Sat & Sun) A vintage bakery-cum–hipster favourite on the Oltrarno.

Mariano (Map p82; ☑055 21 40 67; Via del Parione 19r; panini €3.50-6; ☺8am-3pm & 5-7.30pm Mon-Fri, 8am-3pm Sat) Our favourite for its simplicity, around since 1973. From sunrise to sunset, this brick-vaulted, 13th-century cellar near Via de' Tornabuoni gently buzzes with Florentines propped at the counter sipping coffee or wine or eating salads and *panini*.

Semel (Map p100; Piazza Ghiberti 44r; panini €3.50-5; ☺11.30am-2.30pm Mon-Sat) Locals swear by this pocket-sized sandwich bar opposite Sant'Ambrogio food market. Six gourmet combos are crafted with love by passionate owner and *panino* king Marco Paparozzi.

'Ino (Map p82; ☑055 21 45 14; www.inofirenze.com; Via dei Georgofili 3r-7r; panini €6-10; ☺noon-4.30pm) 🍷 Artisanal ingredients sourced locally and mixed creatively by passionate gourmet Alessandro Frassica are the secret behind this gourmet sandwich bar, handily placed for lunch post-Uffizi.

All'Antico Vinaio (p119) The crowd spills out the door of this noisy Florentine thoroughbred in Santa Croce. Push your way to the tables at the back to taste cheese and salami in situ (advance reservations recommended). Or join the queue at the deli counter for a well-stuffed focaccia wrapped in waxed paper to take away – pour yourself a glass of wine while you wait.

I Due Fratellini (Map p82; ☑055 239 60 96; www.iduefratellini.com; Via dei Cimatori 38r; panini €4; ☺10am-7pm) This hole-in-the-wall near the *duomo* has been in business since 1875. Wash your pick of 30 different types of *panini* down with a beaker of wine and leave the empty glass on the wooden shelf outside.

Shake Café
CAFE

(Map p82; ☑055 21 59 52; www.shakecafe.bio; Via del Corso 28-32; ☺7.30am-8pm) Smoothie bowls with protein powder, kale and goji berries, cold-pressed juices and vitamin-packed elixir shots – to eat in or take away – satisfy wellness cravings at this laid-back cafe on people-busy Via del Corso. International newspapers, mellow music and a relaxed vibe make it a hipster place to hang. All-day wraps, salads and hearty, homemade soups (€6 to €8) too.

Strozzi Caffè
CAFE

(Map p82; ☑055 28 82 36; Piazza degli Strozzi 1; ☺8am-1am Thu-Sat, to 9.30pm Sun-Wed; 🛜) Soul-soaringly high-vaulted ceiling, black Panton chairs, excellent coffee and reasonable prices seduce a mixed crowd at this arty hangout in the seductive, interior courtyard of Palazzo Strozzi on Florence's most designer-chic street. Various tapas-inspired small plates, ranging from Tuscan salamis and cheeses to Mexican spring rolls, make it a great place to linger over that all-essential *aperitivo*.

Fiaschetteria Nuvoli
WINE BAR

(Map p82; ☑055 239 66 16; Piazza dell'Olio 15r; ☺8am-9pm Mon-Sat) Pull up a stool on the street and chat with a regular over a glass of *vino della casa* (house wine) at this old-fashioned *fiaschetteria* (wine seller), a street away from the *duomo*. Food too.

YAB
CLUB

(Map p82; ☑055 21 51 60; www.yab.it/en; Via de' Sassetti 5r; ☺7pm-4am Mon & Wed-Sat Oct-May) Pick your night according to your age and tastes – disco, rock 'n' roll, groove or a 'Un-Yversal' bit of everything – at this hugely popular nightclub with electric dance floor, around since the 1970s, behind Palazzo Strozzi.

🍷 Santa Maria Novella

★ Manifattura
COCKTAIL BAR

(Map p82; ☑055 239 63 67; www.facebook.com/Manifattura-6266; Piazza di San Pancrazio 1; ☺6pm-1am Tue-Thu & Sun, to 2am Fri & Sat) 'Made in Italy' has never been such a pertinent buzzword in the city, hence this trendy cocktail bar – an unabashed celebration of Italian spirits and other drinks, both alcoholic and soft. Behind the bar, Fabiano Buffolini is one of Florence's finest mixologists, tapas-style small plates of traditional Tuscan dishes make wonderful pairings and the music is undeniably retro (think 1950s Italian).

Fabbricato Viaggiatori
BAR

(Map p92; ☑ 055 264 51 14; www.facebook.com/fabbricatoviaggiatori; Piazza del Stazione 50; ☺ 8am-midnight) An experimental 'factory' of people, ideas, food, wine, cocktails and live music is the essence of this funky new hangout, at home in Palazzina Reale di Santa Maria Novella – the striking, white marble Rationalist building from the 1930s adjoining the central train station. Be it breakfast, daytime drinks or dining, DJ sets, wine tasting or late-night dancing, it's an up-coming hybrid to watch.

Tenax
CLUB

(☑ 393 9204279, 335 5235922; www.tenax.org; Via Pratese 46; admission varies; ☺ 10pm-4am Thu-Sun Oct-Apr) The only club in Florence on the European club circuit, with great international guest DJs and wildly popular 'Nobody's Perfect' house parties on Saturday night; find the warehouse-style building out of town near Florence airport. Take bus 29 or 30 from Stazione di Santa Maria Novella.

San Lorenzo & San Marco

★ Caffè del Verone
CAFE

(Map p92; ☑ 392 4982559; www.facebook.com/CaffedelVeroneRooftopFlorence; Piazza della Santissima Annunziata 13, Museo degli Innocenti; ☺ 8.30am-7pm Mon, to 9pm Tue-Sat, 9am-7pm Sun; ☎) At home in Ospedale degli Innocenti's *verone* where linen at the foundling hospital was hung up to dry in the 15th century, this peaceful rooftop cafe on the 5th floor of the Museo degli Innocenti (p93) is one of San Marco's best-kept secrets. Lounging over drinks on the romantic loggia proffers a magnificent vista of Florentine rooftops and Tuscan hills beyond.

PanicAle
COCKTAIL BAR

(Map p92; ☑ 335 5473530; www.facebook.com/PanicAleFirenze; Via Panicale 7-9r; ☺ 5.30pm-1am Mon-Wed & Sun, to 2am Thu-Sat) Still lovingly known as Lo Sverso (its original name) by many a Florentine socialite, this superstylish bar is a gem. In a part of town where hipster addresses are scarce, there's no finer spot for an expertly crafted cocktail mixed with

homemade syrups (try the basil), craft beer on tap or home-brewed ginger ale. DJs spin tunes many a weekend.

Buca 10
WINE BAR

(Map p100; ☑ 055 016 53 28; www.facebook.com/enotecabuca10; Via Fiesolana 10r; ☺ 3.30pm-midnight Tue-Thu, to 2am Fri & Sat; ☎) 'Peace and Wine' is the alluring strapline of this contemporary *enoteca*, run with an arty passion and creativity by Francesca and Daniele. Tasty *taglieri* accompany the excellent wine list, there is a guitar and *cajón* (Peruvian percussion instrument) lying around for anyone to tinkle on, and the modern space hosts occasional photography exhibitions, film screenings and other local happenings.

Bitter Bar
COCKTAIL BAR

(Map p100; ☑ 340 5499258; www.bitterbarfirenze.it; Via di Mezzo 28r; ☺ 9pm-2am Mon-Sat) The 1920s provide the sassy inspiration behind this speakeasy where ordering anything so mundane as a Sex on a Beach is simply not done. Mixologist Cristian Guitti experiments with plenty of unusual bitters, infusions and fresh ingredients to keep cocktail aficionados on their toes, while tasting notes on the tantalising menu – 'sweet smooth', 'fresh and delicate', 'for gin lovers' – pander to the less initiated.

SimBIOsi Caffè
CAFE

(Map p92; ☑ 334 8120188; www.simbiosi.bio; Via de' Ginori 64r; ☺ 8am-10pm Mon-Fri, from 9am Sat & Sun; ☎) As if an organic pizzeria and pasta parlour were not enough, the considerate folk behind SimBIOsi (p126) now run their very own cafe, and it doesn't disappoint. Everything – creative salads, homemade soups, toasty-warm *crostini* – is organic; the natural wine list is outstanding; and the specialist coffee uses beans artisan-roasted in Tuscany and Italy (including Florence's Ditta Artigianale and D612 coffee roasters).

Rex Café
BAR

(Map p100; ☑ 055 248 03 31; www.rexfirenze.com; Via Fiesolana 25r; ☺ 8pm-3am) A firm long-term favourite (since 1990), down-to-earth Rex maintains its appeal. Behind the bar Virginia and Lorenzo shake a mean cocktail, using homemade syrups and artisanal spirits like ginger- or carrot-flavoured vodka, pepper rum and laurel vermouth. The artsy, Gaudí-inspired interior is as much art gallery and nightlife stage as simple bar.

Art. 17 Birreria
CRAFT BEER

(Map p100; ☎055 234 66 94; www.articolo 17birreria.it; Borgo La Croce 64r; ⊙5pm-2am; ☞) Craft-beer aficionados will simply adore this Santa Croce *birreria artigniale* (artisanal brewery) which provides night owls with an edgy fusion of Tuscan, Italian and international craft beer – there are some 50-odd bottled and on tap to choose from – and live music at weekends. 'Happy Hour' kicks in daily from 5pm to 9pm.

🍸 Santa Croce

★ Ditta Artigianale
CAFE

(Map p100; ☎055 274 15 41; www.dittaartigianale.it; Via de' Neri 32r; ⊙8am-10pm Mon-Thu, to midnight Fri, 9am-midnight Sat, to 11pm Sun; ☞) With industrial decor and laid-back vibe, this ingenious coffee roastery is a perfect place to hang at any time of day. The creation of three-times Italian barista champion Francesco Sanapo, it's famed for its first-class coffee and outstanding gin cocktails. If you're yearning for a flat white, cold-brew tonic or cappuccino made with almond milk, come here.

★ Locale
COCKTAIL BAR

(Map p100; ☎055 906 71 88; www.localefirenze.it; Via delle Seggiole 12; ⊙7.30pm-2am) At home in a 13th- to 15th-century *palazzo,* this tucked-away drinking and dining space is designed to stun. From the exquisite craft cocktails (€20 to €30) mixed at the bar, to the beautifully presented modern Tuscan fare and awe-inspiring interior design – a theatrical fusion of original architectural features, period furnishings and contemporary vegetal wall gardens – Locale is a true feast for the eyes (and appetite).

Le Murate
CAFE

(Caffè Letterario Firenze; Map p100; ☎055 234 68 72; www.lemurate.it; Piazza delle Murate; ⊙10.30am-1am Mon-Fri, from 4pm Sat & Sun; ☞) This arty cafe-bar in a former jail is where literati meet to talk, create and perform over coffee, drinks and light meals. The literary cafe hosts everything from readings and interviews with authors – Florentine, Italian and international – to film screenings, debates, live music and art exhibitions. Tables are built from recycled window frames and in summer everything spills outside into the brick courtyard.

Vanilla Club
COCKTAIL BAR

(Map p100; ☎328 9748301; www.vanillaclub.it; Via dei Saponai 14r; ⊙6pm-2am Tue-Sun; ☞) A 1920s speakeasy if ever there was one, Vanilla Club cooks up an astonishing array of craft cocktails – many served in over-sized, vintage-china tea cups – in an atmospheric, fashionably retro setting. The signature house cocktail mixes vanilla-flavoured vodka with fresh grapefruit and Tuscany's very own sweet herbal Galliano liqueur.

Eby's
BAR

(Map p100; www.facebook.com/SeguiLaRana; Via dell'Oriulolo 5r; ⊙11am-2am Mon-Sat) A lively student crowd packs out this young, fun, colourful address with a hipster 'coffee, rum and philosophy' strapline and wooden

---

FAVOURITE PIZZERIA

Santarpia (Map p100; ☎055 24 58 29; www.santarpia.biz; Largo Pietro Annigoni 9c; pizza €8.50-15; ⊙7.30pm-midnight Tue-Sun; ☞) Thin-crust Neapolitan pizza across the street from Mercato di Sant'Ambrogio.

Berberé (Map p104; ☎055 238 29 46; www.berberepizza.it; Piazza dei Nerli 1; pizza €5.90-12.80; ⊙12.30-2.30pm & 7pm-midnight Fri-Sun, 7pm-midnight Mon-Thu) Perfect pizza, craft beer and contemporary interior design in San Frediano.

Gustapizza (Map p104; ☎055 28 50 68; www.facebook.com/GustapizzaFirenze; Via Maggio 46r; pizza €5-8; ⊙11.30am-3.30pm & 7-11.30pm Tue-Sun) Student favourite, Neapolitan-style, on the Oltrarno.

SimBIOsi (Map p92; ☎055 064 01 15; www.simbiosi.bio; Via de' Ginori 56r; pizza €6.50-11; ⊙noon-11pm; ☞) Hipster pizzeria cooking organic pizza, with craft beer and wine by small producers.

Il Pizzaiuolo (Map p100; ☎055 24 11 71; www.ilpizzaiuolo.com; Via dei Macci 113r; pizzas €8-11; ⊙12.30-2.30pm & 7.30pm-midnight Mon-Sat, closed Aug) Cosy pizzeria, lovely for an evening out, in Sant'Ambrogio.

benches tucked outside in a covered alley-way. The kitchen is Mexican, the vibe is party and the barmen are known far and wide for their shots, flaming included.

Babylon Club
CLUB
(Map p100; ✆ 347 3818294; www.facebook.com/BabylonClubOfficialPage; Via dei Pandolfini 26r; ⊙11pm-4am Mon, Tue & Thu-Sat) For late-night dancing in Santa Croce, hit this swish nightclub with sleek black facade and three dance floors playing a mixed bag of sounds: latino, kizomba, reggae and lots of funky hip-hop and R&B. Check Facebook for the week's events.

Blob Club
CLUB
(Map p100; ✆ 324 8043276; Via Vinegia 21r; ⊙10pm-4am) This small and edgy Santa Croce club lures an international crowd with its music theme nights – loads of 1960s, hip-hop, alternative rock; all sounds in fact.

Full Up
CLUB
(Map p100; ✆ 055 29 30 06; www.fullupclub.com; Via della Vigna Vecchia 21r; ⊙11pm-4am Thu-Sat Sep-Jun) A variety of sounds energises the crowd at this popular Florentine nightclub, in the biz since 1958, where 20-somethings dance until dawn.

🍷 Oltrarno

★ Santarosa Bistrot
BAR
(✆055 230 90 57; www.facebook.com/santarosa.bistrot; Lungarno di Santarosa; ⊙8am-midnight; 🛜) The living is easy at this hipster garden-bistro-bar, snug against a chunk of ancient city wall in the flowery Santarosa gardens. Comfy cushioned sofas built from recycled wooden crates sit al fresco beneath trees; food is superb (meals €30); and mixologists behind the bar complement an excellent wine list curated by Enoteca Pitti Gola e Cantina with serious craft cocktails.

★ Mad Souls & Spirits
COCKTAIL BAR
(Map p104; ✆ 055 627 16 21; www.facebook.com/madsoulsandspirits; Borgo San Frediano 38r; ⊙6pm-2am; 🛜) At this ubercool bar in San Frediano, cult alchemists Neri Fantechi and Julian Biondi woo a discerning crowd with their expertly crafted cocktails, served in a tiny aqua-green and red-brick space that couldn't be more spartan. A potted cactus decorates each scrubbed wood table and the humorous cocktail menu is the height of irreverence. Check the 'Daily Madness' blackboard for specials.

SILVER-SPOON DINING

For an utterly unique dining experience reserve a table well in advance at In Fabbrica (✆347 5145468; http://restaurant.pampaloni.com; Via del Gelsomino 99; meals €45; ⊙8-10.30pm Wed-Sat), 1.5km south of Porto Romana along Via Senese on the Oltrarno. Fusing Florence's outstanding tradition of craftsmanship with equally fine cuisine, In Fabbrica – meaning 'In the Factory' – is just that. By day, workers from third-generation Florentine silver house Pampaloni lunch here but come dusk, the speakeasy canteen opens its doors to culturally curious diners. Tables are laid with silver cutlery and majestic candelabras, waiters wear white gloves and the cuisine is Tuscan.

★ Enoteca Pitti Gola e Cantina
WINE BAR
(Map p104; ✆ 055 21 27 04; www.pittigolaecantina.com; Piazza dei Pitti 16; ⊙1pm-midnight Wed-Mon) Wine lovers won't do better than this serious wine bar opposite Palazzo Pitti, run with passion and humour by charismatic trio Edoardo, Manuele and Zeno – don't be surprised if they share a glass with you over wine talk. Floor-to-ceiling shelves of expertly curated, small-production Tuscan and Italian wines fill the tiny bar, and casual dining is around a handful of marble-topped tables. Look forward to excellent cured meats and pasta *fatta in casa* (housemade).

The team has its own fully fledged restaurant, Osteria dell'Enoteca (Map p104; ✆055 21 27 04; www.osteriadellenoteca.com; Via Romana 70r; meals €30; ⊙noon-2.30pm & 7-11pm Wed-Mon), nearby.

Il Santino
WINE BAR
(Map p104; ✆ 055 230 28 20; http://ilsantobevitore.com; Via di Santo Spirito 60r; ⊙12.30-11pm) Kid sister to top-notch restaurant Il Santo Bevitore (p121) two doors down the same street, this intimate wine bar with exposed stone walls and marble bar is a stylish spot for pairing cured meats, cheeses and Tuscan staples with a carefully curated selection of wine – many by local producers – and artisanal beers.

La Cité
BAR
(Map p104; www.facebook.com/lacitelibreriacafe; Borgo San Frediano 20r; ⊙10am-2am Mon-Sat, from 2pm Sun; 🛜) A hip cafe-bookshop with

FLORENCE DRINKING & NIGHTLIFE

an eclectic choice of vintage seating, La Cité makes a wonderful, intimate venue for book readings, after-work drinks and fantastic live music – jazz, swing, world music. Check its Facebook page for the week's events.

Gosh
COCKTAIL BAR

(Map p104; ☑055 046 90 48; www.facebook. com/goshfirenze; Via Santo Spirito 46r; ☺7pm-midnight Tue-Thu, 6pm-2am Fri-Sun) Whimsical flamingo wallpaper, funky music, DJ sets and a subtle NYC vibe lures Florence's fashionable set to this buzzing cocktail bar across the river. Expect lots of fun variations of classic cocktails – blueberry mojitos, dozens of different Moscow mules and sensational basil-infused creations.

Love Craft
COCKTAIL BAR

(Map p104; ☑055 269 29 68; www.facebook.com/ lovecraftfirenze; Borgo San Frediano 24r; ☺6pm-2am) Florence's first dedicated whisky bar – named after illustrious American horror writer HP Lovecraft – has proved a hit from day one with a staunchly local crowd who flock here for a break from the norm. Two hundred-odd whiskies from around the globe jostle for the limelight with mixologist Manuel Petretto's Scotch whisky–based craft cocktails (from €7) and craft beers on tap.

Rasputin
COCKTAIL BAR

(Map p104; ☑055 28 03 99; www.facebook.com/ rasputinfirenze; Borgo Tegolaio 21r; ☺8pm-2am) The 'secret' speakeasy everyone knows about, it has no sign outside: disguised as a chapel of sorts, look for the tiny entrance with the two-seat wooden pew, crucifix on the wall, vintage pics and tea lights flickering in the doorway. Inside, it's back to the 1930s with period furnishings, an exclusive vibe and bar staff mixing Prohibition-era cocktails.

Archea Brewery
CRAFT BEER

(Map p104; www.facebook.com/archea.brwry; Via dei Serragli 44; ☺6pm-1am Mon-Thu, to 2am Fri & Sat, 4.30pm-1am Sun) Craft-beer devotees will enjoy this dimly lit, hole-in-the-wall drinking joint, a step away from the tourist crowds with knowledgeable bartenders at the helm and locals firmly planted around the L-shaped bar. Pick from an interesting range of home and guest brews, bottled and on tap, from Italy and Europe. Four-beer tasting flights too.

SUMMER ROOFTOPS & RIVERSIDE SHACKS

Summer in the city all too often translates as hot, frenetic, overcrowded days when, quite frankly, the only place any savvy urbanite strives to be is by a pool or on a rooftop – away from the crowds.

Breezy (if you're lucky) hotspots up high to catch a brief respite from summertime's sizzling temperatures – over drinks and a dip during the day or after dusk – include Three Sixty at Grand Hotel Minerva (Map p82; ☑055 2 72 30; www.grandhotelminerva. com; Piazza di Santa Maria Novella 16; d €374; ❄️🛜🏊) and American rooftop bar Empireo (Map p100; ☑055 262 35 00; www.hotelplazalucchesi.it; Lungarno della Zecca Vecchia 38; ☺7.30am-midnight; 🛜) at Plaza Hotel Lucchesi. Both seasonal bars open June to September, lure an insanely fashionable crowd, and come with cooling rooftop pool and weekly live jazz soirées.

Summer rooftop bar La Terrazza Lounge Bar (p123) at Hotel Continentale doesn't have a pool but the five-star view of Ponte Vecchio dished up with sophisticated cocktails at sunset is pretty damn good. By Santa Maria Novella train station, fashionistas while away sultry summer nights over drinks at the B-Roof bar atop Grand Hotel Baglioni (Map p82; ☑055 2 35 80; www.hotelbaglioni.it; Piazza dell'Unità Italiana 6; d €130-615; ❄️🛜). Across the river on Piazzale Michelangelo, Florentine sophisticates dress up to the nines to lounge, drink, dance until dawn – and swoon at the city by night beautifully laid out at their feet – at hilltop Flò.

On the banks of the Arno, riverside shacks mushroom after the rain during the sweltering summer months. Year-round snack shack Easy Living (p122) in San Niccolò morphs into an urban beach complete with sand, sun loungers, beach volleyball, sunset yoga classes, DJ sets and weekend beach parties. Watch for seasonal newcomers each year both here and directly across the water where, on the grassy riverbanks, you might also spot cherry-red food truck La Toraia (p120).

Boboli & San Miniato al Monte

★ **Le Volpi e l'Uva**   WINE BAR
(Map p106; ☑055 239 81 32; www.levolpieluva.com; Piazza dei Rossi 1; ⊙11am-9pm Mon-Sat) This humble wine bar remains as appealing as the day it opened in 1992. Its food and wine pairings are first class – taste and buy boutique wines by small Italian producers, matched perfectly with cheeses, cold meats and the finest crostini in town; the warm, melt-in-your-mouth *lardo di cinta senese* (wafer-thin slices of aromatic of pork fat) is absolutely extraordinary.

Flò   LOUNGE
(Map p106; ☑334 1080164, 334 1080164 055 65 07 91; www.flofirenze.com; Piazzale Michelangelo 84; ⊙7.30pm-4am late May-Sep) Without a doubt the hottest spot to be seen on sultry summer nights is Flò, a glitzy lounge bar that pops up each May on Piazzale Michelangelo. Different themed lounge areas include a dance floor and VIP area (where you have no chance of reserving a table – €18 per head – unless you're in the Florentine in-crowd).

☆ Entertainment

Hanging out on warm summer nights on cafe and bar terraces aside, Florence enjoys a vibrant entertainment scene thanks in part to its substantial foreign-student population. The city has highly regarded theatres, a bounty of festivals and – from around midnight once *aperitivo* and dinner are done – a fairly low-key but varied dance scene.

★ **Manifattura Tabacchi**   ARTS CENTRE
(https://eventi.manifatturatabacchi.com; Via delle Cascine 35; ⊙hours vary) A work in progress, this ex-industrial plant near Parco della Cascine hosts some of the city's edgiest contemporary art events and happenings. The complex – a stunning example of Rationalist architecture – was built between 1933 and 1940 as a tobacco-processing plant and cigarette factory, operational until 2001. Today creative arts venues, cultural spaces, coworking spaces, artist residencies and startups are mushrooming inside the derelict buildings. Cycling and walking trails are also injecting new zest into the revitalised 'hood.

Stazione Leopolda   ARTS CENTRE
(☑055 21 26 22; www.stazione-leopolda.com; Viale Fratelli Rosselli 5) Be it an exhibition celebrating 50 years of the moon boot, a Pitti Immagine fashion show, lavish food and wine tastings, DJ sets or a festival dedicated to digital arts and electronic music, events held at Florence's premier exhibition centre – a former 19th-century train station – are big, bold and often an essential date in any self-respecting Florentine's calendar.

Teatro del Maggio Musicale Fiorentino   PERFORMING ARTS
(☑055 200 12 78; www.maggiofiorentino.com; Piazzale Vittorio Gui 1; ⊙box office 10am-6pm Mon-Sat) This strikingly modern theatre with glittering contemporary geometric facade sits on the green edge of city park Parco delle Cascine. Its three thoughtfully designed and multifunctional concert halls can seat an audience of 5000 in total and play host to opera, theatre, ballet, dance and classical-music performances.

Odeon Cinehall   CINEMA
(Map p82; ☑055 21 40 68; www.odeonfirenze.com; Piazza degli Strozzi 2; adult/reduced €8.50/7) This lovingly restored early-20th-century theatre, complete with intact balcony seats and Tiffany-style cupola, shows films in their original language.

Pinocchio Jazz Club   JAZZ
(☑055 68 33 88; www.facebook.com/pinocchio jazz; Viale Donnato Giannotti 13; €12) Live jazz and blues lures a loyal crowd to this atmospheric jazz club across the river. Concerts kick off most nights at 9.45pm and under 25s get free admission; advance table reservations recommended. Check its Facebook page for event listings.

Auditorium Flog   CONCERT VENUE
(☑055 48 71 45; www.facebook.com/Auditorium FlogFirenze; Via Michele Mercati 24b; ⊙9.30pm-3.30am Fri & Sat) Hotspot for live music, international DJs and alternative bands since the 1970s, Auditorium Flog is an essential weekend port of call for Florentine music fans and party animals. Sounds cover every genre. Watch for festivals, sports events, summertime film screenings and other cultural happenings too; check its agenda on Facebook.

To get here, ride the T1 tramline from Piazza della Unità to the Poggetto stop.

🛍 Shopping

Tacky mass-produced souvenirs (boxer shorts emblazoned with *David*'s packet) are everywhere, not least at city market **Mercato Nuovo** (Map p82; Piazza del Mercato

FLORENCE ENTERTAINMENT

FLORENCE SHOPPING

HISTORICAL CAFES

Caffè Gilli (Map p82; ✆ 055 21 38 96; www.gilli.it; Piazza della Repubblica 39r; ⊘ 7.30am-1am) Popular with locals who sip coffee standing up at the long marble bar, this is the most famous of the historic cafes on the city's old Roman forum. Gilli has been serving delectable cakes, chocolates, fruit tartlets and *millefoglie* (lighter-than-light vanilla or custard slice) since 1733. It moved to this square in 1910 and has a beautifully preserved art nouveau interior.

Procacci (Map p82; ✆ 055 21 16 56; www.procacci1885.it; Via de' Tornabuoni 64r; ⊘ 10am-9pm Mon-Sat, 11am-8pm Sun, closed 3 weeks Aug) The last remaining bastion of genteel old Florence on Via de' Tornabuoni, this tiny cafe was born in 1885 as a delicatessen serving truffles in its repertoire of tasty morsels. Bite-sized *panini tartufati* (truffle-pâté rolls) remain the thing to order, best accompanied by a glass of prosecco (sparkling wine).

Caffè Rivoire (Map p82; ✆ 055 21 44 12; www.rivoire.it; Piazza della Signoria 4; ⊘ 7am-midnight Tue-Sun summer, to 9pm winter) This golden oldie with an unbeatable people-watching terrace has produced some of the city's most exquisite chocolate since 1872 (sadly only available in winter). Black-jacketed barmen with ties set the formal tone. Save several euros by joining the local Florentine crowd standing at the bar rather than sitting down at a table.

Nuovo; ⊘ 8.30am-7pm Mon-Sat), awash with cheap imported handbags and other leather goods. But for serious shoppers keen to delve into a city synonymous with craftsmanship since medieval times, there are plenty of workshops and boutiques to visit.

🔒 Duomo & Piazza della Signoria

This is prime shopping terrain: Via de' Tornabuoni is Florence's smartest shopping strip, bejewelled with Gucci, Salvatore Ferragamo et al. Small fashion boutiques and touristy craft and souvenir shops pepper the maze of narrow, pedestrian lanes ensnaring Piazza della Signoria.

★**Benheart** FASHION & ACCESSORIES
(Map p82; www.benheart.it; Via dei Calzaivoli 78; ⊘ 10am-7.30pm) This flagship store of local superstar Ben, a Florentine-based fashion designer who set up the business with schoolmate Matteo after undergoing a heart transplant, is irresistible. The pair swore that if Ben survived, they'd go it alone – which they did, with huge success. For real-McCoy handcrafted leather designs – casual shoes, jackets and belts for men and women – there is no finer address.

Around €200 is the price you pay for a pair of shoes with soft buffalo leather, stitched before being dyed with natural pigments. Find smaller Benheart boutiques around the **corner** (Map p82; ✆ 055 046 26

38; Via dei Cimatori 25r; ⊘ 10am-7.30pm) and in **Santa Maria Novella** (Map p82; ✆ 055 239 94 83; Via della Vigna Nuova 95-97r; ⊘ 9am-8pm).

★**Luisa Via Roma** FASHION & ACCESSORIES
(Map p82; ✆ 055 906 41 16; www.luisaviaroma.com; Via Roma 19-21r; ⊘ 10.30am-7.30pm Mon-Sat, from 11am Sun) The flagship store of this historic store (think: small 1930s boutique selling straw hats) turned luxury online retailer is a must for the fashion-forward. Eye-catching window displays woo with giant screens, while seasonal themes transform the interior maze of rooms into an exotic Garden of Eden. Shop here for lesser-known designers as well as popular luxury-fashion labels.

Pre- or post-shop, hob-nob with the city's fashionista set over fair-trade coffee, organic cuisine and creative cold-press juices in Luisa's chic 1st-floor cafe-bar **Floret** (Map p82; ✆ 055 29 59 24; www.floret-bar.com; salads & bowls €12-16; ⊘ 10.30am-7.30pm Mon-Sat, from 11am Sun; 🛜) 🌿.

Boutique Nadine FASHION & ACCESSORIES
(Map p82; ✆ 055 28 78 51; www.boutiquenadine.com; Lungarno degli Acciaiuoli 22r; ⊘ 10am-7.30pm Mon-Sat, to 7pm Sun) For exquisite vintage clothing, jewellery and stylish knick-knacks for the home curated by inquisitive travellers and Florentines Irene and partner Matteo, browse this old-world boutique on the riverside near Ponte Vecchio. Look out for Irene's own label, Odette, embracing romantic print dresses evocative of old-world Florence.

Angela Caputi JEWELLERY

(Map p82; ☑ 055 29 29 93; www.angelacaputi.
com; Borgo SS Apostoli 42-46; ⊘10am-1pm &
3.30-7.30pm Mon-Sat) The bold and colourful
resin jewellery of Angela Caputi, at work in
Florence since the 1970s, is much loved by
Florentines. Eye-catching costume gems and
jewels are her forté, shown off to perfection
against one-of-a-kind women's labels uncovered during her worldwide travels.

La Bottega dell'Olio FOOD

(Map p82; ☑ 055 267 04 68; www.labot
tegadelloliofirenze.it; Piazza del Limbo 4r; ⊘2.30-
6.30pm Mon, 10am-1pm & 2-6.30pm Tue-Sat) This
bijou boutique takes great care with its displays of olive oils, olive-oil soaps, platters
made from olive wood and skincare products made with olive oil (the Lepo range is
particularly good).

Santa Maria Novella

The web of streets immediately west of de-
signer-studded Via de' Tornabuoni (p69)
offers superstylish shopping for fashion,
crafts, homewares and unique design: Via
della Vigna Nuova and Via della Spada are
lined with superb boutiques.

**★ Officina Profumo-Farmaceutica
di Santa Maria Novella** GIFTS

(Map p82; ☑ 055 21 62 76; www.smnovella.it; Via
della Scala 16; ⊘9am-8pm) In business since
1612, this exquisite perfumery-pharmacy
began life when Santa Maria Novella's Dominican friars began to concoct cures and
sweet-smelling unguents using medicinal
herbs cultivated in the monastery garden.
The shop, with an interior from 1848, sells
fragrances, skincare products, ancient herbal remedies and preparations for everything
from relief of heavy legs to improving skin
elasticity, memory and mental energy.

★ Mio Concept HOMEWARES

(Map p82; ☑ 055 264 55 43; www.mio-concept.
com; Via della Spada 34r; ⊘10am-1.30pm & 2.30-
7.30pm Mon-Sat) Design objects for the home
– made in Italy and many upcycled – as well
as jewellery, bags and belts crafted from old
bicycle tyres and inner tubes by Turinese
designers Cingomma, and so on, cram this
stylish boutique created by German globe-
trotter Antje. Don't miss the prints of iconic
designs by Italian street artists Blub and
Exit Enter, and street-sign artworks by Florence's Clet (p111).

Pineider ARTS & CRAFTS

(Map p82; ☑ 055 28 46 56; www.pineider.com; Piazza de' Rucellai 4-7r; ⊘10am-7pm) 'Writing the
Future' is the inspired strapline of this iconic
stationery company, in business in Florence
since 1714. Stendhal, Byron, Shelley and
Dickens are among the literary luminaries
who have chosen to purchase its beautifully crafted, top-quality paper products, pens
and leather goods.

Aprosio & Co FASHION & ACCESSORIES

(Map p82; ☑ 055 21 01 27; www.aprosio.it; Via del
Moro 75-77r; ⊘10.30am-6.30pm Mon-Sat) Or-
nella Aprosio fashions teeny-tiny Murano
glass and crystal beads into dazzling pieces
of jewellery, hair accessories, animal-shaped
brooches, handbags, even glass-flecked cash-
mere. It is all quite magical.

Grevi FASHION & ACCESSORIES

(Map p82; ☑ 055 26 41 39; www.grevi.it; Via della
Spada 11-13r; ⊘10am-2pm & 3-8pm Mon-Sat)
It was a hat made by Siena milliner Grevi
that actress Cher wore in the film *Tea with
Mussolini* (1999); ditto Maggie Smith in *My
House in Umbria* (2003). So if you want
to shop like a star for a hat by Grevi, this
hopelessly romantic boutique is the address.
Hats range in price from €30 to possibly
unaffordable.

Richard Ginori HOMEWARES

(Map p82; ☑ 055 21 00 41; www.richardgi
nori1735.com; Via de' Rondinelli 17r; ⊘10am-7pm
Mon-Wed, 10am-7.30pm Thu-Sat, noon-7pm Sun)
The maze of beautiful period rooms at this
elegant porcelain shop is well worth exploring. Showcasing tableware produced
by Richard Ginori, a Tuscan company established in 1735, the showroom is one of
the city's most beautiful retail spaces: think
original parquet flooring, moulded ceilings,
papered walls and an 18th-century glass
conservatory filled with plants.

La Bottega della Frutta FOOD & DRINKS

(Map p82; ☑ 055 239 85 90; Via dei Federighi 31r;
⊘8.30am-7.30pm Mon-Sat, closed Aug) Follow
the trail of knowing Florentines, past the
flower-and-veg-laden bicycle parked outside, into this enticing food shop bursting
with boutique cheeses, organic fruit and
veg, biscuits, chocolates, conserved produce,
wine et al. Fresh mozzarella oozing raw milk
arrives from Sicily every Tuesday, and this is
the place to taste and buy olive oil. Ask Elis-
abeta or her husband, Francesco.

San Lorenzo & San Marco

San Lorenzo being the market 'hood of town, this is the obvious place to shop for fresh fruit, veg, olive oil, salami and so on to take home. Otherwise, there are a couple of interesting gourmet shops. The neighbourhood also has a thin sprinkling of fun independent fashion boutiques.

★ Street Doing
VINTAGE

(Map p92; ☑ 055 538 13 34; www.streetdoing vintage.it; Via dei Servi 88r; ⊙ 10.30am-7.30pm Mon-Sat, from 2.30pm Sun) Vintage couture for men and women is what this extraordinary rabbit warren of a boutique – surely the city's largest collection of vintage – is about. Carefully curated garments and accessories are in excellent condition and feature all the top Italian designers: beaded 1950s Gucci clutch bags, floral 1960s Pucci dresses, Valentino shades from every decade. Fashionistas, *this* is heaven.

Sbigoli Terrecotte
CERAMICS

(Map p100; ☑ 055 247 97 13; www.sbigoliter recotte.it; Via Sant'Egidio 4r; ⊙ 9.30am-1pm & 2.30-7pm Mon-Sat) This family-run ceramics workshop and showroom, founded by the Sbigoli family in 1857, is littered with hundreds of handmade and painted tableware pieces. Traditions are kept alive by Antonella Chini Adami, who in her 80s is still painting and firing up her delicate creations in the on-site kiln alongside daughter Lorenza.

Penko
JEWELLERY

(Map p82; ☑ 055 21 16 61; www.paolopenko.com; Via Ferdinando Zannetti 14-16r; ⊙ 9.30am-7pm Mon-Sat) Renaissance jewels and gems inspire the designs of third-generation jeweller Paolo Penko, who works with his son in the atelier his grandfather opened in the 1950s. Everything is handmade, as the mass of vintage tools strewn on the workbench attests. Drop in at the right moment and Paolo can mint you your very own Florentine florin in bronze, silver or gold.

Eataly
FOOD & DRINKS

(Map p82; ☑ 055 015 36 01; www.eataly.net; Via de' Martelli 22r; ⊙ 10am-10.30pm; 🛜) Eataly is a one-stop food shop for everything Tuscan. Peruse beautifully arranged aisles laden with oils, conserved vegetables, pasta, rice, biscuits and so on. There are fresh bakery and deli counters, fridges laden with seemingly every cheese under the Italian sun and a coffee bar with outdoor seating. Many products are local and/or organic; most are by small producers.

Santa Croce

Santa Croce is definitely a neighbourhood for atmospheric open-air market meanderings more than window shopping for chic designer goods.

★ Aquaflor
COSMETICS

(Map p100; ☑ 055 234 34 71; www.aquaflorexpe rience.com; Borgo Santa Croce 6; ⊙ 10am-1pm & 2-7pm) This elegant Santa Croce perfumery in a vaulted 15th-century *palazzo* exudes romance and exoticism. Artisanal scents are crafted here with tremendous care and precision by master perfumer Sileno Cheloni, who works with precious essences from all over the world, including Florentine iris. Organic soaps, cosmetics and body-care products make equally lovely gifts to take back home.

★ C.BIO
FOOD & DRINKS

(Map p100; ☑ 055 247 92 71; www.cbeo.it; Via della Mattonaia 3a; ⊙ 8.30am-8.30pm Mon-Sat) Be it bread baked in situ that morning, organic fruit, veg or wine made by a small Tuscan producer, homemade pasta or a white-truffle *panino* to take away, this artisanal grocery and deli is essential viewing for foodies. A fabulous showcase of Tuscany's rich bounty of seasonal produce, C.BIO is the brainchild of celebrated chef Fabio Picchi of Cibrèo (Map p100; www.cibreo.com; Via dei Macci 122r; meals €30-35; ⊙ 12.50-2.30pm & 6.50-11pm, closed Aug) fame.

Mercato dei Fiori
MARKET

(Flower Market; Map p100; Piazza del Ciompi; ⊙ 9am-3pm Fri) Each Friday a colourful fresh-flower market spills across spruced-up Piazza del Ciompi, a historic market square once home to Florence's fish market and, for decades, an antique market. Flower fans in town on other days can make a beeline for the permanent, racing-green flower kiosk, open daily on the same square.

Oltrarno

A delight to mooch around in, vintage lanes hide tiny workshops with Florentine artisans at work, art galleries and unique independent boutiques. Shopping strips Borgo San Jacopo and Via Santo Spirito are top for avant-garde fashion, and jewellery shops fill Ponte Vecchio. Watch for new openings on upcoming hotspot Via Maggio.

★**Uashmama**   HOMEWARES

(Map p106; ☑ 055 21 62 23; www.uashmama.com; Borgo San Jacopo 30r; ⊙ 10.30am-7.30pm) Modern craftsmanship shines out of this loveable boutique, the pride and joy of the Marconi family, whose washable paper bags – tanned just like leather and, indeed, looking like leather too – are all the rage in contemporary Florence. Handbags, backpacks, sleek clutch bags and purses tempt fashionistas alongside a sleek array of paper tableware, cushions and lampshades.

★**Obsequium**   WINE

(Map p104; ☑ 055 21 68 49; www.obsequium.it; Borgo San Jacopo 17/39; ⊙ 11am-9pm Mon-Sat, from noon Sun) Tuscan wines, wine accessories and gourmet foods, including truffles, in one of the city's finest wine shops – on the ground floor of one of Florence's best-preserved medieval towers to boot. Not sure which wine to buy? Linger over a glass or indulge in a three-wine tasting (€12 to €100) and an accompanying *taglieri* of mixed cheese and salami (€13).

Bjørk   FASHION & ACCESSORIES

(Map p104; ☑ 333 9795839; www.facebook.com/bjorkflorence; Via della Sprone 25r; ⊙ 2.30-7.30pm Mon, 10.30am-1.30pm & 2.30-7.30pm Tue-Sat) Cutting-edge fashion is what this trendy concept store, incongruously wedged between tatty old artisanal workshops on an Oltrarno backstreet, sells. It is the creation of well-travelled Florentine and fashionista Filippo Anzaione, whose taste in Italian and other contemporary European designers is impeccable.

Avavav   FASHION & ACCESSORIES

(Map p104; www.avavav.com; Via Maggio 15; ⊙ 10am-6pm Mon-Fri, hours vary Sat & Sun) 🍃 Affordable luxury and Tuscan craftsmanship are perfect bed companions at this sustainable-fashion boutique for women. Swedish couple Linda and Adam Friberg, at home in Florence, are the creative pair behind the fast-growing, elegant and functional label. Think slinky silky pantsuits, flowery flowing frocks, vintage print scarves, a smattering of faux fur and the occasional recycled fabric from a top-end brand.

Scicc'Art   ARTS & CRAFTS

(Map p104; ☑ 349 6336069; www.facebook.com/sciccart.florentia; Via dello Sprone 9/11r; ⊙ 11am-7.30pm Wed-Mon) Pop into this pocket-sized

boutique and artist studio to shop for 'made in Tuscany' crafts and admire the colourful, floral-inspired contemporary jewellery of Sara Amrhein, a Florence-based American designer and co-founder of the dynamic artists collective, **Creative People in Florence** (www.creativepeopleinflorence.com).

Laboratorio Jane Harman   ARTS & CRAFTS

(Map p104; ☑ 329 0704920; www.harmanjane.it; Via L Bartolini 1r; ⊙ 8am-12.30pm & 2-6pm Mon-Fri) Florence resident since the '80s, British-born Jane Harman is an antiques restorer with more than 30 years' experience. She's opened this quaint store by her south-of-the-river workshop selling contemporary items, all made of wood, from jewellery to mini versions of the local church of Santo Spirito. Her handmade pieces make unique souvenirs.

🅐 Boboli & San Miniato al Monte

★**Lorenzo Villoresi**   PERFUME

(Map p106; ☑ 055 234 11 87; www.lorenzovilloresi.it; Via de' Bardi 14; ⊙ 10am-7pm Mon-Sat) Artisanal perfumes, bodycare products, scented candles and stones, essential oils and room fragrances crafted by Florentine perfumer Lorenzo Villoresi meld distinctively Tuscan elements such as laurel, olive, cypress and iris with essential oils and essences from around the world. His bespoke fragrances are highly sought after and visiting his elegant boutique, at home in his family's 15th-century *palazzo,* is quite an experience.

Watch this space for a new perfume museum and academy scheduled to open in 2019; highlights will include an aromatic courtyard garden scented with plants used in perfumery, and perfume-making workshops and courses.

Il Torchio   ARTS & CRAFTS

(Map p106; ☑ 055 234 28 62; www.legatoriailtorchio.com; Via de' Bardi 17; ⊙ 10am-1.30pm & 2.30-7pm Mon-Fri, 10am-1pm Sat) Peek into Erin Ciulla's workshop for a contemporary insight into traditional Florentine bookbinding. Among the treasure trove of gifts to buy are hand-sewn leather books, marbled-paper photo frames and journals in the shape of musical instruments. Personalised items can be ordered in advance.

FIESOLE DAY TRIPPER

The bijou hilltop village of Fiesole has seduced for centuries with its cooler air, olive groves, scattering of Renaissance-styled villas and spectacular views of the plain. Boccaccio, Marcel Proust, Gertrude Stein and Frank Lloyd Wright, among others, raved about it. Perched in the hills 9km northeast of Florence, Fiesole makes an easy escape when a break from city life beckons.

10am

Founded in the 7th century BC by the Etruscans, Fiesole was the most important city in northern Etruria and its Area Archeologica (☑ 055 596 12 93; www.museidifiesole.it; Via Portigiani 1; adult/reduced €7/5; ☺ 9am-7pm summer, shorter hours winter), off central square Piazza Mino di Fiesole, provides the perfect flashback. Buy a ticket from the tourist office (☑ 055 596 13 11; www.fiesoleforyou.it; Via Portigiani 3; ☺ 10am-1pm & 4-6pm Fri-Mon summer, shorter hours winter) a couple of doors away, then meander around the ruins of an Etruscan temple and Roman baths, and an archaeological museum. Later, pause for thought on the stone steps of the 1st-century-BC Roman amphitheatre, the summer stage for Italy's oldest open-air festival, Estate Fiesolana (www.estatefiesolana.it; ☺ Jun-Aug).

Afterwards pop into neighbouring Museo Bandini (☑ 055 596 12 93; www.museidifiesole.it; Via Giovanni Dupré; adult/reduced €5/3; ☺ 9am-7pm summer, shorter hours winter) to view early Tuscan Renaissance art, including fine medallions (c 1505–20) by Giovanni della Robbia and Taddeo Gaddi's luminous *Annunciation* (1340–45).

Noon

From the museum, a 300m walk along Via Giovanni Dupré brings you to the Museo Primo Conti (☑ 055 59 70 95; www.fondazioneprimoconti.org; Via Giovanni Dupré 18; adult €3; ☺ 9am-1pm Mon-Fri), where the eponymous avant-garde 20th-century artist lived and worked. Inside hang more than 60 of his paintings and the views from the garden are inspiring. Ring to enter.

1pm

Meander back to Piazza Mino di Fiesole, host to an antiques market on the first Sunday of each month, where cafe and restaurant terraces tempt. The pagoda-covered terrace of Villa Aurora (☑ 055 5 93 63; www.villaaurorafiesole.com; Piazza Mino da Fiesole 39; meals €30; ☺ noon-2.30pm & 7-10.30pm), around since 1860, is the classic choice for its view. For rustic Tuscan partaken at a shared table: Vinandro (☑ 055 5 91 21; www.vinandro.it; Piazza Mino da Fiesole 33; meals €25; ☺ noon-midnight) is popular, but not a patch on La Reggia degli Etruschi (☑ 055 5 93 85; www.lareggiadeglietruschi.com; Via San Francesco; meals €30; ☺ 7-9.30pm Mon-Wed, 12.30-1.30pm & 7-9.30pm Thu-Sun), an outstanding spot with swoon-worthy views where in-the-know Florentines lunch on Sunday.

3pm

Wander around Cattedrale di San Romolo (Piazza Mino da Fiesole; ☺ 7.30am-noon & 3-5pm) FREE, begun in the 11th century. A glazed terracotta statue of San Romolo by Giovanni della Robbia guards the entrance inside. After, make your way up steep walled Via San Francesco and be blown away by the staggeringly beautiful panorama of Florence that unfolds from the terrace adjoining 15th-century Chiesa e Convento di San Francesco (☺ 9am-noon & 3-6pm). Grassy-green afternoon-nap spots abound and the tourist office has brochures outlining walking trails (1km to 3.5km) from here.

5pm

Enjoy an *aperitivo* at JJ Hill (☑ 055 5 93 24; Piazza Mino da Fiesole 40; ☺ 6pm-2.30am summer, shorter hours winter), an Irish pub with tip-top beer, burgers and pub grub. Or fire up the romantic in you with a 2½-hour, 21km guided bike ride (€50 including bike hire) at sunset back to Florence with FiesoleBike (☑ 345 3350926; www.fiesolebike.it), a bike-rental and guiding outfit. The 'sunset' tour departs daily from Piazza Mino di Fiesole at 5pm in season; book in advance online.

ⓘ Information

EMERGENCY

Police Station (Questura; ☑ 055 4 97 71, English-language service 055 497 72 68; http://questure.poliziadistato.it/it/Firenze; Via Zara 2; ⊙24hr, English-language service 9.30am-1pm Mon-Fri)

MEDICAL SERVICES

24-Hour Pharmacy (☑ 055 21 67 61; Stazione di Santa Maria Novella; ⊙24hr) Inside Florence's central train station; at least one member of staff usually speaks English.

Dr Stephen Kerr: Medical Service (☑ 335 8361682, 055 28 80 55; www.dr-kerr.com; Piazza Mercato Nuovo 1; ⊙3-5pm Mon-Fri, or by appointment 9am-3pm Mon-Fri) Resident British doctor.

Hospital (Ospedale di Santa Maria Nuova; ☑ 055 6 93 81; www.asf.toscana.it; Piazza di Santa Maria Nuova 1; ⊙24hr)

TOURIST INFORMATION

Tourist Office (Map p82; ☑ 055 21 22 45; www.firenzeturismo.it; Piazza della Stazione 4; ⊙9am-7pm Mon-Sat, to 2pm Sun) Florence's main tourist office, handily located across from the Santa Maria Novella train station, sells the Firenzecard, has accommodation lists and helps with bookings for organised tours.

Airport Tourist Office (☑ 055 31 58 74; www.firenzeturismo.it; Via del Termine 11, Florence Airport; ⊙9am-7pm Mon-Sat, to 2pm Sun)

Infopoint Bigallo (Map p82; ☑ 055 28 84 96; www.firenzeturismo.it; Piazza San Giovanni 1; ⊙9am-7pm Mon-Sat, to 2pm Sun)

ⓘ Getting There & Away

AIR

Florence Airport (Aeroporto Amerigo Vespucci; ☑ 055 306 18 30, 055 3 06 15; www.aeroporto.firenze.it; Via del Termine 11) Also known as Amerigo Vespucci or Peretola airport, 5km northwest of the city centre; domestic and European flights.

BUS

Services from the **bus station** (Autostazione Busitalia-Sita Nord; Map p82; ☑ 800 373760; www.fsbusitalia.it; Via Santa Caterina da Siena 17r; ⊙5.45am-8.40pm Mon-Sat, 6.25am-8.30pm Sun), just west of Piazza della Stazione, are limited; the train is better. Bus company **Autolinee Chianti Valdarno** (www.acvbus.it) operates hourly buses to/from Greve in Chianti (line 365; €4.50 or €7 direct from the driver, one hour), and Siena is served with at least hourly buses by **Tiemma SpA** (www.tiemmespa.it; €7.80, 1¾ hours).

Flixbus (www.flixbus.com) buses to/from Florence and Siena (€4.99; 45 minutes) are cheaper and faster, but arrive/depart from the stop at Parcheggio Villa Costanza on Via della Costituzione, linked by tramline T1 to Stazione Santa Maria Novella in the town centre.

TRAIN

Florence's central train station is **Stazione di Santa Maria Novella** (www.firenzesantamari" novella.it; Piazza della Stazione). Leave luggage at well-organised **KiPoint Left Luggage** (Deposito Bagagliamano; ☑ 055 933 77 49; www.kipoint.it; 1st 5hr €6, then per hr €1 up to 12hr, then per hr €0.50; ⊙6am-11pm) on platform 16. Tickets for all trains are sold in the main ticketing hall, at staffed counters and touch-screen automatic ticket-vending machines.

Florence is on the Rome–Milan line. Services include the following:

DESTINA-TION	FARE (€)	TIME	FREQUENCY
Bologna	29	35-40min	every 15-30min
Lucca	9.90	1½-1¾hr	twice hourly
Milan	56	1¾-2hr	at least hourly
Pisa	8.70	45min-1¼hr	every 15min
Pistoia	4.60	45min-1hr	every 10min
Rome	50	1¾-4¼hr	at least twice hourly
Venice	53	2hr	at least hourly

ⓘ Getting Around

TO/FROM THE AIRPORT

Bus

ATAF (www.ataf.net) operates a **Volainbus** (☑ 800 373760; www.fsbusitalia.it; single/return €6/10) shuttle (20 to 30 minutes) between Florence airport and Florence bus station every 30 minutes between 5am and 8.30pm, then hourly until 12.10am (from 5.30am to 12.30am from the airport). Bus drivers sell tickets.

Taxi

A taxi between Florence Airport and the city centre costs a flat rate of €22 (€24 on Sundays and holidays, €25.30 between 10pm and 6am), plus €1 per bag and €1 supplement for a fourth passenger. Exit the terminal building, bear right and you'll come to the taxi rank.

To call a taxi, dial ☑ 055 42 42, ☑ 055 43 90 or ☑ 055 47 98.

Tram

Tram line T2 links Florence Airport with Piazza della Unità and Stazione di Santa Maria Novella – a swift 22-minute journey – every few minutes between 5am and 12.30am Sunday to Thursday and until 2am on Friday and Saturday. A single ticket costs €1.50 from ticket-dispensing machines at tram stops or €2.50 on board from the driver.

Note passengers can only take one suitcase or bag weighing up to 10kg on board for free; each piece of luggage over 10kg (max 20kg) requires its own ticket.

CAR & MOTORCYCLE

Nonresident traffic is banned from central Florence for most of the week and our advice is to avoid the whole irksome bother of having a car in the city.

BICYCLE

Florence by Bike (☑ 055 48 89 92; www.florencebybike.com; Via San Zanobi 54r; 1hr/5hr/1 day €3/9/12; ☺ 9am-1pm & 3.30-7.30pm Mon-Sat, 10am-7pm Sun) Top-notch bike shop with rental (city, mountain, touring and road bikes), itinerary suggestions and organised tours (two-hour photography tours of the city by bike, and day trips to Chianti).

Florence Station Rental (☑ 055 045 07 05; www.florencestationrental.com; Via XXVII Aprile 37-41r; ☺ 9.30am-7pm summer, to 5pm winter)

BUS

Buses and electric minibuses run by public-transport company ATAF serve the city. Most buses – including bus 13 to Piazzale Michelangelo – start/terminate at the ATAF bus stops opposite the southeastern exit of Stazione di Santa Maria Novella.

Buy tickets at the **ATAF ticketing window** (☑ 800 424500; ☺ 6.45am-8pm) inside the main ticket hall at Stazione di Santa Maria Novella, and at kiosks and tobacconists around town. Upon boarding, time stamp your ticket (punch on board) or risk an on-the-spot €50 fine.

Tickets, valid for 90 minutes (no return journeys), cost €1.50 from the window or ticket machines (€2.50 onboard or €1.80 via SMS with an Italian SIM card); children shorter than 1m travel for free. A 10-ticket carnet/monthly travel pass is €14/35.

TAXI

For a taxi, call ☑ 055 42 42 (www.4242.it) or ☑ 055 43 90 (www.4390.it), or use the IT Taxi smartphone app.

TRAM

Tram line T1 crosses the city from north to south, a 11.5km-long journey in total, although visitors in town for just a few days will have little reason to use it.

Line T2 links Piazza della Unità, in front of Stazione di Santa Maria Novella, with Florence Airport via the predominantly residential Novoli neighbourhood.

Two more tram lines are planned.

Trams use the same tickets (€1.50; valid for 90 minutes, no return journeys) as buses, available at ticket-dispensing machines at every tram stop or directly from the driver (€2.50). Trams run from 4.30am or 5am until 12.30am (1.40am or 2am Friday and Saturday). For timetables and itineraries, see www.gestramvia.com.

Siena & Central Tuscany

Includes ➡

Siena 140
Greve in Chianti 156
Badia a Passignano 158
San Casciano
in Val di Pesa 162
Castellina in Chianti ...163
Radda in Chianti 164
Gaiole in Chianti 165
San Gimignano 167
Monteriggioni 174
Volterra 175
Montalcino................. 180
Pienza 184
Montepulciano............187
Chiusi 193

Why Go?

When people imagine classic Tuscan countryside, they usually conjure up images of central Tuscany. However, there's more to this popular tourist region than silver-green olive groves, sloping fields of golden wheat gently rippling in the breeze, sun-kissed vineyards and artistically planted avenues of cypress tress. The real gems are the historic towns and cities, most of which are medieval and Renaissance time capsules magically transported to the modern day.

This privileged pocket of the country has maintained a high tourist profile ever since the Middle Ages, when Christian pilgrims followed the Via Francigena from Canterbury to Rome. Towns on the route catered to the needs of those pilgrims and prospered as a result. Today not a lot has changed: tourism remains the major industry, closely followed by wine and olive-oil production.

Best Places to Eat

➡ Il Leccio (p184)

➡ L'Osteria di Casa Chianti (p163)

➡ Il Grillo è Buoncantore (p194)

Best Places to Stay

➡ La Bandita (p180)

➡ Pensione Palazzo Ravizza (p151)

➡ Castello di Ama (p166)

Road Distances Chart

	Montepulciano	Siena	San Gimignano	Volterra
Siena	70			
San Gimignano	112	46		
Volterra	120	50	30	
Greve in Chianti	102	48	33	53

Siena & Central Tuscany Highlights

1 **Siena** (p140) Gorging on Gothic architecture, sublime art and sweet almond biscuits.

2 **Chianti** (p156) Eating, drinking and sleeping in style while exploring one of the most famous wine regions in the world.

3 **San Gimignano** (p167) Wandering the streets of this magically preserved medieval city.

4 **Montepulciano** (p187) Savouring Vino Nobile and locally raised Chianina beef in this atmospheric hilltop wine town.

5 **Volterra** (p175) Discovering Etruscan artefacts and alabaster workshops in this fortified hill town.

6 **Montalcino** (p180) Taste-testing Brunello, Tuscany's most famous wine, at one of the many local wine estates.

7 **Val d'Orcia** (p179) Detouring onto scenic back roads in this World Heritage–listed landscape.

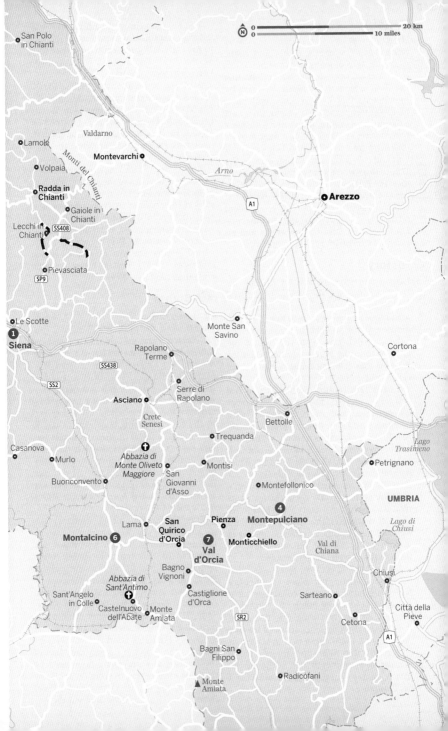

SIENA

📌 0577 / POP 53.901

Siena is a city where the architecture soars, as do the souls of many of its visitors. Effectively a giant, open-air museum celebrating the Gothic, Siena has spiritual and secular monuments that have retained both their medieval forms and their extraordinary art collections, providing the visitor with plenty to marvel at. The city's historic *contrade* (districts) are marvellous too, being as close-knit and colourful today as they were in the 17th century when their world-famous horse race, the Palio, was inaugurated. And within each *contrada* lie vibrant streets populated with artisanal boutiques, sweet-smelling *pasticcerie* (pastry shops) and tempting restaurants. It's a feast for the senses and an essential stop on every Tuscan itinerary.

History

Legend tells us Siena was founded by the son of Remus, and the symbol of the wolf feeding the twins Romulus and Remus is as ubiquitous in Siena as it is in Rome. In reality the city was probably of Etruscan origin, although it didn't begin growing into a proper town until the 1st century BC, when the Romans established a military colony here called Sena Julia.

In the 12th century, Siena's wealth, size and power grew along with its involvement in commerce and trade. Its rivalry with neighbouring Florence grew proportionately, leading to numerous wars during the 13th century between Guelph Florence and Ghibelline Siena. In 1230 Florence besieged Siena and catapulted dung and donkeys over its walls. Siena's revenge came at the Battle of Montaperti in 1260, when it defeated its rival decisively. But victory was short-lived. Only 10 years later, the Tuscan Ghibellines were defeated by Charles of Anjou and Siena was forced to ally with Florence, the chief town in the Tuscan Guelph League.

In the ensuing century, Siena was ruled by the Consiglio dei Nove (Council of Nine), a bourgeois group constantly bickering with the feudal nobles. It enjoyed its greatest prosperity during this time, and the Council commissioned many of the fine buildings in the Sienese-Gothic style that give the city its striking appearance, including lasting monuments such as the duomo (p142), Palazzo Pubblico (p145) and Piazza del Campo.

The Sienese school of painting also had its origins at this time and reached its peak in the early 14th century, when artists such as Duccio di Buoninsegna and Ambrogio Lorenzetti were at work.

A plague outbreak in 1348 killed 55,000 of Siena's 100,000 inhabitants, leading to a period of decline that culminated in the city being handed over to Florence's Cosimo I de' Medici. He barred inhabitants from operating banks, thus severely curtailing the city's power.

But this centuries-long economic downturn was a blessing in disguise, as the lack of funds meant that Siena's city centre was subject to very little redevelopment or new construction. In WWII the French took Siena virtually unopposed, thankfully sparing it discernible damage. This historically fallow period allowed the historic centre's listing on Unesco's World Heritage list as the living embodiment of a medieval city.

◉ Sights

★ Museo Civico   MUSEUM
(Civic Museum; Map p150; 📌 0577 29 26 15; Palazzo Pubblico, Piazza del Campo 1; adult/reduced €10/9; ⊙10am-6.15pm mid-Mar–Oct, to 5.15pm Nov–mid-Mar) Entered via the Palazzo Pubblico's Cortile del Podestà (Courtyard of the Chief Magistrate), this wonderful museum showcases rooms richly frescoed by artists of the Sienese school. Commissioned by the city's governing body rather than by the Church, some of the frescoes depict secular subjects – highly unusual at the time. The highlights are two huge frescoes: Ambrogio Lorenzetti's *Allegories of Good and Bad Government* (c 1338–40) and Simone Martini's celebrated *Maestà* (*Virgin Mary in Majesty;* 1315).

After buying your ticket, head upstairs to the Sala del Risorgimento, where late-19th-century frescoes serialise key events in the Risorgimento (reunification period). Continue through to the Sala di Balìa (Military Court), where frescoes by father and son Spinello and Parri Aretino recount episodes in the life of Pope Alexander III (the Sienese Rolando Bandinelli), including his clashes with the Holy Roman Emperor Frederick Barbarossa. Straight ahead is the Sala del Concistoro (Hall of the Council of Clergymen), dominated by the allegorical ceiling frescoes (1529–35) by the Mannerist painter Domenico (di Pace) Beccafumi. Through a vestibule to the left

THREE PERFECT DAYS IN CENTRAL TUSCANY

Day One

On the first day, prime your palate by touring the ultramodern Antinori nel Chianti Classico (p162) winery (perhaps lunching at Rinuccio 1180; p163) before exploring a historic one; try Badia a Passignano (p159) or Vignamaggio (p156). Next, navigate vine-lined back roads to Panzano in Chianti, visiting the Pieve di San Leolino (p165), dining at a Dario Cecchini eatery (such as Officina della Bistecca, p165) or at Ristoro di Lamole (p164) then checking into a local *agriturismo* (home-stay accommodation) or villa hotel.

Day Two

On day two, explore Volterra's (p175) cobbled streets, admiring artefacts in the Museo Etrusco Guarnacci (p176) and visiting the workshops of alabaster artisans. Lunch might be at fine-dining Ristorante-Enoteca Del Duca (☑ 0588 8 15 10; www.enoteca-delduca-ristorante.it; Via di Castello 2; meals €45; ☺ 12.30-3pm & 7.30-10pm Wed-Mon, closed Jan-early Mar; 📓) or cafe-style L'Incontro (p178). Next, head to the perfectly preserved medieval town of San Gimignano (p167) for art that balances the gravitas of the old (Collegiata, p167) with the exhilaration of the new (Galleria Continua, p168).

Day Three

Third day, visit the majestic medieval abbey of Sant'Antimo (p186) then drive past ranks of Sangiovese grapes for lunch alongside local winemakers at Il Leccio (p184). Next comes Montalcino (p180), home to blockbuster Brunello wines; climb the Fortezza's (p180) battlements, taste vintages in the town's many *enoteche* (wine bars), then enjoy a modern Tuscan dinner at Re di Macchia (p184).

---

are the Anticappella (Chapel entrance hall) and Cappella (Chapel). The Anticappella features frescoes painted in 1415 by Taddeo di Bartolo. These include figures representing the virtues needed for the proper exercise of power (Justice, Magnanimity, Strength, Prudence, Religion), and depictions of some of the leading Republican lights of ancient Rome. The Cappella contains a fine wooden choir and a fresco of the *Holy Family* and *St Leonard* by Giovanni Antonio Bazzi (aka Il Sodoma). Next to the Anticappella is the Vestibolo (Vestibule), whose star attraction is a bronze wolf, the symbol of the city.

The vestibule leads into the Sala del Mappamondo (Hall of the World Map), which houses Simone Martini's powerful and striking *Maestà*. This depicts the Madonna beneath a canopy surrounded by saints and angels, and is one of Martini's first known works, painted when he was only 21 years old. On the other side of the room is Martini's oft-reproduced fresco (1328–30) of Guidoriccio da Fogliano, a captain of the Sienese army. Also here is *The Conquest of the Giuncarico Castle,* attributed to Duccio (di Boninsegna) and painted in the early 14th century.

The next room, the Sala dei Pace, is where the ruling Council of Nine once met. It's decorated with Ambrogio Lorenzetti's fascinating fresco cycle, the *Allegories of Good and Bad Government*, often described as the most important secular painting of the Renaissance. The central allegory portrays scenes with personifications of Justice, Wisdom, Virtue and Peace, all unusually depicted as women, along with scenes of criminal punishment and rewards for righteousness. Set perpendicular from it are the frescoes *Allegory of Good Government* and *Allegory of Bad Government,* which feature intensely contrasting scenes clearly set around Siena. The good depicts a sunlit, idyllic, serene city, with joyous citizens and a countryside filled with crops; the bad city is filled with vices, crime and disease.

Before leaving the museum, be sure to visit the recently restored Loggia dei Nove at the rear of the building, which commands a panoramic view to the Orto de' Pecci (p145) and the south of the city.

★ **Piazza del Campo**   PIAZZA

(Map p150) Popularly known as 'Il Campo', this sloping piazza has been Siena's social centre since being staked out by the ruling

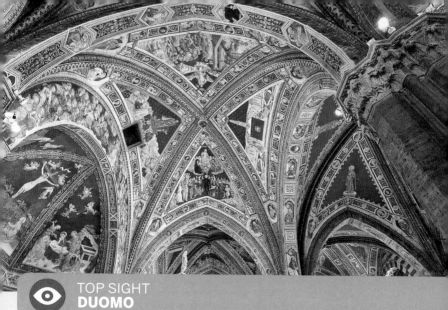

TOP SIGHT
DUOMO

One of Italy's greatest Gothic churches, Siena's *duomo* (cathedral) is the focal point of an important ecclesiastical complex that includes a museum, baptistry and crypt. All are embellished with wonderful art – Giovanni and Nicola Pisano, Pinturicchio, Jacopo della Quercia, Ghiberti, Donatello and (most famous of Sienese painters) Duccio di Buoninsegna are among the artists whose works glorified their city and their god.

Main Building

Construction of the *duomo* started in the 12th century and work continued well into the 14th century. The magnificent facade of white, green and red marble was designed by Giovanni Pisano; the statues of philosophers and prophets are copies; you'll find the originals in the Museo dell'Opera. The interior is truly stunning, with walls and pillars continuing the black-and-white-stripe theme of the exterior.

Libreria Piccolomini

Through a door from the north aisle of the *duomo* is this enchanting **library** (Piccolomini Library; Map p150; €2, built to house the books of Enea Silvio Piccolomini, better known as Pope Pius II. Its walls are decorated with richly detailed frescoes painted between 1503 and 1508 by Bernardino (di Betto) Pinturicchio and depicting events in the life of Piccolomini, including his ordination as pope.

Pisano's Pulpit

The *duomo's* exquisitely crafted marble-and-porphyry pulpit was created between 1265 and 1268 by Nicola Pisano, who had previously carved the famed pulpit in Pisa's

DON'T MISS

➡ Libreria Piccolomini

➡ Battistero di San Giovanni

➡ Cripta

➡ Museo dell'Opera

➡ Panorama del Facciatone

PRACTICALITIES

➡ Cattedrale di Santa Maria Assunta

➡ Map p150

➡ ☎ 0577 28 63 00

➡ www.operaduomo. siena.it

➡ Piazza Duomo

➡ Mar-Oct €5, Nov-Feb free, when floor displayed €8

➡ ⊙ 10.30am-6.30pm Mon-Sat & 1.30-5.30pm Sun Mar-Oct, 10.30am-5pm Mon-Sat & 1.30-5pm Sun Nov-Feb

duomo. Assisted by his son Giovanni and assistant Arnolfo di Cambio, Pisano depicted powerful scenes including the Last Judgement.

Floor Panels

The inlaid-marble floor, decorated with 56 panels by about 40 artists and executed from the 14th to the 19th centuries, depicts historical and biblical subjects. Unfortunately, about half of the panels are obscured by protective covering, and are revealed only between mid-August and late October each year (an extra fee applies).

Battistero di San Giovanni

Behind the *duomo,* down a steep flight of steps, is the frescoed baptistry (pictured; Map p150; Piazza San Giovanni; adult/child €6/1; ⊙10.30am-6.30pm Mon-Sat & 1.30-5.30pm Sun Mar-Oct, 10.30am-5pm Mon-Sat & 1.30-5pm Sun Nov-Feb). At its centre is a hexagonal marble font (c 1417) by Jacopo della Quercia, with bronze panels depicting the life of St John the Baptist by artists including Lorenzo Ghiberti (*Baptism of Christ* and *St John in Prison;* 1427) and Donatello (*The Head of John the Baptist Being Presented to Herod;* 1427).

Cripta

This space (Map p150; Piazza San Giovanni; adult/child €6/1) beneath the cathedral's pulpit was rediscovered and restored in 1999 after having been filled to the roof with debris in the 1300s. The walls are completely covered with *pintura a secco* ('dry painting', better known as 'mural painting') dating back to the 1200s. There are some 180 sq metres worth, depicting biblical stories, including the Passion of Jesus and the Crucifixion.

Museo dell'Opera

The collection in this museum (Map p150; adult/child €6/1;) showcases artworks that formerly adorned the *duomo,* including the 12 statues of prophets and philosophers (1285–87) by Giovanni Pisano that decorated its facade. Pisano designed these to be viewed from ground level, which is why they look so distorted as they crane uncomfortably forward. Also notable is the vibrant stained-glass window designed and painted by Duccio di Buoninsegna (1287–90).

Panorama del Facciatone

In 1339 the city's leaders decided to transform the cathedral into one of Italy's biggest churches, but the plague of 1348 scotched their plan to build an immense new nave with the present church as the transept. Known as the Duomo Nuovo (New Cathedral), all that remains of the project is this panoramic terrace, accessed through the museum.

PORTA DEL CIELO

To enjoy spectacular bird's-eye views of the interior and exterior of Siena's cathedral, buy a ticket for the 'Gate of Heaven' escorted tour (Gate of Heaven; Map p150; adult/child €20/5; ⊙10.30am-7pm Mon-Sat, 1.30-5.30pm Sun Mar-late Aug & late Oct-early Jan, 10.30am-7pm Mon-Sat, 9.30am-5.30pm Sun late Aug-late Oct) up, into and around the building's roof and dome. Tour groups are capped at 18 participants and depart at fixed times throughout the day – purchase your ticket from the office in the Complesso Museale di Santa Maria della Scala (p144). Arrive at the meeting point at least five minutes before your allocated tour time.

You'll save money by purchasing a combined OPA SI or Acropoli Pass, valid for three days, rather than individual sight tickets.

GUIDED TOURS

Walking tours offered by Centro Guide Turistiche Siena e Provincia (p149) and Associazione Centro Guide (p149) include a tour of the *duomo.*

Consiglio dei Nove in the mid-12th century. Built on the site of a Roman marketplace, its paving is divided into nine sectors representing the members of the *consiglio,* and these days acts as a carpet on which young locals meet and relax. The cafes around its perimeter are the most popular coffee and *aperitivo* (predinner drinks) spots in town.

The Fonte Gaia (Happy Fountain; Map p150) is located in the upper part of the square.

★ Complesso Museale di Santa Maria della Scala MUSEUM

(Map p150; ✆0577 28 63 00; www.santamaria dellascala.com; Piazza Duomo 2; adult/reduced €9/7; ⊙10am-7pm Fri-Wed, to 10pm Thu mid-Mar–mid-Oct, to 5pm Mon, Wed & Fri, to 8pm Thu, to 7pm Sat & Sun mid-Oct–mid-Mar) Built as a hospice for pilgrims travelling the Via Francigena, this huge complex opposite the *duomo* dates from the 13th century. Its highlight is the upstairs Pellegrinaio (Pilgrim's Hall), featuring vivid 15th-century frescoes by Lorenzo di Pietro (aka Vecchietta), Priamo della Quercia and Domenico di Bartolo. All laud the good works of the hospital and its patrons; the most evocative is di Bartolo's *Il governo degli infermi* (Caring for the Sick; 1440–41), which depicts many activities that occurred here.

There's so much to see in the complex that devoting half a day is barely adequate. Don't miss the hugely atmospheric National Archaeological Museum set in the basement tunnels; the medieval fienile (hayloft) on level three, which showcases Jacopo della Quercia's original 1419 sculptures from Siena's central Fonte Gaia; and the Sagrestia Vecchia (Old Chapel) of the Chiesa SS Annunziata to the right near the main entrance, which houses di Bartolo's *Madonna della misericordia* (1444–45) and a fresco cycle by di Pietro illustrating the Articles of the Creed.

There's an excellent gift shop on-site, as well as a pleasant cafe that can be accessed from Piazza Duomo. Entry is included in the Acropoli and joint Museo Civico/Santa Maria della Scala passes.

Pinacoteca Nazionale GALLERY

(Map p150; ✆0577 28 11 61; http://pinacotecana zionale.siena.it; Via San Pietro 29; adult/reduced €8/2, free 1st Sun of month Oct-Mar; ⊙8.15am-7.15pm Tue-Sat) Siena's recently renovated art gallery, housed in 14th-century Palazzo Buonsignori since 1932, is home to an extraordinary collection of Gothic masterpieces from the Sienese school. These include works by Guido da Siena, Duccio (di Buoninsegna), Simone Martini, Niccolò di Segna, Lippo Memmi, Ambrogio and Pietro Lorenzetti, Bartolo di Fredi, Taddeo di Bartolo and Sano di Pietro. The museum's re-opening date is yet to be announced.

The collection demonstrates the gulf cleaved between artistic life in Siena and Florence in the 15th century. While the Renaissance flourished 70km to the north, Siena's masters and their patrons remained firmly rooted in the Byzantine and Gothic precepts born of the early 13th century. Religious images and episodes predominate, typically pasted lavishly with gold and partially lacking the advances in painting (perspective, emotion, movement) that artists in Florence were exploring. That's not to say that the works here are second-rate – many

---

THE PALIO

Dating from the Middle Ages, Siena's spectacular Palio (⊙2 Jul & 16 Aug) includes a series of colourful pageants and a wild horse race in Piazza del Campo. Ten of Siena's 17 *contrade* (town districts) compete for the coveted *palio* (silk banner). Each *contrada* has its own traditions, symbol and colours, plus its own church and palio museum.

From about 5pm on race days, representatives from each *contrada* parade in historical costume, all bearing their individual banners. For scarcely one exhilarating minute, the 10 horses and their bareback riders tear three times around a temporarily constructed dirt racetrack with a speed and violence that makes spectators' hair stand on end.

The race is held at 7.45pm in July and 7pm in August. Join the crowds in the centre of the Campo at least four hours before the start if you want a place on the rails, but be aware that once there you won't be able to leave for toilet or drink breaks until the race has finished. Alternatively, the cafes in the Campo sell places on their terraces; these cost between €280 and €400 per ticket. The tourist office (p155) can supply information about how to book tickets; this should be done up to one year in advance.

GREEN ESCAPES

Orto Botanico dell'Università (Botanical Garden of the University; Map p146; ☑0577 23 20 76; www.simus.unisi.it/musei/mb; Via Pier Andrea Mattioli 4; adult/reduced €5/2.50; ⊙10am-7pm Jul-Sep, to 5pm Mar-Jun, to 4pm Oct-Feb) The tranquil terraces of Siena's university-owned botanical garden (1856) provide gorgeous views across the verdant Sant'Agostino Valley and a welcome escape from the tourist crowds. Enjoy three greenhouses filled with tropical and subtropical species, a citrus house and gardens planted with ornamental, medicinal and food plants.

Orto de' Pecci (Map p150; ☑0577 22 22 01; www.ortodepecci.it; Via Porta Giustizia; ⊙8.30am-10pm summer, reduced hr winter; ♿) FREE Operated by a social cooperative that gives support and employment to people with disabilities or dependency problems, this urban oasis shelters a small vineyard with clones of medieval vines, a cooperative organic farm that supplies the on-site restaurant (Map p146; pizza €6-9, meals €22; ⊙noon-2.30pm & 7.30-10pm Tue-Sun) 🍴 with fruit and vegetables, plenty of animals (geese, goats, ducks and donkeys) and a scattering of site-specific contemporary artworks.

are among the most beautiful and important creations of their time.

Artworks to hunt out include Duccio's *Madonna and Child* and *Madonna with Child and Four Saints;* Simone Martini's *Madonna della misericordia* and *Madonna with Child, Madonna and Child* and *Blessed Agostino* altarpiece; Bartolo di Fredi's huge and utterly magnificent *Adoration of the Magi;* Lippo Memmi's *Madonnna col Bambino;* Ambrogio Lorenzetti's luminous *Annunciation* and *Madonna with Child;* Pietro Lorenzetti's *Madonna Enthroned with Saint Nicholas and the Prophet Elijah;* Taddeo di Bartolo's *The Annunciation of the Virgin Mary;* and Jacopo della Quercia's *Angelo annunciante.*

Palazzo Pubblico   HISTORIC BUILDING
(Palazzo Comunale; Map p150; Piazza del Campo) Built to demonstrate the enormous wealth, proud independence and secular nature of Siena, this 14th-century Gothic masterpiece is the visual focal point of the Campo, itself the true heart of the city. Architecturally clever (notice how its concave facade mirrors the opposing convex curve) it has always housed the city's administration and been used as a cultural venue. Its distinctive bell tower, the Torre del Mangia (Map p150; ☑0577 29 26 15; ticket@comune.siena.it; adult/family €10/25; ⊙10am-6.15pm Mar–mid-Oct, to 3.15pm mid-Oct–Feb), provides magnificent views for those who brave the steep climb to the top.

The municipal offices are closed to visitors, but the major historical *sale* (halls) and rear loggia now form the unmissable Museo Civico (p140).

Sinagoga di Siena   SYNAGOGUE
(Museo Ebraico di Siena; Map p150; ☑0577 27 13 45; www.jewishtuscany.it; Vicolo delle Scotte; adult/reduced €4/3; ⊙10.45am-4.45pm Sun, Mon & Thu) Sheltering behind an anonymous facade, this Ashkenazi synagogue in Siena's former Ghetto once serviced a community of 500. Sadly, a mere 50 Jews now live in the city. Functioning since 1731, the synagogue's rococo-style interior with its distinctive green-and-white colour scheme resembles an ornate church and can be visited on an enjoyable guided tour in which the history of the building and of Jews in Siena is recounted. Tours depart every 30 minutes.

Museo delle Tavolette di Biccherne   MUSEUM
(Map p150; ☑0577 24 71 45; www.archiviodista to.siena.it; 4th fl, Via Banchi di Sotto 52; ⊙guided tours 10am, 11am & noon Mon-Sat) FREE Housed in the Renaissance-era Palazzo Piccolomini, Siena's State Archive isn't a usual stop on the standard tourist itinerary, but it provides ample reward for those who choose to visit. The small on-site museum takes its name from the pride of the archive's collection: 103 small late-13th-century painted and gilded wooden panels known as the 'Tavolette di Biccherna'. Created as covers for the municipal accounts books, the *biccherne* were painted by Sienese artists including Ambogio Lorenzetti and Taddeo di Bartolo.

Chiesa di San Martino   CHURCH
(Map p150; www.sanmartinosiena.it; Via del Porrione 41; ⊙hours vary) FREE The baroque facade of this church dates from 1613, but

Siena

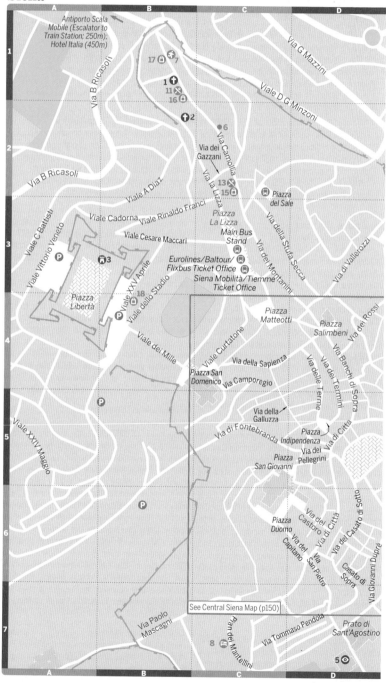

Siena

⊙ Sights

1 Chiesa di San Pietro alla Magione......B1
2 Chiesa di Santa Maria in Portico
   a Fontegiusta.....................................B2
3 Fortezza Medicea B3
4 Oratorio di San Bernardino E4
5 Orto Botanico dell'Università.............D7

➌ Activities, Courses & Tours

6 Fonte Giusta Cooking School.............C2
7 Siena Urban Running B1

🛏 Sleeping

8 Pensione Palazzo Ravizza C7

⊗ Eating

9 La Prosciutteria....................................F5
10 Lievito M@dre......................................E5
11 Osteria Il Vinaio..................................B1
12 Ristorante All'Orto de' Pecci..............E7
13 Ristorante Enzo....................................C2

⊙ Drinking & Nightlife

14 Bottega Roots E5

🛍 Shopping

15 Alessandro Stella................................C2
16 Casa della Pelle B1
17 Il Maratoneta B1
18 Wednesday Market.............................B4

the church itself is much older, having been constructed in the 12th century. Inside are works by Guido Reni and Domenico Beccafumi. Adjacent to the church is the Renaissance-style **Logge del Papa** (Map p150; btwn Via Porrione & Via Pantaneto).

Palazzo Chigi Saracini   MUSEUM
(Map p150; ☑ 333 9180012, 0577 2 20 91; http://eng.chigiana.it; visite@chigiana.it; Via di Città 89; guided tours adult/student €7/5, picture gallery €1; ⊙tours 11.30am Mon-Wed, 11.30am & 4pm Thu & Fri) Few buildings have pedigrees as splendid as this 13th-century palace. Home of the Piccolomini family (of which Pope Pius II was the most prominent member) during the Renaissance, it was acquired by the powerful Saracini family in the 18th century and inherited a century later by a scion of the wealthy Roman Chigi family. Today it houses the **Fondazione Accademia Musicale Chigiana** and its art-adorned interiors are a testament to the wealth, erudition and taste of the Saracini and Chigi families.

ℹ MUSEUM PASSES

If you're planning to visit Siena's major monuments (and we highly recommend that you do), several combined passes will save you money:

OPA SI Pass Covers the duomo (p142), Libreria Piccolomini (p142), Museo dell'Opera (p143), Battistero di San Giovanni (p143), Cripta (p143) and Oratorio di San Bernardino; €13 March to mid-August and last week of October, €8 November to February, valid for three days.

OPA SI + Pass Covers the list above plus Porta del Cielo (p143) tour; €20 March to December, valid for three days.

Acropoli Pass Covers the *duomo,* Libreria Piccolomini, Museo dell'Opera, Battistero di San Giovanni, Cripta, Oratorio di San Bernardino and Complesso Museale di Santa Maria della Scala (p144); €18 March to mid-August and last week of October, €20 from mid-August to late October, €13 November to February, valid for three days.

Acropoli + Pass Covers the list above, plus Porta del Cielo tour; €25 March to October, valid for three days.

A Museo Civico (p140) and Complesso Museale di Santa Maria della Scala combined icket costs €14. A ticket to Museo Civico, Complesso Museale di Santa Maria della Scala and Torre del Mangia (p145) costs €20, tickets available at the museums.

All of the passes can be purchased at the **Duomo Ticket Office** (☑ 0577 28 63 00; www.operaduomo.siena.it; Santa Maria della Scala, Piazza del Duomo; ⊘ 10am-6.30pm summer, to 5pm winter). Note that children under six receive free entry at the *duomo* sites and children under 11 are admitted free to Santa Maria della Scala.

Basilica Cateriniana di San Domenico
CHURCH

(Map p150; www.basilicacateriniana.com; Piazza San Domenico; ⊘ 7am-6.30pm Mar-Oct, 9am-6pm Nov-Feb) FREE St Catherine was welcomed into the Dominican fold within this huge and austere 13th-century basilica. Inside, the Cappella di Santa Caterina (halfway down the wall to right of the altar) contains frescoes by Giovanni Antonio Bazzi (aka Il Sodoma) and Andrea Vanni depicting events in the saint's life. Also here are 15th-century reliquaries containing Catherine's head and one of her fingers, as well as a nasty-looking chain that she is said to have flagellated herself with.

Biblioteca Comunale degli Intronati
LIBRARY

(Map p150; ☑ 0577 292666; www.bibliotecasiena.it; Via della Sapienza 3; ⊘ 9am-7pm Mon-Fri, to 1.45pm Sat; 🌐) FREE Occupying 13th-century buildings once used by the University of Siena, this municipal library was established in the 1750s. Its labyrinthine structure reflects the fact that it was cobbled together by constructing interlinking structures over medieval streets. A popular working space for students, it also has a large kids' zone for junior readers aged under 10 years, a hand-some 15th-century lecture hall lined with historic volumes and a periodicals room.

Oratorio di San Bernardino
GALLERY

(Map p146; ☑ 0577 28 63 00; http://operaduomo.siena.it; Piazza San Francesco 10; adult/child €6/1; ⊘ 1.30am-6.30pm Mar-Oct) Nestled in the shadow of the huge Gothic church of San Francesco, this 15th-century oratory is dedicated to St Bernardino and decorated with Mannerist frescoes by Il Sodoma, Domenico (di Pace) Beccafumi and Girolamo del Pacchia. Upstairs, the small Museo Diocesano di Arte Sacra has some lovely paintings, including *Madonna del latte (Nursing Madonna; c* 1340) by Ambrogio Lorenzetti. Entry is included in the OPA SI and Acropoli passes.

Chiesa di Santa Maria in Portico a Fontegiusta
CHURCH

(Map p146; Via di Fontegiusta; ⊘ hours vary) FREE This three-aisled 15th-century church was built on the site of Porta Fontegiusta, one of the original gates in the city walls, to thank the Virgin Mary for the Sienese victory over the Florentines in the Battle of Poggio Imperiale (1479). Inside, to the right of the altar, is Francesco Vanni's painting *The Blessed Ambrogio Sansedoni Asking the Virgin for Protection of Siena* (1590).

Chiesa di San Pietro alla Magione   CHURCH
(Map p146; cnr Via Camollia & Via Malta; ⊘hours vary) **FREE** Serenely beautiful, this Romanesque church was built in the 10th century and used by the Knights Templar in the 12th century. It then passed to the Knights of Malta after the Templar order was dissolved. The current facade dates from the 13th century. The dimly lit interior is austere, with a 15th-century crucifix being one of the few adornments. To the church's immediate south are hospice buildings where pilgrims on the Via Francigena once rested.

🏃 Activities & Courses

⭐ Fonte Giusta Cooking School   COOKING
(Fonte Giusta Scuola di Cucina; Map p146; ☑0577 4 05 06; http://scuoladicucinafontegiusta.com; Via Camollia 78; per person €100; ⊘4.30-7pm) The best cooking school in Siena is operated by the ultrafriendly Chiarelli family who own the adjacent trattoria of the same name. During the 2½-hour late-afternoon class, which can be gluten-free or vegetarian on request and is followed by dinner with local wines, you'll have plenty of opportunities for hands-on cooking of famous Tuscan dishes. Highly recommended.

Siena Urban Running   RUNNING
(Map p146; ☑0577 4 42 77; maratoneta.sport@libero.it; Via Camollia 201; run €25; ⊘7.45am Mon, Wed & Fri mid-May–Oct, 6pm Thu Nov–mid-May) Guided 90-minute run through the historic centre organised by Il Maratoneta (Maratoneta Sport; Map p146; www.facebook.com/siena.ilmaratonetasport; ⊘9.30am-8pm Mon-Sat) walking and running shop. Running kits are available for €35.

Tuscan Wine School   WINE
(Map p150; ☑333 5707011; www.tuscanwineschool.com; Via di Stalloreggi 26) Two-hour wine-tasting classes introducing Tuscan wines (€45) from 4pm to 6pm Monday to Saturday. Also offers a two-hour foodie walking tour (€45) from noon to 2pm Monday, Wednesday and Saturday, and daily tours into neighbouring wine regions (from €140) from March to December. Advance bookings essential.

👉 Tours

Associazione Centro Guide   CULTURAL
(AGT; ☑0577 4 32 73; www.guidesiena.it/en) One of three official local guides' associations. Operates two-hour tours to the Complesso Museale di Santa Maria della Scala (p144) and the Museo Civico (p140) from 3pm every Monday, Friday and Saturday between mid-April and October (adult/child under 11 €25/free). This departs from outside the tourist office (p155) in the Santa Maria della Scala complex. Other tours are detailed on its website.

Centro Guide Turistiche Siena e Provincia   CULTURAL
(☑0577 4 32 73; www.guidesiena.it) Accredited guides offer guaranteed daily departures of a two-hour 'Classic Siena' Walking Tour (adult/child seven to 12/child under seven €20/10/free) at 11am between April and October. This features key historical and cultural landmarks and includes entrance to the duomo (p142) or Santa Maria della Scala (p144). Tours in English and Italian depart from outside the tourist-information office in Santa Maria della Scala (p144).

🎉 Festivals & Events

Accademia Musicale Chigiana   MUSIC
(www.chigiana.it; ⊘Nov-May, Jul & Aug) The Accademia Musicale Chigiana presents two highly regarded concert series featuring classical musicians from around the world: Micat in Vertice from November to May and the Chigiana International Festival in July and August. Venues include the *duomo,* Teatro dei Rozzi in Piazza Indipendenza, Chiesa di Sant'Agostino and Palazzo Chigi Saracini.

🛏 Sleeping

Siena is blessed with a wide variety of accommodation types. Note that prices skyrocket and minimum-stay requirements are implemented during the Palio (p144).

Ostello Casa delle Balie   HOSTEL €
(Map p150; ☑347 6137678; ostellosms@operalaboratori.com; Vicolo di San Girolamo 2; dm €18; ⊘reception 11am-4.30pm & 7-9.15pm; ❄@🛜) Siena's historic centre sorely lacks backpacker accommodation, so we were thrilled when this hostel just off Piazza Duomo opened in 2017. Though primarily catering to pilgrims walking the Via Francigena, it also welcomes others – book in advance. Rooms have bunk beds and small lockers (sheets and blankets provided); hot showers cost €0.50. Laundry facilities (charged), but no kitchen or lounge.

Central Siena

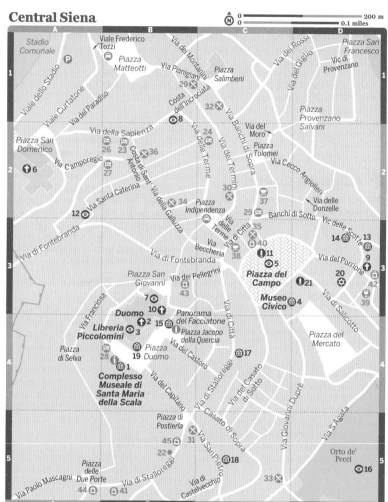

Albergo Bernini PENSION €

(Map p150; ☎0577 28 90 47; www.albergobernini.com; Via della Sapienza 15; d €100, without bathroom €80; 🐭) The tiny terrace alone might prompt you to stay at this welcoming, family-run hotel – it sports grandstand views across to the *duomo* and is a captivating spot for a drink at sunset. The 10 bedrooms are traditional affairs and only a couple have air-con. Cash payment only.

Hotel Alma Domus HOTEL €

(Map p150; ☎0577 4 41 77; www.hotelalmadomus.it; Via Camporegio 37; s €46-55, d €72-140; ❃🐭) Your chance to sleep in a convent:

Alma Domus is owned by the church and is still home to several Dominican nuns. The economy rooms, although comfortable, are styled very simply and aren't as sound-proofed as many would like. But the superior ones are lovely, with stylish decor and modern fittings; many have minibalconies with uninterrupted *duomo* views.

B&B Il Corso B&B €€

(Map p150; ☎392 1045505, 0577 28 42 48; www.ilcorsosiena.it; Via Banchi di Sopra 6; s €85-98, d €120-145, ste €150-200; 🐭) Located on the 1st floor of a 16th-century *palazzo* (mansion), this boutique B&B offers six small

Central Siena

⊙ Top Sights
1 Complesso Museale di Santa
  Maria della Scala............................ B4
2 Duomo.. B4
3 Libreria Piccolomini........................... B4
4 Museo Civico...................................... D3
5 Piazza del Campo.............................. C3

⊙ Sights
6 Basilica Cateriniana di San
  Domenico.. A2
7 Battistero di San Giovanni................ B3
8 Biblioteca Comunale degli
  Intronati... B1
9 Chiesa di San Martino....................... D3
10 Cripta... B3
11 Fonte Gaia.. C3
12 Fontebranda...................................... A2
13 Logge del Papa................................ D3
14 Museo delle Tavolette di
  Biccherne... D3
15 Museo dell'Opera............................. B4
16 Orto de' Pecci.................................. D5
17 Palazzo Chigi Saracini..................... C4
  Palazzo Pubblico......................(see 4)
18 Pinacoteca Nazionale...................... C5
19 Porta del Cielo................................. B4
20 Sinagoga di Siena........................... D3
21 Torre del Mangia............................. D3

⊙ Activities, Courses & Tours
22 Tuscan Wine School......................... B5

⊚ Sleeping
23 Albergo Bernini................................ B2
24 Antica Residenza Cicogna.............. C2
25 B&B Il Corso..................................... C2
26 Campo Regio Relais......................... B2
27 Hotel Alma Domus........................... B2
28 Ostello Casa delle Balie................... B4

⊗ Eating
29 Consorzio Agrario di Siena.............. B1
30 Enoteca I Terzi................................. C2
31 La Vecchia Latteria.......................... B5
32 Morbidi.. C1
33 Osteria La Taverna di San
  Giuseppe.. C5
34 Ristorante Grotta di Santa
  Caterina da Bagoga.......................... B2
35 Te Ke Voi?... C3
36 Zest Ristorante & Wine Bar............. B2

⊙ Drinking & Nightlife
37 Bar Pasticcerie Nannini................... C2
38 Caffè Fiorella................................... C3
39 UnTUBO.. D3

⊙ Shopping
40 Antica Siena..................................... C3
41 Bottega d'Arte................................. B5
42 Brocchi... D3
43 Il Magnifico...................................... B3
44 Pasticceria Bini............................... A5
45 Sator Print....................................... B5

rooms with wooden beams, modern bathrooms and stylish decor. Its location near the Campo is convenient but can be noisy.

Antica Residenza Cicogna B&B €€
(Map p150; ☑0577 28 56 13; www.antica residenzacicogna.it; Via delle Terme 76; s/d/ste €90/110/150; ❄@⑳) You'll get a true feel for Siena's history in this 13th-century *palazzo* close to the Campo. Tiled floors, ornate lights and painted ceilings meet tones of yellow ochre and (suitably) burnt sienna. All of the rooms are charming, but we were particularly taken with the Stanza dei Paesaggi, which is named after the frescoed landscapes that decorate it.

Hotel Italia HOTEL €€
(☑0577 4 42 48; www.hotelitalia-siena.it; Viale Cavour 67; s €70-122, d €140-175; P❄@⑳) Close to both the train station and the busy shopping and eating strip of Via Camollia, this well-priced modern hotel offers a range of accommodation, including worn-but-comfortable standard rooms and swish, newly built executive rooms. Parking costs

€10 per night, the breakfast buffet is generous and guests can use the swimming pool at a nearby hotel in the same group.

★Campo Regio Relais BOUTIQUE HOTEL €€€
(Map p150; ☑0577 22 20 73; www.camporegio. com; Via della Sapienza 25; r €220-450; ☉mid-Mar–early Jan; ❄⑳) Siena's most charming boutique hotel has only six rooms, each individually decorated and luxuriously equipped (opt for deluxe room five, which has a private terrace). An excellent breakfast is served in the sumptuously decorated lounge or on the main terrace, which has a sensational view across the Fontebranda Valley and across to the Torre del Mangia and the *duomo*.

★Pensione Palazzo Ravizza BOUTIQUE HOTEL €€€
(Map p146; ☑0577 28 04 62; www.palazzoraviz za.it; Pian dei Mantellini 34; r €170-330; P❄⑳) Occupying a Renaissance-era *palazzo* located in a quiet but convenient corner of Siena, the Ravizza offers rooms perfectly melding traditional decor and modern amenities; the best face the large rear garden, which has

LOCAL KNOWLEDGE

TOP FIVE: QUICK LUNCH BITES

Lievito M@dre (Map p146; 📞0577 151 54 51; www.facebook.com/LievitoMadreSiena; Via di Pantaneto 59; meal deal €6.90, pizzas €6-12; ⏰7.30am-11pm Sun-Thu, to midnight Fi & Sat; 🛜🍴) Close to the Campo, this popular bakery and cafe offers filled *panini* (sandwiches) and pizza slices to take away or enjoy at one of the inside tables.

La Prosciutteria (Map p146; 📞0328 541 43 25; www.laprosciutteria.com; cnr Via Pantaneto & Vicolo Magalotti; panini €4-7, tasting boards from €10; ⏰11.30am-3.30pm & 5.30pm-midnight Mon-Thu, 11.30am-12.30am Sat; 🛜) Prosciutto is the focus here, served in *panini* or on a *taglieri* (tasting board); cheese is an optional extra. Order to take away – the Orto de' Pecci is close by – or claim a street table.

Consorzio Agrario di Siena (Map p150; 📞0577 23 01; www.capsi.it; Via Pianigiani 9; ⏰8am-8.30pm Mon-Sat, 9.30am-8pm Sun) Operating since 1901, this farmer's co-op is a rich emporium of food and wine, with a bar area serving *panini* and freshly cooked pizza.

Morbidi (Map p150; 📞0577 28 02 68; www.morbidi.com; Via Banchi di Sopra 75; lunch buffet €12; ⏰8am-8pm Mon-Wed, to 9pm Thu & Fri, to 3pm Sat) Famed for its top-quality produce, Morbidi's excellent-value basement lunch buffet includes freshly prepared antipasti, salads, risotto, pasta and dessert. Buy your ticket upstairs before heading down.

Te Ke Voi? (Map p150; 📞0577 4 01 39; Vicolo di San Pietro 4; burgers €10-14, pizza €7-10, focaccias €4.50-5.50; ⏰noon-3.30pm & 6.30pm-midnight Mon-Thu, noon-1am Fri & Sat, noon-midnight Sun; 🍴) The name means 'Whaddya want?' and the answer is simple – cheap and tasty food prepared fast and served in pleasant surrounds. Beloved of local students, the *pasta cresciuta* (fried pasta) goes down a treat with a cold beer or glass of wine.

a panoramic terrace. The breakfast buffet is generous, on-site parking is free if you book directly with the hotel and room rates are remarkably reasonable (especially in low season).

🍴 Eating

There are plenty of dining options in Siena, ranging from budget bakeries, *enoteche* and cafes popular with local university students, to long-established, elegant and expensive restaurants that are the choice of cashed-up locals and visitors. What all of these share is a strict adherence to regional cuisine.

Among the many traditional local dishes served in Siena are *panzanella* (summer salad of soaked bread, basil, onion and tomatoes), *ribollita* (a rich vegetable, bean and bread soup), *pappardelle alla lepre* (ribbon pasta with hare), *panforte* (a rich cake of almonds, honey and candied fruit) and *ricciarelli* (sugar-dusted chewy almond biscuits). Keep an eye out for dishes featuring the region's signature *cinta senese* (indigenous Tuscan pig).

★ **La Vecchia Latteria**　　　　　GELATO €
(Map p150; 📞0577 05 76 38; www.facebook.com/GelateriaYogurteriaLaVecchiaLatteria; Via San Pietro 10; gelato €2-4.50; ⏰noon-11pm, to 8pm winter) Sauntering through Siena's historic centre is always more fun with a gelato in hand. Just ask one of the many locals who are regular customers at this *gelateria artigianale* (maker of handmade gelato) near the Pinacoteca Nazionale. Using quality produce, owners Fabio and Francesco concoct and serve fruity fresh or decadently creamy iced treats – choose from gelato or frozen yogurt.

Osteria Il Vinaio　　　　　TUSCAN €
(Map p146; 📞0577 4 96 15; Via Camollia 167; dishes €6.50-13; ⏰10am-10pm Mon-Sat) Wine bars are thin on the ground here in Siena, so it's not surprising that Bobbe and Davide's neighbourhood *osteria* (casual tavern) is so popular. Join the multigenerational local regulars for a bowl of pasta or your choice from the generous antipasto display, washed down with a glass or two of eminently quaffable house wine.

Enoteca I Terzi　　　　　TUSCAN €€
(Map p150; 📞0577 4 43 29; www.enotecaiterzi.it; Via dei Termini 7; meals €42; ⏰12.30-3pm & 7.30-11pm Mon-Sat) Close to the Campo but off the well-beaten tourist trail, this *enoteca* is located in a vaulted medieval building but has a contemporary feel. It's popular with sophisticated locals, who linger over working

lunches, *aperitivo* sessions and slow-paced dinners featuring Tuscan *salumi* (cured meats), delicate handmade pasta, grilled meats and wonderful wines (many available by the glass).

Zest Ristorante & Wine Bar TUSCAN €€

(Map p150; ☑ 0577 4 71 39; http://zestsiena.com/en; Costa di Sant'Antonio 13; meals €38; ⊘noon-2.30pm & 6.30-10pm; ☞ ✍) There are more vegetarian, seafood and gluten-free options on the menu of this contemporary eatery than is usual in Siena, and the cuisine is less traditional than the norm, featuring plenty of colour and fresh flavours. Sit inside or at one of the tables on the steep street.

Ristorante Grotta di
Santa Caterina da Bagoga TUSCAN €€

(Map p150; ☑ 0577 28 22 08; www.bagoga.it; Via della Galluzza 26; meals €35; ⊘12.30-3pm & 7-10pm Tue-Sat, 12.30-3pm Sun) Pierino Fagnani ('Bagoga'), one of Siena's most famous Palio jockeys, swapped his saddle for an apron in 1973 and opened this much-loved restaurant. Now operated by his son Francesco, it serves traditional Tuscan palate-pleasers that are lauded by Slow Food Italia (this is one of only two Slow Food–accredited restaurants in the city). The set menus (€25 to €55) offer good value.

★Osteria La Taverna
di San Giuseppe TUSCAN €€€

(Map p150; ☑ 0577 4 22 86; www.tavernasangiuseppe.it; Via Dupré 132; meals €49; ⊘noon-2.30pm & 7-10pm Mon-Sat) Any restaurant specialising in beef, truffles and porcini mushrooms attracts our immediate attention, but not all deliver on their promise. Fortunately, this one does. A favoured venue for locals celebrating important occasions, it offers excellent food, an impressive wine list with plenty of local, regional and international choices, a convivial traditional atmosphere and efficient service.

★Ristorante Enzo TUSCAN €€€

(Map p146; ☑ 0577 28 12 77; www.daenzo.net; Via Camollia 49; meals €52; ⊘noon-2.30pm & 7.30-10pm Tue-Sun) The epitome of refined Sienese dining, Da Enzo, as it is popularly called, welcomes guests with a complimentary glass of prosecco (sparkling wine) and follows up with Tuscan dishes made with skill and care. There's plenty of fish on the menu, as well as excellent handmade pasta and non-standard meat dishes. The setting

is equally impressive, with quality napery and glassware.

Drinking & Nightlife

Via Camollia and Via di Pantaneto are Siena's major bar and coffee strips. Though atmospheric, the bars lining the Campo (p141) are expensive if you sit at a table – consider yourself warned.

Bar Pasticcerie Nannini CAFE

(Map p150; ☑ 0577 23 60 09; www.pasticcerienannini.it/en; Via Banchi di Sopra 24; ⊘7.30am-10pm Mon-Thu, to 11pm Fri & Sat, to 10pm Sun) Established in 1886, Nannini's good coffee and location near the Campo ensure that it remains a local favourite. It's a great place to sample Sienese treats including *cantuccini* (crunchy, almond-studded biscuits), *cavallucci* (chewy biscuits flavoured with aniseed and other spices), *ricciarelli*, *panforte* and *panpepato* (*panforte* with the addition of pepper and hazelnuts).

Caffè Fiorella CAFE

(Torrefazione Fiorella; Map p150; www.torrefazionefiorella.it; Via di Città 13; ⊘7am-6pm Mon-Sat) Squeeze into this tiny, heart-of-the-action space to enjoy some of Siena's best coffee. In summer, the coffee *granita* with a dollop of cream is a wonderful indulgence.

Bottega Roots BAR

(Map p146; ☑ 0577 89 24 82; www.facebook.com/bottegarootssiena; Via di Pantaneto 58; ⊘10.30am-2am; ☞) Located in Siena's student quarter, this bar stages live-music acts in a vaulted interior with a mezzanine area. Artisan beer is the tipple of choice. Check its Facebook page for the performance schedule.

UnTUBO CLUB

(Map p150; ☑ 0577 27 13 12; www.untubo.it; Vicolo del Luparello 2; cover charge varies; ⊘6.30pm-3am Tue-Sat) Live jazz acts regularly take the stage on Thursday and Friday nights at this intimate club near the Campo, which is popular with students and the city's boho set. Check the website for a full events program – blues, pop and rock acts drop in for occasional gigs too. Note that winter hours are often reduced.

Shopping

★Il Magnifico FOOD

(Map p150; ☑ 0577 28 11 06; www.ilmagnifico.siena.it; Via dei Pellegrini 27; ⊘7.30am-7.30pm Mon-Sat) Lorenzo Rossi is Siena's best baker,

Text along right margin: SIENA & CENTRAL TUSCANY SIENA

ℹ️ SIENA FOR CHILDREN

This is a great choice of destination for those travelling with children. Toddlers will enjoy running around the Piazza del Campo (p141), climbing the ramparts of a castle – the Fortezza Medicea (Map p146; Piazza Caduti delle Forze Armate; ⊙ 24hr) FREE – and exploring the Orto de' Pecci (p145) with its grassy lawns, outdoor artworks, trees and farm animals.

They will also adore playing the unique Palio-inspired *barberi* game, which involves an exciting race of wooden balls around a tiered circular stone course called a *pista*. The *barberi* balls, painted in the colours of the city's 17 *contrade*, can be purchased at shops including Antica Siena (Map p150; ☑ 0577 4 64 96; Piazza del Campo 28; ⊙ 9am-8.30pm) in the Campo and there are marble *pistas* at the Fortezza Medicea and opposite the Fontebranda (Map p150; Vicolo del Tiratoio). For some quiet time, head to the kids' zone in the Biblioteca Comunale degli Intronati (p148).

There is a dedicated breastfeeding room (open 8am to 7.30pm) that can be used by members of the public on the ground floor of Palazzo Pubblico (look for the entrance with a security guard, to the right of the museum entry).

and his *panforte, ricciarelli* and *cavallucci* (chewy biscuits flavoured with aniseed and other spices) are a weekly purchase for most local households. Try them at his bakery and shop behind the *duomo*, and you'll understand why.

Pasticceria Bini   FOOD
(Map p150; ☑ 0577 28 02 07; www.facebook.com/Bini1944; Via di Stalloreggi 91-93; ⊙ 8am-1pm & 4.30-7pm Tue-Sat, to 1pm Sun) You'll be assailed by the most wonderful smell when entering this *pasticceria* next to the medieval Arco delle Due Porte. Established in 1944, it's famed for its *cantuccini* (crunchy, almond-studded biscuits) and *ricciarelli*. A large glass window onto the street allows passersby to watch *biscotti* (biscuits) being made in the modern, squeaky-clean kitchen.

Brocchi   ANTIQUES
(Map p150; ☑ 347 4346393; brocchi1815@libero.it; Via del Porrione 41-43; ⊙ 4-7.30pm Mon-Fri) A brass door knocker may seem a strange choice of souvenir, but the examples made by Laura Brocchi are attractive, well priced and authentically Sienese. Continuing a family tradition (Brocchi has been in business since 1815), Laura works from a historic nearby forge and is known throughout the city for the traditional pieces she makes for the city's *contrade*.

Sator Print   ART
(Map p150; ☑ 340 4689286; www.satorprint.com; Via di Stalloreggi 20; ⊙ hours vary) Maestro d'arte Bertolozzi Caredio presides over this atelier, creating works on paper featuring richly coloured and finely detailed calligraphic works in both English and Hebrew. Small illuminations cost from €50. There are also attractive printed cards available (from €3).

Bottega d'Arte   ART
(Map p150; www.arteinsiena.it; Via di Stalloreggi 47; ⊙ hours vary) Inspired by the works of Sienese masters of the 14th and 15th centuries, artists Chiara Perinetti Casoni, Paolo Perinetti Casoni and Michelangelo Attardo Perinetti Casoni create exquisite icons in tempera and 24-carat gold leaf. Expensive? Yes. Worth it? You bet.

Alessandro Stella   SHOES
(Map p146; ☑ 0349 530 20 42; stellaale59@gmail.com; Via Camollia 45; ⊙ hours vary) Sienese males are a particularly dapper lot, and their sartorial splendor owes much to local artisans such as Alessandro Stella. His handmade men's shoes, belts and wallets are sold from this small store in front of his workshop and are most definitely worth seeking out.

Casa della Pelle   FASHION & ACCESSORIES
(Map p146; ☑ 0577 28 74 75; info@CasaDellaPelle.it; Via Camollia 153; ⊙ 9am-7pm Mon-Sat) Everything at the House of Leather is made by master craftsman Paolo Infunti on-site, including the extraordinary medieval-style armour that *Game of Thrones* and *Lord of the Rings* devotees will adore (it's sure to take role-play games to a whole new level). Purses, handbags and belts are more orthodox purchases, but no less alluring.

Wednesday Market
(Map p146; ⊙7.30am-2pm) FREE Spreading around Fortezza Medicea and towards the Stadio Comunale, this is one of Tuscany's largest markets and is great for cheap clothing; food is also sold.

❶ Information
Tourist Office (Map p150; ✆0577 28 05 51; www.terresiena.it; Piazza Duomo 2, Santa Maria della Scala; ⊙10am-6pm mid-Mar–Oct, to 4.30pm Nov–mid-Mar) Can provide free maps of the city. The entrance is on the right (western) side of the museum building.

❶ Getting There & Away
BUS
Siena Mobilità (✆800 922984; www.siena mobilita.it), part of the Tiemme network, links Siena with the rest of Tuscany. It has a **ticket office** (Map p146; Piazza Antonio Gramsci; ⊙6.30am-7.30pm Mon-Fri, from 7am Sat) underneath the **main bus station** (Map p146) in Piazza Antonio Gramsci; there's also a daytime-only left-luggage office here (€5.50 per bag between 7am and 7pm).

Tickets for bus services operated by Eurolines, Baltour and Flixbus to Bologna, Milan, Rome, and elsewhere in Italy are also available from a **ticket office** (Map p146; ✆0861 1991900; ⊙8.30am-1.30pm & 2-5.30pm Mon-Sat) underneath the bus station in Piazza Antonio Gramsci.

TRAIN
Siena's rail links aren't that extensive; buses are usually a better option. There are direct *regionale* services to Florence (€9.30, 1½ to two hours, hourly) and Grosseto (€9.90, 1½ hours, nine daily). Rome requires a change of train at Chiusi-Chianciano Terme. For Pisa, change at Empoli.

A free *scala mobile* (escalator) connects the **train station** (Piazza Carlo Rosselli) with Viale Vittorio Emanuele II, near Porta Camollia in the historic centre.

❶ Getting Around
BUS
Within Siena, **Tiemme** (✆7am-7pm 199 16 81 82; www.tiemmespa.it) operates *pollicino* (city centre), *urbano* (urban) and *suburbano* (suburban) buses (€1.20 per 70 minutes). Buses 3 and 7 run between the train station and Piazza del Sale in the historic centre.

CAR & MOTORCYCLE
There's a ZTL (Zona a Traffico Limitato; Limited Traffic Zone) in Siena's historic centre, although visitors can often drop off luggage at their hotel; ask reception to report your licence number in advance, or risk a hefty fine.

There are large car parks operated by **Siena Parcheggi** (✆0577 22 87 11; www.sienapar cheggi.com) at the Stadio Comunale and around the Fortezza Medicea, both just north of Piazza San Domenico (the website is a useful resource). Hotly contested free street parking (look for white lines) is available in Viale Vittorio Veneto

SIENA BUS TRAVEL
Routes operated by Siena Mobilità from Monday to Saturday include the following:

DESTINATION	FARE (€)	TIME	FREQUENCY	NOTES
Arezzo	7.60	90min	8 daily	
Colle di Val d'Elsa	3.90	30-40min	hourly	Onward connections for Volterra (€2.75, four daily)
Fiumicino Airport (Rome) via Grosseto	22	3¾hr	2 daily	
Florence (*Corse Rapide*/Express service via the *autostrada*)	8.40	75min	frequent	*Corse Ordinarie* services don't use the *autostrada*; add at least 20min
Montalcino	5.60	75min	6 daily	Departs train station
Montepulciano	7.60	90min	2 daily	Departs train station
Monteriggioni	2.60	25min	frequent	
Pienza	6.20	70min	2 daily	Departs train station
San Gimignano	6.20	60-90min	10 daily	Often changes in Poggibonsi (€4.35, 1hr, hourly)

LOCAL KNOWLEDGE

GO LOCAL

Organised by a group of Central Tuscan municipalities, Be Tuscan for a Day (www.betuscanforaday.com) cooks up a varied programme of curated experiences that offers visitors a chance to taste 'authentic' local life on local farms, in the kitchen, in artisans' studios and outdoors. It includes cooking classes, vineyard and photography tours, horse riding, trekking and cycling.

on the Fortezza Medicea's southern edge. The paid car parks at San Francesco and Santa Caterina (aka Fontebranda) each have a free *scala mobile* going up into the centre.

Most car parks charge €2 per hour between 7am and 8pm.

TAXI

Call **Radio Taxi Siena** (📞0577 4 92 22; www.taxisiena.it) to order a cab, or head to the stands on **Piazza Independenza** (Map p150) or **Piazza Matteotti** (Map p150).

CHIANTI

The vineyards in this picturesque part of Tuscany produce the grapes used in namesake Chianti and Chianti Classico: world-famous reds sold under the Gallo Nero (Black Cockerel/Rooster) trademark. It's a landscape where you'll encounter historic olive groves, honey-coloured stone farmhouses, dense forests, graceful Romanesque *pievi* (rural churches), handsome Renaissance villas and imposing stone castles built in the Middle Ages by Florentine and Sienese warlords.

Though now part of the province of Siena, the southern section of Chianti (Chianti Senese) was once the stronghold of the Lega del Chianti, a military and administrative alliance within the city-state of Florence that comprised Castellina, Gaiole and Radda. Chianti's northern part sits in the province of Florence (Chianti Fiorentino) and is a popular day trip from that city. The major wine and administrative centres are Greve in Chianti, Castellina in Chianti and Radda in Chianti.

For regional information, including festivals and special events, see www.wechianti.com and www.chianti.com.

Greve in Chianti

📞0558 / POP 13,814

The main town in the Chianti Fiorentino, Greve is a hub of the local wine industry and has an amiable market-town air. It's not picturesque (most of the architecture is modern and unattractive), but it does boast an attractive, historic central square and a few notable businesses. The annual wine fair Expo del Chianti Classico (Chianti Classico Expo; www.expochianticlassico.com) is held in early September – if visiting at this time, book accommodation here and throughout the region well in advance.

⊙ Sights & Activities

Vignamaggio WINERY
(📞0558 54 66 24; www.vignamaggio.com; Via Petriolo 5; ⊗guided tours daily Apr-Oct) Mona Lisa Gherardini, subject of Leonardo da Vinci's world-famous painting, married into the family that built this villa in the 14th century. After a major restoration, the villa and its magnificent formal garden can be visited on a one-hour tour of the garden and historic cellars (€10), for a wine tasting (two wines plus local cheese and cured meats, €15) or for a combined tour and tasting experience (€29). Bookings essential.

Enoteca Falorni WINE
(📞0558 54 64 04; www.enotecafalorni.it; Piazza delle Cantine 2-6; tastings by glass €0.60-30; ⊗10.30am-7.30pm Apr-May, to 8pm Jun-Sep, 10am-7pm Thu-Mon Oct-Mar, closed 3 weeks Jan) A perfect place to let your palate limber up before visiting individual wineries, this *enoteca* stocks more than 1000 wines and offers 100 for tasting, including a huge array of Chianti Classico, IGTs and other Tuscan favourites. Leave your credit-card as a guarantee or buy a non-refundable prepaid wine card (€5 to €100) to test your tipples of choice.

Castello di Verrazzano WINE
(📞0558 5 42 43; www.verrazzano.com; Via Citille, Greti; tours €21-68; ⊗9.30am-6pm Mon-Sat, 10am-1pm & 3-6.30pm Sun) This hilltop castle 3km north of Greve was once home to Giovanni da Verrazzano (1485–1528), who explored the North American coast and is commemorated in New York by the Verrazzano-Narrows Bridge. Today it presides over a 225-hectare wine estate offering a wide range of tours.

📖 Sleeping & Eating

⭐ Borgo del Cabreo   AGRITURISMO €€€
(📞347 1174065, 0553 98 50 32; www.borgo delcabreo.it; Via Montefioralle Case Sparse 9; d €260-280, q villa €400; 🅿✳🛜🖥) Manager Michele works hard to ensure that guests enjoy their stay at this boutique *agriturismo* owned by the Tenuta di Nozzole winery, offering an efficient check-in, pouring a complimentary *aperitivo* on arrival and organising everything from restaurant bookings to bicycle hire. Rooms are classically elegant and extremely comfortable; facilities include a fabulous pool terrace overlooking the estate's olive groves.

La Cantina   PIZZA €
(📞0558 5 40 97; www.pizzerialacantina.it; Piazza Trento 3; pizzas €6-12, pastas €9-18; ⊘noon-midnight) Head to this popular local hangout to feast on thin-crust pizzas that are so huge they hang over the rims of the plates they are served on – bring a big appetite or share with your dining companion. Gluten-free options are available, as are dirt-cheap bottles of house wine. Menu alternatives include equally gargantuan bowls of pasta.

Bistro Falorni   DELI €
(📞0558 5 30 29; www.falorni.it; Piazza Giacomo Matteotti 71; taglieri €7-9, panini €4-5, lasagne €6; ⊘10am-7pm; 🛜) Italians do fast food differently, and what a wonderful difference it is. Greve's famous *macelleria* (butcher) and gourmet-provision shop operates this cafeteria attached to the *macelleria*, and it's popular with both locals and tourists. You can choose from the range of *taglieri*, *panini* and meat or vegetable lasagnes on offer, and enjoy a glass of wine (€4) too.

❶ Information

The **tourist office** (📞0558 54 62 99, 0558 5 36 06; www.helloflorence.net; Piazza Matteotti 11; ⊘10.30am-1.30pm late Mar–mid-Oct, to 6.30pm Easter-Aug) is located in Greve's main square.

❶ Getting There & Around

BUS
Buses travel between Greve in Chianti and Florence (€4.50, one hour, hourly) and between Greve and Panzano in Chianti (€1.50, 15 minutes, frequent). The bus stop is on Piazza Trento, 100m from Piazza Giacomo Matteotti. Purchase tickets from the tourist office or from **Caffè Annando** (open Thursday to Tuesday) in Galleria delle Cantine next to the Coop Supermarket on the main road.

CAR & MOTORCYCLE
Greve is on the Via Chiantigiana (SR222). Find parking in the underground carpark next to Enoteca Falorni on the main road through town (€2/1 per 1st/subsequent hours 8am-8pm, €1/0.50 8pm-8am) or in the two-level, open-air car park on Via Luca Chini, on the opposite side of the main road to Piazza Matteotti, which is free on the top level. On Fridays, don't park overnight in the paid spaces in Piazza Matteotti – your car will be towed away to make room for Saturday market stalls.

DON'T MISS

CYCLING CHIANTI

Exploring Chianti by bicycle is a true highlight. The Greve in Chianti tourist office can supply information about local cycling routes, and the town is home to the well-regarded Discovery Chianti (📞328 6124658; www.discoverychianti.com; Via I Maggio 32, Greve in Chianti; ⊘Mar-Oct), which runs guided cycling tours. It's also possible to rent bicycles from Ramuzzi (📞055 85 30 37; www.ramuzzi.com; Via Italo Stecchi 23; mountain or hybrid bike per day/week €20/130, e-bike/scooter per day €35/€65; ⊘9am-1pm & 3-7pm Mon-Fri, 9am-1pm Sat) in Greve's town centre.

A number of companies offer guided cycling tours (including by Discovery Chianti) leaving from Florence:

Florence by Bike (📞0554 8 89 92; www.florencebybike.it; Chianti guided bike tour adult/ reduced €83/75; ⊘daily Mar-Oct)

I Bike Italy (📞342 9352395; www.ibikeitaly.com; 2-day Chianti guided bike tour road bike/ e-bike €450/550; ⊘Mon, Wed & Fri mid-Mar–Oct)

We Bike Tuscany (📞USA 1-800-850-6832; www.webiketuscany.com; prices on application)

Chianti

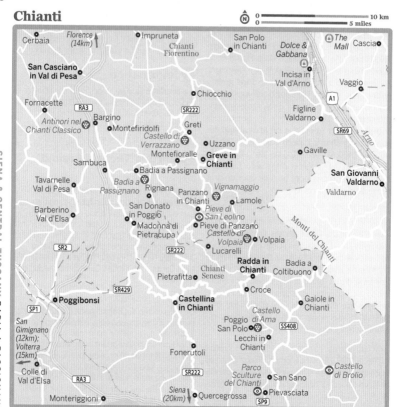

Badia a Passignano

Chianti doesn't get much more atmospheric than Badia a Passignano, a Benedictine Vallombrosan abbey set amid vineyards run by the legendary Antinori dynasty. Head here to visit the historic church and abbey buildings, admire the views over the vineyards, and taste wines in the Antinori *enoteca* or in one of a number of good eateries located here.

◎ Sights & Activities

Badia a Passignano's Chiesa di San Michele Arcangelo and adjoining monastery can officially be visited every day except Thursday, though opening hours can be unpredictable.

Chiesa di San Michele Arcangelo   CHURCH
(Abbey of Passignano; Via di Passignano; ⊙10am-noon & 3-5pm Mon-Wed, Fri & Sat, 3-5pm Sun) An 11th-century church on this site was destroyed in the 13th century and replaced by this structure, which was subsequently heavily altered over the centuries. Dedicated to St Michael the Archangel (look for the 12th-century statue of him slaying a dragon next to the high altar), it is home to frescoes and paintings of varying quality – the best are by Domenico Cresti (known as 'Il Passignano') on the side walls of the transept.

**Abbazia di San Michele
Arcangelo a Passignano**   MONASTERY
(☑English 0558 07 23 41, Italian 0558 07 11 71; Via di Passignano; by donation; ⊙tours by reservation) The four Vallombrosan monks who call this medieval abbey home open their quarters to visitors on regular guided tours. The highlight is the refectory, which was remodelled in the 15th century and is presided over by Domenico Ghirlandaio's utterly marvellous, recently restored 1476 fresco *The Last Supper*. The tours also visit the monastery's garden cloister and historic

kitchen. It's best to book in advance, as tour times can vary.

La Bottega di Badia a Passignano · WINE

(☑ 0558 07 12 78; www.osteriadipassignano.com; Via di Passignano 33; ⊙ 10am-7.30pm Mon-Sat) Taste or purchase Antinori wine in this *enoteca* beside the prestigious Osteria di Passignano restaurant. A tasting of three wines by the glass will cost between €20 and €50, and there is a variety of guided tours of the cellars and vineyards on offer – check the website for details. Wines by the glass cost between €6 and €23.

🛏 Sleeping

Torre di Badia · B&B €€

(☑ 0550 16 41 60; www.torredibadia.com; Via Passignano 22; r €110-180; 🅿 🖧 🛜) Offering five comfortable rooms, this B&B in a recently restored medieval tower on the Badia di Passignano estate is a good choice for those wanting to explore the local area. In winter, the open fire and honesty bar in the lounge make for a welcoming retreat; in summer the garden terrace overlooking the Antinori vineyard beckons.

Fattoria di Rignana · AGRITURISMO €€

(☑ 0558 5 20 65; www.rignana.it; Via di Rignana 15, Rignana; d from €95; ⊙ Apr-Nov; 🅿 @ 🛜 🌊) The historic *fattoria* (farmhouse) of this wine estate has its very own chapel and bell tower, which reveal themselves after you brave a long, rutted access road. You'll also find glorious views, a large swimming pool and a nearby eatery. Sleep in rustic en suite rooms in the *fattoria*. Find it 4km from Badia a Passignano.

🍴 Eating & Drinking

★ L'Antica Scuderia · TUSCAN €€

(☑ 0558 07 16 23, 335 8252669; www.ristorolanti cascuderia.com; Via di Passignano 17; meals €45, pizza €12-20; ⊙ 12.30-2.30pm & 7.30-10.30pm Wed-Mon; 🖧 🛜 🍴) The large terrace at this restaurant overlooks one of the Antinori vineyards and is perfect for summer dining. In winter, the elegant dining room comes into its own. Lunch features antipasti, pastas and traditional grilled meats, while dinner sees plenty of pizza-oven action. Kids love the playground set; adults love the fact that it keeps the kids occupied. Huge wine list.

MONTEFIORALLE

Surrounded by olive groves and vineyards, medieval Montefioralle was home to Amerigo Vespucci (1415–1512), an explorer who followed Columbus' route to America. Vespucci wrote so excitedly about the New World that he inspired cartographer Martin Waldseemüller (creator of the 1507 Universalis Cosmographia) to name the new continent in his honour.

The village crowns a rise just east of Greve, and can be accessed via a 2km walking path from the town centre (head up Via San Francesco, off Via Roma).

La Cantinetta di Rignana · TUSCAN €€

(☑ 0558 5 26 01, 347 4534884; www.lacantinettadi rignana.com; Rignana; meals €38; ⊙ 12.30-2.30pm & 7-10pm Wed-Mon summer, hours vary winter) You might wonder, as you settle onto the terrace here, whether you've found your perfect Chianti lazy-lunch location. A historic mill forms the backdrop, vine-lined hills roll off to the horizon and rustic dishes are full of local ingredients and packed with flavour. It's 4km from Badia a Passignano at the end of an unsealed, rutted road.

Osteria di Passignano · ITALIAN €€€

(☑ 055 807 12 78; www.osteriadipassignano.com; Via di Passignano 33; meals €85, tasting menus €90, wine pairing €140; ⊙ 12.15-2.15pm & 7.30-10pm Mon-Sat; 🅿 🛜 🍴) This elegant Michelin-starred eatery in the centre of Badia a Passignano has long been one of Tuscany's best-loved dining destinations. Intricate, Tuscan-inspired dishes fly the local-produce flag and the wine list is mightily impressive, with Antinori offerings aplenty. Vegetarians are well catered for, with a dedicated tasting menu available.

La Cantinetta di Passignano · SEAFOOD €€€

(☑ 0558 07 19 75; www.lacantinettadipassignano. it; Strada di Greve 1a; meals €46; ⊙ 12.30-3pm & 7.30pm-midnight Tue-Sun, 7.30pm-midnight Mon, closed Dec-Feb; 🛜) Tuscan menus are dominated by meat dishes, so the existence of this upmarket *cantinetta*, which focuses on seafood, comes as a pleasant surprise. We recommend booking a table on the vineyard-facing terrace and settling in to enjoy a feast of antipasti (much of it *crudo* – uncooked), pastas and mains accompanied by your choice from a champagne-dominated wine list.

WINE TOUR OF CHIANTI

Tuscany has its fair share of highlights, but few can match the indulgence of a drive through its wine country – an intoxicating blend of scenery, acclaimed restaurants and ruby-red wine.

❶ Castello di Verrazzano

Some 26km south of Florence, the Castello di Verrazzano (p156) lords it over a 230-hectare estate where Chianti Classico, Vin Santo, grappa, honey, olive oil and balsamic vinegar are produced. In a previous life, the castle was home to Giovanni di Verrazzano (1485–1528), an adventurer who explored the North American coast and is commemorated in New York by the Verrazzano-Narrows Bridge linking Staten Island to Brooklyn.

At the *castello*, you can choose from a range of guided tours, which include a tasting and can also include lunch with the estate wines. Book ahead.

The Drive > From the castello it's a simple 10-minute drive to Greve in Chianti. Double back to the SR222 in Greti, turn right and follow for about 3km.

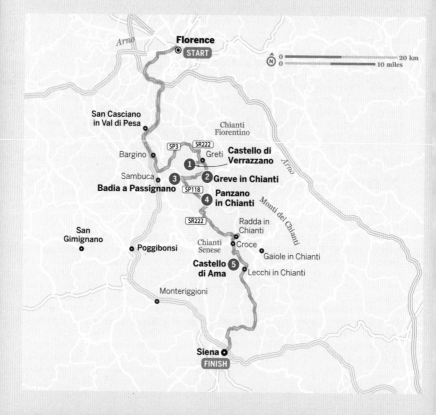

Four Days 150km

Great for... Food & Drink, Outdoors

Best Time to Go May to October

② Greve in Chianti

The main town in the Chianti Fiorentino, the northernmost of the two Chianti districts, Greve in Chianti has been an important wine centre for centuries. It has an amiable market-town air, and several eateries and *enoteche* that showcase the best Chianti food and drink. To stock up on picnic supplies, head to **Antica Macelleria Falorni** (☑ 0558 5 30 29; www.falorni.it; Piazza Giacomo Matteotti 71; ⊙ 9am-1pm & 3-7pm Mon-Sat, from 10am Sun), an atmospheric butcher's shop-cum-bistro that the Bencistà Falorni family have been running since the early 19th century and which specialises in delicious *finocchiona briciolona* (pork salami made with fennel seeds and Chianti wine). The family also run the Enoteca Falorni (p156), the town's top cellar, where you can sample all sorts of local wine.

The Drive > From Greve turn off the main through road, Viale Giovanni di Verrazzano, near the Esso petrol station, and head up towards Montefioralle. Continue on as the road climbs past olive groves and through woods to Badia a Passignano, about 15 minutes away.

③ Badia a Passignano

Encircled by cypress trees and surrounded by swaths of olive groves and vineyards, the 11th-century Chiesa di San Michele Arcangelo (p158) at Passignano sits at the heart of a historic wine estate run by the Antinoris, one of Tuscany's oldest and most prestigious winemaking families. The estate offers a range of guided tours, tastings and cookery courses. Most require prior booking, but you can just turn up at the estate's wine shop, La Bottega (p159), to taste and buy wines and olive oil.

The Drive > From Badia a Passignano, double back towards Greve and pick up the signposted SP118 for a pleasant 15-minute drive along the narrow tree-shaded road to Panzano.

④ Panzano in Chianti

The quiet medieval town of Panzano is an essential stop on any gourmet's tour of Tuscany. Here you can stock up on meaty picnic fare at L'Antica Macelleria Cecchini (p165), a celebrated butcher's shop run by the poetry-spouting guru of Tuscan meat, Dario Cecchini. Alternatively, you can eat at one of his three eateries: the Officina della Bistecca (p165), which serves a simple set menu based on steak; Solociccia (p165), where guests share a communal table to sample meat dishes other than bistecca; and Dario DOC (p165), a casual daytime eatery. Book ahead for the Officina and Solociccia.

The Drive > From Panzano, it's about 20km to the Castello di Ama. Strike south on the SR222 towards Radda in Chianti, enjoying views off to the right as you wend your way through the green countryside. At Croce, just beyond Radda, turn left and head towards Lecchi and San Sano. The Castello di Ama is signposted after a further 7km.

⑤ Castello di Ama

To indulge in some contemporary-art appreciation between wine tastings, make for Castello di Ama (p165) near Lecchi. This highly regarded wine estate produces a fine Chianti Classico and has an original sculpture park showcasing 14 site-specific works by artists including Louise Bourgeois, Chen Zhen, Anish Kapoor, Kendell Geers and Daniel Buren. Book ahead.

The Drive > Double back to the SP408 and head south to Siena.

ⓘ CHEAP SLEEPS

The countryside west of Badia e Passignano hides away a trio of excellent-value accommodation options – all as easily accessible from nearby Florence as from Chianti.

Ostello del Chianti (☑0558 05 02 65; www.ostellodelchianti.it; Via Roma 137, Tavarnelle Val di Pesa; dm €16, s €35, d €50, d without bathroom €39; ☺Apr-Oct; Ⓟ🛜) This is one of Italy's oldest hostels and though it occupies an ugly building in a less-than-scenic town, the bargain prices compensate. Dorms max out at six beds, a simple breakfast is available and there are basic cooking facilities. Florence is easily accessed by ACV/Busitalia bus (€3.50, one hour).

La Locanda di Pietracupa (☑0558 07 24 00; www.locandapietracupa.com; Via Madonna di Pietracupa 31, San Donato in Poggio; s €85, d €108; Ⓟ🛜) It's difficult to access inexpensive accommodation in Chianti, so the four rooms at this inn come as a wonderful surprise. Though at the budget end of the price scale, they are elegant, comfortable and beautifully maintained. Breakfast is served in the downstairs restaurant, which also serves modern Tuscan cuisine at lunch and dinner (meals €50).

Castello di Gabbiano (☑0558 2 10 53; www.castellogabbiano.it; Via di Gabbiano 22, Mercatale Val di Pesa; r/ste/apt per day from €120/185/140; Ⓟ❄🛜🏊) Vines were first planted here in the 12th century, and this 100-hectare estate with its medieval castle has been producing vintages ever since. Only 22km from Florence, it offers comfortable rooms in the castle and self-catering apartments in estate farmhouses. On-site facilities include a restaurant (open April to November) and a scenically sited swimming pool with adjacent hot tub.

ⓘ Getting There & Away

There is no public transport connection to Badia a Passignano. The easiest road access is via Strada di Badia off the SP94.

San Casciano in Val di Pesa

☑0588 / POP 17,171

Almost totally destroyed by Allied bombs in 1944, San Casciano in Val di Pesa, to the south of Florence, was fully rebuilt and is now a busy hub for the local wine and olive-oil industries. There are no sights of note within the town itself, but the surrounding countryside is home to a number of impressive *agriturismi* (farmstay accommodation) and villas.

◉ Sights & Activities

★**Antinori nel Chianti Classico**   WINE

(☑0552 35 97 00; www.antinorichianticlassico.it; Via Cassia per Siena 133, Località Bargino; tours & tastings from €35; ☺10am-5pm Mon-Fri, to 5.30pm Sat & Sun winter, to 6.30pm Sat & Sun summer) Marco Casaminti's sculptural building set into the hillside is a landmark sight from the *autostrada* just south of Florence, and is one of the world's most impressive examples of contemporary winery design. Daily guided tours (in English and Italian) include a short film presentation, a visit to the winemaking

and fermentation areas and a guided tasting; in the 'Bottaia' tour, the latter is often held in a glass tasting room cantilevered over the barriques in the cathedral-like ageing cellar. Bookings essential.

The Antinori family has been in the winemaking business since 1180. You can taste or purchase their wines in the stylish *enoteca* or enjoy a glass or two over lunch in the Rinuccio 1180 restaurant. Alternatively, book for the 'Bottaia Cru' tour (€160), which includes tastings of seven of the vineyard's wines as well as lunch.

Bargino is 7km south of San Casciano in Val di Pesa and 20km northwest of Greve.

Tuscany Ballooning   BALLOONING

(☑335 6454036, 055 824 91 20; www.tuscanyballooning.com; Via del Masso 14, San Casciano in Val di Pesa; per person €250; ☺Apr-Nov) Offers dawn flights followed by breakfast around Florence, Siena and Chianti.

🛏 Sleeping

★**Villa I Barronci**   HOTEL €€

(☑0558 2 05 98; www.ibarronci.com; Via Sorripa 10; s/d/ste from €165/185/330; Ⓟ❄@🛜🏊) Exemplary service, superb amenities and high comfort levels ensure this country hotel on the northwestern edge of San Casciano is one to remember. You can relax in the bar, rejuvenate in the spa, laze by the pool, dine in the excellent restaurant (meals €36) or take day trips to Pisa, Lucca, Florence, Volterra, San Gimignano and Siena. Amazing low-season rates.

Il Paluffo   AGRITURISMO €€
(📞0571 66 42 59; www.paluffo.com; Via Citerna 144, Località Fiano; B&B r from €125, apt from €170; P ❄ @ 🛜 🌊) 🚗 Hidden in the hills 14km southwest of San Casciano, this clever conversion of a centuries-old olive farm has seen the former fermentation room transformed into a comfortable guest lounge, farm buildings into self-catering apartments, and upstairs rooms of the frescoed farm villa into elegant B&B rooms with modern bathrooms. Views from the terraces stretch as far as San Gimignano's towers.

Staff can arrange wine tasting and truffle hunting, while cookery courses cover everything from pasta making to Tuscan dinner parties. Add a luscious bio-filtered swimming pool, an honesty bar stacked with Tuscan wines and a delicious breakfast featuring organic local produce (included in B&B room cost, charge levied for apartment guests). There's a two-night minimum stay.

🍴 Eating & Drinking

⭐ **L'Osteria di Casa Chianti**   TUSCAN €€
(📞0571 66 96 88; www.osteriadicasachianti.it; Località Case Nuove 77, Fiano; meals €38; ⊙7-10pm Tue-Sat, 12.30-2.30pm & 7-10pm Sun; 🚗) The type of restaurant that fuels fantasies of moving permanently to Tuscany, Massimiliano Canton's ultrafriendly *osteria* bakes its own bread, makes pasta by hand, grills *bistecca* on a wood fire, specialises in truffle and porcini dishes, and has an exceptional wine list. Families appreciate the keenly priced kids' menu (€5 to €12) too. Book ahead.

You'll find it on the SP79 between Fiano and Certaldo, 14km southwest of San Casciano in Val di Pesa.

Rinuccio 1180   TUSCAN €€
(📞0552 35 97 20; www.antinorichianticlassico.it; Via Cassia per Siena 133, Bargino; meals €42; ⊙noon-4pm) Built on the rooftop of the sleek Antinori winery, this restaurant seats diners on an expansive outdoor terrace with a 180-degree Dolby-esque surround of hills, birdsong and pea-green vines. In cooler weather, the dining action moves into a glass dining space. Cuisine is Tuscan, modern, seasonal and sassy (Chianti burger, anyone?). Book ahead.

ℹ️ Getting There & Away

San Casciano is on the SP92, just off the Florence–Siena *autostrada*. **Busitalia/Autolinee Chianti Valdarno** (ACV; www.acvbus.it) operates services between the town and Florence (€3.50, 35 minutes, frequent).

Castellina in Chianti
📞0577 / POP 2852

Established by the Etruscans and fortified by the Florentines in the 15th century as a defensive outpost against the Sienese, sturdy Castellina in Chianti is now a major centre of the wine industry, as the huge silos brimming with Chianti Classico on the town's approaches attest. The town's medieval *rocca* (fortress) safeguards Etruscan archaeological finds from the local area in the small **Museo Archeologico del Chianti Senese** (📞347 6790752; www.museoarcheologicochianti.it; Piazza del Comune 17-18; adult/child €5/3; ⊙10am-6pm daily Apr, May, Sep & Oct, 11am-7pm Jun-Aug, 10am-5pm Sat & Sun Nov, Dec, closed Jan-Mar). Castellina in Chianti's location on the SR222 makes it a convenient overnight or meal stop for those travelling between Florence and Siena.

Il Colombaio   B&B €
(📞0577 74 04 44; www.albergoilcolombaio.it; Via Chiantigiana 29; s/d/tr €90/100/130; P 🛜 🌊) This 14th-century farmhouse on the edge of Castellina has been tastefully converted into a welcoming *albergo* (hotel) with 15 rooms and a rich heritage feel: tapestry-covered chairs frame lace curtains and oil paintings;

ℹ️ OUTLET SHOPPING

Follow local bargain-hunters to the Valdarno area in northeast Chianti to unleash your inner fashionista (and your credit cards). Bargains from the previous season's collections can be sourced at the **Mall** (📞055 865 77 75; www.themall.it; Via Europa 8; ⊙9.30am-7.30pm Jun-Aug, 10am-7pm Sep-May) in Leccio Regello; **Dolce & Gabbana** (📞055 833 13 00; Via Pian dell'Isola 49, Località Santa Maria Maddalena; ⊙10.30am-7.30pm), off the SR69 near Incisa Val d'Arno; and **Prada** (📞0559 19 65 28; Space Factory Outlets, Via Aretina 403; ⊙10.30am-7.30pm Mon-Fri & Sun, 9.30am-7.30pm Sat), in Levanella off the SR69 on the southern edge of Montevarchi.

WORTH A TRIP

LUNCH WITH A VIEW
....

Family-run Ristoro di Lamole (☎0558 54 70 50; www.ristorodilamole.it; Via Lamole 6, Lamole; meals €40; ⊙noon-3pm & 7-9.30pm Apr-Oct, noon-3pm Thu, Fri, Mon & Tue, 7-9.30pm Fri & Sat Nov-Mar), 8km east of Panzano and 9km southeast of Greve, offers its diners one of the most spectacular panoramic views in Chianti. Book well in advance to score a table on the terrace, where you can enjoy delicious contemporary riffs on traditional Tuscan dishes. The wine list is excellent, as is the service.

wood-beamed ceilings and iron bedheads add plenty of character. Breakfast is served in the vaulted wine cellar or in the garden, where there is also a pool.

Palazzo Squarcialupi HOTEL €€

(☎0577 74 11 86; www.squarcialupirelaxinchianti.com; Via Ferruccio 22; r €138-175; ⊙closed Nov-early Apr; P @ ⊛ ⊚ ⊠) You've gotta love a hotel that offers four-star facilities for three-star prices. And that's what this well-run hotel in a 15th-century *palazzo* in Castellina's historic centre does. Rooms are comfortable and well sized; those in the superior category have views. Facilities include an excellent restaurant, bar, large swimming pool, panoramic terrace and spa (free for guests).

Ristorante Taverna Squarcialupi TUSCAN €€

(☎0577 74 14 05; www.tavernasquarcialupi.it; Via Ferruccio 26; meals €40; ⊙noon-3pm Thu-Tue, 7-10pm Thu-Mon) Interesting and highly successful flavour combinations characterise the menu at this huge *taverna* (tavern) in the centre of Castellina. The handmade pasta dishes are delicious – grab a seat on the panoramic rear terrace and enjoy one with a glass or two of wine from the nearby La Castellina wine estate.

Ristorante Albergaccio TUSCAN €€€

(☎0577 74 10 42; www.ristorantealbergaccio.com; Via Fiorentina 63; meals €55, set menus €43-60; ⊙12.30-2.30pm & 7.30-9.30pm Mon-Sat, closed parts of Dec-Mar; ☑) Albergaccio bills its culinary approach as 'the territory on the table', and local seasonal produce certainly holds sway here. Once the proud possessor of a Michelin accolade, its star has waned (literally) in recent times, but it's still a satisfying albeit pricey place to dine. Find it 1km

northeast of Castellina on the San Donato in Poggio road.

ⓘ Getting There & Away

BUS

Tiemme (p155) buses link Castellina in Chianti with Radda in Chianti (€2.60, 10 minutes, three to five daily Monday to Saturday) and with Siena (€3.50, 40 minutes, seven daily Monday to Saturday). The most convenient bus stops are on the main road near Via delle Mura; buy tickets from **Tabacchi Piattellini** in Via Ferruccio (open Monday to Saturday).

CAR & MOTORCYCLE

Castellina is on the Via Chiantigiana (SR222). The most convenient car park is at the southern edge of town off Via IV Novembre (€1 per hour 8am to 8pm).

Radda in Chianti

☑0577 / POP 1581

The age-old streets in pretty Radda in Chianti fan out from its central square, where the heraldic shields of the 16th-century Palazzo del Podestà add a touch of drama to the scene. A historic wine town, it's the home of the Consorzio di Chianti Classico and is an appealing albeit low-key base for visits to some classic Tuscan vineyards.

There is a limited number of sleeping options in Radda, most at the top end. The best is Palazzo Leopoldo (☎0577 73 56 05; www.palazzoleopoldo.it; Via Roma 33; s from €120, d from €135, ste from €240; P ⊛ ⊚ ⊠).

Casa Chianti Classico MUSEUM

(☎0577 73 81 87; www.chianticlassico.com; Monastery of Santa Maria al Prato, Circonvallazione Santa Maria 18; self-guided tour with glass of wine €7; ⊙tours & tastings 11am-7pm Tue-Sat, to 5pm Sun mid-Mar–Oct) FREE Occupying an 18th-century convent complex attached to a 10th-century church, this facility is operated by the Consorzio di Chianti Classico and pays homage to the region's favourite product. Self-guided tours of the Wine Museum on the 1st floor introduce the terroir and history of the denomination and include an enjoyable multimedia quiz in which participants test their newly acquired oenological knowledge by analysing a glass of local wine (included in tour price).

Bistro Casa Chianti Classico TUSCAN €

(☎0577 73 81 87; www.chianticlassico.com; Monastery of Santa Maria al Prato, Circonvallazione Santa Maria 18; meals €23; ⊙noon-5pm Tue-Sun mid-

WORTH A TRIP

TUSCANY'S CELEBRITY BUTCHER

The small town of Panzano in Chianti, 10km south of Greve in Chianti, is known throughout Italy as the location of L'Antica Macelleria Cecchini (0558 5 20 20; 9am-4pm), a butcher's shop owned and run by the ever-extroverted Dario Cecchini (www.dario cecchini.com; Via XX Luglio 11). This Tuscan celebrity has carved out a niche for himself as a poetry-spouting guardian of the *bistecca* (steak) and other Tuscan meaty treats, and he operates three eateries clustered around the *macelleria*: Officina della Bistecca (0558 5 20 20; set menu adult/child under 10 €50/25; sittings at 1pm & 8pm), with a set menu built around his famous *bistecca*; Solociccia (0558 5 27 27; set meat menu adult/child under 10 €30/15; sittings at 1pm, 7pm, 8pm & 9pm), where guests sample meat dishes other than steak; and Dario DOC (0558 5 21 76; burgers €10 or €15 Mon-Fri, €15 Sat, meat sushi €20; noon-3pm Mon-Sat), his casual lunchtime-only eatery. Book ahead for the Officina and Solociccia.

Don't leave Panzano in Chianti without visiting one of Chianti's most beautiful religious buildings, the Pieve di San Leolino (Strada San Leolino, Località San Leolino; 10am-7pm, reduced hr winter, mass 10am Sun). Located on a hilltop just outside the village, the Romanesque *pieve* safeguards a 1421 polyptych behind the high altar by Mariotto di Nardo (1421), two glazed terracotta tabernacles by Giovanni della Robbia, and a luminous 13th-century triptych by the master of Panzano depicting the Virgin and Child next to saints – including St Catherine of Alexandria, the patron saint of philosophers.

Panzano in Chianti is on the SR222 from Florence to Siena. Buses travel between it and both Greve in Chianti (€1.50, 15 minutes, frequent) and Florence (€4.50, 70 minutes, frequent). The most central bus stop is on Piazza Gastone Bucciarelli.

Mar–Oct) Offering a seasonally driven menu and boasting (of course) a wonderful wine list, this bistro in the Chianti complex seats diners in the former kitchen and cloisters of an 18th-century convent, as well as in a downstairs *enoteca* with a terrace overlooking an adjoining vineyard. Try the signature *pici del convento* (pasta with confit tomato, almonds, olives and herbs).

La Botte di Bacco   TUSCAN €€€
(0577 73 90 08; www.ristorantelabottedibacco. it; Viale XX Settembre 23; meals €50; 12.30-2.30pm & 7.30-10.30pm Fri-Wed mid-Apr–late Oct;) A long-standing favourite, this romantic choice on the main road through Radda has a traditional interior but the menu has an untraditional tinge, probably because chef Flavio D'Auria hails from Naples and isn't afraid to make unobtrusive tweaks to Tuscan classics. The impressive wine list is dominated by local drops.

Information

Tourist Office (0577 73 84 94; www.face book.com/proradda; Piazza del Castello 2; 10am-1pm Mon-Sat;) Radda's pro-loco tourist office can book accommodation and tours for this pocket of Chianti, and also supplies information about walks in the area.

Getting There & Away

Radda is linked with Siena by the SP102 and with Castellina in Chianti by the SR429. Tiemme (p155) buses link the town with Castellina (€2.60, 10 minutes, three to five daily Monday to Saturday) and with Siena (€4.50, one hour, four daily Monday to Saturday). Buses stop on Via XX Settembre (SR429) near La Botte di Bacco restaurant; buy tickets at **Porciatti Alimentari** on Piazza IV Novembre.

Gaiole in Chianti

0577 / POP 2758

Surrounded by majestic medieval castles and atmospheric *pievi*, this small town has few attractions but is sometimes visited en route to Castello di Brolio (p166) or Castello di Ama.

Sights & Activities

★ Castello di Ama   WINERY
(0577 74 60 69; www.castellodiama.com; Località Ama; guided tours adult/child under 16yr €15/free; enoteca 10am-7pm, tours by appointment) At Castello di Ama, centuries-old winemaking traditions meet cutting-edge contemporary art in a 12th-century *borgo* (agricultural estate). As well as vineyards and a winery producing internationally acclaimed wines such

---

WORTH A TRIP

VOLPAIA

Wines, olive oils and vinegars have long been produced at Castello di Volpaia (☑0577 73 80 66; www.volpaia.it; ⊙ enoteca 9am-1pm & 2.30-5pm Mon-Fri Apr-Nov), an estate based in the medieval hamlet of Volpaia, 7km north of Radda in Chianti. Book ahead to enjoy a tasting of four wines in the *enoteca* (€14) inside the hamlet's main tower, or for a tour of the cellars followed by a tasting (€24, 90 minutes).

Post-tour, consider a light lunch of *bruschette or* cheese-and-*salumi* plates washed down with local wine at Bar Ucci (☑0577 73 80 42; www.bar-ucci.it; Piazza della Torre 9; ⊙ 9am-11pm Tue-Sun late Mar-early Jan) on Volpaia's pretty piazza. Otherwise, herbs and vegetables from the estate's organic garden are used to excellent advantage in the dishes served at the estate's highly regarded Osteria Volpaia (☑0577 73 80 66; www.osteriavolpaia.com; Vicolo della Torre 2; meals lunch €34, dinner €46; ⊙ 12-2.30pm & 7-9.30pm Thu-Tue) 🍴. Order a four-course lunch menu (€41) or tasting menu (€37 to €59) to fully appreciate chef Marco Lagrimino's refined take on modern Tuscan cuisine.

---

as 'L'Apparita' merlot, the estate also features a boutique hotel, a restaurant and a sculpture park showcasing 14 impressive site-specific pieces by artists including Louise Bourgeois, Chen Zhen, Anish Kapoor, Kendell Geers and Daniel Buren. This can be visited on a guided tour; advance bookings essential.

Castello di Brolio   CASTLE
(☑0577 73 02 80; www.ricasoli.it; Località Madonna a Brolio; garden, chapel & crypt €5, museum €3, guided tours with tasting adult/teenager from €30/20; ⊙10am-5.30pm mid-Mar–Oct) The ancestral estate of the aristocratic Ricasoli family dates from the 11th century and is the oldest winery in Italy. Currently home to the 32nd baron, it opens its formal garden, panoramic terrace and small but fascinating museum to day trippers, who often adjourn to the excellent on-site *osteria* for lunch after enjoying a morning tour and tasting.

Parco Sculture del Chianti   SCULPTURE
(Chianti Sculpture Park; ☑0577 35 71 51; www.chiantisculpturepark.it; Località La Fornace; adult/child €10/5; ⊙10am-dusk; 👶) Site-specific contemporary artworks created by artists from over 20 countries are scattered throughout this 7-hectare wood, including a glass labyrinth by Jeff Saward that children in particular will adore. Between June and August weekly sunset jazz, classical and opera concerts are staged in the park's marble-and-granite amphitheatre.

The park is 11km southwest of Gaiole in Chianti. When here, be sure to visit the neighbouring village of Pievasciata, which is full of site-specific outdoor artworks.

🛏 Sleeping & Eating

The in-house Il Pievano restaurant in the ritzy Hotel Castello di Spaltenna (www.spaltenna.it) on the edge of Gaiole is one of the relatively few restaurants in Chianti to possess a Michelin star. Outside town, the best options are the *osteria* at Castello di Brolio and the restaurant at Castello di Ama.

Osteria del Castello   TUSCAN €€
(☑0577 73 02 90; Località Madonna a Brolio; meals €40; ⊙ noon-2.30pm 2nd half of Mar–Oct and Sun-Wed Nov-Dec, 7-10pm Apr-Oct and Fri-Sat 2nd half of Mar, closed Jan–mid-Mar) Modern twists on classic Tuscan dishes are the focus at this *osteria* on the Castello di Brolio estate. The food here is light and full of flavour, made with seasonal ingredients (including vegetables grown in the restaurant's kitchen garden). Settle in for a five-course tasting menu (€50), which can be paired with estate wines for an extra €15.

★ Castello di Ama   BOUTIQUE HOTEL €€€
(☑0577 74 60 31; www.castellodiama.com; Località Ama; ste €345-490; ⊙ closed Dec–mid-Mar; 🅿🛜) These five luxurious suites filled with art, antiques and sleek contemporary furnishings are set in an 18th-century villa on the Castello di Ama (p165) wine estate and are particularly alluring for a romantic getaway. A tour of the estate's internationally acclaimed sculpture garden is offered to all guests, and its wines can be enjoyed over dinner at the on-site restaurant (☑0577 74 61 91; www.castellodiama.com; Castello di Ama, Località Ama; meals €30; ⊙ noon-3pm & 7-10pm Wed-Mon).

🅘 Getting There & Away

Gaiole is on the SP408 between Siena and Montevarchi. Tiemme (p155) bus 127 travels between Gaiole and Via Lombardi behind Siena's railway station (€3.50, 40 minutes, seven daily Monday to Saturday). The bus stop in Gaiole is on the main road, opposite the elementary school.

SAN GIMIGNANO

🅙 0577 / POP 7774

As you crest the nearby hills, the 14 towers of the walled town of San Gimignano rise up like a medieval Manhattan. Originally an Etruscan village, the settlement was named after the bishop of Modena, San Gimignano, who is said to have saved the city from Attila the Hun. It became a *comune* (local government) in 1199, prospering in part because of its location on the Via Francigena. Building a tower taller than their neighbours' (there were originally 72 of them) became a popular way for prominent families to flaunt their power and wealth. In 1348 plague wiped out much of the population and weakened the local economy, leading to the town's submission to Florence in 1353. Today, not even the plague would deter the swarms of summer day trippers, who are lured by a palpable sense of history, an intact medieval streetscapes and the enchanting rural setting.

⊙ Sights

San Gimignano's triangular Piazza della Cisterna is named after the 13th-century cistern at its centre. In Piazza del Duomo, the cathedral looks across to the late-13th-century Palazzo Vecchio del Podestà (Piazza del Duomo) and its tower, the Torre della Rognosa.

★ Collegiata   CHURCH

(Duomo; Basilica di Santa Maria Assunta; 🅙 0577 28 63 00; www.duomosangimignano.it; Piazza del Duomo; adult/reduced €4/2; ⊙ 10am-7pm Mon-Sat, 12.30-7pm Sun Apr-Oct, 10am-4.30pm Mon-Sat, 12.30-4.30pm Sun Nov-Mar, closed 2nd half Jan & 2nd half Nov) Parts of San Gimignano's Romanesque cathedral were built in the second half of the 11th century, but its remarkably vivid frescoes, depicting episodes from the Old and New Testaments, date from the 14th century. Look out too, for the Cappella di Santa Fina, near the main altar – a Renaissance chapel adorned with naive and touching frescoes by Domenico Ghirlandaio depicting the life of one of the town's patron saints. These featured in Franco Zeffirelli's 1999 film *Tea with Mussolini*.

★ Palazzo Comunale   MUSEUM

(🅙 0577 28 63 00; www.sangimignanomusei.it; Piazza del Duomo 2; combined Civic Museums ticket adult/reduced €9/7; ⊙ 10am-7pm Apr-Sep, 11am-5pm Oct-Mar) The 13th-century Palazzo Comunale has always been the centre of San Gimignano's local government; its magnificently frescoed Sala di Dante is where the great poet addressed the town's council in 1299 and its Camera del Podestà and Pinacoteca (Art Gallery) once housed government offices – now they are home to wonderful artworks. Be sure to climb the 218 steps of the *palazzo's* 54m Torre Grossa for a spectacular view over the town and surrounding countryside.

SIENA & CENTRAL TUSCANY SAN GIMIGNANO

CHIANTI WINES

Chianti's blockbuster wines are the ruby-red Chianti and Chianti Classico DOCGs, both of which have a minimum Sangiovese component (75% for Chianti and 80% for Chianti Classico).

The biggest wine-producing estates have *cantine* (cellars) where you can taste and buy wine, but few vineyards – big or small – can be visited without reservations. For a comprehensive list and map of wine estates, buy a copy of *Le strade del Gallo Nero* (€2.50) at the tourist offices in Greve in Chianti (p157) or Radda in Chianti (p165).

A high-profile consortium of local producers, the Consorzio Vino Chianti Classico (www.chianticlassico.com), operates Casa Chianti Classico (p164) in Radda in Chianti, which is home to a small wine museum, *enoteca* and bistro. The *corsorzio's* website has plenty of information on its members (96% of local producers), the wines themselves and wine-related events.

DON'T MISS

A VINTAGE BIKE RIDE

The original event in a now-global phenomenon, Chianti's famous cycling race Eroica (www.eroicagaiole.com; ⊘1st Sun Oct) was launched in 1997 to raise funds and awareness for the protection and preservation of gravel roads in Tuscany. Cyclists follow five routes of varying difficulty throughout Chianti and the Crete Senese; these start and end in Gaiole in Chianti and range in distance from 45km to 209km. The Eroica Montalcino (www.eroicamontalcino.it; ⊘May) in May sees hardy cyclists hit unpaved roads in the Val d'Orcia, with routes ranging from a 27km family ride to a hardcore 171km.

Both events are hugely popular, so you'll need to register well in advance to participate. Riders ride 'vintage' bikes – no modern racing, mountain or e-bikes are allowed.

★Vernaccia di San Gimignano
Wine Experience   MUSEUM

(⌨0577 94 12 67; www.sangimignanomuseovernaccia.com; Via della Rocca 1; ⊘11.30am-7.30pm Apr-Oct, to 6.30pm Nov & Mar, closed Dec-Feb) FREE San Gimignano's famous wine, Vernaccia, is celebrated at this museum and *enoteca* next to the rocca (Via della Rocca; ⊘24hr) FREE. Interactive exhibits on the 1st floor trace the history of the product and the surrounding land, and the ground-floor *enoteca* offers both tastings (tasting card €10 to €25, leftover credit refunded) and Vernaccia master classes. It's also possible to buy a glass of wine (€4 to €7) to enjoy on the terrace, which has a panoramic view.

Galleria Continua   GALLERY

(⌨0577 94 31 34; www.galleriacontinua.com; Via del Castello 11; ⊘10am-1pm & 2-7pm) FREE It may seem strange to highlight contemporary art in this medieval time capsule of a town, but there's good reason to do so. This is one of the best commercial art galleries in Europe, showing the work of big-name artists such as Ai Weiwei, Daniel Buren, Antony Gormley and Mona Hatoum. Spread over four venues (an old cinema, a medieval tower, a vaulted cellar and an apartment on Piazza della Cisterna), it's one of San Gimignano's most compelling attractions.

San Lorenzo in Ponte   MUSEUM

(⌨0577 28 63 00; www.sangimignanomusei.it; Via del Castello; combined Civic Museums ticket adult/reduced €9/7; ⊘10am-7.30pm summer, 11am-5.30pm winter) The name of this 13th-century church refers to its original location next to a drawbridge (*ponte* means bridge) leading to the bishop's castle. The drawbridge has long since gone, but the castle still stands (now empty, it has functioned as a monastery and as a prison). Inside, a cycle of recently restored frescoes depicts scenes of St Benedict and a large 15th-century fresco by Cenni di Francesco di Ser Cenni shows Christ in Glory with the Virgin and 12 apostles.

Chiesa di Sant'Agostino   CHURCH

(Piazza Sant'Agostino; ⊘10am-noon & 3-7pm Apr-Oct, to 6pm Nov & Dec, 4-6pm Mon, 10am-noon & 3-6pm Tue-Sun Jan-Mar) FREE This late-13th-century church is best known for Benozzo Gozzoli's charming fresco cycle (1464–65) illustrating the life of St Augustine. You'll find it in the choir behind the altar. Gozzoli also painted the fresco featuring San Sebastian on the north wall, which shows the saint protecting the citizens of San Gimignano during the 1464 plague. What makes the image highly unusual is that he's helped by a bare-breasted Virgin Mary; this symbolises her maternal love for humanity.

Polo Museale Santa Chiara   MUSEUM

(Santa Chiara Museum Centre; ⌨0577 28 63 00; www.sangimignanomusei.it; Via Folgore da San Gimignano 11; combined Civic Museums ticket adult/reduced €9/7; ⊘10am-7pm Apr-Sep, 11am-5pm Oct-Mar) There are three museums in this complex. The ground floor is home to a part-reconstructed 15th- to 18th-century pharmacy known as the Speziera di Santa Fina, which features shelves stacked with brightly painted ceramic jars and half-empty potion bottles. Next to it is an Archaeological Museum showcasing Roman finds, including tiny bronze figurines, etched mirrors and piles of brightly coloured mosaic tiles. Upstairs, the Gallery of Modern and Contemporary Art features works by Italian artists.

Museo d'Arte Sacra   MUSEUM

(⌨0577 94 01 52; www.duomosangimignano.it; Piazza Pecori 1; adult/child €3.50/2; ⊘10am-7pm Mon-Sat, 12.30-7pm Sun Apr-Oct, 10am-4.30pm Mon-Sat, 12.30-4.30pm Sun Nov-Mar, closed 2nd half Jan & 2nd half Nov) Works of medieval religious art from San Gimignano's key churches are on display in this modest museum. Particularly beautiful items made from precious metals include crafted chalices and thuribles (censers); there are also some exquisitely embroidered textiles.

Torre e Casa Campatelli
HOUSE

(Campatelli Tower & House; ✆0577 94 14 19; www.torrecampatelli.it; Via San Giovanni 15; adult/reduced €7/4; ⏱10am-7pm Tue-Sun Apr-Oct, 10.30am-5.30pm Thu-Sun Nov-early Jan, to 5pm Sat & Sun early Jan-Feb, to 5.30pm Wed-Sun Mar) Protected and opened to the public by the Fondo Ambiente Italiano (FAI), the Italian National Trust equivalent, this art- and antique-filled tower house was the home of the wealthy Campatelli family and has been preserved exactly as it was when its last resident, Lydia Campatelli, bequeathed it to the FAI in 2005. The main – and extremely compelling – reason for a visit is the 'Thousand Years of San Gimignano' audiovisual presentation about the history of the city (in English and Italian).

Activities

The tourist office (p174) takes bookings for a range of English-language guided nature walks amid the hills surrounding San Gimignano, along 6km to 9km stretches of the Via Francigena and through the Riserva Naturale di Castelvecchio to the southwest of town. These run according to demand and cost between €15 and €25.

Vernaccia Master Classes
WINE

(Via della Rocca 1; class €15-60; ⏱Mar-Nov) Held at the Vernaccia di San Gimignano Wine Experience, these daily master classes include wine tastings; all but the 'Mini Master Class' (€15) also include typical local foods. Advance bookings are possible on la rocca@vernaccia.it, but it's usually possible to sign up on the day of your visit.

Festivals & Events

Ferie delle Messi
CULTURAL

(www.cavalieridisantafina.it; ⏱3rd weekend Jun) San Gimignano's medieval past is evoked through re-enacted battles, archery contests and plays.

Festival Barocco di San Gimignano
MUSIC

(www.accademiadeileggieri.org; tickets adult/reduced €10/8; ⏱Sep) A high-quality season of baroque music concerts staged in the historic Teatro Leggieri and Palazzo Comunale.

🛌 Sleeping

There is a limited number of accommodation options in San Gimignano, so it's a good idea to book well in advance.

Foresteria del Monastero di San Girolamo
HOSTEL €

(✆0577 94 05 73; www.monasterosangirolamo.it; Via Folgore da San Gimignano 26; s/tw/tr €32/60/90; ℗) This is a first-rate backpacker choice. Run by friendly Benedictine Vallumbrosan nuns, it has basic but comfortable and impeccably clean rooms sleeping two to four people in single beds; all have attached bathrooms. Parking costs €4 per night, breakfast costs €3 and there are two rooms set up for guests in wheelchairs (a rarity in town). Sadly, no wi-fi.

Hotel L'Antico Pozzo
BOUTIQUE HOTEL €€

(✆0577 94 20 14; www.anticopozzo.com; Via San Matteo 87; s €95, d €120-190; ⏱closed mid-Jan–mid-Feb; ❄@🛜) The sense of heritage here is palpable: stone arches and winding stairs lead to a handsome breakfast salon, and some rooms have frescoes and period furniture. The sun-drenched rear courtyard is a great retreat from the madding crowds. Room types are named after Italian poets – those in the Boccaccio category are cramped but the Dante suites are elegant and extremely desirable.

⭐ Locanda dell' Artista
AGRITURISMO €€€

(✆0577 94 60 26; www.locandadellartista.com; Lucignano 43, Canonica; r €325, ste €450; ⏱mid-Mar–mid-Oct; ℗❄🛜🏊) American Baker Bloodworth left a career in Hollywood to open this boutique retreat with his Italian partner Cristian Rovetta, the culinary force behind the property's Michelin-starred restaurant, Al 43 (menus €85 to €95). The seven rooms and suites are as elegant as they are comfortable, and facilities include a pool terrace with wonderful views over olive groves towards nearby San Gimignano. No children under 14.

🍴 Eating

Many San Gimignano restaurants focus on the tourist trade and serve mediocre food at inflated prices. Higher-standard eateries gravitate toward fresh local produce, including the town's famous *zafferano* (saffron). Purchase meat, vegetables, fish and takeaway food at the **Thursday morning market** (⏱8am-1.30pm) on and around Piazzas Cisterna, Duomo and delle Erbe. A small

1. Duccio di Buoninsegna's *Maestà* 2. Palazzo Pubblico (p145)
3. Fresco in Collegiata (p167) 4. Abbazia di Sant'Antimo (p186)

Medieval Masterpieces

We reckon the Middle Ages get a bad rap in the history books. This period may have been blighted by famines, plagues and wars, but it also saw an extraordinary flowering of art and architecture. Cities such as Siena, San Gimignano and Volterra are full of masterpieces dating from this time.

Palazzo Pubblico, Siena

Built on the cusp of the Middle Ages and the Renaissance, Siena's city hall (p145) is a triumph of Gothic secular architecture. Inside, the Museo Civico (p140) showcases a collection that is modest in size but monumental in quality.

Abbazia di Sant'Antimo, Castelnuovo dell'Abate

Benedictine monks have been performing Gregorian chants in this Romanesque abbey (p186) near Montalcino ever since the Middle Ages. Dating back to the time of Charlemagne, its austere beauty and idyllic setting make it an essential stop on every itinerary.

Collegiata, San Gimignano

Don't be fooled by its modest facade. Inside, the walls of this Romanesque cathedral (p167) are adorned with brightly coloured frescoes resembling a vast medieval comic strip.

Duccio di Buoninsegna's Maestà, Siena

Originally displayed in Siena's *duomo* (cathedral) and now the prize exhibit in the Museo dell'Opera (p143), Duccio's altarpiece portrays the Virgin surrounded by angels, saints and prominent Sienese citizens of the period.

San Gimignano

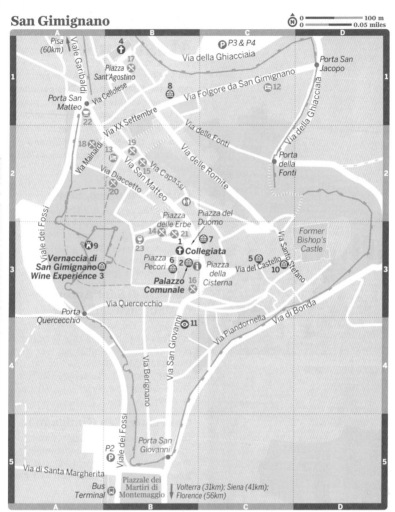

produce market also operates on the latter on Saturday morning.

★ Gelateria Dondoli
GELATO €

(📞0577 94 22 44; www.gelateriadipiazza.com; Piazza della Cisterna 4; gelato €2.50-5; ⊙9am-11pm summer, to 7.30pm winter, closed mid-Dec–mid-Feb) Think of it less as ice cream, more as art. Former gelato world champion Sergio Dondoli is known for creations including Crema di Santa Fina (saffron cream) gelato and Vernaccia sorbet. His creations are so delicious that some devotees even sign up for a two-hour gelato-making workshop (www.dondoli gelatoclass.com, price on application).

Dal Bertelli
SANDWICHES €

(📞348 3181907; Via Capassi 30; panini €4-6, glass of wine €3; ⊙1-7pm Apr-Dec) The Bertelli family has lived in San Gimignano since 1779, and its current patriarch is fiercely proud of both his heritage and his sandwiches. Salami, cheese, bread and wine are sourced from local artisan producers and is sold in generous portions in a determinedly ungentrified space with marble work surfaces, wooden shelves and curious agricultural implements dangling from stone walls.

San Gimignano

⊙ Top Sights
1 Collegiata	B3
2 Palazzo Comunale	B3
3 Vernaccia di San Gimignano Wine Experience	A3

⊙ Sights
4 Chiesa di Sant'Agostino	B1
5 Galleria Continua	C3
6 Museo d'Arte Sacra	B3
7 Palazzo Vecchio del Podestà	C3
8 Polo Museale Santa Chiara	B1
9 Rocca di Montestaffoli	A3
10 San Lorenzo in Ponte	C3
11 Torre e Casa Campatelli	B4

⊙ Activities, Courses & Tours
Vernaccia Master Classes	(see 3)

⊙ Sleeping
12 Foresteria del Monastero di San Girolamo	C1
13 Hotel L'Antico Pozzo	B2

⊗ Eating
14 Caffè delle Erbe	B3
15 Dal Bertelli	B2
16 Gelateria Dondoli	B3
17 Locanda di Sant'Agostino	B1
18 Osteria delle Catene	A2
19 Perucà	B2
20 Ristorante La Mandragola	B2
21 Thursday Morning Market	B3

⊙ Drinking & Nightlife
22 Bar Piazzetta	A1
23 D!Vineria	B3

★Ristorante La Mandragola TUSCAN €€
(☑348 3023766; www.locandalamandragola.it; Via Diaccetto 26; meals €38; ⊙12.15-2.30pm & 7-9.30pm; 🐾) Nestled beneath the crumbling walls of the rocca (p168), La Mandragola (The Mandrake) is deservedly popular – book ahead, especially if you're keen to dine in the gorgeous courtyard. It's not exactly tourist-free, but the welcome is genuine and the food is delicious, especially the hand-made pasta dishes, which feature unusual sauces and stuffings.

Osteria delle Catene TUSCAN €€
(☑0577 94 19 66; www.osteriadellecatene.it; Via Mainardi 18; mains €30; ⊙noon-2pm & 7-9pm Thu-Tue, closed Sun dinner Nov-Mar) 'The Prison' is as popular with San Gimignano locals as it is with visitors, something that can't be said of many places in this tourist-driven town. The menu is full of delightful surprises – dishes are seasonally focused and many utilise local saffron and Vernaccia wine. Set menus (€15.50 to €25) offer good value.

Locanda di Sant'Agostino TUSCAN €€
(☑0577 94 31 41; g.pompei@me.com; Piazza Sant'Agostino 15; meals €45; ⊙11.30am-11pm Mar–mid-Jan, closed Wed Mar, Apr, Nov & Dec) Family run, this trattoria next to the church of the same name has a dining room made distinctive by its bright colour scheme, a profusion of tables on the handsome piazza and a menu of Tuscan favourites. Home-made *pici* (thick, hand-rolled pasta) is a speciality.

Perucà TUSCAN €€
(☑0577 94 31 36; www.peruca.eu; Via Capassi 16; meals €38; ⊙noon-2.30pm & 7-10.30pm Fri-Wed) Set in an atmospheric vault under an ancient city arch, this trattoria serves modern cuisine inspired by local ingredients – try the *fagottini* (pasta filled with *pecorino* and pear) topped with a saffron and pine-nut cream.

Drinking & Nightlife

There are plenty of wine bars in San Gimignano's centre where you can sip a glass of chilled Vernaccia. For coffee, head to Bar Piazzetta (☑0577 94 06 09; Piazzetta Filippo Buonaccorsi 5; ⊙7am-10pm Thu-Tue) or Caffè delle Erbe (☑0577 94 04 78; Piazza delle Erbe; panini €5.50-7.50, bruschette €8.50-10, salads €6.50-9.50; ⊙8.30am-6pm Apr-Oct, reduced hr Nov & Feb-Mar, closed Dec & Jan).

D!Vineria WINE BAR
(☑0577 94 30 41; www.divineria.it; Via della Rocca 2c; ⊙10am-10pm mid-Mar–Oct) Massimo Delli, the owner of this tiny wine bar on the street leading up to the rocca (p168), will enthusiastically suggest local wines to try (consider ordering Montenidoli's Fiore or Rubicini's Etherea – both excellent Vernaccias). A glass costs between €3.50 and €25, and Massimo also stocks a good range of local salami and cheese (*taglieri* €20).

ⓘ Information

Tourist Office (☑0577 94 00 08; www.sangimignano.com; Piazza del Duomo 1; ⊙10am-1pm & 3-7pm Mar-Oct, 10am-1pm &

ⓘ MUSEUM PASSES

Three combined tickets can save you money in San Gimignano:

Civic Museums Ticket (adult/reduced €9/7) Gives admission to the Palazzo Comunale (p167), the Polo Museale Santa Chiara (p168) and San Lorenzo in Ponte (p168). Valid 48 hours; one visit per site.

San Gimignano Pass (adult/child €13/10) Includes all of the above plus the Collegiata (p167) and Museo d'Arte Sacra (p169). Valid 48 hours; one visit per site.

Collegiata & Museo d'Arte Sacra (adult/child €6/3)

2-6pm Nov-Feb) Organises tours, supplies maps and books accommodation. It also has information on the Strada del Vino Vernaccia di San Gimignano (Wine Road of the Vernaccia di San Gimignano).

ⓘ Getting There & Away

BUS

San Gimignano's **bus station** (Piazzale dei Martiri di Montemaggio) is next to the *carabinieri* (police station) at Porta San Giovanni. The tourist office sells bus tickets.

Florence (€6.80, 1¼ to two hours, 14 daily) Change at Poggibonsi.

Monteriggioni (€4.50, 55 minutes, eight daily Monday to Saturday)

Poggibonsi (€2.60, 30 minutes, frequent)

Siena (€6.20, one to 1½ hours, 10 daily Monday to Saturday)

Head to Colle di Val d'Elsa (€3.50, 35 minutes) to take a connecting bus to Volterra (€3.50, 50 minutes). These run four times daily from Monday to Saturday.

CAR & MOTORCYCLE

To arrive in San Gimignano from Florence and Siena, take the Siena–Florence autostrada, then the SR2 and finally the SP1 from Poggibonsi Nord. From Volterra, take the SR68 east and follow the turn-off signs north to San Gimignano on the SP47.

Parking is expensive here. The cheapest option (€1.50/6/1 per hour/day/night) is at Parcheggio Giubileo (P1) on the southern edge of town; the most convenient is at Parcheggio Montemaggio (P2) next to Porta San Giovanni (€2.50/2/15/5 per hour/subsequent hours/day/night). Full charges apply between 8am and

8pm daily; reduced night rates apply between 8pm and 8am.

TRAIN

The closest train station to San Gimignano is Poggibonsi (by bus €2.60, 30 minutes, frequent).

MONTERIGGIONI

📞 0577 / POP 9937

The local tourism office markets Monteriggioni as a 'Gateway to the Middle Ages', and though hackneyed, the description fits. Enclosed by monumental walls with ramparts and 14 watchtowers, the physical structure of this fortified village has changed little since it was established in the 13th century and became a popular stop on the Via Francigena. Sights include the walls and the 13th-century Church of Santa Maria Assunta. There are also plenty of touristy boutiques to browse. In July, the streets are full of colourfully clad characters participating in one of Italy's oldest medieval festivals.

Ramparts   CASTLE

(adult/child under 8yr €4/free; ⊙ 10am-1.30pm & 2-7pm summer, to 4pm mid-Sep–Oct, closed Tue winter) Built by the Republic of Siena in the 13th century as a defensive outpost against Florence, Monteriggioni's castle resisted a number of sieges and attacks but fell into disrepair after Siena fell to its rival in the 16th century. Reconstructed in the 19th century, the ramparts can now be accessed from two locations within the town and offer wonderful views over the countryside.

The ticket also includes entry to the four-room **armour museum** in the tourist office building.

Abbadia a Isola   ABBEY

(📞 335 6651581; SP74; donation requested; ⊙ 9am-1pm Mon-Fri, to 1pm & 3-6pm Sat & Sun summer) 🆓 The name (*isola* means island) reflects the fact that until the 18th century, this 11th-century abbey was surrounded by swampland. It has hosted many pilgrims on the Via Francigena over the centuries and a modern hostel continues that tradition. Its **Chiesa di San Salvatore** features a 14th-century fresco by Taddeo di Bartolo and a polyptych by 15th-century painter Sano di Pietro. An Etruscan sarcophagus to the right of the altar contains the bones of St Chirino, the church's patron saint.

The abbey is 4km from the Monteriggioni fortress, and it is possible to walk between the two on an original stretch of the Via Francigena.

Slow Travel Fest
CULTURAL

(Festival della Viandanza; www.slowtravelfest.it; ⊙ Jun, Sep & Oct) Celebrating the culture of travel on foot and by bicycle, this annual event held in various summer and autumn months features cultural events and plenty of peregrination on the local stretch of the Via Francigena.

Medieval Festival
CARNIVAL

(Festa Medievale; ☑ 0577 30 48 34; www.monter iggionimedievale.com; daily pass adult €11-13, reduced €9-11; ⊙ Jul) This popular festival held over two long weekends in July includes feasts, jousts, a market, musical performances, falconry and battle re-enactments.

Casa per Ferie Santa Maria Assunta
HOSTEL €

(☑ 0577 30 42 14, 335 6651581; www.monterig gioniviafrancigena.it; Piazza Roma 23; dm €30, s €40, d €75, d without bathroom €55) Located behind the tourist office inside the medieval fortress, this old-fashioned church-owned hostel welcomes pilgrims walking the Via Francigena as well as other travellers. It offers two dorms sleeping four and five, plus two double rooms (sheet hire €7). Bathrooms are squeaky clean, with torrents of hot water, and it has a well-equipped kitchen and lounge for guest use. No breakfast.

★ Bar dell'Orso
TUSCAN €

(☑ 0577 30 50 74; www.bardellorso.it; Via Cassia Nord 23, La Colonna di Monteriggioni; meals €24, panini €2-4.50; ⊙ 5am-midnight) Known throughout the region for the affordability and excellence of its food, the Bear Bar bustles from morning to night and is a great place to grab a quick *panino* or a lunch of handmade pasta or hearty stew. Later in the day, order a *merende* (afternoon snack) of cured meats, cheese and pickled vegetables – best enjoyed with a glass of *vino*.

ⓘ Information

Tourist Office (☑ 0577 30 48 34; www.mon teriggioniturismo.it; Piazza Roma 23; ⊙ 9.30-1.30 & 2-7.30pm daily summer, 10am-1.30pm & 2-4pm Wed-Mon winter) Located inside Monteriggioni's walls. Supplies plenty of info about the town and surrounding area.

ⓘ Getting There & Away

Buses link Monteriggioni with Florence (€7.60, 75 minutes, frequent services Monday to Saturday, two daily Sunday), San Gimignano (€4.50, 55 minutes, eight daily Monday to Saturday) and Siena (€2.60, 25 minutes, frequent services Monday to Saturday), stopping at the roundabout at Colonna di Monteriggioni.

Trains between Monteriggioni and Siena (€2.60, 15 minutes, hourly) stop at Castellina Scalo, on the SR2 and 2.6km from the castle. Change at Empoli for Florence.

VOLTERRA

☑ 0588 / POP 10,290

Volterra's well-preserved medieval ramparts give the windswept town a proud, forbidding air. Fortunately, the reality is considerably more welcoming, as a wander through the winding cobbled streets dotted with Roman, Etruscan and medieval structures attests. Known for its artisanal heritage – alabaster carving in particular – the town is a particularly satisfying stop for those seeking to stock up on Tuscan art and handicrafts.

History

The Etruscan settlement of Velathri was an important trading centre and senior partner of the Dodecapolis group of Etruscan cities. It's believed that as many as 25,000 people lived here in its Etruscan heyday. Partly because of the surrounding inhospitable

Volterra

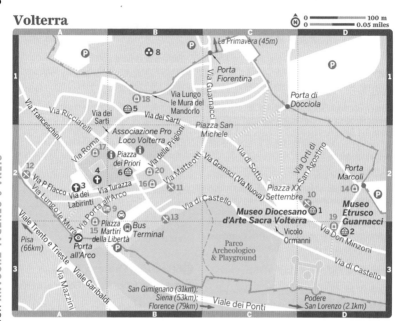

terrain, the city was among the last to succumb to Rome – it was absorbed into the Roman confederation around 260 BC and renamed Volaterrae. The bulk of the old city was raised in the 12th and 13th centuries under a fiercely independent free *comune*. The city first entered Florence's orbit in 1361, but the people of Volterra fought hard against Medici rule – their rebellion was brought to a brutal end when Lorenzo Il Magnifico's soldiers sacked the city in 1472. There was another rebellion in 1530 – again brutally crushed by the Florentines – but Volterra would never again achieve self-government, moving from Florentine rule to that of the Grand Duchy of Tuscany before Italian unification in 1860.

◎ Sights & Activities

The Volterra Card (adult/reduced/family €16/13/24, valid 72 hours) gives admission to Volterra's Museo Etrusco Guarnacci, the Pinacoteca Comunale, Ecomuseo dell'Alabastro, Palazzo dei Priori (☑ 0588 8 60 50; www.comune.volterra.pi.it/Palazzo_dei_Priori; Piazza dei Priori 1; adult/reduced €6/4; ☉ 10.30am-5.30pm mid-Mar–Oct, 10am-4.30pm Nov–mid-Mar), Acropoli and Teatro Romano. It's available at all of the museums.

★ Museo Etrusco Guarnacci   MUSEUM
(☑ 0588 8 63 47; www.volterratur.it/en/come/arts-culture/the-museum/guarnacci-etruscan-museum; Via Don Minzoni 15; adult/reduced €8/6; ☉ 9am-7pm mid-Mar–Oct 10am-4.30pm Nov–mid-Mar) The vast collection of artefacts exhibited here makes this one of Italy's most impressive Etruscan collections. Found locally, they include some 600 funerary urns carved mainly from alabaster and tufa – perhaps the pick is the *Urna degli sposi* (Urn of the Spouses), a strikingly realistic terracotta rendering of an elderly couple. The finds are displayed according to subject and era; the best examples (those dating from later periods) are on the 2nd and 3rd floors.

★ Museo Diocesano d'Arte
Sacra Volterra   MUSEUM
(Sacred Art Museum; ☑ 0588 8 77 33; Piazza XX Settembre; adult/reduced €5/3; ☉ 11am-6pm Tue-Sun Easter-Oct, to 5pm Fri-Sun Oct-Easter) Offering an innovative and particularly satisfying museum experience, this collection of sacred art is housed in the still-functioning Chiesa di San Agostino, ensuring that works are presented in a proper context. Drawn from the churches of the diocese of Volterra, they include three magnificent *Madonnas Enthroned with Child*: 15th-century versions

Volterra

◎ **Top Sights**
1 Museo Diocesano d'Arte Sacra
Volterra... D2
2 Museo Etrusco Guarnacci.................. D3

◎ **Sights**
3 Baptistry...A2
4 Cattedrale di Santa Maria
Assunta..A2
5 Ecomuseo dell'Alabastro B1
6 Palazzo dei Priori B2
Pinacoteca Comunale .... (see 5)
7 Porta all'Arco.......................................A3
8 Teatro Romano B1

🛌 **Sleeping**
9 Hotel Volterra In....................................A2

🍴 **Eating**
10 La Carabaccia D2
11 L'Incontro B2
12 Osteria Fornelli....................................A2
13 Ristorante-Enoteca Del Duca B2

🛍 **Shopping**
14 Alab'Arte.. D2
15 Alabastro Federico Pruneti................ A3
16 Boutique del Tartufo............................B2
17 Centro di Restauro CPRCA.................A2
18 Fabula Etrusca B1
19 Gloria Giannelli.................................... D3
20 Società Cooperativa Artieri
Alabastro B2

by Neri di Bicci and Taddeo di Bartoli, and a 16th-century example from Rosso Fiorentino. Don't miss the particularly beautiful 14th-century carved wooden *Madonna of the Annunciation.*

**Cattedrale di
Santa Maria Assunta**   CATHEDRAL
(Duomo di Volterra; Piazza San Giovanni) A handsome coffered ceiling is the standout feature of Volterra's *duomo,* which was built in the 12th and 13th centuries and remodelled in the 16th. The Chapel of Our Lady of Sorrows, to the left as you enter from Piazza San Giovanni, has two sculptures by Andrea della Robbia and a small fresco of the *Procession of the Magi* by Benozzo Gozzoli. The *duomo* was closed for restoration work when we last visited but was due to reopen in late 2019.

Ecomuseo dell'Alabastro   MUSEUM
(☎0588 8 75 80; www.volterratur.it/en/come/arts-culture/the-museum/ecomuseum-of-alabaster; Via dei Sarti 1; adult/reduced €8/6; ☺9am-7pm mid-Mar–Oct, 10am-4.30pm Nov–mid-Mar)

As befits a town that's hewn the precious material from nearby quarries since Etruscan times, Volterra is the proud possessor of an alabaster museum. It's an intriguing exploration of everything related to the rock, from production and working to commercialisation. Contemporary creations feature strongly; there are also choice examples from Etruscan times onwards, as well as a recreated artisan's workshop. The ticket includes entrance to the Pinacoteca Comunale in the same building.

Pinacoteca Comunale   GALLERY
(☎0588 8 75 80; www.volterratur.it/en/come/arts-culture/the-museum/art-gallery; Via dei Sarti 1; adult/reduced €8/6; ☺9am-7pm mid-Mar–Oct, 10am-4.30pm Nov–mid-Mar) Local, Sienese and Florentine art holds sway in this modest collection in the Palazzo Minucci Solaini. Taddeo di Bartolo's *Madonna Enthroned with Child* (1411) is exquisite, while Rosso Fiorentino's *Deposition from the Cross* (1521) appears strikingly modern. The ticket includes entrance to the Ecomuseo dell'Alabastro, which is attached.

Teatro Romano   ARCHAEOLOGICAL SITE
(☎0588 8 63 47; Via Francesco Ferrucci; adult/reduced €5/3; ☺10.30am-5.30pm mid-Mar–Oct, 10am-4.30pm Sat & Sun Nov–mid-Mar) The grassy ranks of seating and towering columns of Italy's finest and best-preserved Roman theatre makes this a particularly evocative archaeological site. It was commissioned in the 1st century BC and could hold up to 2000 spectators. Today the *cavea* (sloping seating area), orchestra pit and stage are still clearly discernible. Note that there's also a good – and free – view of the theatre from Via Lungo Le Mura del Mandorlo.

🎊 Festivals & Events

Volterra AD 1398   CULTURAL
(☎0588 8 72 57; www.volterra1398.it; day pass adult/reduced €10/6; ☺Aug) The citizens of Volterra roll back the calendar some 600 years, take to the streets in period costume and celebrate all the fun of a medieval fair on the second and third Sundays in August.

🛏 Sleeping

⭐ **La Primavera**   B&B €
(☎0588 8 72 95; www.affittacamere-laprimavera.com; Via Porta Diana 15; s/d/tr €50/75/100; ☺mid-Apr–mid-Nov; ⓟ🛜) This home-style B&B in a former alabaster workshop is a cosy affair, with a knick-knack-adorned

lounge, a pretty garden, polished parquet floors and meticulously presented bedrooms featuring soothing pastel colour schemes. It's in an excellent location just outside the city walls, a 10-minute walk from Piazza dei Priori. The free on-site parking is a definite plus. No credit cards.

Podere San Lorenzo   AGRITURISMO €
(☑0588 3 90 80; www.agriturismo-volterra.it; Via Allori 80; B&B d €100, 2-/3-/4-bed apt without breakfast €105-165; ☞▣) In this tranquil model of slow tourism you dip straight into a rural idyll. An alluring spring-fed swimming pool is located next to an enviable veggie garden; apartments sleep between two and four (some have private terraces) and rooms are quiet. Dinners (per person €30 including wine) are served in a former 12th-century chapel.

Hotel Volterra In   HOTEL €
(☑0588 8 68 20; www.hotelvolterrain.it; Via Porta all'Arco 37-41; s €75, d €90-110, ste €160-170; ▧☞) There are no top-end or boutique hotels in the centre of Volterra, so the recent opening of this small three-star establishment close to the Porta all'Arco (Via Porta all'Arco) is to be applauded. Though it doesn't deserve its self-claimed boutique label, the rooms are pleasant and have bathrooms so clean they gleam. Guests rave about the quality of the breakfast.

🍴 Eating & Drinking

Decent dining options are somewhat limited in Volterra. Those we've recommended tend to serve local specialities including white Marzuolo truffles, mushrooms (porcini and ovuli), *zuppa volterrana* (thick vegetable and bread soup), *pappardelle* with hare or wild boar sauce, *trippa alla volterrana* (tripe cooked with tomato, sausage and herbs) and *ossi di morto* (bones of the dead) almond biscuits.

★L'Incontro   CAFE €
(☑0588 8 05 00; Via Matteotti 18; panini €2-4, biscuits €1.50-2.50; ☺6am-midnight, to 2am summer, closed Wed winter; ☞) L'Incontro's rear *salone* is a top spot to grab a quick antipasto plate or *panino* for lunch, and its front bar area is always crowded with locals enjoying a coffee or *aperitivo*. The house-baked biscuits are noteworthy – try the chewy and nutty *brutti mai buoni* (ugly but good) or its alabaster-coloured cousin, *ossi di morto*.

La Carabaccia   TUSCAN €€
(☑0588 8 62 39; www.lacarabacciavolterra.it; Piazza XX Settembre 4-5; meals €26; ☺12.30-2.30pm Tue-Sun, 7.30-9.30pm Tue-Sat, reduced hours winter; ☞▨) Mother and daughters Sara, Ilaria and Patrizia put their heart and soul into this charming trattoria with a country-style interior and attractive front terrace. Named after a humble Tuscan vegetable soup (one of the

ABBAZIA DI SAN GALGANO

About 45km southwest of Siena via the SS73 are the evocative ruins of the 13th-century Cistercian Abbazia di San Galgano (www.sangalgano.info; San Galgano; adult/reduced €3.50/3; ☺9am-7pm Jun & Sep, to 6pm Apr & May, to 8pm Jul & Aug, to 5.30pm Oct-Mar), in its day one of the country's finest Gothic buildings. Today, the abbey's roofless ruins are a compelling sight, with remarkably intact walls interspersed with soaring arches and empty, round spaces where windows would have been.

On a hill overlooking the abbey is the tiny, round Romanesque Cappella di Monte Siepi, dedicated to Galgano Guidotti, a saint who lived his final years here as a hermit. In the middle of the chapel is a sword embedded in a rock – legend tells us that San Galgano, a soldier by profession, drove his weapon into the stone to symbolise his renunciation of worldly life. In a room off the chapel, three badly damaged early-14th-century frescoes by Sienese artist Ambrogio Lorenzetti depict scenes from the saint's life.

Near the approach to the abbey is a *fattoria* with a cafe (*panino* €4 to €5) and restaurant (meals €24).

San Galgano is a popular weekend day-trip destination for locals – come mid-week to beat the crowds.

If you are heading towards Siena, Montalcino, Pienza or Montepulciano after your visit here, be sure to take the SS73 south and then veer east onto the SP delle Pinete (direction San Lorenzo a Merse), a scenic drive through protected forest.

house specialities), it's the city's best lunch option. The small seasonal menu changes daily and always features fish on Fridays.

Osteria Fornelli
ITALIAN €€€

(☑ 0588 8 86 41; www.osteriafornelli.it; Piazzetta dei Fornelli 3; meals €50; ☉ noon-3pm & 7-10pm Wed-Mon) Contemporary cuisine is the exception rather than the rule here in Volterra, so the existence of this modern bistro next to the town's walls is cause for celebration. Order à la carte or opt for one of the five-course *degustazione* menus (€50) – one is traditional but the other showcases inventive dishes and includes vegetarian and seafood choices. Excellent wine list.

🛍 Shopping

Volterra's centuries-old heritage as a town that mines and works alabaster ensures plenty of shops that specialise in hand-carved alabaster items. The Società Cooperativa Artieri Alabastro (☑ 0588 8 61 35; www.artierialabastro.it; Piazza dei Priori 4-5; ☉ 10.30am-6pm) showcases the impressive work of 23 local alabaster artisans, while ateliers include Alab'Arte (☑ 340 9816908, 340 7187189; www.alabarte.com; Via Orti di San Agostino 28; ☉ 10am-12.30pm & 3-6pm Mon-Sat), Alabastro Federico Pruneti (☑ 348 6546514; Via Porta all'Arco; ☉ hours vary) and Gloria Giannelli (☑ 0588 8 40 30; www.gloriagiannellialabastri.it; Via Don Minzoni 13; ☉ 10am-1pm & 3-7pm Mar-Oct).

For information about local artisans, see www.arteinbottegavolterra.it.

Boutique del Tartufo
FOOD

(☑ 348 7121883; www.boutiquedeltartufo.it; Via Matteotti 5; ☉ 10.30am-7.30pm Wed-Mon summer, 10.30am-12.30pm & 2.30-6.30pm winter) Stefania Socchi's husband Daniele is a professional truffle hunter, and sources the tasty fungi that are used to produce the products sold in this shop near Piazza dei Priori. Purchase whole truffles or opt for honey, polenta, pasta, oil or pastes made or infused with them. You can also order a *panino* made with truffle paste or truffle-infused cheese (€6).

Centro di Restauro CPRCA
STATIONERY

(☑ 0588 8 12 67; www.facebook.com/restaurocarta; Via Roma 9; ☉ 8.30am-12.30pm & 3.30-7.30pm Mon-Fri, 8.30am-12.30pm Sat) This paper and parchment restoration laboratory is used by major cultural organisations and institutions around the country. It offers short courses on artistic book binding and also has some hand-made paper products for sale.

Fabula Etrusca
JEWELLERY

(☑ 0588 8 74 01; www.fabulaetrusca.it; Via Lungo Le Mura del Mandorlo 10; ☉ 10am-7pm Easter-Christmas) Distinctive pieces in 18-carat gold – many based on Etruscan designs – are handmade in this workshop on Volterra's northern walls.

ℹ Information

Associazione Pro Loco Volterra (☑ 0588 8 61 50; www.provolterra.it; Piazza dei Priori 10; ☉ 9am-12.30pm & 3-6pm Mon-Sat, 9am-12.30pm Sun) Helpful, volunteer-run service gives tourist advice, sells bus tickets and provides luggage storage (two hours/extra hour/day €3/1/6).

Tourist Office (☑ 0588 8 60 99; www.volterratur.it; Piazza dei Priori 19; ☉ 9.30am-1pm & 2-6pm) Extremely efficient and friendly, this office provides free maps, books hotels and tours, and rents out an audio guide tour of the town (€5).

ℹ Getting There & Away

BUS

Volterra's **bus station** is in Piazza Martiri della Libertà. Buy tickets at *tabacchi* or Associazione Pro Loco Volterra. Note bus services are greatly reduced on Sundays.

CTT (☑ 800 570530; www.pisa.cttnord.it) buses connect Volterra with Pisa (€6.90, two to 2½ hours, 11 daily Monday to Saturday, one Sunday) via Pontedera (€5.60, 1½ hours).

You'll need to go to Colle di Val d'Elsa (€3.50, 50 minutes, four Monday to Saturday) to catch a connecting Tiemme (p155) service (four Monday to Saturday, one Sunday) to San Gimignano (€3.50, 35 minutes), Siena (€3.90, 30 to 40 minutes) or Florence (€6.80, 65 minutes).

CAR & MOTORCYCLE

Volterra is accessed via the SR68, which runs between Cecina on the coast and Colle di Val d'Elsa, just off the Siena–Florence autostrada.

A ZTL applies in the historic centre. The most convenient car park is beneath Piazza Martiri della Libertà (€2/15 per hour/day). Whether charges apply in other car parks encircling the town is seasonal and subject to change. The tourist office can give updates.

VAL D'ORCIA

The picturesque agricultural valley of Val d'Orcia is a Unesco World Heritage Site, as is the historic centre of Pienza (on its northeastern edge, and a good base for exploring the Val d'Orcia). The valley's distinctive landscape features flat chalk plains, out of which rise almost conical hills topped with fortified settlements and magnificent abbeys that were once important staging points on the Via Francigena. Pretty as a picture, the medieval hilltop village of Monticchiello, 10km south of Pienza, makes an alternative tranquil base for exploring the Val d'Orcia.

For information about places, activities and events in the Val d'Orcia see www.par codellavaldorcia.com.

Montalcino
📞 0577 / POP 5919

Known globally as the home of one of the world's great wines, Brunello di Montalcino, the attractive hilltop town of Montalcino has a remarkable number of *enoteche* lining its medieval streets and is surrounded by hugely picturesque vineyards. There's history to explore too: the town's efforts to hold out against Florence even after Siena had fallen earned it the title 'the Republic of Siena in Montalcino', and there are many well-preserved medieval buildings within the historic city walls.

◉ Sights & Activities

To save a couple of euros for your wine fund, purchase a combined ticket (adult/reduced €6/4.50) for entry to the Fortezza's ramparts and the Museo Civico e Diocesano d'Arte Sacra. These are available from the tourist office (p184).

Fortezza di Montalcino · HISTORIC BUILDING
(📞0577 84 92 11; Piazzale Fortezza; courtyard free, ramparts adult/reduced €4/2; ⊙9am-8pm Apr-Oct, 10am-6pm Nov-Mar) This imposing 14th-century structure was expanded under the Medici dukes and now dominates Montalcino's skyline. You can sample and purchase local wines in its enoteca (www.enotecala fortezza.com; ⊙9am-8pm, 10am-6pm in winter) and also climb up to the fort's ramparts. Buy a ticket for the ramparts at the bar.

Museo Civico e Diocesano d'Arte Sacra MUSEUM
(📞0577 84 60 14; www.facebook.com/museo civicoediocesanoearcheologicamontalcino; Via Ricasoli 31; adult/reduced €4.50/3; ⊙10am-1pm & 2-5.40pm Tue-Sun Sep-Mar, 10am-1pm & 2-5.50pm Apr-Oct) Occupying the former convent of the neighbouring Chiesa di Sant'Agostino, this collection of religious art from the town and surrounding region includes a triptych

by Duccio and a *Madonna and Child* by Simone Martini. Other artists represented include the Lorenzetti brothers, Giovanni di Paolo and Sano di Pietro.

🛏 Sleeping

Central Montalcino cooks up a couple of solid midrange options; otherwise, the dreamiest addresses are a short drive away.

Albergo Il Giglio HOTEL €€
(📞0577 84 81 67; www.gigliohotel.com; Via Soccorso Saloni 5; s €95, d €150; ﷽🖳) There's a real old-world feel at this family-run place, something enhanced by the traditional Tuscan fireplace in the lounge and the brass bedsteads and arched ceilings in the 12 comfortable rooms. The views from upstairs windows are captivating – try to score room 1, which has its own panoramic terrace.

Hotel Vecchia Oliviera HOTEL €€
(📞0577 84 60 28; www.vecchiaoliviera.com; Via Landi 1; r €145-180; 🅿﷽🖳🏊) Chandeliers, polished wooden floors and rugs lend this converted oil mill a refined, albeit slightly worn, air. Of the 11 rooms on offer, opt for one in the superior category as these have great views (number 9 is best). The pool is in an attractive garden setting and the terrace has wrap-around views. Breakfast is disappointing.

★ La Bandita BOUTIQUE HOTEL €€€
(📞333 4046704; www.la-bandita.com; Podere La Bandita, Località La Foce; r €250-550, self-contained ste €550; ⊙Apr-early Nov; 🅿﷽@🖳🏊) Sophisticated urban style melds with stupendous scenery at this rural retreat in one of the most stunning sections of the Val d'Orcia. Owned and operated by a former NYC music executive and his travel-writer wife (non–Lonely Planet, we hasten to add), it offers spacious rooms, amenities galore (we love the Ortigia toiletries), communal dinners (set menu €45 per person) and personalised service.

★ Foresteria Podere Brizio AGRITURISMO €€€
(📞0577 04 10 72; www.poderebrizio.it; Località Podere Brizio; r €230-255; ⊙closed Dec-Easter; 🅿﷽🖳🏊) A huge amount of thought has gone into the design and construction of this splendid hotel on a wine estate 8km southwest of Montalcino, near Tavernelle. Room rates are relatively restrained considering the comfort and amenity levels in the spacious rooms and the wide array of facilities (huge swimming pool, restaurant, tennis court, spa).

EXPLORING BRUNELLO COUNTRY

One of Italy's most prized wines, Brunello di Montalcino is produced using 100% locally grown Sangiovese grapes. One of the first Italian wines awarded a Denominazione di Origine Controllata e Garantita (DOCG) designation, it must be aged a minimum of 24 months in oak barrels and four months in bottles, and cannot be released until five years after the vintage. Brunello Riserva – produced with the best grapes from the best harvests – must age for a minimum of 24 months in barrels and six months in bottles, and cannot be released until six years after the vintage. Brunello's substantially cheaper but eminently drinkable sibling is the Rosso di Montalcino DOC, which only needs to be aged for one year.

Brunello is currently produced by 200 or so wineries, using grapes grown within a 24,000-hectare region surrounding the medieval hilltop town of Montalcino and bordered by the rivers Ombrone, Asso and Orcia. Vineyards within the territory are planted in a variety of soils, including limestone, clay, schist, volcanic soil and a crumbly marl known as *galestro*. Altitudes range from 149m to 500m. North-facing slopes receive fewer hours of sunlight and are generally cooler than the south-facing slopes, meaning that their grapes ripen more slowly and tend to produce wines that are light and elegant. Vineyards on the southern and western slopes receive more sun and more maritime wind, which lead to wines with more power and complexity.

Many of the wine estates in Brunello country offer visitors the chance to taste and purchase their wines in on-site *cantine*. Those particularly well set-up for wine tourism include the following:

Cantina di Montalcino (☑0577 84 87 04; www.cantinadimontalcino.it; Località Val di Cava, off Strada Provinciale del Brunello; ⊙8.30am-6.30pm) Located 6km north of Montalcino, this cooperative is known for its distinctive modern winery building designed by Arezzo-based architecture firm Corrado Prosperi. Offers a 30-minute tour and tasting (€18 to €25, Monday to Saturday) as well as casual tastings (2/3/4 wines €6/9/12).

Castello Banfi (Castello di Poggio alle Mura; ☑0577 840111; https://castellobanfi.com; off SP117, Poggio alle Mura; tour & tasting €35, with 3-/4-/5-course lunch with matched wine €80/90/100; ⊙wine shop 10am-8pm late Mar-early Nov, to 6.30pm early Nov-late Mar) Huge American-owned estate built around an imposing medieval castle and incorporating a wine shop, two restaurants, luxury accommodation and a small museum of bottles and glass. Offers daily 75-minute guided tours (€35) that visit the vineyards, winery and *balsameria* (cellar where balsamic vinegar is aged) and include a guided tasting.

Ciacci Piccolomini d'Aragona (☑0577 83 56 16; www.ciaccipiccolomini.com; Località Molinello; ⊙9am-7pm Mon-Fri, 10.30am-6.30pm Sat Apr-Oct, 9am-6pm Mon-Fri Nov-Mar) Located near the Abbazia di Sant'Antimo, this 17th-century estate has a stylish modern tasting room that commands wonderful views over the vine-dominated landscape. Tastings are free with purchase; alternatively, book for a tour with a tasting and light lunch (€20).

Fattoria dei Barbi (☑0577 84 11 11; www.fattoriadeibarbi.it; Località Podernuovi 170; ⊙10am-7pm May-Sep, 11am-1.30pm & 2.30-5pm Oct-Apr) The Cinelli Colombini family has owned land in this part of Tuscany since 1352 and has been producing wine at this estate 4km southeast of Montalcino since 1790. They welcome visitors to their historic *cantina* for tastings (€2 to €10) and also have an on-site **restaurant** (☑0577 84 71 43; meals €30; ⊙12.30-2.30pm & 7-9pm Thu-Tue late Feb-early Jan; P) and **Brunello museum** (☑0577 84 61 04; www.fattoriadeibarbi.it/museo-del-brunello; adult/reduced €5/2.50; ⊙10am-12.30pm & 2.30-6pm Thu-Tue Easter-late Nov).

Poggio Antico (☑0577 84 80 44; www.poggioantico.com; Località Poggio Antico, off SP14; ⊙10am-7pm) Located 5km southwest of Montalcino, this 200-hectare estate welcomes visitors for a tour of the winery building and a paid tasting in its *cantina* (€15 to €25).

For more information about visiting wineries in the Montalcino region, go to the website of the **Consorzio del Vino Brunello di Montalcino** (www.consorziobrunellodimontalcino.it), which includes a handy list and map of producers.

EXPLORING THE VAL D'ORCIA

Few valleys are as magnificent as this – but then, the valley is a Unesco World Heritage Site. Stitched from vine-covered rolling hills, medieval abbeys and celebrity wine towns, the Val d'Orcia is among Tuscany's most beautiful road trips. Pilgrims following the Via Francigena to Rome trod the same route in medieval times and most rewards remain unchanged: peace, serenity, soul-soaring views, plus sensational food and wine...

❶ Abbazia di Sant'Antimo

From the medieval town of Montalcino, cruise along the SP55 south past vineyard after vineyard planted with the grapes used

in Tuscany's most-famous wine, Brunello. Arriving in Castelnuovo dell'Abate 11km later, get set for the ultimate swoon: the village looks down on the hauntingly beautiful, Romanesque church of Abbazia di Sant'Antimo

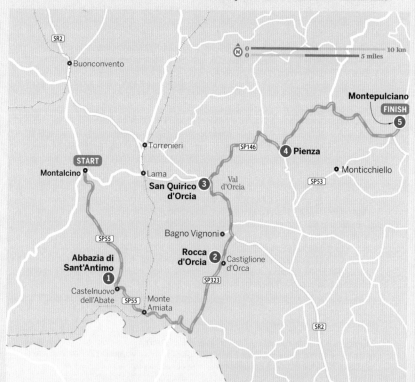

One Day 70km

Great for... Outdoors, History & Culture, Food & Drink

Best Time to Go May to October

(p186). Built in pale travertine stone, the abbey church positively glistens in the sunlight. If you're lucky, you might catch monks singing Gregorian chants.

❷ Rocca d'Orcia

Continue south on the SP55 and north on the SP323 towards Castiglione d'Orcia, admiring the sight of Tuscany's highest mountain, Monte Amiata, in the distance. These roads ride a ridge providing sweeping Val d'Orcia views, before twisting down then up through a quintessentially Tuscan landscape: honey-yellow farmhouses set amid rows of cypress trees and vines. Near Castiglione d'Orcia the stern mass of the **Rocca d'Orcia** (also called the Rocca di Tentennano) looms into view. This part-13th-century fortress clings to a limestone spur: follow signs to park beneath it and clamber up for a closer look, both at the castle and the landscape laid out like a living map far below.

❸ San Quirico d'Orcia

From the Rocca, the SP323 swoops down and joins the SR2, which leads to the charming hill town of San Quirico d'Orcia. Once a well-known stop on the Via Francigena pilgrimage route, the town is home to five medieval churches, a scattering of artisanal boutiques and a popular craft brewery, the Birrificio San Quirico (p185), where you should pause to sample one of the house brews. Leaving town, follow the SP146, one of Tuscany's most stupendously scenic roads. The views here are so postcard perfect that stopping for a photography session is obligatory.

❹ Pienza

Soon, the *duomo*-dominated skyline of the town of Pienza (p184) comes into view. Stop to admire its World Heritage–listed Piazza Pio II, take a guided tour of Palazzo Piccolomini and enjoy a coffee or *aperitivo* while admiring the panorama from the terrace of Bar Il Casello or Idyllium.

❺ Montepulciano

Head to your final destination: the enchanting medieval town of Montepulciano (p187), teetering on a narrow ridge of volcanic rock and seducing hordes of visitors with its exceptional portfolio of accommodation, dining options and wine-tasting opportunities – most with spectacular views over the Val di Chiana and Val d'Orcia.

DON'T MISS

PERFECTION ON A PLATE

Sometimes simple dishes are the hardest to perfect – and perfection is the only term to use when discussing Il Leccio (☑ 0577 84 41 75; www.illeccio. net; Via Costa Castellare 1/3, Sant'Angelo in Colle; meals €30; ⊙ noon-3pm & 7-10pm Thu-Tue; ☑), an unforgettable trattoria in Brunello heartland. Watching the chef make his way between his stove and kitchen garden to gather produce for each order puts a whole new spin on the word 'fresh', and both the results and the house Brunello are spectacular. Be sure to order the *grande antipasti* (large enough for two to share) and ask about daily specials.

Sant'Angelo in Colle is 10km southwest of Montalcino along Via del Sole (or 10km west of the Abbazia di Sant'Antimo along an unsealed but signed road through vineyards).

✗ Eating & Drinking

For a small town, Montalcino has a surprisingly large number of eateries. You'll have no trouble sourcing a good meal here. The town's weekly market is held on Friday mornings in the streets near the fortress and showcases plenty of local produce.

Trattoria L'Angolo   TUSCAN €

(☑ 0577 84 80 17; Via Ricasoli 9; meals €22; ⊙ noon-3pm Wed-Mon Sep-Jun, noon-3pm & 7-11pm Wed-Mon Jul & Aug) We thought about keeping shtum about this place (everyone loves to keep a secret or two), but it seemed selfish not to share our love for its pasta dishes. Be it vegetarian (ravioli stuffed with ricotta and truffles) or carnivorous (*pappardelle* with wild-boar sauce), the handmade *primi* (first courses) here are uniformly excellent. *Secondi* aren't as impressive.

★ Re di Macchia   TUSCAN €€

(☑ 0577 84 61 16; redimacchia@alice.it; Via Soccorso Saloni 21; meals €35, set menus €27; ⊙ noon-2pm & 7-9pm Fri-Wed; ☑) Husband-and-wife team Antonio and Roberta run this relaxed eatery in the centre of town with great aplomb. Roberta's cooking is much more sophisticated than the Tuscan average but retains the usual laudable focus on local, seasonal produce. Antonio's excellent and affordable wine list is one of the best in town.

Enoteca Osteria Osticcio   TUSCAN €€€

(☑ 0577 84 80 46; www.osticcio.it; Via Giacomo Matteotti 23; meal €75; ⊙ 12.30-2.30pm & 7.30-10pm Tue-Sun mid-Feb–mid-Dec; ☀) In a town overflowing with *enoteche*, this is definitely one of the best. Choose a bottle from a huge selection of Italian and European wines on offer (including loads of Brunello) and then relax over a selection of well-executed modern Tuscan dishes. You can order à la carte or opt for a six-course set menu with wine match (€130).

Drogheria Franci   ITALIAN €€€

(☑ 0577 84 81 91; www.locandafranci.com; Piazzale Fortezza 6; meals €46; ⊙ 12.30-3pm & 7.15-9.45pm, later in Jul & Aug; ☀ ☎) A perfect example of the sleekly styled wine bar that is trending in Tuscany today, Franci offers a menu that takes more than a few liberties when presenting traditional dishes – think exciting flavour combinations, refined plating and pared-back serving sizes. Seating is in an old *drogheria* (grocery store) that has been given a modern makeover, or on two outdoor terraces.

ⓘ Information

Tourist Office (☑ 0577 84 93 31; www.prolocomontalcino.com; Costa del Municipio 1; ⊙ 10am-1pm & 2-5.40pm, closed Mon winter) Just off the main square, this office can supply free copies of the *Consorzio del Vino Brunello di Montalcino* map of wineries and also books cellar-door visits and winery accommodation.

ⓘ Getting There & Away

BUS

Tiemme (p155) buses run between Montalcino and Siena (€5.60, 75 minutes, six daily Monday to Saturday, two daily Sunday). The bus stop is near the Hotel Vecchia Oliviera (p180).

CAR & MOTORCYCLE

To reach Montalcino from Siena, take the SS2 (Via Cassia); after Buonconvento, turn off onto the SP45. There's plenty of parking around the *fortezza* and in Via Pietro Strozzi (€1.50 per hour, 8am to 8pm).

Pienza

☑ 0578 / POP 2082

Once a sleepy hamlet, pretty Pienza was transformed when, in 1459, Pope Pius II began turning his home village into an ideal Renaissance town. The result is magnificent – the church, papal palace, town hall and accompanying buildings in and around Piazza Pio II went up in just three years and haven't been remodelled since. In 1996 Unesco added the town's historic centre to its World Heritage list, citing the revolutionary vision of urban space. On weekends, Pienza draws big crowds; come midweek if you possibly can.

⊙ Sights

A cumulative ticket (adult/student €5/3.50) covers access to both the Museo Diocesano and the baptistry.

★ Duomo   CATHEDRAL
(Concattedrale di Santa Maria Assunta; Piazza Pio II; ⊙7.30am-1pm & 2-7pm) Pienza's *duomo* was built on the site of the Romanesque Chiesa di Santa Maria, of which little remains. The Renaissance church with its handsome travertine facade was commissioned by Pius II, who was so proud of the building that he issued a papal bull in 1462 forbidding any changes to it. The interior is a strange mix of Gothic and Renaissance styles and contains a superb marble tabernacle by Rossellino housing a relic of St Andrew the Apostle, Pienza's patron saint.

Piazza Pio II   PIAZZA
Stand in this magnificent square and spin 360 degrees. You've just taken in an overview of Pienza's major monuments. Gems of the Renaissance constructed in a mere three years between 1459 and 1462, they're arranged according to the urban design of Bernardo Rossellino, who applied the principles of Renaissance town planning devised by his mentor, Leon Battista Alberti.

Palazzo Borgia   PALACE
(Palazzo Vescovile; Piazza Pio II) The future Pope Alexander VI, then just Cardinal Roderigo Borgia, was gifted this palace by Pius II and subsequently modified and enlarged it in 1492. It's home to the Museo Diocesano (☑0578 74 99 05; www.palazzoborgia.it; Corso il Rossellino 30; adult/reduced €4.50/3; ⊙10.30am-1.30pm & 2.30-6pm Wed-Mon mid-Mar–Oct, 10am-1pm & 2-5pm Sat & Sun Nov–mid-Mar) and the tourist office (p187). Enter via the courtyard onto Corso il Rossellino.

Palazzo Piccolomini   PALACE
(☑0577 28 63 00; www.palazzopiccolominipienza.it; Piazza Pio II; adult/reduced with guided tour €7/5; ⊙10am-6pm Tue-Sun mid-Mar–Oct, to 4pm mid-Oct–mid-Mar, closed mid-Jan–mid-Feb & 2nd half Nov) This magnificent palace was the residence of Pope Pius II, and is considered Bernardo Rossellino's masterpiece. Built on the site of the pope's family houses, it features a fine courtyard, a handsome staircase and the former papal apartments, which are filled with period furnishings and minor art. To the rear, a three-level loggia offers a spectacular panorama over the Val d'Orcia far below. Visitors follow a multilanguage audio tour; peeking into the courtyard is free.

LOCAL KNOWLEDGE

CRAFT BEER
When wine tires, recharge your tastebuds at Birrificio San Quirico (☑347 2646227; www.birrificiosanquirico.it; Via Dante Alighieri 93, San Quirico d'Orcia; ⊙9am-midnight summer, reduced hr rest of yr), a sleek but petite brewery and tap room run by craft-beer devotee Roberto Rappuoli. You'll find it in the fortified medieval hill town of San Quirico d'Orcia, 10km southwest of Pienza along the SP146. Specialising in wheat beers, he offers eight varieties including the Iris, a blonde ale named after writer Iris Origo (p191), and the Giulitta, an English-style pale ale named after San Quirico's patron saint.

For dedicated craft-beer aficionados, Central Tuscany's other key tipple is brewpub Vapori di Birra (☑328 2334464, 0588 2 61 56; www.vaporidibirra.it; Via dei Lagoni 25, Sasso Pisano; ⊙11am-11pm daily Easter-Oct, closed Mon-Thu Nov-Easter; ⊛) ⌀, 47km south of Volterra (and 24km north of Massa Marittima in Southern Tuscany) in the Val de Cecina. A member of the Comunità del Cibo a Energie Rinnovabili della Toscana (www.comunitadelciboenergierinnovabili.it), a network of food producers in the Val di Cecina that use the area's renewable geothermal energy in their production processes, this brewpub is a popular local hangout on summer evenings and weekends. Its talented female brewers make eight beers, including the eminently drinkable Geyser Pale Ale.

Sleeping

⭐ **La Bellavita**   B&B €€
(☑ 391 4392068; www.labellavitapienza.it; Via della Chiochina 1; r €90-140; ⊗ closed Christmas; ❄ 🛜) Host Elisabetta goes out of her way to make guests feel at home in her cute four-room B&B. It can be hard to find – enter through the arch next to 81 Corso il Rossellino – but once you've arrived you'll be charmed by the clean and comfortable rooms, panoramic terrace and cute attic where a delicious buffet breakfast is served.

⭐ **La Bandita Townhouse**   BOUTIQUE HOTEL €€€
(☑ 0578 74 90 05; www.la-bandita.com/townhouse; Corso il Rossellino 111; r €350-€595; ⊗ mid-Mar–early Jan; ❄ @ 🛜) Aiming to provide their guests with a taste of Tuscan village life and Pienza with a world-class boutique hotel, the American owners of this boutique hotel purchased and renovated a Renaissance-era convent close to Piazza Pio – the result is both sensitive and supremely stylish. Facilities include a communal lounge with an honesty bar and a restaurant with a garden terrace.

 Eating

Townhouse Caffè   ITALIAN €€
(☑ 0578 74 90 05; www.la-bandita.com/townhouse/the-restaurant; Via San Andrea 8; meals €40; ⊗ noon-2.30pm Tue-Sun, 7.30-10pm daily mid-Mar–early Jan; 🛜 ☑) The menu at this chic eatery is pared back in more ways than one: there are around four choices per course, presentation is minimalist and the emphasis is on the quality of the produce rather than clever culinary tricks – bravo! In summer, guests dine in an atmospheric medieval courtyard; in winter, the action moves into a two-room space with open kitchen.

La Terrazza del Chiostro   ITALIAN €€€
(☑ 349 5676148, 0578 74 81 83; www.laterrazzadelchiostro.it; Via del Balzello; meals €55; ⊗ 12.15-2.45pm & 7.15-10pm Thu-Tue, closed mid-Nov–mid-Mar, open Wed in high summer; ❄ 🛜) Dining on this gorgeous terrace with its panoramic view is the stuff of which lasting travel memories are made, and the food also has plenty of pizzazz – to fully appreciate it, opt for a set menu (from €45) and choose a wine match from the restaurant's impressive wine selection.

🍷 **Drinking & Nightlife**

Coffee breaks in Pienza are best spent at one of the cafes around Piazza Pio II.

⭐ **Idyllium**   BAR
(☑ 0578 74 81 76; www.facebook.com/idylliumbar; Via Gozzante 67; ⊗ 11am-2am summer, reduced hours rest of year) Located underneath Palazzo Piccolomini and accessed via the staircase between the palace and the *duomo*, this hybrid cafe and cocktail bar in the former palace stables has a terrace with wonderful views over the Val d'Orcia and towards Monte Amiata. Owners Bledar Ndoci and Federico Fioravanti learned their mixology art in Milan and definitely make the best cocktails in town.

OFF THE BEATEN TRACK

ABBAZIA DI SANT'ANTIMO

This serenely beautiful, Romanesque abbey (☑ 0577 28 63 00; www.antimo.it; ⊗ 10am-7pm Apr-Oct, to 5pm Nov-Mar) FREE lies in an isolated valley just below the village of Castelnuovo dell'Abate, 11km from Montalcino.

Tradition tells us that Charlemagne founded the original monastery here in 781. The exterior of the abbey's church, built in pale travertine stone, is simple except for the stone carvings, which include various fantastical animals. Inside, study the capitals of the columns lining the nave, especially the one representing Daniel in the lion's den (second on the right as you enter). Below it is a particularly intense polychrome 13th-century *Madonna and Child* and there's a haunting 12th-century *Crucifixion* above the main altar. The church, crypt, upper loggia, chapel, pharmacy and garden can be visited with a rented videoguide (€6), and there is also a dedicated videoguide to the church (€3).

It's a two- to three-hour walk from Montalcino to the abbey. The route starts next to the police station near the main roundabout in town; many visitors choose to walk to the abbey and return by bus (€1.50, 10 minutes, four daily) – check the timetable with the tourist office (p184) in Montalcino.

Bar Il Casello   BAR

(📞 0578 74 91 05; Via del Casello 3; ⏱ noon-8pm Wed, Thu & Sun, 6pm-midnight Fri, noon-midnight Sat) A local secret that we hereby expose, this bar next to the *belvedere* (scenic viewpoint) behind Piazza Pio II is a perfect place to enjoy an *aperitivo* – the sunset vistas are simply stupendous. It's also a popular spot for an afternoon coffee.

🛈 Information

Tourist Office (📞 0578 74 99 05; info.turismo @comune.pienza.si.it; Corso il Rossellino 30; ⏱ 10.30am-1.30pm & 2.30-6pm Wed-Mon mid-Mar–Oct, 10am-1pm & 2-5pm Sat & Sun Nov–mid-Mar) Located off the ground-floor courtyard in Palazzo Borgia. It supplies a town map but offers few other services.

🛈 Getting There & Away

Four Tiemme (p155) buses run Monday to Saturday between Siena and Pienza (€6, 70 minutes, two daily) and eight travel to/from Montepulciano (€2.60, 20 minutes). The bus stops are on Via della Madonnina, near the police station. Buy tickets at Pancaffè Il Chicco nearby.

MONTEPULCIANO

📞 0578 / POP 13,984

Exploring the medieval town of Montepulciano, perched on a reclaimed narrow ridge of volcanic rock, will push your quadriceps to failure point. When this happens, self-medicate with a generous pour of the highly reputed Vino Nobile while also drinking in the spectacular views over the Val di Chiana and Val d'Orcia.

⊙ Sights

Il Corso   STREET

Montepulciano's main street – called in stages Via di Gracciano, Via di Voltaia, Via dell'Opio and Via Poliziano – climbs up the eastern ridge of the town from Porta al Prato and loops to meet Via di Collazzi on the western ridge. To reach the centre of town (Piazza Grande), take a dog-leg turn into Via del Teatro.

In Piazza Savonarola, up from the Porta al Prato, is the Colonna del Marzocca, erected in 1511 to confirm Montepulciano's allegiance to Florence. The late-Renaissance Palazzo Avignonesi is at No. 91 Via di Gracciano nel Corso. Other notable buildings include the Palazzo di Bucelli at No. 73 (look for the recycled Etruscan and Latin inscriptions and reliefs on the lower facade) and Palazzo Cocconi at No. 70.

Continuing uphill, you'll find Michelozzo's Chiesa di Sant'Agostino (Piazza Michelozzo; ⏱ 9am-noon & 3-6pm), with its lunette above the entrance holding a terracotta Madonna and Child, John the Baptist and St Augustine. Opposite, the Torre di Pulcinella, a medieval tower house, is topped by the town clock and the hunched figure of Pulcinella (Punch, of Punch and Judy fame), which strikes the hours. After passing historic Caffè Poliziano (p192), the Corso continues straight ahead and Via del Teatro veers off to the right.

Piazza Grande   PIAZZA

Elegant Piazza Grande is the town's highest point and main meeting place. If you think it looks familiar, it might be because it featured in *New Moon*, the second movie in the *Twilight* series based on Stephenie Meyer's vampire novels. They shot the main crowd scene here, despite the book being set in Volterra. More recently, it features in episodes of the television series *Medici: Masters of Florence*.

Palazzo Comunale   PALACE

(Piazza Grande; terrace & tower adult/reduced €5/2.50, terrace only €2.50; ⏱ 10am-6pm Apr-Christmas) Built in the 14th century in Gothic style and remodelled in the 15th century by Michelozzo, the Palazzo Comunale still functions as Montepulciano's town hall. Head up the 67 narrow stairs to the tower to enjoy extraordinary views – you'll see as far as Pienza, Montalcino and even, on a clear day, Siena.

Duomo   CATHEDRAL

(Cattedrale di Santa Maria Assunta; www.mon tepulcianochiusipienza.it; Piazza Grande; ⏱ 8am-7pm) Montepulciano's 16th-century *duomo* is striking, largely because its unfinished facade gives the building a stern, heavily weathered look. Inside, don't miss Taddeo di Bartolo's ornate *Assumption* triptych (1401) behind the high altar and Sano di Pietro's *Madonna del pilastro* (Madonna of the Pillar; 15th century) on the eastern wall of the nave.

Museo Civico &
Pinacoteca Crociani   MUSEUM

(📞 0578 71 73 00; www.museocivicomontepul ciano.it; Via Ricci 10; adult/reduced €6/4; ⏱ 10am-6.30pm Wed-Mon Apr-Oct, to 6pm Sat & Sun Nov-Mar) It was a curatorial dream come true: in 2011 a painting in the collection of this modest art gallery was attributed to Caravaggio.

Montepulciano

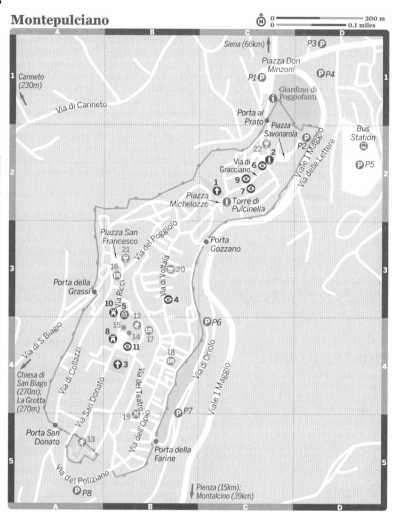

The work, *Portrait of a Man,* is thought to portray Cardinal Scipione Borghese, the artist's patron. It's now accompanied by a touch-screen interpretation that allows you to explore details of the painting, its restoration and diagnostic attribution. Other works here include two terracottas by Andrea Della Robbia, and Domenico Beccafumi's painting of the town's patron saint, Agnese.

Chiesa di San Biago CHURCH
(☑ 0577 28 63 00; www.tempiosanbiago.it; Via di San Biago; incl audio guide €3.50; ⊙ 10am-6pm Mar-May & Oct, 9.30am-7pm Jun-Sep, 10am-5pm Sat & Sun Nov-Feb) Designed by Antonio da

Sangallo (Sangallo il Vecchio) and constructed in the late-16th century, this splendid Renaissance church in the valley below the upper town has a distinctive central dome and pyramid-topped bell tower. The church is dedicated to San Biago (St Blaise), the Armenian-born martyred patron saint of wool combers.

🏃 Activities

Enoliteca Consortile WINE
(www.enolitecavinonobile.it; Fortezza di Montepulciano, Via San Donato 21; ⊙ 2-6pm Mon, Wed & Thu, 11am-6pm Fri, 10.30am-7pm Sat & Sun) Operated

Montepulciano

⊙ Sights
1 Chiesa di Sant'Agostino C2
2 Colonna del Marzocca C2
3 Duomo B4
4 Il Corso B3
5 Museo Civico & Pinacoteca Crociani ... B3
6 Palazzo Avignonesi C2
7 Palazzo Cocconi C2
8 Palazzo Comunale B4
9 Palazzo di Bucelli C2
10 Palazzo Ricci B3
11 Piazza Grande B4

⊕ Activities, Courses & Tours
    Cantina de' Ricci .... (see 10)
12 Cantina Storica Talosa B4
13 Enoliteca Consortile A5

14 Strada del Vino Nobile di
    Montepulciano e dei Sapori
    della Valdichianna Senese B4
15 Urban Bikery B4

⊜ Sleeping
16 Camere Bellavista B3
17 Meublè Il Riccio B4
18 Palazzo Carletti B4

⊗ Eating
19 Osteria Acquacheta B5

⊙ Drinking & Nightlife
20 Caffè Poliziano B3
21 E Lucevan Le Stelle B3
22 La Vineria C2

by Montepulciano's consortium of local wine producers, this recently opened showcase of Vino Nobile on the ground floor of the Medicean fortress has a modern tasting room offering over 70 wines for tasting and purchase. Buy a €10 or €15 card, use it to pour the tipples of your choice and direct your own tasting.

Cantina de' Ricci   WINE

(✆0578 75 71 66; www.cantinadericci.it; Via Ricci 11; ⊘10.30am-7pm mid-Mar–early Jan, Sat & Sun only early Jan–mid-Mar) **FREE** The most evocative of Montepulciano's wine cellars, this *cantina* lies at the foot of a steep winding staircase in the Renaissance-era Palazzo Ricci (✆0578 75 60 22; www.palazzoricci.com). Immense vaulted stone encasements surround two-storey-high barrels. Dimly lit and hushed, it's like a cathedral of wine. Entry is free, as will be your first two tastings.

Cantina Storica Talosa   WINE

(✆0578 75 79 29; www.talosa.it; Via Talosa 8; ⊘10.30am-7pm, reduced hr Jan & Feb) **FREE** The underground tunnels in this *cantina* were hewn out of tufa by the Etruscans and are now filled with huge oak barriques. Look out for the sea fossils in the tufa – they're five million years old. There's also an Etruscan tomb dating from the 6th century BC to visit. Tastings are free, but the expectation is that you'll purchase a bottle.

Canneto   WINE

(✆0578 757 737; www.canneto.com; Via dei Canneti 14; tasting of 4 wines €15, tour & tasting €25; ⊘10am-7pm Mon-Fri Apr-Oct, 9am-5pm Mon-Fri Nov-Mar) An easy walk from Montepulciano's upper town, this winery has 50 hectares of prime agricultural land planted with grapes and olive trees. It produces a Nobile, three IGTs (including two whites) and a Rosso, all of which can be tasted in Canneto's modern *cantina*. After tasting, buy a bottle and a tasting plate of local produce (€15) and enjoy the lovely vineyard view.

🏃 Out of Town

★ Avignonesi Winery – Le Capezzine   WINE

(✆0578 72 43 04; www.avignonesi.it; Via Colonica 1, Valiano; ⊘10am-6pm Mon-Fri Mar & Apr, 10am-7pm Mon-Sat, noon-6pm Sun May-Sep, 10am-6pm Mon-Sat Oct, 10am-5pm Mon-Fri Nov & Dec, closed Jan & Feb) Part of the legendary Avignonesi company, this 19-hectare organic estate is known for its 'Round Vineyard', which was designed to establish to what extent the quality of wine is influenced by planting density. No bookings are needed to enjoy a guided tasting (from €15), glass of wine (from €5 per glass) and tasting board (€25) in the *cantina*.

★ Palazzo Vecchio Winery   WINE

(✆0578 72 41 70; www.vinonobile.it; Via Terra Rossa 5, Valiano; ⊘10am-5pm) Idyllic is the first word that comes to mind when describing this wine estate. Its large 14th-century stone farmhouse is surrounded by fruit trees, the winery is in converted outbuildings, and 25 hectares of vineyards planted with Sangiovese, Canaiolo and Mammolo grapes cascade down the hillsides. A tour and tasting (€20 to €35 per person, €60 to €70 with lunch) are by reservation only.

☞ Tours

★ Urban Bikery
CYCLING

(☑ 377 5453297; www.urbanbikery.it; Via Ricci 2; per 2hr/half-day/day €40/45/65; ⊙ 9.30am-7pm Mar-Oct, 11am-6pm Nov-Feb) What a clever idea! This recently established outfit rents out specially customised off-road e-bikes with attached GPS devices that have been programmed with cycling routes in the Montepulciano area. It also offers two guided tours: a four-hour, 22km e-bike experience that includes tastings at two wine estates (€110) and a four-hour, 22km experience passing through local landscapes immortalised in cinema (€99).

Strada del Vino Nobile di Montepulciano e dei Sapori della Valdichiana Senese
TOURS

(☑ 0578 71 74 84; www.stradavinonobile.it; Piazza Grande 7; ⊙ 9.30am-1.30pm & 2.30-6pm Mon-Fri, 10am-1pm & 2-5pm Sat, 10am-1pm Sun, closed Sat & Sun Jan-Mar) This organisation of local wine and food producers, hospitality businesses and municipalities organises a huge range of tours and courses, including cooking courses (€115 to €170), vineyard tours (€69 to €115) and vineyard walking tours that culminate in wine tasting (€49 to €69). Book in advance online or at its information office.

⚝ Festivals & Events

Montepulciano Calici di Stelle
WINE

(Glasses of Stars; www.calicidistellemontepulciano.it; ⊙ Aug) Organised by the Strada del Vino Nobile di Montepulciano e dei Sapori della Valdichiana Senese, this popular evening

---

BAGNI SAN FILIPPO

Medieval pilgrims walking the Via Francigena from Canterbury to Rome loved pausing in this part of central Tuscany to enjoy a long therapeutic soak in its thermal springs. If you're keen to do the same, consider avoiding the famous thermal institute in Bagno Vignoni and instead head to the open-air cascades (⊙ 24hr) FREE in this tiny village 16km south of Pienza. You'll find them just uphill from Hotel le Terme – follow signs to 'Fosso Bianco' down a lane for about 150m. Your destination is a series of mini pools, fed by hot, tumbling cascades of water. A free al fresco spa!

---

event features wine tastings, live music and performances of traditional flag throwing and drumming in Piazza Grande.

Bravio delle Botti
CULTURAL

(www.braviodellebotti.com; ⊙ Aug) Members of Montepulciano's eight *contrade* push 80kg wine barrels uphill in this race held on the last Sunday in August. There are also Renaissance-themed celebrations during the week before.

🛏 Sleeping

There are plenty of accommodation choices within Montepulciano and in the surrounding countryside.

Camere Bellavista
HOTEL €

(☑ 0578 75 73 48; www.camerebellavista.it; Via Ricci 25; r €70-120; ᴘ 🅢) As this budget hotel is four storeys tall and sits on the edge of the old town, the views live up to its name. The styling is heritage rustic with exposed beams, hefty wooden furniture, brass bedsteads and smart new bathrooms. The owner isn't resident, so phone ahead to be met with the key. No breakfast; cash only.

Agriturismo Nobile
AGRITURISMO €€

(☑ 340 7904752, 347 7252853; www.agriturismonobile.it; Strada per Chianciano, Località San Benedetto; d €100, apt €150-220; ᴘ🅟🅢🅧) In the 15th century they were sheds and hen houses; now they're five rustic-chic self-contained apartments. Some have big open fireplaces and many feature grandstand views of Montepulciano, which is only 1km away. There are also five cheaper, simpler rooms in the 15th-century farmhouse; rates for these include breakfast. In high season there's a three-night minimum stay. Very kid friendly.

Meublè Il Riccio
B&B €€

(☑ 0578 75 77 13; www.ilriccio.net; Via Talosa 21; s €80, d €100-110, ste €150-180; ᴘ🅟@🅢) Owned by the same family for over 800 years, this atmospheric B&B offers a choice of comfortable standard and superior rooms with tea/coffee set-up and satellite TVs – opt for a superior with a balcony if possible. It has a large breakfast salon and a terrace with a spectacular view. An indifferent breakfast costs €8 – you're better off heading to Caffè Poliziano (p192).

Palazzo Carletti
BOUTIQUE HOTEL €€€

(☑ 0578 75 60 80; www.palazzocarletti.it; 1st fl, Via dell'Opio nel Corso 3; s €150-225, d €205-240, ste €220-280; ᴘ🅢) Occupying the *piano nobile*

IRIS ORIGO & THE GARDENS AT LA FOCE

Of the many foreigners who chose to make Tuscany their home in the early decades of the 20th century, Iris Origo made one of the greatest impacts. Born in 1902, her wealthy American father died when she was only seven years old and she was raised by her neurotic Anglo-Irish mother, Sybil. Choosing to live in Fiesole, Sybil rented a villa built by the Medicis and threw herself into the intellectual and artistic circles of the Anglo-Florentines, which were dominated by the charismatic figure of art historian Bernard Berenson. Iris grew up in a privileged and artistic milieu populated with expats, extroverts and eccentrics. By the time she turned 21, she had decided to marry an urbane Florentine, Antonio Origo, and settle down permanently in the countryside with him to lead a more meaningful life.

In 1924, Iris and Antonio purchased a run-down farm estate called La Foce in the Val d'Orcia and set about restoring its main 16th-century building and improving the long-neglected farm. Having grown up in one of Fiesole's most beautiful villas, Iris was keen to make improvements to her new house, which had originally been used as an inn for pilgrims walking the Via Francigena. She engaged one of her oldest friends, fashionable English architect Cecil Pinsent (1884–1963), to first renovate the house and then – over a period of 15 years – create a series of splendid landscaped gardens that have been lovingly maintained and can now be visited on guided tours (☑ 0578 6 91 01; www.lafoce.com; Strada della Vittoria 61, off SP40; adult/child under 12 €10/free; ⊙ tour & entry 3pm, 4pm, 5pm & 6pm Wed, 11.30am, 3pm & 4.30pm Sat & Sun last weekend Apr-Oct). The tours visit the elegant *limonaia* (greenhouse where lemon trees are protected over winter); the fountain garden with its travertine water feature, manicured hedges and flower beds; a fragrant wisteria walk; and a stunning lower garden with geometric plantings of cypress trees, double box hedges and a distant backdrop of Monte Amiata.

In the tours, guides describe the lives of Iris and Antonio; their collaboration with Pinsent; their experiences at La Foce during WWII, when they sheltered and aided partisans, refugees and allied troops (recounted by Iris in her celebrated 1947 memoir *War in Val d'Orcia*); and their socially progressive initiatives in education and health care for the estate's workers. As extraordinary as it sounds, Iris was able to do all of this, raise two children (a third died in his infancy), travel across the globe, conduct two passionate extra-marital affairs and write 12 books across a wide variety of subjects, including an autobiography, *Images and Shadows* (1970). Her last work, a book of essays titled *A Need to Testify,* was published in 1984, only a few years before her death in 1988, aged 86.

Post-tour, indulge in a long and lazy lunch at Dopolavoro La Foce (☑ 0578 75 40 25; www.dopolavorolafoce.it; Strada della Vittoria/SP40 90; meals €30, sandwiches €5-9; ⊙ 8am-11pm Tue-Sun late Mar-Oct; ᴘ 🛜 ✍), a *dopolavoro* (recreational club) from 1939 recently transformed into a stylish space with a contemporary vibe. The rear garden is a textbook exercise in Tuscan chic – perfect for summer dining – and the menu is equally on trend: vegetarian pastas, burgers, flatbread sandwiches, craft beers and organic juices.

(main floor) of an 18th-century *palazzo* on Montepulciano's major pedestrian thoroughfare, this elegant option offers three rooms and two suites melding original features (frescoes, antiques, parquet flooring) with modern amenities (swish bathrooms, coffee and tea facilities, satellite TV). An excellent breakfast is served in the magnificent communal lounge, which has huge windows commanding panoramic views.

Eating

When dining here, opt for the local Chianina beef washed down with a glass or two of the famous Vino Nobile. Many of the *agriturismi* in the surrounding countryside have good on-site restaurants.

Osteria Acquacheta   TUSCAN €
(☑ 0578 71 70 86; www.acquacheta.eu; Via del Teatro 22; meals €24; ⊙ 12.30-3pm & 7.30-10.30pm Wed-Mon mid-Apr–Dec) Hugely popular with locals and tourists alike, this bustling

SACRED SOLITUDE, WITH WINE

Concealed amid dense forest on the edge of the Castelnuovo Berardenga region, 14th-century abbey Abbazia di Monte Oliveto Maggiore (☑ 0577 70 76 11; www.monteolivetomaggiore.it; Monte Oliveto Maggiore; ☺ 9.15am-noon & 3.15-5pm, to 6pm summer; P) FREE was founded by Giovanni Tolomei – later Saint Bernardo Tolomei – and is still a retreat for Benedictine monks. The cloister features a fresco series by Luca Signorelli and Giovanni Antonio Bazzi (aka Il Sodoma) illustrating events in the life of St Benedict, founder of the order. There is also a church with magnificent choir stalls of inlaid wood and a refectory frescoed by Fra' Paolo Novelli.

Mass on Sundays (11am) features Gregorian chanting. A donation is requested to visit the abbey's library, museum and pharmacy; visits to the historic cantina (☑ 0577 70 76 47; ☺ 10am-1pm & 2.30-6.30pm mid-Mar–Oct, closed weekdays Nov–mid-Mar) FREE, where you can enjoy a wine tasting, are free. Parking costs €1.

Should you fancy staying nearby, luxurious Castello delle Serre (☑ 0577 70 50 18, 338 5040811; www.castellodelleserre.com; Piazza XX Settembre 1, Serre di Rapolano; r €245-275, ste €300-450; P ✳ @ ☎ ☒) on the very edge of the Chianti Senese is the place to be. Meticulously restored by the Italian-American Gangale family, the medieval castle-turned-boutique hotel features huge rooms, swish pool area and magnificent views.

osteria specialises in *bistecca alla fiorentina* (chargrilled T-bone steak), which comes to the shared tables in huge, lightly seared and exceptionally flavoursome slabs (don't even *think* of asking for it to be served otherwise). Phone to book ahead.

★ La Grotta   TUSCAN €€

(☑ 0578 75 74 79; www.lagrottamontepulciano.it; Via di San Biagio 15; meals €43; ☺ 12.30-2pm & 7.30-10pm Thu-Tue, closed mid-Jan–late Mar) Located just below Montepulciano, overlooking the Renaissance splendour of the Chiesa di San Biago (p188), the town's best restaurant serves traditional dishes with refined flavour and presentation. Service is exemplary, and the courtyard garden is a lovely place to enjoy a six-course tasting menu (€53) or your choice from the à la carte menu. Bookings advisable.

★ La Dogana   ITALIAN €€

(☑ 339 5405196; www.ladoganaenoteca.it; Strada Lauretana Nord 75, Valiano; 3-/5-course set lunch €25/40, meals €34; ☺ 11am-3.30pm & 6-10pm Wed-Mon, closed Jan) Chef and cookbook writer Sunshine Manitto presides over the kitchen of this chic *enoteca* overlooking the Palazzo Vecchio Winery, 13km northeast of Montepulciano. Windows frame vistas of vines and cypress trees, but the best seats in the house are on the grassed rear terrace. The casual menu showcases seasonal produce (much of it grown in the kitchen garden).

🍷 Drinking & Nightlife

★ Caffè Poliziano   CAFE

(☑ 0578 75 86 15; www.caffepoliziano.it; Via di Voltaia 27; ☺ 7am-9pm Mon-Fri, to 10.30pm Sat, to 9pm Sun; ☎) Established in 1868, Poliziano was lovingly restored to its original form 20 years ago and is the town's most atmospheric cafe. It serves excellent coffee but is most atmospheric for *aperitivo*, when the view of the sun setting over the Val di Chiana from the tables near the rear windows is simply magnificent.

La Vineria   WINE BAR

(☑ 0578 85 01 53; www.facebook.com/lavineriadimontepulciano; Via di Gracciano nel Corso 101; ☺ 10am-10pm) Specialising in local produce, this tiny place near the Porta al Prato is an excellent choice if you are keen to try a glass or two of Nobile or Rosso di Montepulciano, accompanied by a generously sized tasting board of *crostini* (toasts with toppings), *pecorino* cheese and cured meats (€15). It also offers filled *panini* at lunch.

E Lucevan Le Stelle   WINE BAR

(☑ 0578 75 87 25; www.locandasanfrancesco.it; Piazza San Francesco 3; ☺ 10am-midnight Easter-Oct, to 11pm Sat & Sun Nov-Easter, closed 2 weeks Nov & 2 weeks Jan; ☎) The decked terrace of this ultrafriendly *osteria* is the top spot in Montepulciano to watch the sun go down. Inside, squishy sofas, modern art and jazz on the sound system give the place a chilled-out vibe. Snacks include *piandine* (filled flatbreads; €8), pastas (€9) and antipasto boards (€10 to €28).

ℹ️ Information

**Strada del Vino Nobile di Montepulciano
Information Office** (p190) Books accommodation in Montepulciano and arranges a wide
range of courses and tours.

Tourist Office (📞 0578 75 73 41; www.pro
locomontepulciano.it; Piazza Don Minzoni 1;
🕐 9.30am-1pm & 3-7pm Apr-Sep. 9.30am-1pm
& 3-6pm Mon-Sat Oct-Mar; 📶) This office in
the car park opposite the Giardino Poggiofanti
near the main gate to the upper town reserves
last-minute accommodation (in person only),
supplies town maps (€0.50) and sells bus and
train tickets.

ℹ️ Getting There & Away

BUS

The Montepulciano **bus station** (Piazzo Pietro
Nenni) is next to Car Park No. 5, behind the
Giardino di Poggiofanti. Tiemme (p155) runs
four buses to/from Siena's train station daily
from Monday to Saturday (€7.60, 1½ hours)
stopping at Pienza (€2.60, 20 minutes) en route.
There are also four extra services solely to/from
Pienza.

CAR & MOTORCYCLE

To reach Montepulciano from Florence, take
the Valdichiana (Val di Chiana) exit off the A1
(direction Bettolle–Sinalunga) and then follow
the signs; from Siena, take the Siena–Bettolle–
Perugia Super Strada.

A 24-hour ZTL applies in the historic centre
between May and September; in October and
April it applies from 8am to 8pm, and from
November to March it applies from 8am to
5pm. Check whether your hotel can supply a
permit. Otherwise, there are plenty of paid car
parks circling the historic centre (€1.50/10 per
hour/day).

CHIUSI

📞 0578 / POP 8558

Located in Tuscany's Etruscan heartland, in
territory where archaeologists still regularly unearth tombs, Chiusi's history stretches
back as far as the 2nd millennium BC. Originally called Clevsin, the town was particularly prosperous during the rule of King
Porsenna, a powerful character who waged
a war against the city of Rome in the 6th
century BC. Local archaeologists – some
professional and others amateur – regularly excavate in the local area searching for
Porsenna's burial place. They haven't yet
been successful, but the fruits of many past
archaeological digs grace the display cases

in the town's major tourism draw, the extraordinary Museo Archeologico Etrusco di
Chiusi.

The **Città di Chiusi Card** (adult/reduced
€10/5), sold at participating sights, gives
discounted entry to the town's three key
museums.

⭐ Museo Archeologico
Etrusco di Chiusi   MUSEUM

(📞 0578 2 01 77; www.facebook.com/museoetrus
co.dichiusi; Via Porsenna 93; adult/reduced €6/3;
🕐 9am-8pm) Small but outstanding, Chiusi's
Etruscan museum boasts a bevy of ceramics,
pottery, jewellery and cinerary urns (for cre-
mation ashes) dating from between the 9th
and 2nd centuries BC. Don't miss the extraordinary *pietra fetida* (sulphur stone) funerary
sphinx and bust of a grieving woman, both of
which date from the 6th century BC, or the
7th-century-BC canopic urn from Dociano,
with its bronze body and terracotta head.

Museo della Cattedrale e
Labirinto di Porsenna   MUSEUM

(📞 0578 22 69 75; www.facebook.com/labirintoc
attedrale; Piazza Duomo 7; adult/reduced €5/3.50;
🕐 10am-12.30pm & 2.30-5pm Tue-Sun mid-Apr–
mid-Oct, 10am-12.30pm Tue-Fri, 10am-12.30pm &
2.30-4.30pm Sat & Sun mid-Oct–mid-Apr) This
church museum houses the usual array of
religious artefacts, but differentiates itself
with its Labirinto di Porsenna, a series of
tunnels (not for the claustrophobic) dating from Etruscan times that formed part
of Chiusi's water-supply system. Guided
tours of the labyrinth (in Italian or English,
depending on the crowd), leave at 10am,
10.45am, 11.30am, 12.15pm, 2.30pm, 3.15pm,
4pm and 4.45pm in high season, less regularly at other times.

Museo Civico 'La Città
Sotterranea'   ARCHAEOLOGICAL SITE

(📞 0578 2 09 15; Via I Ciminia 2; adult/reduced
€4/3; 🕐 guided tours 10.10am, 11.10am & 12.10pm
Thu & Fri, 10.10am, 11.10am, 12.10pm, 3.10pm,
4.10pm & 5.10pm Sat & Sun) Subterranean
passages filled with the city museum's collection of monumental inscriptions (mainly urns and grave tiles) can be accessed on
guided visits.

⭐ Residenza dei Ricci   B&B €€

(📞 0578 22 65 39; www.residenza-deiricci.com; Via
Lavinia 13; 🕐 s €150, d €177; 🅿️❄️📶) Overnighting in this 13th-century *palazzo* is a real
treat. There are only four rooms, and each is
as elegant as it is comfortable, with modern

bathrooms, large beds and tasteful furnishings; one room is accessed from the large flower-filled rear garden. Owner Donatella is a trained pastry chef, and her breakfasts are renowned.

★ Il Grillo è Buoncantore   TUSCAN €€
(☎ 0578 2 01 12; https://ilgrilloebuoncantore. wixsite.com/ristorante; Piazza XX Settembre 10; meals €30, pizzas €6-10; ⊙ noon-2.30pm & 7-11pm, closed Mon winter; 🖟 🖉) Chef and sommelier Tiziana Tacchi is passionate about the cuisine and wine of the Chiusi region and showcases both in this acclaimed Slow Food destination. The menu is grounded in local tradition but Tiziana's creations are executed with a contemporary sensibility and the results are truly delectable (the antipasti are a knockout). No pizzas at lunch.

ⓘ Information

Tourist Office (☎ 0578 22 76 67; www.proloco chiusi.it; Via Porsenna 79; ⊙ 9am-1pm & 3-5pm Mon-Sat, 9am-1pm Sun Apr-Sep, 9.30am-12.30pm Tue-Sun Oct-Mar) Located near the *duomo* and Museo Archeologico Etrusco di Chiusi.

ⓘ Getting There & Away

BUS

Tiemme (www.tiemmespa.it) runs frequent buses to/from Montepulciano's bus station from Monday to Saturday (€3.50, 45 minutes). These stop at both the Chiusi-Chianciano Terme railway station and on Via della Pietriccia in the historic centre, close to the Museo Archeologico Etrusco di Chiusi.

TRAIN

Chiusi-Chianciano Terme railway station is in Chiusi Scalo, 3km southeast of Chiusi's historic centre. There are 12 daily *regionale* services to/from Siena (€8.60, 90 minutes) and Rome (€9.95, 1¾ hours). Six additional intercity services connect the station with Orvieto (€9, 20 minutes) and Rome (€21, 1¼ hours). A new fast train line between Rome and Florence stopping at Chiusi-Chianciano Terme station was due to be inaugurated in late 2019. A bus ticket between the railway station and the historic centre costs €1.20.

Southern Tuscany

Includes ➡

Massa Marittima........ 198
Monte Amiata 202
Vetulonia 203
Pitigliano 204
Sovana 207
Sorano 208
Grosseto..................... 212
Parco Regionale
della Maremma.......... 213
Orbetello 215
Monte Argentario........ 215

Best Places to Eat

➡ Hostaria del Ceccottino (p206)

➡ Taverna del Vecchio Borgo (p201)

➡ Antica Trattoria Aurora (p215)

➡ Il Tufo Allegro (p206)

Best Places to Stay

➡ Conti di San Bonifacio (p200)

➡ Hotel della Fortezza (p208)

➡ Il Pellicano (p216)

Why Go?

This is an intriguing part of Tuscany, home to wild scenery and evocative reminders of Italy's Etruscan heritage. Usually referred to as the Maremma, its highlights include the intensely atmospheric Città del Tufo archaeological park, a network of Etruscan tombs and mysterious sunken roads known as *vie cave* in the countryside around the towns of Pitigliano, Sovana and Sorano. Further north, more Etruscan heritage can be explored at the archaeological sites of Roselle and Vetulonia, and in the archaeological museum at one of Tuscany's most charming Renaissance-era hilltop towns, Massa Marittima.

An embarrassment of natural riches takes you past wildlife-packed marshes and vine-covered slopes, or from sandy beaches to snowy mountains, in just a few hours. Swim, hike, horse ride and mountain bike by day before recharging on flavoursome Maremmese food and wine in *agriturismi* (farm-stay accommodation) at night.

Road Distances Chart

	Vetulonia	Massa Marittima	Grosseto	Pitigliano
Massa Marittima	38			
Grosseto	52	48		
Pitigliano	129	120	75	
Parco Regionale della Maremma	28	67	20	56

Southern Tuscany Highlights

1 **Parco Regionale della Maremma** (p213) Hiking, bicycling, horse riding and swimming in this wild and wonderful national park.

2 **Massa Marittima** (p198) Joining the *passeggiata* (evening stroll) in one of Tuscany's most magnificent piazzas.

3 **Parco Archeologico 'Città del Tufo'** (p204) Walking in the footsteps of Etruscans along the mysterious sunken roads known as *vie cave*.

4 **Pitigliano** (p204) Visiting the fascinating historic Jewish enclave in this hilltop stronghold hewn out of volcanic rock.

5 **Monte Amiata** (p202) Discovering medieval abbeys, mineral museums and a sculpture garden amid dense forests of beech and chestnut.

6 **Il Giardino dei Tarocchi** (p213) Marvelling at Niki de Saint Phalle's fantastical sculpture garden inspired by the tarot deck.

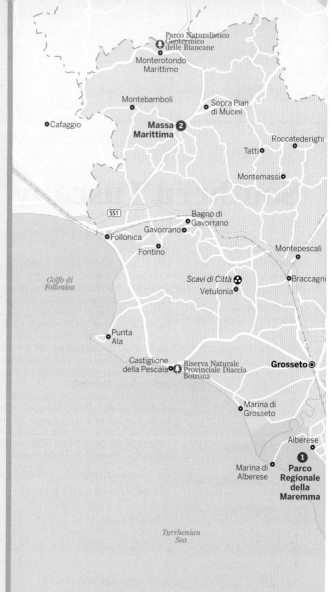

Parco Naturalistico Geotermico delle Biancane

Monterotondo Marittimo

Montebamboli

Sopra Pian di Mucini

Cafaggio

Massa Marittima **2**

Roccatederighi

Tatti

Montemassi

SS1

Bagno di Gavorrano

Gavorrano

Follonica

Fontino

Montepescali

Golfo di Follonica

Scavi di Città **3**

Braccagni

Vetulonia

Punta Ala

Castiglione della Pescaia

Riserva Naturale Provinciale Diaccia Botrona **6**

Grosseto

Marina di Grosseto

Alberese

Marina di Alberese

1 **Parco Regionale della Maremma**

Tyrrhenian Sea

Porto Santo Stefano

Isola de Giglio

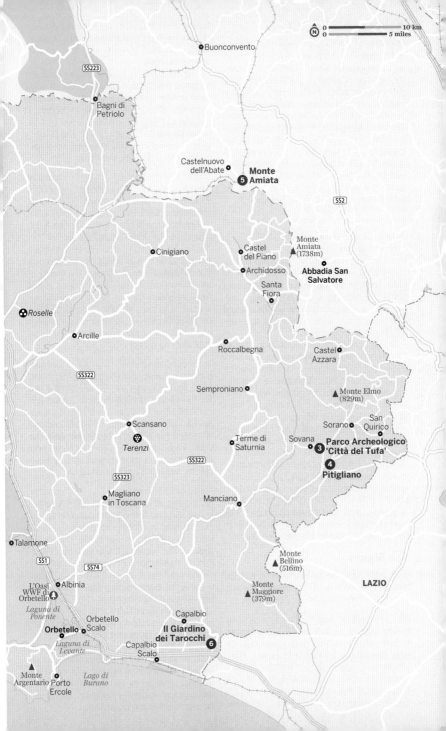

ALTA MAREMMA

The Alta (Upper) Maremma starts south of Livorno and continues down to Grosseto, incorporating Massa Marittima and the surrounding Colline Metallifere (or 'metal-producing hills'). The ancient mining history and unique landscape of these hills have been acknowledged by inclusion in Unesco's European Geoparks Network, and the surrounding area is rich in Etruscan history too. Inland territory includes the hill towns south of the Crete Senesi and the mountainous terrain surrounding Monte Amiata, all of which make excellent stops for those travelling between Southern and Central Tuscany.

Massa Marittima

☑ 0566 / POP 8286

Drawcards at this tranquil hill town in Tuscany's Colline Metallifere (metal-producing hills) include an eccentric yet endearing jumble of museums, an extremely handsome central piazza (Piazza Garibaldi) and largely intact medieval streets that are blessedly bereft of tour groups.

Briefly under Pisan domination, Massa Marittima became an independent *comune* (city-state) in 1225 but was swallowed up by Siena a century later. A plague in 1348 was followed by the decline of the region's lucrative mining industry, reducing the town to the brink of extinction, a situation made even worse by the prevalence of malaria in surrounding marshlands. Fortunately, the draining of marshes in the 18th century and the re-establishment of mining shortly afterwards brought it back to life.

The town is divided into three districts: the Città Vecchia (Old Town), Città Nuova (New Town) and Borgo (Borough). The medieval Arco Senese marks the boundary between the Città Vecchia and Città Nuova.

◉ Sights

A cumulative ticket (adult/reduced €12/10) gives access to all of Massa Marittima's museums and monuments.

★**Cattedrale di San Cerbone**   CATHEDRAL
(Piazza Garibaldi; ⊙ 8am-noon & 3-7pm summer, to 6pm winter) Presiding over photogenic Piazza Garibaldi (aka Piazza Duomo), Massa Marittima's asymmetrically positioned 13th-century *duomo* (cathedral) is dedicated to St Cerbonius, the town's patron saint, always depicted surrounded by a flock of geese.

Inside, don't miss the free-standing *Maestà* (Madonna and Child Enthroned in Majesty; 1316), attributed by some experts to Duccio di Buoninsegna.

The other treasures of the *duomo* include a carved marble urn known as the *Arca di San Cerbone* (St Cerbone's Ark; 1324) behind the high altar and an early-14th-century polychrome wooden crucifix carved by Giovanni Pisano on the altar itself. The facade's main doorway is topped by carved panels depicting scenes from St Cerbonius' life.

Museo di Arte Sacra   MUSEUM
(Complesso Museale di San Pietro all'Orto; ☑ 0566 90 22 89; www.museidimaremma.it; Corso Diaz 36; adult/reduced €5/3; ⊙ 10am-1pm & 4-7pm Tue-Sun Jul-Sep, 11am-1pm & 3-5pm Tue-Sun Apr-Jun & Oct, 3-5pm Fri & 10am-1pm & 3-5pm Sat & Sun Nov-Mar) A splendid *Maestà* (c 1335–37) by Ambrogio Lorenzetti, as well as sculptures by Giovanni Pisano that originally adorned the facade of the *duomo,* are the major attractions at this small museum housed in the former convent of San Pietro all'Orto in the Città Nuova. The collection of primitive grey-alabaster bas-reliefs also came from the *duomo,* but date from an earlier era.

Torre del Candeliere   TOWER
(Candlestick Tower; ☑ 0566 90 65 25; Piazza Matteotti; adult/reduced €3/2; ⊙ 10am-1pm & 4-7pm Tue-Sun Jul-Sep, 11am-1pm & 3-5pm Tue-Sun Apr-Jun & Oct, 3-5pm Fri & 10am-1pm & 3-5pm Sat & Sun Nov-Mar) Climb to the top of this 13th-century, 30m-high tower on the border between the Città Vecchia and Città Nuova for views over the old town. It's the only part of the medieval city walls that can be walked on.

Fonte dell'Abbondanza   MONUMENT
(Via Ximenes, off Piazza Garibaldi) FREE A rather risqué surprise lurks in the street-level loggia (balcony) of a 13th-century former wheat store close to Piazza Garibaldi. The loggia shelters the Fonte dell'Abbondanza (Fountain of Abundance), a now-decommissioned public drinking fountain built in 1265 that features an extraordinary fresco known as the *Albero della Fecondità* (Fertility Tree). This portrays a tree laden with penises hanging like fruit and shows women fighting each other for those fruits that have fallen.

The 270m-long *cunicolo* (underground tunnel) along which spring water once flowed to the fountain can be explored on occasional tours led by members of the town's speleological society – bookings are made through the Museo Archeologico.

THREE PERFECT DAYS IN SOUTHERN TUSCANY

Day One

Explore Etruscan necropolises and walk along mysterious *vie cave* in the Parco Archeologico 'Città del Tufo' (p204) before visiting the *duomo* and museum in Sovana (p207) and then heading to Pitigliano (p204) to wander centuries-old streets, visit an ancient Jewish enclave and dine in one of the town's excellent restaurants.

Day Two

Your destination today is the Parco Regionale della Maremma (p213), where you can walk, cycle, horse ride or canoe through wild scenery and have a beach break at Marina di Alberese. At the end of the day, relax over a bottle of Morellino di Scansano at the welcoming *agriturismo* on the Terenzi (p209) wine estate.

Day Three

Head north to Massa Marittima (p198) to admire its handsome piazzas and the Cattedrale di San Cerbone (p198), eating lunch at one of its Slow Food–accredited restaurants. Work off some calories exploring the Etruscan sites in and around Vetulonia (p203) and then check into the Montebelli Agriturismo & Country Hotel (p204), one of the region's best *agriturismo* options.

Museo Archeologico MUSEUM

([✒] 0566 90 65 25; www.museidimaremma.it; Piazza Garibaldi 1; adult/reduced €3/2; ⊙ 10am-1pm & 4-7pm Tue-Sun Jul-Sep, 11am-1pm & 3-5pm Tue-Sun Apr-Jun & Oct, 3-5pm Fri & 10am-1pm & 3-5pm Sat & Sun Nov-Mar) Housed in the 13th-century **Palazzo del Podestà**, the historic residence of the town's chief magistrate, this archaeological museum has a small collection of artefacts dating from the Palaeolithic to Etruscan eras. The most noteworthy exhibit is *La stele di vado all'arancio,* a simple but compelling stone stela (funeral or commemorative marker) dating from the 3rd millennium BC.

Arco Senese ARCHITECTURE

(Sienese Arch; Piazza Matteotti) Massa Marittima's immense, medieval Arco Senese soars overhead as you pass between the Città Vecchia and Città Nuova.

🏃 Activities

In summer, **Lago dell'Accesa** (Accesa Lake; SP Accesa) 9km south of Massa Marittima is a popular, free-of-charge swimming spot.

Mountain biking is growing in popularity and a number of *agriturismi* in the area offer bike rental and guided bike tours; the tourist office (p202) can supply details.

🎉 Festivals & Events

Balestro del Girifalco CULTURAL

(Contest of the Falcon's Heart; www.societaterzierimassetani.it; ⊙ May & Aug) This crossbow competition is held twice yearly on the fourth Sunday of May and on 14 August.

Twenty-four competitors from the town's three *terzieri* (districts) dress in medieval costume and compete for a golden arrow. Tickets are sold at the Museo Archeologico in Piazza Garibaldi in the week before the event.

Lirica in Piazza MUSIC

(www.liricainpiazza.it; Piazza Garibaldi; ⊙ early Aug) Three operas are staged under the stars.

🛏 Sleeping

The town's clutch of hotels leave a lot to be desired – consider staying in a B&B or *agriturismo* in the surrounding area. The area's proximity to the coast means that accommodation is always heavily booked in August.

⭐ **Casa della Pia** PENSION €

([✒] 333 9777614; www.casadellapia.eu; Via della Libertà 15; r €82; 🛜) The marital home of tragic Pia dei Tolomei, immortalised in Dante's *Divine Comedy,* this pension in a 13th-century *palazzo* (mansion) just off Piazza Garibaldi is run by the charming Costanza, who goes out of her way to make guests feel at home. One spacious and well equipped room is on offer, providing extremely comfortable accommodation. No breakfast.

Il Bell'Arco APARTMENT €€

([✒] 351 8982588; www.ilbellarco.com; Vicolo Butigni 5; d/tr/q €155/225/295; ❄🛜) Tucked behind the *duomo*, this spacious two-bedroom apartment makes a perfect base for visitors wanting to immerse themselves

Massa Marittima

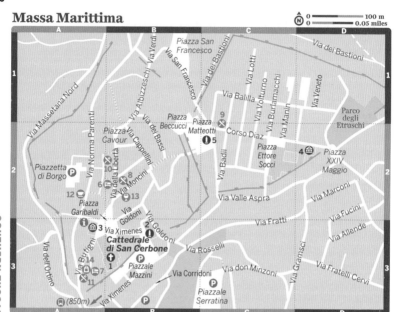

in local life. Its panoramic terrace atop one of Massa's historic walls is a huge draw, as are the fully equipped kitchen and comfortable lounge. American-born owner Janie Holstein can supply plenty of information to assist in exploring the region. Three-night minimum stay.

Out of Town

The countryside around Massa Marittima squirrels away some wonderfully restful B&Bs and farm stays.

La Fattoria di Tatti
B&B €

(☑ 0566 91 20 01; www.tattifattoria.it; Via Matteotti 10, Tatti; r €95-110; ☺ closed Nov–mid-Mar; P ☎) A stately Tuscan farmhouse positioned at the summit of the hilltop village of Tatti, 25km southeast of Massa Marittima, this excellent choice offers eight simple but stylish rooms, a generous breakfast buffet and mesmerising valley views from the guest terrace and some rooms. Families appreciate the on-site playground and nearby restaurant/pizzeria.

Podere Riparbella
AGRITURISMO €€

(☑ 0566 91 55 57; www.riparbella.com; Località Sopra Pian di Mucini; s/d €68/116; ☺ closed early Jan–mid-Apr; P) ✎ The Swiss owners of this 46-hectare estate, 5km out of town, have built an ecologically sustainable farm operation where

they cultivate grapes and olives and host guests in 11 small and simple guest rooms. Facilities include a communal lounge and a terrace. Meals featuring home-grown and local produce can be arranged (fully vegetarian on request). No credit cards and no wi-fi.

Pieve di Caminino
AGRITURISMO €€

(☑ 0564 56 97 36, 393 3356605; www.caminino. com; Via Provinciale di Peruzzo, Località Roccatederighi; ste €120-185, 4-person apt €190-220; P ✳ ☎ ☒) Few sleeping options can boast a historic atmosphere to equal this now-decommissioned 11th-century monastery, set on a 500-hectare estate planted with olive trees and vines. It offers six charmingly decorated two-person suites and three apartments sleeping three or four. Each has a panoramic terrace, sitting area and kitchen; some also have air-conditioning. Weekly rates are discounted. Roccatederighi is 27km southeast of Massa Marittima.

Conti di San Bonifacio
RESORT €€€

(☑ 0566 8 00 06; www.contidisanbonifacio.com; Località Casteani 1; r €450-540, ste €630-850; P ✳ ☎ ☒) Set on a wine estate 18km southeast of Massa Marittima, this boutique resort offers both room and suite accommodation (the suites overlooking the vineyard are particularly alluring). Guests can laze by the saltwater swimming pool, dine in the

Massa Marittima

◉ Top Sights
1 Cattedrale di San Cerbone................. B3

◉ Sights
Arco Senese .... (see 5)
2 Fonte dell'Abbondanza B3
3 Museo Archeologico........................... A3
4 Museo di Arte Sacra D2
5 Torre del Candeliere C2

◉ Sleeping
6 Casa della Pia B2
7 Il Bell'Arco A3

◉ Eating
8 La Tana dei Brilli................................ B2
9 Le Fate 'Briache C2
10 L'Osteria da Tronca B2
11 Taverna del Vecchio Borgo................ A3

◉ Drinking & Nightlife
12 Bar Torrefazione................................ A2
13 Il Bacchino B2

◉ Shopping
14 Cantina Moris.................................... A3

restaurant, relax on the vineyard-facing terrace or sign up for one of the many activities on offer.

Eating

Three restaurants in the old town are recognised as Slow Food destinations; all serve local specialities including *tortelli alla maremma* (pasta parcels filled with ricotta and spinach).

La Novella
DELI €
(📞 0566 91 90 05; www.lanovella.it; SR439, Località Il Cilindro, Valpiana; filled panini €2.50-5, taglieri €7.50-13; ☺8am-7.30pm) Located on the road between Massa Marittima and the coast, this local favourite is a great place to source picnic provisions including filled *panini* (sandwiches) and dirt-cheap wine. It's also possible to eat *merende* (snacks) in the basic attached trattoria, where offerings include pasta, salads and *abbuffata* (€12.60), a huge platter of *bruschette*, *salumi* (cured meats), cheese and veggies.

Taverna del Vecchio Borgo
TUSCAN €€
(📞 0566 90 21 67; taverna.vecchioborgo@libero.it; Via Norma Parenti 12; meals €32; ☺7.30-10pm Tue-Sun summer, 7.30-10pm Tue-Sat, 12.30-2.30pm Sun winter) Massa's best restaurant is as atmospheric as it is delicious. You'll sit in a dimly lit brick-vaulted wine cellar dating from the 16th century and dine on top-quality beef

grilled on the wood-fired oven, fresh mushrooms in season or unusual dishes such as *testaroli* pasta with a pistachio sauce. The set four-course menu (€30) is a steal.

Le Fate 'Briache
TUSCAN €€
(📞 0566 90 10 10; www.facebook.com/lefatebriache; Corso Diaz 3; meal €26; ☺7.30-9.30pm Tue-Sun summer, 7.30-9.30pm Tue-Sat, 12.30-2.30pm Sun winter; 📞) Talented chef Caterina creates tasty dishes using local, seasonal produce, sensibly limiting the size of her menu and focusing on creative vegetarian choices, excellent pasta dishes and home-style desserts. There are only five tables so booking ahead is highly advised.

La Tana dei Brilli
TUSCAN €€
(📞 0566 90 12 74; www.facebook.com/latanadeibrilli; Vicolo del Ciambellano 4; meals €26; ☺noon-2.30pm & 7-10pm Thu-Tue Dec-Oct) Seating a mere 10 people at four tables (another six can squeeze onto tiny alley tables outside), this friendly place operated by Raffaella Cecchelli ticks every box on the Slow Food checklist, featuring authentic Maremmese dishes made with local products.

L'Osteria da Tronca
TUSCAN €€
(📞 0566 90 19 91; Vicolo Porte 5; meals €28; ☺7-9.45pm Thu-Tue Mar–mid-Dec) Squeezed into a side street, this stone-walled restaurant specialises in the rustic dishes of the Maremma. Specialities include *acquacotta* (a hearty vegetable soup with bread and egg), *tortelli alla maremma* and *coniglio in porchetta* (roasted stuffed rabbit).

Drinking & Nightlife

★ Il Bacchino
WINE BAR
(📞 0566 94 02 29; www.facebook.com/pages/Il-Bacchino/140075709522677; Via Moncini 8; ☺10am-noon & 4-7pm Mon-Sat, 10am-noon Sun, closed Mon Nov-Feb) Owner Magdy Lamei may not be a local (he's from Cairo), but it would be hard to find anyone else as knowledgeable and passionate about local artisanal produce. Come to his classy *enoteca* (wine bar) to taste and buy local wines (€3.50 to €25 per glass), or to stock up on picnic provisions including jams, cheese and cured meats.

Bar Torrefazione
CAFE
(Via Norma Parenti 35; ☺7.30am-12.30pm & 5-7.30pm Mon-Fri, 7.30am-12.30pm Sat) Gloria Dini makes the best coffee in town, which is why her Bar Torrefazione (Bar and Roastery) is always busy. The fact that it's the cheapest cup in town probably helps too.

THE COLLINE METALLIFERE

Massa Marittima's handsome buildings and artistic treasures are the legacy of the town's location in the centre of Tuscany's Colline Metallifere. Mining occurred here for three millennia, and has shaped the region's physical and cultural landscapes – something acknowledged by the addition of the Parco delle Colline Metallifere (www. parcocollinemetallifere.it) to Unesco's European Geoparks Network.

The national park incorporates many sites, including **Parco delle Biancane** (⏹0566 91 70 39; Strada Provinciale Bagnolo; ⊗24hr) FREE in Monterotondo Marittimo, a geothermal park 21km north of Massa Marittima where steam has been transformed into power by vapour turbines since 1916, supplying electricity to one million Tuscan households (and meeting 25% of Tuscany's energy needs). Visitors can take a two-hour walk through wooded terrain, where steam belches from the earth's crust and clumps of sulphur crystals form.

🛍 Shopping

Cantina Moris   WINE
(⏹0566 91 91 35, 0566 91 80 10; www.morisfarms. com; Via Butigni 1; ⊗8.30am-12.30pm & 4-7.30pm Thu-Tue) The best-known winery in the area, Morisfarms has a hugely atmospheric 15th-century *cantina* (wine cellar) in town where you can purchase wines, including its signature Avvoltore, a sophisticated Sangiovese, cabernet sauvignon and syrah blend. Call ahead to enjoy a tasting of seven wines (€20 per person, Monday to Saturday Easter to October) at its equally atmospheric *fattoria* (farm) in nearby Cura Nuova.

ℹ Information

Tourist Office (⏹0566 90 65 54; www.turis momassamarittima.it; Via Todini 5; ⊗10am-1pm & 3-5pm Wed-Mon Apr-Jun & Sep-Oct, 10am-1pm & 4-7pm daily Jul & Aug, 10am-1pm & 3-5pm Fri-Sun Nov-Mar; 🅟) Down a side street beneath the Museo Archeologico. The website has plenty of information.

ℹ Getting There & Away

BUS

The bus station is in Piazza XXIV Maggio, near the Museo di Arte Sacra; the bus stop closest to Piazza Garibaldi is in Via Corridoni. **Tiemme** (www.tiemmespa.it) operates buses to Grosseto (€5.60, one hour, four daily) and Siena (€7.60, two hours, one daily) from Monday to Saturday. To get to Volterra you'll need to change at Monterotondo Marittimo. **Massa Veternensis** (Piazza Garibaldi 18) sells bus and train tickets.

CAR & MOTORCYCLE

There's a convenient car park (€1 per hour during the day, free at night) close to Piazza Garibaldi; head up the hill and you'll find it on your left.

TRAIN

The nearest train station is in Follonica, 22km southwest of Massa Marittima; Tiemme buses (€3.50, 25 minutes, frequent Monday to Saturday, two services Sunday) travel between the station and the town.

Monte Amiata

Circling the extinct volcano of Mt Amiata (1738m), the heavily forested region of Monte Amiata links the Maremma with the Val d'Orcia and is an intriguing off-the-beaten-track destination for those travelling between Southern and Central Tuscany.

🔘 Sights

★**Il Giardino di Daniel Spoerri**   GARDENS
(Garden of Daniel Spoerri; ⏹0564 95 00 26; www.danielspoerri.org; Strada Provinciale Pescina, Seggiano; adult/reduced €10/8; ⊗11am-6pm Tue-Sun Easter-Nov, closed Mon Easter–mid-Jun & mid-Sep–Nov) Set in the wild surrounds of Seggiano, this sculpture garden is the passionate project of Romanian–Swiss artist Daniel Spoerri (b 1930), who created many of the 112 artworks spread over its 16 hectares. The landscape here is glorious – wildflowers carpet the fields and olive groves surround the property – and the site-specific works address the theme of how art should complement nature rather than overwhelm it. The standout piece is Olivier Estoppey's 2001 work *Dies Irae* (Judgement Day).

There's a cafe and snack bar on-site, as well as three self-contained apartments to rent.

Mineral Park Museum   MUSEUM
(Parco Museo Minerario di Abbadia San Salvatore; ⏹0577 77 83 24; www.museominerario.it; Piazzale Renato Rossaro 6, Abbadia San Salvatore; adult/

reduced €12/10; ☺9.30am-12.30pm & 3.30-6.30pm mid-Mar–Oct, 9.30am-12.30pm & 3.30-6.30pm Sat & Sun Nov–mid-Mar) Cinnabar, the red-coloured mineral from which mercury is extracted, was mined in the hills around Abbadia San Salvatore from Etruscan times until quite recently. This now-defunct mine was once the largest employer in Monte Amiata and it has now been converted into a fascinating museum documenting the mine's role in shaping both the local economy and the life of the community. It offers displays, artworks, audiovisual presentations and even a train ride through the mine tunnels.

Abbadia San Salvatore   ABBEY

(⚡0577 77 73 52; www.abbaziasansalvatore.it; Via del Monastero; donation to enter crypt €2; ☺8am-1pm & 3-7pm winter, to 6pm summer) Founded by the Lombards in the 8th century, this abbey was originally entrusted to the Benedictines but later passed to the Cistercians. An important stop on the Via Francigena, it is notable primarily for its hugely atmospheric crypt, which has a forest of 44 columns, each featuring unique decorations on their capitals.

🏃 Activities

Dzogchen Community & Cultural Association   YOGA

(⚡0564 96 68 37; www.dzogchen.it; Merigar West; prices on application) A community of Tibetan Buddhists in rural Tuscany? Yes, you read that correctly. This Buddhist centre near Archidosso was established in 1981 and offers workshops in Yantra yoga, meditation and sacred and modern Tibetan dancing to those interested in investigating techniques for living in a more mindful way. These are held in the centre's richly decorated temple.

The community has also opened an extremely impressive multimedia Museum of Asian Art and Culture (MACO; ⚡0564 164 32 39; http://maco.arcidosso.museum; Piazza Castello 1; combined ticket with Archidosso Castle adult/reduced €7/5; ☺9.30am-12.30pm & 3.30-6.30pm Sat & Sun), near the medieval castle in Archidosso, 5km away.

🛏 Sleeping & Eating

There are plenty of *agriturismi* and B&Bs in the area, as well as a number of top-end spa hotels at Bagno Vignoni.

Borgo Tepolini   B&B €

(⚡349 4752477; www.borgotepolini.it; Località Tepolini 16, Castel del Piano; s/d from €70/95; P🅿🛜🏊) Antonio and Pino's cute B&B has two comfortable if old-fashioned rooms, but what makes their B&B so exceptional is the warm welcome, delicious breakfast and wonderful swimming pool, which is set in a large garden with fantastic vistas over the surrounding countryside.

❶ Getting There & Away

Local bus services are extremely limited. You'll need a car to explore the area.

Vetulonia

⚡0564

Originally an important Etruscan settlement, this windswept hilltop village 23km northwest of Grosseto was colonised by the Romans in 224 BC. It retains important traces of both eras, which can be investigated at the Museo Civico Archeologico and by visiting the Scavi di Città archaeological site and a scattering of Etruscan tombs nearby.

👁 Sights

Museo Civico Archeologico 'Isidoro Falchi'   MUSEUM

(⚡0564 94 80 58; www.museoisidorofalchi.it; Piazza Vatluna; adult/reduced €5/2.50; ☺10am-2pm & 3-7pm daily Jul & Aug, 10am-2pm & 3-7pm Tue-Sun Jun & Sep, 10am-4pm Tue-Sun Oct-Feb, 10am-6pm Tue-Sun Mar-May) Piazza Vatluna off Vetulonia's main street boasts spectacular views over the surrounding countryside and is also home to this small museum, which brings Etruscan history to life through a display of artefacts excavated from local Etruscan tombs and settlements. Highlights include a 7th-century-BC bronze helmet, shield and leggings in Room B upstairs, and bronze statues of the domestic *divinità* (divinities) dating from the third to first centuries BC on the ground floor.

Scavi di Città   ARCHAEOLOGICAL SITE

(☺10am-2pm & 3-7pm daily Jul & Aug, 10am-2pm & 3-7pm Tue-Sun Jun & Sep, 10am-6pm Tue-Sun Mar-May) FREE In 2009 a small team of archaeologists began excavating these foundations of a 2300-year-old Etruscan *domus* (house), on the main road just below Vetulonia. The team uncovered dry-stone walls, a brick floor, a small terracotta altar, plenty of amphorae (tall, two-handled jars) and a small fragment of wall fresco. It's thought this is the most intact Etruscan–Roman-era villa in existence, and there may be other undiscovered sites nearby.

🛏 Sleeping & Eating

There's a snack bar on the main street near the Museo Civico (p203) and one restaurant on Piazza Stefani; neither merit a recommendation. Make sure your accommodation offers meals.

Montebelli Agriturismo & Country Hotel
AGRITURISMO €€

(📞 334 2206929; www.montebelli.com; Località Molinetto, Caldana; agriturismo d €132-170, country hotel d €210, ste €240, f €300; ⊙ closed Nov-Mar; 🅿 ❋ 🛜 🐕) A country-club feel prevails on this sprawling biodynamic wine and olive-oil estate 7km north of Vetulonia. The facilities are sensational: tennis court, two swimming pools (one indoor, one outdoor), horse-riding lessons, restaurant (five-course dinner adult/child €27/15) and sleek wellness centre. Choose between cheaper (but more atmospheric) rooms in the *agriturismo* or deluxe air-con rooms in the modern 'country hotel'.

ⓘ Getting There & Away

Tiemme (www.tiemmespa.it) buses travel once per day between Grosseto's train station and Vetulonia (€4.50, 35-40 minutes) but the schedule is of no use for day trippers.

CITTÀ DEL TUFO
📞 0564

The picturesque towns of Pitigliano, Sovana and Sorano form a triangle enclosing a dramatic landscape where local buildings have been constructed from the volcanic porous rock called 'tufo' since Etruscan times. This area is known as the Città del Tufo (City of the Tufo) or, less commonly, the Paese del Tufo (Land of the Tufo), and is protected as an archaeological park, Parco Archeologico 'Città del Tufo' (www.leviecave.it).

Pitigliano
📞 0564 / POP 3757

Perched atop a volcanic rocky outcrop towering over the surrounding countryside, this spectacularly sited hilltop town is surrounded by gorges on three sides, constituting a natural bastion completed to the east by a fort. Within the town, twisting stairways disappear around corners, cobbled alleys bend tantalisingly out of sight beneath graceful arches, and reminders of the town's once-considerable Jewish community remain in the form of a 16th-century synagogue and a unique Jewish-flavoured local cuisine.

⊙ Sights

A combined ticket (adult/reduced €6/3) gives entry to the Museo Civico Archeologico di Pitigliano and the Museo Archeologico all'Aperto 'Alberto Manzi' outside town. Another ticket (adult/reduced €10/8) gives entry to both of these as well as Sovana's Museo di San Mamiliano, the Parco Archeologico 'Città del Tufo' outside Sovana, and the Fortezza Orsini in Sorano.

La Piccola Gerusalemme
MUSEUM

(Little Jerusalem; 📞 0564 61 42 30; www.lapicco lagerusalemme.it; Vicolo Manin 30; adult/reduced €5/4; ⊙ 10am-1pm & 2.30-6pm Sun-Fri summer, 10am-12.30 & 2-3.30pm Sun-Fri winter) Head down Via Zuccarelli and turn left at a sign indicating 'La Piccola Gerusalemme' to visit this fascinating time capsule of Pitigliano's historic but sadly near-extinct Jewish culture. It incorporates a tiny, richly adorned synagogue (established in 1598 and one of only five in Tuscany), ritual bath, kosher butcher, bakery, wine cellar and dyeing workshops.

Interpretative panels recount the history: in the course of the 16th century, a Jewish community settled in Pitigliano, increasing notably when Pope Pius IV banned Jews from Rome in 1569. Under Medici rule, its members were moved into this tiny ghetto, where they remained until 1772. From then until well into the following century, the local community of 400 flourished, forming the largest Jewish community in Italy and leading to the town being dubbed 'Little Jerusalem'. By the time the Fascists introduced the race laws in 1938, most Jews had moved away; only 80 or so were left and precious few survived the war. Those who did were hidden from the Fascists by locals.

Museo Civico Archeologico di Pitigliano
MUSEUM

(📞 389 5933592; Piazza della Fortezza; adult/reduced €3/2; ⊙ 10am-6pm Fri-Sun Jun, 10am-7pm Tue-Sun Jul-Sep, 9am-5pm Fri-Sun Oct, 10am-5pm Sat & Sun Nov, hours vary rest of year) Head up the stone stairs to this small but well-run museum, which has rich displays of finds from local Etruscan sites. Highlights include some huge intact *bucchero* (black earthenware pottery) urns dating from the 6th century BC and a collection of charming pinkish-cream clay oil containers in the form of small deer.

VIE CAVE

There are at least 15 *vie cave* (sunken roads) hewn out of tufa in the valleys below Pitigliano. These enormous passages – up to 20m deep and 3m wide – are popularly believed to be sacred routes linking Etruscan necropolises and other religious sites. A more mundane explanation is that these strange ancient corridors were used to move livestock or as some kind of defence, allowing people to flit from village to village unseen. The Torciata di San Giuseppe is a procession through the Via Cava di San Giuseppe to mark the end of winter.

Two particularly good examples of *vie cave*, the Via Cava di Fratenuti FREE and the Via Cava di San Giuseppe FREE, are found 500m west of Pitigliano on the road to Sovana. Fratenuti has high vertical walls and Etruscan markings, and San Giuseppe passes the Fontana dell'Olmo, a fountain carved out of solid rock. From it stares the sculpted head of Bacchus, the god of wine and fertility.

There's a fine walk from Pitigliano to Sovana (8km) that incorporates parts of the *vie cave*. There's also an enjoyable 2km walk from the small stone bridge in the gorge below Sorano along the Via Cava San Rocco FREE to the Necropoli di San Rocco, another Etruscan burial site.

The open-air Museo Archeologico all'Aperto 'Alberto Manzi', south of Pitigliano on the road to Saturnia, contains sections of *vie cave* and several necropolises.

For up-to-date information about the *vie cave*, see www.facebook.com/pg/Parco -Archeologico-Città-del-Tufo-179178385473482.

Museo Archeologico all'Aperto 'Alberto Manzi' ARCHAEOLOGICAL SITE
(Alberto Manzi Open-Air Archaeology Museum; ✍0564 61 40 67, 389 5933592; SP127 Pantano, off SR74; adult/reduced €4/2; ⊙10am-6pm Fri-Sun May & Jun, 10am-7pm Thu-Sun Jul, 10am-7pm Tue-Sun Aug, 10am-6pm Fri-Sun Sep) This open-air museum south of Pitigliano on the road to Saturnia contains sections of *vie cave* and several Etruscan necropolises. The *vie cave* are impressive feats of construction that sit comfortably in the landscape and endow the site with a palpable sense of mystery and majesty.

Cattedrale dei Santi Pietro e Paolo CATHEDRAL
(Duomo di Pitigliano; Piazza San Gregorio 7; ⊙7.30am-noon & 3.30-7.30pm) Construction of Pitigliano's *duomo* commenced in the late 13th century; the campanile was added a century later and the facade and interior were given baroque makeovers in the early 18th century. Inside, Francesco Vanni's painting of the *Madonna del rosario* (1609), which shows the Madonna with Saints Catherine of Siena, Dominic and Pio V, is on the immediate left as you enter.

Museo di Palazzo Orsini MUSEUM
(✍0564 61 60 74; www.palazzo-orsini-pitigliano. it; Piazza della Fortezza 25; adult/child €4.50/3; ⊙10am-1pm & 3-6.30pm Tue-Sun summer, to 5.30pm winter) Enlarged by the ruling Orsinis in the 16th century, this 13th-century castle later became the residence of the local bishop and is now a museum. Its rooms are filled with an eclectic collection of artworks and local ecclesiastical oddments. Don't miss the 15th-century painted wooden sculpture of the Madonna with baby Jesus by Jacopo della Quercia.

★ Festivals & Events

Torciata di San Giuseppe CULTURAL
(⊙19 Mar) Every spring on the night of the equinox there is a torch-lit procession down the Via Cava di San Giuseppe, which culminates in a huge bonfire in Pitigliano's Piazza Garibaldi. The procession serves as a symbol of purification and renewal marking the end of winter.

🛏 Sleeping

La Casa degli Archi APARTMENT €€
(✍349 4986298; www.lacasadegliarchi.com; r €129-149; 🕲) These apartment rentals, sleeping between two and six guests across three properties, make great bases for those visiting the region. Casa degli Archi is highly recommended and two of the three apartments in a second building, Case Nuove, are also good – the third, Casa Capitano, has a strangely sloping low roof and isn't as comfortable. Reception is in Via Roma 106.

SATURNIA HOT SPRINGS

The sulphurous thermal baths at Terme di Saturnia (☑ 0564 60 08 14; www.termedi saturnia.it; pool park access Mon-Fri €26, Sat & Sun €31, after 2pm €21; ☺ 9.30am-7pm summer, to 5pm winter, closed Jan) are some 2.5km downhill from the village of Saturnia, which is 25km west of Pitigliano. You can happily replicate the Romans and spend a whole day indulging in bathing and spa treatments at this luxury resort, or take the econo-bather option at the Cascate del Gorello (Cascate del Mulino; SP10; ☺ 24hr) FREE, 1.8km south on the opposite side of the highway, where a cluster of gratis, open-air pools with temperatures at a constant 37.5°C can be found. These pools are hugely popular, but before you opt to bathe in them consider the fact that the pools are filled with water that has been expelled from the *terme* upriver, so they aren't particularly clean. And be sure not to leave any valuables in your car when bathing – thefts are a regular occurrence. Alternatively, overnight in the Hotel Saturno Fonte Pura (☑ 0564 60 13 13; www.hotelsaturn ofontepura.com; Località la Croce; d with half-board 2/3 nights €400/594; P ❋ 🛜 ☒), a spa resort with its own thermal pool.

Le Camere del Ceccottino
PENSION €€

(☑ 0564 61 42 73; www.ceccottino.com; Via Roma 159; r €100-130; ❋ 🛜) Owned and operated by the extremely helpful Chiara and Alessandro, who also run the nearby restaurant of the same name, this *pensione* boasts an excellent location near the *duomo* and five immaculately maintained and well-equipped rooms. Opt for a superior room if possible, as the standard versions are cramped. No breakfast.

✖ Eating

When here, try to sample Jewish specialities such as *sfratto pitiglianese* (a sweet made with honey and walnuts).

La Rocca
TUSCAN €

(☑ 0564 61 42 67; Piazza della Repubblica 12; meals €30, pizzas €6-8.50; ☺ 9.30am-10pm, closed Mon in winter) Generous pourings of local wine are on offer at this cavernous restaurant and wine bar next to one of the panoramic viewpoints on Piazza della Repubblica. There are far more seafood options on the menu than is usual, which is a refreshing change in rural Tuscany. In summer, the terrace seating is popular.

Il Tufo Allegro
TUSCAN €€

(☑ 0564 61 61 92; www.facebook.com/iltufoallegro; Vicolo della Costituzione 5; meals €42; ☺ 12.30-2.30pm & 7.30-9.30pm Wed-Sun) The aromas emanating from the kitchen door off Via Zuccarelli should be enough to draw you down the stairs and into the cosy dining rooms, which are carved out of tufa. Chef Domenico Pichini's menu ranges from traditional to modern and all of his creations rely heavily on local produce for inspiration. It's near La Piccola Gerusalemme (p204).

★ Hostaria del Ceccottino
TUSCAN €€€

(☑ 0564 61 42 73; www.ceccottino.com; Piazza San Gregorio VII 64; meals €53; ☺ 12.30-3pm & 7-10pm Fri-Wed mid-Mar–mid-Jan; 🛜) Specialising in *piatti tipici* (typical dishes), Ceccottino serves delicious versions of Tuscan classics such as *spezzatino di cinghiale* (wild-boar stew), but also offers less-common dishes inspired by local produce. There might be a *tagliatelle* (ribbon pasta) made with *bottarga* (salted dried cod roe) from Orbetello, or a *tortelli* stuffed with fresh ricotta and *ortica* (nettles). Excellent local wine list too.

🍷 Drinking & Nightlife

There are a few wine bars on and around Piazza della Repubblica and a popular cafe on Piazza Francesco Petruccioli near the main gate to the historic centre. The local DOC wine, Bianco di Pitigliano, is a crisp white with a good balance of floral and mineral notes.

Angiolina Vineria
WINE BAR

(☑ 0564 61 52 91; www.facebook.com/angiolinaeno teca; Piazza della Repubblica 209; ☺ noon-8.30pm Mon-Fri, to midnight Fri & Sat Easter-Oct) It may be modest in size, but this wine bar is ambitious in its aspirations. There's a small but stellar list of wines by the glass (order the Roccapesta Morellino di Scansano if it's on offer), and a similarly styled food menu. Try the *merenda toscana* platter of local delicacies.

ℹ Information

Tourist Office (☑ 0564 61 71 11; www. comune.pitigliano.gr.it; Piazza Garibaldi 12;

🕒 9am-12.30pm & 3.30-6.30pm Tue-Sat, 9am-12.30pm Sun, extended hours summer) In the piazza just inside the the main gate to the historic centre.

❶ Getting There & Away

Tiemme (www.tiemmespa.it) buses leave from Via Santa Chiara, just off Piazza Petruccioli. Some routes operate Monday to Saturday only; buy tickets at the newsagent next to La Rocca restaurant in Piazza della Repubblica. Services include the following:

Grosseto (€8.40, two hours, three daily)

Orbetello (€6.90, 90 minutes, one daily)

Siena (€12.20, three hours, one daily)

Sorano (€1.50, 15 minutes, three daily)

Sovana (€1.50, 20 minutes, one daily)

Sovana

📞 0564

The main attractions at this postcard-pretty village are a cobbled main street that dates from Roman times, two austerely beautiful Romanesque churches and a museum showcasing a collection of ancient gold coins.

⊙ Sights & Activities

★ **Necropoli di Sovana**   ARCHAEOLOGICAL SITE
(📞0564 61 40 74; www.leviecave.it; €5; 🕒10am-7pm summer, to 6pm Oct, to 5pm Sat & Sun Nov-Mar; ℗) At Tuscany's most significant Etruscan tombs, part of the Parco Archeologico 'Città del Tufo', signs in Italian and English guide you around four elaborate burial sites. The headline exhibit is the **Tomba Ildebranda**, named after Pope Gregory VII, which preserves traces of its carved columns and stairs. The **Tomba dei Demoni Alati** (Tomb of the Winged Demons) features a recumbent headless terracotta figure.

The carving of a sea demon with huge wings that was the original centrepiece of that tomb is now protected in a roofed enclosure nearby. The **Tomba del Tifone** (Tomb of the Typhoon) is about 300m down a trail running alongside a rank of tomb facades cut from the rock face. Two arresting lengths of *vie cave* (one known as 'Cavone' and the other 'Poggio Prisca') are nearby.

On the opposite side of the site is the **Tomba della Sirena** and another *via cava*, **San Sebastiano**. The latter can be accessed at all times, not just within the Necropoli's official hours.

Find the Necropoli 1.5km east of town.

Cattedrale di San Pietro   CATHEDRAL
(Via del Duomo; adult/child 12-17/child under 12 €2/1/free; 🕒10am-1pm & 2.30-7pm Apr-Oct, 10am-1pm & 2.30-5.30pm Nov–early Jan, 10am-1pm & 2.30-6pm mid-Feb–Mar, weekends only early-Jan–mid-Feb) Built over a 200-year period starting in the 12th century, this Romanesque–Gothic cathedral was commissioned by local boy-made-big Pope Gregory VII (Hildebrand of Sovana; c 1015–85). Its strangely positioned doorway is decorated with carvings of people, animals and plants, and its huge interior has a beauty that owes nothing to artworks and everything to the genius of its unknown architect.

Museo di San Mamiliano   MUSEUM
(📞0564 61 40 74; www.leviecave.it; Piazza del Pretorio; adult/child €2/free; 🕒10am-1pm & 3-7pm Thu-Tue Apr-Oct, 10am-1pm & 2-5pm Sat & Sun Nov & Dec, 10am-1pm & 3-6pm Sat & Sun Mar) In 2004 archaeologists excavating beneath the ruined 9th-century Church of St Mamiliano made the discovery of a lifetime – a cache of 498 gold coins buried in a vase under the church floor in the 5th century AD. Most are now displayed in this small museum of Roman times, which occupies the now-restored church.

Santa Maria Maggiore   CHURCH
(Piazza del Pretorio; 🕒9am-5pm) Designed in a Romanesque–Gothic transitional style, the 16th-century frescoes in the apse of this church are perhaps the main reason to head inside; there's also an unusual stone *ciborium* (vaulted canopy over the altar) dating from the 9th century.

La Biagiola   WINE
(📞366 676 64 00; www.labiagiola.it; Località Pianetti; 🕒by appointment) Those interested in wine and archaeology might want to combine the two by visiting this wine estate 7km north of Sovana. In 2004 the remains of an imperial Roman villa were discovered in the vineyard; the archaeologists leading an ongoing excavation welcome visitors to join them for hands-on experiences assisting on the dig in summer. See www.culturaterritorio.org for details.

🛏 Sleeping

Sovana Hotel & Resort   HOTEL €€
(📞338 5802977, 0564 61 70 30; www.sovanahotel.it; Via del Duomo 66; r €125-145; ℗ 🖥 ➰) The huge garden surrounding this hotel is nothing less than extraordinary, featuring a maze, Etruscan ruin, olive grove and

swimming pool grand enough for a Roman emperor's villa. Rooms aren't quite as swish, but they are perfectly comfortable and offer good value. There's also a bar, restaurant and communal lounge with open fire. Special two-night deals (weekdays/weekends €298/328) include dinner.

PoggioBa   B&B €€

(☑ 347 3639147, 0564 61 57 37; www.poggioba.it; C S Pian della Madonna 17a; s/d/tr €100/110/145; P ☜) If you're after a hefty dose of Tuscan tranquillity, this is the place to come. Only 3km from Sovana, PoggioBa offers two rooms with private entrances; the tower room with its spectacular views is the best. Host Stefania has used antique furniture and objets d'art to give her B&B loads of character; she also provides an excellent breakfast.

Eating

★ **Vino al Vino**   TUSCAN €

(☑ 0564 61 71 08; www.facebook.com/enoteca. vinoalvino; Via del Duomo 10; cheese & salumi plates €15, soup €8; ☺ 10.30am-9pm Wed-Mon mid-Mar–Dec, 10.30am-9pm Sat & Sun Jan–mid-Mar; ☑) Mellow jazz plays on the soundtrack, art adorns every wall and the vibe is friendly at this hybrid cafe and *enoteca* on Sovana's main street. The speciality-roast coffee is good; cakes (sourced in Pitigliano) are even better. At lunch or dinner, glasses of wine and tasting plates of local produce reign supreme. Vegan and vegetarian soups and *bruschette* are available.

ⓘ Information

The extremely helpful **tourist office** (☑ 0564 61 40 74; www.facebook.com/pg/Parco-Ar cheologico-Città-del-Tufo-179178385473482/; Piazza del Pretorio; ☺ 10am-1pm & 3-7pm Fri-Wed mid-Mar–Oct, 10am-1pm & 2-5pm Sat & Sun Nov & Dec) is in the Palazzo Pretorio on the main piazza.

ⓘ Getting There & Away

Between Monday and Saturday, **Tiemme** (www. tiemmespa.it) buses travel to Pitigliano (€1.50, 30 minutes, five daily) and Sorano (€1.50, 15 minutes, two daily).

Sorano

☑ 0564 / POP 3322

Sorano's setting is truly dramatic – sitting astride a rocky outcrop, its weatherworn stone houses are built along a ridge overlooking the Lente river and gorge. Below the ridgeline are *cantine* (cellars) dug out of tufa, as well as a series of terraced gardens, many part-hidden from public view.

◉ Sights & Activities

Fortezza Orsini   FORT

(☑ 0564 63 34 24; adult/reduced €5/3.50; ☺ 10am-1pm & 3-7pm Tue-Sun summer, 10am-1pm & 2-5pm Sat & Sun Nov & Dec) Work on this massive fortress started in the 11th century. Today it still stands sentinel over the town, its sturdy walls linking two bastions surrounded by a dry moat. The highlight of any visit is undoubtedly a guided tour of the evocative subterranean passages (tour schedule varies), which are noticeably chilly even in the height of the Tuscan summer.

Area Archeologica di Vitozza   ARCHAEOLOGICAL SITE

(☺ 10am-dusk) FREE More than 200 caves pepper a high rock ridge here, making it one of the largest troglodyte dwellings in Italy. The complex was first inhabited in prehistoric times. To explore the site, you'll need two hours and sturdy walking shoes. It's 4km due east of Sorano; there's a signed walking path between Sorano and the site.

🛏 Sleeping

★ **Sant'Egle**   AGRITURISMO €€

(☑ 329 4250285; www.santegle.it; Case Sparse Sant'Egle 18; r €170-280, glamping €150; ☺ closed mid-Jan–mid-Mar; P ☜ ☒) ✿ If only all accommodation could be as sustainable and comfortable as this. Set on an organic multi-crop farm, it offers individually designed bedrooms in a carefully renovated 17th-century customs house, one luxury glamping tent and a wonderfully tranquil garden environment in which to de-stress and relax. Four-night minimum stay in August.

Almost everything here is organic, from the bedding and the toiletries (made with extra-virgin olive oil) to the gourmet breakfast buffet. There's also a tiny bio-pool, a yoga pavilion (bi-weekly classes May to September) and two al fresco hot tubs.

Hotel della Fortezza   HOTEL €€

(☑ 0564 63 35 49; www.hoteldellafortezza.com; Piazza Cairoli 5; s/d/ste €104/109/139; ☺ closed mid-Nov–Mar; P ☜) Fancy the idea of sleeping in a medieval castle? If so, this comfortable hotel inside one of the fortress' bastions is for you. Many of its 16 rooms have spectacular views, but some are cramped – the best are the three recently renovated rooms in the tower. There's a lovely breakfast room with panoramic views and an attached restaurant. Limited wi-fi.

Eating & Drinking

La Cantina dei Sapori
TUSCAN €
(☑ 0564 63 37 48; Via della Madonnina 2/4; taglieri $8.50-10, soup €7, lasagne €8; ☺10am-8pm Wed-Mon) A popular local hangout, this laid-back *enoteca* offers a limited menu of soup, lasagna and *taglieri* (cheese-and-meat boards). There's a good choice of local wines by the glass and bottle, as well as a few artisanal beers.

Hosteria del Borgo
TUSCAN €€
(☑ 0564 63 84 31; www.hosteriadelborgo.it; Via del Borgo 46; meal €37; ☺noon-4pm & 6-10pm) The view from the terrace of this friendly *osteria* (casual tavern) is simply spectacular, making it a particularly popular choice in fine weather. The menu is traditionally Maremmese – your best bet is to order a pasta such as the hand-made *pappardelle* with wild-boar sauce, or opt for one of the rustic dishes made with locally grown beans and lentils. Good house wine too.

Ristorante Fidalma
TUSCAN €€
(☑ 0564 63 30 56; www.ristorantefidalma.com; Piazza Busatti 5; meals €27; ☺12.30-3.30pm & 7.30-10.30pm Thu-Tue; ✱) There's a lot to like at this barn-like restaurant just off Sorano's main piazza. The menu is dominated by home-style Maremmese dishes (expect lots of meat), the pasta is handmade by nonna, and the waiters are incredibly friendly. There's even a well-priced set menu of two courses, *contorno* (side dish) and a coffee for €20. Avoid the house wine.

Cantina L'Ottava Rima
WINE BAR
(☑ 349 8024196; www.cantinaottavarima.com; Via del Borgo 25; ☺noon-3pm & 6pm-midnight Thu-Sun summer, reduced hours winter) Here you'll sip your drink surrounded by carved rock walls – this casual *cantina* has been hacked out of the tufo. Add rickety tables and it's an atmospheric spot to sample local wines and simple dishes that highlight quality Maremmese produce. It's on a terraced walkway towards the foot of town.

ⓘ Information

The main **tourist office** (☑ 0564 63 30 99; ☺10am-1pm & 3-7pm Thu-Tue Apr–Sep, 10am-1pm & 2-5pm Sat & Sun Oct-Dec) is in Piazza

A WINE LOVER'S RETREAT

A highly regarded local wine producer, Terenzi (☑ 0564 59 96 41; www.terenzi.eu; Località Montedonico, Scansano; ☺9.30am-7.30pm Apr-Oct, 9.30am-5.30pm Mon, Thu & Fri, 9.30am-1pm & 2-5.30pm Wed, 10am-6pm Sat, 9.30am-12.30pm Sun Nov-Mar) is best known for its Madrechiesa Morellino di Scansano DOCG Riserva, a ruby-red Sangiovese with berry and violet overtones. Call ahead to book a free tour of the vineyards and winery, or visit the *cantina* for a tasting (€9-30, noon-3pm).

You'll find the vineyard on a scenic road just outside the town of Scansano, on a secondary route between Pitigliano and Grosseto. Its lovely on-site inn, the eight-room, pool-clad Locanda Terenzi (☑ 0564 59 96 01; d €145-155, ste €175; ☺closed Jan; P� ☎ ✱), makes a perfect base for travellers wanting to soak up wonderful views – row after row of vines arranged on the hillside running down to the valley – and wine over a few days.

Busatti, next to the belvedere with its scenic viewpoints and plaque commemorating the liberation of the town from the Nazis.

ⓘ Getting There & Away

From Monday to Saturday, **Tiemme** (www.tiemmespa.it) operates five daily services to Pitigliano (€1.50, 20 minutes); there are three services from Pitigliano. There are three services each way on Sundays.

BASSA MAREMMA

☑ 0564

The Bassa (Lower) Maremma starts at Grosseto and sweeps along the coast, incorporating the peninsula of Monte Argentario and the mountains and marshes of the Parco Regionale della Maremma. It's a wonderland for nature lovers, full of pristine landscapes with abundant local flora and fauna, and it's also a hugely popular spot for outdoor activities including walking, horse riding and birdwatching.

This is where Tuscany's famed Maremmana cows are raised, so the local beef is among Italy's best. Seafood is also plentiful and fresh – try the famed *bottarga* and *anguilla sfumata* (spicy, smoked eel) from Orbetello.

ERMESS/SHUTTERSTOCK ©

VALERIOMEI/SHUTTERSTOCK ©

MILOSK50/SHUTTERSTOCK ©

SCOTT YELLOX/SHUTTERSTOCK ©

1. Via Cava (p205)
Etruscan *vie cave* (sunken roads) near Pitigliano.

2. Cascate del Gorello (p206)
Thermal pools in Saturnia.

3. Cattedrale di San Cerbone (p198), Massa Marittima
A 13th-century cathedral on pretty Piazza Garibaldi.

4. Pitigliano (p204)
A spectacularly located hilltop town.

Grosseto

☎ 0564 / POP 82,036

The provincial capital of the Maremma, Grosseto's major drawcard is its proximity to the wonderful nature reserves that line the nearby coast. One of the last Sienese-dominated towns to fall into Medici hands (in 1559), its bastions, fortress and hexagonal-shaped, 2.5km-long walls were raised by the Florentines in order to protect what was then an important grain and salt depot for the grand duchy.

Though a pleasant-enough city, Grosseto's lack of headline tourist attractions and infrastructure means that there is a good reason why it is usually relegated to a mere navigational marker for those taking the coastal highway to or from Rome.

The city is renowned for its heavy winter rainfalls, which have caused catastrophic floods in the past.

The main bar and cafe strips are Via San Martino, Via Ricasoli and Via degli Aldobrandeschi in the *centro storico* (historic centre).

★ **Museo Archeologico e d'Arte della Maremma**   MUSEUM

(MAAM; ☎ 0564 48 87 50; http://maam.comune.grosseto.it; Piazza Baccarini 3; adult/reduced €5/2.50; ☺10am-7pm Tue-Fri, 10am-1pm & 5-8pm Sat & Sun summer, reduced hours rest of year) Grosseto's major tourist drawcard features an archaeological museum on the ground floor and a museum of ecclesiastical art upstairs. Items unearthed from Roselle are given pride of place downstairs – don't miss the statues of the family of Emperor Augustus. There's also an impressive collection of Etruscan funerary urns. The 2nd floor is home to artworks spanning the 13th to 19th centuries, including Stefano di Giovanni's *Madonna delle ciliege* (Madonna with Cherries; c 1445), which originally hung in the city's *duomo*.

Roselle   ARCHAEOLOGICAL SITE

(☎ 0564 40 24 03; SS223; adult/reduced €4/2; ☺8.15am-4.45pm Tue-Sun) In the 7th century BC Roselle (Rusellae) was already an Etruscan town; it fell under Roman control in the 3rd century BC. Although there are no great monuments, you do get a clear idea of the town's layout from the remaining Roman defensive walls, amphitheatre, and traces of houses and baths, forum, workshops and streets. When here, be sure to take the 1km walk alongside the settlement's massive, still intact 8000-year-old walls. It's located 11km northeast of Grosseto off the E78.

Guided Tours   WALKING

(☎ 0564 48 85 73) FREE In an excellent initiative, Grosseto's tourist office has introduced a programme of free one-hour guided walking tours in and around the city. Choose from themed tours highlighting Grosseto's 19th-century architecture, its walls, its churches, its museums, the marina and Roselle. Entry fees apply at the archaeological museum, Roselle and the walls. Advance bookings essential.

Grand Hotel Bastiani   HOTEL €€

(☎ 0564 2 00 47; www.hotelbastiani.com; Piazza Gioberti 64; budget/standard s from €76/87, budget/standard d from €86/97, ste from €97; ❄ ☎) Housed within an imposing but worn old building, the Bastiani offers dark budget rooms, comfortable and airy standard options, and an excellent breakfast buffet. It's set just inside the main gate into the *centro storico*, and there are charged public car parks close by.

Al Numero Nove   TUSCAN €

(☎ 0564 42 76 98; Via degli Aldobrandeschi 9; meals €24; ☺noon-3pm & 6-10pm Tue-Sun; ☑) Ultrafresh ingredients and budget pricing are the hallmarks at this hybrid restaurant and wine bar near the *duomo*. There are fish and vegetarian options aplenty, as well as *bruschette* to graze on if you don't feel like a full meal. No *coperto* (cover charge).

L'Uva e il Malto   ITALIAN €€

(☎ 0564 41 12 11; www.facebook.com/Uva.Malto; Via Mazzini 165; meals €42; ☺noon-2pm & 7pm-midnight Mon-Sat, noon-2pm Sunday) Chef Moreno Cardone takes great pride in his dishes, using quality local produce to create tasty, attractively presented meals. There are fish and meat options aplenty, but few vegetarian choices. Wife Samantha runs front of house and is always happy to guide you through the predominantly local wine list.

ⓘ Information

There is a **tourism information point** (☎ 0564 48 85 73; www.quimaremmatoscana.it; Corso Carducci 5; ☺9.30am-1.30pm & 2-6pm Apr-Sep, 10am-1pm Wed-Mon Oct-Mar), near the *duomo* (cathedral).

ⓘ Getting There & Away

BUS

Buses usually leave from the train station. Buy tickets at the **Tiemme ticket office** (Grosseto Train Station; ⏰7.30am-6.45pm Mon-Sat) next door. Monday to Saturday services include the following:

Florence (€14.10, two hours, six daily)
Massa Marittima (€5.60, one hour, four daily)
Pitigliano (€8.40, two hours, three daily)
Rome Airport (€17, two hours, two daily)
Siena (€8.40, 80 minutes, 10 daily)

CAR & MOTORCYCLE

A Zona a Traffico Limitato (ZTL; Limited Traffic Zone) applies in the *centro storico*. There's plenty of paid car parking surrounding the city walls; the most convenient is at Porta Corsica, in front of the children's playground next to the city gate on Viale Zimenes (€0.60 per hour, 9am-1pm & 4-8pm Monday to Saturday).

TRAIN

The main coastal train line runs between Pisa, Livorno and Rome via Grosseto. Services include the high-speed *(Alta Velocità) Frecciabianca*. Regular (roughly hourly) connections from Grosseto include the following:

Genoa (Intercity €36, four hours)
Livorno (*Regionale* €11.70, 1¾ hours)
Pisa (*Regionale* €13.10, two hours)
Rome (Intercity €24, 1¾ hours)

Parco Regionale della Maremma

📍0564

Hundreds of acres of forests, pristine coasts, countless activities and your chance to be a cowboy are all on offer in this wild and wonderful national park (📍0564 39 32 38; www.parco-maremma.it; adult/reduced from €6/4; ⏰8.30am-4pm Apr–mid-Jun, to 6pm mid-Jun–Oct, to 2pm Nov-Mar). It's also a popular destination for beachgoers, who enjoy safe swimming at the 8km-long sandy beach at Marina di Albarese.

OFF THE BEATEN TRACK

NIKI DE SAINT PHALLE'S GIARDINO DEI TAROCCHI

Driving inland from the Via Aurelia (SS1) towards Pescia Fiorentina, an extraordinary sight catches the eye. In an abandoned quarry set amidst flat expanses of farmland and olive groves are the monumental multicoloured sculptures that make up the Giardino dei Tarocchi (The Tarot Garden; www.ilgiardinodeitarocchi.it; Località Garavicchio-Capalbio; adult/reduced €12/7; ⏰2.30-7.30pm Apr–mid-Oct; P), a fantastical sculpture garden conceived and constructed by Franco-American artist Niki de Saint Phalle (1930-2002).

A sculptor, painter and filmmaker, de Saint Phalle commenced her artistic career in her twenties, while working as an occasional fashion model and leading an itinerant bohemian life in Europe with her husband, American writer Harry Mathews, and their two children. Her early works were paintings in the naïve style but from the late 1950s she began to make assemblages from household objects and castoffs. After her marriage to Mathews disintegrated she began a relationship with Swiss sculptor Jean Tinguely, whom she eventually married in 1971; they amicably divorced in 1991.

Throughout her artistic career De Saint Phalle explored the various roles of women in society, often in monumental sculptural form. Her *Nanas* series (1964-73) features colourful archetypal female figures dancing or using their bodies in uninhibited and joyous ways. In 1978, she began to plan her most ambitious work, this sculpture garden in the Maremma. Influenced by Antoni Gaudí's Parc Güell in Barcelona, she designed a group of oversized figures representing characters from the tarot pack (including the High Priestess, Wheel of Fortune and Justice). Construction on the site, which was donated by the Agnelli family of Fiat fame, commenced in 1980 and de Saint Phalle lived inside one of the sculptures – *The Empress* – when working here. Her bedroom was inside one breast, and her kitchen inside the other.

The garden was officially opened in May 1998, when its structures built from welded steel frameworks covered in cement and decorated with multicoloured mosaic glass, ceramic tiles, mirrors and polished stones were unveiled to the public. De Saint Phalle was working on designs for new garden features when she died in La Jolla, California, in 2002.

BIRDWATCHING PARADISE

The marshes surrounding the coastal town of Castiglione della Pescaia are an important shelter for migrating birds, and the 12.7-sq-km nature reserve, Riserva Naturale Provinciale Diaccia Botrona (☑ 389 003 13 69, 348 774 32 01; www.maremma-online.it), off the SS322 is a wonderful chance to explore this flat yet fascinating landscape. Boat tours (adult/child €12/6; 5pm, 6pm and 7pm Tuesday to Sunday mid-June to mid-September) enable you to spot waterfowl, heron, flamingo and other species; book in advance. Tours leave from Casa Rossa Ximenes, a handsome sluice-house commissioned in the mid-18th century by Grand Duke Pietro Leopoldo I of Lorraine to help reclaim the marshes for agriculture and reduce the area's horrifyingly high levels of malaria.

Activities

Park Access is limited to 12 signed walking trails ranging in length from 2.5km to 13km; seven leave from the main Alberese visitor centre, three from the seasonal visitor centre in Talamone and two from Collecchio, near Alberese Scalo. The most popular routes are the easy 7km A2 ('Le Torri') and the demanding A1, a 7.8km uphill hike to San Rabano Abbey and the Torre Uccellina. From mid-June to mid-September you can only visit on a guided tour, because of possible bushfires; call ahead to check times.

The park's main visitor centre can organise guided horseback-riding excursions for both novice and experienced riders (€46-100); advance bookings are essential. Experienced riders can also sign up for a 4½-hour experience with the famed *butteri* (traditional Maremmese cowboys) at Tenuta di Alberese (☑ 0564 40 71 00; www.alberese.com; Strada del Mare 25, Spergolaia, Alberese; ☺ 10am-1pm Thu Jul & Aug, other times by reservation), a 400-hectare cattle farm.

Silva Società Cooperativa (☑ 375 5828328; www.silvacoop.com; guided tours adult/child 6-14yr/child under 6yr €18/10/free) conducts tranquil 2½-hour guided canoe tours along peaceful waterways, with the chance of seeing ducks, geese and even beaver.

MBM Bike Store (☑ 339 4609310; www.noleggiobicimaremma.it; Via del Bersagliere; one-day city/mountain bike hire €10/25, one-day e-bike hire €35-40) operates a stand next to the Alberese visitor centre and rents city, mountain and e-bikes for those who are keen to follow well-graded bike trails through the park.

Visitor centres can provide maps showing all bike and hiking trails.

Sleeping & Eating

There are quite a few *agriturismi* within and around the park.

La Bottega Maremmana   DELI €
(Via del Bersagliere, Alberese; panini €2.50-4, pizza slice €1.50; ☺ 8am-2pm Mon-Thu, 7am-2pm & 4-8pm Fri & Sat, 7am-3pm Sun Apr-Sep, 8am-3pm Oct-Mar) This store opposite the park's Alberese visitor centre stocks a range of groceries, wine and local produce. It also sells *panini* and pizza slices. Coffee is available at the attached cafe.

Osteria Il Mangiapane   TUSCAN €€
(☑ 0564 40 72 63, 340 5345770; Strada Cerretale 9, Alberese; meals €28; ☺ 12.30-2pm & 7.30-9.30pm Fri-Wed Easter-Sep; ⛄) You can't get more Maremmese than this place. There are tables inside, but everyone prefers to sit in the garden, where there are trees and a children's play area. The cuisine is solidly traditional – try the beef, which is sourced from the Terre Regionali Toscani farm.

Shopping

★ **La Bottega di Alberese**   FOOD & DRINKS
(☑ 0564 40 72 65; Via dell'Artigliere 4, Alberese; ☺ 8.30am-1pm & 4-7pm, closed Mon, Wed & Sun Oct-May) Showcasing produce from the local farm of the same name, this shop is manna from heaven for self-caterers – look out for top-quality Maremmana beef, honey, dried pasta made with wheat grown on the farm, olive oils, *pecorino* (sheep's-milk cheese), *salumi* and cheap DOCG wines.

ⓘ Information

Main Visitor Centre (☑ 0564 39 32 38; Via del Bersagliere 7-9, Alberese; ☺ 8am-6pm mid-Jun–mid-Sep, to 4pm mid-Sep–mid-Nov, to 2pm mid-Nov–mid-Jun)

Seasonal Visitor Centre (☑ 0564 88 71 73; Via Nizza 12, Talamone; ☺ 9am-noon & 3-5pm Jul & Aug) A summer-only visitor centre that adjoins the Talamone Aquarium at the park's southern edge (the aquarium showcases the local lagoon environment and works to safeguard local turtles).

Getting There & Away

Tiemme (www.tiemmespa.it) buses travel between Alberese and Grosseto (€2.60, eight daily). Buy tickets at Caffè Hawaii near the bus stop.

Orbetello

📞 0564 / POP 14,744

Set on a balance-beam isthmus running through a lagoon south of the Parco Regionale della Maremma, Orbetello is a relatively laid-back destination with some appealing, if low-key, historic buildings and a bird-packed nature reserve.

Restaurants are scattered on and around Corso Italia and Via Roma.

Oasi WWF Laguna di Orbetello   NATURE RESERVE
(📞0564 89 88 29; www.wwf.it; SS Aurelia, Località Ceriolo; ⊙guided visits 9.30am & 3.30pm Sat & Sun Sep-Apr) FREE An extraordinary 140 species of birds have been seen on Orbetello Lagoon. The best place to spot some of them is at the L'Oasi WWF north of town. As well as winter weekend visits, you can also explore the reserve in July and August (by appointment only) on Tuesday and Saturday at 5.30pm.

I Pescatori   SEAFOOD €€
(📞0564 86 06 11; www.facebook.com/IPescatoriOrbetello; Via Leopardi 9; meals €30; ⊙12.30-2.30pm & 7.30-10pm Sat, 12.30-2.30pm Sun, extended hours summer) Orbetello's fish co-operative restaurant may lack frills but it makes amends with the freshness of its lagoon-caught seafood. Grab a ticket, tick off your choices on the menu printouts, order at the counter, then claim a table. The mixed fisherman's antipasti, *anguilla sfumata* and seafood pastas are popular orders. In summer, bookings are advisable.

Information

Tourist Office (📞0564 86 04 47; www.proloco-orbetello.it; Piazza della Repubblica 1; ⊙10am-noon & 4-6pm) Diagonally opposite the *duomo*.

Getting There & Away

Frequent **Tiemme** (www.tiemmespa.it) buses connect Orbetello-Monte Argentario train station in Orbetello Scalo with Orbetello's port (€1.50, 5 minutes) and with both Porto Santo Stefano and Porto Ercole on Monte Argentario (€2.60, 20 minutes).

Frequent train services also travel between Grosseto and Orbetello-Monte Argenteria (*regionale* €4.60, 25 minutes).

Monte Argentario

📞 0564 / POP 12,455

Once an island, this rugged promontory became linked to the mainland by three slender, 6km-long accumulations of sand, one of which now forms the isthmus of Orbetello. Overdevelopment has spoiled the promontory's northern side, particularly around crowded Porto Santo Stefano. Porto Ercole on the promontory's less-frenetic southern side is a smaller and more attractive harbour, with three historic forts and a long sandy beach known as Feniglia. Traffic on the promontory is simply horrendous and accommodation prices head into the stratosphere during August – avoid visiting at this time.

Sights & Activities

Old Town   HISTORIC SITE
(Porto Ercole) Porto Ercole's *centro storico* stretches up the hillside, past the sandwiched-in Chiesa di Sant'Erasmo and up towards the largest of the three Spanish forts that surround the town.

Forte Stella   FORT
(Porto Ercole; adult/reduced €2/1; ⊙5-9pm daily Jul-Aug, 10.30am-12.30pm & 4-8pm Sat & Sun late Apr-Jun & Sep) Built by the Spanish, this

WORTH A TRIP

MAGLIANO IN TOSCANA

A 23km drive inland from Orbetello leads to this hilltop town, fortified by monumental walls built between the 14th and 16th centuries. Specific sights are limited to the Romanesque churches of San Martino and San Giovanni Battista (the latter has a remodelled Renaissance facade), but the trip is well rewarded by lunch at one of the Maremma's best restaurants. Refined modern cuisine at Antica Trattoria Aurora (📞0564 59 27 74; Via Chiasso Lavagnini 12; meals €43; ⊙noon-2.30pm & 7.30-10pm Thu-Tue Mar-Dec) is refreshingly untraditional – try burrata cream with anchovies, mullet eggs and breadcrumbs if it's on the menu. In summer, tables in the pretty rear garden are popular so book ahead.

16th-centry fort, an unusual star shape (hence its name), is the only Porto Ercole fort open to the public.

Caravaggio's Tomb   TOMB
(Via Caravaggio, Porto Ercole) One of the greatest painters of the Renaissance, Michelangelo Merisi Caravaggio, died in Porto Ercole on 18 July 1610 after a tempestuous and short life. In 2014, authorities 'found' his bones in a local crypt and DNA tested them to prove their authenticity. They then constructed this extremely strange tomb in the centre of town. Not everyone approved – many locals were shocked at the reliquary-like structure, which they deemed more suited to a saint than the sinner Caravaggio undoubtedly was.

Via Panoramica   SCENIC DRIVE
Signs point you towards this narrow route that encircles the entire Monte Argentario promontory. It offers sweeping sea views across to the hazy whaleback of the Isola de Giglio. The road can get dangerously busy in summer.

🛏 Sleeping & Eating

Most accommodation options close from late October to late April. During August, everything is solidly booked months or even a year in advance.

Il Pellicano   HOTEL €€€
(☑ 0564 85 81 11; www.hotelilpellicano.com; Località Lo Sbarcatello, Porto Ercole; r/ste from €650/1800; ☺ mid-Apr–mid-Oct; 🅿 ❄ @ 🛜 🏊) One of Italy's most famous hotels, Il Pellicano is perched on a clifftop overlooking the Tyrrhenian Sea and certainly makes the most of its location – the pool, restaurant terraces and many rooms command spectacular views. Rooms are amenity-packed, and common areas are superswish. Levels of service are exactly as one would expect from a hotel of this reputation (ie stellar).

Pozioni di Neve   GELATO €
(☑ 0564 81 08 40; www.pozionidineve.it; Piazza Vittorio Emanuele 16, Porto Santo Stefano; gelato €2.50-5; ☺ 2-8pm Mon-Sat, noon-8pm Sun, extended hours summer; ☑) Its name means 'snow potions', and there are plenty of delectable icy concoctions (granita or crushed ice with natural flavour, sorbet and gelato) on offer at this artisanal gelateria. Fresh organic ingredients are the focus, and the results

are popular with locals and tourists alike. Vegan choices available.

★ Bar/Caffè Giulia   CAFE
(Via del Molo 16, Porto Santo Stefano; ☺ 7am-2.30am daily summer, closed Mon rest of year) Overlooking a small harbour framed by slopes of colourfully painted buildings, Giulia is a popular locals' haunt. Its waterside terrace is a picturesque spot for a morning coffee, panino (€4) or late-afternoon aperitivo. Find it at the far (western) end of the lungomare (seafront promenade).

ℹ Information

There are tourist offices in both Porto Santo Stefano and Porto Ercole. Both can supply the handy Hiking Through Argentario map, which outlines 27 hiking trails on Monte Argentario.

Porto Santo Stefano Tourist Office (☑ 0564 81 42 08; www.prolocomonteargentario.it; Piazzale del Valle, Porto Santo Stefano; ☺ 3-6pm Fri, 9.30am-12.30pm & 4-7pm Sat, 9.30am-12.30pm Sun Easter–mid-Jun & Oct, 9.30am-12.30pm & 4.30-7.30pm daily mid-Jun–Sep) Set at the far eastern end of the port.

Porto Ercole Tourist Office (☑ 0564 81 19 79; www.prolocomonteargentario.it; Piazza Roma, Porto Ercole; ☺ 10am-1pm & 4-7pm Sat, 10am-1pm Sun mid-Apr–early Jun, 9.30am-1pm & 5-7.30pm daily mid-Jun–Sep, 9am-noon & 3-6pm Sat, 9am-noon Sun Oct) Near the port.

ℹ Getting There & Away

BOAT
Maregiglio (www.maregiglio.it) and **Toremar** (www.toremar.it) operate year-round ferry services between Porto Santo Stefano and the island of Giglio, one hour away. Fares cost around €30 return per passenger and €115 return per car.

BUS
Tiemme (www.tiemmespa.it) buses connect Orbetello-Monte Argentario train station with Porto Santo Stefano (€2.60, 20 minutes, frequent) and Porto Ercole (€2.60, 20 minutes, seven services Monday to Saturday, 11 services Sunday).

CAR & MOTORCYCLE
Follow signs for Monte Argentario from the SS1, which connects Grosseto with Rome. In Porto Ercole, park in Piazza Roma or Piazza Amerigo Vespucci; in Porto Santa Stefano park on the lungomare. Street parking costs €0.50 per hour in both towns.

Central Coast & Elba

Includes ➡
Livorno 220
Castiglioncello 227
Bolgheri......................228
San Vincenzo 229
Suvereto.....................232
Golfo di Baratti...........233
Elba 234
Giglio, Gorgona &
Pianosa 246
Capraia.......................246

Best Places to Eat

➡ La Pineta (p232)

➡ Scom Posto (p225)

➡ Alle Vettovaglie (p226)

➡ La Barrocciaia (p225)

➡ Enoteca Tognoni (p228)

Best Places to Stay

➡ Agriturismo Due Palme (p239)

➡ Hotel Ilio (p240)

➡ Belvedere di Suvereto (p233)

➡ Hotel Hermitage (p242)

Why Go?

Despite possessing the types of landscapes that dreams are made of, much of this part of Tuscany feels far away from well-beaten tourist trails. Here you can investigate the multicultural past and extraordinary cuisine of port-city Livorno, then follow the Strada del Vino e dell'Olio Costa degli Etruschi south, visiting vineyards, olive groves, medieval villages and scenic archaeological sites along the way.

And then there's Elba: ripe for al fresco frolics, this Mediterranean island has a landscape dotted with orange trees, palms, vineyards and sandy coves begging you to lay down a beach towel. It's the perfect place to wind down after a stretch of busy Tuscan travelling. Dedicated island-philes, meanwhile, will most certainly get a kick out of sailing to the tiny but intriguing Tuscan islets of Pianosa, Giglio and faintly more developed Capraia.

Road Distances Chart

	Suvereto	Livorno	Piombino	Bogheri
Livorno	79			
Piombino	24	86		
Bolgheri	39	50	38	
Portoferrario	24+1hr	86+1hr	1hr	38+1hr

Central Coast & Elba Highlights

1 Livorno
(p220) Sampling superb seafood and investigating Tuscany's multi-cultural past in this historic port city.

2 Strada del Vino e dell'Olio Costa degli Etruschi
(p230) Taste-testing local drops at wineries and *enoteche* (wine bars) while following this scenic wine route along the Etruscan Coast.

3 Parco Archeologico di Baratti e Populonia
(p233) Picnicking between Etruscan tombs and enjoying majestic sea views.

4 Elba (p234)
Emulating Napoleon and spending a far-too-brief sojourn on

Ligurian Sea

Gorgona

TYRRHENIAN SEA

Livorno 1

Antignano

Montenero
Gabbro

Quercianella

Castelnuovo
Misericordia

Fortullino

Rosignano
Solvay

Castiglioncello

Rosignano
Marittimo

Vada

Cecina

Marina di
Cecina

Marina di
Bibbona

Forte di
Bibbona

Bibbona

Vada

Crespina

Lorenzana

Lari

Casciana
Terme

Chianni

Riparbella

Montescudaio

San Guido

Bolgheri 2

Strada del
Vino e dell'Olio
Costa degli
Etruschi

Donoratico

Castagneto
Carducci

Sassetta

Monteverdi
Marittimo

Terme di
Sassetta 6

A12

SS206

A12

SS1

SS68

SS243

SS1

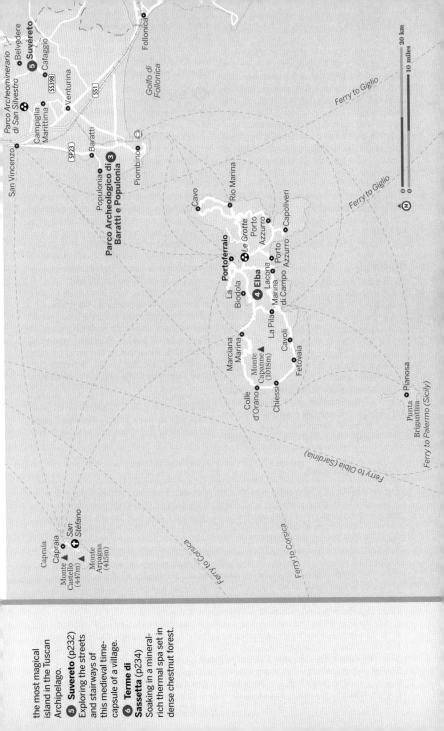

the most magical
island in the Tuscan
Archipelago.

5 Suvereto (p232)
Exploring the streets
and stairways of
this medieval time-
capsule of a village.

**6 Terme di
Sassetta** (p234)
Soaking in a mineral-
rich thermal spa set in
dense chestnut forest.

Capraia
Capraia ●
Monte ▲ *San*
Castello *Stefano* ✚
(447m) ▲
Monte
Arpagna
(415m)

Parco Archeominerario
di San Silvestro
Belvedere ●
5 Suvereto ⊗
Cafaggio ●
Campiglia ⊗
Marittima ● Venturina ●
[SS398]
[SS1]
San Vincenzo ●
[SP23]
Baratti ●
Populonia ●
**Parco Archeologico di 3
Baratti e Populonia**
Piombino ● ◉

*Golfo di
Follonica*
Follonica ●

Ferry to Giglio
Ferry to Giglio

⊙ 0   20 km
⊙ 0   10 miles

◄ N

Cavo ●
Rio Marina ●
Porto
Le Grotte ⊗ Azzurro ●
Portoferraio
Porto ●
La Azzurro
Biodola ● Lacona ●
4 Elba Marina ●
di Campo
Marciana La Pila ●
Marina ● Cavoli ●
Monte
Capanne ▲ Fetovaia ●
(1018m)
Colle
d'Orano ●
Chiessi ●
Capoliveri ●

Ferry to Olbia (Sardinia)
Ferry to Corsica
Ferry to Corsica

Punta ● Pianosa
Brigantina
Ferry to Palermo (Sicily)

LIVORNO

📞 0586 / POP 161,893

Tuscany's third-largest city is a quintessential port town with a colourful history and cosmopolitan heritage. A free port from the 17th century, Livorno (Leghorn in English) attracted traders from across the globe, who brought with them new customs and habits, exotic goods, slaves and foreign forms of worship. The result was a city famed throughout Europe for its multiculturalism. Today its seafood is the best on the Tyrrhenian coast, its shabby historic quarter threaded with Venetian-style canals is full of character, and its elegant belle-époque buildings offer reminders of a prosperous past. An easy train trip from Florence, Pisa and Rome, it makes an understated but undeniably worthwhile stop on any Tuscan itinerary.

History

The earliest references to Livorno date from 1017. The port was ruled by Pisa and Genoa for centuries, until Florence took control in 1421. It was still tiny; by the 1550s it had only 480 residents. But all that changed under Cosimo I de' Medici, who converted the settlement into a heavily fortified bastion – to the point that even today it's known throughout Italy as a 'Medici town'.

The 17th-century declaration of Livorno as a free port sparked swift development and the 19th century saw even more. But as parts of the local community became increasingly prosperous, issues of social inequity arose, leading to the 1921 founding of the Italian Communist Party.

As one of fascist Italy's main naval bases, Livorno was bombed heavily during WWII and many of its historic buildings were destroyed.

⊙ Sights

★ **Santuario della Madonna di Montenero** CHRISTIAN SITE

(📞 0586 57 96 27; www.santuariomontenero.org; Piazza di Montenero 9; ⊙ 6.30am-12.30pm & 2.30-7pm summer, to 6pm winter) The story goes like this: in 1345, the Virgin Mary appeared to a shepherd, who led her to *monte nero* (black mountain), a haven of brigands. The brigands immediately saw the error of their ways and built a chapel on the mountain. Soon pilgrims arrived and the chapel was extended in stages; it reached its present form in 1774. Rooms and corridors surrounding the church house a fascinating collection of 20,000 historic ex-votos thanking the Virgin for miracles.

The best time to visit is on 8 September, for the Festa della Madonna. To get here by public transport, take the LAM Rosso bus to Montenero (€1.50 or €2 on board, every 10 to 20 minutes) and get off at the last stop on Piazza delle Carrozze in Montenero Basso. From there, take the historic funicular (€2, every 10 to 20 minutes) up to the sanctuary.

Acquario di Livorno AQUARIUM

(Aquarium; Map p222; 📞 0586 26 91 11; www. acquariodilivorno.com; Piazzale Mascagni 1; adult €10-17, child €5-11; ⊙ 10am-7pm Jul & Aug, to 6pm

---

CITY OF NATIONS

Livorno's status as a free port in the 17th century made it a magnet for British, Dutch and other merchants trading between Europe and the Middle East. The long and prosperous involvement of these merchants with the city is reflected in the churches still standing in the town's centre: the Greek community's Chiesa dei Greci Uniti (Chiesa della Santissima Annunziata; Map p224; Via della Madonna 22); the Armenian community's Chiesa di San Gregorio degli Armeni (Map p224; Via della Madonna 32); the Dutch-German community's Chiesa Olandese-Alemanna (Map p224; Scali degli Olandesi 20); and multinational Chiesa della Madonna (Map p224; Via della Madonna 22; ⊙ hours vary). Sadly, the original 17th-century synagogue where the city's then-300-strong Jewish community worshipped was destroyed during WWII; a modern concrete synagogue (Map p224; 📞 0586 89 62 90; Piazza Elijah Benamozegh 1) was built as a replacement after the war.

The traders weren't the only foreigners to live in Livorno: the Medicis were involved in the slave trade, and African slaves formed part of the labour force that built the canal system in Piccola Venezia and feature in the 17th-century Monumento dei Quattro Mori (Monument of the Four Moors; Map p224; Piazza Giuseppe Micheli) opposite the port. Though commissioned to commemorate the victories of Grand Duke Ferdinand I of Tuscany over the Ottomans, its depiction of the grand duke elevated above the chained, subjected African slaves is a disturbing reminder of this dark episode in the city's history.

THREE PERFECT DAYS ON THE CENTRAL COAST

Day One

Livorno does seafood like nowhere else in Tuscany. Examine raw specimens bright and early at the Mercato Centrale (p226), stay around for lunch at Alle Vettovaglie (p226) or La Barrocciaia (p225), then head to the waterfront to join the *passeggiata* (evening stroll) along the black-and-white chequered Terrazza Mascagni before dinner and a glass or two of vino at friendly Cantina Nardi (p226).

Day Two

From Livorno head south, wending your way through a rolling hinterland strung with medieval villages and vines. Famous foodie stops include Bolgheri (p228), where Enoteca Tognoni (p228) in the village and Bolgheri Green (p229), 7km south, are top picks. Next, pop into Tenuta Argentiera (p229) and Petra Wine (p232) to taste local Val di Cornia DOC wines before overnighting in postcard-perfect Suvereto (p232).

Day Three

On day three, head across the water to the paradisiacal island of Elba (p234). Catch the ferry from Piombino to Portoferraio, explore the waterfront, visit Napoleon-related sites and lunch in the Old Town. You might also squeeze in a trip up Monte Capanne (p240) before enjoying a farmhouse dinner at Ristoro Agricolo Montefabbrello (p239) and checking into a nearby hotel.

mid-Apr–Jun & early-mid Sep, 10am-6pm Sat & Sun mid-Sep–Mar) Livorno's seafront aquarium swims with black-tip reef and zebra sharks, seahorses, Madagascan spider tortoises, moon jellyfish and impressive green sea turtles. Among the 33 tanks on the ground floor, there is also a touching pool – a favourite with kids. Upstairs, the 1st floor showcases insects, amphibians and reptiles, including a chameleon and glorious green iguana. End your visit on the panoramic terrace with sweeping sea views.

Terrazza Mascagni   STREET
(Map p222; Viale Italia) ⓕⓡⓔⓔ No trip to Livorno is complete without a stroll along this seafront terrace with its dramatic black-and-white chessboard-style pavement. When it was built in the 1920s, it was called Terrazza Ciano after the leader of the Livorno fascist movement; it now bears the name of Livorno-born opera composer Pietro Mascagni (1863–1945).

Piccola Venezia   AREA
(Little Venice; Map p224) Piccola Venezia is a tangle of small canals built during the 17th century, using Venetian methods of reclaiming land from the sea. At its heart sits the remains of the Medici-era Fortezza Nuova (New Fort; Map p224; Scali della Fortezza Nuova; ⊘8am-8pm mid-Apr–mid-Sep, reduced hours rest of year) ⓕⓡⓔⓔ. Canals link this with the slightly older, waterfront Fortezza Vecchia (p227).

The waterways can be explored by canalside footpaths but a boat tour is the best way to see its shabby-chic panoramas of faded, peeling apartments draped with brightly coloured washing, interspersed with waterside cafes and bars.

Il Parterre   PARK
(Parco Pertini; Viale Giosuè Carducci 2; ⊘8.30am-8pm mid-Apr–mid-Sep, reduced hours rest of year) Laid out in 1854 to prettify the wasteland around the city's great water cistern (unveiled in 1842), this lush public park is a peaceful green oasis of towering palm trees, statues of mythological gods and nymphs, fountains and Livornese dog walkers aplenty. A slowly expanding collection of beast-themed open-air art by local artists evokes the exotic animals kept here during the park's late-19th-century heyday (including a dancing bear named Gigi who local singer Bobo Rondelli penned a song about in 1993).

Chiesa di Santa Caterina   CHURCH
(Map p224; ☑0586 89 40 90; Piazza dei Domenicani; ⊘9am-12.30pm & 3-6.30pm Mon-Sat, 9am-12.30pm Sun) This early-18th-century Domenican church with its thick stone walls and prominent dome stands sentry on the western side of Piazza dei Domenicani as it did for the Medicis, who commissioned its construction. Sadly, they ran out of money before the facade could be covered in marble. The main altar features a painting of

Livorno

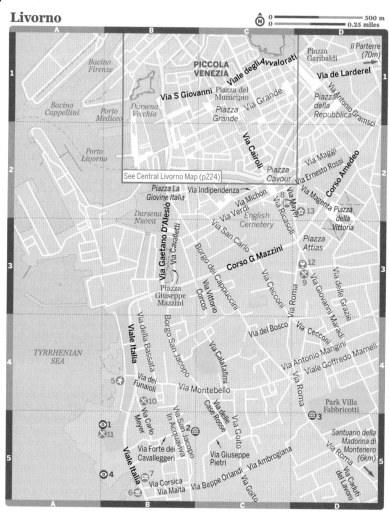

The Coronation of the Virgin by Giorgio Vasari, and there's a gallery of ex-votos to its right.

Chiesa di San Ferdinando Re CHURCH
(Map p224; ☑ 0586 88 85 41; Piazza Anita Garibaldi 1; ☺ hours vary) Constructed between 1704 and 1714 but extensively damaged during WWII and subsequently rebuilt, this church was named after the King of Castile. Its ornate interior features stucco and marble decoration, as well as statues by Giovanni Baratta. The main marble altar includes Baratta's sculpture of an angel freeing two slaves and acknowledges the role of this congregation in paying the ransom for Christian slaves in North Africa during the 17th century.

Museo Civico Giovanni Fattori GALLERY
(Map p222; ☑ 0586 82 46 20; www.museofattori. livorno.it; Via San Jacopo in Acquaviva 65; adult/reduced €6/4; ☺ 10am-1pm & 4-7pm Tue-Sun) The highlight of a visit here is the 19th-century building, Villa Mimbelli. It has an ornately decorated interior featuring an extraordinary staircase with balustrades in the form of naked cherubs. Works in the collection include a few medieval and Renaissance pieces, but the main focus is on works by the 19th-century

Livorno

◎ **Sights**
1 Acquario di Livorno B5
2 Museo Civico Giovanni Fattori B5
3 Museo di Storia Naturale del
   Mediterraneo D5
4 Terrazza Mascagni B5

◎ **Activities, Courses & Tours**
5 Bagni Nettuno B4
6 Bagni Pancaldi B5

◎ **Sleeping**
7 Grand Hotel Palazzo B5
8 Hotel al Teatro C2

◎ **Eating**
9 Cantina Nardi D3
10 Gelateria Populare 2 .... B4
11 Surfer Joe B5

◎ **Drinking & Nightlife**
12 Sketch D3

◎ **Entertainment**
13 Teatro Goldoni D2

Italian Impressionist Macchiaioli school led by Livorno-born Giovanni Fattori (1825–1908). Artists in this group worked directly from nature, emphasising naturalness through patches, or *macchia* (stains) of colour.

**Museo di Storia Naturale
del Mediterraneo** MUSEUM
(Natural History Museum; Map p222; ☑0586 26 67 11; http://musmed.provincia.livorno.it; Via Roma 234; adult/child €10/5; ☺9am-1pm Wed & Fri, 9am-7pm Tue, Thu & Sat, 3-7pm Sun) Livorno's Natural History Museum is beloved of school groups and families. The highlight of the permanent collection is a 20m-long whale skeleton called Annie, which occupies pride of place in a dedicated Sala del Mare (Sea Room) building including hands-on displays. Other displays focus on invertebrates, minerals, geology and palaeontology, and include old-fashioned dioramas.

🕴 Activities

The city's beach clubs open from May to September.

Bagni Nettuno BEACH
(Map p222; ☑333 2006215; www.bagninettuno.it; Viale Italia 16; ☺hours vary) Handily placed across the street from a cluster of beachfront cafes and snack bars, this elegant bathing establishment with baby-blue paintwork

and parasol-shaded deckchairs on the sand oozes retro charm. It was opened in the 1950s by a certain Signore Domenico Scanzi, and today his granddaughters, Monica and Cristiana, are proudly at the helm.

Free wi-fi and a toasty-warm hot tub are among its millennial perks.

Bagni Pancaldi SWIMMING
(Map p222; ☑0586 80 55 66; www.pancaldiacquaviva.it; Viale Italia 56; adult/child €7/5; ☺8am-8pm May-Sep, later in high summer) These old-fashioned, buttermilk-yellow-and-racing-green baths on the seafront are a summertime hotspot for swimming, renting a vintage wooden changing cabin and lounging under rented parasols. When they first opened in 1840 the baths were the height of sophistication, hosting tea dances and musical soirées, and in season they're still a popular place to play in the sun.

🕝 Tours

Livorno in Battello BOATING
(Map p224; ☑333 1573372; www.livornoinbattello.it; adult/child €12/5) One of a handful of local companies to offer daily one-hour guided tours of Livorno's Medicean waterways by boat, Livorno in Battello operates year-round (up to four departures daily in summer, limited departures December to February). The main departure jetty for boats is the pier opposite the Monumento dei Quattro Mori (p220), but check online or at the tourist office when buying tickets.

🛌 Sleeping

Camping Miramare CAMPGROUND €
(☑0586 58 04 02; www.campingmiramare.it; Via del Littorale 220; standard/seafront tent pitch €15/48, campsite adult/child/car €15/7/10; ☺reception 8am-10pm Jul & Aug, reduced hours rest of year; ▣🈺🐕) Be it a tent pitched beneath trees or the deluxe version with wooden terrace and sun lounges on the pebble beach, this pool-clad campground by the sea – open year-round thanks to its village of mobile homes, maxi caravans and bungalows – has it all. Rates outside of July and August are at least 50% lower. Find the campground 8km south of town in Antignano, near Montenero.

Hotel al Teatro BOUTIQUE HOTEL €€
(Map p222; ☑0586 89 87 05; www.hotelalteatro.it; Via Mayer 42; s €78-85, d €99-115, tr 110-128; ▣🈺🐕) The eight rooms in this hotel near the Goldoni Theatre (Map p222; ☑0586 20 42 90; www.goldoniteatro.it; Via Carlo

CENTRAL COAST & ELBA LIVORNO

Central Livorno

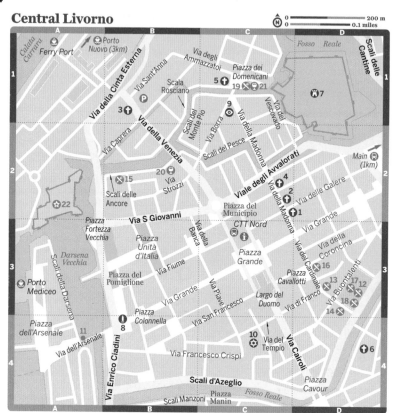

Goldoni 83) are comfortable and clean, if a tad frumpy, but the real draw is the hidden garden out back. Here, guests can breakfast or lounge over coffee on wicker furniture beneath a breathtakingly beautiful, 300-year-old magnolia tree.

Grand Hotel Palazzo HISTORIC HOTEL €€€
(Map p222; ☎0586 26 08 36; www.grandhotel palazzo.com; Viale Italia 195; d from €225; P ✳ @ ☎ ⓢ) Livorno's grand dame of a belle-époque hotel, part of the MGallery by Sofitel, looks out to sea from its waterfront perch. The finest of its 123 spacious, elegant rooms enjoy big blue sea views – or simply head up to the rooftop infinity pool and restaurant-bar with panoramic balcony. There is no lovelier spot for a sunset *aperitivo* (predinner drink).

✗ Eating

Livornese cuisine – particularly traditionally prepared seafood – is known throughout Italy for its excellence. Indeed, sampling the city's signature dish of *cacciucco* (pronounced kar-*choo*-ko), a mixed seafood stew, is reason enough to visit the city. Preferably made using the local Slow Food–accredited San Vincenzo tomatoes, it packs more than its fair share of flavour.

★**Antica Torteria
Al Mercato da Gagarin** SANDWICHES €
(Map p224; ☎0586 88 40 86; Via del Cardinale 24; sandwich €2.50-3.20; ⊙8am-2pm & 4.30-8.30pm Mon-Sat) There is no finer blast to old-world Livorno than this retro snack bar, little changed since its 1959 opening. Push through the plastic fly-net veiling the unmarked door and order the house speciality: a sensational 'five and five' sandwich (ask for a *cinque e cinque*) stuffed with scrumptious *torta di ceci* (chickpea pancake, fried in peanut oil and salted).

Central Livorno

⬤ Sights

1	Chiesa dei Greci Uniti	C2
2	Chiesa della Madonna	C2
3	Chiesa di San Ferdinando Re	B1
4	Chiesa di San Gregorio degli Armeni	C2
5	Chiesa di Santa Caterina	C1
6	Chiesa Olandese-Alemanna	D4
7	Fortezza Nuova	D1
8	Monumento dei Quattro Mori	B4
9	Piccola Venezia	C1
10	Sinagoga di Livorno	C4

⬤ Activities, Courses & Tours

11	Livorno in Battello	A4

⬤ Eating

12	Alle Vettovaglie	D3
13	Antica Friggitoria	D3
14	Antica Torteria Al Mercato da Gagarin	D3
15	Il Mercato del Pesce	B2
16	La Barrocciaia	D3
17	Mercato Centrale	D3
18	Pastificio Chiesa	D3
19	Scom Posto	C1

⬤ Drinking & Nightlife

20	Bad Elf	B2
21	Le Botteghe & Makutu Tiki Bar	C1

⬤ Entertainment

22	Fortezza Vecchia	A2

★ **Scom Posto**   TUSCAN €

(Map p224; ☎ 0586 88 75 96; www.dascomposto. it; Piazza dei Domenicani 17; sandwiches & platters €5-7, tartare €14; ⊗ 11am-3.30pm & 6pm-midnight Sun-Thu, to 2am Fri & Sat; ☎) Everything about this water-edge bistro is sassy, fresh and on trend. Plump for a place around one huge long shared table outside or enjoy the romance of a candlelit, vaulted red-brick interior. Furnishings are crafted from chipboard and the dining choice is simple: Chianina beef tartare, cheese and salami platters, or gourmet *schiacciate* (sandwiches) already assembled or served loose on a wooden board.

La Barrocciaia   OSTERIA €

(Map p224; ☎ 0586 88 26 37; www.labarrocciaia. it; Piazza Cavallotti 13; meals €25, panini €5.50-8; ⊗ 12.30-3pm & 7.30-11pm Tue-Sat) Locals speak of La Barrocciaia with great fondness – partly because of a homely interior that's alive with banter, but also because of its simple but flavour-packed food. Stews fluctuate between wild boar and *cacciucco,* there's always a choice of *mare* (sea) or *terra* (land) antipasti and it's perfectly acceptable to drop in for a simple *panino* (sandwich) and glass of wine.

Gelateria Populare 2   GELATO €

(Map p222; ☎ 0586 26 03 54; www.gelateria popolare2.it; Via Carlo Meyer 11; gelato €2.50-4; ⊗ 8am-midnight summer, 8am-8pm Tue-Sun winter; ☎) Join locals at this local institution for a sweet sugar hit after enjoying a late-afternoon *passeggiata* on the Terrazza Mascagni. Made fresh each day, the gelato here is undoubtedly the best in town.

Favourite flavours include almond, banana and nutty-chocolate Ferrero Rocher.

Il Mercato del Pesce   SEAFOOD €

(Map p224; ☎ 327 8881444; www.facebook.com/ ilmercatodelpescebylaraffineria; Scali delle Ancore; ⊗ 11am-11pm summer, reduced hours in winter) For affordable seafood waterside, make a beeline for this sea-blue shack with plastic tables and chairs overlooking a canal in 'Little Venice'. A Marshall speaker on the bar injects an on-trend retro vibe and the Fish Market's simple menu includes old-school classics like *polpo e patate* (octopus and potatoes), *baccalà* (salted cod) and ink-black *riso al nero di seppia* (cuttlefish-ink risotto).

Antica Friggitoria   SWEETS €

(Map p224; ☎ 0586 88 45 71; www.antica friggitoria.it; Via del Cardinale 9; doughnut €1; ⊗ 8.30am-12.30pm & 4-7.30pm Mon-Sat) It's rare to encounter a Livornese who isn't a fan of the delectable *frati* (doughnuts) and *scagliozzi* (fried polenta) that have been made at this simple place on the city's major market square since 1920. In the lead-up to the Festa di San Giuseppe in March, customers flock here to buy *frittelle di riso* (sweet fried-rice balls).

Surfer Joe   AMERICAN €

(Map p222; ☎ 0586 80 92 11; www.surferjoe.it; Terrazza Mascagni; meals €20; ⊗ 11am-midnight Sun-Thu, to 1am Fri & Sat summer, reduced hours in winter; ☎ ♿) American burgers, onion rings, pancakes and all-day breakfasts are cooked up at this 1950s-styled surf bar and American diner adjoining Livorno's aquarium on the seafront. The huge shaded terrace licked by the sea breeze is a favourite

MARKET MEANDERS

The largest covered market in Italy, Mercato Centrale (Mercato Centrale detto Vettovaglie; Map p224; www.facebook.com/mercato.centralecoperto; Via Buontalenti; ⊙5.30am-3pm Mon-Thu, 5.30am-3pm & 6-11pm Fri & Sat) is housed in a 95m-long neoclassical building that miraculously survived Allied WWII bombing. Arresting both gastronomically and architecturally, its central hall with emerald-green painted steelwork is a real feast for the eyes. Italian painter Amedeo Modigliani (1184–1920) once had his studio on the upper floor (now offices).

Owned by three sommeliers, wine bar Alle Vettovaglie (Map p224; ☑347 7487020; www.allevettovaglie.com; Scali Saffi 27; dishes €6.50-12; ⊙10am-3pm Tue-Thu, 10am-3pm & 7-11pm Fri & Sat) is in the Mercato Centrale. It has a menu that changes according to what produce is fresh and plentiful on the day – it's just as likely to feature *triglie alla livornese* (mullet in tomato sauce) as it is pasta with an aromatic pesto. It also – unsurprisingly – offers an impressive selection of wine.

Also in the Mercato Centrale, Pastificio Chiesa (Map p224; ☑0586 88 46 97; www.thekingofpasta.com; Via del Cardinale 24; meal €5-7; ⊙8am-1pm Mon-Sat) is a family *pastificio* that has been in business since 1969, crafting fresh pasta to cook at home or eat in at bar stools. A B&W photograph of grandmother Giuseppina hangs on the wall; parents Roberto and Salvatorica serve behind the counter, while charismatic son Valerio chit-chats with faithful regulars. Count on €5 to €7 for a lunchtime plate of the day's pasta special with pesto, *ragù* (sauce) or tomato sauce. The family business also, bizarrely, makes luxurious *tortelli* (type of pasta cushion) filled with 24-carat gold leaf and lobster or black truffle. A single *tortello* weighs 15g and costs €250. Watch them being made in the glass-walled kitchen adjoining their small shop.

family hangout and come dark, a younger crowd flocks here for DJ and jam sessions, concerts and hip surf-music happenings.

Out of season, Surfer Joe only cooks up dinner and late-night drinks at weekends; weekdays, the place is shut up by 6pm.

★ Cantina Nardi   TUSCAN €€
(Map p222; ☑0586 80 80 06; www.cantina nardi.com; Via Leonardo Cambini 6-8; meals €20-30; ⊙8am-4pm & 5-9.30pm Mon-Thu, to 10.30pm Fri & Sat) They've been in business since 1965, so the friendly Nardis know how to keep their customers happy. As much an *enoteca* (wine bar) as Slow Food–hailed eatery, Cantina Nardi has a 400-bottle wine list and an amazing 100 wines are offered by the glass. It is one of the city's best *aperitivo* spots, so come sit between bottle-filled shelves inside, or at a streetside table.

🍷 Drinking & Nightlife

Piazza Grande and Piazza Cavour are surrounded by cafes where locals meet for coffee or an *aperitivo*. Waterfront snack bars and cafes dot the seafront around the Terrazza Mascagni. In Piccola Venezia watch for new bar openings on and around Scali delle Ancore.

★ Le Botteghe & Makutu Tiki Bar   BAR
(Map p224; ☑346 6217884; www.facebook.com/lebotteghelivorno; Piazza dei Domenicani 20; ⊙7.30pm-1.30am Sun-Thu, to 2am Fri & Sat) Live music, craft beer, creative bar cuisine and fabulous cocktails lure a local party set to this red-brick cellar bar, right by a canal in Piccola Venezia. Sultry summer nights are particularly fun when the drinking and dancing action spills onto the quayside in front.

Bad Elf   CRAFT BEER
(Map p224; ☑351 8456007; www.badelfpub.it; Scali delle Ancore 1d; ⊙6.30pm-late summer, reduced hours in winter) A couple of hip waterfront bars speck the canals in Piccolo Venezia – hugely atmospheric in summer when the drinking action spills outside. 'Food, Beer & Vinyls' is the thrust behind the Bad Elf where craft-beer lovers can agonise over some 90 different brews to try, including homegrown labels from Tuscany and several from independent Belgian and British breweries.

Sketch   COCKTAIL BAR
(Map p222; ☑333 7541200; Via Leonardo Cambini 3; ⊙6pm-1am; 🐾) With a cocktail menu designed like a beautiful book featuring hand-drawn illustrations, and a dynamic

mixologist happy to also create off-list, cocktail lovers won't be disappointed. Craft cocktails (€8-12) mix homemade syrups and some unusual bitters with bespoke spirits.

☆ Entertainment

★ **Fortezza Vecchia**   ARTS CENTRE
(Old Fort; Map p224; Piazzale dei Marmi; ⊙ hours vary) FREE Close to the waterfront, the 'Old Fort' was constructed to a design by Antonio de Sangallo the Elder in the 16th century, but incorporates an 11th-century watchtower from a previous fortress on the site. An edgy arts and culture venue today, the fort rocks with 'summer vibe' dance parties, live jazz, contemporary-art exhibitions and all sorts of fun happenings.

ℹ Information

Tourist Office (Map p224; ☑ 0586 89 42 36; Via Pieroni 18; ⊙ 9am-4pm summer, to 3pm winter) Hands out free maps and books boat tours.

ℹ Getting There & Away

BOAT

Livorno is a major port. Regular ferries for Sardinia, Corsica and Sicily depart from the **ferry port** (Map p224; Calata Carrara); ferries to Capraia use the smaller **Porto Mediceo** (Map p224; Via del Molo Mediceo) near Piazza dell'Arsenale. Boats to Spain use Porto Nuovo, 3km north of the city.

Corsica Ferries (www.corsica-ferries.co.uk) Up to seven ferries per week to Bastia, Corsica (from €60, four hours) and Golfo Aranci, Sardinia (from €90, 9½ hours).

Grimaldi Lines (www.grimaldi-lines.com) Daily sailings to/from Olbia, Sardinia (from €34, nine hours) and Palermo, Sicily (from €45, 18 hours).

Moby (www.moby.it) Year-round at least two services a day to Olbia, Sardinia (from €32, seven to 10 hours). Plus in the summer, several crossings a week to Bastia, Corsica (from €25, four hours).

Toremar (www.toremar.it) Several weekly crossings year-round to Capraia (€22, 2¾ hours).

CAR & MOTORCYCLE

The A12 runs past the city; the SS1 connects Livorno with Rome. There are several car parks near the waterfront; these charge between €0.30 (Nuovo Mercatale Americano) and €1 (Piazza Mazzini) per hour.

TRAIN

From the central **train station** (Piazza Dante) walk westwards (straight ahead) along Viale Carducci, Via de Larderel and Via Grande to access Piazza Grande, Livorno's central square.

Services include:

Castiglioncello (€3.60, 20 minutes, at least hourly)

Florence (€9.90, 1¼ hours, hourly).

Pisa (€2.60, 15 minutes, frequent).

Rome (€22.85, 3¾ hours, at least seven daily).

San Vincenzo (€6.10, 40 minutes to one hour, at least hourly)

ETRUSCAN COAST

The coastline south from Livorno to just beyond Piombino lives up to its historically charged name, the Costa degli Etruschi (Etruscan Coast), thanks to the Etruscan tombs unearthed on its shores. Its basic bucket-and-spade beaches are often unstartling, but those who venture inland will discover a swathe of pretty hilltop villages and some lesser-known but very good wines.

Castiglioncello

☑ 0586 / POP 3800

Diminutive Castiglioncello, 30km south of Livorno, is an agreeably unpretentious seaside resort where Italian art-critic Digo Martelli held court in the late 19th century. He played host to the Florentine Impressionist artists of the period, giving birth to the artistic movement known as La Scuola di Castiglioncello (Castiglioncello School). These days, the town is popular with summer visitors who flock to its sandy beaches; the best of these are on the town's northern fringe. Vineyards lace its scenic surrounds.

Seafood is the thing to eat. There are plenty of restaurants on Via Aurelia and along the seafront at Punta Righini. Otherwise, head out of town to a tasty farm or vineyard restaurant.

★ **Agrilandia**   WINE
(☑ 0586 75 90 07; www.agrilandia.eu; Strada Vicinale delle Spianate; ⊙ guided visits 10am & 2pm Mon-Fri, 10am Sat Mar-Sep) One of the Etruscan Coast's most appealing wineries accessible to visitors, this well-established farm 3.5km north of Castiglioncello offers fantastic guided visits of its wine cellars (€25). Tours include tastings of both its ruby-red Fortulla wines made from hand-picked cabernet sauvignon and cabernet franc grapes, and other typical local products, including estate-made olive oil and floral acacia honey.

CENTRAL COAST & ELBA CASTIGLIONCELLO

Albergo Pensione Bartoli
PENSION €

(☑ 0586 7 52 05; www.albergobartoli.com; Via Diego Martelli 9; s/d/tr €65/80/100; ᴾ 🛜) For bags of character and superb value, head to this impeccably kept villa with an old-fashioned 'let's stay with grandma' atmosphere and 17 basic but comfortable rooms (five with sea views). The shaded garden is a treat. You'll need to book well in advance for July and August, when it's half- or full-board only and a minimum three-day stay applies.

Grand Hotel Villa Parisi
DESIGN HOTEL €€

(☑ 0586 75 16 98; www.villaparisi.com; Via Romolo Monti 10; s/d/tr from €146/185/220; ⊙ Apr-Sep; ᴾ ❄ 🛜 ≋) With its chic cream facade and racing-green wooden shutters, this 1905 clifftop villa wouldn't look amiss in a glossy design mag. Refined elegance holds sway inside, and most of the rooms have sea views; some even have private balconies. You won't be spending much time in your room, though, as every guest gravitates to the magnificent sea-facing terrace and pool.

Casale del Mare
TUSCAN €€€

(☑ 0586 75 90 07; www.casaledelmare.it; Strada Vicinale delle Spianate; meals €35-50; ⊙ noon-2pm & 7-11pm Sat & Sun, 7-11pm Thu & Fri; ᴾ 🛜 🍴) Fine wine, wood-aged grappa, olive oil, honey and other gourmet treats produced on the restaurant's farm and vineyard go into the sensational cuisine of chef Marco Parillo at this out-of-town restaurant, 3.5km north of the centre. Summertime dining is around parasol-shaded tables on the lawn and big blue sea views are magnificent. Expect lots of fish dishes on the refined menu.

Should you desire to stay longer, Casale del Mare has self-catering accommodation (double from €600/1070 per week in winter/summer).

ⓘ Information

The **tourist office** (☑ 0586 75 32 41; www.prolococastiglioncello.it; Via Aurelia 632; ⊙ 10am-1pm & 5-8pm Jul & Aug, reduced hours in winter) is at the train station and can provide free town maps.

ⓘ Getting There & Away

There are hourly train services between Castiglioncello and Livorno (€3.60, 20 minutes).

Bolgheri
☑ 0565 / POP 160

Every serious wine buff knows the name Bolgheri, largely due to the fact that it is where the first of the internationally famous 'Super Tuscans', Sassicaia, was produced. The bijou town approached via a spectacular 5km-long avenue of 2540 cypress trees, made famous by Tuscan poet Giosuè Carducci in his 1874 poem *Davanti a San Guido*. It is dominated by a storybook-style castle which incorporates the main town gate and the part-Romanesque Chiesa di SS Giacomo e Cristoforo. The main – really only – reason to head here is to taste local wines and dine on seasonal produce in one of its excellent *enoteche*.

Most sleeping options are in the countryside outside the town.

There are a number of eateries on or near Via Giulia – tasting wine is an inevitable part of any meal.

Agriturismo DallOlivo
AGRITURISMO €

(☑ 0565 76 51 23, 347 5423060; www.dallolivo.it; Località Magazzino 273; 4-person apt per night/week €140/840 summer; ᴾ ❄ 🛜) Splashes of yellow and red lend these two modern holiday apartments a jaunty air; their terraces, framed by narrow olive groves, have a chilled-out feel – helped by the BBQs and sun lounges. Kitchens are well-equipped and there may even be a bottle of zero-kilometre olive oil for you. DallOlivo is 5km south of Bolgheri, just off the road to Castagneto Carducci.

Castello di Bolgheri
APARTMENT €€

(☑ 0565 76 21 10; www.castellodibolgheri.eu; Via Lautetta 7b; 2-/8-person apt per week €1085/3000; ᴾ ❄ 🛜) The aristocratic owners of this wine and olive-oil estate offer six luxurious apartments – some with gardens overlooking olive groves – in three converted farmhouses in or around Bolgheri. Properties sleep two to eight people, and sport kitchens and washing machines. Guests are offered a free tour of the estate's wine cellars in town.

★ Enoteca Tognoni
TUSCAN €

(☑ 0565 76 20 01; www.enotecatognoni.it; Via Lauretta 5; meals €15-20; ⊙ noon-2.30pm & 7-10pm Thu-Tue) This wine-lined *enoteca* is a temple to taste, both gastronomic and oenological. Sassicaia is among dozens of local wines available to sample – some more affordable than others. The menu is limited but delectable, changing daily according to what is fresh at the market: its *pappardelle* (flat pasta ribbons) laced in wild-boar *ragù* is an unmissable autumnal classic.

⭐ **Bolgheri Green**   TUSCAN €

(☑ 348 8913766; www.poderearduino.com; Strada Provinciale Bolgherese 16b, Località Magazzino 210, Castagneto Carducci; meals €15-25; ⊙ noon-3pm & 5.30-9.30pm) Tuscan romance oozes out of this stylish wooden shack, framed by lawns peppered with tables and Persian picnic rugs. The short but sweet menu features seasonal dishes loaded with organic produce, including tangy olive oil from the restaurant's organic olive and fruit farm, Podere Arduino.

ⓘ Getting There & Away

Between Monday and Saturday, one daily **Tiemme** bus (www.tiemmespa.it) travels between Castagneto Carducci and Bolgheri (€2.60, 30 minutes), continuing and terminating in San Guido. There is a car park on Via degli Orti, downhill from the main gate.

San Vincenzo

☑ 0565 / POP 6992

Italian visitors flock to this moderately attractive seaside town in summer to flop on sandy beaches backed by herb-scented *macchia* (Mediterranean shrubbery) and pine forest. Yachties moor their vessels in the town's smart modern Marina di San Vincenzo, while the plains inland are rich in industrial heritage and soothing thermal springs.

Parco Archeominerario
di San Silvestro   ARCHAEOLOGICAL SITE

(www.parchivaldicornia.it; Via di San Silvestro 34b, Campiglia Marittima; entire park adult/reduced €20/15, Rocca di San Silvestro and Temperino mine €10/8, Temperino mine by train €12/9; ⊙ 10am-7pm Tue-Sun Jun & early Sep, 9.30am-7.30pm daily Jul & Aug, reduced hours Oct-May) The area's 3000-year mining history is explored at this intriguing industrial site, approximately 10km inland from San Vincenzo. Here you can explore the ruins of the 14th-century mining town Rocca di San Silvestro and the Temperino copper and lead mines, one of which is accessed via an underground train. Guided tours, taking in either Rocca di San Silvestro or Temperino mines or both, depart roughly hourly.

Calidario Terme Etrusche   HOT SPRINGS

(☑ 0565 85 15 04; www.calidario.it; Via del Bottaccio 40, Venturina; pool entry weekday/weekend €20/22, half-day spa package €29-43; ⊙ 9am-mid-

A WINE-FUELLED PIT STOP

When motoring from Castiglioncello to Bolgheri along the SS1, it's worth breaking for tastings at one of the region's many innovative, often organic, wineries: 16km south of Castiglioncello, turn left (east) onto the SR68 to uncover La Regola (☑ 0586 69 81 45; www.laregola.com; Località Altagrada; tour with 4-/5-wine tastings €15/25-35; ⊙ wine boutique 10am-1pm & 3-6pm, tastings Tue, Thu & Sat, shorter hours winter) in Riparbella.

Brothers Flavio and Luca Nuti bottled their first vintage in 1997, and now their 25-hectare organic vineyard in the Cecina Valley yields more than 1000 bottles of wine per year. A location close to the sea on mineral-rich soil gives their wines a distinctive taste that can be appreciated during a 20-minute tour and choice of tastings in the modern winery building. A highlight is seeing (and hearing) Stefano Tonelli's evocative multimedia artwork *Somnium* (2016) in the ageing cellar. It's one of a number of site-specific artworks on the estate.

night Jul & Aug, 9.30am-9.30pm May-Jun & Sep, 9.30am-8.30pm Oct-Dec & Mar-May) What a treat: a thermal spa, 15km south of San Vincenzo, where you can enjoy a swim in the natural spring-water pool or pamper yourself with a spa package including use of the sauna, the Turkish bath and frigidarium with multisensory shower and chromotherapy. Magnesium- and calcium-rich waters, at a toasty 36°C, flow into a minilake where bathers take relaxing and therapeutic dips.

Tenuta Argentiera   WINE

(☑ 0565 77 45 81; www.argentiera.eu; Via Aurelia 412, Località Pianali; ⊙ 10am-6pm Mon-Sat, to 5pm Nov-Mar) Known for its Bordeaux-style cabernet sauvignon, franc and merlot, this sprawling estate on the coastal road 6.5km north of San Vincenzo is among the region's largest wine producers, with 75 hectares of vineyards. Tours and tastings include the estate's flagship Bolgheri Superiore.

Podere San Michele   AGRITURISMO €

(☑ 335 7809881; www.poderesanmichele.it; Via della Caduta 3a; d €70-80; P ❋ 🐾) The warmth of the welcome at this wine estate is superb. Wicker furniture, huge beds and

ETRUSCAN WINE & OIL ROAD

Tasting wine on coastal estates and motoring along avenues lined with olive groves and cypress trees strikes at the essence of the Strada del Vino e dell'Olio Costa degli Etruschi (www.lastradadelvino.com). The 150km-long tourist route stretches south from Livorno to Piombino, and across to Elba, and passes wineries and farms offering wine and olive-oil tastings (book in advance), and enticing places to eat.

❶ Bolgheri

Wine map and other information from the San Guido **visitor centre** (☎0565 74 97 68; www.lastradadelvino.com; Castagneto Carducci 45; ⊙10am-1pm & 2-5pm Mon-Sat summer, 10am-5pm Mon-Fri winter) in hand, hit the road in San Guido along the famous 5km-long **Cypress Alley** (Viale dei Cipressi, SP16d) to bijou Bolgheri. Park in the car park on Via degli

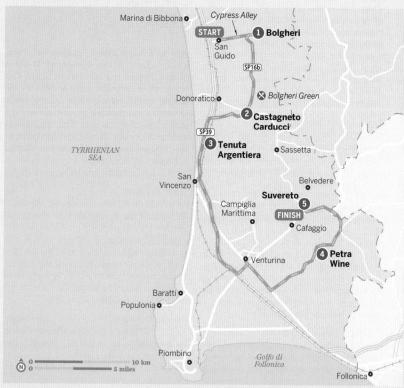

One Day 60km

Great for... Food & Drink, Outdoors

Best Time to Go Spring, summer or autumn

Orti, then stroll through the fortified arch to explore this historic town where the first of the internationally famous 'Super Tuscans', Sassicaia, was produced. Consider staying for a wine tasting (including a couple of IGT tipples) at Enoteca Tognoni (p228).

❷ Castagneto Carducci

Next, head 1km back down the Cypress Alley before taking the SP16b south past neatly planted vineyards and scattered olive groves. Gourmets should consider lunch at Bolgheri Green (p229). A series of switch-backs later, the pale-yellow buildings of Castagneto Carducci appear ranged on the ridge above. Park on the village edge and follow one of the lanes heading upwards. Most lead to the 13th-century Propositura di San Lorenzo, a dimly lit affair with faded frescoes and ornate beams inside and a view of the sun-dappled Etruscan Coast from the terrace.

❸ Tenuta Argentiera

Continue west towards the coast, turning left (south) and heading down the SP39 for 5km to reach Tenuta Argentiera (p229), one of this region's largest, best-known and most spectacularly sited wineries – 75 hectares of majestic vineyards extend from forested hills down to the sea. Enjoy a tasting in the *cantina* or in the fortress-like hilltop winery with its views to the coast; book ahead for the latter.

❹ Petra Wine

Continue south towards Venturina and on to the architecturally distinctive Petra Wine (p232) in San Lorenzo Alto, a temple-like modern structure built into the side of a hill. The impressively environmentally sustainable winery produces 100% organic wines. Learn all about the hi-tech winery and its extraordinary vintages on guided a tour, ending with a tasting; again, you'll need to book in advance.

❺ Suvereto

Finish your tour in the miraculously intact medieval hamlet of Suvereto, where you can explore the cobbled streets and hike up to the 15th-century Rocca Aldobrandesca (p232) to admire a sweeping panorama of the medieval village and surrounding vineyard-clad lands. Given the accolades of 'Slow Food town', 'wine town' and 'oil town' that it bears, Suvereto is a predictably wonderful place to discover local Val di Cornia DOC wines and to dine well. Come dusk, relax over a delectable dinner of modern Tuscan cuisine Slow Food–style at Osteria di Suvereto da l'Ciocio (p233) or Ristorante dal Cacini (p233).

DON'T MISS

SEASIDE GLAMPING & SPLURGING

Campers and glampers visiting the Etruscan Coast won't beat a pitch (or bubble tent) with sea view at Camping Casa di Caccia (☑ 329 8826009, 0586 60 00 00; www.camp ingcasadicaccia.com; Via del Mare 40, Marina di Bibbona; tent pitch 2 adults & car €48.50, Bubble Room d €250; ⓟ @ ⓢ), 25km south of Castiglioncello and 10km west of Bolgheri. The glitzy highlight of this seaside campground is its tent pitches backing onto a generous swathe of golden-sand beach and – drum roll – its glamper-chic Bubble Room (www. bubbleroomtuscany.it). This is a part-transparent bubble tent (perfect for stargazing) cocooning a luxurious round double bed inside, real toilet, romantic outdoor shower, coffee machine and private hammock-strung terrace. Guests also get free use of a parasol and two sun-loungers on the beach.

Glampers all out for the ultimate splurge should reserve a table at La Pineta (☑ 0586 60 00 16; www.lapinetadizazzeri.it; Via dei Cavalleggeri Nord 27; meals €55-90; ☺ 8-10pm Tue, 12.30-2pm & 8-10pm Wed-Sun; ⓢ), a Michelin-starred seafood and fish restaurant in Marina di Bibbona. Tasting menus (€65 to €80) marry the catch of the day with top-quality local produce, invariably organic and bursting with sun-filled flavours. The setting – a wooden hut with turquoise shutters on the sand – is vintage chic.

swish bathrooms define bedrooms, breakfast is a vast spread and you can organise tastings of the wine grown from the estate's grapes. The setting, on the plains just south of San Vincenzo, isn't as picturesque as some, but it's well placed for exploring both hills and coast.

Zanzi Bar
BAR

(☑ 0565 179 43 53; www.facebook.com/zanzibar sanvincenzo; Piazza del Porto 2; ☺ 6pm-3am Fri & Sat, to 2am Sun-Thu) Those in the know remain staunchly loyal to shabby-chic Zanzi Bar, drawn by vintage decor, designer nourishment and DJ sets after dark. It's in a former fisherman's hut at the northern end of the marina. Watch for live music and weekend DJ sets.

❶ Getting There & Away

Frequent trains link San Vincenzo and Livorno (€6.10, 40 minutes to one hour).

Suvereto

☑ 0565 / POP 3129

On weekends and over summer, day-trippers flock to this almost magically preserved medieval village to meander along its narrow cobbled streets and climb its steep, cream-stone stairways brightened by balconies brimming with flowers. Surrounded by countryside planted with olive trees, vineyards and the *suvere* (cork oak) trees that give the village its name, it's one of the most delightful destinations on the Etruscan Coast.

◉ Sights & Activities

There are 80km of signed walking, biking and horse-riding trails in the countryside around Suvereto. Access 18 dedicated itineraries at www.suveretotrekking.com.

Rocca Aldobrandesca
CASTLE

(Via Corta; ☺ 9am-dusk) Suvereto's crowning glory is this part-15th-century *rocca* (castle), abandoned in the 1600s and slowly being restored. The climb to it is steep but rewards with a magnificent panorama of surrounding fields and olive groves. On dusky pink summer evenings it's particularly enchanting.

★ Petra Wine
WINE

(☑ 0565 84 53 08; www.petrawine.it, visit@petra wine.it; Località San Lorenzo Alto 131; ☺ daily by appointment) On first sight, Petra resembles a huge pink Mayan temple that has been mysteriously transported to this rural pocket of Tuscany. Designed by acclaimed Swiss architect Mario Botta, the building is inserted into the hillside and houses an environmentally sustainable winery producing 100% organic wines under the Petra and Belvento labels. Email to book a tour (in English) of the building, which features an extraordinary purple-lit underground ageing tunnel among other state-of-the-art features, followed by a tasting of the company's wines.

★☆ Festivals & Events

Le Serate Medievali
CULTURAL

(Medieval Evenings; http://suvereto.net/serate-me dievali; ☺ mid-Jul) For two nights each year in mid-July the Serate Medievali transforms the Romanesque cloister of the Convento di San Francesco into a medieval marketplace, complete with locals dressed in traditional costume, fire eaters, minstrels, a medieval banquet, and plenty of art, craft and food stalls.

Eating & Drinking

Given the accolades of 'Slow Food town', 'wine town' and 'oil town' that it bears, Suvereto is a predictably wonderful place to discover local Val di Cornia DOC wines and dine well.

Most restaurants are closed in January and February.

Il Gallo Golosone   GELATO €

(☑ 320 3123030; www.facebook.com/gallogolos one; Via Roma 4; gelato €2-4; ⊙ 6.30am-7.30pm Mon, Tue & Thu, to 8pm Fri-Sun) On busy weekends, staff here do an excellent job filling cups and cones with the house-made gelato. They also make coffee and serve it to customers on the small streetside terrace.

Dal Cacini   TUSCAN €€

(☑ 0565 82 83 13; www.ilcacini.it; Via del Crocifisso 3; set menu €30-55; ⊙ 12.30-2.30pm & 7-9.30pm Wed-Mon) The chef here buys fish fresh every day and cooks it however his fancy dictates – hence the compulsory set menu rather than an à la carte array. Tables sport driftwood and filmy drapes, while the vine-shaded terrace and garden have sea glimpses – the perfect spots to linger over lunch.

★**I'Ciocio**   TUSCAN €€€

(Osteria di Suvereto; ☑ 0565 82 99 47; www.face book.com/osteriadisuvereto; Piazza dei Giudici 1; meals €45; ⊙ noon-2pm & 7.30-10.30pm Tue-Sat, noon-2pm Sun) Worthy recipient of a Slow Food accolade (the only Suvereto eatery so honoured), this *osteria* (casual tavern) opposite the handsome 13th-century *palazzo comunale* (town hall) has a beautiful terrace lined by honey-coloured stone walls and a stylish dining room adorned with modern art. The menu, meanwhile, is aimed firmly at foodies – modern dishes that also manage to respect centuries-old local food traditions.

Enoteca dei Difficili   WINE BAR

(☑ 0565 82 70 87; Via San Leonardo 2; ⊙ 6pm-2am Mon-Wed, to 3am Fri-Sun; 🛜) Suvereto's younger generation loves this spirited *osteria*. No wonder: the brick ceiling and vintage chairs ensure it's stylish, there's live music on weekends and plenty of local drops on the wine list.

ⓘ Information

The **tourist information point** (☑ 0565 82 93 04; www.facebook.com/ufficioturistico.suvere to; Via Magenta 14; ⊙ hours vary Easter-1 Jan) shares a building with the Museo Artistico della Bambola (Doll Museum).

ⓘ Getting There & Away

Regular **Tiemme** (www.tiemmespa.it) buses link Suvereto with the Campiglia Marittima train station at Venturina (€2.60, 20 minutes), where regular trains to/from Livorno (€7, 40 minutes to one hour) stop.

Golfo di Baratti

☑ 0565

The crescent-shaped Baratti Gulf sits at the southern tip of the Etruscan Coast, at the end of a 12km dead-straight road lined by sandy beaches and sky-high parasol pines. The main draws here are the beaches, which are packed in summer, and the sprawling Parco Archeologico di Baratti e Populonia, which is set on a promontory overlooking the sea.

There are beach bars and cafes along the road linking the main highway and Porto di Baratti, as well as at the port and in Baratti itself. There's also an eatery in the archaeological park's reception building.

★**Parco Archeologico di Baratti e Populonia**   ARCHAEOLOGICAL SITE

(Archaeological Park of Baratti & Populonia; ☑ 0565 22 64 45; www.parchivaldicornia.it; Baratti; Acropolis adult/reduced €12/9, Necropoli €10/8, Acropolis & Necropoli €17/13, entire park €20/15; ⊙ 9.30am-7.30pm Jul & Aug, 10am-7pm Jun & early Sep, reduced hours late Sep-May) The Etruscan sites on display here are some of Tuscany's finest.

CENTRAL COAST & ELBA GOLFO DI BARATTI

WORTH A TRIP

A ROOM WITH A VIEW

Its name and location says it all. Belvedere di Suvereto (☑ 0565 82 70 61; www.belvederedisuvereto.it; Piazza San Tommaso 33, Belvedere; s/d/tr/q €58/90/120/140) is a stylish B&B and bistro in a tiny hilltop hamlet, 3km north of Suvereto. Rooms sport fresh white walls, rustic roof supports, minimalist country-crafted furnishings and a blockbuster *belvedere* (viewpoint) of sweet Suvereto far, far below.

TERME DI SASSETTA

Head to **Terme di Sassetta** (☑338 1851877 0565 79 43 52; www.termedi sassetta.it; Via Campagna Sud 143, Pian delle Vigne; 4hr/day adult/child €35/50; ☺10am-8pm daily Jun-Aug, shorter hours Sept-May) to spend a therapeutic hour or two relaxing in these popular *terme* (baths) in a chestnut wood outside the tiny settlement of Sassetta. It features a cascade of indoor and outdoor rock pools filled with hyperthermal water that springs from the ground at a constant temperature of 51°C. Children aged under five years of age aren't admitted. There's also rustic accommodation on the property in farmhouse **La Cerreta** (www.lacerreta.it).

Four marked walking trails lead through a vast green park, revealing a ruined town and well-preserved prehistoric tombs. The gigantic circular tumulus tombs in the **Necropoli di San Cerbone** are among the most impressive and are visited on a one-hour Italian-language guided tour that enters the **Tomba dei Carri**, which is a whopping 28m in diameter. The **Acropolis** can be visited on a self-guided 90-minute tour.

Canessa SEAFOOD €€
(☑0565 2 95 30, 320 9328353; www.ristorante canessa.com; Località Baratti 43; meals €35-40; ☺12.30-2.30pm & 7.30-10pm Apr-Nov) What makes this seafood restaurant at Porta di Baratti so unique is the 15th-century watchtower that the modern building is wrapped around. The freshly made pasta is delicious, as are the many fishy choices. Best of all is the view, with huge windows overlooking the lapping waves.

❶ Getting There & Away

Buses operated by **Tiemme** (www.tiemmespa.it) travel between Piombino and Baratti every day except Sunday (€2.60, 30 minutes).

TUSCAN ARCHIPELAGO

POP 34,389

A local legend says that when Venus rose from the waves seven precious stones fell from her tiara, creating seven islands off the Tuscan coast. These little-known gems range from tiny Gorgona, just 2.23 sq km in size, to the biggest and busiest island, 224-sq-km Elba (Isola d'Elba), best known as the place where Napoleon was exiled.

Elba

Napoleon would think twice about fleeing Elba today. Dramatically more congested than when the emperor was exiled here in 1814 (he managed to engineer an escape within a year), the island is an ever-glorious paradise of beach-laced coves, vineyards, azure waters, hairpin-bend motoring, a 1018m mountain (Monte Capanne) and mind-bending views. It's all supplemented by a fine seafaring cuisine, lovely island wines, and land and seascapes just made for hiking, biking and sea kayaking.

With the exception of high season (actually only August), when the island's beaches and roads are jam-packed, Elba is something of a Robinson Crusoe paradise. In springtime, early summer and autumn, when grapes and olives are harvested, there are plenty of tranquil nooks on this stunningly picturesque, 28km-long, 19km-wide island.

There is a wealth of information about the island at www.infoelba.com.

History

Elba has been inhabited since the Iron Age and the extraction of iron ore and metallurgy were the island's principal sources of economic wellbeing until well into the second half of the 20th century. In 1917 some 840,000 tonnes of iron were produced, but in WWII the Allies bombed the industry to bits.

Ligurian tribespeople were the island's first inhabitants, followed by Etruscans and Greeks. Centuries of peace under the Pax Romana gave way to more uncertain times during the barbarian invasions, when Elba became a refuge for those fleeing mainland marauders. By the 11th century, Pisa (and later Piombino) was in control and built fortresses to help ward off attacks by Arab raiders and pirates operating out of North Africa.

In the 16th century, Cosimo I de' Medici grabbed territory in the north of the island, where he founded the port town of Cosmopolis, today's Portoferraio.

TUSCANY'S ARCHIPELAGO NATIONAL PARK

The Parco Nazionale dell'Arcipelago Toscano (Tuscan Archipelago National Park; www.islepark.it) safeguards the delicate ecosystems of Tuscany's seven islands as well as the 600 sq km of sea that washes around them. It's Europe's largest protected marine area and is home to rare species such as the Neptune's shaving brush seaweed, unique to the archipelago.

Monk seals, driven from other islands by humans, still gambol in the deep underwater ravines off Montecristo. The islands serve as an essential rest stop for birds migrating between Europe and Africa. The shy red partridge survives on Elba and Pianosa and the archipelago supports more than a third of the world's population of the Corsican seagull, adopted as the national park's symbol.

On Elba, the park runs a visitor centre (Info Park; ☑ 0565 90 82 31; www.parcoarcipela go.info; Calata Italia 4; ☺ 9am-7pm Apr-Oct, to 10pm Tue & Thu Aug, 9am-4pm Mon-Sat, to 3pm Sun Nov-Mar) in Portoferraio. In April and again in late September/early October, it hosts a popular Walking Festival (☑ 0565 90 82 31; www.tuscanywalkingfestival.it). Guided hikes across the island range from two to five hours and are graded easy, medium and challenging.

❶ Getting There & Away

AIR

Elba's airstrip, **Aeroporto Isola d'Elba** (☑ 0565 97 60 11; www.elbaisland-airport.it), is 2km north of Marina di Campo in La Pila. **Silver Air** (www. silverairtravels.com), with a ticketing desk at the airport, operates seasonal flights mid-June to September to/from Lugano (Switzerland).

BOAT

Getting to Elba involves a ferry crossing from Piombino or San Vincenzo on the mainland. Ferry companies include **Moby** (www.mobylines. com), **Toremar** (www.toremar.it), **Blu Navy** (www.blunavytraghetti.com) and **Aquavision** (www.aquavision.it). Most passengers arrive in Portoferraio (at least hourly, foot passenger/car and driver from €14/30 one way) or Marina di Campo (adult/child €20/10 one way; 1½ hours; one daily) on ferries from Piombino. There are also boat services to/from Cavo and Rio Marina.

Aquavision also runs seasonal ferries between Portoferraio and Bastia on Corsica (adult/child return 40/25; 2¼ hours; one weekly), departing on Sundays in July and August.

In season Aquavision runs a twice-weekly 'island tour' boat service departing from San Vincenzo on the mainland at 8.30am, with subsequent prolonged stops in Porto Azzurro, Marciana Marina and Portoferraio, before docking back in San Vincenzo at 7.30pm. Count on €40/25 per adult/child for the complete round trip.

❶ Getting Around

BUS

CTT Nord (www.livorno.cttnord.it) runs reasonably regular services linking all of Elba's main towns (€1.50 to €2.60). In Portoferraio, buses leave from the bus station, opposite the main Piombino ferry jetty.

CAR & MOTORCYCLE

Car is the easiest way to get around Elba, except in August when roads are jammed. The island's southwest coast offers the most dramatic and scenic motoring. With no traffic, expect to take one hour to motor the 35km from Procchio to Cavoli. Parking in blue bays on the island costs between €1 and €1.50 per hour and fees usually only apply between June and September.

TWN Rent (☑ 329 2736412, 0565 91 46 66; www.twn-rent.it; Viale Elba 32) has an office next to the port in Portoferraio and also in Marina di Campo, Lacona and Porto Azzurro, which rents cars and scooters. Otherwise, try **Rent Procchio** (☑ 338 7185735; www. rentprocchio.it; Via Provinciale di Procchio) in Procchio, 10km west of Portoferraio.

Portoferraio

☑ 0565 / POP 12,029

Portoferraio can be a hectic place, especially in August when holidaymakers pour off the ferries from Piombino on the mainland every 20 minutes or so. But wandering the streets and steps of the historic centre, indulging in the exceptional eating options and haggling for sardines with fishermen more than makes up for the squeeze.

Known to the Romans as Fabricia and later Ferraia (an acknowledgement of its important role as a port for iron exports), this small harbour was acquired by Cosimo I de' Medici in the mid-16th century, when its distinctive fortifications took shape.

Elba

0   5 km
0   2.5 miles

Piombino
Piombino
Piombino
Capraia
Montecristo (35km)

Tyrrhenian Sea

Cavo
Rio Marina
Rio dell'Elba
Ortano
Spiaggia dello Stagnone
Spiaggia di Naregno
Nispotino
Nisporto
Bagnaia
Ottone
Magazzini
Schiopparello
Cima del Monte (516m)
Porto Azzurro
Capoliveri
Calamita: Miniere di Capoliveri
Monte Calamita (413m)
Punta della Calamita
Spiaggia di Morcone
Spiaggia di Barabarca
Spiaggia di Pareti
Spiaggia dell'Innamorata
Spiaggia di Zuccale
Portoferraio
Le Grotte
San Giovanni
Spiaggia la Padulella
Spiaggia di Capo Bianco
Spiaggia di Sansone
Spiaggia di Sorgente
Capo d'Enfola
Enfola
Viticcio
Spiaggia della Biodola
La Biodola
Spiaggia di Spartaia
Golfo della Biodola
Spiaggia della Paolina
Procchio
Marmi
La Pila
San Martino
Museo
Villa Napoleonica di San Martino
Aeroporto Isola d'Elba
Acquario dell'Elba
Via Colle Reciso
Lacona
Golfo della Lacona
Golfo di Campo
Marina di Campo
Sant'Ilario in Campo
San Piero in Campo
Cavoli
Le Piscine
Seccheto
Fetovaia
Punta di Fetovaia
Spiaggia di Fetovaia
Spiaggia delle Tombe
Chiessi
Pomonte
Marciana Marina
Poggio
Monte Perone (630m)
SP37
Monte Maolo (749m)
Marciana
Monte Capanne (1018m)
Santuario della Madonna del Monte
Colle d'Orano
Capo Sant'Andrea
Spiaggia di Patresi
Tyrrhenian Sea

⊙ Sights

The Old Town's spiderweb of narrow streets and alleys staggers uphill from the old harbour to Portoferraio's twinset of forts, Forte Falcone and Forte Stella (☑ 0565 91 69 89; Via della Stella; adult/reduced €2/1.50; ⊙ 10am-1pm & 3-6pm Easter-Sep), revealing deserted 16th-century ramparts to wander and seagulls freewheeling overhead.

From waterside square Piazza Cavour head uphill along Via Garibaldi to the foot of the monumental Scalinata Medici, a fabulous mirage of 140 wonky stone steps cascading up through every sunlit shade of amber to the dimly lit, 17th-century Chiesa della Misericordia (Via della Misericordia; ⊙ 8am-5pm). Inside is Napoleon's death mask. Continue to the top of the staircase to reach the forts and Villa dei Mulini, where Napoleon lived when in Portoferraio.

★ Museo Villa Napoleonica di San Martino   MUSEUM

(☑ 0565 91 58 46; San Martino; adult/reduced €5/2; ⊙ 8.30am-1.30pm Tue, Thu, Sat & Sun, 2-5.30pm Wed & Fri summer, 9am-3pm Tue-Sun winter) Napoleon personally supervised the transformation of what had been a large farmhouse in the hills 5km southwest of Portoferraio into an elegant villa where he could escape the summer heat. Romanticism and hubris both came into play as he sought to give his new residence a Parisian sheen – the pretty Room of the Love Knot and grand Egyptian Room were particular triumphs. In the 1850s, a Russian nobleman purchased the villa and built a grandiose gallery at its base.

Museo Nazionale della Residenze Napoleoniche   MUSEUM

(Villa dei Mulini; ☑ 0565 91 58 46; Piazzale Napoleone; adult/reduced €5/2; ⊙ 8.30am-7.30pm Mon-Sat, 8.30am-1.30pm Sun summer, 8.30am-1.30pm daily winter) Villa dei Mulini was home to

Napoleon during his stint in exile on this small isle. With its Empire-style furnishings, splendid library, fig-tree-studded Italianate gardens and unbeatable sea view, the emperor didn't want for creature comforts – contrast this with the simplicity of the camp bed and travelling trunk he used when on campaigns. While that history lesson is nice, the dearth of actual Napoleonic artefacts here is a tad disappointing.

Forte Falcone   FORT

(☑ 0565 94 40 24; www.visitaportoferraio.com; Via del Falcone; €5; ⊙ 10am-8pm mid-June–mid-Sep, 10am-6pm mid-Apr–mid-June & mid-Sep–early Nov) Portoferraio's loftiest highest hill is crowned by this largely intact, 16th-century fort (1548) – a key point, together with Fort Stella and Torre del Martello, in the defensive ring built around the town by Cosimo 1 de' Medici. From Piazzale Napoleone head uphill along Via del Falcone then bear right along a small winding path that leads to the fort.

Villa Romana delle Grotte   ARCHAEOLOGICAL SITE

(☑ 327 8369680; www.villaromanalegrotte.it; Le Grotte, Punta delle Grotte; adult/reduced €4/3; ⊙ 10am-12.30pm & 5-8pm daily mid-Jun–mid-Sep, 10am-12.30pm & 2.30-6.40pm Fri-Sun mid-Apr–mid-June & mid-Sep–early Nov) About 5km out of Portoferraio town, wander through the ruins of this 1st-century-BC Roman villa overlooking the sea at Punta delle Grotte and you will be able to evoke the privileged lifestyle of its original owners, the noble Valerii family. Foundations, walls and columns are scattered over two levels, first excavated in the 1960s and still being studied by archaeologists.

Area Archeologica della Linguella   ARCHAEOLOGICAL SITE

(Torre della Linguella; ☑ 0565 94 40 24; Calata Buccari; adult/reduced €7/5; ⊙ 10am-12.30pm & 2.30-6.40pm late-Apr–early Nov) The 16th-century Torre del Martello was where Napoleon was 'imprisoned' at the start of his fleeting exile on Elba in 1814 and the russet-red, hexagonal tower remained a prison until 1877. It and the archaeological ruins next door (part of a luxurious Roman villa known as 'La Linguella' built between the 1st and 5th centuries AD) are now part of this museum. Also of interest are terracotta friezes from the Villa de Romana delle Grotte in the main museum building.

❶ PORTOFERRAIO DISCOUNTS

The Cosmopoli Card (adult/reduced €14/10; www.visitaportoferraio.com) is valid for seven days and covers admission to Forte Falcone, Area Archeologica della Linguella, Villa Romana delle Grotte, Teatro dei Vigilanti and other smaller sights.

CENTRAL COAST & ELBA ELBA

🛏 Sleeping & Eating

Accommodation options in central Portoferraio are lacklustre – you're better off sleeping elsewhere on the island; Schiopparello, Magazzini and Otone are all handily close by.

Restaurants in town aren't among the island's best, although they're always packed to the gills in August – reserve your table well in advance of dining.

B&B Porta del Mare
PENSION €

(☑ 328 8261441; www.bebportadelmarelba.com; Piazza Cavour 34; d €70-140, tr €90-170; 🐕) If you like being in the heart of things, the 4th-floor rooms in this elegant town house could work a treat. Three light, bright bedrooms have tall ceilings and filmy drapes; two have cracking harbour views. It's right in the middle of Portoferraio's main square (so expect some noise after dark). Owners Rossella and Bruno are gracious hosts.

Il Castagnacciao
PIZZA €

(☑ 0565 91 58 45; www.ilcastagnacciaio.com; Via del Mercato Vecchio 5; pizza €6-10; ⊙ 9.30am-2.30pm & 5pm-midnight daily summer, 10am-2.30 & 4.30-10.30pm Thu-Tue winter) They work the pizza chef so hard here that the dining room sometimes has a smoky tinge. To go local, start with a lip-smacking plate of *torta di ceci*, then watch your rectangular, thin-crust supper go in and out of the wood-fired oven. But save space for dessert – *castagnaccio* (chestnut 'cake') baked over the same flames.

Osteria Libertaria
TUSCAN €€

(☑ 0565 91 49 78; www.facebook.com/osterialibertaria; Calata Giacomo Matteotti 12; meals €35; ⊙ noon-2.30pm & 7-10.30pm, reduced hours winter) Fish drives the menu of this traditional *osteria* – no wonder, as the boats that land it are moored right outside. Traditional dishes such as fried calamari or *tonno in crosta di pistacchi* (pistachio-encrusted tuna fillet) are superfresh and very tasty. Dine at one of two tile-topped tables on the traffic-noisy street or on the back-alley terrace.

Bitta 20
SEAFOOD €€€

(☑ 0565 93 02 70; www.facebook.com/bitta20; Calata Guiseppe Mazzini 20; meals €50; ⊙ noon-3.30pm & 7-10.30pm Easter–mid-Oct) A Portoferraio favourite, this harbourside restaurant has a long terrace overlooking a string of bobbing yachts. White napery and efficient service combine with fresh fish and seafood to make it a good choice for lunch or dinner. Book for the latter.

Drinking & Nightlife

There are plenty of options in the Old Town, especially along Calata Mazzini. The island's hottest nightclub, **Club 64** (☑ 347 3231284; www.facebook.com/Club64Elba; Provinciale dei Marciana, SP24; ⊙ 11.55pm-5am Sat), around since 1964 in a garden-clad white villa, is 6km west of town near Spiaggia della Biodola.

Il Rifrullo
BAR

(☑ 0565 91 54 32; www.facebook.com/rifrullo.ristopub; Via Giuseppe Cacciò 35, SP24; ⊙ 6pm-3am Mon-Sat, to midnight Sun; 🐕) A fun and laid-back mixed bag of a hangout, Il Rifrullo is a well-established spot for listening to live music over a beer, cocktail, grilled meat or tasty pizza cooked in a wood-fired oven. Summer dining is on an attractive, greenery-draped verandah, and a roaring fire in the hearth warms the cockles on cooler nights in the red-brick and beamed-ceiling interior.

HAGGLING FOR FISH

Hanging out with locals, waiting for the fishing boats to come in, is a quintessential Portoferraio pastime. The crowd starts forming on the quay around 9.30am and by the time the first boats dock at 10am there's a line-up of punters waiting to exchange hand-crumpled bank notes for the catch of the day.

The larger industrial fishing boats dock midway between the ferry terminal and the old-town harbour on Banchina d'Alto Fondale. Occasionally they'll catch a huge tuna – which draws a real crowd – but in the main it's wooden crates of sardines, mackerel and anchovies the crews sell from the sides of their boats (€5 for a plastic-bag full).

Smaller vessels with just one or two fishermen moor alongside Calata Giacomo Matteotti at the old harbour each morning any time from 8am onwards. And these are the guys who get the real catch – octopus, lobster, eel and swordfish on good days.

If haggling for fish is simply not your cup of tea, there's always harbourside fishmonger Pescheria del Porto (☑ 0565 91 87 29; www.pescheriadelporto.it; Via delle Galeazze 20; ⊙ 8am-12.30pm Mon-Sat).

ℹ Information

Parco Nazionale dell'Arcipelago Toscana Office (p235) Helpful staff have abundant information on walking and biking on the island. Find the office on the seafront, near the ferry docks.

ℹ Getting There & Away

BOAT

See pxxx for information on ferry services to Portoferraio.

BUS

Bus 118 travels between Portoferraio and Bagnaia (€2.60; 25 minutes) stopping at Schiopparello and Magazzini (€1.50) en route, but services are scant.

More-frequent bus 117 (€2.60) connects Portoferraio with Capoliveri (45 minutes), Porto Azzurro (45 minutes), Rio Elba (65 minutes), Rio Marina (1¼ hours) and Cavo (1½ hours) at least eight times daily.

Schiopparello, Magazzini & Otone

☑ 0565

So close to Portoferraio that they are generally considered to be its suburbs, this cluster of settlements around pebbled coves and on rich agricultural land east of the ferry docks dates from the Roman period, when the powerful owners of the island's iron mines built ornate seaside villas here. These days, the coves shelter hotels and the hinterland is planted with olive trees, grapes, citrus and wheat. It's a much more peaceful and attractive sleeping option than Portoferraio itself.

Tenuta La Chiusa   WINE

(☑ 0565 93 30 46; www.tenutalachiusa.it; Località Magazzini 93, Magazzini; ☺ 8.30am-2.30pm & 3-7pm Mon-Sat summer, to 5pm winter) La Chiusa is idyllically located on the edge of the water at Magazzini, some 8km east of Portoferraio. In the history books because it was where Napoleon stayed on the night he landed on Elba in 1814, it's the oldest and possibly largest wine and olive-oil estate on the island, with 11.5 hectares of vineyards and 700 olive trees. Visitors are welcomed for paid tastings (€5 or free if you buy two bottles of wine) of up to six vintages in the cellar. There is basic farmhouse accommodation (self-catering) on-site.

Rosselba Le Palme   CAMPGROUND €

(☑ 0565 93 31 01; www.rosselbalepalme.it; Località Ottone; campsite adult/child €15/12, tent/car €20/5; ☺ mid-Apr–Sep; P ⚛ ⚛) Set around a botanical garden backed by Mediterranean

forest, few campgrounds are as leafy or large. The beach is a 400m walk between trees while accommodation ranges from simple pitches to 'glamping' tents with bathtubs, or cute wooden chalets to villa apartments. Find the ground 9km east of Portoferraio near Ottone.

★**Agriturismo Due Palme**   AGRITURISMO €€

(☑ 338 7433736, 0565 93 30 17; www.agriturismoelba.it; Via Schiopparello 28, Schiopparello; r €120-140; P ⚛) Utterly tranquil despite being just a few minutes from the Portoferraio–Magazzini road, this *agriturismo* (farm-stay accommodation) is part of the only olive plantation on Elba to produce quality-stamped IGP olive oil. Its six simple but well-maintained self-catering cottages are dotted amid flowerbeds, citrus trees and 100-year-old olive groves. Tree-shaded deckchairs, a barbecue and a tennis court heighten the charm.

Hotel Mare   HOTEL €€

(☑ 0565 93 30 69; www.hotelmare.org; Magazzini; d from €110; ☺ mid-Apr–mid-Oct; ⚛ @ ⚛ ⚛) Set on the edge of a crab-claw harbour 9km east of Portoferraio, this family-friendly hotel has a resort feel. A blue-and-white colour scheme lends things a nautical air, and the rooftop terrace, pool and spectacular bay views mean that many guests stay put rather than heading off to explore the island.

★**Ristoro Agricolo Montefabbrello**   TUSCAN €€

(☑ 338 6183584 0565 94 00 20; www.montefabbrello.it; Località Schiopparello 30; meals €35-40; ☺ 7.30-10pm daily Jun-Sep, 7.30-10pm Fri & Sat, noon-3pm Sun Oct-May) A model of slow and sustainable cuisine, this organic restaurant on the Montefabbrello farm grows its own wheat to make pasta, grapes to make wine and olives to produce oil. Fruit and veggies are homegrown too. Tasty pasta dishes, homemade bread and plenty of rustic meat and game dishes (unusual on Elba) make it an essential stop on every foodie itinerary.

Il Faro   LOUNGE

(☑ 0565 96 12 49; www.ristorantebarilfaro.it; Via della Marina, Spiaggia di Bagnaia; ☺ noon-11pm Easter-Oct) The sunset view from the beach terrace of this bar-restaurant in the cute cove of Bagnaia is the stuff that lasting holiday memories are made of. Head here for a cocktail or beer before dinner, but adjourn elsewhere to eat as the food is disappointing.

ⓘ Getting There & Away

Bus 118 travels between Portoferraio and Bagnaia (€2.60; 25 minutes) stopping at Schiopparello and Magazzini (€1.50) en route, but services are few and far between.

Marciana Marina, Marciana & Poggio

📞 0565 / POP 1975

Unlike many modern, cookie-cutter marinas, the attractive resort of Marciana Marina has character and history to complement its pleasant pebble beaches. The port is 18km west along the coast from Portoferraio. From it, a twisting 9km mountain road winds inland up to Marciana, the island's oldest and highest village (375m).

Marciana's stone streets, arches and stone houses with flower boxes and petite balconies are as pretty as a picture, and it's worth exploring them before heading uphill from the village to Elba's most important pilgrimage site: the Santuario della Madonna del Monte.

Between the two Marcianas, along a twisting and precipitous road, is the mountain village of Poggio. Set on the SP25, it's famous for its spring water and has steep cobblestone alleys and stunning coastal views.

◉ Sights & Activities

The loveliest moment of the day in laidback Marciana Marina is early evening, when the entire town seems to wander beside the waterfront for that oh-so-Tuscan *passeggiata*, gelato in hand. End on **Spiaggia di Capo Nord**, a handsome beach of large smooth pebbles overlooked by a 12th-century Saracen tower, and watch the sun sink over the Tyrrhenian Sea.

★ **Cabinovia Monte Capanne** CABLE CAR

(📞 0565 90 10 20; www.cabinovia-isoladelba.it; Località Pozzatello; adult/reduced return €18/13; ⊙ 10am-1pm & 2.20-5.30pm Jul-Sep, to 5pm Apr-Jun & Oct) Elba's famous cable car transports passengers up to the island's highest point, Monte Capanne (1018m), in open, barred baskets – imagine riding in a canary-yellow parrot cage and you'll get the picture. After a 20-minute ride, passengers alight and can scramble around the rocky peak to enjoy an astonishing 360-degree panorama of Elba, the Tuscan Archipelago, Etruscan Coast, and Corsica 50km away. Keen hikers can buy a cheaper one-way ticket and take the 90-minute walk back down a rocky path.

Santuario della Madonna del Monte CHAPEL

(⊙ 24hr) **FREE** To enjoy an invigorating 40-minute hike, head up through Marciana along Via della Madonna to reach this much-altered hilltop chapel with its 13th-century fresco of the Madonna painted on a slab of granite. A remarkable coastal panorama unfolds as you make your way here, past scented parasol pines, chestnut trees, wild sage and thyme. Once you reach the chapel (627m), emulate Napoleon and drink from the old stone fountain across from the church – a plaque commemorates his visit in 1814.

🛏 Sleeping & Eating

★ **Hotel Ilio** BOUTIQUE HOTEL €€

(📞 0595 90 80 18; www.hotelilio.com; Via Sant'Andrea 5, Capo Sant'Andrea; d/tr from €185/223; ⊙ mid-May–mid-Oct; P ✳ @ 🛜) With a suite splendidly set on the soft sands of Sant'Andrea beach and standard rooms – Contemporary, Mediterranean, Tuscan or Essential in decor – prettily arranged around a courtyard garden, Elba's most chic boutique address can do no wrong. The hotel has a lovely bar and hiking, biking and other outdoor-action activities abound on the surrounding green cape of Capo Sant'Andrea.

La Svolta GELATO €

(📞 0565 9 94 79; www.gelaterialasvolta.it; Via Cairoli 6, Marciana Marina; ⊙ 10.30am-late Tue-Sun Apr-Oct) The philosophy here is laudable: use fresh local produce (organic where possible), ensure that the flavours are as natural as possible, and serve the almost-inevitably delectable result in cones or in biodegradable cups.

Chilli and black pepper, bread with butter and jam, and pumpkin with toasted almonds are among wacky flavours that simply have to be tried…more than once.

★ **Ristorante Salegrosso** SEAFOOD €€

(📞 0565 99 68 62; www.facebook.com/SaleGrossoRistorante; Piazza della Vittoria 14, Marciana Marina; meals €40; ⊙ noon-3pm & 7.30-10pm Wed-Sun Mar-Dec) Those on the hunt for Elba's best fish dish need look no further – the fish stew here is a flavoursome pile of shellfish, tomato and saffron topped by a garlicky slice of *bruschetta*. Delicious! Dine on it or other fishy treats, including excellent homemade pasta, while watching locals take their *passeggiata* along the waterfront.

BEACH TALK

Given the wide range of bays on Elba's 147km-long coast it pays to know your *spiagge* (beaches). You'll find sandy strands on the south coast and in the Golfo della Biodola, on the western side of Capo d'Enfola. Beach town Procchio and adjoining resort La Biodola, 10km west of Portoferraio, also sport beautiful sandy beaches with a couple of luxurious hotels on the sand: Procchio's family-friendly Hotel del Golfo (☑ 0565 90 21; www.hoteldelgolfo.it; Via delle Ginestre 31; d/tr €350/490; ☺ late Apr–early Oct; P ✳ ☎ ✉) with tip-top beachside dining, and La Biodola's designer-chic Baia Bianca Suites (☑ 0565 96 99 16; www.baiabiancarelais.com; La Biodola 16; d from €250; ☺ late Apr–early Oct) and on-trend beach restaurant B.Bistrot. Elba's quietest, prettiest beaches are tucked in bijou rocky coves and often involve a steep clamber down. Parking is invariably roadside and scant.

Colle d'Orano & Fetovaia

The standout highlight of these two beach destinations on Elba's western coast is the dramatic 9km-long drive between the two along the SP25. Legend has it Napoleon frequented Colle d'Orano to sit and swoon over his native Corsica, which is visible across the water. Its rocky pebble beach, Spiaggia di Patresi (Via il Faro, Colle d'Orano), is a beautiful and wild spot to watch the sun set. Heading south, a heavenly scented promontory covered in *maquis* protects the brilliant golden sands of Spiaggia di Fetovaia (SP25, Fetoviaia), popular with families for its beach restaurant and canoe/pedalo/boat rentals on the sand. Not far away, nudists flop on granite rocks known as Le Piscine.

Enfola

Just 6km west of Portoferraio, it's not so much the grey pebbles as the outdoor action that lures crowds to this tiny fishing port. There are pedalos to rent, a beachside diving school (☑ 338 6893949, 347 2713187; www.enfoladivingcenter.it; ☺ 9am–7pm Jun–Sep), and a family-friendly 2.5km-long circular hiking trail around the green cape.

Morcone, Pareti & Innamorata

Find this trio of charming sandy-pebble coves framed by sweet-smelling pine trees some 5km south of Capoliveri in southeast Elba. Rent a kayak and paddle out to sea from Cala dell'Innamorata (SP31), the wildest of the three; or fine-dine and overnight on Pareti beach at Hotel Stella Maris (p244), one of the few three-star hotels to be found on the sand.

Sansone & Sorgente

This twinset of cliff-ensnared, white-shingle and pebble beaches stands out for its crystal-clear, turquoise waters just made for snorkelling and kayaking. A footpath crosses the small rocky promontory dividing Spiaggia La Sorgente (east) from Spiaggia di Sansone (west). By car from Portoferraio, follow the SP24 for 5km towards Enfola. Parking is challenging.

Procchio & La Biodola

Just 10km west of Portoferraio, the beach town of Procchio and adjoining resort area of La Biodola draw the summer-time crowds thanks to one of Elba's longest stretches of golden sand. West from Procchio, the road hugs cliffs above Spiaggia di Spartaia (Via di Spartaia) and Spiaggia della Paolina (SP25), beautiful little beaches requiring a steep clamber down.

Osteria del Noce　　　　SEAFOOD €€
(☑ 0565 90 12 84; www.osteriadelnoce.it; Via della Madonna 19, Marciana; meals €30; ☺ noon–2pm & 7.30–9.30pm late Mar–Sep) This family-run bistro in hilltop Marciana is the type of place where the bread is homemade and flavoured with fennel, chestnut flour and other seasonal treats. The pasta (incredible walnut-pesto sauce!), seafood dishes and sweeping views from the terrace are all truly magnificent. To find it, follow the Madonna del Monte walking signs to the top of the village.

LAZY DAYS IN ELBA

There is no more perfect spot in Tuscany to wind down than Elba, a Mediterranean island of orange and citrus trees, olive groves; and gold-sand beaches requiring nothing more than hardcore relaxation.

GOURMET ESCAPE

Tranquil Agriturismo Due Palme (p239) is located the island's only olive plantation to produce quality-stamped IGP olive oil. Its cottages are simple, well-maintained and have kitchens, and are surrounded by flowerbeds, citrus trees and 100-year-old olive groves. Don't leave without tasting and buying the silky fresh-green oil.

BEACH LIFE

Life is a beach on the island of Elba where snorkellers mingle with wave-frolicking kids in crystal-clear waters, while further out at sea, kayaking couples paddle peacefully from secret cove to secret cove, in search of their own private spot to romance under the hot Tuscan sun. Sun fish, barracudas and eagle rays reward the most of patient of divers. Beach hotspots: Spaggia di Spartaia, Innamorata and Sorgente.

SENSATIONAL SUNSETS

End the day on a sea-facing terrace with a glass of velvety red Aleatico DOCG wine, island-distilled grappa or tangy, Elba-lemon limoncino in hand. Watch the sun sink into the Med in one of the restaurants at the island's swishest James Bond–style address, **Hotel Hermitage** (☏0565 97 40; www.hotelhermitage.it; La Biodola; d €400; ☉late Apr–early Oct; P✳@🛜🏊), by the sand in La Biodola.

1. Porto Azzurro (p245) at sunset
2. Spiaggia di Fetovaia (p241)

ℹ Getting There & Away

Bus 116 links Marciana Marina and Marciana with Portoferraio at least eight times per day (€2.60).

Marina di Campo

☑ 0565 / POP 4679

A small fishing harbour on the south side of the island, Marina di Campo is Elba's second-largest town. Here a curling, picturesque bay dotted with bobbing boats adds personality to what is otherwise very much a holiday-oriented town. Its beach of bright, white sand pulls in holidaymakers by the thousands; coves further west, though less spectacular, are more tranquil. Two kilometres northeast of town, the modest Acquario dell'Elba entertains on rainy days.

Il Cantuccio   TRATTORIA €

(☑ 0565 97 67 75; Largo Garibaldi 6; meals €15-25; ⊙ noon-3pm & 7-11pm) Ignore the waterfront's menu-touting waiters and instead duck down Largo Garibaldi to find this unassuming, no-frills trattoria. In business since 1930, the place is excellent value (a rarity on Elba), serving seafood, homemade pasta, wood-fired pizza and 18 different varieties of olive oil.

Garden Beach   BAR

(☑ 0565 97 60 36; www.facebook.com/Garden BeachMarinadiCampo; Via Venezia 40; ⊙ 7am-2am) Be it breakfast at dawn, mid-morning coffee and artisan pastries, an afternoon gelato, or cocktails at dusk, this beachfront bar has you covered all day and is *the* address in Marina di Campo to party until late. Homemade sushi and various fast-food bites pander to late-night munchies and live music kicks in at weekends.

Da Mario   BAR

(☑ 0565 193 08 06; www.facebook.com/DaMar ioYachtClub; Lungomare Generale Fabio Miribelli 29; ⊙ 8am-11pm) The full name is Yacht Club Da Mario, but everyone shortens this to Da Mario – that's the kind of place it is. Pouring drinks and making coffee since 1952, it's friendly and has decking overlooking a cluster of fishing boats and a long curl of sand. Check its Facebook page for DJ sets, live music and party nights.

Giannino Live Music   CLUB

(☑ 340 3326868, 0565 97 80 34; https://gianni noelba.com; Via per Portoferraio, SP25; incl one drink women €13-16, men €15-20; ⊙ 11pm-5am daily Aug, 11pm-5am Fri & Sat late Jun-Jul & 1st two weeks Sep) An old farmhouse on a hill overlooking Marino di Campo, 4.5km north of town along the SP25, is the on-trend venue for Elba's biggest music club, firmly on the international DJ set circuit since 1980. Check its Facebook page for the month's gigs, concerts and events.

ℹ Getting There & Away

Aquavision (www.aquavision.it) operates a daily ferry in season between Marina di Campo and Piombino (adult/child return €35/20; 1½ hours).

Bus 116 links Marina di Campo with Procchio and Portoferraio at least eight times per day (€2.50).

Capoliveri

☑ 0565 / POP 3846

Picturesque Capoliveri sits in the high hills of Elba's southeast corner. Its steep alleys are lined with narrow houses, while the panorama of rooftops and sea that fans out from the old stone terrace on its central square, Piazza Matteotti, is utterly riveting.

There are one or two *pensiones* in the old town, but it's best to sleep somewhere near the beach. Book well in advance.

Calamita: Miniere di Capoliveri   MINE

(☑ 0565 93 54 92; www.minieredicalamita.it; museum adult/reduced €2.50/1.50, tours adult €18 & €24, reduced €12 & €18; ⊙ hourly tours from 10am-4.30pm late May-Aug, reduced tours & hours late Apr & Sep-Nov) Guided tours take visitors from a small site museum in Vallone, 11km south of Capoliveri, to the Genevro mine where magnetite was extracted until the operation closed in 1981. You'll walk through dark underground tunnels to see huge cathedral-like caverns where the metal was extracted.

Hotel Stella Maris   HOTEL €

(☑ 0565 96 84 25; www.albergostellamaris.it; Località Pareti; half-board per person d €70-100; P ✳ 🛜) Set bang on the gravelly beach at Pareti, this is one of the few three-star hotels in Elba with a location right on the seashore. Appealing facilities include a restaurant and bar with sea views, parasol-shaded sun-loungers on the sand, and pedalo/boat rental.

★ Locanda Lo Sgarbo   SEAFOOD €

(☑ 348 2987970; Via Silvio Pellico 3; meals €20-25; ⊙ 7.30-10.30pm) No resort-style glamour or pretension at this popular *spaghetteria*,

HIKING & BIKING ON ELBA
....

A dizzying network of walking and mountain-biking trails blankets Elba. Many start in Portoferraio, but some of the best, far-flung trailheads kick off elsewhere.

Monte Capanne Circular A three-hour, 20km adventure on the slopes of Elba's highest mountain, which sees you cycling on paved and unpaved routes past scented *maquis* (herbal scrubland) and pines. Total climb: 540m.

Marciana to Chiessi A 12km (six-hour) hike starts high up in Marciana and dribbles downhill past ancient churches, sea vistas and granite boulders to the seaside in Chiessi.

The Great Elba Crossing This three- to four-day, 60km east–west island crossing includes Monte Capanne, Elba's highest point (1018m), before overnighting on the coast (camping isn't allowed beside paths). The highlight is the final 19km leg from Poggio to Pomonte, passing the Santuario della Madonna del Monte (p240) and the **Masso dell'Aquila** rock formation.

just friendly down-to-earth service and exceptionally tasty seafood pasta served in a small dining room or at one of the outdoor tables. Everything is fishy and superfresh, and the homemade *dolci* (desserts) are legendary. Ending with a slice of chocolate-and-chilli-pepper cake is a Capoliveri essential.

La Taverna dei Poeti TUSCAN €€
(2347 6633395, 347 6633395 0565 96 83 06; www.latavernadeipoeti.com; Via Roma 14; meals €35-45; ⊙7.30-11.30pm summer) Much-loved by locals, this traditional address sees chef Massimo cook up the very best of Tuscan produce with a generous peppering of simplicity. The menu splits dishes into *mare* (sea) and *terra* (literally 'earth', meaning meat), and tasting menus can be paired with different wines. To ensure a sensational start to your meal, order the *baccalà* (salted cod) cheesecake with a green olive tapenade, cocoa beans and orange sauce.

★ **Fandango** WINE BAR
(2389 8407711; www.facebook.com/fandango.ca poliveri.3; Via Cardenti 1; ⊙10pm-4am Easter-Oct) Steps lead down from the panoramic terrace at the far end of the central Piazza Matteotti to this party-hot *enoteca,* a strictly after-dinner address cooking up well-made cocktails, excellent local wines, live music and *piccola cucina* (little snacks) made with local, often organic produce. Kudos for the atmospheric al fresco seating beneath a vine-clad pergola.

ⓘ Getting There & Away

Bus 117 connects Capoliveri with Porto Azzurro (€1.50; six minutes), Rio Elba (€2.60; 25 minutes), Rio Marina (€2.60; 35 minutes), Cavo

(€2.60; 50 minutes) and Portoferraio (€2.60; 40 minutes) at least eight times daily (€2.60).

Porto Azzurro
⌚ 0565 / POP 3885

Fittingly (considering its name), Porto Azzurro's glittering blue harbour fronts a palm-dotted pedestrianised square; a compact maze of flower-framed lanes, lined with restaurant and cafe terraces, spreads out behind. It makes for an atmospheric place to sample local seafood and wine, and a sweep of good beaches is found nearby.

There are few if any sleeping options in the centre of town, but a reasonable number on the busy seaside road in and out of town.

L'Osteria dei Quattro Gatti SEAFOOD €€
(2 0565 9 52 40; Piazza del Mercato 4; meals €35-45; ⊙7.30-10.10pm Tue-Sun, closed Mon mid-Sep–May) In the maze of lanes leading off from the main square (Piazza Matteotti), hunt out the flower-framed deck of this *osteria,* which sets the scene for excellently executed fish-themed dishes, often featuring treats such as *bottarga* (mullet roe). There aren't many tables, so it's a good idea to make a reservation.

ⓘ Getting There & Away

Aquavision (www.aquavision.it) operates a weekly ferry in season to/from San Vincenzo on the mainland and Porto Azzurro (adult/child return €35/20; 1¼ hours).

Bus 117 connects Porto Azzurro with Capoliveri (€1.50; six minutes), Portoferraio (€2.60; 45 minutes), Rio Elba (€1.50; 20 minutes), Rio Marina (€2.60; 30 minutes) and Cavo (€2.60; 45 minutes) at least eight times daily (€2.60).

BIKING MONTE CALAMITA

Keen cyclists gravitate to this scenic neck of the Elba woods to zip up, down and along 100km of biking paths through a stunning variety of landscapes on the slopes of Monte Calamita: from dusty, fire-red dirt tracks through former open-cast mineral mines to sandy beachside paths and shady trails through scented holm-oak forest. Five mapped off-road itineraries in the Capoliveri Bike Park (www.capoliveribikepark.it) range from an easy 19km loop for families to a more demanding, 41km through steep, hair-raising terrain at times. Rent moun-tain bikes, pick up maps and/or join a guided bike tour at Capoliveri Legend Park (✆392 9606114; www.rentelbabike.it; Piazza del Cavatore 1), the park's info and rental point in town.

Giglio, Gorgona & Pianosa

Giglio (population 1436) is the second-largest of the seven islands in the Tuscan Archipel-ago. Located south of Elba, it comprises 21 sq km of predominantly hilly terrain and is a popular hiking destination. There are also a number of sheltered bays popular with swimmers and it is a lovely place to spend a day. Sail here by ferry (50 minutes) from Porto Santo Stefano on Monte Argentario – Maregiglio (www.maregiglio.it) and Toremar (www.toremar.it) operate year-round services (adult/child/car €26/17/92 return). In season Aquavision (www.aquavision.it; adult/child return €35/20, two hours) operates boat trips on Wednesday from Elba's Porta Azzurro to Giglio, with a five-hour stop on the island (adult/child €35/20 return).

Pinprick Pianosa, southwest of Elba, served as a penal colony until 1997. It's not geared to tourism so there's no compelling reason to visit. Should you have the urge, hop aboard a seasonal daily boat run by Aquavision from Elba's Marino di Cam-po (adult/child €30/15 return; 40-minute crossing) or Piombino (adult/child €40/25 return; two-hour crossing).

North of Elba, the island of Gorgona (pop-ulation 220) holds a high-security prison and is pretty well off-limits to day-trippers. The other islands in the group are Capraia and teeny-tiny Montecristo and Giannutri, each home to no more than a handful of islanders.

Capraia

✆0586 / POP 404

This tiny island in the Tyrrhenian Sea is a mere 31km from the French island of Corsi-ca. Only 8km long and 4km wide, its highest point is Monte Castello (447m). It is a pop-ular day-tripping destination in summer, when its few hotels and restaurants open, but is eerily quiet at other times of the year.

The island's great walks include the trail to Lake Stagnone – Capraia's tourist of-fice has maps of hiking and biking routes around the island. A chequered history has seen Genoa, Sardinia, the Saracens from North Africa and Napoleon all have a bash at running Capraia.

Ultima Spiaggia WATER SPORTS

(✆392 7951508; Cala del Frate; ⊙mid-May–Oct) Immediately north of the port, the cove of Cala del Frate squirrels away the small peb-ble beach of Spiaggia del Frate with wood-en sunbathing deck, a ladder into the sea and the island's only stand-up paddleboard outfit. Rent a board to explore the coastline or sign up for a lesson.

Capraia Diving DIVING

(✆333 3172333, 0586 90 51 37; www.capraia diving.it; Via Assunzione 100) The island's well-established diving school offers baptism dives, diving lessons and courses as well as less technical, lots-of-fun snorkelling expedi-tions. Rent all the gear at its port-side shop.

ⓘ Information

The friendly **tourist office** (✆338 1509312; www.prolococapraiaisola.it; Via Assunzione 72; ⊙9.30am-12.30pm & 5.30-6.30pm summer) is a summer-only affair.

ⓘ Getting There & Away

Once a week, **Aquavision** (www.aquavision.it) runs a day trip (adult/child return €35/20, 2½ hours each way) from Portoferraio and Marciana Marina on Elba to Capraia, which leaves you five hours to explore the island. It also runs twice-weekly ferries from San Vincenzo on the mainland to the island (adult/child return €35/20, two hours), with a seven-hour stop.

Toremar (www.toremar.it) operates ferries between Livorno and Capraia (adult/child €43/30 return, 2¾ hours each way, one or two daily in summer, less frequently in winter); in high season schedules can allow a return trip in a day, but triple-check before setting out.

Northwestern Tuscany

Includes ➡

Pisa.............................250
Lucca...........................261
Pistoia 270
San Miniato................ 277
Castelnuovo di
Garfagnana................ 279
Barga...........................281
Bagni di Lucca 283
Carrara.......................284
Pietrasanta 287
Viareggio.....................289
Pontremoli 292

Best Places to Eat

➡ Filippo (p289)

➡ La Parte degli Angeli (p267)

➡ Osteria Vecchia Mulino (p280)

➡ Pepenero (p279)

Best Places to Stay

➡ Barbialla Nuova (p278)

➡ Palazzo Puccini (p276)

➡ Al Benefizio (p282)

➡ Albergo Pietrasanta (p288)

Why Go?

There's far more to this green corner of Tuscany than Italy's iconic Leaning Tower. Usually hurtled through en route to Florence and Siena's grand-slam queue-for-hours sights, this is the place to take your foot off the accelerator and go slowly – on foot or by bicycle or car. Allow for long lunches of regional specialities to set the pace for the day, before meandering around a medieval hilltop village or along an ancient pilgrimage route.

University hub Pisa and 'love at first sight' Lucca – with its 16th-century walls ensnaring a labyrinth of butter-coloured buildings, Romanesque palaces and gracious piazzas – have an air of tranquillity and tradition that begs the traveller to linger. Lesser-known Pistoia, Prato and Pietrasanta, all off the beaten tourist track, provide a welcome reprieve in high season from the crowds (dead-easy half- or full-day trips by train from Florence, incidentally). This is snail-paced Italy, and is impossible not to love.

Road Distances Chart

	Pistoia	Pisa	Lucca	San Miniato
Pisa	55			
Lucca	40	23		
San Miniato	64	47	70	
Pietrasanta	68	31	30	77

North-western Tuscany Highlights

❶ Lucca (p261) Pedalling and picnicking on delicious local treats atop this handsome city's Renaissance city walls.

❷ Leaning Tower (p252) Meandering through medieval Pisa and scaling its iconic tower at sunset.

❸ Truffle hunts (p279) Hunting white truffles with a dog in autumnal woods near outrageously foodie San Miniato.

❹ Pistoia (p270) Fleeing the crowds by delving into the treasure trove of museums in this quiet provincial town.

❺ Pietrasanta (p287) Revelling in exciting contemporary art, cuisine and boutique shopping in this gem of a small art town.

❻ Garfagnana (p279) Losing yourself in green rural Tuscany in chestnut-rich forests.

❼ Carrara (p284) Seeing where Michelangelo sourced his marble and visiting the extraordinary quarries.

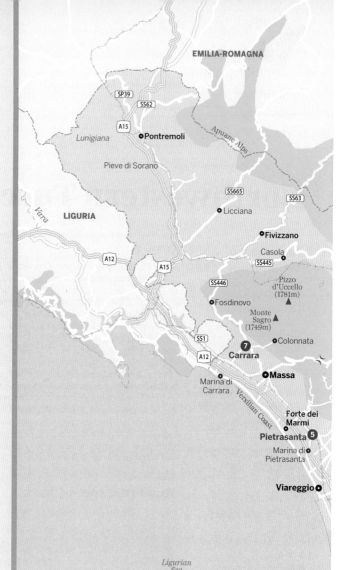

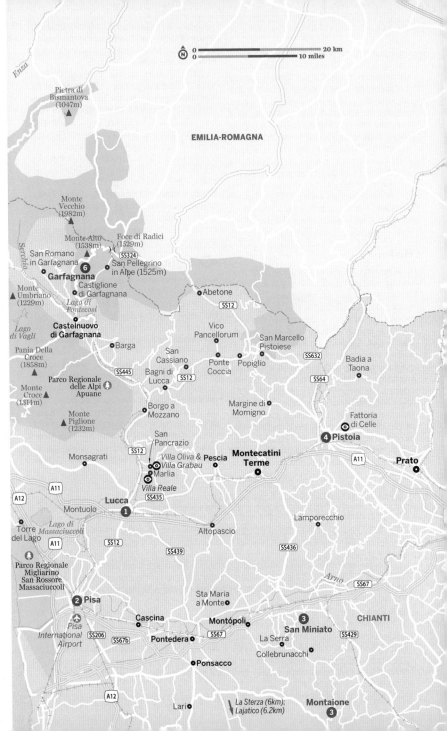

PISA

📌 050 / POP 90,500

Once a maritime power to rival Genoa and Venice, modern Pisa is best known for an architectural project gone terribly wrong. But the world-famous Leaning Tower is just one of many noteworthy sights in this compelling city. Education has fuelled the local economy since the 1400s, and students from across Italy compete for places in its elite university. This endows the centre of town with a vibrant cafe and bar scene, balancing an enviable portfolio of well-maintained Romanesque buildings, Gothic churches and Renaissance piazzas with a lively street life dominated by locals rather than tourists – a charm you will definitely not discover if you restrict your visit to Piazza dei Miracoli.

History

Pisa became an important naval base and commercial port under Rome and remained a significant port for centuries. The city's golden days began late in the 10th century, when it became an independent maritime republic and a formidable rival of Genoa and Venice. A century on, the Pisan fleet was sailing far beyond the Mediterranean, successfully trading with the Orient and bringing home new ideas in art, architecture and science. At the peak of its power (the 12th and 13th centuries), Pisa controlled Corsica, Sardinia and the Tuscan coast. Most of the city's finest buildings date from this period, when the distinctive Pisan-Romanesque architectural style with its use of coloured marbles and subtle references to Andalucian architectural styles flourished. Many of these buildings sported decoration by the great father-and-son sculptural team of Nicola and Giovanni Pisano.

Pisa's support for the imperial Ghibellines during the tussles between the Holy Roman Emperor and the pope brought the city into conflict with its mostly Guelph Tuscan neighbours, including Siena, Lucca and Florence. The real blow came when Genoa's fleet inflicted a devastating defeat on Pisa at the Battle of Meloria in 1284. After the city fell to Florence in 1406, the Medici court encouraged great artistic, literary and scientific endeavours and re-established Pisa's university, where the city's most famous son, Galileo Galilei, taught in the late 16th century. During WWII about 40% of old Pisa was destroyed.

⊙ Sights

Many visitors to Pisa arrive by train at Pisa San Rossore and don't get any further than neighbouring Piazza dei Miracoli; those in the know arrive or depart using the central train station, Stazione Pisa Centrale, allowing casual discovery of the *centro storico* (historic centre).

Away from the crowded heavyweights of Piazza dei Miracoli, along the Arno river banks, Pisa comes into its own. Splendid *palazzi,* painted a multitude of hues, line the southern *lungarno* (riverside embankment), from where shopping boulevard Corso Italia legs it to Stazione Pisa Centrale. Don't miss the waterside, triple-spired Chiesa di Santa Maria della Spina

---

❶ HOW TO FALL IN LOVE WITH PISA

Sure, the iconic Leaning Tower is the reason everyone wants to go to Pisa. But once you've put yourself through the Piazza dei Miracoli madness (littered lawns, football-playing school groups, photo-posing pandemonium...) most people simply want to get out of town.

To avoid leaving Pisa feeling oddly deflated by one of Europe's great landmarks, save the Leaning Tower and its oversized square for the latter part of the day – or, better still, an enchanting visit after dark (mid-June to late August or early September) when the night casts a certain magic on the glistening white monuments and the tour buses have long gone.

Upon arrival, indulge instead in peaceful meanderings along the Arno river, over its bridges and through Pisa's medieval heart. Discover the last monumental wall painting (p259) Keith Haring did before he died, enjoy low-key architectural and artistic genius at the Chiesa di Santa Maria della Spina and Palazzo Blu, and lunch with locals at Sottobosco (p259) or Osteria Bernardo (p258). Scale and stroll atop Pisa's ancient city walls for a privileged bird's-eye view of the city.

Only once you've fallen in love with the other Pisa should you head for the tower.

Cappella di San Cappella Ranieri. Arab-sculpted decorative elements in the chapel demonstrate how influential the Islamic world was on Pisa at this time; the 11th-century bronze griffin that stood atop the cathedral until 1828 was booty, probably Egyptian in origin.

Giovanni Pisano's Pulpit
The extraordinary octagonal pulpit in the north aisle was sculpted from Carrara marble by Pisano between 1302 and 1310; it was inspired by his father's pulpit in the *battistero* and also features nude and heroic figures. With it, Pisano brought a new pictorial expressionism and life to Gothic sculpture.

Battistero
Construction of the cupcake-style battistero (Battistero di San Giovanni; €5, combination ticket with Camposanto or Museo delle Sinopie €7, Camposanto & Museo delle Sinopie €8; 8am-8pm Apr-Oct, 9am-6pm or 7pm Nov-Mar) began in 1152, but the building was remodelled and continued by Nicola and Giovanni Pisano more than a century later and finally completed in the 14th century. Don't leave without climbing to the Upper Gallery to listen to the custodian demonstrate the double dome's remarkable acoustics and echo effects.

Camposanto
Soil shipped from Calvary during the Crusades is said to lie within the white walls of this hauntingly beautiful cloistered quadrangle (€5, combination ticket with Battistero or Museo delle Sinopie €7, Battistero & Museo €8; 8am-8pm Apr-Jul, Sep & Oct, 8am-10pm Aug, 9am-7pm Nov, Dec & Mar, 9am-5pm Jan & Feb), where prominent Pisans were once buried. It's a peaceful sanctuary after the selfie mayhem on the square outside. Some of the sarcophagi here are of Graeco-Roman origin, recycled during the Middle Ages. During WWII, Allied artillery destroyed many of the 14th- and 15th-century frescoes that once covered the cloister walls. Those in the southern cloister have been beautifully restored.

Museo delle Sinopie
Home to some fascinating frescoes, this museum (€5, combination ticket with Battistero or Camposanto €7, Battistero & Camposanto €8; 8am-8pm Apr-Nov, 9am-6pm or 7pm Nov-Feb) safeguards several *sinopie* (preliminary sketches) drawn by artists in red earth pigment on the walls of the Camposanto in the 14th and 15th centuries before frescoes were painted over them. It offers a compelling study in fresco painting technique, with short films and scale models filling in the gaps.

TOP TIPS
Book Leaning Tower tickets in advance online or grab the first available slot when you arrive at ticket desks behind the tower or in the Museo delle Sinopie. *Duomo* admission is free, but you need a ticket – for another sight or a *duomo* coupon distributed at ticket offices.

The *battistero* highlight is a hexagonal marble pulpit (1260) by Nicola Pisano. Inspired by the Roman sarcophagi in the Camposanto, Pisano used powerful classical models to enact scenes from biblical legend. His figure of Daniel, supporting the pulpit on his shoulders, is extraordinary.

THE TRIUMPH OF DEATH
Among the Camposanto's frescoes are Buonamico Buffalmacco's remarkable illustrations of hell (1336–41). In *Inferno* (second fresco to the right of main entrance) observe the artist's monstrous portrait of Lucifer in hell greedily devouring sinners and excreting them, while ape-like demons dance around him in torment. In *Triumph of Death* (fourth fresco on right) the damned are being roasted alive on spits.

Why Pisa Leans

In 1160 Pisa boasted 10,000-odd towers, but no *campanile* (bell tower) for its cathedral. Loyal Pisan, Berta di Bernardo, righted this in 1172 when she died and left a legacy of 60 pieces of silver in her will to the city to get cracking on a *campanile*.

Ironically, when Bonnano Pisano set to work on the world's most famous *campanile* in 1173, he did not realise what shaky ground he was on: beneath Piazza dei Miracoli's lawns lay a treacherous mix of sand and clay, 40m deep. And when work stopped five years on, with just three storeys completed, Italy's stump of an icon had already tilted. Building resumed in 1272, workers compensating for the lean by building straight up from the lower storeys to create a subtle banana curve. By the 19th century, many were convinced the tower

was a mere whimsical folly of its inventors, built deliberately to lean.

In 1838 a clean-up job to remove muck oozing from the base of the tower exposed, once and for all, the true nature of its precarious foundations. In the 1950s the seven bells inside the tower, each sounding a different musical note and rung from the ground by 14 men since 1370, were silenced for fear of a catastrophic collapse. In 1990 the tower was closed to the public. Engineers placed 1000 tonnes of lead ingots on the north side to counteract the subsidence on the south side. Steel bands were wrapped around the 2nd storey to keep it together.

Then in 1995 the tower slipped a whole 2.5mm. Steel braces were slung around the 3rd storey of the tower and attached to heavy hydraulic A-frame anchors some

1. Leaning Tower (p252)
2. Battistero di San Giovanni (p253) 3. Bell tower, Chiesa di San Nicola

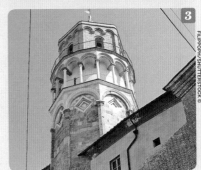

way from the northern side. The frames were replaced by steel cables, attached to neighbouring buildings. The tower held in place, engineers gingerly removed 70 tonnes of earth from below the northern foundations, forcing the tower to sink to its 18th-century level – and correct the lean by 2011 to 43.8cm. Success...

Every year scientists carry out tests on Pisa's pearly white leaning tower to measure its lean and check it's stable. Ironically, results in 2013 showed that the world's most famous leaning tower had, in fact, lost 2.5cm of its iconic lean, with some scientists even predicting a complete self-straightening by the year 2300. Let's hope not.

LEANING CITY

Duomo & Battistero (p252 & p253) The tower's neighbours lean 25cm and 51cm, respectively.

Chiesa di San Nicola (Via Santa Maria) Nicola Pisano's octagonal *campanile* (bell tower) is another sacred edifice that is not dead straight.

Chiesa di San Michele degli Scalzi (Via San Michele degli Scalzi) Note the wonky red-brick square tower.

Pisa

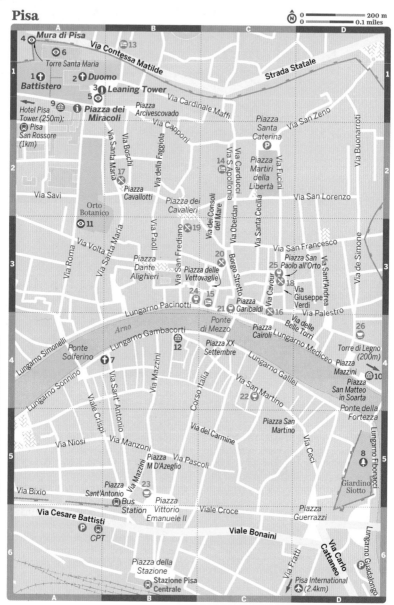

N ⊙ 0 ▬▬▬▬▬▬▬▬▬▬ 200 m
      0 ▬▬▬▬▬▬▬▬▬▬ 0.1 miles

✿ Festivals & Events

Palio delle Quattro
Antiche Repubbliche Marinare   CULTURAL
(Regatta of the Four Ancient Maritime Republics;
⊙early Jun) The four historical maritime rivals – Pisa, Venice, Amalfi and Genoa – take
turns to host this historic regatta. The regatta next sails into Pisa in 2021.

Luminaria di San Ranieri   LIGHT SHOW
(⊙16 Jun) The night before the day of Pisa's
patron saint is magical: thousands upon
thousands of candles and blazing torches

Pisa

◎ **Top Sights**
| | |
1 Battistero A1
2 Duomo A1
3 Leaning Tower A1
4 Mura di Pisa A1
5 Piazza dei Miracoli A1

◎ **Sights**
6 Camposanto A1
7 Chiesa di Santa Maria della
    Spina B4
8 Giardino Siotto D5
9 Museo delle Sinopie A1
10 Museo Nazionale di San
    Matteo D4
11 Orto e Museo Botanico A3
12 Palazzo Blu B4

◎ **Sleeping**
13 Hostel Pisa Tower B1
14 Hotel Di Stefano C2
15 Royal Victoria Hotel C3

◎ **Eating**
16 Chilometro Toscano C3
    Gelateria De' Coltelli .... (see 24)
17 L'Ostellino B2
18 Osteria Bernardo C3
19 Osteria dei Cavalieri B3
20 Pizzeria Il Montino C3

◎ **Drinking & Nightlife**
21 Bazeel C3
22 Caffè Letteraria Volta Pagina ... C4
23 Keith B5
24 La Stafetta B3
25 Sottobosco C3
26 Wood Coffee D4

light up the river and riverbanks while fireworks dazzle in the night sky.

Gioco del Ponte　　　　　CULTURAL
(◎ last Sun Jun) During Gioco del Ponte (Game of the Bridge), two teams in medieval costume battle it out over the Ponte di Mezzo.

🛏 Sleeping

Pisa is people- and traffic-busy, and quality accommodation is limited: hotels are predominantly midrange. Instead consider day-tripping to Pisa from lovely Lucca (p261), a farm around San Miniato (p277) or a stylish art gem in Pietrasanta (p287).

Hostel Pisa Tower　　　　HOSTEL €
(☑ 050 520 24 54; www.hostelpisatower.it; Via Piave 4; dm €25; @ 🛜) This super-friendly hostel occupies a suburban villa a only couple of minutes' walk from Piazza dei Miracoli. It's bright and cheery, with colourful decor, both female and mixed dorms, a communal kitchen and a summer-friendly terrace overlooking a small grassy garden. Dorms are named, meaning you can sleep with Galileo, Mona Lisa, Leonardo or Michelangelo.

Hotel Di Stefano　　　　HOTEL €
(☑ 050 55 35 59; www.hoteldistefanopisa.com; Via Sant'Apollonia 35; d/q €140/160; P ❄ @ 🛜) This three-star hotel has been in business since 1969 for good reason. Partly tucked in a medieval town house, it fuses vintage charm with no-frills functionality and a warm, family-run ambience. Deluxe rooms have beamed ceilings, exposed brickwork and a balcony overlooking the small back garden. The rooftop terrace, with armchairs and stunning sunset views, is accessible – fabulously so – to all.

★ **Hotel Pisa Tower**　　　HOTEL €€
(☑ 050 520 00 19; www.hotelpisatower.com; Via Pisano 23; d/tr/q from €109/134/149; P ❄ 🛜) For peace, tranquillity and sundown drinks in a romantic walled garden after a busy day navigating the Pisa crowds, this outstanding three-star hotel hits the spot. Its 14 rooms are spacious, with high ceilings and country-style furnishings. Chandeliers, marble floors and framed antique prints adorn the lounge, and breakfasting al fresco on the elegant terrace is the perfect start to any Tuscan day.

Five cheaper rooms that sleep four (€139) languish in the hotel annexe. Find the hotel a two-minute walk from Pisa San Rossore train station. The hotel rents out bicycles and runs daily shuttles to Pisa Centrale train station/Pisa International Airport (€5/6 per person).

Royal Victoria Hotel　　　HOTEL €€
(☑ 050 94 01 11; www.royalvictoria.it; Lungarno Pacinotti 12; d/tr €100/110; ❄ 🛜) This doyen of Pisan hotels, run by the Piegaja family since 1837, offers old-world luxury accompanied by warm, attentive service. Its 38 rooms exude a shabby-chic spirit with their Grand Tour antiques – some peep out onto the murky river. Don't miss an *aperitivo* flopped on a sofa on the 4th-floor terrace, packed with potted plants. Garage parking per day is €20.

✕ Eating

Pisa has a good range of eating places, especially around Borgo Stretto, the university on cafe-ringed Piazza Dante Alighieri, and south of the river in the trendy San Martino quarter. Avoid the touristy restaurant strip on Via Santa Maria.

Local specialities include fresh *pecorino* (sheep's-milk cheese) from San Rossore, *zuppe di cavolo* (cabbage soup), *pan ficato* (fig cake) and *castagnaccio* (chestnut-flour cake enriched by nuts).

★ **Gelateria De' Coltelli**   GELATO €

(☑ 345 4811903; www.decoltelli.it; Lungarno Pacinotti 23; small/medium/large €2.50/3/4.30; ⊙ 11.30am-10.30pm Sun-Thu, to 11.30pm Fri & Sat) Follow the crowd to this world-class gelateria, famed for its sensational artisanal, organic and 100% natural gelato. Flavours are as zesty and appealing as its bright-orange interior. The hard part is choosing: ginger, Sicilian orange, ricotta cheese with candied orange peel and chocolate chips, candied chestnuts, cashew with Maldon salt, kiwi, pear and pink pepper...

L'Ostellino   SANDWICHES €

(Piazza Cavallotti 1; panini €4-7; ⊙ noon-4.30pm Mon-Fri, to 7pm Sat & Sun) For a gourmet *panino* (sandwich) wrapped in crunchy waxed paper, this minuscule deli and *panineria* delivers. Take your pick from dozens of different combos written by hand on the blackboard (*lardo di colonnata* with figs or cave-aged *pecorino* with honey and walnuts are sweet favourites), await construction, then hit the green lawns of Piazza dei Miracoli to picnic with the crowds.

Pizzeria Il Montino   PIZZA €

(☑ 050 59 86 95; Vicolo del Monte 1; pizza €6-8.50, foccacine €2.50-5, cecina €2; ⊙ 11am-3pm & 5.30-10.30pm Mon-Sat) There's nothing fancy about this down-to-earth pizzeria, an icon among Pisans, students and sophisticates alike. Take away or order at the bar then grab a table, inside or out, and munch on house specialities such as *cecina* (chickpea pizza), *castagnaccio* (chestnut cake) and *spuma* (sweet, nonalcoholic drink). Or go for a *focaccine* (small flat roll) filled with salami, pancetta or *porchetta* (suckling pig).

Osteria dei Cavalieri   TUSCAN €€

(☑ 050 58 08 58; www.osteriacavalieri.pisa.it; Via San Frediano 16; meals €25-30; ⊙ 12.30-2pm & 7.45-10pm Mon-Fri, 7.45-10pm Sat) When an *osteria* cooks up a tripe platter for *antipasto*, bone marrow with saffron-spiced rice as *primo* and feisty T-bone steaks as *secondo*, you know you've struck Tuscan foodie gold. A trio of inspired *piatti unico* (single dishes) promise a quick lunch, or linger over themed multicourse menus (including, unusually, a vegetarian menu) packed with timeless Tuscan faves.

Chilometro Toscano   TUSCAN €€

(☑ 331 3214164; www.chilometrotoscano.it; Via Cavour 9; meals €20-30; ⊙ 10.30am-3.30pm & 6-11pm Mon-Sat; ☎) With its soul-soaringly high stone-vaulted ceiling and lavish deli display of Tuscan cheeses and salamis, this contemporary wine bar and eatery is hard to resist. Build your own tasting platter or opt for a daily special chalked on the board such as *testaroli* (triangle-cut pasta) with walnut sauce and crispy prosciutto. *Torta di farro* with organic ricotta is among the vegetarian dishes.

Osteria Bernardo   TUSCAN €€

(by Il Giardino Nascosto; ☑ 050 57 52 16; www.facebook.com/osteriabernardobygiardinonascosto; Piazza San Paolo all'Orto 1; meals €40; ⊙ 12.30-3pm & 7-11pm Tue-Sun) This small bistro on a pretty square, well away from the Leaning Tower crowd, is the perfect fusion of easy dining and gourmet excellence. Its menu is small – just four or five dishes per course – and the cuisine is creative. Think pistachio-crusted lamb, beef in beer sauce or a tasty risotto with Stilton cheese, lettuce and crisp leek. Reservations recommended.

🍺 Drinking & Nightlife

Most drinking action takes place on and around Piazza delle Vettovaglie and student-packed Piazza Dante Alighieri. Sun-dashed Piazza Cairoli is another favourite for lingering al fresco over *un caffè* or gelato. Try to taste local wines produced in the Pisan hills under the DOCG Chianti delle Colline Pisane label.

Wood Coffee   COFFEE

(☑ 050 622 37 38; www.facebook.com/woodcoffeepisa; Via Santa Bibbiana 10; ⊙ 7.30am-6.30pm Mon-Sat; ☎) Chill in peace over a love heart-topped cappuccino, French-press coffee, Nutella-flavoured frappuccino or iced americano at this speciality coffee shop. Fittings and furnishings are recycled from wooden pallets and coffee bean sacks, and the kitchen cooks up a tasty selection of cookies,

GREEN ESCAPE

Lap up the peace and tranquillity of local Pisan life in one of the city's (picnic-perfect) urban gardens.

Orto e Museo Botanico (Botanical Garden & Museum; ☑ 050 221 13 10; www.ortomuseo bot.sma.unipi.it; Via Roma 56; adult/reduced €4/2; ☺ 8.30am-8pm Apr-Sep, 9am-5pm Mon-Sat, to 1am Sun Oct-Mar) For a Zen-like respite from the Piazza dei Miracoli crowd, explore this peaceful walled garden laced with centurion palm trees, flora typical to the Apuane Alps, a fragrant herb garden, vintage greenhouses and 35 orchid species. Showcasing the botanical collection of Pisa University, the garden dates from 1543 and was Europe's first university botanical garden, tended by the illustrious botanist Luca Ghini (1490–1556). The museum, inside **Palazzo della Conchiglie**, explores the garden's history, with exquisite botanical drawings, catalogues, maquettes etc.

Giardino Siotto (Cittadella Nuova; Lungarno Fibonacci 2; ☺ 8am-8.30pm Jul & Aug, shorter hr rest of year) Straddling the southern bank of the River Arno, this attractive city park – complete with children's playground and benches aplenty – is ensnared within the ancient walls of Pisa's fortified Citadella Nuova (New Citadel), built here between 1440 and 1475 following Florence's victory over Pisa, but swiftly destroyed by the Pisans in 1495. Two towers, the western wall and escarpment remain today.

muffins, creatively stuffed bagels (€5 to €6) and sassy lunchtime salads (€4 to €6.50).

English breakfasts (€6), omelettes, pancakes and French toast too.

La Stafetta CRAFT BEER
(www.lastaffetta.com; Lungarno Pacinotti 24; ☺ 6pm-1am Mon-Thu, 7pm-2am Fri & Sat, 4-11pm Sun) Squat on a bench outside or grab a pew inside this funky riverside tap room, the creation of three ale-loving Pisan students: Matteo, Davide and Francesco. Inside, order one of the small microbrewery's own brews: taste English hops in Wilson (a dark-red bitter with hints of coffee, chocolate and liquorice) or go for a light and golden May Ale.

Caffè Letteraria Volta Pagina BAR
(☑ 328 0025526; Via San Martino 71; ☺ 3pm-midnight Tue-Sun) Kick back with Pisan cool cats at this edgy literary cafe with a red-brick vaulted ceiling, achingly cool vintage furnishings and a laid-back lounge vibe. Watch for weekly readings, concerts and other cultural happenings that set the place buzzing. Check its Facebook page for what's on.

Sottobosco BAR
(☑ 050 314 20 84; www.facebook.com/sottobosco. libricafe; Piazza San Paolo all'Orto 3; ☺ 6pm-midnight Sat-Thu, to 1am Fri, shorter hours winter) Tuck into an end-of-day sugar doughnut and cappuccino or an early-evening *aperitivo* at a glass-topped table filled with artists'

crayons perhaps, or a button collection. Salads, *panini,* salami or cheese *taglieri* (tasting boards) and oven-baked cheese are simple and homemade. Come dark, jazz bands play or DJs spin tunes.

Bazeel BAR
(☑ 349 0880688; www.bazeel.it; Lungarno Pacinotti 1; ☺ 7am-1am Sun-Thu, to 2am Fri & Sat) A dedicated all-rounder, Bazeel is a hotspot from dawn to dark. Laze over breakfast, linger over a pizza or hang out with the A-list crowd over a generous *aperitivo* spread, live music and DJs. Its chapel-like interior is nothing short of fabulous, as is its pavement terrace out the front. Check its Facebook feed for what's on.

Keith CAFE
(☑ 050 50 31 35; www.facebook.com/keithcafe; Via Zandonai 4; ☺ 7am-11pm summer, to 9pm winter; ☎) This trendy cafe stares face to face with *Tuttomondo* (1989), a mural on the facade of a Pisan church – and the last mural American pop artist Keith Haring painted just months before his death. Sip a coffee or cocktail on the terrace and lament the fading, weather-beaten colours of Haring's 30 signature prancing, dancing men.

Free wi-fi, occasional contemporary-art exhibitions, superb coffee and a student-friendly €5 *apericena* buffet all keep Keith buzzing.

WORTH A TRIP

VESPA TOUR

There's a certain romance to touring Tuscany on the back of a Vespa, Italy's iconic scooter, which revolutionised travel when Piaggio launched it from its factory in Pontedera, 25km southeast of Pisa, in 1946. The 'wasp', as the two-wheeled utility vehicle was affectionately known, has been restyled 120 times since, culminating most recently in Piaggio's vintage-inspired GTV and LXV models. Yet the essential design remains timeless.

The complete Vespa story, from the Genovese company's arrival in Tuscany in 1921 to its manufacturing of four-engine aircraft and hydroplanes, to its WWII destruction and rebirth as Europe's exclusive Vespa producer, is grippingly told in Pontedera's Museo Piaggio ([📞] 0587 2 71 71; www.museopiaggio.it; Viale Piaggio 7; ⊙10am-6pm Tue-Sat & 2nd & 4th Sun of month) FREE, in a former factory building.

Should Vespa's free-wheeling, carefree spirit take hold, hook up with Tuscany by Vespa (www.tuscanybyvespa.com) – operated by Florence Town (p110) in Florence – for your very own Hepburn-style Vespa tour.

ⓘ Information

Tourist Office ([📞] 050 55 01 00; www.turismo. pisa.it/en; Piazza del Duomo 7; ⊙9.30am-5.30pm Mar-Oct, 9am-5pm Nov-Feb; 🛜)

ⓘ Getting There & Away

AIR

Pisa International Airport (Galileo Galilei Airport; [📞] 050 84 93 00; www.pisa-airport. com) Tuscany's main international airport is a 10-minute drive south of Pisa.

BUS

From its **bus station** (Piazza Sant'Antonio 1) hub, Pisan bus company **CPT** ([📞] 050 520 51 00; www.cpt.pisa.it; Via Cesare Battisti 53; ⊙ticket office 7.20am-7.40pm) runs buses to/from Volterra (€6.40, two hours, up to 10 daily) with change of bus in Pontedera.

CAR & MOTORCYCLE

Parking costs around €2 per hour; don't park in the historic centre's Limited Traffic Zone (ZTL). There's a free car park outside the zone on Lungarno Guadalongo, near Fortezza di San Gallo on the south side of the Arno.

TRAIN

There is a handy **left-luggage counter** (Deposito Bagagli; [📞] 050 2 61 52; www.deposito bagaglipisa.it; bag per day €5; ⊙7am-9pm) at **Pisa Centrale** (Piazza della Stazione) train station – not to be confused with north-of-town **Pisa San Rossore** (Via Giunta) station. Regional train services to/from Pisa Centrale include the following:
Florence (€8.70, 50–80 minutes, frequent)
Livorno (€2.60, 15 minutes, frequent)
Lucca (€3.60, 30 minutes, every 30 minutes)
Viareggio (€3.60, 15 minutes, every 20 minutes)

ⓘ Getting Around

TO/FROM THE AIRPORT

Fully automated, super-speedy PisaMover (http://pisa-mover.com) trains link Pisa International Airport with Pisa Centrale train station (€5, five minutes, every five minutes from 6am to midnight).

The LAM Rossa (red) bus line (€1.20, 10 minutes, every 10 to 20 minutes) run by CPT passes through the city centre and by the train station en route to/from the airport. Buy tickets from the blue ticket machine next to the bus stops to the right of the train station exit.

A taxi between the airport and city centre should cost no more than €10. To book, call **Radio Taxi Pisa** ([📞] 050 54 16 00; www.cotapi.it).

BICYCLE

Some hotels lend bikes to their guests. Otherwise pedal around town on a silver bicycle courtesy of Pisan bike-sharing scheme Cicopli, with an **info point** ([📞] 800 005640; www.ciclopi.eu; Piazza del Duomo 7; 1st hour free, 2nd/3rd/4th half-hour €0.90/1.50/2; ⊙9.30am-5.30pm Mar-Oct, 9am-5pm Nov-Feb) inside the tourist office. Pick-up/drop-off at 15 stations dotted around the city, including at Pisa Centrale and Pisa San Rossore train stations, Pisa airport and Piazza Manin (adjoining Piazza dei Miracoli).

Toscana In Tour ([📞] 333 2602152; www. toscanaintour.it; Via della Faggiola 41; ⊙hours vary) rents out decent bicycles (€16 to €25 per day), scooters and stylish vespas (€50 to €65). Touristy stands at the northern end of Via Santa Maria and other streets off Piazza dei Miracoli rent out bicycles (€5 per hour) and touristy four-wheel rickshaws for up to six people (from €15 per hour).

LUCCA

📞 0583 / POP 89,240

Lovely Lucca endears itself to everyone who visits. Hidden behind imposing Renaissance walls, its cobbled streets, handsome piazzas and shady promenades make it a perfect destination to explore by foot – as a day trip from Florence or in its own right. At the day's end, historic cafes and restaurants tempt visitors to relax over a glass or two of Lucchesi wine and a slow progression of rustic dishes prepared with fresh produce from nearby Garfagnana.

If you have a car, the hills to the east of Lucca demand exploration. Home to historic villas and belle époque Montecatini Terme (p264), where Puccini lazed in warm spa waters, they are easy and attractive day-trip destinations from Lucca.

⊙ Sights

Stone-paved Via Fillungo, with its fashion boutiques and car-free mantra, threads its way through the medieval heart of the old city. East is one of Tuscany's loveliest piazzas: oval cafe-ringed Piazza Anfiteatro, named for the amphitheatre that was here in Roman times. Spot remnants of the amphitheatre's brick arches and masonry on the exterior walls of the medieval houses ringing the piazza.

⭐ City Wall   WALLS

Lucca's monumental *mura* (wall) was built around the old city in the 16th and 17th centuries and remains in almost perfect condition. It superseded two previous walls, the first built from travertine stone blocks in the 2nd century BC. Twelve metres high and 4.2km long, today's ramparts are crowned with a tree-lined footpath looking down on the historic centre and – by the Baluardo San Regolo (San Regolo Bastion) – the city's

---

vintage Orto Botanico (p265) with its magnificent centurion cedar trees.

The wall-top path is a favourite location for the locals' sacrosanct *passeggiata* (evening stroll). Childen's climbing frames, swings and picnic tables beneath shady plane trees add a buzz of weekend activity to Baluardo San Regolo, Baluardo San Salvatore and Baluardo Santa Croce – a trio of 11 bastions studding the way. Older kids kick footballs around on the green lawns of Baluardo San Donato; and a mix of knowing fashionistas and tourists gather for sundown drinks at lounge bar San Colombano (p269) in Baluardo San Colombano.

⭐ Cattedrale di San Martino   CATHEDRAL

(📞 0583 49 05 30; www.museocattedralelucca. it; Piazza San Martino; €3; ⊙ 9.30am-6.30pm Mon-Fri, to 6.45pm Sat, noon-6.30pm Sun) Lucca's predominantly Romanesque cathedral dates from the 11th century. Its stunning facade was constructed in the prevailing Lucca-Pisan style and designed to accommodate the pre-existing *campanile* (bell tower). The reliefs over the left doorway of the portico are believed to be by Nicola Pisano, while inside, treasures include the Volto Santo (literally, Holy Countenance) crucifix sculpture and a wonderful 15th-century tomb in the sacristy. The cathedral interior was rebuilt in the 14th and 15th centuries with a Gothic flourish.

Legend has it that the *Volto Santo*, a simply fashioned image of a dark-skinned, life-sized Christ on a wooden crucifix, was carved by Nicodemus, who witnessed the crucifixion. In fact, it has been dated to the 13th century. A major object of pilgrimage, the sculpture is carried through the streets every 13 September at dusk during the Luminaria di Santa Croce, a solemn torch-lit procession marking its miraculous arrival in Lucca.

The cathedral's many other works of art include a magnificent *Last Supper* by Tintoretto above the third altar of the south aisle, and Domenico Ghirlandaio's 1479 *Madonna Enthroned with Saints*. This impressive work by Michelangelo's master is currently located in the sacristy. Opposite lies the exquisite, gleaming marble tomb of Ilaria del Carretto carved by Jacopo della Quercia in 1407. The young second wife of the 15th-century lord of Lucca, Paolo Guinigi, Ilaria died in childbirth aged only 24. At her feet lies her faithful dog.

ℹ️ DISCOUNT TICKETS

If you plan to visit the Museo della Cattedrale, Chiesa e Battistero dei SS Giovanni e Reparata and the sacristy inside Cattedrale di San Martino, buy a cheaper combined ticket (adult/reduced €9/5) at any of the sights.

A combination ticket covering the Torre Guinigi, Torre del'Ore or the Orto Botanico is €6/4 for two of the sights or €9/6 for all three.

Lucca

200 m
0.1 miles

Baluardo San Salvatore

Via dei Bacchettoni

Baluardo della Libertà

Villa Lucrezia (150m)

Strada del Vino e dell'Olio

Porta Elisa

Baluardo San Regolo

Via della Quarquonia

Via Paoli

Via Elisa

9

16

Piazza San Francesco

Via Santa Chiara

Via San Michetto

11

Via del Fosso

Via del Fosso

Via San Nicolao

Porta San Gervasio

7

Via Santa Gemma Galgani

Via della Fratta

Via della Quarquonia

Piazza San Pietro Somaldi

Via dell'Angelo Custode

Porta San Gervasio

Via del Giardino Botanico

Via Filungo

Via Canuleia

Via Guinigi

Via della Rosa

Piazza degli Scalpellini

Piazza Anfiteatro

Torre Guinigi 3

Piazza Santa Croce

37

Via Mordini

Piazza dei Servi

Via Vallisneri

Piazza del Collegio

Via dell'Anfiteatro

Piazza del Carmine

Via Sant'Andrea

Piazza Bernardini

Piazza Antelminelli

Cattedrale di San Martino 1

35

29 8

San Colombano (100m); (A)(350m)

City Wall 2

Via Battisti

Via degli Angeli

17

24

22

34 26 21 36 38

Via del Moro

Via Buia

14

Via Fillungo

Piazza San Giovanni 5

Via del Molinetto

Via del Battistero

Piazza San Martino

Via del Duomo

12

23

Via Santa Lucia

Via Cenami

Via San Giusto

Piazza San Michele

Via San Girolamo

Piazza Sant'Agostino

30

Via Calderia

32 27

4

Via Roma

Piazza San Giusto

18 27

31

15

Via degli Asili

19

20

Corte Campana

Via Veneto

Piazza XX Settembre

Piazza del Giglio

Via San Giorgio

Via del Loreto

Via Tegrini

28

13

Via di Poggio

Piazza Cittadella

Via della Cervia

Piazza San Romano

Piazza Napoleone

Via San Giustina

Via del Toro

Via Galli Tassi

25 33

10

Via Vittorio Emanuele II

Passeggiata della Mura

Via delle Conce

Piazza Sant'Agostino

Via San Paolino

Piazza San Donato

Porta San Donato

Baluardo Santa Croce

Piazzale San Donato

6

Piazzale Verdi

Piazzale Boccherini

Porta Sant'Anna

Lucca

Top Sights
1 Cattedrale di San Martino D4
2 City Wall C1
3 Torre Guinigi E2

Sights
4 Chiesa di San Michele in Foro C3
5 Chiesa e Battistero dei SS
   Giovanni e Reparata D4
6 La Cavallerizza A2
7 Lucca Center of Contemporary Art E2
8 Museo della Cattedrale D4
9 Museo Nazionale di Palazzo Guingi G1
10 Museo Nazionale di Palazzo Mansi B2
11 Orto Botanico F4
12 Palazzo Pfanner C1
13 Puccini Museum C3
14 Torre del'Ore D2

Activities, Courses & Tours
15 Chronò C4
16 Tuscany Ride A Bike F3

Sleeping
17 Alla Corte degli Angeli C2
18 Grand Universe Lucca C4
19 Piccolo Hotel Puccini C3

Eating
20 Buca di Sant'Antonio C3
21 Forno Amedeo Giusti C2
22 Gustevole C2
23 La Parte degli Angeli C2
24 L'Hamburgheria di Eataly C2
25 Osteria del Bastian Contrario B3
26 Pizza Da Felice C2
27 Ristorante Giglio C4
28 Trattoria da Leo C2

Drinking & Nightlife
29 Bistrot Undici Undici D4
30 Bollicine d'Autore C2

Entertainment
31 Teatro del Giglio C4

Shopping
32 Antica Farmacia Massagli C3
33 Barsanti e Marlia B3
34 Benheart C2
35 De Cervesia D2
36 La Bodega di Prospero C2
37 Le Sorelle D2
38 Taddeucci C3

⭐ **Torre Guinigi**   TOWER

(Via Sant'Andrea 45; adult/reduced €4/3; ⊗ 9.30am-7.30pm Jun-Sep, to 6.30pm Apr & May, to 5.30pm Oct & Mar, to 4.30pm Nov & Dec) The bird's-eye view from the top of this medieval, 45m-tall red-brick tower adjoining 14th-century Palazzo Guinigi is predictably magnificent. But what impresses even more are the seven oak trees planted in a U-shaped flower bed at the top of the tower. Legend has it that upon the death of powerful Lucchese ruler Paolo Guinigi (1372–1432) all the leaves fell off the trees. Count 230 steps to the top.

Palazzo Pfanner   PALACE

(📞 0583 95 21 55; www.palazzopfanner.it; Via degli Asili 33; palace or garden adult/reduced €4.50/4, both €6.50/5.50; ⊗ 10am-6pm Apr-Nov) Fire the romantic in you with a stroll around this beautiful 17th-century palace where parts of *Portrait of a Lady* (1996), starring Nicole Kidman and John Malkovich, were shot. Its baroque-styled garden – the only one of substance within the city walls – enchants with ornamental pond, lemon house and 18th-century statues of Greek gods posing between potted lemon trees. Summertime chamber-music concerts hosted here are absolutely wonderful.

La Cavallerizza   CULTURAL CENTRE

(Piazzale Verdi; ⊗ hours vary) Abandoned for decades, this grandiose building was built as stables in 1876 for the adjoining 'Prato del Marchese' – the nickname given to today's Piazzale Verdi where equestrian displays, shows and other forms of entertainment took place in the 19th century. Recently restored and renovated, former stables now host exciting exhibitions and cultural events, opening in 2018–19 with the brilliant Museo della Follia – an itinerant 'Museum of Madness' exploring the notion of madness and its effect on creativity through art and history.

Museo della Cattedrale   MUSEUM

(Cathedral Museum; 📞 0583 49 05 30; www.museocattedralelucca.it; Piazza San Martino; adult/reduced €4/3; ⊗ 10am-6pm) The cathedral museum safeguards elaborate gold and silver decorations made for the cathedral's *Volto Santo,* including a 17th-century crown and a 19th-century sceptre.

**Chiesa e Battistero dei
SS Giovanni e Reparata**   CHURCH

(📞 0583 49 05 30; www.museocattedralelucca.it; Piazza San Giovanni; adult/reduced €4/3; ⊗ 10am-6pm) The 12th-century interior of this

TRAILING PUCCINI

Lucca has a particular lure for opera buffs: it was here, in 1858, that the great Giacomo Puccini was born, and baptised the following day in the Chiesa e Battistero dei SS Giovanni e Reparata (p263). The maestro, who came from a long line of Lucchesi musicians, grew up in an apartment at Corte San Lorenzo 9, now the house-museum **Puccini Museum** (Casa Natale; ☑ 0583 58 40 28; www.puccinimuseum.org; Corte San Lorenzo 9; adult/reduced €7/5; ⊙ 10am-7pm Apr-Sep, to 6pm Mar & Oct, 10am-1pm & 3-5pm Wed-Mon Nov-Feb) – look for the imposing statue of the maestro at the front. During his teenage years, Puccini played the organ in Cattedrale di San Martino (p261) and performed as a piano accompanist at **Teatro del Giglio** (☑ 0583 4 65 32; www.teatrodelgiglio.it; Piazza del Giglio 13-15; ⊙ box office 10.30am-1pm & 3-6pm Wed-Sat plus 1hr before performances), the 17th-century theatre where the curtain would later rise on some of his best-known operas: *La Bohème* (1896), *Tosca* (1900) and *Madame Butterfly* (1907).

In 1880 Puccini left Lucca to study at Milan's music conservatory. After his studies, he returned to Tuscany to rent a lakeside house in **Torre del Lago**, 15km west of Lucca on the shore of Lago di Massaciuccoli. Nine years later, after the successes of *Manon Lescaut* (1893) and *La Bohème*, he had a villa built on the same lakeshore, undertaking the Liberty-style interior decoration himself. It was here that Puccini with his wife, Elvira, spent his time working, hunting on the lake and carousing with a diverse group of hunters, fishermen and bohemian artists. *Madame Butterfly, La fanciulla del West* (1910), *La Rondine* (1917) and *Il Trittico* (1918) were composed on the Forster piano in his front study, and he wrote his scores on the walnut table in the same room.

Villa di Torre del Lago, now the **Museo Villa Puccini** (☑ 0584 34 14 45; www.giacomopuccini.it; Viale Puccini 266, Torre del Lago; adult/reduced €7/3; ⊙ 3-6pm Mon, 10am-12.40pm & 3-6pm Tue-Sun Apr-Oct, shorter hr rest of yr), has been preserved as it was during Puccini's residence and is hence fascinating to visit (by guided tour every 40 minutes). In summer the villa grounds and lakeshore buzz with the world-famous **Puccini Festival** (www.puccinifestival.it), which sees three or four of the great man's operas performed in a purpose-built outdoor theatre. Tickets are like gold dust and sell out months in advance.

Puccini was a frequent visitor to **Montecatini Terme**, a charming spa resort 56km east, known for its mineral-rich waters. From May to October, spa lovers still flock here to wallow in warm waters and indulge in beauty treatments at its *terme* (thermal baths) in grand old buildings overlooking a beautiful park. The Montecatini Terme **tourist office** (☑ 0573 77 22 44; Viale Verdi 66-68; ⊙ 9am-12.30pm & 3-6pm Mon-Sat, plus 9am-noon Sun summer) has details.

In 1921 Puccini and Elvira moved to a villa in nearby **Viareggio** where the composer became a regular fixture at **Gran Caffè Margherita** (☑ 0584 58 11 43; www.ristorante margherita.info; Viale Regina Margherita 30; ⊙ 8am-midnight). He worked on his last opera, the unfinished *Turandot*, here. After Puccini's death in 1924, Elvira and son Antonio added a chapel to the Torre del Lago villa; Puccini's remains were interred there in 1926.

deconsecrated church is a hauntingly atmospheric setting for summertime opera and concert recitals (www.puccinielasualucca.com), staged daily at 7pm; buy tickets (adult/reduced €25/20) in advance inside the church or at a cheaper rate before 6pm from the tourist office (p269) – €20 instead of €25.

In the north transept, the Gothic baptistry crowns an archaeological area comprising five building levels going back to the Roman period. Don't miss the hike up the red-brick bell tower.

Chiesa di San Michele in Foro   CHURCH
(Piazza San Michele; ⊙ 9am-6pm) FREE One of Lucca's many architecturally significant churches, this glittering Romanesque edifice marks the spot where the city's Roman forum was. The present building with exquisite wedding-cake facade was constructed over 300 years on the site of its 8th-century precursor, beginning in the 11th century. Crowning the structure is a figure of the archangel Michael slaying a dragon. Inside, its plain, dimly lit interior comes as something as a shock: don't miss Filippino Lippi's

1479 painting of Sts Helen, Jerome, Sebastian and Roch (complete with plague sore) in the south transept.

Orto Botanico
GARDENS

(Botanical Garden; ☑ 0583 58 30 86; www.lemuradilucca.it/orto-botanico; Casermetta San Regolo; adult/reduced €4/3; ☉ 10am-7pm Jul-Sep, to 6pm May & Jun, to 5pm Mar, Apr & Oct) Tucked across the walkway from the Baluardo San Regolo are Lucca's pretty botanical gardens, well worth a meander and a contemplative moment in the shade of its magnificent Lebanese cedar tree planted in 1820.

Museo Nazionale di Palazzo Guingi
MUSEUM

(☑ 0583 49 60 33; www.luccamuseinazionali.it; Via della Quarquonia; adult/reduced €4/2; ☉ admission 9.30am, 11.30am, 3.30pm & 5.30pm) Lucchese history from the 8th century BC to late 18th century AD is evoked through archaeological objects, paintings and other artworks at this small museum, at home in a late-Gothic *palazzo* (mansion) with striking porticoed facade, built between 1413 and 1430 as a summer residence for Paolo Guinigi (1372–1432), Lord of Lucca until his arrest by rival Florentine troops and subsequent death in captivity.

Museo Nazionale di Palazzo Mansi
MUSEUM

(☑ 0583 5 55 70; www.luccamuseinazionali.it; Via Tassi 43; adult/reduced €4/2; ☉ admission 9.30am, 11.30am, 2.30pm & 4.30pm Tue-Sat) This 16th-century mansion built for a wealthy Luccan merchant is a wonderful piece of rococo excess. The private apartments are draped head to toe in tapestries, paintings and chintz. The elaborate, gilded bridal suite must have inspired many high jinks in its time.

Check the website for details of the current temporary exhibition. If you plan on visiting sister museum Museo Nazionale di Palazzo Guingi too, buy a combo ticket for €6.50/3.25 (valid three days).

Lucca Center of Contemporary Art
MUSEUM

(☑ 0583 49 21 80; www.luccamuseum.com; Via della Fratta 36; adult/reduced €11.50/9.50; ☉ 10am-7pm Tue-Sun) FREE Lucca's contemporary-art museum hosts some riveting exhibitions; check its website for details.

Torre del'Ore
TOWER

(Via Fillungo; adult/reduced €4/3; ☉ 9.30am-7.30pm Jun-Sep, to 6.30pm Apr & May, to 5.30pm Oct & Mar) Legend has it that Lucca's 13th-century clock tower – at 50m tall, the highest of the city's 130 medieval towers – is inhabited by the ghost of Lucida Mansi, a Lucchese lass who sold her soul to the devil in exchange for remaining young and beautiful for three decades. On 14 August 1623 the devil came after her to pay her debt, only for Lucida to climb up the clock tower to try to stop time. The devil caught her and took her soul.

☞ Tours

★ Chronò
CYCLING

(☑ 0583 49 05 91; www.chronobikes.com; Corso Garibaldi 93; per day €20) Up-to-speed bike-rental shop, with top-quality road bikes for serious cyclists (and a handy little grocery store directly opposite to pick up picnic supplies before you pedal off). Daily rates include spare inner tube, pump and helmet.

The shop's touring arm, ChronoPlus (www.chronoplus.com), offers fantastic multiday bike tours in Tuscany and beyond, including a scenic seven-day roam through vineyards, olive and cypress groves, forests and medieval hamlets around Lucca.

Tuscany Ride A Bike
CYCLING

(☑ 0583 47 17 79; www.tuscanbike.it; Via Elisa 28; ☉ 9.30am-7.30pm) Explore the city or region by bike with a guided tour, ranging from a 10km-long urban pedal (three hours; €25) to a half-day bike ride to Pisa (34km; from €60) or to an organic farm (20km; €70), or an exhilarating bike ride along back roads to the Versilian Coast (90km; from €64).

Bike and wine tours too and regular bike rental (from €5/15 per hour/day).

🛏 Sleeping

From charm-rich B&Bs to small boutique hotels on quiet cobbled lanes, Lucca delivers. The tourist office has accommodation lists and, if you visit in person, can make reservations for you (free of charge). For accommodation amid vines, consider a winery along the idyllic Strada del Vino e dell'Olio (☑ 0583 49 51 69; www.stradavinoeoliolucca.it; Porta Elisa; ☉ 9.30am-7pm).

Piccolo Hotel Puccini
HOTEL €

(☑ 0583 5 54 21; www.hotelpuccini.com; Via di Poggio 9; s/d €75/100; ✳ 🛜) In a brilliant central location, this welcoming three-star hotel

A VILLA TOUR

Between the 15th and 19th centuries, successful Lucchesi merchants flaunted their success to the world by building opulent summer residences in the hills around the city, and though a few have crumbled away or been abandoned, many are still inhabited.

Villa Reale (☑0583 3 01 08; www.parcovillareale.it; Via Fraga Alta 2, Marlia, Capannori; adult/reduced €9/7; ⊙10am-6pm Mar-Oct) Elisa Bonaparte, Napoleon's sister and short-lived ruler of Tuscany, once lived in handsome Villa Reale, 7km north of Lucca. The house isn't open to the public, but the statuary-filled gardens can be visited. Bring a picnic.

Villa Grabau (☑0583 40 60 98; www.villagrabau.it; Via di Matraia 269, San Pancrazio; guided tour adult/child €7/free; ⊙10am-1pm & 2.30-6pm Tue-Sun summer, 11am-1pm & 2.30-5.30pm winter) Neoclassical Villa Grabau, 11km north of Lucca, sits among a vast parkland with sweeping traditional English- and Italian-styled gardens, splashing fountains, more than 100 terracotta pots with lemon trees, and a postcard-pretty lemon house – host to fashion shows, concerts and the like – dating from the 17th century. It even has a clutch of self-catering properties to rent in its grounds should you happen to fall in love with the estate. Guided villa and garden visits last 45 minutes.

Villa Oliva (☑330 446252, 0583 40 64 62; www.villaoliva.it; Via delle Ville, San Pancrazio; ⊙9.30am-12.30pm & 2-6pm mid-Mar–early Nov) `FREE` Eleven kilometres north of Lucca, the gardens of Villa Oliva, surrounding a 15th-century country residence designed by Lucchesi architect Matteo Civitali, demand a springtime stroll. Retaining its original design, the fountain-rich park staggers across three levels and includes a romantic cypress alley and stables reckoned to be even more beautiful than those at Versailles. Watch out for summertime concerts here.

To reach these villas, take the SS12 northeast from Lucca (direction Abetone) and exit onto the SP29 to Marlia. From Marlia, San Pancrazio is a mere 1.2km north.

hides behind a discreet brick exterior. Its small guest rooms are attractive with wooden floors, vintage ceiling fans and colourful, contemporary design touches. Breakfast, optional at €3.50, is served at candlelit tables behind the small reception area. Rates are at least 30% lower in winter.

Villa Lucrezia
B&B €

(☑0583 95 42 86; www.luccainvilla.it; Viale Cadorna 30; d/q €98/150; P ﹖) A particularly handy address for those arriving by car, this 10-room B&B is a two-minute walk from the city walls, inside a graceful 19th-century villa with a jasmine-scented garden. Rooms are spacious and light-filled, with big windows, contemporary design furnishings and sharp en suite bathrooms. Complimentary tea, coffee and cakes are at hand throughout the day in the basement breakfast room.

The villa also lends guests free bicycles to pedal into town. Free courtyard parking too.

2italia
APARTMENT €€

(☑392 9960271; www.2italia.com; apt for 2 adults & up to 4 children per night/week €240/1250; ﹖) Not a hotel but a handful of family-friendly self-catering apartments in the historic centre. Available on a nightly basis (minimum two nights), the project is the brainchild of well-travelled parents-of-three, Kristin (English) and Kaare (Norwegian). Spacious apartments sleep five to 10 people, have a fully equipped kitchen and washing machine, and come with sheets and towels.

★Alla Corte degli Angeli
BOUTIQUE HOTEL €€€

(☑0583 46 92 04; www.allacortedegliangeli.com; Via degli Angeli 23; d from €180; ﹡@﹖) This four-star boutique hotel sits in a couple of terraced 15th-century town houses on a peaceful lane. Its 24 sunny suites and doubles – named after flowers – feature frescoed ceilings, patches of exposed brick, romantic landscape murals and some lovely pieces of period furniture. Up-to-the-minute bathrooms have hot tubs and power-jet showers. The hotel restaurant and cocktail bar is an address in its own right.

The stylish lounge begs relaxation beneath yet another vintage beamed ceiling. It also hosts fantastic wine-tasting workshops with the hotel sommelier (30-minute/one hour class €25/50), and fun two-hour cooking classes kicking off with a bike ride with the chef through town to shop for the ingredients (€50).

Grand Universe Lucca   LUXURY HOTEL €€€
(☑0583 49 36 78; www.granduniverselucca.com; Piazza del Giglio; @🛜) Luxury accommodation arrives in Lucca with the opening of this on-trend hotel, part of the Marriott Group's Autograph Collection, in a 16th-century *palazzo* that once was home to the historic Hotel Universo (1857). Tech-smart rooms (think iPad room directory, video on demand, Netflix and so on) enjoy soft colour schemes typical to earthy Tuscany – rust, gold, terracotta and peach – and beautiful fabrics.

🍴 Eating

Lucca is known for its traditional cuisine and prized olive oil. Garfagnana is not far away and local chestnuts, porcini mushrooms, honey, *farro* (spelt), sheep's-milk cheese and *formenton* (ground corn) are abundant – and perfect with a white Colline Lucchesi or red Montecarlo di Lucca wine. Lucca's dining scene covers everything from formal restaurants to affordable, casual trattorias and fantastic takeaway places.

★ Gustevole   GELATO €
(☑366 8960346; www.facebook.com/gelateria gustevolelucca; Via Buia 14; cones & tubs €2.30-3.50; ⊙12.30-7pm Mon-Sat, 3-7pm Sun) With enticing flavours like liquorice and mint, ricotta with fig and walnut, or pine kernel made with local Pisan kernels (nuts in sweet, crunchy caramelised clumps), this pocket-sized gelateria is pure gold. The artisanal gelato is organic, natural and gluten-free. The key to entering gelato heaven: ask for a dollop of thick whipped cream on top.

Pizza Da Felice   PIZZA €
(☑0583 49 49 86; www.pizzeriadafelice.it; Via Buia 12; focaccia & pizza slices €1-5; ⊙11am-8.30pm Mon, 10am-8.30pm Tue-Sat) This buzzing spot behind Piazza San Michele is where the locals come for wood-fired pizza, *cecina* (salted chickpea pizza) and *castagnacci* (chestnut cakes). Eat in or take away, *castagnaccio* comes wrapped in crisp white paper, and my, it's good married with a chilled bottle of Moretti beer.

L'Hamburgheria di Eataly   BURGERS €
(☑0583 42 92 16; www.facebook.com/ham burgheriadieatalylucca; Via Fillungo 91a; burgers €9.80-13.80; ⊙noon-3pm & 6.30-11pm Mon-Fri, noon-11pm Sat & Sun; 🛜) A clever mix of fast

and slow food, this modern Eataly eatery cooks up gourmet burgers crafted from Tuscany's signature Chianina beef alongside a tantalising mix of hot dogs, grilled meats and *taglieri* (wooden chopping boards) loaded with salami, cold meats and cheeses (€10.50 to €17). Begin with a focaccia (€10.50) to share beneath red-brick vaults inside, or among potted lemon trees in the courtyard.

Trattoria da Leo   TRATTORIA €
(☑0583 49 22 36; Via Tegrimi 1; meals €25; ⊙12.30-2pm & 7.30-10.30pm Mon-Sat) Veteran Leo is famed for its friendly ambience and cheap food – ranging from plain-Jane acceptable to grandma delicious. Enticing sides include baked fennel with parmesan, oven-baked baby onions and *peperonata* (stewed peppers). Arrive early to snag one of a handful of tables squashed beneath parasols on the street outside. Otherwise it's noisy dining inside amid 1970s decor. No credit cards.

★ La Parte degli Angeli   TUSCAN €€
(☑346 8079791, 0583 46 92 04; www.facebook. com/lapartedegliangeli; Via degli Angeli 23; meals €30-40; ⊙7pm-midnight Tue-Sun) For a stylish cocktail with a herb-infused gin perhaps, followed by dinner amid romantic frescoes, look no further than 'The Angels' Share', an intimate restaurant named after the portion of whisky lost to evaporation during the ageing process. Mixologist, chef and owner Leonardo is a huge whisky fan, works with his own homemade syrups and cooks creative Tuscan in the kitchen.

★ Ristorante Giglio   TUSCAN €€
(☑0583 49 40 58; www.ristorantegiglio.com; Piazza del Giglio 2; meals €40-50, 4-/5-course tasting menus €45/55; ⊙12.15-2.45pm & 7.30-10.30pm Thu-Mon, 7.30-10.30pm Wed) Splendidly at home in frescoed 18th-century Palazzo Arnolfini, Giglio is stunning. Sip a complimentary prosecco, watch the fire crackle in the marble fireplace and savour traditional Tuscan fare with a modern twist: think fresh artichoke salad served in an edible parmesan-cheese wafer 'bowl', or risotto simmered in Chianti. End with Lucchese *buccellato* (sweet bread) filled with ice cream and berries.

In summer dining spills out onto Giglio's pretty terrace overlooking the town's historic theatre.

Osteria del Bastian Contrario TUSCAN €€
(☏0583 08 29 92; www.facebook.com/Bastian
ContrarioLucca; Via San Paolino 90; meals €25-35;
⊙noon-3.30pm & 7-11pm;) With an outside
terrace open year-round (heated and covered
in winter) and a huge choice of dishes on the
multilingual menu, this down-to-earth *osteria* is a much-loved crowd-pleaser. The local
speciality, *tordelli Lucchesi* (meat-filled pasta cushions), comes in at least a dozen different varieties and there are ample chicken,
steak and tripe dishes for meat lovers. Inside, bar tables are made from recycled vintage suitcases.

In winter, the full-page menu featuring
specialita' al tartufo nero fresco (fresh
black-truffle specialities) is the one to pick
from.

Buca di Sant'Antonio TUSCAN €€€
(☏0583 5 58 81; www.bucadisantantonio.com;
Via della Cervia 3; meals €40-50; ⊙12.30-3pm &
7.30-10pm Tue-Sat, 12.30-3pm Sun) Gosh, what a
fabulous collection of copper pots is strung
from the wood-beamed ceiling! This atmosphere-laden restaurant has wooed romantic
diners since 1782 and is still going strong.
The Tuscan cuisine does not quite live up
to the exceptional wine list, but it remains

a favourite nonetheless. Service is formal –
think gents of a certain age in black suits
and dicky bows – and opens with a glass of
prosecco on the house as aperitif.

🍷 Drinking & Nightlife

At almost every turn within the walls there
is a pavement terrace to sit down at and savour a coffee or *aperitivo* – those on Piazza
San Frediano, Piazza Cittadella (lorded over
by a bronze Puccini in waistcoat and bow
tie) and Piazza Napoleone are not quite as
tourist-packed as the terraces on iconic Piazza Anfiteatro.

★Bistrot Undici Undici CAFE
(☏0583 189 27 01; www.facebook.com/undiciundi
cill.11; Piazza Antelminelli 2; ⊙10am-8pm Tue-Thu,
to 1am Fri-Sun) With a giant canvas cream parasol providing shade and a tinkling stone
fountain the atmospheric soundtrack, cafe
terraces don't get much better than this.
And then there is the view from this bucolic
cafe on Piazza San Miniato of the almighty
facade of Lucca's lovely cathedral. Kick back
over an Aperol spritz at sundown and enjoy
occasional live music after dark.

A WALL-TOP PICNIC

When in Lucca, picnicking atop its city walls – on grass or at a wooden picnic table – is
as lovely (and typical) a Lucchesi lunch as any.

Buy fresh-from-the-oven pizza and focaccia with a choice of fillings and toppings from
fabulous bakery Forno Amedeo Giusti (☏0583 49 62 85; www.facebook.com/Pan
ificioGiusti; Via Santa Lucia 20; pizzas & filled focaccias per kg €10-15; ⊙7am-7.30pm Mon-Sat,
to 1.30pm Sun), then nip across the street for a bottle of Lucchesi wine and Garfagnese
biscotti al farro (spelt biscuits) at La Bodega di Prospero (☏0583 49 48 75; Via Santa
Lucia 13; ⊙9am-7pm); look for the old-fashioned shop window stuffed with sacks of
beans, lentils and other local pulses.

Complete the perfect picnic with a slice of *buccellato*, a traditional sweet bread loaf
with sultanas and aniseed seeds, baked in Lucca since 1881. Devour the rest at home,
either with butter, dipped in egg and pan-fried, or dunked in sweet Vin Santo. Buy it at
pastry shop Taddeucci (☏0583 49 49 33; www.buccellatotaddeucci.com; Piazza San Michele
34; buccellato loaf per 300/600g €4.50/9; ⊙8.30am-7.45pm, closed Thu winter).

Swill down the picnic with your pick of Italian craft beers from microbrewery De
Cervesia (☏0583 49 30 81; www.decervesia.it; Via Fillungo 92; ⊙noon-midnight Wed-Fri,
noon-1am Sat, 5pm-midnight Sun), which has a small shop on Lucca's main shopping
street and a tap room for serious tasting (open 5pm to 10pm Tuesday to Sunday) a few
blocks away at Via Michele Rosi 20. Should a shot of something stronger be required to
aid digestion, nip into historic Antica Farmacia Massagli (☏0583 49 60 67; Piazza San
Michele 36; ⊙9am-8pm Mon-Sat) for a bottle of China elixir, a heady liqueur of aromatic
spices and herbs first concocted in 1855 as a preventive measure against the plague.
Lucchese typically drink the natural alcoholic drink (no colouring or preservatives) at the
end of a meal.

Bollicine d'Autore BAR

(☑347 7655596; https://bollicinedautore.com; Via Calderia 12; ⊙10am-midnight Fri-Wed) Food pairings with fine wine and bubbles is the speciality of this glamorous *enoteca* (wine bar), *champagneria* (champagne cellar) and bistro in central Lucca. Pick from Italy's top sparkling wines – an Uberti or Bellavista Franciacorta Brut from Lombardy perhaps, a Ferrari Trento from Trentino-Alto Adige or a timeless prosecco DOC – or go French with a Pommery or Laurent Perrier champagne.

San Colombano LOUNGE

(☑0583 46 46 41; www.ristorantesancolombanolucca.it; Rampa Baluardo San Colombano; ⊙9am-1am daily summer, Thu-Sun winter; 🛜🍴) With an unexpected view of the cathedral's crenellated bell tower and tree-shaded tables snug against ancient red-brick walls, this wall-top lounge bar is a lovely spot for an *aperitivo* with generous complimentary canapés in the early evening sun. The wall's steady stream of after-work joggers and cyclists provides people-watching fun and the extensive menu includes tapas dishes, pizza and pasta.

🛍 Shopping

⭐**Le Sorelle** FASHION & ACCESSORIES

(Uashmama; ☑0572 77 18 80; www.uashmama.com; Piazza Anfiteatro 31; ⊙10am-7pm Feb-Dec) Be it a metallic-gold table bag for wine, a stone to keep your paper bread basket's contents warm, body-care products made from olive oil or beautiful linen for your table, family-run Uashmama is constantly innovating. All its bags, wallets, pencil cases etc are made from washable paper in a rainbow of colours, and beauty products are organic.

⭐**Benheart** SHOES

(☑0583 152 43 85; www.benheart.it; Via Santa Lucia 5; ⊙10.30am-6.30pm Mon-Fri, to 8pm Sat & Sun) For an exquisite pair of handmade leather shoes (men and women), jackets and leather accessories, delve into the fashionable boutique of Florentine designer Ben. The young designer went into business with friend and business partner Matteo after surviving a heart transplant – hence the shop's name.

Barsanti e Marlia HOMEWARES

(Ferramenta e Mesticheria; ☑0583 5 59 62; Via San Paolino 88; ⊙8.30am-12.30pm & 2-7pm Mon-Sat) Included in many a guided walking tour of the city, this hardware shop has been in biz since 1949 and sells everything from traditional truffle, oyster and chestnut knives to spaghetti and *tagliatelli* 'rolling pins', chocolate thermometers and mushrooming tools. Its window display, strung with rather fierce-looking machetes and knives, is particularly eye-catching.

ℹ Information

Tourist Office (☑0583 58 31 50; www.turismo.lucca.it; Piazzale Verdi; ⊙9.30am-6.30pm)

ℹ Getting There & Away

BUS

From the **bus stops** around Piazzale Verdi, **CTT Lucca** (www.lucca.cttnord.it) runs services throughout the region, including the following:

Bagni di Lucca (€3.60, 50 minutes, eight daily)

Castelnuovo di Garfagnana (€4.40, 1½ hours, eight daily)

Pisa airport (€4, 45 minutes to one hour, 30 daily)

CAR & MOTORCYCLE

It's easiest to park at Parcheggio Carducci, just outside Porta Sant'Anna. Within the walls, most car parks are for residents only, indicated by yellow lines. Blue lines indicate where anyone, including tourists, can park (€2 per hour). If you are staying within the city walls, contact your hotel ahead of your arrival and enquire about the possibility of getting a temporary resident permit during your stay.

TRAIN

The train station is south of the city walls: take the path across the moat and through the (dank and grungy) tunnel under Baluardo San Colombano. Regional train services include the following:

Florence (€7.80, 1¼ to 1¾ hours, hourly)

Pietrasanta (€4.60, 50 minutes, hourly)

Pisa (€3.60, 30 minutes, half-hourly)

Pistoia (€5.70, 45 minutes to one hour, half-hourly)

Viareggio (€3.60, 25 minutes, hourly)

ℹ Getting Around

Pedalling the 4.2km circumference of Lucca's romantic city walls is always fun. There are plenty of outlets, ranging from touristy to those aimed squarely at serious cyclists, to rent wheels.

Biciclette Poli (☑0583 49 37 87; www.biciclettepoli.com; Piazza Santa Maria 42; per hr/day €4/16; ⊙9am-7pm summer)

Cicli Bizzarri (☑ 0583 49 66 82; www.cicli bizzarri.net; Piazza Santa Maria 32; per hr/day €4/16; ⊙ 8.30am-12.30pm & 2-7.30pm)
Tourist Center Lucca (☑ 0583 49 44 01; www. touristcenterlucca.com; Piazzale Ricasoli 203; bike per 3hr/day €8/12; ⊙ 9am-7pm)

PISTOIA

☑ 0573 / POP 90,200

Pretty Pistoia sits snugly at the foot of the Apennines. An easy day trip from Pisa, Lucca or Florence, it thoroughly deserved its 2017 status as European City of Culture. A town that has grown well beyond its medieval ramparts, its *centro storico* (historic centre) is well preserved and stands guardian to striking contemporary art.

On Wednesdays and Saturdays a morning **market** transforms Pistoia's main square, Piazza del Duomo, and seemingly every surrounding street into a lively sea of colourful awnings and busy shoppers. From Monday to Saturday, peruse open-air stalls heaped with seasonal fruit and vegetables on tiny Piazza della Sala.

⊙ Sights

Pistoia's key sights are clustered around its beautiful cathedral square, Piazza del Duomo, hemmed by a maze of narrow pedestrian streets made for peaceful meandering. Avoid Monday – and weekday afternoons – when many of the key sights are shut.

★ Cattedrale di San Zeno   CATHEDRAL
(☑ 0573 2 50 95; Piazza del Duomo; cathedral free, chapel adult/reduced €5/3.50, bell tower €8/5.50, chapel & bell tower €12/10; ⊙ 8.30am-6pm, chapel 10.30am-noon & 3-5.30pm) FREE This cathedral with beautiful Pisan-Romanesque facade safeguards a lunette of the Madonna and Child between two angels by Andrea della Robbia. Its other highlight, in the gated chapel **Cappella di San Jacopo** off the north aisle (right of the main entrance), is the dazzling **Altare d'Argento di San Giacomo** (Silver Altarpiece of St James), begun by silversmiths by hand in 1287 and finished two centuries later by Brunelleschi. Buy chapel tickets, visited with an audio guide, in the Battistero di San Giovanni.

★ Antico Palazzo dei Vescovi   MUSEUM
(☑ 0573 2 87 82; www.fondazionepistoiamusei.it; Piazza del Duomo; adult/reduced €5/3; ⊙ 10.15am-4pm Tue, Thu & Fri, to 6pm Sat & Sun) The bishops' palace, wedged next to the cathedral, provides a fascinating tour of Pistoia's urban history, ranging from touchable scale models of architectural gems such as the cathedral and the baptistry on the 1st floor to archaeological treasures in the basement. The indisputable highlight is *L'Arazzo Mille Fiori* (Thousand Flowers Tapestry; 1530), a rare, late-Gothic tapestry originally laid in front of the main altar in the cathedral on Good Friday, upon which a crucified Christ would be venerated.

Chiesa del Tau   CHAPEL
(☑ 0573 2 42 12; Corso Fedi 70; ⊙ 8.15am-1.30pm Mon-Sat) FREE This tiny 14th-century chapel, frescoed Gothic-style from bottom to top by the School of Giotto, is a dramatic guardian to Marino Marini's monumental equestrian sculpture *The Miracle* (1952). The frescoes illustrate tales from the New and Old Testaments and the story of St Anthony Abbot, depicted as an old man with white beard, staff and pig by his side. On his feast day, 17 January, local farmers used to bring their animals to the chapel to get them blessed by their patron saint.

Fattoria di Celle   GARDENS
(☑ 0573 47 99 07; www.goricoll.it; Via Montalese 7, Santomato di Pistoia; ⊙ by appointment only, guided tours 9.30am & 2.30pm Mon-Sat May-Jun & Sep, 9.30am Jul & Aug) FREE A teahouse, an aviary and other romantic 19th-century follies mingle with cutting-edge sculptures and art installations created by top contemporary artists here at Fattoria di Celle, 5km west of Pistoia. The extraordinary private collection and passion of local businessman Giuliano Gori, this unique estate showcases 70 site-specific installations sprinkled around his vast family home. Visits – reserved for serious art lovers able to walk four to five hours with no rest stops – require an email reservation six to eight weeks in advance.

Campanile della Cattedrale   TOWER
(Cathedral Bell Tower; ☑ 334 1689419; Piazza del Duomo; adult/reduced €8/5.50; ⊙ 10am-6pm Apr–mid-Oct, 10am-1pm & 3-5pm mid-Oct–Mar) Scale the sky-high, red-brick *campanile* (bell tower) of the Cattedrale di San Zeno for a wonderful bird's-eye view of Pistoia's iconic cathedral square. Visits are by guided tour only; buy tickets at the battistero across the square.

ℹ COMBO TICKETS

For visitors planning to take in several of Pistoia's museums and churches, there are a couple of combination-ticket options. Admission to the cathedral and baptistry are free, but individual or combo tickets (adult/reduced €12/10) are available for the Capella di San Jacobo (inside the cathedral) and its bell tower *(campanile)*.

A combination ticket, valid for three days and covering two/three city-run museums (http://musei.comune.pistoia.it/) – Museo Civico, Museo Marino Marini, Museo dello Spedale del Ceppo and Palazzo Fabroni – costs €6/9 (reduced €3/5) and is sold in any participating museum.

The privately run Fondazione Pistoia Musei (www.fondazionepistoiamusei.it) groups together four art venues (including Piazza del Duomo's neighbouring Antico Palazzo dei Vescovi), with a strong focus on modern and contemporary artists. Palazzo de' Rossi and Palazzo Buontalenti host seasonally changing exhibitions; Chiesa di San Salvatore explores local history. Admission to all four costs €15.

Battistero di San Giovanni   CHRISTIAN SITE

(Baptistry; ☑ 334 1689419; Piazza del Duomo; ☺10am-6pm Apr–mid-Oct, 10am-1pm & 3-5pm mid-Oct–Mar) **FREE** Across the square from the cathedral is its 14th-century octagonal baptistry, elegantly banded in green-and-white marble to a design by Andrea Pisano. An ornate square marble font and soaring dome enliven the otherwise bare, red-brick interior. Buy tickets here for the Capella di San Jacopo and bell tower, both inside Cattedrale di San Zeno.

Museo Civico   MUSEUM

(☑0573 37 12 96; http://musei.comune.pistoia. it; Piazza del Duomo 1; adult/reduced €3.50/2; ☺10am-2pm Tue-Fri, to 6pm Sat & Sun) Pistoia's Gothic **Palazzo Communale** is strung with works by Tuscan artists from the 13th to 20th centuries. Don't miss Bernardino di Antonio Detti's *Madonna della Pergola* (1498) with its modern treatment of St James, the Madonna and Baby Jesus; spot the mosquito on Jesus' arm.

Chiesa di San Salvatore   MUSEUM

(☑0573 97 42 66; www.fondazionepistoiamusei. it; Via San Tomba di Catilina; adult/reduced €5/3; ☺10am-6pm Thu-Tue) Just steps from Piazza del Duomo is this beautiful gem of a Romanesque church, thought to date from the 8th to 10th centuries within the ancient city walls (spot the small section of cobblestone wall) and reconstructed to gain its current appearance in 1270. The church was abandoned in 1784 and subsequently used as a warehouse and artist's studio. Following lengthy renovations, it reopened in late 2019 as a small modern museum on local history.

Piazzetta degli Ortaggi   PIAZZA

Don't miss this beautiful small square, with its laid-back cafe life and striking, life-size sculpture of three blindfolded men, **Giro di Sole** (Around the Sun; Piazzetta degli Orgaggi) (Around the Sun; 1996), by contemporary Pistoia artist Roberto Barni (b 1939). In the 18th century the market square, adjoining Piazza della Sala, was the entrance to Pistoia's Jewish ghetto.

Chiesa di San Giovanni Fuorcivitas   CHURCH

(☑0573 2 47 84; Via Crispi 2; ☺9-11am & 5.15-6.30pm) **FREE** Gargantuan black-and-white striped marble facade aside, the star turn of this striking Romanesque church fronting Via Cavour is Luca della Robbia's glazed terracotta *Visitation* (1445), portraying Elizabeth, about to become mother to John the Baptist, affectionately kneeling in front of a younger pregnant Mary. The women's blue eyes provide a powerful contrast to the milky-white terracotta.

Palazzo Fabroni   MUSEUM

(Museo del Novecento e del Contemporaneo; ☑0573 37 12 96; http://musei.comune.pistoia. it; Via Sant'Andrea 18; ☺10am-2pm Tue-Fri, to 6pm Sun & Sun) Take a breather from the ancient with this airy modern- and contemporary-art museum, host to riveting temporary exhibitions and a permanent collection amassed through donated works from exhibiting artists. Highlights include the shadow wall painting *Scultura d'Ombra* (2007) by iconoclastic Italian artist Claudio Parmiggiani (b 1943) and rooms dedicated to Pistoia-born artists Mario Nigro (1917–1992) and Fernando Melani

NORTHWESTERN TUSCANY PISTOIA

Pistoia

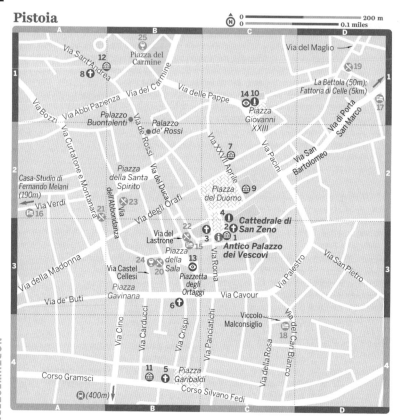

(1907–85). Don't miss the photo of sculptor Marino Marini on the beach with his horse at Forte dei Marmi in 1973.

Should you get completely hooked, upon advance request it is possible to visit the nearby casa-studio (al.giachini@comune. pistoia.it; Corso Gramsci 159; ⊙by appointment) FREE of Fernando Melani where the abstract artist lived and worked.

Chiesa di Sant'Andrea Apostolo CHURCH
(Via Sant'Andrea 21; ⊙8.30am-6.30pm Mon-Sat, 8.30-10am, 11.45am-4.30pm & 5.45-6.30pm Sun) FREE This 12th-century church was built outside the original city walls, hence its windowless (fortified) state. The partly white-and-green striped marble facade is enlivened by a relief of the *Journey and Adoration of the Magi* (1166) by Gruamonte and Adeodato. But the highlight – Pistoia's most prized artwork – is within its dark interior: an imposing marble pulpit carved by Giovanni Pisano (1298–1301). Two lions and

a bent human figure bear the heavy load of the seven-columned masterpiece, and sibyls and the Prophets decorate the capitals.

Museo dello Spedale del Ceppo MONUMENT
(☑0573 37 12 96; http://musei.comune.pistoia. it; Piazza Giovanni XXIII; adult/reduced €3/2.50; ⊙10am-2pm Tue-Fri, to 6pm Sat & Sun) The beautifully restored facade of this former hospital, operational from 1277 until 2013, stuns with its 16th-century polychrome terracotta frieze by Giovanni della Robbia. It depicts the *Sette Opere di Misericordia* (Seven Works of Mercy), and the five medallions represent the *Virtù Teologali* (Theological Virtues). Inside, a small museum explores both the fine art of glazed terracotta in the early Renaissance and the history of public healthcare in the 13th-century hospital. 'Gruesome' best describes some of the historic surgical tools exhibited.

Pistoia

⊚ Top Sights
1 Antico Palazzo dei Vescovi....................C3
2 Cattedrale di San Zeno C3

⊚ Sights
3 Battistero di San Giovanni.....................C3
4 Campanile della Cattedrale..................C2
5 Chiesa del Tau.......................................B4
6 Chiesa di San Giovanni Fuorcivitas......B3
7 Chiesa di San Salvatore........................C2
8 Chiesa di Sant'Andrea Apostolo............A1
   Giro di Sole....................................(see 13)
9 Museo Civico...C2
10 Museo dello Spedale del Ceppo C1
11 Museo Marino Marini.............................B4
12 Palazzo Fabroni....................................A1
13 Piazzetta degli Ortaggi.........................B3
14 Pistoia Sotteranea................................C1

⊜ Sleeping
15 Battistero Residenza d'Epoca B3
16 Lo Studio A2
17 Locanda San Marco D1
18 Palazzo Puccini.....................................C4

⊗ Eating
19 Baldovino.. D1
   Bonodinulla ....(see 15)
20 I Salaioli...B3
21 Magno Gaudio.......................................A2
22 Osteria La BotteGaia............................B3
23 Trattoria dell'Abbondanza B2

⊙ Drinking & Nightlife
   Caffètteria Marino Marini............. (see 11)
24 Fiaschetteria La Pace B3
25 Il Carbonile B1

Pistoia Sotteranea　　　　　　　　TUNNEL
(☑ 0573 36 80 23; www.irsapt.it/it/pistoia-sot
terranea/; Piazza Giovanni XXIII 15; adult/reduced
€10/8; ☺10am-5pm) Delve into the underbelly
of subterranean Pisa with a one-hour guided trek (in English) of passageways snaking
beneath 13th-century hospital Ospedale del
Ceppo, famed for its colourful Della Robbia
ceramics on Piazza Giovanni XXIII.

The dark, dank, barrel-vaulted tunnels
follow the course of a subterranean river,
diverted underground in the 13th century in
order for the hospital above ground to increase in size and so care for Black Death
victims. The passageways later served as a
laundry, oil mill and public grain mill pow-
ered by the underground river. Not recommended for the claustrophobic.

Museo Marino Marini　　　　　　　MUSEUM
(☑ 0573 3 02 85; www.fondazionemarinomarini.it;
Corso Fedi 30; adult/reduced €7/5; ☺11am-6pm
Tue-Sat, 2.30-7.30pm Sun) This gallery inside
Palazzo del Tau is devoted to Pistoia's most
famous modern son, sculptor and painter Marino Marini (1901–80). Dozens of his
drawings and paintings – mainly of female
nudes (pear-shaped, evoking goddess of fertility Pomona) and horses – hang here.

⁂ Festivals & Events

Pistoia Blues　　　　　　　　　　　MUSIC
(www.pistoiablues.com; tickets €25-50; ☺Jul)
Going strong for at least three decades, Pis-
toia's annual blues festival lures big names.
BB King, Miles Davis, Sting, Santana, Ben
Harper, Robert Plant, Father John Misty,
Damien Rice and Noel Gallagher have all

taken to the stage here – an electrical fresco
affair that packs out Piazza del Duomo.

🛏 Sleeping

Locanda San Marco　　　　　　　　B&B €
(☑ 0573 2 19 13, 393 8170317; www.lsmpistoia.
it; Via Porta San Marco 26-28; s/d/tr/q from
€65/95/105/125; ❄ @ 🛜) This utterly irresistible guesthouse, run by the same creative
team behind Palazzo Puccini (p276), oozes
Italian chic. Terracotta herringbone-tiled
floors, period furnishings and fabrics in natural hues lend it a rustic 'country chic' vibe.
Some rooms have original wall frescoes and
beamed ceilings, and the courtyard garden
and roof terrace are real summertime treats.

Lo Studio　　　　　　　　　　　　　B&B €
(☑ 0573 194 16 66; www.lostudiobb.it; Via Verdi 56;
d €70-100; @ 🛜) A romantic, sea-blue front
door welcomes guests to this stylish B&B,
tucked discreetly away on a quiet backstreet
off Via della Madonna. Host Cristina, an
artist, charms the socks off every guest, and
artistically arranged rooms comfortably mix
ancient wood beams, exposed red brick and
frescoes with contemporary artworks and
decorative touches. Kudos for the delicious
Italian breakfast.

**Battistero Residenza
d'Epoca**　　　　　　　　　　　GUESTHOUSE €
(☑ 0573 07 92 20; www.residenzabattistero.it; Vicolo dei Fuggiti 4; s/d €80/100; ❄ 🛜) This stylish
guesthouse in a 13th-century town house
is the fabulous joint creation of a local coffee roaster and a baker. Nine comfortable
rooms and four suites enjoy a contemporary
decor, with coffee machine and romantic

MICHAEL R EVANS/ SHUTTERSTOCK ©

1. Lucca (p261)
A beautiful city ringed by city walls.

2. Castelnuovo di Garfagnana (p279)
Delightful narrow lanes and local Slow Food dining.

3. Piazza della Sala (p276), Pistoia
Fresh produce market open six days a week.

4. Marble Quarry (p285) near Carrara
One of 188 quarries where white Carrara marble is extracted.

STEFANO_VALERI/SHUTTERSTOCK ©

D-VISIONS/SHUTTERSTOCK ©

MARTIN BOND/ALAMY ©

3

ⓘ THE PERFECT TUSCAN PICNIC

Shop for the perfect Tuscan picnic on Piazza della Sala, an ancient square that's hosted a market since the 11th century. From Monday to Saturday open-air stalls are heaped with of small purple artichokes, juicy sun-rich strawberries, cherries, golden courgette flowers, peppers and other local seasonal produce. Round off any picnic shop with cheese and salami from I Salaioli (☑ 0573 2 02 25; www.isalaioli.it; Piazza della Sala 20-22; meals €30; ⊙ 7.30am-midnight) deli, and sensational bread – studded with marinated anchovies and cherry tomatoes perhaps, or flat bread topped with olives and sausage – from the only baker in town, Bonodinulla. This is also the spot to buy the finest *schiacciata* (flat-bread sandwiches; €3.50) in northwestern Tuscany.

views of the bustling market on Piazza della Sala or Pistoia's eye-catching baptistry and burnt-red rooftops beyond. Delicious breakfasts are served in the ground-floor bakery-cafe-pizzeria Bonodinulla.

★ **Palazzo Puccini**   B&B €€
(☑ 0573 2 58 62; www.lsmpistoia.it; Vicolo Malconsiglio 4; s/d/tr/q €70/90/100/120; ❄ @ 🕏) This boutique guesthouse is everything one would expect of an address in the family *palazzo* where wealthy Pistoian philanthropist and merchant Niccolò Puccini was born in 1799. Eight elegant rooms lie beneath majestic high ceilings, some with original frescoes, and all are fitted with tasteful period furnishings and smart contemporary en suite bathrooms. Some overlook a peaceful courtyard, others a quiet backstreet.

Tenuta di Pieve a Celle   AGRITURISMO €€
(☑ 0573 91 30 87; www.facebook.com/tenutadipieveacelle/; Via di Pieve a Celle Nuova 158; d €160; P ❄ 🌊) In the hills 3km outside Pistoia, this 1850s country estate with olive grove and pool is approached along a driveway lined with cypress trees. Five pretty rooms, each named after a different flower, sport canopy beds and views of the estate's expansive gardens. Host Fiorenza cooks evening meals on request (Monday to Saturday) using seasonal produce fresh from her organic vegetable garden.

✕ Eating

Pistoia's foodie street is pedestrian-only Via del Lastrone, lined with cafes, wine bars and traditional restaurants serving *carcerato* (a type of offal), *frittata con rigatino* (omelette with salt-cured bacon), *farinata con cavalo* (chickpea pancake with cabbage), *migliacci* (fritters made with pig's blood) and other local specialities. End with *berlingozzo*, a sweet traditionally served with a glass of local Vin Santo.

La Bettola   TRATTORIA €
(☑ 0573 2 96 62; www.facebook.com/la.bettola.79; Via Porta San Marco 69; meals €20; ⊙ 7.30-10.30pm Tue, 12.30-2.30pm & 7-11pm Wed-Sat, 12.30-2.30pm & 7-10pm Sun) A backstreet treasure that you really won't find unless you know about it, this stalwart no-frills trattoria cooks up some of the most traditional and tastiest Tuscan cuisine in town beneath age-old, red-brick vaults. Just as remarkable are its low prices. Try the once-eaten-never-forgotton *zuppa del carcerato* (a local offal soup) followed by *collo di pollo ripieno* (stuffed chicken neck) perhaps or the *lampredotto con salse* (tripe with salsa).

★ **Magno Gaudio**   ITALIAN €€
(☑ 0573 2 69 05; Via Curtatone e Montanara 12; meals €30; ⊙ 7am-11pm Mon-Sat; 🕏) If it is local Pistoians you're looking for, snag a table at this tasty all-rounder. Be it breakfast, brunch, dinner or an *aperitivo* on the street terrace, this hybrid delivers with creative cuisine and friendly, unpretentious service. Choose between fish and vegetarian dishes aplenty, meal-sized salads, imaginative pasta, springtime artichokes deep-fried, and sublime, sesame-seed-encrusted tuna carpaccio.

Bonodinulla   PIZZA €€
(☑ 0573 35 87 92; www.bonodinulla.it; Via del Lastrone 21; meals €20-30; ⊙ 8am-2.30pm & 7-10.30pm Sun, Mon, Wed & Thu, to 11pm Fri & Sat; 🕏 🍴) Given one of the owners is a sixth-generation baker, a dish involving bread is the only sensible choice at this millennial pizzeria-osteria-cafe-bakery hybrid overlooking Piazza del Sala. Enjoy drinks with crostini – a mix of walnut bread, spicy red-pepper bread and multigrain with various toppings – followed by a half-meter chopping board of pizza to share.

Baldovino   TUSCAN €€
(☑ 0573 2 15 91; www.enotecabaldovino.it; Piazza San Lorenzo 5; meals €25-35; ⊙ 12.30-2.30pm & 7.30pm-midnight Mon-Fri, 7.30pm-midnight Sat) A

timeless faithful, Pistoia's traditional *enoteca* (wine bar) promises hearty Tuscan fare in the company of excellent wine and a staunchly local crowd every time. Be it beef tartare, a brilliantly blue T-bone or wholesome bowl of pasta you crave, this kitchen delivers. Daredevils should try the *tagliatelle* with pureed peas and osso buco (bone marrow).

Trattoria dell'Abbondanza   TRATTORIA €€

(☑ 0573 36 80 37; www.trattoriadellabbondanza. it; Via dell'Abbondanza 10; meals €25; ☺ noon-2.30pm & 7-10.30pm Thu-Tue) Dine al fresco in a quiet street or plump for a table inside where homey collections of doorbells, pasta jars et al catch the eye at this enchanting Slow Food favourite. Cuisine is seasonal Tuscan: begin perhaps with spelt with green peas and goat's-cheese fondue, followed by stewed octopus in tomato sauce or a meaty mix of fried beef tongue and cheek.

Osteria La BotteGaia   OSTERIA €€

(☑ 0573 36 56 02; www.labottegaia.it; Via del Lastrone 17; meals €30; ☺ noon-3pm & 7-11pm Tue-Sat, 7-11pm Sun) Dishes range from traditional to experimental at this Slow Food–hailed *osteria*, famed for its finely butchered cured meats and interesting wine list. Asparagus-laced risotto and artichoke flan in a cheesy parmesan sauce are among the interesting vegetarian options. Reserve in advance or opt for wine-fuelled snacks at La BotteGaia's *vineria* (wine bar) on the same street.

Drinking & Nightlife

Car-free market square Piazza della Sala (and its surrounding web of narrow streets) is the hotspot in town for atmospheric drinks in trendy bars – wonderfully al fresco in summer.

★ Caffètteria Marino Marini   CAFE

(☑ 0573 36 59 88; www.facebook.com/caffetteria. marini; Corso Fedi 32; ☺ 7am-9pm Mon-Thu, to 11pm Fri & Sat) This warm, vibrant cafe has its own bakery that bakes superb breads, and a flowery courtyard garden that buzzes with local life. Sip an espresso at the bar, chat with friends over cappuccino at one of four tables in the cosy interior, or flop on a country-style sofa in the covered porch and admire the blooming hydrangeas in the fabulous cloister garden – it's utterly gorgeous in summer.

Il Carbonile   LOUNGE

(The Bunker; ☑ 340 3259281; www.facebook.com/ ilcarbonile; Piazza del Carmine 6b; ☺ 8pm-2am Thu & Fri, 7pm-2am Sat) This retro 'bunker' lures a fashionable set with its vintage furnishings. Everything, from the colourful 1950s formica tables to travelling chests doubling as low tables, is actually for sale. Its outdoor deck, complete with creaky wooden floorboards and old-fashioned bunting, is a lovely space for drinks, and come dusk an eclectic mix of music kicks in.

Fiaschetteria La Pace   WINE BAR

(☑ 0573 2 31 39; www.fiaschetteriapistoia.com; Via dei Fabbri 7; ☺ 5.30-11pm) 'Everything is going to be all right' is the strapline of this hip bar and bistro. And indeed, be it shelling free peanuts around a wooden table in the vintage interior or perching on a stone slab of a window sill outside, everything *is* good at this trendy eating-drinking address. Creative Tuscan cuisine and traditional tasting boards of salami and cheese keep everyone happy any time of day.

Information

Tourist Office (☑ 0573 2 16 22; turismo. pistoia@comune.pistoia.it; Piazza del Duomo 4; ☺ 9am-1pm & 3-6pm) Dedicated, ever-charming Paolo is a mine of information. He also distributes free city maps, and walking and cycling itineraries, and takes bookings for themed walking tours of both the city and key monuments (€10; two hours).

Getting There & Away

From the train station, head straight along Viale XX Settembre, across the roundabout, and beyond along Via Vannucci (which becomes Via Cino) to get to the old town. Regional train services include the following:

Florence (€4.60, 45 minutes, every 20 minutes)

Lucca (€5.70, 45 minutes to one hour, half-hourly)

Pisa (€7 to €9.90, two hours, change in Florence or Lucca)

Prato (€2.60, 15 minutes, every 20 minutes)

Viareggio (€7, one hour, hourly)

SAN MINIATO

☑ 0571 / POP 27,530

There is one delicious reason to visit this enchantingly sleepy, medieval hilltop town almost equidistant (50km) between Pisa and

LARI: DESTINATION SPAGHETTI

Built around the base of an 11th-century castle acquired and fortified by the Medicis, the medieval village of Lari (pop 8780), 35km south of Pisa, is home to an address no gastronome should miss: the **Martelli Pasta Factory** (☑ 0587 68 42 38; www.famigliamartelli.it; Via dei Pastifici 3; ☺ 9am-1pm & 3-5pm Mon, Tue & Thu-Sat, closed 2 weeks Aug) FREE. Established in 1926, this tiny family-run pasta factory exports internationally (Germany and Australia are the biggest importers) and is happy to give curious visitors a free 10-minute tour showcasing its hands-on production methods – the best days to visit are Tuesday and Friday, when spaghetti is made.

Chewier and coarser in texture than many, Martelli's pasta marries particularly well with meat sauces and game. In Lari itself, buy Martelli's trademark canary-yellow paper packets of pasta for €4.50 per kilogram at village cafe and tobacconist **La Bottega delle Specialità** (☑ 0587 68 71 12; Via Diaz 12-14; ☺ 7.30am-8pm Mon-Sat; ☎) or eat the pasta for lunch at **Antica Osteria Al Castello** (☑ 329 2088155; Piazza Matteotti 13; meals €35; ☺ 12.30-2pm & 7.30-10pm Wed-Sun, also Mon Jun-Aug) in the main piazza.

Florence: to eat, hunt and dream about the *Tuber magnatum pico* (white truffle).

San Miniato town's ancient cobbled streets, burnt soft copper and ginger in the hot summer sun, are a delight to meander along. Savour a harmonious melody of magnificent palace facades, 14th- to 18th-century churches and an impressive Romanesque cathedral with 12th-century bell tower (Piazza del Duomo; adult/child €2.50/free; ☺ 11am-2pm Mon-Fri, 11am-2pm & 3-6pm Sat & Sun Apr-Sep, 10am-1pm & 2-5pm Sat, 2-5pm Sun Oct-Mar) to scale, ending with the stiff hike up San Miniato's reconstructed medieval fortress tower, Torre di Frederico II (Tower of Frederick II; Via di Rocca; €3.50; ☺ 11am-6pm Tue-Sun), to enjoy a great panorama. Before setting off, buy a combined ticket covering both towers and a few other minor sites (adult/reduced €5/4) at the tourist office.

With an abundance of exceptional local produce, dining out in San Miniato is second to none, whatever your budget. Devour *carciofo San Miniatese* (locally grown artichokes) in April and May; chestnuts and wild mushrooms in autumn; and *formaggio di capra delle colline di San Miniato* (the local goat's cheese) and locally raised Chianina beef whatever the month.

★ Barbialla Nuova   FARMSTAY €
(☑ 0571 67 70 04; www.barbialla.it; Via Casastada 49, Montaione;   2-/4-/6-/8-person apt €110/190/240/350, minimum 2/7 nights winter/summer; ☺ Mar-Dec; ⓟ ☎ ⚟) ⚟ Creamy Chianina cows graze on the hillside and wild boars ferret for white truffles between tree roots on this heavily wooded, 500-hectare biodynamic farm with just the right mix

of adventure (unpaved roads) and panache (stylish decor). Apartments in old farmhouses dotted around the property offer self-catering accommodation and, most memorably, guests can buy fresh truffles in season at the farm shop.

Staying here is all about feeding the pigs, admiring the livestock, walking (guests get a map of trails around the estate), stocking up on fresh organic produce and truffles at the farm shop – and cooking them up! Barbialla is 20km south of San Miniato on the SP76; look for the white sign on your right 3km after the village of Corrazano.

Sergio Falaschi   TUSCAN €
(☑ 0571 4 31 90; www.sergiofalaschi.it; Via Augusto Conti 18-20; meals €25; ☺ 7.30am-3pm & 4-8pm Mon-Tue & Thu-Sat, 9am-3pm Sun; ☎) The most famous *macelleria* (butcher's shop) in town, run by the same family since 1925, is where most local restaurants buy their outstandingly excellent meat. Forge your way past the counter into the back of the ceramic-tiled shop to feast on feisty dishes of the day made from local Chianina beef and *cinta senese* (indigenous Tuscan pork from Siena).

Try to sample local Slow Food favourite *mallegato* (blood sausage) and arrive on the dot to snag the best table in the house – on a bijou covered terrace with a panoramic valley view.

★ Pepenero   TUSCAN €€€
(☑ 0571 41 95 23; www.pepenerocucina.it; Via IV Novembre 13; meals €50; ☺ 12.30-2pm & 7.30-10pm Wed-Fri & Sun, 7.30-10pm Sat) Chef and TV star Gilberto Rossi is one of the new breed of innovative Tuscan chefs using traditional

products to create modern, seasonally driven dishes at this much-lauded restaurant. To experience the best of his cooking, indulge in a themed tasting menu (€30 to €50), with optional wine pairings. Vegetarians are catered for with their own *degustazione* menu too. Reservations essential.

Peperino TUSCAN €€€

(🍽 0571 41 95 23; Via IV Novembre 1; menu incl bottle champagne & wine €250; ⊙ by appointment) Book the only table – a table for two – at Peperino, the world's smallest restaurant plum in the heart of Tuscany's most gourmet village, next to big brother, Pepenero. Decor is in-your-face romantic (think pink silk), furnishings are period and the waiter only comes when diners ring the bell. Reserve months in advance.

ℹ Information

Tourist Office (🍽 0571 4 27 45; www.sanmini atopromozione.it; Piazza del Popolo 1; ⊙ 9am-1pm Mon, 9am-5pm Tue-Sun)

ℹ Getting There & Away

Take a train to San Miniato-Fuecchio, then take a shuttle bus (€1, every 20 minutes) to the old town.

Regional train services include the following:

Florence (€5.70, 40 minutes, hourly)

Pisa (€4.60, 30 minutes, hourly)

APUANE ALPS & GARFAGNANA

Rearing up inland from the Versilian Riviera are the Apuane Alps, a rugged mountain range protected by the Parco Regionale delle Alpi Apuane (Apuane Alps Regional Park; www.parcapuane.it) that beckons hikers with a trail of isolated farmhouses, medieval hermitages and hilltop villages.

Continue inland, across the Alps' eastern ridge, and three stunning valleys formed by the Serchio and its tributaries – the low-lying Lima and Serchio Valleys and the higher Garfagnana Valley, collectively known as the Garfagnana – take centre stage. Thickly forested with chestnut and acacia woods, this is a land where fruits of the forest (chestnuts, porcini mushrooms and honey) create a very rustic and fabulous cuisine.

The main gateway to this staunchly rural area is Castelnuovo di Garfagnana, home to the regional park's visitor centre.

Castelnuovo di Garfagnana

🍽 0583 / POP 6030

The medieval eyrie of Castelnuovo crowns the confluence of the Serchio and its smaller tributary, the Turrite. Its heart is pierced by the burnt-red Rocca Ariostesca (Ariosto's

HUNTING WHITE TRUFFLES

An integral part of local culture since the Middle Ages, some 400 *tartufaio* (truffle hunters) in the trio of small valleys around San Miniato snout out the precious fungus, pale ochre in colour, from October to mid-December. The paths and trails they follow are a family secret, passed along generations. The truffles their dogs sniff out are worth a small fortune after all, selling for anything between €1500 and €3000 per kilogram in Tuscany and four times as much in London and other European capitals.

There is no better time to savour the mystique of this cloak-and-dagger truffle trade than during San Miniato's Mostra Mercato Nazionale del Tartufo Bianco (National White Truffle Market), on the last three weekends in November, when restaurateurs and truffle tragics come from every corner of the globe to purchase supplies, sample truffle-based delicacies in the town's shops and restaurants, and breathe in one of the world's most distinctive aromas. San Miniato tourist office has a list of truffle dealers and can help you join a truffle hunt.

The best are the early-morning truffle hunts at Barbialla Nuova, a 500-hectare farm, 20km south of San Miniato near Montaione, run by new-generation farmer Guido Manfredi. Truffle hunts (€60 to €80 per person, 2½ hours, October to mid-December) end with a glass of Chianti and a tasting of local organic cheese and salami – or go to a local restaurant and savour your truffle shaved over pasta followed by a *bistecca alla fiorentina* (chargrilled T-bone steak). Famed far and wide for its enviable success rate when it comes to uncovering these nuggets of 'white' gold, Barbialla's *tartufaio* and its dogs unearth some 20kg or so of edible booty in a season.

Apuane Alps & Garfagnana

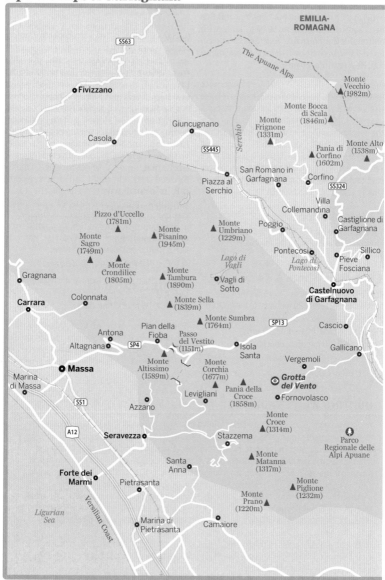

Castle), built in the 12th century and named after Italian poet Ariosto who lived here between 1522 and 1525 as governor of the Garfagnana for the House of Este. The town's quiet narrow lanes, arranged around the city's small *duomo,* are a delight to meander along

and local Slow Food dining is a real treat. Thursday morning is market day.

★ **Osteria Vecchia Mulino**   OSTERIA €
(☎0583 6 21 92; www.facebook.com/vecchiomulino1985; Via Vittorio Emanuele 12; tasting menu €20; ⏱11am-9pm Tue, Wed & Fri-Sun, 7am-9am

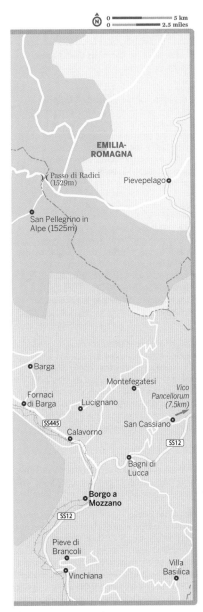

EMILIA-ROMAGNA

Passo di Radici (1529m)

Pievepelago

San Pellegrino in Alpe (1525m)

Barga

Fornaci di Barga

Montefegatesi

Vico Pancellorum (7.5km)

Lucignano

SS445

San Cassiano

Calavorno

SS12

Bagni di Lucca

Borgo a Mozzano

SS12

Pieve di Brancoli

Villa Basilica

Vinchiana

packaged culinary goodies to buy and take home with you.

Fuori dal Centro GELATO €
(☑347 3459847; www.facebook.com/fuoridal centro; Piazza Dini 1f; cones €2.50-4.50; ⊙1-8pm Tue-Sat, 11am-8pm Sun) Dare we say it: having tried and tested dozens of Tuscan gelaterie, this bright modern ice-cream shop comes out tops. Fuori dal Centro's regionally inspired flavours are magnificent. Try chestnut, fig and honey, pine kernel, cinnamon and local Lunigiana honey, meringue (truly sublime!) or – most unusually – *crema di farro*, which really does have grains of *farro* (spelt) in it.

ⓘ Information

Turismo Garfagnana (☑0583 64 84 35, 0583 6 51 69; www.turismo.garfagnana.eu; Piazza delle Erbe 1; ⊙9am-1pm & 3-7pm summer, to 5.30pm winter; 🛜)

ⓘ Getting There & Away

Regional train services include the following:
Lucca (€5.70, one hour, nine daily)
Pisa (€7, 1½ hours, four daily)

Barga

☑0583 / POP 10.150
This chic village, 12km south of Castelnuovo di Garfagnana, is one of those irresistibly slow Tuscan hilltop towns. It is also home to a disproportionately large and dynamic English-speaking community – where else in Tuscany can you find a British, poppy-red telephone box upcycled as a free English book exchange? Churches, artisanal workshops, attractive stone houses and palaces built by rich merchants between the 15th and 17th centuries lace the steep, photogenic streets leading up to Barga's elegant, Romanesque cathedral (☑0583 72 30 31; Piazza Beato Michele 1; ⊙8.30am-6.30pm) [FREE]. Allow plenty of time for tranquil ambling between cafe terraces.

Bijou Barga has a couple of lovely B&Bs and *agriturismi* (farm stays). It's also a prime spot for sampling Garfagnana produce, including *necci* (chestnut crepes) and various local pasta made with sweet chestnut flour, stone-ground from the region's smoke-dried Carpinese chestnuts. A handful of cafes and casual restaurants with pretty pavement terraces pepper its narrow car-free streets.

Thu) Run with passion and humour by the gregarious Andrea Bertucci, this 160-year-old *osteria* has no menu but rather a symphony of cold dishes crafted from local products and brought to shared tables one at a time. Bottles of wine line the walls, floor to ceiling, and there are plenty of local,

0 5 km
0 2.5 miles

OFF THE BEATEN TRACK

THREE SCENIC ROAD TRIPS

If your nerves and stomach are up to it, there are dozens of narrow roads that spaghetti from Castelnuovo into the Garfagnana's rural depths.

Across a Mountain Pass

Spiralling north from Castelnuovo, a concertina of hairpin bends along the SS324 lifts you up to **Castiglione di Garfagnana** and over the scenic **Passo di Radici** mountain pass, across the Apennines and into Emilia-Romagna. A minor parallel road to the south of the pass takes you to **San Pellegrino in Alpe** (www.sanpellegrino.org), a hilltop village at 1525m with a monastery and, in the old hospital, a **Museo Etnografico** (Ethnographic Museum; ☎0583 64 90 72; www.sanpellegrinoinalpe.it; Via del Voltone 14; adult/reduced €2.50/1.50; ⏲10am-1pm & 2-6.30pm summer, closed Mon & shorter hours winter) that brings traditional mountain life, scarcely changed for centuries, to life.

Alpine Flora & Marble Mountain

Head west towards the Med. The first 17km along the SP13 is straightforward, but once you fork right 2km south of Arni (follow signs for Massa along the SP4), motoring becomes a relentless succession of hairpins, unlit tunnels and breathtaking vistas of Carrara's marble quarries as you cross the Apuane Alps over the **Passo del Vestito** (1151m). Stop in **Pian della Fioba** to discover alpine flora in the **Orto Botanico delle Alpi Apuane 'Pietro Pellegrini'** (Apuane Alps Botanical Garden; ☎0585 49 03 49, 348 8809255; www.parcapuane.toscana.it/orto; ⏲9am-1pm & 3-7pm Jun–mid-Sep) FREE. From here the road drops down, through **Antona** and **Altagnana**, clinging to the hillside, to **Massa** on the Versilian Coast. The entire drive is 42km.

Subterranean Rivers & Lakes

The SS445 is a twisting route that leads you through lush green hills pocked with caves – completely worth the drive in itself, broken perhaps with a roadside picnic and plenty of photo stops. Allow time to visit the spectacular **Grotta del Vento** (☎0583 72 20 24; www.grottadelvento.com; Grotta del Vento 1, Vergemoli; adult/reduced 1hr guided visit €9/7, 2hr €14/11, 3hr €20/16; ⏲10am-noon & 2-6pm), 9km west of the SS445 along a very narrow road. Inside is a world of underground abysses, lakes and caverns. From April to October, choose between a one-, two- or three-hour guided tour; if you're up to the 800/1200 steps involved in the two-/three-hour tour, it's worth it. From November to March, the one-hour tour (300 steps) is the only choice.

After dark, **Barga Jazz Club** (☎0583 72 38 60; www.bargajazzclub.com; Via del Pretorio 23; annual membership card €8; ⏲9.30pm-1am Fri & Sat) – at home in a former carpenter's workshop – is the hotspot for live jazz, blues, soul and drinks with Barga's resident Anglophones.

Casa Cordati GUESTHOUSE €
(☎338 1994975, 0583 72 34 50; www.casacordati.it; Via di Mezzo 17; s/d/tr/q €38/54/66/78; ⏲Mar–mid-Nov & mid-Dec–mid-Jan; @ 📶) This atmospheric town house is an ode to art, fittingly so given it's situated in the former home and studio of painter Bruno Cordati (1890–1979). The ground-floor gallery (free admission) shows off some of his works, while stylish rooms above sport wooden floors, period decor and an arty feel. Some bathrooms are shared.

Two-room studios sleeping five (€90), with tiny kitchenettes to prepare your own breakfast, are a particular hit with families.

★ **Al Benefizio** AGRITURISMO €€
(☎347 2703624; www.albenefizio.it; Via Ronchi 4, Ponte di Catagnana; r €120; P @ 📶 🏊) Squeeze your car along the narrow road to this farm, framed by fig trees, olive groves, vines, acacia and chestnut woods on a steeply terraced hillside near Barga, uphill from Ponte di Catagnana. Self-catering apartments with wood stoves, no TV and spectacular views sleep up to four, and the local baker, Maurizio, drives by each morning with fresh bread, pastries and scrumptious focaccia.

But the real reason to stay here is get acquainted with charismatic owner Francesca, a talented chef and beekeeper. With her you can visit the apiary with 100 hives beneath cherry trees, see how honey is extracted (Easter to September), sign up for a cooking course or olive-oil workshop, or help out with the olive harvest (by hand) in late November. In summer guests can swim, mountain bike, barbecue, play table tennis, help themselves to veg and herbs in the vegetable patch, pet the farm donkey Geubi, and collect fresh eggs. Or mingle, memorably so, with other guests at Francesca's wonderfully informal 'pizza parties' around the farm's old stone bread oven. No credit cards.

Trattoria L'Altana   TUSCAN €
(📞0583 72 31 92; www.facebook.com/trattori alaltana; Via di Mezzo 1; meals €20-25; ⊙12.30-2.30pm & 7.30-10.30pm Fri-Tue, 7.30-10.30pm Thu) Dining at this popular trattoria is akin to dining in someone's family home – that of Camilla, Angela and Giulia in this case, who cook up authentic homemade Tuscan fare (fantastic pasta!) in Barga old town. The back room, complete with wall mural of the valley, is winter-cosy and in summer the rooftop terrace is the place to be.

⭐**Sosta dei Diavoli**   TUSCAN €
(📞348 3643550; www.sostadeidiavoli.it; Via Pascoli 140, Ponte di Catagnana; meals €20) It might seem to be just another humble, family-run cafe-bar in rural Tuscany, but the Devils' Stop is wickedly good. Come 7.30pm, owner Lorenzo Giuliani dons his chef's apron

to cook up a small but sensational choice of antipasti and pasta *primi:* his local *pecorino* cheese with fresh pea-green broad beans and a pot of Lunigiana honey is simple, but oh so good.

The 'devils', should you be wondering, were local charcoal burners who, faces black with soot after a hard day's graft making and transporting charcoal, would drop into the veteran bar for a wee nip. Find Sosta dei Diavoli at the bottom of the hill from Barga, 4km north in riverside Ponte di Catagnana.

ℹ Information

Tourist Office (📞0583 72 47 45; Via di Mezzo 47; ⊙9.30am-12.30pm Mon-Sat)

ℹ Getting There & Away

Buses operated by Viabus Lucca (https://lucca. cttnord.it) link Barga with Lucca (€4, one hour, three or four daily).

Bagni di Lucca
📞0583 / POP 6150
The small town of Bagni di Lucca is 28km south of Castelnuovo di Garfagnana on the banks of the Lima river. It was famed in the early 19th century for its thermal waters, which were enjoyed by the Lucca gentry and an international set: Byron, Shelley, Heinrich

OFF THE BEATEN TRACK

AN OPERA BUFF'S DETOUR
Some 35km west of both Barbialla Nuova and San Gimignano, ringed by a natural amphitheatre of soul-stirring hills, is Lajatico (population 1374). This tiny village is the birthplace and family home of opera singer Andrea Bocelli (b 1958) who, each year in July or August, returns to his village to sing – for just one evening. In 2019 the tenor was joined on stage by his pop-star son, Matteo Bocelli.

His stage is the astonishing Teatro del Silenzio (www.teatrodelsilenzio.it), a specially constructed, open-air 'Theatre of Silence' built in a green meadow on the fringe of the village where the natural silence is broken once a year – by the Tuscan tenor and his friends (Placido Domingo, José Carreras, Sarah Brightman and Chinese pianist Lang Lang have all performed here). Each year different sculptures by contemporary artists are added to the ensemble, to striking effect. Listening to the tenor sing to an audience of 10,000 against a backdrop of gently rolling green hills is an overwhelming experience. Tickets, usually released each year in March, cost €98 to €425 and are sold by City Sound Milano (http://citysoundmilano.com).

Opera buffs with a penchant for fine food and wine can continue 5km to La Sterza to drink and dine in style, or buy wine and olive oil, on the Bocelli's family estate at Officine Bocelli (Food Court; 📞0587 39 81 43; www.officinebocelli.it; Via Volterrana 10, La Sterza; meals €25; ⊙noon-3pm Tue, Wed & Sun, noon-3pm & 8-11pm Thu-Sat, shop 10am-8pm Tue & Wed, 10am-midnight Thu-Sun), at the southern end of the village on the SR439.

Heine and Giacomo Puccini were among the celebrity guests to take to the waters. While the spa town today is a pale shadow of its former splendid neoclassical self, it remains a pretty place to meander for a couple of hours. Admire its neoclassical casino (1837) with a music room where Strauss, Puccini and Liszt all performed, its atypically ornate Anglican church (now the municipal library – look for the stucco lion-and-unicorn motif above each window on the vivid burnt-red facade) and the baroque headstones in the small British cemetery.

There are two distinct areas: the smaller casino-clad Ponte a Serraglio, clustered around a bridge that crosses the Lima river; and the main town, 2km east, where most shops, restaurants and hotels are. In the former, you'll find the Sorgente La Cova (Viale Casino Municipale 84), a natural spring spouting out of a roadside wall.

In the tiny riverside hamlet of Borgo a Mozzano, 2km southwest of town, is the medieval stone Ponte del Diarolo – the so-called 'Devils' Bridge' with ancient stone paving dating from the 14th century.

Most visitors overnight at the Bagni di Lucca Terme (☑ 0583 8 60 34; www.termebagnidilucca.it; Via del Paretaio 1; s/d/tr from €69/115/167; P ⓢ ⓧ) to wallow in the town's thermal waters; accommodation options are otherwise limited.

Buca di Baldabò   TUSCAN €

(☑ 0583 8 90 62; www.labucadibaldabo.it; Via Prati 11, Vico Pancellorum; meals €20-30; ⓢnoon-3pm & 7-10pm Jun-Aug, lunch by reservation & 7-10pm Wed-Sun Sep-May) Perched on a hillock above chestnut and walnut forests, this is an iconic address every local foodie knows about. Hidden at the back of the village bar, it has no printed menu. Listen to what's cooking that day and take your pick from homemade pasta and sauces cooked up daily by chef Giovanni. Game is particularly big and side dishes are creative.

To get to Vico Pancellorum from Bagni di Lucca, head 9km northeast along the scenic SS12 towards Abetone and at the northern end of Ponte Coccia take the sharp turning on the left signposted 'Vico Pancellorum'; the restaurant is another 3km from here, at the foot of the hamlet, along a steep, narrow, curving road. Advance reservations are essential.

ⓘ Information

Tourist Office (☑ 0583 80 57 45; www.bagnidiluccaterme.info/en; Viale Umberto I 93; ⓢ10am-1pm Mon & Wed-Sat)

ⓘ Getting There & Away

Bagni di Lucca train station is in Fornoli, 4km southwest of the Bagni di Lucca Terme. Hope a local bus passes relatively soon after your arrival or arrange a taxi in advance through your hotel. Regional train services:

Lucca (€3.60, 30 minutes, seven daily)
Pisa (€5.70, 1¼ hours, five daily)

Carrara

☑ 0575 / POP 64,400

Many first-time visitors assume the white mountain peaks forming Carrara's backdrop are capped with snow. In fact, the vista provides a breathtaking illusion – the lunar white is 2000 hectares of marble gouged out of the foothills of the Apuane Alps in vast quarries, 5km out of town, that have been worked since Roman times.

The texture and purity of Carrara's white marble (derived from the Greek *marmaros,* meaning shining stone) is unrivalled, and it remains the world's most sought-after. Michelangelo selected marble here for masterpieces such as *Pièta* (the veined marble he used for his iconic *David* came from a quarry in neighbouring Pietrasanta), while Carrara marble was used for London's Marble Arch and by Rodin to sculpt *The Kiss.*

Bar the thrill of admiring its marble pavements, marble street benches, decorative marble *putti* (cherubs), marble-clad post office and marble everything else, Carrara doesn't offer much for the visitor.

ⓞ Sights & Activities

The tourist office (p286) has information on marble-carving workshops and walking trails with magnificent quarry views. Keen cyclists will appreciate the three-hour 'Michelangelo in White' biking itinerary – a 24km route that climbs 550m up from Carrara-Avenza train station to the quarries and beyond to tasty Colonnata.

Cava di Fantiscritti   HISTORIC SITE

(Fantiscritti Quarry; Via Miseglia Fantiscritti) Head up the mountain to this dusty, truck-busy *cava de marmo* (marble quarry), through a dramatic series of tunnels used by trains to

MARBLE MOUNTAIN

Zipping down a dank, wet, unlit tunnel in a dusty white minibus, grubby headlights blazing and driver incongruously dolled up in a shiny shocking-pink bomber jacket... It is all somewhat surreal. Five minutes into the pitch-black marble mountain, everyone is told to get out.

It is 16°C (61°F), foggy, dirty and slippery underfoot. And far from being a polished pearly white, it's grey – cold, wet, miserable grey. Rough-cut blocks, several metres long and almost as wide, are strewn about the place like toy bricks and marble columns prop up the 15m-high ceiling, above which a second gallery, another 17m tall, stands. The place is bigger than several football pitches, yet amazingly there is still plenty of marble left for the five workers employed at Cava di Fantiscritti, 5km north of Carrara, to extract. With the aid of water and mechanical diamond-cutting chains that slice through the rock like butter, they take 10,000 tonnes of white marble a month.

To learn how the Romans did it (with chisels and axes – oh my!), visit the surprisingly informative, open-air Cava Museo, adjoining the souvenir shop across from the quarry entrance. Don't miss the B&W shots of marble blocks being precariously slid down the *lizza* (mountain pathway) to the bottom of the mountain where 18 pairs of oxen would haul the marble on carts to Carrara port. In the 1850s a rail network of 24 tunnels and seven bridges was built for trains to do the job – which they did until the 1960s. Cars can drive through many of these defunct train tunnels today (hence the tunnel that quarry tour groups use to drive into the mountain).

Carrara alone exploits 188 marble quarries today: the Apuane Alps safeguard the world's largest marble field, with the best Carrara marble selling for €4000 a tonne (exports alone are worth some €360 million a year). Carrara's quarries employ 1200 workers and another 700 truck drivers who zigzag each day up and down terrifyingly steep, mountain 'roads' transporting giant marble blocks. It's hard, dangerous work and on Carrara's central Piazza XXVII Aprile a monument remembers past workers who lost their lives up on the hills.

transport marble from 1890 until the 1960s when trucks took over. At the Fantiscritti Quarry entrance, pick a 40-minute guided tour by minibus and on foot of the Ravaccione 84 gallery inside the quarry, run by Marmotour (☑ 339 7657470; www.marmotour. com; adult/child €10/free; ⊙ 10am-6pm mid-Jun–mid-Sep, 11am-5pm mid-Sep–early Nov, shorter hr rest of yr), or pick a Bond-style 4WD tour of the open-cast quarries run by various unofficial operators lurking around on-site. Or book ahead with Cave di Marmo Tours (☑ 328 0993322, 0585 62 51 12; www.cavedimar motours.com; Viale G Galilei 122e; ⊙ 9am-5pm).

Yes, the Bond movie *Quantum of Solace* was shot here. Both type of tours are highly dramatic.

Museo Civico del Marmo   MUSEUM
(Marble Museum; ☑ 0585 84 57 46; www.musei. carrara.ms.gov.it/museo-del-marmo; Viale XX Settembre 85; adult/reduced €5/3; ⊙ 11am-8pm Tue-Thu, Sat & Sun, 11am-9pm Fri summer, 10am-12.30pm & 3-5.30pm Tue-Sun winter) Opposite the tourist office, Carrara's Marble Museum tells the full story of the marble quarries

outside town, from the old chisel-and-hammer days to the 21st century's high-powered industrial quarrying. A fascinating audiovisual history presentation documents the lives of quarry workers in the 20th century.

Cava Museo   MUSEUM
(☑ 393 3575925, 334 7870741; www.cavamuseo. com; Cava di Fantiscritti; ⊙ 11am-6pm) FREE To learn how the Romans worked with marble, visit this surprisingly informative, open-air museum adjoining the souvenir shop across from the quarry entrance.

✷ Festivals & Events

White Carrara Downtown   CULTURAL
(www.whitecarraradowntown.it; ⊙ Jun) This annual one-week festival in early June celebrates the town's famous marble. Expect music concerts inside marble quarries (brilliant acoustics), marble-carving workshops, open-air sculpture exhibitions, food and wine tastings, quarry treks on foot and by bike, and al fresco art happenings galore around town.

ⓘ HIKING, BIKING, RAFTING & CULINARY REWARDS

Indulge your passions with one of the following outfits:

Tuscany Walking (www.tuscanywalking.com) This family-run, English-speaking set-up in Barga offers guided and self-guided hikes.

Ecoguide (☑ 340 6778356; www.eco-guide.it) This creative Lucca-based operation offers guided nature tours in the Garfagnana on foot and by bicycle, including magical night walks in the Garfagnana, kids' walks and photography treks.

Garfagnana Rafting (☑ 336 666795, 340 7116974; www.garfagnanarafting.com) Canyoning, kayaking, aqua-trekking and white-water rafting on the Lima and Serchio rivers; small-group hikes in the Apuane Alps too.

Sapori e Saperi (☑ 339 7636321, UK 07768 474 610; www.sapori-e-saperi.com) Embark on a bespoke culinary tour of the Garfagnana with knowledgeable foodie Erica or passionate chef, beekeeper and olive farmer Francesca. Learn how bread is traditionally baked, sausages are made, and *pecorino* cheese is produced as it's been done for generations. Visit olive farms, harvest chestnuts, hunt truffles, meet local cheesemakers and savour age-old recipes in local-endorsed restaurants.

🍽 Sleeping & Eating

Decent accommodation options in Carrara are limited to a few unremarkable B&Bs; the neighbouring art town of Pietrasanta makes an attractive, alternative base.

The most memorable place to lunch is in the hamlet of Colonnata, 2km from the Fantiscritti quarries, where one of Tuscany's greatest gastronomic treats, *lardo di colonnata* (thinner-than-wafer-thin slices of aromatic pig fat) sits ageing in marble vats of herby olive oil. Once you're hooked, purchase a vacuum-packed slab (€15 per kilogram) to take home from one of the many *larderie* (shops selling *lardo*) in the village.

Dalle Zie   TUSCAN €
(☑ 0585 7 07 28; www.facebook.com/DalleZie/; Piazza del Duomo; meals €25; ⊙ 12.45-2.15pm & 8-10pm Tue-Sat, 12.45-2.15pm Sun) Locals rave about this tiny family-run *trattoria* on Cathedral Sq, aptly called 'By Auntie' and with an inviting '*Cibo e Vino*' (food and wine) strapline. Cuisine is strictly local, with plenty of traditional, potato-filled *tordelli* (square pasta cushions, larger than ravioli) and sweet *torta di riso* (rice cake) plumping out the handwritten menu.

Osteria nella Pia'   OSTERIA €
(☑ 0585 75 80 97, 338 8408173; www.osterianellapia.it; Via Fossa Cava 3, Colonnata; meals €20; ⊙ noon-3pm Tue-Thu & Sun, noon-3pm & 7.30-10pm Fri & Sat) It's worth getting lost in Colonnata's tangle of narrow lanes to find this family-run *osteria*, a local favourite for tasty *lardo* platters and imaginative pasta dishes. The *penne con lardo e pesto d'ortica* (penne with *lardo*

and nettle pesto) is nothing short of superb. Kudos for the shaded summertime terrace wedged between old stone village houses and the hulk of marble mountain beyond.

ⓘ Information

Tourist Office (☑ 0585 84 41 36; www.aptmassacarrara.it; Viale XX Settembre 152a; ⊙ 8.30am-2.30pm summer) Located opposite the stadium. Stop here to pick up a map of Carrara, its marble workshops and out-of-town quarries.

ⓘ Getting There & Away

The nearest station is Carrara-Avenza, between Carrara and Marina di Carrara. Regional train services include the following:

Pietrasanta (€2.60, 15 minutes, at least twice hourly)

Viareggio (€3.60, 30 minutes, twice hourly)

VERSILIAN COAST

One of the most surprising joys of the busy Versilian Coast is a trip inland to Pietrasanta, a hinterland town known for its vibrant arts culture and attractive *centro storico*. Sandy, sun-drenched beaches from Viareggio northwards to Liguria are popular with local holidaymakers and get packed out in summer.

Versilia is a major gateway to the Apuane Alps, Garfagnana and Lunigiana; with roads from the coastal towns snaking their way deep into the heart of the mountains and connecting with small villages and walking tracks.

Pietrasanta

📞 0584 / POP 23.660

Often overlooked by Tuscan travellers, this refined art town sports a bijou historic heart (originally walled) peppered with tiny art galleries, workshops and fashion boutiques – perfect for a day's amble broken only by lunch.

Founded in 1255 by Guiscardo da Pietrasanta, the *podestà* (governing magistrate) of Lucca, Pietrasanta was seen as a prize by Genoa, Lucca, Pisa and Florence, all of which jostled for possession of its marble quarries and bronze foundries. Florence won out and Leo X (Giovanni de' Medici) took control in 1513, putting the town's quarries at the disposal of Michelangelo, who came here in 1518 to source marble for the facade of Florence's San Lorenzo. Artists continue to work here, including internationally lauded Colombian-born sculptor Fernando Botero (b 1932), whose work can be seen here.

Pietrasanta, with its outstanding accommodation, is a great base for exploring the Apuane Alps, Pisa and Viareggio.

👁 Sights & Activities

From Pietrasanta train station on Piazza della Stazione head straight across Piazza Carducci, through the Old City gate and onto Piazza del Duomo, the main square, which doubles as an outdoor gallery for sculptures and other seasonal, generally very large works of art.

Via della Rocca   VIEWPOINT
(Piazza del Duomo) Next to Chiesa di Sant'Agostino, a steep path known as Via della Rocca leads up to the remnants of Pietrasanta's ancient fortifications. The crenellated city walls date from the early 1300s and what remains of Palazzo Guinigi was built as a residence for the *signore* of Lucca, Paolo Guinigi, in 1408. Views of the city and the deep-blue Mediterranean beyond are worth the short climb.

Duomo di San Martino   CATHEDRAL
(📞0584 79 01 77; www.duomodipietrasanta.org; Piazza del Duomo; ⊙hours vary) Grandiose white-marble steps flank Pietrasanta's attractive cathedral, built in the 14th century on the site of an earlier church dating from 1250. Its distinctive 36m-tall, freestanding, red-brick bell tower is actually unfinished; the red brick was intended to have a marble

cladding when designed by Donato Benti in the 15th century. The cathedral interior dates from the 17th century, with fine frescoes by Florentine painter Luigi Ademello (1764–1849) in the dome and nave.

Watch for organ concerts in the cathedral and summertime art exhibitions that occasionally open up the bell tower and the unusual helix-shaped staircase hidden inside – a treat not to be missed – to visitors.

Battistero di Pietrasanta   CHRISTIAN SITE
(Baptistry; 📞0584 79 01 77; www.duomodipietrasanta.org; Via Garibaldi 12; ⊙8am-12.30pm & 3.30-midnight summer, to 7pm winter) Around the corner from the cathedral on pedestrian Via Garibaldi is this atmospheric old-world baptistry. The pair of baptismal fonts – one originally in the cathedral in the 16th century and the other a hexagonal tub (1389) used two centuries before for full immersion baptisms – form a dramatic ensemble in the tiny candlelit space.

Museo dei Bozzetti   MUSEUM
(Maquettes Museum; 📞0584 79 55 00; www.museodeibozzetti.it; Via Sant'Agostino 1; ⊙2-7pm Mon & Sat, 9am-1pm & 2-7pm Tue-Fri, 4-7pm Sun) FREE Inside the convent adjoining Chiesa di Sant'Agostino, this small museum explores the evolution of modern sculpture through 700-odd *bozzetti* (maquettes or models) and plaster moulds of famous sculptures cast or carved in Pietrasanta by some 350 artists from all over the world since the early 20th century.

Don't leave without enquiring about the latest additions to the museum's informal Parco della Scultura (Sculpture Park), an open-air trail leading to 70 public works of art in and around town. Check the museum's website for a complete list of artworks.

🛏 Sleeping & Eating

The historic heart spoils for choice with its many arty addresses spilling onto flowerpot-adorned summer terraces. Pedestrian Via Stagio Stagi, parallel to main street Via Mazzini, has several appealing restaurants.

★Hotel Palagi   HOTEL €€
(📞0584 7 02 49; www.hotelpalagi.it; Piazza Carducci 23; s/d/tr €90/140/150; P❄@) The tender love and care lavished on this outstanding three-star hotel by owner Eliza and her friendly staff seeps out of every last perfectly plumped cushion, potted plant and modern artwork. Thirteen rooms in soft

PRATO

It is off the beaten tourist track, yes. But the historical town of Prato (pop 194,270) is conveniently 'on track' when it comes to savouring this unexplored town on a crowd-free foray by train from Pistoia (€2.60, 15 minutes) or Florence (€2.60, 30 minutes).

Tuscany's second-largest town after Florence, this traditional textile-producing centre has a compact old town girded by near-intact city walls. From Prato's Stazione Porta al Serraglio it is a five-minute walk to Piazza del Duomo and 12th-century Cattedrale di Santo Stefano (☑ 0574 2 62 34; www.museidiocesanidiprato.it/it/filippolippi; ⊘ 9am-3pm Mon-Sat) FREE, with its magnificent frescoes by Fra' Filippo Lippi behind the altar and Agnolo's fresco cycle of the *Legend of the Holy Girdle* (1392–95) in the chapel to the left of the entrance. The unusual protruding pulpit (1428) on the cathedral's Pisan-Romanesque facade was designed by Donatello and Michelozzo to publicly display the *sacra cintola*, a deeply venerated girdle believed to have been given to St Thomas by the Virgin and brought to Prato from Jerusalem after the Second Crusade. Brought out five times a year today, the gossamer-fine wool rope brocaded with gold thread is locked away in the chapel in a gold reliquary with three keys.

Learn more about the Virgin's girdle in the cathedral's Museo dell'Opera del Duomo (☑ 0574 2 93 39; www.diocesiprato.it/museo-dellopera-del-duomo; adult/reduced €5/4; ⊘ 10am-1pm & 2-5pm Mon & Wed-Sat, 2-5pm Sun), accessed via the foot of the cathedral bell tower, and at the nearby Museo di Palazzo Pretorio (☑ 0574 193 49 96; www.palazzopretorio.prato.it; Piazza del Commune; adult/reduced €8/6; ⊘ 10.30am-6.30pm Wed-Mon), an impressive hulk of a history museum. The tourist office (☑ 0574 2 41 12; www.pratoturismo.it; Piazza del Commune; ⊘ 10am-2pm & 3-6pm) is just around the corner from here. Dedicated museum buffs can continue to local textile museum Museo del Tessuto (☑ 0574 61 15 03; www.museodeltessuto.it; Via Puccetti 3; adult/reduced €7/5; ⊘ 10am-3pm Tue-Thu, to 7pm Fri & Sat, 3-7pm Sun), at home in the former Campolmi textile mill. If contemporary art is more your cup of tea, head 3km out of town to the dazzling Centro Per l'Arte Contemporanea Pecci (☑ 0574 53 17; www.centropecci.it; Viale della Repubblica 277; adult/reduced €10/7; ⊘ 10am-8pm Tue-Thu, Sat & Sun, to 11pm Fri), a curvaceous gold piece of contemporary architecture by Netherlands-based Indonesian architect Maurice Nio, with exciting art exhibitions.

Post-sightseeing, excite taste buds with a sweet shopping spree at Antonio Mattei (☑ 0574 2 57 56; www.antoniomattei.com; Via Ricasoli 20; ⊘ 8.30am-7.30pm Tue-Fri, 8.30am-1pm & 3.30-7.30pm Sat, 8.30am-1pm Sun), Prato's famed *biscottificio* where the city's signature *biscotti di Prato* (twice-baked almond biscuits made for dunking in sweet wine) have been made since 1858. To see the bakers in action, visit in the morning. The biscuits (€16.50 per kilogram), not sealed but simply wrapped in waxy royal-blue paper and tied with string, are best eaten within five days.

Round off your Prato visit with a local craft beer at artisanal brewery Mostodolce (☑ 0574 06 36 52; www.facebook.com/mostodolcepo; Via dell'Arco 6; ⊘ 7.30pm-2.30am Thu-Sat, to 2am Sun, Tue & Wed) or a memorable glass of wine and lunch, *apericena* (meal-sized *aperitivo* buffet) or dinner at Le Barrique (☑ 0574 3 01 51; www.lebarriquewinebar.it; Corso Mazzoni 19; ⊘ noon-12.30am; 🐾). This fashionable wine bar, with stylish red-brick interior and excellent Tuscan kitchen, is one of the few places in town to taste *mortadella di Prato*, a heavily seasoned, rose-coloured sausage spiced up with Alchermes liqueur and only produced by two butchers in Prato today.

muted hues are spacious with white marble bathrooms, and the shared romantic rooftop terrace is pure gold. Breakfast includes heaps of freshly cut fruit and homemade cakes.

Albergo Pietrasanta   BOUTIQUE HOTEL €€€
(☑ 0584 79 37 26; www.albergopietrasanta.com; Via Garibaldi 35; d from €350; P ✳ @ 🐾) This

chic 17th-century *palazzo* – a perfect fusion of old and new – is Tuscany's luxury address and deliciously boutique to boot. After a day spent sightseeing, its gorgeous interior courtyard, conservatory and beautifully appointed, classically elegant rooms – each different, with sumptuous marble bathrooms – are clearly designed for relaxing and pampering. The finest have canopy beds resting romantically beneath centuries-old frescoed ceilings.

⭐**Filippo** TUSCAN €€
(📞 0584 7 00 10; https://filippopietrasanta.it; Via Barsanti 45; meals €40-50; ⏱ 12.30-2.30pm & 7.30pm-1am, bar 6pm-midnight) This foodie address never disappoints. From the homemade bread and focaccia brought warm to your table, to the industrial-meets-lime-green-velour interior and contemporary part-glass kitchen, this hybrid lounge-bistro-cocktail bar is sensual and chic. Cuisine mixes tripe-type classics with modern dishes (the deep-fried artichoke with creamed potato and bacon is glorious) and, just like the menu, the wall art by the bar changes each season.

Drinking & Nightlife

Piazza del Duomo, with its many cafes, is the al fresco favourite for a coffee or sundowner. Otherwise head to Filippo, a superb cocktail bar and bistro deliciously representative of fashionable Pietrasanta's boutique drinking and dining scene.

⭐**L'Enoteca Marcucci** WINE BAR
(📞 0584 79 19 62; www.enotecamarcucci.it; Via Garibaldi 40; ⏱ 10am-1pm & 5pm-1am Tue-Sun) Taste fine Tuscan wine on bar stools at high wooden tables or beneath big parasols on the street outside. Whichever you pick, the distinctly funky, arty spirit of Pietrasanta's best-loved *enoteca* enthrals.

🛍 Shopping

Window-shopping – or the real thing – is a highlight of any visit to Pietrasanta. Main strip Via Garibaldi is a quaint pedestrian strip dotted with chic fashion boutiques and stylish art galleries. Highlights guaranteed to tempt include fashion designer Paolo Milani (📞 0584 79 07 29; Via Garibaldi 11; ⏱ 10am-1pm & 3.30-7.30pm Tue-Sun summer, shorter hours winter), whose studio is a riot of bold vibrant prints and a wild mix of textures covering the whole sombre-to-sequin spectrum; multibrand fashion queen and trendsetter Zoe (📞 0424 52 21 25; www.zoeboutique.it/en; Via Garibaldi 29-33 & 44-46; ⏱ 10am-1pm & 4-8pm, shorter hours winter); and concept store Dada (📞 0584 7 04 37; www.dadaconcept.it; Via Garibaldi 39; ⏱ 10am-1pm & 3.30-7.30pm Tue-Sun summer, shorter hours winter).

❶ Getting There & Away

Regional train services include the following:
Florence (with change of train in Pisa; €10.80, 1¾ hours, at least hourly)
Lucca (with change of train in Pisa or Viareggio; €4.60, one hour, every 30 minutes)
Pisa (€4.60, 30 minutes, every 30 minutes)
Viareggio (€2.60, 10 minutes, every 10 minutes)

Viareggio

📞 0584 / POP 62,080

This hugely popular sun-and-sand resort is known as much for its flamboyant Mardi Gras Carnevale, second only to Venice for party spirit, as for its dishevelled line-up of once-grand art nouveau facades along its seafront, which recall the town's 1920s and '30s heyday.

Viareggio's vast golden-sand beachfront is laden with cafes, climbing frames and other kids' amusements and, bar the short public stretch opposite fountain-pierced Piazza Mazzini, is divided into *stabilimenti* (individual lots where you can hire cabins, umbrellas, loungers etc). Only a handful of waterfront buildings retain the ornate stylishness of the 1920s and '30s, notably Puccini's favourite cafe, 1929 Gran Caffè Margherita (p264), and neighbouring wooden Chalet Martini (1899).

◉ Sights & Festivals

Literature lovers might like to pass by Piazza Shelley, the only tangible reference to the romantic poet who drowned in Viareggio; his body was washed up on the beach and his comrade-in-arts, Lord Byron, had him cremated on the spot.

La Citadella di Carnevale MONUMENT
(📞 0584 5 30 48; https://viareggio.ilcarnevale.com/en/luoghi/la-cittadella; Via Santa Maria Goretti; ⏱ 4-7pm Sat & Sun) FREE A couple of kilometres from the seafront is 'Carnival City', aka 16 gargantuan hangars that serve as workshops and garage space for the fantastic floats, crafted with passion by each highly skilled and prized *carrista* (float-builder) for Viareggio's annual carnival. Carnevale history and the art of making *teste in capo* (the giant heads worn in processions) and *mascheroni a piedi* (big walking masks) is explained in the on-site Museo del Carnevale (Carnival Museum). Ask about its hands-on papier-mâché workshops.

VIA FRANCIGENA

The medieval pilgrimage route of Via Francigena connected Canterbury with Rome by way of the rural Lunigiana region in northwestern Tuscany. It was so popular with pilgrims that in the 8th century the Lombard kings built churches, hospices and monasteries offering shelter and protection for pilgrims along its Lunigiana length. This tour, perfectly viable by car or bicycle, explores some of them.

① Pieve di Soprano

From Pontremoli pick up the SS62 and follow it 8km towards Filattiera. In a grassy field on the left, admire the Romanesque Pieve di Sorano (1148), with traditional its *piagnaro* (stone slab) roof and a watchtower to signal its presence as a fortified stop on the pilgrimage route. Beyond the church, up high, is the old hilltop village.

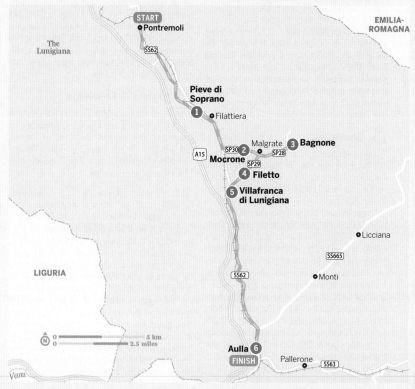

2 to 3 Hours 32km

Great for... Outdoors, History & Culture

Best Time to Go Spring, summer or early autumn

➋ Mocrone

Continue for 2.5km along the SS62 then turn left onto the SP30 (direction Bagnone) and drive 2.3km. In Mocrone enjoy great views of fortified Malgrate teetering on the hillside on your left; break for lunch at Locanda Gavarini (p293), an old-world village inn at the end of the narrowest street you're ever likely to drive along. A rural idyll where the only noise is from birds and the sunrise cry of the village cockerel, this countryside hotel-restaurant is a homage to local Lunigianese culinary tradition.

➌ Bagnone

About 4km after Mocrone, the road brings you into Bagnone, an important trading stop on the Via Francigena and distinctive for its castle, church and eateries. Stretch your legs with a scenic walk above the fiercely gushing river and its dramatic gorges; pick up the easy 15- or 30-minute trail from Piazza Roma and end on main street Via della Repubblica. The final leg across the medieval, stone-paved Ponte Vecchio (Old Bridge) is the stuff of poetry.

➍ Filetto

From Bagnone backtrack towards Mocrone and onwards towards Villafranca, veering slightly left onto the SP29 to reach Filetto.

The walled medieval hamlet derives its name from the Greek word 'filakterion' and goes back in time each August with a fabulous Mercato Medioevale (Medieval Market); locals don medieval garb and set up street stalls selling local wares, demonstrating ancient crafts etc. Park outside its monumental gate and wander through its tiny piazzas and narrow lanes.

➎ Villafranca di Lunigiana

Arriving in Villafranca di Lunigiana 1.5km south, you're on another key stop on the pilgrim route. Set on the Magra river, it is an unassuming place with a small ethnographical museum in an old 15th-century flour mill.

➏ Aulla

End the tour 12km south in Aulla, known for its imposing Fortezza della Brunella (fortress) and abbey founded in AD 884. Originally part of a Benedictine monastery, the abbey served as a shelter to Via Francigena pilgrims on route to Rome for centuries and, to this day, safeguards the remains of St Caprasio, the hermit monk who inspired the spread of monastic life in Provence from the 5th century and subsequently was honoured with the title of patron saint of pilgrims.

Carnevale di Viareggio   CULTURAL
(☑ 0584 58 07 55; http://viareggio.ilcarnevale.com;
☺ Feb & Mar) Viareggio's annual moment of
glory lasts four weeks in February to early
March when the city goes wild during Carnevale – a festival of floats, many featuring
giant satirical effigies of political and other
topical figures. It also includes fireworks
and rampant dusk-to-dawn spirit.

🛏 Sleeping & Eating

The tourist office has a list of (unexceptional) hotels in town; prices rocket during Carnevale and again in July and August when
Italians join the hordes of holiday-makers
on the sandy beach. Lucca and Pietrasanta
are fantastic alternative bases.

La Barchina   FISH & CHIPS €
(☑ 347 7212848; Lungomolo Corraldo del Greco;
meals €8-10; ☺ noon-3pm Mon & Wed-Fri, to 11pm
Sat & Sun summer, shorter hours winter) Join locals standing in line at this small white boat,
moored at the harbour, which cooks up the
morning's catch for lunch. The hot item to
order is *fritto misto,* a mix of squid, prawns
and octopus battered, deep-fried and served
with a huge friendly smile in plastic punnets. Friday cooks up *baccalà* (battered,
salted cod) and veggie lovers are catered for
with punnets of fried mushrooms.
    To find the *barchina* (boat), walk to the
harbour end of seafront promenade Viale
Regina Margherita and duck under the
white iron footbridge crossing the canal.

La Trattoria da Cicero   SEAFOOD €€€
(☑ 0584 39 30 89; Via Michele Coppino 319; meals
€50;   ☺ 12.30-2.30pm & 8-10.30pm Sat-Wed,
8-10.30pm Fri) Ask any local where to find the
freshest and finest fish and seafood in town,
and they'll all direct you to the same address:
this traditional trattoria by the shipyards
with passionate owner Cicero, now in his 70s,
very much at the helm and a fantastic menu
featuring fresh lobster, king prawns, sea bass,
mussels and the season's catch of the day.

ⓘ Information

Tourist Office (☑ 0584 96 22 33; Viale Carducci 10; ☺ 9am-1pm Mon, Fri & Sat, 9am-1pm
& 3-6pm Tue & Thu) Across from the clock on
the waterfront.

ⓘ Getting There & Away

Regional train services include the following:
Florence (€9.90, 1½ hours, at least hourly)

Livorno (€5.70, 45 minutes, 16 daily)
Lucca (€3.60, 17 minutes, every 20 minutes)
Pietrasanta (€2.60, 10 minutes, every 10
minutes)
Pisa (€3.60, 18 minutes, every 20 minutes)
Pontremoli (€7.80, 1¼ hours, hourly)

LUNIGIANA

This landlocked enclave of territory is
bordered to the north and east by the Apennines, to the west by Liguria and to the
south by the Apuane Alps and the Garfagnana. The few tourists who make their way
here tend to be lunching in Pontremoli, a
real off-the-beaten-track gastronomic gem,
or following in the footsteps of medieval pilgrims along the Via Francigena.
    Autumnal visits reward with fresh, in-
tensely scented porcini mushrooms that
sprout under chestnut trees in fecund
woods and hills. Wild herbs cover fields, and
5000 scattered hives produce the region's
famous chestnut and acacia honey. These
fruits of the forest and other regional delicacies – including Zeri lamb, freshly baked
focaccette, crisp and sweet *rotella* apples,
boiled pork shoulder, *caciotta* (a delicate
cow's-milk cheese), *bigliolo* beans, local olive oil and Colli di Luni wines – are reason
enough to visit.

Pontremoli

☑ 0187 / POP 7390
It may be small, but this remote small
town presided over by the impressive bulk
of Castello del Piagnaro (☑ 0187 83 14 39;
www.statuestele.org; adult/reduced €5/4; ☺ 10am-
7.30pm Jun-Sep, 9.30am-5.30pm Oct-May) has a
decidedly grand air – a legacy of its strategic location on the pilgrimage and trading
route of Via Francigena. Its merchants made
fortunes in medieval times, and adorned
the *centro storico* with palaces, piazzas and
graceful stone bridges.
    The *centro storico* is a long sliver
stretching north–south between the Magra
and Verde rivers, which have historically
served as defensive barriers. Meandering
its streets takes you beneath colonnaded arches, through former strongholds of
opposing Guelph and Ghibelline factions,
and past a 17th-century cathedral and an
18th-century theatre.

Locanda Gavarini · HOTEL €

(☑ 0187 49 55 04; www.locandagavarini.it; Via Benedicenti 50, Mocrone; s/d €70/90; ⊙ Mar-Dec; ℗ ✵) This old-world country inn in Mocrone village, 10km south of Pontremoli, at the end of an excruciatingly narrow street, is a rural idyll where the only noise is twittering birds and the sunrise cry of the village cockerel. Five double rooms and a family-friendly apartment enjoy period furniture and plenty of original features (wooden beams, exposed stone and the like).

Its restaurant (meals €25 to €30) is a culinary homage to Lunigianese tradition and the best for miles around.

Trattoria Da Bussè · TRATTORIA €

(☑ 0187 83 13 71; Piazza del Duomo 31; meals €25; ⊙ 7.45-9.45pm Mon-Thu, 12.30-3pm & 7.45-9.45pm Sat & Sun) This Slow Food favourite has been run by the same family since the 1930s, and its original decor is charmingly old world. The regional menu includes *torta d'erbe della Lunigiana* (herb pie cooked over coals in a cast-iron pan lined with chestnut leaves to keep the mixture from sticking) and *testaroli* (thick crepe, cut in diamond shapes, boiled and often served with pesto). No credit cards.

Trattoria Pelliccia · TRATTORIA €€

(☑ 0187 83 05 77; Via Garibaldi 137; meals €30; ⊙ noon-2pm & 7.30-10pm) A wonderful family affair with two generations in the kitchen and Veronica front of house, this staunchly traditional trattoria is an ode to regional cuisine. Start with *testaroli della lunigiana al pesto*, followed by oven-baked lamb.

ⓘ Information

Tourist Office (☑ 0187 83 20 00; www.proloco pontremoli.it; Piazza del Duomo; ⊙ 9am-2pm Mon-Fri, 10am-noon & 3-6pm Sat & Sun)

ⓘ Getting There & Away

Regional train services include the following:
La Spezia (€5.70, 50 minutes, at least hourly)
Pisa (€9.30, 90 minutes, hourly)

Eastern Tuscany

Includes ➡

Arezzo 295
Sansepolcro 303
Casentino Valley 307
Poppi 307
Parco Nazionale delle Foreste Casentinesi ... 309
Val di Chiana 313
Cortona 313

Best Places to Eat

➡ Il Cedro (p308)

➡ Ristorante Da Muzzicone (p312)

➡ Ristorante Al Coccio (p307)

➡ Ristorante La Nena (p302)

➡ Antica Osteria Agania (p301)

Best Places to Stay

➡ Villa Fontelunga (p301)

➡ Borgo Corsignano (p308)

➡ Sugar Rooms (p300)

➡ Il Contado (p308)

➡ Dolce Rosa (p306)

Why Go?

The eastern edge of Tuscany is beloved by both Italian and international film directors, who have immortalised its landscape, hilltop towns and oft-quirky characters in several critically acclaimed and visually splendid films. Despite this, the region remains largely bereft of foreign tourists (Cortona is a notable exception) and so offers uncrowded trails and destinations for those savvy enough to explore here. Attractions are many and varied: spectacular mountain scenery, hidden hermitages and walks in the Casentino; magnificent art and architecture in the medieval destinations of Arezzo, Sansepolcro and Cortona; one of Italy's most significant Catholic pilgrimage sites, La Verna; and Tuscany's best *bistecca alla fiorentina* (T-bone steak) in the Val di Chiana. Here, your travels may be solitary – particularly in the low season – but they'll always be rewarding.

Road Distances Chart

	Assisi	Arezzo	Cortona	Sansepolcro
Arezzo	94			
Cortona	65	29		
Sansepolcro	76	38	52	
Poppi	132	36	62	71

AREZZO

☑ 0575 / POP 99,419

Arezzo may not be a Tuscan centrefold, but those parts of its historic centre that survived merciless WWII bombings are as compelling as any destination in the region – the city's central square is as beautiful as it appears in Roberto Benigni's classic film *La vita è bella* (Life is Beautiful; 1997).

Once an important Etruscan trading post, Arezzo was later absorbed into the Roman Empire. A free republic as early as the 10th century, it supported the Ghibelline cause in the violent battles between pope and emperor and was eventually subjugated by Florence in 1384.

Today the city is known for its churches, museums and fabulously sloping Piazza Grande, across which a huge antiques fair spills each month. Come dusk, Arentini (locals of Arezzo) spill along the length of shop-clad Corso Italia for the ritual late-afternoon *passeggiata* (stroll).

◉ Sights

A combined ticket (adult/reduced €12/8) covers admission to Cappella Bacci, Museo Archeologico Nazionale, Museo di Casa Vasari and Museo Nazionale d'Arte Medievale e Moderna. It's valid for two days and can be purchased at each museum.

★ Cappella Bacci   CHURCH

(☑ 0575 35 27 27; www.pierodellafrancesca.it; Piazza San Francesco; adult/reduced €8/5; ☺ 9am-6pm Mon-Fri, to 5.30pm Sat, 1-5.30pm Sun, extended hours summer) This chapel, in the apse of 14th-century Basilica di San Francesco, safeguards one of Italian art's greatest works: Piero della Francesca's fresco cycle of the *Legend of the True Cross*. Painted between 1452 and 1466, it relates the story of the cross on which Christ was crucified. Only 30 people are allowed in every half hour, making advance booking (by telephone or email) essential in high season. The ticket office is down the stairs by the basilica's entrance.

This medieval legend is as entertaining as it is inconceivable. The illustrations follow the story of the tree that Seth plants on the grave of his father, Adam, and from which the True Cross is made. One scene shows the long-lost cross being rediscovered by Helena, mother of the emperor Constantine; behind her, the city of Jerusalem is pictured as a medieval view of Arezzo. Other scenes show the victory of Heraclius over the Persian king Khosrau, who had been accused of stealing the cross; Constantine sleeping in a tent on the eve of his battle with Maxentius (note Piero's masterful depiction of the dawn light); and Constantine carrying the cross into battle.

THREE PERFECT DAYS IN EASTERN TUSCANY

Day One

Tuscany's most famous family of sculptors, the Della Robbias, took ceramics way beyond teacups in the 15th century, creating magnificent devotional sculptures for churches throughout Tuscany. Devote your first day to visiting the medieval monasteries at Camaldoli (p312) and Santuario della Verna (p309) in the Parco Nazionale delle Foreste Casentinesi (p309), to admire masterpieces in glazed terracotta by the family's most famous member, Andrea (1435–1525).

Day Two

On day two, explore the historic streets and piazzas in Arezzo where Roberto Benigni filmed *La vita è bella* (Life is Beautiful; 1997). Pop into the Duomo (p300) and Chiesa di Santa Maria della Pieve (p298); see where Arezzo-born painter, architect and art historian Vasari lived and worked; and pay homage to Piero della Francesca's genius in Basilica di San Francesco's Cappella Bacci, where Anthony Minghella shot the most memorable scene of *The English Patient* (1996).

Day Three

On day three, dip into Val di Chiana (p313), well placed between Arezzo and Cortona (p313) and also en route to central Tuscany. Home to apple orchards, olive groves and lush pastures where creamy-white Chianina cattle graze, the valley invites off-the-beaten-track meanderings. Explore hilltop town Castiglion Fiorentino (p312), allowing time for a meaty lunch stop at Ristorante Da Muzzicone (p312).

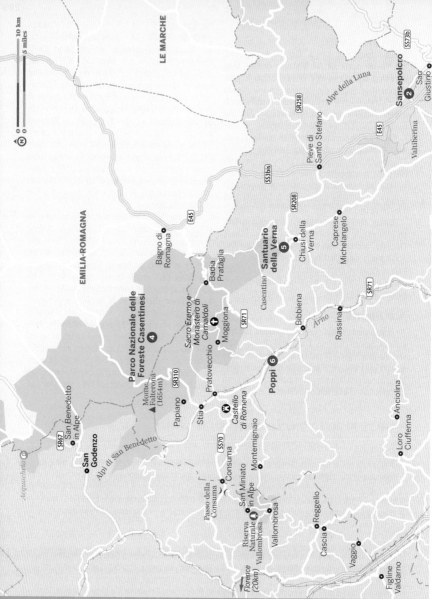

Eastern Tuscany Highlights

1 Arezzo (p295)
Marvelling at the frescoes in the Capella Bacci and visiting the famed antiques fair held in magnificent Piazza Grande.

2 Museo Civico (p303) Admiring the work of Renaissance painter Piero della Francesca in Sansepolcro.

3 Cortona (p313) Viewing the rich collections of the diocesan and archeological museums in this spectacularly sited hilltop town.

4 Parco Nazionale delle Foreste Casentinesi (p309) Communing with nature in this heavily forested, wildlife-rich national park.

LE MARCHE

EMILIA-ROMAGNA

Acquacheta

SR67

San Benedetto in Alpe

San Godenzo

Alpi di San Benedetto

Alpi di San Benedetto

Monte Falterona (1654m)

Papiano

SR310

Bagno di Romagna

E45

Parco Nazionale delle Foreste Casentinesi

4

Sacro Eremo e Monastero di Camaldoli

Badia Prataglia

SS3bis

Moggiona

SR71

Alpe della Luna

Pieve di Santo Stefano

Valtiberina

E45

SR258

Sansepolcro

2

San Giustino

SS73b

SS73b

Stia

Pratovecchio

Castello di Romena

Consuma

SS70

Montemignaio

Passo della Consuma

San Miniato in Alpe

Riserva Naturale Vallombrosa

Vallombrosa

Florence (20km)

Casentino

Casentino

SR208

Santuario della Verna

5

Chiusi della Verna

Caprese Michelangelo

Bibbiena

Arno

Poppi

6

Rassina

SR71

Loro Ciuffenna

Anciolina

Reggello

Cascia

Vaggio

Figline Valdarno

10 km
5 miles

N

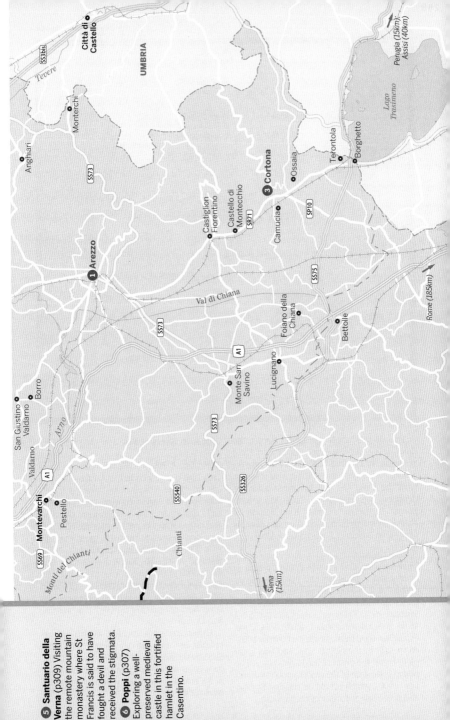

5 Santuario della Verna (p309) Visiting the remote mountain monastery where St Francis is said to have fought a devil and received the stigmata.

6 Poppi (p307) Exploring a well-preserved medieval castle in this fortified hamlet in the Casentino.

1 Arezzo

3 Cortona

UMBRIA

Città di Castello

Monterchi

Anghiari

Monterchi

SS3bis

Tevere

SS73

Castiglion Fiorentino

Castello di Montecchio

SR71

Camucia

Ossaia

Terontola

Borghetto

SP10

Lago Trasimeno

Perugia (15km); Assisi (40km)

Val di Chiana

SS73

SS75

A1

Foiano della Chiana

Bettolle

Monte San Savino

Lucignano

Rome (185km)

San Giustino Valdarno

Borro

Valdarno

Arno

SS73

SS326

Montevarchi

Pestello

SS69

Monti del Chianti

SS540

Chianti

Siena (15km)

Arezzo

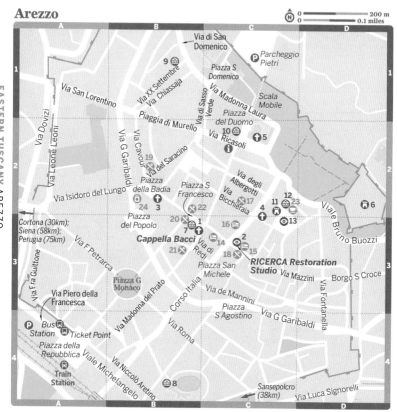

Two of the best-loved scenes depict the meeting of the Queen of Sheba and King Solomon. In the first half she is kneeling on a bridge over the Siloam River and meeting with the king; she and her attendants are depicted wearing rich Renaissance-style gowns. In the second half, King Solomon's palace seems to be modelled on the designs of notable architect Leon Battista Alberti.

Piazza Grande
PIAZZA

This lopsided and steeply sloping piazza is overlooked at its upper end by the porticoes of the **Palazzo delle Logge Vasariane**, completed in 1573. Construction of the churchlike **Palazzo della Fraternità dei Laici** (☑ 0575 2 46 94; www.fraternitadeilaici.it; adult/child €5/free; ⊗10.30am-6pm) in the northwest corner started in 1375 in the Gothic style and was completed after the onset of the Renaissance. The piazza is the hub of the city's famous antiques fair (p300), which is held on the first Sunday and preceding Saturday of each month.

Chiesa di Santa Maria della Pieve
CHURCH

(Corso Italia 7; ⊗8am-12.30pm & 3-6.30pm) **FREE**
This 12th-century church – Arezzo's oldest – has an exotic Romanesque arcaded facade adorned with carved columns, each individually decorated. Above the central doorway are 13th-century carved reliefs called *Cyclo dei Mesi* representing each month of the year. The plain interior's highlight – being restored at the RICERCA Restoration Studio (p300) at the time of research – is Pietro Lorenzetti's polyptych *Madonna and Saints* (1320–24). Below the altar is a 14th-century silver bust reliquary of the city's patron saint, San Donato.

Other treasures include a 13th-century crucifix by Margarito di Arezzo (left of the altar by the door to the sacristy) and a fresco on a column (across from the sacristy door) of Sts Francesco and Domenico by Andrea di Nerio (1331–69).

Arezzo

◎ Top Sights
1 Cappella Bacci........................ B3
2 RICERCA Restoration Studio............... C3

◎ Sights
3 Badia delle Sante Flora e Lucilla.......... B2
4 Chiesa di Santa Maria della Pieve........ C2
5 Duomo di Arezzo....................... C2
6 Fortezza Medicea D2
7 Galleria Comunale D'Arte
    Contemporanea B3
8 Museo Archeologico Nazionale
    'Gaio Cilnio Mecenate'..................... B4
9 Museo di Casa Vasari........................B1
10 Museo Diocesano di Arte Sacra C2
11 Palazzo della Fraternità dei Laici........... C2
12 Palazzo delle Logge Vasariane C2
13 Piazza Grande C3

◎ Sleeping
14 Graziella Patio Hotel C3
15 Palazzo dei Bostoli C3
16 Sugar Rooms C3

◎ Eating
17 Aliciati C2
18 Antica Osteria Agania.......................C3
19 L'Antica Bottega di Primo B2
20 Le Chiavi d'Oro................................B3
21 Officine Panini.................................B3
22 Sunflower B2

◎ Drinking & Nightlife
23 Caffè Vasari....................................C2
No Sugar Please ....(see 16)

◎ Shopping
24 Mercato Logge del Grano.....................B2

Museo Archeologico Nazionale 'Gaio Cilnio Mecenate' MUSEUM

(Gaius Cilnius Maecenas Archeological Museum; ☑0575 2 08 82; www.facebook.com/archeologicoarezzo; Via Margaritone 10; adult/reduced €6/3; ☺8.30am-7.30pm Mon-Sat) Overlooking the remains of a Roman amphitheatre that once seated up to 10,000 spectators, this museum – named after Gaius Maecenas (68–8 BC), a patron of the arts and trusted advisor to Roman Emperor Augustus – exhibits Etruscan and Roman artefacts in a 14th-century convent building. The highlight is the *Cratere di Euphronios,* a 6th-century-BC Etruscan vase decorated with vivid scenes showing Hercules in battle.

Also of note is an exquisite tiny portrait of a bearded man from the second half of the 3rd century AD that was executed in chrysography, a method in which a fine sheet of gold is engraved then encased between two glass panes.

The museum is open occasionally on Sundays; call ahead to confirm dates and times.

Galleria Comunale D'Arte Contemporanea GALLERY

(www.facebook.com/coloartesarezzo; Piazza San Francesco 4; ☺2-6pm Tue & Wed, 10am-6pm Thu, Fri & Sun, 10am-6.30pm Sat) FREE Showcasing the work of contemporary visual artists – many based in the Arezzo region – this multifloor art gallery in a building next to the Basilica di San Francesco embraces innovation and is more impressive than many similar institutions in Tuscany.

Badia delle Sante Flora e Lucilla ABBEY

(Piazza della Badia 3; ☺8am-noon & 4-7pm Mon-Sat, 7.15-9.15am & 10.15am-12.30pm Sun) This 13th-century abbey was rebuilt to a design by Vasari in the 16th century, and its austerely elegant Romanesque exterior stands in extreme contrast to the inappropriately oversized altar inside, which Vasari designed as his family tomb. His too-clever-by-half trompe-l'œil feature over the altar, which simulates a dome, is equally discordant. Vasari's recently restored painting *La Pala Albergotti* (c 1567), which depicts the Assumption and coronation of the Virgin with Saints Donato and Francesco, is to the right as you enter.

Museo Diocesano di Arte Sacra MUSEUM

(MuDAS; ☑0575 402 72 68; www.diocesiarezzo.it; Piazza del Duomo 1; adult/reduced €3/2; ☺10am-2pm Sat & Sun) Located inside a stunning 13th-century *palazzo* where the bishop of Arezzo lived from 1256, this museum exhibits 12th- to 16th-century works of sacred art originally displayed in churches now destroyed or shut. At the top of the grandiose staircase, on the 1st floor, a series of beautifully frescoed rooms showcase the art collections of various resident bishops over the centuries.

Museo di Casa Vasari MUSEUM

(Vasari House Museum; ☑0575 29 90 71; www.museistataliarezzo.it/museo-casa-vasari; Via XX Settembre 55; adult/reduced €4/2; ☺8.30am-7.30pm Mon & Wed-Sat, to 1.30pm Sun) Built and sumptuously decorated by Arezzo-born painter,

DON'T MISS

BEHIND THE SCENES

Art lovers will adore visiting RICERCA Restoration Studio (☑ 0575 2 86 70, 333 2851179; www.ricercarestauro.word press.com; Via Mazzini 1; by donation; ⊘ by appointment). The base of Art Angels Arezzo (www.artangelsarezzo.org), a group of professional art historians and conservators dedicated to restoring important Arentini works of art, this conservation laboratory welcomes visitors interested in learning about restoration techniques and seeing the painstaking process underway. Past projects have included Vasari's *La Pala Albergotti* from the Badia; when we visited, Pietro Lorenzetti's exquisite *Madonna and Saints* altarpiece from the Pieve was being returned to its original glory.

architect and art historian Giorgio Vasari (1511–74), this museum is where Vasari lived and worked, and where the original manuscript of his *Lives of the Most Excellent Painters, Sculptors and Architects* (1550) – still in print under the title *The Lives of the Artists* – is kept. End on the bijou, Renaissance-style roof garden with flower beds, box hedges and a fountain in its centre. To access the museum, ring the bell.

The most important room in this Mannerist residence is the Sala della Virtu (Room of Virtue), which Vasari decorated in 1548 while writing *Lives*. It features episodes in the lives of the most famous painters of antiquity.

Vasari's contemporaries are celebrated in the Camera della Fama con le Quattro Arti (Room of Fame and the Four Arts), where the seven portraits include Michelangelo, Andrea del Sarto and – in a display of hubris – Vasari himself.

Duomo di Arezzo   CATHEDRAL
(Cattedrale di SS Donato e Pietro; Piazza del Duomo; ⊘ 7am-12.30pm & 3-6.30pm) **FREE** Construction of Arezzo's cathedral started in the 13th century, but wasn't completed until 1511. In the northeast corner, next to the vestry door left of the intricately carved main altar, is Piero della Francesca's fresco of *Mary Magdalene* (c 1459). Also notable are five glazed terracottas by Andrea della Robbia and his studio in the Cappella della Madonna del Conforto.

Behind the cathedral is the pentagonal Fortezza Medicea (Viale Bruno Buozzi) (1560) atop the crest of one of Arezzo's two hills – the *duomo* was built on the crest of the other.

🎎 Festivals & Events

Fiera Antiquaria di Arezzo   FAIR
(Arezzo Antique Fair; www.fieraantiquaria.org; ⊘ 9am-7pm) Tuscany's most famous antiques fair is held in Piazza Grande (p298) on the first Sunday and preceding Saturday of every month.

Giostra del Saracino   CULTURAL
(Joust of the Saracino; www.giostradelsaracinoarez zo.it; tickets standing €10, seated €30-50; ⊘ Jun & Sep) This medieval jousting competition, held on Piazza Grande (p298) on the third or fourth Saturday of June at night and the first Sunday of September during the day, sees each of the city's four *quartieri* (quarters) put forward a team of 'knights'. Tickets are available from an office in Via della Bicchieraia one week prior to the event.

🛏️ Sleeping

Palazzo dei Bostoli   B&B €
(☑ 334 1490558; www.palazzobostoli.it; Via Mazzini 1; s €60, d €70-110; ❄ 🛜) This well-located option offers three simple but comfortable rooms on the 2nd floor of a 13th-century *palazzo* near Piazza Grande (p298); the cheapest has an external (albeit private) bathroom. Breakfast – a coffee and a *cornetto* (croissant) – is served at a bar on nearby Corso Italia.

Graziella Patio Hotel   BOUTIQUE HOTEL €€
(☑ 0575 40 19 62; www.hotelpatio.it; Via Cavour 23; d €160-180, ste €210-285; ❄ @ 🛜) Each of the 10 rooms at this central hotel has decor inspired by Bruce Chatwin's travel books. Pink-kissed Arkady is the 'Australia room', Fillide exudes a distinctly Moroccan air and Cobra Verde is a green Amazon-inspired loft. Every room has a Macbook for guests to go online; wi-fi access on smartphones is pretty well nonexistent.

⭐ Sugar Rooms   BOUTIQUE HOTEL €€€
(☑ 0575 35 46 31; www.sugar.it; Corso Italia 60; r/ste €200/250; ❄ 🛜) Occupying the floors above the designer clothing retailer of the same name, this recently opened boutique B&B in a 15th-century *palazzo* (mansion) is the town's best accommodation option. Arezzo-based architectural firm Baciocchi

Associates has given the 12 rooms a minimalist yet theatrical makeover that melds designer furniture, sleek bathroom fittings and original 18th-century frescoes. The best rooms overlook the rear garden.

Breakfast is served in Sugar's chic courtyard cafe, No Sugar Please (☺4-8pm Mon, 10am-8pm Tue-Sat).

★ Villa Fontelunga   BOUTIQUE HOTEL €€€
(☑0575 66 04 10; www.fontelunga.com; Via Cunicchio 5, Foiano della Chiana; d €240-410, villa per week €2730-4830; ☺mid-Mar–Oct; P ✽ 🛜 ≋) Gorgeous is the only word to use when describing this 19th-century villa in Foiano della Chiana, 35km southwest of Arezzo. Its nine rooms are the perfect balance of traditional Tuscan elegance and jet-set pizzazz. Leisure facilities include a tennis court, gorgeous pool and mountain-bike use. Dinner (€39 including wine) is offered twice weekly.

🍴 Eating & Drinking

Dining in Arezzo is a real treat, with a fantastic choice of restaurants offering top-notch traditional and modern Tuscan cuisine. In warm weather, the dining action spills out onto the pavements.

★ Antica Osteria Agania   TUSCAN €
(☑0575 29 53 81; www.agania.com; Via Mazzini 10; meals €20; ☺noon-3pm & 6-10.30pm Tue-Sun) Operated by the Ludovichi family since 1905,

Agania serves the type of diehard traditional fare that remains the cornerstone of Tuscan dining. Specialities include sensational antipasti (with lots of vegetarian options), rustic soups, homemade pasta and *secondi* ranging from *lumache* (snails) to *grifi* (lambs' cheeks) with polenta, *baccalà* (cod) with chickpeas, and sausages with beans.

L'Antica Bottega di Primo   SANDWICHES €
(☑0575 04 01 24; https://it-it.facebook.com/Bottegadiprimo; Via Cavour 92; panini €2.50-4; ☺7.30am-9pm Mon-Thu, to 11pm Fri-Sun; 🛜) A delectable array of local cheese and cured meats awaits at this popular *alimentari* (grocery store), which fills fresh *panini* (sandwiches) and foccacias to order and also sells delicious freshly baked biscuits and pastries. Eat in or take away.

Officine Panini   SANDWICHES €
(☑0575 08 10 01; www.facebook.com/officinepaninigourmet; 2 Via della Madonna del Prato; panini €10-14; ☺12.30-3pm & 7-11pm Tue-Sat, 12.30-3pm Sun; ✒) Tucked behind the Cappella Bacci (p295), this gourmet *panini* bar has Zen-styled decor and a choice of sandwiches filled with fish, cheese, meats (pork, rabbit), fresh tuna tataki or prawns. Vegans will enjoy the 'Green Vegg', chickpea and spirulina bread filled with pea hummus, chicory and almond-milk ricotta. Tables are limited and communal.

WORTH A TRIP

DAY TRIP: ASSISI

Thanks to St Francis, who was born here in 1182, the medieval hilltop town of Assisi in the neighbouring region of Umbria is a major destination for millions of pilgrims. Its major draw is its Basilica di San Francesco (www.sanfrancescoassisi.org; Piazza Superiore di San Francesco; ☺basilica superiore 8.30am-6.50pm, basilica inferiore 6am-6.50pm summer, shorter hours winter) FREE comprising two churches filled with magnificent Renaissance art. The tomb of St Francis lies in the crypt.

The basilica has its own information office (☑075 819 00 84; ☺9am-5.30pm Mon-Sat winter, to 6pm summer), opposite the entrance to the lower church, where you pick up an audio guide or join a guided tour led by a resident Franciscan friar; book in advance by email, or contact the tourist office (☑075 813 86 80; www.visit-assisi.it; Piazza del Comune 10; ☺9am-7pm).

For lunch, consider seasonal Umbrian cuisine peppered with Med-Asian touches at Osteria La Piazzetta dell'Erba (☑075 81 53 52; www.osterialapiazzetta.it; Via San Gabriele dell'Addolorata 15a; meals €30-35; ☺12.30-2.30pm & 7.30-10pm Tue-Sun; 🛜) or local cheese and salumi platters with lovingly curated local wines at Bibenda Assisi (☑075 815 51 76; www.bibendaassisi.it; Vicolo Nepis 9; wines by the glass from €3.50; ☺11.30am-11pm Wed-Mon; 🛜).

Regular trains connect Assisi with Arezzo (€8.70, 1½ hours) and Florence (€15.80, 2½ hours). Find parking outside the old town on Piazza Giovanni Paolo II.

ANGHIARI: A MEDIEVAL PIT STOP

The unspoilt medieval hill town of Anghiari (population 5636) looms over the plain where the army of the Italian League, spearheaded by the Republic of Florence, famously defeated the numerically superior forces of Milan on 29 June 1440. Enclosed by massive walls, it is an easy detour for those travelling between Arezzo and Sansepolcro. The walls encircle steep cobbled lanes lined by houses, shops, churches including the **Chiesa di San Agostino** (Via Giuseppe Garibaldi 47) `FREE` with its unusual Matteo di Giovanni triptych, the **Museo della Battaglia e di Anghiari** (☑ 0575 78 70 23; www.battaglia.anghiari. it; Piazza Mameli 1-2; adult/reduced €4/3; ☺ 9.30am-1pm & 2.30-6.30pm Apr-Oct, to 5.30pm Nov-Mar) with its exhibits about the battle, and the **Museo Statale di Palazzo Taglieschi** (☑ 0575 78 80 01; www.polomusealetoscana.beniculturali.it; Piazza Mameli 16; adult/reduced €4/2; ☺ 9am-5.15pm Tue-Thu, 10am-6.15pm Fri-Sun), which has a modest collection of 15th- and 16th-century sculptures and paintings.

Much-loved **Ristorante La Nena** (☑ 0575 78 94 91; www.ristorantenena.it; Corso Giacomo Matteotti 10-14; meals €40; ☺ noon-2.30pm & 7.30-10pm Tue-Sun) is the old-world address for a diehard traditional Tuscan lunch: *zuppa di pane* (bread soup), seasonal mushrooms and truffles, and a range of homemade pastas are the mouth-watering house specialities. Reservations are recommended, especially for Sunday lunch.

Sunflower   GELATO €

(☑ 338 4161464; Piazza San Francesco 11; gelato €2-4, frozen yogurt €1.50-3; ☺ noon-10pm Thu & Sun-Tue, noon-midnight Fri & Sat Oct-May, to 1am Jun-Sep; ✍) No artificial flavourings, emulsifiers, preservatives or food dyes are used in the creation of the gelato and frozen yogurt here, and this, combined with the budget prices, makes it the most popular *gelateria* in town.

★**Aliciati**   ITALIAN €€

(☑ 0575 2 72 41; www.aliciati.com; Via Bicchieraia 16-18; meals €38; ☺ 12.30-2.30pm & 7.30-10pm Tue-Sun) At his eponymous restaurant, chef Giovanni Aliciati reimagines classic Italian dishes using top-quality ingredients and incorporating French and Spanish techniques and flavours. The refined results are as good to taste as they are to look at. The interior of the restaurant, which is near Piazza Grande (p298), is equally impressive, with contemporary glass light fittings throwing golden light on stone walls.

Le Chiavi d'Oro   ITALIAN €€

(☑ 0575 40 33 13; www.ristorantelechiavidoro.it; Piazza San Francesco 7; meals €45; ☺ 12.30-2.30pm & 7.30-10.30pm Tue-Sat, 12.30-2.30pm Sun) Contemporary Italian cooking is on offer at this game-changing restaurant in central Arezzo. Design lovers are wooed by the minimalist interior with part-resin, part-parquet floor and stylish 1960s Danish chairs, while foodies are quickly won over by the menu, which balances seafood and meat choices and is

strictly seasonal. There are few options for vegetarians, though.

Caffè Vasari   CAFE

(☑ 0575 04 36 97; Piazza Grande 15; ☺ 7.30am-9pm summer, 8.30am-6pm winter) Bathed in Tuscan sunrays from dawn to dusk, this cafe is the perfect spot for lapping up the ancient elegance and beauty of Piazza Grande (p298) over a coffee or *aperitivo* (predinner drink). Find it enviably squirrelled beneath the cinematic porticoes of Palazzo delle Logge Vasariane (p298).

🛍 Shopping

★**Mercato Logge del Grano**   FOOD & DRINKS

(☑ 0575 2 06 46; www.facebook.com/loggedel grano; Piazzetta a delle Loggia del Grano; ☺ 9am-2.30pm & 4.30-8pm Mon-Sat) A treasure trove of locally grown and produced foodstuffs, this organic market sells a wonderful variety of fresh meat, fruit and vegetables, olive oil, dried pasta and legumes, bread, wine and dairy products including milk and cheese. It's a sensational resource for self-caterers. Free tastings are offered every Saturday and also at special openings on the first Sunday of each month.

ℹ Information

The city's **tourist office** (Centro Accoglienza Turistica; ☑ 0575 40 19 45; www.arezzointuscany. it; Piazza della Libertà; ☺ 10am-4pm) is housed in the Palazzo Comunale (Town Hall), diagonally opposite the *duomo*.

The local association of tourist guides, **Centro Guide Arezzo e Provincia** (☑ 0575 40 33 19; www.centroguidearezzo.it), has members fluent in English, French, German, Spanish and Russian.

❶ Getting There & Away

BUS

Buses operated by **Tiemme** (www.tiemmespa.it) travel to/from Siena (€7.60, 1½ hours, eight daily Monday to Saturday, four Sunday), Sansepolcro (€5.60, one hour, hourly Monday to Saturday, two Sunday), Anghiari (€4.50, 45 minutes, hourly Monday to Saturday, two Sunday) and Cortona (€4.50, 65 minutes, 10 daily Monday to Saturday). Buy tickets from the **ticket point** (Via Piero della Francesca 1; ☺ 6.10am-8pm Mon-Sat year-round, 6.30am-noon Sun summer, 8am-12.30pm Sun winter) to the left as you exit the train station; buses leave from the **bus bay** (Via Piero della Francesca) opposite.

CAR & MOTORCYCLE

To drive here from Florence, take the A1; the SS73 heads west to Siena. Parking at the train station costs €1.30/8 per hour/day, but the best parking option is Parcheggio Pietro (€0.70/5 per hour/day), which is connected to Piazza Duomo by a free *scala mobile* (escalator).

TRAIN

Arezzo is on the Florence–Rome train line, and there are frequent services to Florence (*regionale* €8.60, 45 minutes to 1½ hours) and Rome (Intercity €27.50, 2¼ hours; *regionale* €15.15, 2¾ hours) from the train station in Piazza della Repubblica on the southwest edge of the city centre. There are also twice-hourly regional trains to Camucia-Cortona (€3.60, 20 minutes).

SANSEPOLCRO

☑ 0575 / POP 15,876

This hidden gem is a town that truly deserves that description. Dating from the year 1000, Sansepolcro (called 'Borgo' by locals) reached its current size in the 15th century and was walled in the 16th century. Its historic centre is littered with *palazzi* (mansions) and churches squirrelling away Renaissance works of art or bejewelled with exquisite terracotta Andrea della Robbia medallions. Spend a day wandering from dimly lit church to church, following in the footsteps of Sansepolcro's greatest son, Renaissance artist Piero della Francesca.

◉ Sights

★ Museo Civico   MUSEUM

(☑ 0575 73 22 18; www.museocivicosansepolcro.it; Via Niccolò Aggiunti 65; adult/reduced €10/8.50, with Casa di Piero della Francesca €11/9.50; ☺ 10am-1.30pm & 2.30-6.40pm mid-Jun–mid-Sep, reduced hours est of year) The town's flagship museum is home to a small but top-notch collection of artworks, including two Piero della Francesca masterpieces – *Resurrection* (1458–74) and the *Madonna della Misericordia* (Madonna of Mercy; 1445–56) polyptych – as well as two fresco fragments portraying *San Ludovico* (Saint Ludovic; 1460) and *San Giuliano* (Saint Julian; 1460). Also of note are works from the studio of Andrea della Robbia, including a beautiful tondo (circular sculpture) known as the *Virgin and Child with Manetti Coat of Arms* (1503).

Aboca Museum   MUSEUM

(☑ 0575 73 35 89; www.abocamuseum.it; Via Niccolò Aggiunti 75; adult/reduced €8/4; ☺ 10am-1pm & 3-7pm Apr-Sep, 10am-1pm & 2.30-6pm Tue-Sun Oct-Mar) When you tire of magnificent art and churches, take a break in this medicinal plant museum inside 18th-century Palazzo Bourbon del Monte. Exhibits provide a fascinating insight into our relationship with herbs from prehistoric times to the present, with rooms dedicated to mortars, weighing scales, glassware and antique books chronicling ancient remedies. In the Poison Cellar, see how deadly ingredients were skillfully crafted into medicinal remedies.

Casa di Piero della Francesca   MUSEUM

(☑ 0575 74 04 11; www.facebook.com/LaCasa diPierodellaFrancesca; Via Niccolò Aggiunti 71; adult/reduced €5/3, with Museo Civico €11/9.50;

❶ **SANSEPOLCRO DISCOUNTS**
....

A cumulative ticket (adult/reduced/under yr 18 €11/9.50/5) gives entrance to both the Museo Civico and the Casa di Piero della Francesca and is available at both venues.

The Valtiberina Casentino Card (www.valtiberinacasentinocard.it, €19, valid 3 days) gives admission to the Museo Civico, Casa di Piero della Francesca, Aboca Museum and Museo Madonna del Parto, as well as many others in the region. Purchase it online or at the tourist office (p307) in Sansepolcro.

EASTERN TUSCANY SANSEPOLCRO

1. Eremo Francescano Le Celle (p313), Cortona 2. Great Cloister, Abbazia di Monte Oliveto Maggiore (p192), near Siena 3. Basilica di San Francesco (p301), Assisi 4. Santuario della Verna (p309), Tuscany

Magnificent Monasteries

Consider yourself warned: after visiting these medieval monasteries in Tuscany and nearby Umbria, you may well find yourself entertaining serious thoughts about leaving your fast-paced urban existence to embrace the contemplative life.

Basilica di San Francesco, Assisi

Every year, more than five million pilgrims make their way to the medieval hilltop town of Assisi, St Francis' birthplace in the Umbria region, to visit the huge basilica (p301) and monastery that is dedicated to his legacy. Don't miss his ornamental tomb in the basilica crypt.

Santuario della Verna

St Francis of Assisi is said to have received the stigmata at this spectacularly located monastery (p309) on the southeastern edge of the Casentino. Pilgrims flock here to worship in the Cappella delle Stimmate and to admire the Andrea della Robbia artworks in the church.

Sacro Eremo e Monastero di Camaldoli

Deep in the forest of the Casentino, amid a landscape that has changed little for centuries, lies this Benedictine monastery and hermitage (p312). Treasures include paintings by Vasari and Bronzino, as well as one of Andrea della Robbia's greatest terracotta sculptures.

Abbazia di Monte Oliveto Maggiore

The Benedictine monks living in this medieval abbey (p192) southeast of Siena tend the vineyard and olive grove, study in one of Italy's most important medieval libraries and walk through a cloister frescoed by Luca Signorelli and Il Sodoma.

Eremo Francescano Le Celle

A babbling stream, old stone bridge and terraces of olive trees contribute to the fairy-tale feel of this picturesque Franciscan hermitage (p313) just outside Cortona.

PIERO DELLA FRANCESCA

Though many details about his life are hazy, it is believed that the great Renaissance painter Piero della Francesca was born around 1420 in Sansepolcro and died there in 1492. Trained as a painter from the age of 15, his distinctive use of perspective, mastery of light and skilful synthesis of form and colour set him apart from his artistic contemporaries, and the serene grace of his figures remains unsurpassed to this day. In his book *The Lives of the Artists*, Piero's fellow Tuscan Giorgio Vasari called him the 'best geometrician of his time' and lamented the fact that so few of his works were preserved for posterity, leading to him being 'robbed of the honour that [was] due to his labours'.

Piero's most famous works are the *Legend of the True Cross* in Arezzo's Cappella Bacci (p295), his *Resurrection* in Sansepolcro's Museo Civico (p303) and his panel featuring *Federico da Montefeltro and Battista Sforza, the Duke and Duchess of Urbino* in Florence's Uffizi (p70). But he is perhaps most fondly remembered for his luminous *Madonna del Parto* showcased in Museo Madonna del Parto (Pregnant Madonna Museum; ☑ 0575 7 07 13; www.madonnadelparto.it; Via della Reglia 1; adult/reduced €6.50/5; ⊘ 9am-1pm & 2-7pm Apr-Oct, to 5pm Wed-Mon Nov-Mar) in Monterchi, a village in the remote Tiber Valley between Sansepolcro (15km north) and Arezzo (28km west). During the time Piero lived in Sansepolcro, the painter had a home studio at Via Niccolò Aggiunti 71 – this now houses the Casa di Piero della Francesca (p303) museum where multimedia displays profile the great man's life and work.

⊘ 10am-12.30pm & 3-5pm) Sansepolcro's most famous son, Renaissance painter Piero della Francesca, lived and worked at this modest 15th-century house in central Sansepolcro. Between lengthy visits to Italian courts, he slowly restored the house in a Renaissance style. These days, it houses informative multimedia exhibits about his life and work.

Cattedrale di San Giovanni Evangelista
CATHEDRAL

(Duomo di Sansepolcro; Via Giacomo Matteotti 4; ⊘ 10am-noon & 4-7pm) The original parts of Sansepolcro's Romanesque-Gothic *duomo* (cathedral) date from the 11th century. Inside, look for the *Ascension* by Perugino, a *Resurrection* by Raffaellino del Colle and a polyptych by Niccolò di Segna (1348) that is thought to have influenced Piero's *Resurrection*. Left of the main altar is the striking *Il Volto Santo* (Sacred Face), a wooden crucifix with a wide-eyed Christ in a blue gown that dates from the 9th century.

Leaving the cathedral, turn right onto Piazza Garibaldi to admire the 16 medallions by Andrea della Robbia on the facade of Palazzo Preterio.

🎯 Festivals & Events

Palio della Balestra CULTURAL
(www.balestrierisansepolcro.it; tickets €15; ⊘ 2nd Sun Sep) A crossbow tournament between local archers and rivals from nearby Gubbio, with contestants and onlookers in medieval costumes. It usually takes place on Piazza Torre di Berta.

There's another tournament in mid-April, for which tickets aren't required.

🛏 Sleeping

There's a scattering of B&Bs and pensions to ensure a decent night's sleep here. The Guidi, Da Ventura and Fiorentino (☑ 0575 74 20 33; www.ristorantefiorentino.it; Via Luca Pacioli 60; meals €35; ⊘ noon-3pm & 7.30-10.30pm Thu-Tue) eateries all offer a couple of B&B rooms as well as memorable dining.

⭐ **Dolce Rosa** PENSION €
(☑ 366 3973527; www.dolcerosa.it; Via Niccolò Aggiunti 74; s/d €45/60; ❄) It's rare to find budget accommodation that is well located, super-clean and extremely comfortable, but that's what's on offer at this excellent pension near the Museo Civico (p303). Host Rodolfo looks after his guests well, providing kettles and mini-fridges stocked with complimentary water and soft drinks. No breakfast, but at these prices, who's quibbling?

🍴 Eating & Drinking

Sansepolcro has some delightful places to dine. Cuisine is staunchly Tuscan and faithful to its roots – no deviating from Nonna's cookbook in this traditional small town. Foodie street Via Niccolò Aggiunti, peppered with eating options, is a good starting point.

Pasticceria Chieli CAFE €

(☑ 0575 74 20 26; www.pasticceriachieli.it; Viale Vittorio Veneto 35; ⊙ 6am-8pm Tue-Fri, to 8.30pm Sat, 6.30am-1.30pm Sun; ❄) Just outside the historic town walls, Sansepolcro's best cafe bustles at all times of the day. It's a go-to destination whether you're after a morning coffee and pastry, a lunchtime *panino*, a cake in the afternoon or an *aperitivo*. Staff are friendly and there's plenty of seating too.

Borgo Antico TUSCAN €

(☑ 0575 75 02 08; Via Giulia Boninsegni Buitoni 46; meals €25; ⊙ 11.30am-3.30pm & 6.30-10.30pm Wed-Mon) Serving rustic dishes from Lazio and Tuscany, this frills-free tavern is an excellent lunch stop. The small menu includes tasty *antipasti* such as *la burratina* (burrata served on *pappa pomodoro*), Roman-style carbonara and *cacio e pepe* (*pecorino* and pepper) pastas, and succulent steaks.

★Ristorante Da Ventura TUSCAN €€

(☑ 0575 74 25 60; www.albergodaventura.it; Via Niccolò Aggiunti 30; meals €30; ⊙ 12.30-2.15pm & 7.30-9.45pm Tue-Sat, 12.30-2.15pm Sun; ☑) This old-world eatery is a culinary joy. Trolleys laden with feisty joints of pork, beef stewed in *chianti classico* and roasted veal shank are pushed from table to table, the bow-tied waiters intent on piling plates high. Vegetarians are well catered for with a feast of a mixed house antipasti followed by black truffle omelette or buttered *tagliatelle* (ribbon pasta).

Ristorante Al Coccio TUSCAN €€

(☑ 0575 74 14 68; www.alcoccio.com; Via Niccolò Aggiunti 83; meals €40; ⊙ 12.30-2.30pm & 7.30-9.30pm Wed-Mon; ❄) 🍴 Sisters Sara and Loide Battistelli head the kitchen and dining room of this elegant restaurant, which serves organic produce and plenty of gluten-free choices. The locally sourced beef is a highlight – order a *tagliata* of dry-aged Chianina or a carpaccio topped with shaved black truffle and *parmigiano reggiano*. Great desserts too.

Enoteca Guidi WINE BAR

(☑ 0575 73 65 87; www.locandaguidi.com; Via Luca Pacioli 44; meals €20; ⊙ 11.30am-3pm & 6pm-midnight Thu-Tue) Owner Saverio presides over this convivial *enoteca* (wine bar) and rear dining space where simple meals are served. Enjoy a local artisanal beer or *vino* (everything from local drops to fashionable Super Tuscans). Should you be unable to drag yourself away at the end of the night, the bar has a handful of simple rooms upstairs (single €45, double €80).

ℹ Information

Tourist office (☑ 0575 74 05 36; www.valtiberinaintoscana.it; Via Giacomo Matteotti 8; ⊙ 10am-1pm & 2.30-6.30pm mid-Mar–Oct, shorter hours winter; ☎) Opposite the *duomo*.

ℹ Getting There & Away

Tiemme (www.tiemmespa.it) operates buses to/from Arezzo (€5.60, one hour, hourly Monday to Saturday, two Sunday), stopping in Anghiari (€1.50, 15 minutes) en route. **Sulga** (www.sulga.it) operates a daily service to Rome and Leonardo da Vinci Airport (€19.50, 3½ to 4¼ hours); check schedules and buy tickets for this service online. All buses use the **bus interchange** on Via Guglielmo Marconi, near Porta Fiorentina; purchase tickets at Bar Autostazione here.

CASENTINO VALLEY

The northeastern corner of Tuscany is home to spectacular mountains, historic monasteries and hamlets where traditional customs and cuisine are proudly maintained. It's a popular destination for hikers and cyclists, and also has a proud reputation for its distinctive cuisine, which draws on local forest produce such as game, porcini mushrooms, chestnuts and truffles.

Poppi

☑ 0575 / POP 6153

Seeming to float in the clouds above the Arno plain, Poppi Alta (the historic upper section of the town) is crowned by the commanding presence of the Castello dei Conti Guidi. The 13th-century fortress was built by Count Simone da Battifolle, head of the Guidi family, and shelters a fairy-tale courtyard, handsome staircase, library full of medieval manuscripts and chapel with fresco fragments by Taddeo Gaddi. The scene of Herod's Feast shows Salome apparently clicking her fingers as she dances, accompanied by a lute player, while John the Baptist's headless corpse lies slumped in the corner.

The kiosk in the piazza outside the castle is the social hub during the summer months; at other times locals tend to socialise in Ponte a Poppi (the lower town).

CUCINA TIPICA CASENTINESE: IL CEDRO

Utterly fantastic, 100% homemade *cucina tipica Casentinese* (typical Casentino cuisine) is the draw of Il Cedro (☑ 0575 55 60 80; www.ristoranteilcedro.com; Località Moggiona; meals €24; ⏱ 12.30-2pm & 7.30-9pm Tue-Sun Jun-Aug, 12.30-2pm Fri-Sun Sep-Nov & Mar-May; ☑), a gem of a family-run village bistro, squirreled away for the last 45 years in the tiny hamlet of Moggiona, 10km north of Poppi on the winding road (SP67) to Camaldoli. There is no menu – rather, seasonal, traditional dishes of the day are chalked on the board.

Expect Casentino's signature *tortelli di patate* (potato-filled pasta cushions) or a hearty plate of pappardelle pasta laced with a hare or goat *ragù* (meat and tomato sauce), followed by local Chianina beef or autumnal game with porcini mushrooms from the nearby forest. Its *capriolo* (roe deer venison cooked in white wine) and *cianghiale in umido* (wild boar, slowly braised in red wine with juniper berries and red peppers) are local legends. Lots of veggie choices too.

🛏 Sleeping

The best places to stay in this area are a short drive our of town, amid rolling countryside, rendering your own wheels – two or four – essential for exploring.

I Tre Baroni   HOTEL €

(☑ 0575 55 62 04; www.itrebaroni.it; Via di Camaldoli 52, Moggiona; s €65-75, d €75-85, ste €110-280; ⏱ Easter-Oct; [P][🖥][🏊]) Panoramic views of Poppi village and forested hills frame this bucolic hotel, deep in the Casentino countryside. Its 24 rooms are spacious, if slightly dated, and some open onto terraced gardens perfumed with beds of thyme. Modern suites have four-poster bed, sauna and hot tub with a view. Gastronomic dining in the hotel's Matar restaurant (menus from €65) spills outside in summer. Find the hotel 9km north of Poppi, on the SP67 towards Camadoli.

★ Borgo Corsignano   AGRITURISMO €€

(☑ 0575 50 02 94; www.borgocorsignano.it; Via Corsignano, Corsignano; d/q from €150/300; [P][@][🖥][🏊]) In a *borgo* (medieval hamlet) once home to Camaldoli monks, this gorgeous country hotel is the Casentino's finest accommodation option. A 5km drive from Poppi, it has a mix of self-catering apartments and houses spread lavishly among 13 old stone properties. Voluptuous sculptures collected by the art-loving owners pepper the vast grounds, and sweeping mountain views are magnificent.

★ Il Contado   BOUTIQUE HOTEL €€

(☑ 0575 52 01 34; www.contadospa.com; Viale dei Pini 2; r €140-160, apt per week €800-1300; [P][🖥][🏊]) This newcomer is attracting rave reviews, and no wonder. Replete with amenities (kettles, robes, satellite TV), its six rooms and four two-bedroom apartments are impeccably clean and extremely comfortable. Facilities include a spa with hot tub, sauna and hammam (€15/20 per 2 hours/day, included in room charge during high season) and a large outdoor swimming pool.

Fattorie de Celli   AGRITURISMO €€

(☑ 0575 52 99 17; www.borgocorsignano.it; Via de Becarino 32a, Celli; d/q from €150/260; ⏱ May-Oct; [P][🖥][🏊]) For a complete Tuscan getaway, this vast green estate offers seven villas and 18 self-catering suites in the countryside 5km northwest of Poppi. Self-catering properties sleep two to 11 guests, and mix traditional with contemporary Tuscan decor. Sustainable Villa Chimera is built solely from natural materials and has its own pool staring smugly at the entire Casentino Valley.

🍴 Eating

There are a couple of dining options in Poppi, but the best choices are found in nearby Pratovecchio and Moggiona.

Osteria Il Porto   TUSCAN €

(☑ 0575 52 92 33; www.osteriailporto.it; Via Roma 226, Ponte a Poppi; meals €24; ⏱ 7-11.30pm Mon, Tue, Thu & Fri, 12.30-3pm & 7-11.30pm Sat & Sun late Nov; [P][🖥][🍴]) Follow the locals to this wildly popular eatery, which has a large summer garden that's perfect for summer dining. Cuisine is staunchly Tuscan, with lots of regional dishes: the *tortelli di patate* (potato-filled pasta cushions) made with local red Cetica potatoes, the wild boar stew and herb-stuffed rabbit are all hearty and delicious. Craft beer is the thing to drink.

La Vite TUSCAN €€

(☑ 0575 56 09 62; www.ristorantelavite.net; Piazza della Repubblica, Soci; meals €25; ☺ noon-2.30pm & 6.30-10.30pm Wed-Mon) This easy dine in Soci, 5km east of Poppi, is run by young dynamic sommelier Barbara and chef Cesare. It's a real favourite with locals – and travellers – hungry for a good-value feast of top-quality Tuscan food in the company of great wine. Under no circumstances skimp on *dolci* (dessert) – all homemade and fabulous. Kudos for the pretty summertime patio garden.

❶ Getting There & Away

Frequent trains run by **Trasporto Ferroviario Toscano** (TFT; www.trasportoferroviariotoscano.it) link Poppi with Arezzo (€4.80, one hour) and Pratovecchio (€2.50, 15 minutes).

Parco Nazionale delle Foreste Casentinesi

One of three national parks in Tuscany, the Parco Nazionale delle Foreste Casentinesi (Casentino Forests National Park; www.parcoforestecasentinesi.it/en) straddles the Tuscany–Emilia-Romagna border and protects scenic stretches of the Apennines and Italy's largest forest and woodlands.

One of the highest peaks, Monte Falterona (1654m), marks the source of the river Arno. The park is home to a rich assortment of wildlife, including nearly 100 bird species. Nine self-guided nature trails criss-cross the park: the most popular is the 4.5km uphill hike (4½ hours return) from San Benedetto in Alpe to the spectacular Acquacheta Waterfall, made famous by Dante's *Divine Comedy*.

The major settlement in the park is Badia Prataglia, a small village in the Alpe di Serra mountain range, near the border with Emilia-Romagna.

◉ Sights

★ **Santuario della Verna** MONASTERY

(☑ 0575 53 41; www.laverna.it; Via del Santuario 45, Chiusi della Verna; ☺ sanctuary 6.30am-10pm summer, to 7.30pm winter, Cappella delle Stimmate 8am-7pm summer, to 5pm winter, Museo della Verna 10am-noon & 1-4pm Sat & Sun, daily Jul & Aug) FREE This remote Franciscan monastic complex is where St Francis of Assisi is said to have received the stigmata and is a major pilgrimage destination. The Corridoio delle Stimmate, decorated with modern frescoes recounting St Francis' life, leads to the Cappella delle Stimmate, built in 1263 on the spot where the saint supposedly received the stigmata two years before his death, aged 44. The monumental *Crucifixion* (c 1481) by Andrea della Robbia here is magnificent.

Across from the door to the chapel, steps lead outside to the Precipicio, the precipice – literally – from which the devil supposedly tried to hurl Francis down onto the rocks below. The narrow path is not for the vertiginously challenged.

The monastery basilica houses remarkably fine polychrome glazed ceramics by Andrea della Robbia and his studio: a

(margin, vertical) EASTERN TUSCANY PARCO NAZIONALE DELLE FORESTE CASENTINESI

WORTH A TRIP

PRATOVECCHIO: A DELICIOUS DETOUR

The town itself is unremarkable, but Pratovecchio (population 5697) does have two tasty addresses well worth the 8km drive north from Poppi along the SR70 and SP310.

La Tana degli Orsi (☑ 0575 58 33 77; Via Roma 1; meals €40; ☺ 7.30pm-1am Thu-Tue, to 2am Fri & Sat) In the evening the dozen tables at La Tana degli Orsi (The Lair of the Bear), an unusual chalet-style building, are hotly contested, making advance reservations essential. Decor hovers between classy and kitsch, but cuisine is top-quality Tuscan, with many traditional Casentino dishes created here with local produce. An outstanding wine list lures oenophiles.

Toscana Twist (☑ 0575 58 21 20; toscana.twist@libero.it; Via della Libertà 3; panini/cakes/meals €2.50/1.50/30; ☺ 6.30am-7.30pm Tue-Thu, to 10pm Fri, to 9pm Sat) Toscana Twist is a rare and wonderful breed in rural Tuscany – a contemporary bistro-cafe-wine bar hybrid serving creative Tuscan cuisine packed with fresh seasonal veggies. Located near the train station, its day begins with breakfast – delicious cakes, biscuits and pastries that are a particular strength of chef Patrizia Vignati – and closes with dinner on Friday and an *aperitivo* banquet (from 6.30pm) on Saturday.

GO SLOW IN THE VALLE DEL CASENTINO

Time seems to stand still in the remote Valle del Casentino (Casentino Valley). Ancient Etruscan strongholds, Romanesque churches and isolated farmsteads have scarcely changed over the centuries, while the pace of local life – slow – follows the hypnotic beat of the seasons and the land. When the romantic call of the Tuscan wild beckons, this road trip – easily done in a day from Florence – is the one to take.

❶ Castello di Romena

From Florence head southeast (direction Firenze Sud) and drive alongside the Arno river through Pontassieve and over the Passo della Consuma (SS70), a scenic mountain pass over this Tuscan section of the Apennine Mountains (follow the signs for Consuma and Bibbiena). The road eventually brings you to the turn-off to the Castello di

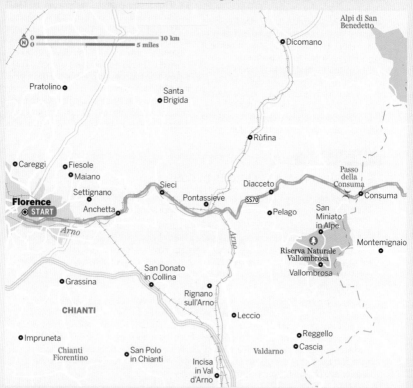

6 Hours 59km

Great for... Outdoors, History & Culture

Best Time to Go Spring, summer or early autumn

Romena, on the left-hand side of the road. Wander around this ruined 11th-century castle and let your imagination run riot Dantesque-style. Yes, Dante was a regular visitor from Florence.

② Pieve di Romena

Walk or drive the 1.5km downhill to the Pieve di Romena, an exquisite Romanesque church built in the mid-12th century. Inside, capitals are sculpted with primitive carvings of human and animal figures. To gain entry, try knocking on the door of the adjoining building.

③ Stia

Follow road signs to Stia, the town where the Arno River meets its first tributary, the Staggia. The town was for many years the centre of the local wool industry and is now home to the **Museo dell'Arte della Lana – Lanificio di Stia** (☎ 0575 58 22 16; www.museodellalana.it; Via Sartori 2; adult/reduced €5/3; ⊙ 10am-1pm Tue, Wed & Fri, 10am-1pm & 3-6pm Thu & Sun, 3-6pm Sat), an impressive wool museum that occupies a handsome, centuries-old mill. The mill was the Casentino Valley's major employer from the 19th century until 2000 when it closed down. Near the museum's entrance is **Tessilnova**, a shop selling examples of the brightly coloured and 'nubby' woollen blankets and clothing that the Casentino is famous for, as well as other top-quality, Italian-made woollen clothing.

④ Santuario di Santa Maria delle Grazie

Drive 4km northwest along the P556 (towards Fornace and Londa) to the Santuario di Santa Maria delle Grazie, a beautiful Renaissance church dating from 1432 and built, so local lore says, to commemorate the apparition of the Virgin Mary to a local peasant called Giovanna. If the church is not open, try to find a local who might be able to let you inside to admire its treasure chest of sacred art: a fresco by Ghirlandaio and two colourful ceramic lunettes by Benedetto Buglioni. The cloister adjoining the church is all that remains of a neighbouring monastery.

⑤ Poppi

Backtracking to Stia, proceed south through Pratovecchio and continue on to the regional centre of Poppi (p307), where you can visit the magnificent 13th-century **Castello dei Conti Guidi** (☎ 0575 52 05 16; www.buonconte. com; Piazza della Repubblica 1; adult/reduced €7/4; ⊙ 10am-4.30pm Thu-Sun, extended hours summer) and wander the picturesque streets of the upper town before heading to your accommodation for the night.

CASTIGLION FIORENTINO: THE PERFECT STEAK

Driving from Arezzo to Cortona, take a break in Castiglion Fiorentino (population 13,228), a picturesque walled town crowned with a bulky medieval fortress with panoramic views of the Val di Chiana from both its grassy green grounds and atop its half-ruined tower, the Torre del Cassero (☑0575 65 94 57; www.museicastiglionfiorentino.it; Via del Tribunale 8; ⊙hours vary) FREE. Next door, the Museo Archeologico (☑Mon-Fri 0575 65 94 57; www.museicastiglionfiorentino.it; Via del Tribunale 8; ⊙10.30am-1pm & 4.30-7.30pm Thu-Sun May-Sep) FREE is a well-put-together archaeological museum incorporating medieval prison cells and the subterranean remains of a 6th-century-BC Etruscan temple and an Etruscan house from the late 4th century BC.

Sampling locally produced Chianina beef, however, is the real reason to visit Castiglion Fiorentino. Ask any local where to sink your teeth into the perfect T-bone and the answer is always Ristorante Da Muzzicone (☑0575 65 84 03, 348 9356616; Piazza San Francesco 7; meals €30; ⊙12.15-2.15pm & 7.30-9.30pm Thu-Mon, 7.30-9.30pm Wed), famed for its succulent, cooked-to-perfection beef (€45 per kg) grilled above a wood fire. In summer, tables spill onto the pretty square outside. Advance reservations essential.

Madonna and Child Enthroned between Saints to your right as you enter the church; a *Nativity* on the right before the altar; an *Adoration* in the small chapel to the right of the altar; saints on either side of the altar; a huge *Ascension* in the chapel to the left of the altar; and a beautiful *Annunciation* in the second chapel to the left.

Don't miss the Cappella delle Reliquie, a small chapel on the right side of the basilica, safeguarding the habit that Francis wore when he received the stigmata in 1224. Other relics include the saint's girdle, a blood-stained cloth used to clean his stigmatic wounds, a whip used by Francis as an instrument of penance, and the stick he walked with when roaming the mountains.

In the interesting Museo della Verna, monastic life is evoked by artefacts such as ancient Bibles and song books, manuscripts, sacred art, the recreation of an old pharmacy and a huge cauldron above the old kitchen chimney and so on.

By car, follow signs just outside the hamlet of Chiusi della Verna for the monastery complex or take the way of the pilgrims along the taxing 30-minute uphill footpath from Chiusi della Verna – it is 23km east of Bibbiena, accessed via the SP208. There is a pilgrim guesthouse (s/tw €35/55, with full board €63/106) with a refectory (⊙8am-8.30pm, panino €2.50-3, set breakfast/lunch/dinner €4.50/16.50/16), and a cafe-bar selling monk-made products (chocolate, honey, liqueur, jams, conserved fruit) on-site. Parking costs €1.50/10 per 75 minutes/day.

Sacro Eremo e Monastero di Camaldoli
MONASTERY

(Camaldoli Hermitage & Monastery; ☑eremo 0575 55 60 21, monastery 0575 55 60 12; www.camaldoli.it; Località Camaldoli 14, Camaldoli; ⊙hermitage 6-11am & 3-6pm, monastery 8am-noon & 2.30-6pm, pharmacy 9am-12.30pm & 2-6pm) FREE Hidden in the dense forest of the national park are the Benedictine hermitage and monastery of Camaldoli, founded between 1024 and 1025 by St Romualdo and now home to a small community of monks. From Poppi, follow Via Camaldoli (SR67) up through the forest; the *eremo* (hermitage), 6km uphill to the left where the road splits, and *monastero* (monastery), 2km straight downhill, are both clearly signposted.

At the remote hermitage, you can visit the baroque Chiesa del Sacro Eremo (1658) with its Bronzino altarpiece of the *Crucifixion and Four Saints*, and the Cappella di San Antonio Abate, left of the main entrance, with an exquisite ceramic altarpiece depicting the *Virgin, Child and Saints* by Andrea della Robbia. In the courtyard, opposite the church, is the 11th-century Cella di San Romualdo Abate (cell) where St Romualdo lived, worked and prayed. Before leaving the hermitage complex, admire the Porta Speciosa, a black bronze set of doors to the right of the main entrance chillingly adorned with a skull, headstone, cranium of a billy goat and a tree, all representing death; an owl represents a solitary monk praying at night, and the bell strung from the tree is a symbol of life. The unusual artwork is a contemporary piece by Claudio Parmiggiani (b 1943).

Continuing to the monastery, a 3km drive away through thick forest, admire a trio of paintings by Vasari in the Chiesa dei Monastero di Camaldoli (1501–24), restored in 1772. Don't miss the 15th-century Antica Farmacia (1450), an old-world pharmacy with beautiful wood-panelled cabinets stocked with soap, perfumes, cosmetics and ancient natural remedies made by the 20 resident monks. A small museum displays wooden hand presses, stone milling machines, earthenware oil jars, copper alembics and other tools used by the monks since the 15th century.

An albergo, trattoria and bakery selling freshly made *schiacciata* (flat bread made with olive oil) are located opposite the monastery.

ⓘ Information

National Park Tourist Office (☑ 0575 50 30 29; www.parcoforestecasentinesi.it; Via Guido Brocchi 7, Pratovecchio; ☺ 9am-1pm Mon-Fri)

ⓘ Getting There & Away

Your own vehicle is essential for exploring the thickly forested and mountainous national park, and for visiting both the Santuario della Verna (p309) and the Sacro Eremo e Monastero di Camaldoli. Main access roads are the narrow and sinuous SR71 linking Bibbiena with Badia Pratáglia, and the hairpin-laced SP208 driving east from Bibbiena to Chiusi della Verna.

VAL DI CHIANA

This wide green valley stretches south from Arezzo into the province of Siena in central Tuscany, and is punctuated by gently rolling hills crowned with medieval villages. Its agricultural land is rich in orchards and olive groves, but it is primarily known as the home of Tuscany's famed Chianina cows, one of the oldest breeds of cattle in the world and the essential ingredient in Tuscany's signature dish, *bistecca alla fiorentina* (T-bone steak).

If you're in the valley on the third Sunday in June, don't miss the Palio dei Rioni that sees jockeys on horseback race around Piazza Garibaldi in Castiglion Fiorentino – like Siena's *palio* on a smaller scale.

Cortona

☑ 0575 / POP 22,057

Rooms with a view are the rule rather than the exception in this spectacularly sited hilltop town. At the beginning of the 15th century Fra' Angelico lived and worked here,

and fellow artists Luca Signorelli and Pietro da Cortona were both born within the walls – all three are represented in the Museo Diocesano's small but sensational collection. Large chunks of *Under the Tuscan Sun,* the 2003 film of the book by Frances Mayes, were shot here and the town has been a popular tourist destination ever since.

⊙ Sights

★ **Museo Diocesano di Arte Sacra**   MUSEUM
(☑ 0575 6 28 30; Piazza del Duomo 1; adult/reduced €5/3; ☺ 10am-6.30pm Apr-Oct, 11am-4pm Tue-Fri, 10am-5pm Sat & Sun Nov-Mar) Highlights of this small museum in the decommissioned 16th-century Chiesa del Gesù include a number of works by Pietro Lorenzetti, a *Madonna and Child* (c 1336) by Niccolò di Segna and two beautiful works by Fra' Angelico: *Annunciation* (1436) and *Madonna with Child and Saints* (c 1438). Upstairs, the Sala Signorelli is home to two paintings by the Cortona-born artist, including *Lamentation Over the Dead Christ* (1502).

Museo dell'Accademia Etrusca e della Città di Cortona   MUSEUM
(MAEC; ☑ 0575 63 04 15; www.cortonamaec. org; Piazza Signorelli 9; adult/reduced €10/7; ☺ 10am-7pm Apr-Oct, to 5pm Tue-Sun Nov-Mar) Spread over five floors and 40 rooms in the 13th-century Palazzo Casali, the collection here includes substantial local Etruscan and Roman finds, Renaissance globes, 18th-century decorative arts and an eclectic array of paintings. The Etruscan collection is the highlight – don't miss the extraordinary hanging bronze lamp on the 2nd floor. Paintings to look out for include Luca Signorelli's sinister *Madonna with Child and Saint Protectors of Cortona* (1512) and Gino Severini's exquisite *Maternità* (1916).

After admiring the museum's collection of Etruscan artefacts excavated from the tombs at Sodo, you may wish to visit the tombs themselves, which are part of the MAEC Archeological Park just outside town on the road to Arezzo (open 10am to 2pm Friday to Sunday; free at the time of research but €5 charge to be levied at some time in the future).

Eremo Francescano Le Celle   MONASTERY
(☑ 0575 60 33 62; Strada dei Cappuccini 1; ☺ 7am-7pm) This Franciscan hermitage hides in dense woodland 3km north of Cortona. Its buildings sit next to a picturesque stream

Cortona

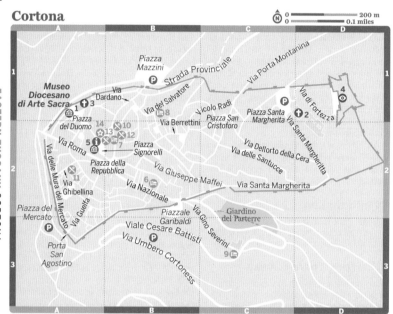

with an 18th-century stone bridge, and the only sounds to disturb the tranquil atmosphere are the bells that call the resident friars to vespers and Mass in the cave-like Chiesa Cella di San Francesco.

Cattedrale di
Santa Maria Assunta CHURCH
(Piazza del Duomo; ⊗ hours vary) The views of the Val di Chiana from the terrace in front of Cortona's 15th-century *duomo* (cathedral) are spectacular, but the church itself is undistinguished. Its original artworks are today displayed in the neighbouring Museo Diocesano (p313).

Basilica di Santa Margherita CHURCH
(Piazza Santa Margherita; ⊗ 8am-noon & 3-7pm summer, 9am-noon & 3-6pm winter) For an effective cardiovascular workout, hike up to this largely 19th-century church through Cortona's warren of steep cobbled lanes. Inside, the remains of St Margaret, patron saint of Cortona, lie in a 14th-century glass-sided tomb above the altar.

Fortezza del Girifalco LANDMARK
(www.fortezzadelgirifalco.it; Via di Fortezza; adult/reduced €5/3; ⊗ 10am-6pm mid-Mar–mid-Apr & Oct, to 7pm mid-Apr–mid-Jun & Sep, to 8pm mid-Jun–Aug) Lap up the stupendous view over the Val di Chiana to Lago Trasimeno in Umbria from

the remains of this Medici fortress, atop the highest point in town – count on a good 15 minutes for the steep hike up. Check the website for its fabulous season of events including exhibitions, concerts and workshops.

✷ Festivals & Events

Cortona Jazz MUSIC
(www.cortonajazz.eu; ⊗ late Apr) Popular jazz festival featuring performances by Italian musicians and international guests. Venues include the fortezza. Buy tickets from the info point in the loggia of Teatro Signorelli (✆ 0575 60 18 82; www.teatrosignorelli.it; Piazza Signorelli).

Cortona on the Move ART
(www.cortonaonthemove.com; ⊗ mid-Jul–Sep) International festival of contemporary photography. Venues include the Fortezza del Girifalco.

🛏 Sleeping

Cortona has some lovely places to stay, ranging from stylish boutique hotels to luxurious B&Bs.

La Corte di Ambra B&B €€
(✆ 0575 178 82 66; www.cortonaluxuryrooms.com; Via Benedetti 23; d €160, ste €190-400; ✳ 🖨) Tucked away in Palazzo Fierli-Petrella, this

Cortona

◉ **Top Sights**
  1 Museo Diocesano di Arte Sacra A1

◉ **Sights**
  2 Basilica di Santa Margherita D1
  3 Cattedrale di Santa Maria Assunta A1
  4 Fortezza del Girifalco D1
  5 Museo dell'Accademia Etrusca e
    della Città di Cortona A2

⌂ **Sleeping**
  6 Casa Chilenne B2

  7 La Corte di Ambra B2
  8 Monastero di Cortona Hotel & Spa B1
  9 Villa Marsili C3

⊗ **Eating**
  10 Fiaschetteria Fett'unta B2
  11 La Bucaccia A2
  12 Osteria del Teatro B2
  13 Taverna Pane e Vino B2

⊛ **Entertainment**
  14 Teatro Signorelli A2

contemporary guesthouse has five attractively decorated rooms with modern bathrooms; one is genuinely wheelchair friendly. There's a lift (unusual for a Renaissance Tuscan palace) and a downstairs salon where a delicious breakfast is served. Parking costs €20.

The same owners operate Casa Ambra at number 14 in the same street, where four self-catering apartments with air-conditioning (double/triple/quadruple room €100/150/250) and a few double rooms with fans (€70/95 without/with breakfast) are available.

Casa Chilenne   B&B €€
(☑0575 60 33 20; www.casachilenne.com; Via Nazionale 65; s/d €85/110; ❄@☎) Run by San Francisco–born Jeanette and her Cortonese husband Luciano, this welcoming B&B scales a narrow town house on Cortona's main pedestrian street. Five spacious rooms with satellite TV and double-glazed windows have access to a small rooftop terrace and a lounge complete with microwave oven, fridge and espresso machine.

Villa Marsili   HOTEL €€
(☑0575 60 52 52; www.villamarsili.net; Viale Cesare Battisti 13; s €75-85, d €110-220; ⊗Apr-Nov; P❄☎) Service is the hallmark at this attractive villa wedged against the city walls and a short walk downhill from Cortona centre. Guests rave about the helpful staff, lavish breakfast buffet and early-evening *aperitivo* served in the garden. Pricier suites have hot tubs and wonderful views across the Val di Chiana to Lago Trasimeno. Advance, non-refundable rates are considerably reduced.

**Monastero di Cortona
Hotel & Spa**   LUXURY HOTEL €€€
(☑0575 178 58 39; www.monasterodicortona.com; Via del Salvatore; r €195-300, ste €350; P❄☎❄) The monks who once called this monastery home wouldn't recognise their quarters

these days, as a 2018 makeover transformed the heritage building into an alluring luxury hotel. Rooms are elegant and well equipped, and facilities include an atmospheric spa with indoor pool, garden with plunge pool, and bar with 17th-century frescoes.

✕ Eating & Drinking

Pedestrian main street Via Nazionale has plenty of places to linger over coffee, cocktails or a refreshing craft beer. At its western end, cafe terraces spill across pretty Piazza della Repubblica.

Fiaschetteria Fett'unta   TUSCAN €
(☑0575 63 05 82; www.winebarcortona.com; Via Giuseppe Maffei 5; meals €24; ⊗11am-10.30pm Thu-Tue) Hanging baskets of flowers mark the entrance to this tiny, deli-style *fiaschetteria* (simple wine bar), which is known for its budget dining and convivial atmosphere. The menu focuses on cold cuts, creative salads, pastas and *bruschette* (toasted bread with assorted toppings).

Taverna Pane e Vino   TUSCAN €
(☑0575 63 10 10; www.pane-vino.it; Piazza Signorelli 27; bruschette €4, cheese & meat boards €7-13; ⊗noon-11pm Tue-Sun) Simple seasonal dishes are the trademark of this vaulted cellar, a hotspot with local bon vivants who come to indulge in their pick of Tuscan and Italian wines in the company of *bruschette* and generous platters of local cheese and cured meats.

La Bucaccia   TUSCAN €€
(☑0575 60 60 39; www.labucaccia.it; Via Ghibellina 17; meals €38; ⊗12.30-2.30pm & 7-10.30pm Tue-Sun) Occupying the medieval stable of a Renaissance *palazzo*, Cortona's best-regarded restaurant has close-set tables where diners enjoy refined versions of Cortonese specialities – beef, game and

OFF THE BEATEN TRACK

CAPRESE MICHELANGELO

David's creator was born in the hilltop village of Caprese (renamed Caprese Michelangelo in the 19th century in his honour), 17km south of Chiusi della Verna, and the small stone house where he spent the first six months of his life now houses the Museo Casa Natale di Michelangelo Buonarroti (📞 0575 79 37 76; www.casanatalemichelangelo. it; Via Capoluogo 1; adult/reduced €4/2.50; ⏰ 9.30am-1pm & 3-6.30pm Apr-Oct, 10am-1pm & 3-5.30pm Sat & Sun Nov-Mar), a small museum celebrating his art as well as work by modern Italian sculptors.

So deeply was Michelangelo inspired by the landscape of his birthplace that he later used the silhouette of Mt Penna, as seen from Chiusi della Verna, as the backdrop for the *Tondo Doni* in Florence's Uffizi (p70) and the *Creation of Adam* fresco in Rome's Sistine Chapel. Driving downhill from the Santuario della Verna towards Chiusi della Verna village, look for a brown sign on the left indicating 'La Roccia di Adamia'. Adam's Rock is just that – the rock that Michelangelo painted, and on which he set a reclining Adam holding out his left arm, fingers almost touching, towards a bearded God.

When visiting, consider stopping for lunch at Buca di Michelangelo (📞 0575 79 39 21; www.bucadimichelangelo.it; Via Capoluogo 51; meals €25; ⏰ 12.45-2pm & 8-10pm Fri-Tue), where the panoramic views over the countryside are as good as the pasta and meat dishes on the menu, which incorporate seasonal delights such as chestnuts, porcini mushrooms and black truffles. In October, Tuscans flock here to celebrate the annual chestnut festival, where the Marroni di Caprese Michelangelo DOP (aka the Caprese chestnut) takes pride of place.

For more information about the village, see www.capresesmichelangelo.net.

handmade pasta feature on the menu. Owner Romano Magi ripens his own cheeses and starting or ending your meal with a cheese course is recommended. There's an excellent wine list too. Reservations essential.

Osteria del Teatro ITALIAN €€

(📞 0575 63 05 56; www.osteria-del-teatro.it; Via Giuseppe Maffei 2; meals €37; ⏰ 12.30-2.30pm & 7.30-9.30pm Thu-Tue; ❄) The interior walls of this long-standing favourite are adorned with B&W snaps of actors who've dined here after performing in the nearby theatre, and service is a performance in motion – efficient and good-humoured. The menu relies heavily on seasonal produce, with local Chianina beef being a speciality.

ℹ Information

Tourist office (📞 0575 63 72 23; www.comunedicortona.it/turismo-e-cultura/info-cortona; Piazza Signorelli 9; ⏰ 10am-7pm Apr-Oct, 9am-1pm Mon-Thu, 10am-5pm Fri-Sun Nov-Mar) Helpful office that can assist with hotel reservations, provide information and book tours.

ℹ Getting There & Away

BUS

Tiemme (www.tiemmespa.it) buses connect the town with Arezzo (€4.50, 65 minutes, 10 daily Monday to Saturday) via Castiglion Fiorentino (€2.60, 35 minutes). There are bus stops in Piazzale Garibalidi and Piazzale del Mercato.

CAR & MOTORCYCLE

Car is by far the easiest way to access hilltop Cortona. The city is on the north–south SR71 that runs to Arezzo. It's also close to the Siena–Bettolle–Perugia autostrada, which connects to the A1. There are paid car parks around the circumference of the city walls and a free car park at Parcheggio dello Spirito Santo that is connected to the historical centre by a *scala mobile* (escalator). A Zona a Traffico Limitato (ZTL; Limited Traffic Zone) applies inside the walls.

TRAIN

The nearest train station is 6km southwest in Camucia, accessible via bus (€1.40, 15 minutes, hourly); buy bus and train tickets at the bar in the station. Destinations include the following:
Arezzo (€3.60, 20 minutes, hourly)
Florence (€10.80, 1½ to two hours, hourly)
Rome (€12.15, 2½ hours, eight daily)

Understand Tuscany

HISTORY 318

Plagues, plotting and patronage – Tuscany's wild and wonderful history is stranger than any fiction.

TUSCAN WAY OF LIFE 329

Family, fashion and tradition reign supreme in this privileged pocket of Italy.

THE TUSCAN TABLE 333

Food in Tuscany is seasonally driven, flavour charged and best savoured slowly.

TUSCANY ON PAGE & SCREEN 341

A comprehensive look at books and films to enjoy before your trip or while you are on the road.

ART & ARCHITECTURE 344

Its Gothic glories and Renaissance masterpieces give Tuscany an artistic heritage unmatched anywhere in the world.

History

Tuscan history is an opera that quietly opens with the wine-loving Etruscans around the 9th century BC, staccatos with feisty clashes between medieval city states, and crescendos with Florence's powerful Medici dynasty and the birth of the Renaissance. To this day, it is the Renaissance, with its extraordinary art and architecture, that defines the region's largest city and remains the region's greatest moment; Tuscany has not been at the cusp of such momentous change since.

The Etruscans

No one knows exactly why the ancient Etruscans headed to Tuscany in the 9th century BC, but Etruscan artefacts give clues as to why they stayed: dinner. The wild boar roaming the Tuscan hills was a favourite on the menu, and boar hunts are a recurring theme on Etruscan ceramics and tomb paintings. In case the odd boar bristle tickled the throat while eating, Etruscans washed down their meals with plenty of wine, thereby introducing viticulture to Italy.

Tomb paintings show Etruscan women keeping pace with men in banquets so decadent they scandalised even the orgy-happy Romans. Many middle-class and aristocratic women had the means to do what they wished, including indulging in music and romance, participating in politics and overseeing a vast underclass of servants. Roman military histories boast of conquests of Etruscan women along with Etruscan territory starting in the 3rd century BC. According to recent genetic tests, Etruscans did not mingle much with their captors – their genetic material is distinct from that of modern Italians, who are the descendants of ancient Romans.

Etruscans didn't take kindly to Roman authority, nor were they keen on being enslaved to establish Roman plantations. They secretly allied with Hannibal to bring about the ignominious defeat of the Romans – one of the deadliest battles in all Roman history – at Lago Trasimeno in neighbouring Umbria: 16,000 Roman soldiers were lost in approximately three hours.

Etruscan Ruins

vie cave (p205; Pitigliano)

Parco Archeologico di Baratti e Populonia (p233; Golfi di Baratti)

Necropoli (p207; Sovana)

TIMELINE	9th century BC	265 BC	88 BC
	Etruscans bring highly civilised wine, women and song to the hills of Tuscany – never has life been so good. Unfortunately they fail to invite the Romans and war ensues.	Etruria falls to Rome, but it remains unruly and conspires with Hannibal against Rome during the Punic Wars.	The Romans establish the province of Tuscia (Tuscany), grant Etruscans citizenship and give them a free hand to run the province as they see fit.

After that Rome took a more hands-off approach with the Etruscans, granting them citizenship in 88 BC to manage their own affairs in the new province of Tuscia (Tuscany) and in return securing safe passage along the major inland Roman trade route via the Via Flaminia. Little did the Romans realise when they paved the road that they were also paving the way for their own replacements in the 5th to 8th centuries AD: first came German emperor Theodoric, then Byzantine emperor Justinian, then the Lombards and finally Charlemagne in 800.

Medieval Scandal

Two notorious women wielded power effectively against a shifting backdrop of kings and popes in medieval Tuscany. The daughter of a Roman senator and a notorious prostitute-turned-senatrix, Marozia already had one illegitimate son by her lover Pope Sergius III and was pregnant when she married the Lombard duke of Spoleto, Alberic I, in AD 909. He was hardly scrupulous himself: he'd achieved his position by murdering the previous duke, and he soon had Sergius III deposed. When Alberic was in turn killed, Marozia married Guy of Tuscany and conspired with him to smother Pope John X and install (in lethally rapid succession) Pope Leo VI and Stephen VIII.

After Guy's death, she wooed his half-brother Hugh of Arles, the new king of Italy. No matter that he already had a wife: his previous marriage was soon annulled. But at the wedding ceremony, Marozia's son, Alberic II, who had been named Pope John XI, had the happy couple arrested. Marozia spent the rest of her life in prison, but her legacy lived on: five popes were her direct descendants.

Countess Matilda of Tuscany (1046–1115) was another power woman. Rumour has it that she was more than just an ally to Pope Gregory VII. To consolidate her family's Tuscan holdings, she married her own stepbrother, Godfrey the Hunchback. She soon arranged for him to be sent off to Germany, annulling the marriage and marrying a powerful prince 26 years her junior.

When Matilda's ally Pope Gregory VII excommunicated Holy Roman Emperor Henry IV in 1077 for threatening to replace him with an antipope, the emperor showed up outside her castle barefoot and kneeling in the snow to beg the pope's forgiveness. Gregory, who was Matilda's guest, kept him waiting for three days before rescinding the excommunication. Henry retaliated for what he saw as Matilda's complicity in his humiliation by conspiring with Matilda's neighbours to seize her property, and even turned her trophy husband against her – but Matilda soon dislodged Henry's power base in the north with the support of his son Conrad. Disgraced by his own family and humbled on the battlefield by a woman, Henry died in 1106.

Best Roman Relics

Area Archeologica (p134; Fiesole)

Roman theatre (p177; Volterra)

Vetulonia (p203)

Medieval Tuscany was violent: leaders of powerful families were stabbed by rivals while attending Mass; peasants were ambushed by brigands; and bystanders were maimed in neighbourhood disputes that all too easily escalated into murderous brawls. Petty crimes were punished with steep fines, corporal punishment and public flogging or mutilation.

59 BC	AD 570–774	773–74	1080
After emerging victorious from a corrupt election campaign for the position of Roman consul, Julius Caesar establishes a soldier-retiree resort called Florentia.	The Lombards rule Italy as far south as Florence and manage to turn the tiny duchy of Spoleto into a booming trade empire.	Charlemagne crosses the Alps into Italy, fighting the Lombards and having his ownership of Tuscany, Emilia, Venice and Corsica confirmed by Pope Hadrian I.	Henry IV deposes Pope Gregory VII for the second time, installing Clement III in his place and marching against Gregory's supporter Matilda of Tuscany, confiscating her territory.

A New Law & Order

By the 13th century Tuscans wanted change. Farmers who had painstakingly reclaimed their fields wanted to survive getting their produce to market; merchants needed peaceful piazzas in which to conduct their business; and the populace at large began to entertain hopes of actually living past the age of 40.

In a bid to reorganise their communities in a more civilised fashion, *comuni* (town councils) were established in Florence, Siena and other towns. In this new power-sharing arrangement, representatives were drawn from influential families, guilds and the merchant classes. Building projects were undertaken to give citizens a new sense of shared purpose and civic identity. Hospitals and public charities helped serve the needy, and new public squares, marketplaces and town halls became crucial meeting places.

Law and order was kept by a *podestà*, an independent judiciary often brought in from outside the city for limited terms of office to prevent corruption. Each *comune* (city state) developed its own style of government: Siena's was the most imaginative. To curb bloody turf battles among its *contrade* (neighbourhoods), Siena channelled its fighting spirit into organised boxing matches, bullfights and Il Palio, an annual horse race. Anyone who breached the peace was fined and the city's coffers soon swelled with monies collected in the city's *osterie* (casual tavern or eatery presided over by a host) for cursing.

After Florence won yet another battle against Siena by cutting off the town's water supply, Siena's *comune* was faced with a funding choice: build an underground aqueduct to fend off Florence or a cathedral to establish Siena as the creative capital of the medieval world. The council voted unanimously for the latter.

FLAGELLATING MONKS & NUNS

The first known case of religious self-flagellation dates from the mid-13th century in Perugia in Tuscany's neighbour Umbria, when a strange, spontaneous parade of believers began whipping themselves while singing. By 1260 roving bands of Flagellants appeared in major Tuscan cities, stripped to the waist, hooded and ecstatically whipping themselves while singing *laudi* (songs about the passion of Christ).

The Church remained neutral on the issue until the fledgling Flagellants claimed that their activities could grant temporary relief from sin. The Flagellant movement was banned in 1262, only to regain momentum a century later during the plague and recur periodically until the 15th century, when the Inquisition subjected Flagellants to the ultimate mortification of the flesh: burning at the stake.

1082	1136	1167	1296
Florence picks a fight with Siena over ownership of the Chianti region, starting a bitter rivalry that will last the next 400 years.	Scrappy, seafaring Pisa adds Amalfi to its list of conquests, which includes Jerusalem, Valencia, Tripoli and Mallorca, and colonies in Constantinople and Cairo.	Siena's *comune* (town council) establishes a written constitution, declaring that elected terms should be short and money should be pretty; it's soon amended to guarantee Sienese public boxing matches.	Building work begins on Florence's *duomo*. The cathedral takes 150 years to complete and, once capped with the largest dome in Italy since antiquity, becomes the ultimate symbol of Renaissance Florence.

Dante's Circle of Hell

In Dante Alighieri's *Inferno,* 1300 is an ominous year: our hero Dante (1265–1321) escapes from one circle of hell only to tumble into the next – as was the case for the writer and his fellow Tuscans, who endured a hellish succession of famine, economic collapse, plague, war and tyranny throughout the 14th century.

Approximately two-thirds of the population was lost in cities across Tuscany in the bubonic-plague outbreak of 1348, and since the carriers of the plague (fleas and rats) weren't identified or eradicated, the Black Death ravaged the area for decades. Entire hospital and monastery populations were wiped out, leaving treatment to opportunists promising miracle cures. Flagellation, liquor, sugar and spices were prescribed, as was abstinence from bathing, fruit and olive oil.

Renaissance Belligerence & Beauty

The Renaissance was a time of great art and great tyrants, and there was an uneasy relationship between the two. The careful balance of power of the *comuni* became a casualty of the plague in the 14th century; political control was mostly left to those who survived and were either strong enough or unscrupulous enough to claim it. In *comuni* such as Florence and Siena, powerful families assumed control of the *signoria,* the city council ostensibly run by guild representatives and merchants.

Cities, commercial entities and individual families took sides with either the Rome-backed Guelphs or the imperial Ghibellines, loyalists of the Holy Roman Empire. Since each of these factions was eager to put itself on the map, this competition might have meant a bonanza for artists and architects – but shifting fortunes in the battlefield meant funds for pet art projects could disappear just as quickly as they appeared.

Tuscany began to resemble a chess game, with feudal castles appearing only to be overtaken, powerful bishops aligning with nobles before being toppled, and minor players backed by key commercial interests occasionally rising to power. Nowhere was the chess game harder to follow than in the Ghibelline *comune* of Pistoia: first it was conquered by the Florentine Guelphs, then it split into White and Black Guelph splinter groups, then it was captured by Lucca (which was at that time Ghibelline backed) before being reclaimed by the Florentines.

The Medicis

The Medici family were not exempt from the usual failings of Renaissance tyrants, but early on in his rise to power Cosimo the Elder (1389–1464) revealed a surprisingly enlightened self-interest and an exceptional eye for art. Although he held no elected office, he served as ambassador for the Church, and through his behind-the-scenes diplomatic skills

Relive 14th-century Florence at Dante's Florentine home, with a tripe shop and the chapel where he met his muse, Beatrice Portinari. For pop-culture Dante, read Sandow Birk and Marcus Sanders' *The Divine Comedy,* which sets the *Inferno* in Los Angeles, *Purgatorio* in foggy San Francisco and *Paradiso* in New York.

1348–50	1375–1406	1378	1478–80
Black Death ravages Tuscany, wiping out approximately two-thirds of the population in dense urban areas, and it doesn't stop there: further outbreaks are recorded until 1500.	Coluccio Salutati serves as chancellor of Florence, promoting a secular civic identity to trump old feudal tendencies; it's a bold, new model of citizenship for Europe that occasionally even works.	The Florentine *signoria* (city council) ignores a petition from the city's *ciompi* (wool carders), who want guild representation: cue the Revolt of Ciompi, an ultimately unsuccessful democratic uprising.	A confusing set of overlapping wars breaks out among the papacy, Siena, Florence, Venice, Milan and Naples, as individual families broker secret pacts and the dwindling Tuscan population pays the price.

managed to finagle a rare 25-year stretch of relative peace for Florence. When a conspiracy led by competing banking interests exiled him from the city in 1433, some of Cosimo's favourite artists split town with him, including Donatello and Fra' Angelico.

But they weren't gone long: Cosimo's banking interests were too important to Florence, and he returned triumphant after just a year to crush his rivals, exert even greater behind-the-scenes control and sponsor masterpieces such as Brunelleschi's legendary dome for Florence's *duomo* (cathedral).

But sponsorship from even the most enlightened and powerful patrons had its downside: their whims could make or break artists and they attracted powerful enemies. Lorenzo de' Medici (Lorenzo Il Magnifico; 1449–92) was a legendary supporter of the arts and humanities, providing crucial early recognition and support for Leonardo da Vinci, Sandro Botticelli and Michelangelo, among others.

But after Lorenzo escaped an assassination attempt arising from a conspiracy among the rival Florentine Pazzi family, the king of Naples and the pope, the artists he supported had to look elsewhere for sponsorship until Lorenzo could regain his position. Religious reformer Savonarola took an even darker view of Lorenzo and the classically influenced art he promoted, viewing it as a sinful indulgence in a time of great suffering. When Savonarola ousted the Medici in 1494, he decided that their decadent art had to go too, and works by Botticelli, Michelangelo and others went up in flames in the massive 'Bonfire of the Vanities' on Florence's Piazza della Signoria.

You can see the preserved middle finger (and other body parts) of Galileo Galilei in Florence's superb and wholly interactive Museo Galileo, next to the Uffizi. Online, explore Galileo's life, times, religious context and scientific advances in The Galileo Project (http://galileo. rice.edu).

Galileo Galilei

One of the most notable faculty members at the revitalised University of Pisa was a professor of mathematics named Galileo Galilei (1564–1642). To put it in mathematical terms, Galileo was a logical paradox: a Catholic who fathered three illegitimate children; a man of science with a poetic streak who lectured on the dimensions of hell according to Dante's *Inferno;* and an inventor of telescopes whose head was quite literally in the clouds but who kept in close contact with many friends who were the leading intellectuals of their day.

Galileo's meticulous observations of the physical universe attracted the attention of the Church, which by the 16th century had a difficult relationship with the stars. Research into the universe's guiding physical principles was entrusted by Pope Paul III to his consulting theologians, who determined from close examination of the scriptures that the sun must revolve around the earth.

Equipped with telescopes that he'd adjusted and improved, Galileo came to a different conclusion. His observations supported Nicolaus

1494	1497	1498	1527–30
The Medici are expelled by Charles VIII of France, and friar Savonarola declares a theocratic republic with his Consiglia di Cinquecento.	Savonarola sets fire to art in Florence. Books, paintings and musical instruments go up in flames on the pious preacher's 'Bonfire of the Vanities' on Florence's Piazza della Signoria.	To test Savonarola's beliefs, rival Franciscans invite him to a trial by fire. He sends a representative to be burned instead, but is eventually tortured, hanged and burned as a heretic.	Florentines run the Medici out of town. The Republic of Florence holds out for three years, until the emperor's and pope's combined cannon power reinstalls the Medici.

Copernicus' theory that the planets revolved around the sun, and a cautious body of Vatican Inquisitors initially allowed him to publish his findings as long as he also presented a case for the alternative view. But when Galileo's research turned out to be dangerously convincing, the Vatican reversed its position and tried him for heresy. Under official threat of torture, Galileo stated in writing that he may have overstated the case for the Copernican view of the universe, and he was allowed to carry out his prison sentence under house arrest. Pope Urban VIII alternately indulged his further studies and denied him access to doctors, but Galileo kept on pursuing scientific research even after he began losing his sight.

HOW MACHIAVELLIAN...

Few names have such resonance as that of Niccolò Machiavelli (1469–1527), the Florentine scholar and political thinker who said 'the times are more powerful than our brains'. He was born into a poor offshoot of one of Florence's leading families and his essential premise – 'the end justifies the means' – is one that continues to live with disturbing vitality five centuries on.

Impoverished as Machiavelli's family was, his father had a well-stocked library, which the young Machiavelli devoured. When he was 29 Machiavelli landed a post in the city's second chancery. By 1500 he was in France on his first diplomatic mission in the service of the Florentine Republic. Indeed, so impressed was he by the martial success of Cesare Borgia and the centralised state of France that Machiavelli concluded Florence, too, needed a standing army – which he convinced the Republic to do in 1506. Three years later it was bloodied in battle against the rebellious city of Pisa.

The return to power of the Medici family in 1512 was a blow for Machiavelli. Suspected of plotting against the Medici, he was thrown into Florence's Le Stinche (the earliest known jail in Tuscany, dating from 1297 and among the first in Europe) in 1513 and tortured with six rounds of interrogation on the prison's notorious rack. Yet he maintained his innocence. Once freed, he retired a poor man to a small property outside Florence.

But it was during these years that Machiavelli did his greatest writing. Il Principe (The Prince) is his classic treatise on the nature of power and its administration, a work reflecting the confusing and corrupt times in which he lived and his desire for strong and just rule in Florence and beyond. He later wrote an official history of Florence, the Istorie Fiorentine.

In 1526 Machiavelli joined the papal army in its futile fight against imperial forces. By the time the latter had sacked Rome in 1527, Florence had again rid itself of Medici rule. Machiavelli hoped he would be restored to a position of dignity, but to no avail. He died frustrated and, as in his youth, impoverished.

1633	1656	1737	1760s
Galileo Galilei is condemned for heresy in Rome. True to his observations of a pendulum in motion, the Inquisition's extreme measures yield an opposite reaction: Enlightenment.	The plague kills at least 300,000 people across central and southern Italy.	Habsburg Maria Theresa ends the Medici's dynastic rule by installing her husband as grand duke of Tuscany. She remains the brains of the operation, reforming Tuscany from behind the scenes.	Florence, along with Venice, Milan and Turin, becomes an essential stop for British aristocrats on the Grand Tour, a trend that continues until the 1840s.

Foreigners Come Calling

With his astrologers on hand, the pope might have seen Italy's foreign domination coming. Far from cementing the Church's authority, the Inquisition created a power vacuum on the ground while papal authorities were otherwise occupied with lofty theological matters. While local Italian nobles and successful capitalists vied among themselves for influence as usual, the Austrian Holy Roman Empress Maria Theresa took charge of the situation in 1737, and set up her husband, Francis, as the grand duke of Tuscany.

Napoleon Bonaparte took over swaths of Tuscany in 1799, and so appreciative was he of the area's cultural heritage that he decided to take as much as possible home with him. What he couldn't take he gave as gifts to various relatives – never mind that all those Tuscan villas and church altarpieces were not technically his to give. Following Napoleon's fall from grace in 1814, the emperor was exiled to the island of Elba in the Tuscan Archipelago and Habsburg Ferdinando III took over the title of grand duke of Tuscany. However, Napoleon's sister Elisa Bonaparte and various other relations refused to budge from the luxe Lucchesi villas they had usurped, so concessions were made to accommodate them all.

Still more upmarket expats arrived in Tuscany with the inauguration of Italy's cross-country train lines in 1840. Soon no finishing-school education would be complete without a Grand Tour of Italy, and the landmarks and museums of Tuscany were required reading. Trainloads of debutantes, dour chaperones and career bachelors arrived, setting the stage for EM Forster novels and Tuscan time-share investors.

Red & Black: A Chequered Past

While an upper-crust expat community was exporting Romantic notions about Italy, the country was facing harsh realities. Commercial agriculture provided tidy sums to absentee royal Austrian landlords while reducing peasants to poverty and creating stiff competition for small family farms. In rural areas, three-quarters of the family income was spent on a meagre diet of mostly grains. The promise of work in the burgeoning industrial sector lured many to cities, where long working hours and dangerous working conditions simply led to another dead end, and 70% of family income was still spent on food. Upward mobility was rare, since university admissions were strictly limited, and the Habsburgs were cautious about allowing locals into their imperial army or bureaucratic positions. Increasingly, the most reliable means for Tuscans to support their families was emigration to the Americas.

Austrian rule provided a common enemy that united Italians across provinces and classes. The Risorgimento (reunification period) was not

America was named after Amerigo Vespucci, a Florentine navigator who, from 1497 to 1504, made several voyages of discovery in what would one day be known as South America.

1765–90	1796–1801	1805–14	1861
Enlightenment leader Leopold I continues his mother Maria Theresa's reforms. Moved by Cesare Beccaria's case for criminal-justice reform, he makes Tuscany the first sovereign state to outlaw the death penalty.	Italy becomes a battleground between Napoleon, the Habsburgs and their Russian allies: Tuscans witness much of their cultural patrimony divvied up as the spoils of war.	Napoleon establishes himself as king of Italy, with the military assistance of Italian soldiers he'd conscripted; when his conscripts desert, Napoleon loses Tuscany to Grand Duke Ferdinando III in 1814 and is exiled to Elba.	Two decades of insurrections culminate in a new Italian government, with a parliament and a king. Florence becomes Italy's capital in 1865, despite extensive poverty and periodic bread riots.

so much a reorganisation of some previously unified Italian states (which hadn't existed since Roman times) as a revival of city-state ideals of an independent citizenry. The secret societies that had flourished right under the noses of the French as a local check on colonial control formed a network of support for nationalist sentiment. During 1848 and 1849 revolution broke out, and a radical government was temporarily installed in Florence.

Nervous that the Austrians would invade, conservative Florentine leaders invited Habsburg Leopold II to return as archduke of Tuscany. But when rural unrest in Tuscany made Austria's return to power difficult, Austrian retaliation and brutal repression galvanised nationalist sentiment in the region. Although the country was united under one flag in 1861, this early split between radicals and conservatives would define the region's future political landscape.

Unification didn't end unemployment or unrest; only 2% of Italy's population gained the right to vote in 1861. Strikes were held to protest working conditions, and their brutal suppression gave rise to a new Socialist Party in 1881. The new Italian government's money-making scheme to establish itself as a colonial power in Abyssinia (modern-day Ethiopia and Eritrea) proved a costly failure: 17,000 Italian soldiers were lost near Adowa in 1896. When grain prices were raised in 1898, many impoverished Italians could no longer afford to buy food, and riots broke out. Rural workers unionised, and when a strike was called in 1902, 200,000 rural labourers came out en masse.

Finally Italian politicians began to take the hint and initiated some reforms. Child labour was banned, working hours set and the right to vote extended to all men over the age of 30 by 1912 (women would have to wait until 1945). But as soon as the government promised the Socialists to fund an old-age pension scheme, it reneged, and opted to invade Tunisia instead.

Italy got more war than it had budgeted for in 1914 when WWI broke out. A young, prominent Socialist firebrand named Benito Mussolini (1883–1945) led the call for Italy to intervene in support of the Allies, though most Socialists were opposed to such an action. As a result, Mussolini was expelled from the Socialist Party and went on to join the Italian army. After being injured and discharged, he formed the Italian Combat Squad in 1919, the forerunner of the National Fascist Party.

Inter-War Blues

Though Italy had been on the winning side in WWI, Tuscans were not in the mood to celebrate. In addition to war casualties, 600,000 of their countrymen served time as prisoners of war, and 100,000 died, primarily due to the Italian government's failure to send food, clothing and medical

1871	1915	1921	1940–43
After French troops are withdrawn from Rome, the forces of the Kingdom of Italy defeat the Papal States to take power in Rome; the capital moves there from Florence.	Italy enters WWI fighting a familiar foe: the Austro-Hungarian Empire. War casualties, stranded POWs, heating-oil shortages and food rationing make for a hard-won victory by 1918.	Mussolini forms the Fascist Party, and Tuscan supporters fall in line by 1922. The 1924 elections are 'overseen' by Fascist paramilitary groups, and the Fascists win a parliamentary majority.	The Fascist Italian Empire joins Germany in declaring war on Great Britain and France. Italy surrenders in 1943; Mussolini refuses to comply and war continues.

supplies to its own soldiers. Wartime decrees that extended working hours and outlawed strikes had made factory conditions in industrial centres so deplorable that women led mass strikes. Bread shortages and bread riots spread, and in 1919 violent uprisings broke out in the industrial towns of Viareggio and Piombino: the dismissal of 500 workers at the Piombino steel mills sparked a general strike that rapidly degenerated into full-scale bloodshed between workers and armed forces.

Mussolini had clearly found support for his call to order in disgruntled Tuscany, and by 1922 his black-shirted squads could be seen parading through Florence, echoing his call for the ousting of the national government and the purging of socialists and communists from all local positions of power. In 1922 the Fascists marched on Rome and staged a coup d'etat, installing Mussolini as prime minister.

No amount of purging prevented the country from plunging into recession in the 1930s after Mussolini demanded a revaluation of the Italian lira. While the free fall of wages won Mussolini allies among industrialists, it created further desperation among his power base. New military conquests in Libya and Ethiopia initially provided a feeble boost to the failing economy, but when the enormous bill came due in the late 1930s, Mussolini hastily agreed to an economic and military alliance with Germany. Contrary to the bold claims of Mussolini's propaganda machine, Tuscany and the rest of Italy was ill-prepared for the war it entered in 1940.

WWII & Tuscan Resistance

Contrary to the deep-rooted Florentine belief that a city brimming with so many artistic treasures could not possibly be targeted, Florence was badly damaged during WWII. Ironically, it was not until the end of the war, however, following the occupation of the city by German troops on 11 September 1943, that the first bombs were dropped. Allied forces broke through the German line south of Rome in May 1944 and promptly rushed north to liberate Rome and all the territory in between. Forced to retreat, the Germans built a new defensive line using forced labour further north: the Gothic Line ran east from the Pisan coast – via Pisa, Lucca, Florence and eastern Tuscany – to the Adriatic Coast.

A powerful resistance movement emerged in Tuscany during WWII, but not soon enough to prevent hundreds of thousands of Italian casualties, plus a still-unknown number of Italians shipped to death camps in Germany and 23 Italian concentration camps, including one near Arezzo; in Florence a stone in front of the city synagogue memorialises the 248 Jews from Florence who died in the camps. Similar fates were shared by Jews in Siena, Pisa and other Tuscan towns.

Historical Reads

Renaissance Florence on Five Florins a Day (2010), Charles FitzRoy

Tuscany: A History (2011), Alistair Moffat

Queen Bee of Tuscany: The Redoubtable Janet Ross (2013), Ben Downing

1943–45	1946	1966	1970s–'80s
The Italian Resistance joins the Allies against Mussolini and the Nazis; Tuscany is liberated. When civil warfare ends in 1945, a coalition government is formed.	Umberto II is exiled after a referendum to make Italy a republic is successful; 71.6% of Tuscans vote for a republic.	The Arno bursts its banks, submerging Florence in metres of mud and water. Some 5000 people are left homeless and thousands of artworks and manuscripts are destroyed.	The Anni di Piombo (Years of Lead) terrorise the country with extremist violence and reprisals; police kill anarchist Franco Serantini in Pisa, and the Red Brigades kill Florence's mayor in 1986.

German forces' final gift to the city of Florence before leaving in August 1944 was to destroy all the bridges across the River Arno in order to slow advancing Allied troops. Every bridge was blown up except for the Ponte Vecchio, which Hitler ordered to be spared: the timelessly seductive view down the Arno from the new window Mussolini had specially punched in the bridge section of the Vasari Corridor in anticipation of Hitler's visit to Florence in 1941 had obviously made a lasting impression on the Nazi leader.

Rise of the Tuscan Left

A new Italian government surrendered to the Allies in 1943, but Mussolini refused to concede defeat, and dragged Italy through two more years of civil war and German occupation. Tuscany emerged from these black years redder than ever and a staunch Socialist power base.

Immediately after the war, three coalition governments succeeded one another. Italy became a republic in 1946 and the newly formed right-wing Democrazia Cristiana (Christian Democrats) won the first elections under the new constitution in 1948.

Until the 1980s the Partito Comunista Italiano (Italian Communist Party), despite being systematically kept out of government, played a crucial role in Tuscany's social and political development. The party was founded in the Tuscan port town of Livorno in 1921, and its huge popularity prompted the so-called Anni di Piombo (Years of Lead) in the 1970s, dominated by terrorism and social unrest. In 1978 the Brigate Rosse (Red Brigades, a group of young left-wing militants responsible for several bomb blasts and assassinations) claimed their most important victim – former Christian Democrat prime minister Aldo Moro. He was kidnapped in Rome, kept hostage for 54 days, then shot.

The 1970s enjoyed positive change: divorce and abortion became legal, and legislation was passed allowing women to keep their own names after marriage. The Regione Toscana was one of 15 regional governments with limited powers to be formed across the country. And, in predictable Tuscan centre-left fashion, from the moment of its creation, it was the red left in Tuscany that dominated local political debate.

Banca Monte dei Paschi di Siena Scandal

Europe's ailing economy limped from bad to dire from 2012 in a financial crisis considered to be the worst since the 1930s Great Depression. The Tuscan crunch came with a bank scandal. In 2013 the Banca Monte dei Paschi di Siena – Italy's third-largest lender and the world's longest-operating bank, at home in a wonderful old *palazzo* in Siena since 1472 – revealed losses of €730 million on a trio of derivative deals made between 2007 and 2009 and hidden from regulators. While former high-ranking officials at

Tuscany's regional government is headed by the president, elected every five years. The president is aided by 10 ministers and a legislative regional council comprising 65 members, also elected by proportional representation for the same five-year term. Keep tabs on the regional government and council at www.regione.toscana.it and www.consiglio.regione.toscana.it.

HISTORY RISE OF THE TUSCAN LEFT

1993	1995	2005	2008
A car bomb at the Uffizi kills six and causes US$10 million damage to artworks. The mafia is suspected but never indicted. The same year 200,000 people protest mafia violence.	Maurizio Gucci, heir to the Florence-born Gucci fashion empire, is gunned down outside his Milan offices. Three years later, his estranged wife, Patrizia Reggiani, is jailed for ordering his murder.	Regional elections in Tuscany see incumbent centre-left president Claudio Martini win a second term in office, reconfirming Tuscany as Italy's bastion of the left.	Silvio Berlusconi and his right-wing allies, in power since 2001, win the national election and a second seven-year term in office. Tuscany's traditional support of leftist candidates and parties is diluted.

the pedigree bank grappled with corruption, fraud and bribery allegations, the government came to the rescue with a €4.1 billion bailout and a €5 billion share sale 12 months later to raise capital. Amid increased fears of the bank's complete collapse, the EU accepted a massive rescue plan put forward by the Italian government in 2017 that effectively saw the state bail out the bank in return for EU-approved, cutthroat restructuring. Shares in the Banca Monte dei Paschi nonetheless plummeted in value by 69% between late 2017 and early 2019.

Hundreds of the bank's 1900 countrywide branches subsequently closed. But the fallout of the scandal reached far beyond job cuts. For decades 'il Monte' (as Tuscans know the bank) sustained Siena's vibrant cultural life. Through its foundation, the Fondazione Monte dei Paschi di Siena, it funded part of the city's university, hospital, football team, Palio horse race and so on – effectively providing around 10% of Siena's local-government budget. For Siena (and Tuscany) the social and economic impact of their historic sugar daddy's dramatic fall from grace was grave cause for concern.

Arrivederci Red Tuscany

General elections in Italy in 2018 saw a notable rise in far-right populism, echoing similar trends elsewhere in Europe. The incumbent, centre-left Democratic Party (PD) was heavily defeated by the right, with the anti-illegal-migrant League party and anti-establishment Five Star Movement forming a new coalition government. Municipal elections three months later saw the Democratic Party lose several traditionally left strongholds – Pisa, Siena and Massa included – to Interior Minister Matteo Salvini's right-wing alliance, leaving the Democratic Party governing just three (Florence, Lucca and Prato) of the 11 Tuscan provincial capitals. This dramatic loss – the centre-left party held 10 out of the 11 in 2013 – confirmed once that the right's populist, anti-immigrant, Eurosceptic message had made notable inroads in an Italian region known for decades as 'Red Tuscany'.

European elections in May 2019 coincided with local elections in Florence. Among the nine candidates running was left-wing Antonella Bundu – born in Florence to an Italian mother and father from Sierra Leone. She was the first black woman in Italy to run for a mayorship. Key points in her manifesto were the promotion of an inclusive, multicultural city and improving the rights of migrants and women. She was defeated at the polls by incumbent mayor, Dario Nardella of the Democratic Party, who won a second five-year term in office. In European elections, meanwhile, the far-right Northern League waltzed away with the lion's share of votes in both Tuscany and Italy. *Arrivederci* Red Tuscany.

2012	2015	2018	2019
Italian cruise ship *Costa Concordia* sinks off the Tuscan coast, claiming 32 lives. The eventual removal of the wreckage in 2015 from the island of Giglio is the most costly in maritime salvage history.	The left emerges stronger than ever in Tuscany in regional elections. Incumbent centre-left president Enrico Rossi's Democratic Party (PD) lands 48.03% of votes, ensuring a second term in office for Rossi.	Italy's general election and subsequent municipal elections witness a dramatic rise in right-wing populism. Tuscany's traditional left-wing strongholds of Siena, Pisa and Massa fall to the right.	A year-long party of art and cultural happenings throughout Tuscany celebrates the 500th anniversary of Leonardo da Vinci's death.

The Tuscan Way of Life

Romanticised the world over, Tuscany has impassioned more writers, designers and film-makers than any other region. Yet what is it that makes the birthplace of Gucci, Cavalli and the Vespa scooter so inspiring, so *dolce* (sweet)? Florence takes the lead with its artistic heritage and tradition of master artisanship, but Tuscan style, grace and appreciation of beauty find expression in an extraordinary attention to detail, a quest for perfection and a dauntless pride in local dialect and history.

Rural Roots

Deeply attached to their patch of land, people in this predominantly rural neck of the woods, with only a dusting of small towns, are not simply Italian or Tuscan. Harking back to centuries of coexistence as rival political entities with their own style of architecture, school of painting, bell tower and so on, it is the *paese* (home town) or, in the case of Siena and other towns, the *contrada* (neighbourhood) in which one is born that reigns supreme. For most, such *campanilismo* (literally, 'loyalty to one's bell tower') is all-consuming. 'Better a death in the family than a Pisan at the door' says an old Florentine proverb with reference to the historic rivalry between the Tuscan towns.

Being passionate, proud, reserved, hard-working, family-oriented, fond of food and wine, thrifty, extremely self-conscious and careful in their appearance are characteristics attributed to Tuscans across the board.

Brash? No, but in Florence Florentines like to make it known where they stand in society. From oversized doorknobs to sculpted stonework, overt statements of wealth and power are everywhere in this class-driven city, whose dialect – penned for the world to read by literary greats Dante, Boccaccio and Petrarch in the 14th century – is deemed the purest form of Italian.

> No title better delves into the essence of Tuscan life than *The Wisdom of Tuscany: Simplicity, Security and the Good Life – Making the Tuscan Lifestyle Your Own* by Ferenc Màté.

A PEASANT'S LIFE

Mezzadria (sharecropping), a medieval form of land management in place until 1979, was the key to success in the Tuscan countryside. *Contadini* (peasants) lived and worked on the land, receiving in return a home for their traditionally large families (typically consisting of 10 people – the more hands the better) and 50% of the crops or profit reaped from the land they worked. The other half went to the *padrone* (land owner), who often did not live on his *fattoria* (agricultural estate) but in the city.

Post-WWII industrialisation saw the birth of the tractor and the first shift in the equal balance between landowner and peasant: farmers had no money to buy tractors, obliging owners to invest instead and so upsetting the apple cart in terms of who gave how much. Gradually farm workers gravitated towards towns in search of better-paid jobs, the 1960s witnessing a particularly large exodus and prompting the eventual collapse of sharecropping and many a Tuscan farm with it.

Titled Florentines are still alive and well, accounting for a tiny fraction of contemporary Florentine society. From the 12th century until the Renaissance, when wealth and ability overtook aristocratic ranking, titles – prince, duke, marques, count, viscount, baron, patrician and noble – ruled the roost. Florentine nobility derived mainly from bankers and merchants, and many of the city's most wonderful properties and countryside estates remain in the hands of counts and barons – Europe's largest private walled garden, the Giardini di Torrigiani, is a prime example.

In the city, elderly nobles still gather each week at Florence's exclusive, elusive Circolo dell' Unione (aka 'club of nobles'), enthroned since 1852 in a *palazzo* on Florence's most aristocratic street, Via de' Tournabuoni. Membership is not hereditary and costs a (large) fee. Some 60% of the club's 400-odd members (of which just a handful are female) bear a title – though titles have not been recognised by the Italian state since 1948, following the fall of the Italian monarchy.

La Dolce Vita

Life is *dolce* (sweet) for this privileged pocket of Italy, one of the country's wealthiest enclaves, where the family reigns supreme, and tradition and quality trump quantity. From the great names in viticulture to the flower-producing industry of Pescia and the small-scale farms of rural Tuscany, it is family-run businesses handed down generations that form the backbone of this proud, strong region.

In Florence – the only city with a faint hint of the cosmopolitan – daily life is the fastest paced. Florentines rise early, drop their kids at school by 8am, then flit from espresso to the office by 9am. Lunch is a lengthy affair for these food- and wine-loving people, as is the early-evening *aperitivo*, enjoyed in a bar with friends to whet the appetite for dinner. For younger Florentines, who bear the brunt of Florence's ever-rising rent and salaries that scarcely increase, it is quite common to treat the lavish *aperitivo* spread like dinner – enter *apericena*. Smokers, fast dwindling, puff on pavements outside.

There is no better time of day or week than late Sunday afternoon to witness the *passeggiata* (early-evening stroll), a wonderful tradition that sees Tuscans in towns don a suitable outfit and walk – to get a gelato, chat, meet friends, mooch, contemplate the sunset and, quite simply, relish the close of the day at an exceedingly relaxed pace.

Theatre, concerts, art exhibitions (the free opening on Thursday evenings at Florence's Palazzo Strozzi is always packed) and *il calcio* (football) entertain after hours. Tuscany's top professional football club, ACF Fiorentina, has a fanatical fan base (check the memorabilia in Florence's Trattoria Mario).

Weekends see many flee their city apartments for less urban climes, where the din of *motorini* (scooters) whizzing through the night lessens and there's more space and light. Green countryside is a mere 15-minute getaway from lucky old Florence, unlike many urban centres where industrial sprawl really sprawls.

Casa Dolce Casa

By their very nature, family-oriented Tuscans travel little (many live all their lives in the town of their birth) and place great importance on *casa dolce casa* (home, sweet home) – the rate of home ownership in Tuscany is among Europe's highest.

The rural lifestyle is driven by close-knit, ancient communities in small towns and villages, where local matters and gossip are more important than national or world affairs. Everyone knows everyone to the point of being clannish, making assimilation for outsiders hard – if not impossible. Farming is the self-sufficient way of life, albeit one that is

Italians Dance and I'm a Wallflower by Florence-based author Linda Malcone provides a cracking insight into local behaviour and cultural expression. It's published by the Florentine Press (www.thefloren tinepress.com), a fabulous resource for publications (print and e-book) in English covering everything from arts and culture to politics, travel and humour.

Tuscan Icons

Vespa scooter

Gucci

Chianti wine

Michelangelo's David

Renaissance art

becoming increasingly difficult – hence the mushrooming of *agriturismi* (farm-stay accommodation), as farmers stoically use every resource they have to make ends meet.

At one time the domain of Tuscany's substantial population of well-off Brits (there's good reason why playwright John Mortimer dubbed Chianti 'Chiantishire' in his 1988 novel and 1989 TV adaptation *Summer's Lease*), the region's bounty of stylish stone villas and farmhouses with terracotta floors, wood-burning fireplaces and terraces with views are now increasingly passing back into the hands of Tuscans eagerly rediscovering their countryside.

In both urban and rural areas, children typically remain at home until they reach their 30s, often only leaving the nest to wed. In line with national trends, Tuscan families are small, with one or two kids; around 20% of households are childless and 25% are single. Despite increasing numbers of working women, chauvinistic attitudes remain well entrenched in more rural areas.

La Festa

Delve into the mindset of a Tuscan and a holy trinity of popular folklore, agricultural tradition and religious rite of passage dances before your eyes – which pretty much translates as *la festa* (party!). No cultural agenda is more jam-packed with ancient festivities than theirs: patron saints alone provide weeks of celebration, given that every village, town, profession, trade and social group has a saint to call its own and venerate religiously.

La festa climaxes – not once but twice – with Siena's soul-stirring Il Palio (2 July), a hot-blooded horse race conceived in the 12th century to honour the Virgin Mary and revamped six centuries on to celebrate the miracles of the Madonna of Provenzano and the Assumption (16 August). Deeply embroiled in its religious roots is a fierce *contrada* rivalry, not to mention a penchant for dressing up and a respect for tradition that sees horses blessed before the race, jockeys riding bareback and the silk banner for the winner of August's race ritually designed by Sienese artists and the July banner by non-Sienese. (Legend says that a Sienese bride marrying in far-off lands took earth from her *contrada* to put beneath the legs of her marital bed to ensure that her offspring would be conceived on home soil.)

Although it's by no means the social force it once was, Catholicism (the religion of 85% of the region) and its rituals nevertheless play a key role in daily lives: first communions, church weddings and religious feast days are an integral part of Tuscan society.

Unesco World Heritage Sites

Florence's historic centre

Pisa's Piazza dei Miracoli

Siena's historic centre

Val d'Orcia

San Gimignano's historic centre

Pienza's historic centre

Medici villas and gardens

COFFEE CULTURE

Coffee is not just a drink but a way of life for Tuscans, whose typical day is punctuated with caffeine, the type of coffee depending wholly on time of day and occasion.

The number-one cardinal rule: cappuccino (espresso topped with hot, frothy milk), *caffè latte* (milkier version with less froth) and *latte macchiato* (warmed milk 'stained' with a spot of coffee) are only ever drunk at breakfast or in the early morning. If you're truly Tuscan, though, the chances are you'll probably grab a speed espresso (short, sharp shot of strong, black coffee) or *caffè doppio* (double espresso) standing up at the bar with everyone else at your favourite cafe on the way to work.

Lunch and dinner only end one way: with *un caffè* (literally 'a coffee', meaning an espresso and nothing else), although come dusk it is quite acceptable to finish with *un caffè corretto* (espresso with a dash of grappa or another spirit).

Sitting down at a table in a cafe to have a coffee is four times more expensive than drinking it standing at the bar.

Vintage Vespa in Arezzo (p295)

Bella Figura

A sense of style is vital to Tuscans, who take great pride in their dress and appearance to ensure their *bella figura* (good public face). Dressing impeccably comes naturally, and for most Florentines chic is a byword. Indeed it was in Florence that the Italian fashion industry was born and bred.

Guccio Gucci and Salvatore Ferragamo got the haute-couture ball rolling in the 1920s with boutiques in Florence. And in 1951 a well-heeled Florentine nobleman called Giovanni Battista Giorgini held a fashion soirée in his Florence home that spawned Italy's first prêt-à-porter fashion shows. The catwalk quickly shifted to Florence's Palazzo Pitti, where Europe's most prestigious fashion shows dazzled until 1971 (when the women's shows moved to Milan). The menswear shows stayed put, though, and top designers still leg it to Florence twice a year to unveil their menswear collections at the Pitti Immagine Uomo fashion shows and their creations for *bambini* (kids) at Pitti Bimbo.

Lose yourself in the culinary and cultural beauty of the Tuscan home with Emiko Davies' most recent book, *Tortellini at Midnight* (2019), an inspirational collection of heirloom recipes with exquisite photography, a 'romantic nostalgia' vibe and plenty of astute musings on Italian life.

Tuscan Design

Never was Italian design so expressive as in 1963, when Piaggio in Pontedera, 25km east of Pisa, launched the Vespa 50, a motorised scooter requiring no driving licence. Overnight it became a 'must-have' item as Italy's young things snapped up the machine and the freedom and independence it gave. All of Europe's Vespas are still made in the Tuscan plant where the original 'wasp' was born in 1946.

While Audrey Hepburn was cruising around Rome side-saddle on a Vespa for Hollywood, a group of anti-establishment artists and architects was busy building a reputation for Florence as the centre of 1960s avant-garde design. The groups Radical Design, Archizoom and Superstudio were all founded in Florence in 1966, and included hotshot Florentines Massimo Morozzi (b 1941; buy his pasta set from Alessi) and Andrea Branzi (b 1938), whose furniture designs are timeless.

As with fashion, the design scene moved to Milan in the 1970s, starving Tuscany of its cutting edge.

The Tuscan Table

Whether sinking your teeth into a beefy blue *bistecca alla fiorentina* (chargrilled T-bone steak), wine tasting in Chianti, savouring Livorno fish stew or devouring white truffles unearthed around San Miniato near Pisa, travelling in Tuscany is a memorable banquet of gastronomic and viticultural experiences.

A Country Kitchen

It was above an open wood fire in *la cucina contadina* (the farmer's kitchen) that Tuscan cuisine was cooked up. Its basic premise: don't waste a crumb.

During the 13th and 14th centuries, when Florence prospered and the wealthy started using silver cutlery instead of fingers, simplicity remained the hallmark of dishes served at lavish banquets thrown by feuding families as a show of wealth. And while the Medici passion for flaunting the finer things in life during the Renaissance gave Tuscan cuisine a fanciful kick, with spectacular sugar sculptures starring alongside spit-roasted suckling pig, ordinary Tuscans continued to rely on the age-old *cucina povera* (poor dishes) to keep hunger at bay.

Contemporary Tuscan cuisine remains faithful to these humble roots, using fresh local produce and eschewing fussy execution.

GO SLOW TUSCANY

Born out of a desire to protect the world from McDonaldisation, Slow Food (www.fondazioneslowfood.com) preserves local food traditions and encourages interest in the food we eat, its origins and how it tastes. Created by Italian wine writer Carlo Petrini, it works in over 130 countries and has also given rise to Slow City (www.cittaslow.blogspot.com). Slow City towns in Tuscany – Anghiari, Barga, Castelnuovo Berardenga, Civitella in Val di Chiana, Greve in Chianti, Massa Marittima, Pratovecchio, San Miniato, San Vincenzo and Suvereto – have a visible and distinct culture; rely on local resources rather than mass-produced food and culture; work to reduce pollution; and increasingly rely on sustainable development, such as organic farming and public transport.

Industrialisation, globalisation and environmental dangers threaten traditional, indigenous edibles. Enter Slow Food's **Ark of Taste**, a project born and headquartered in Florence that aims to protect and promote endangered food products, including, in Tuscany: Chianina beef, *lardo di colonnata*, Certaldo onions, Casola chestnut bread, Cetica red potatoes, Garfagnana potato bread and *farro* (spelt), Carmignano dried figs, *cinta senese* (the indigenous Tuscan pig), Londa Regina peaches, Pistoian Mountain *pecorino* cheese, Orbetello *bottarga* (salted mullet roe) and Zeri lamb. Among the many cured meats that make the list: San Miniato *mallegato,* Prato *mortadella* (smooth-textured pork sausage made dull pink with drops of alkermes liqueur and speckled white with cubes of fat), Sienese *buristo* (a type of pork salami made in the province of Siena), Valdarno *tarese* (a 50cm- to 80cm-long pancetta spiced with red garlic and orange peel and covered in pepper), Florentine *bardiccio* (fresh fennel-flavoured sausage encased in a natural skin of pig intestine and eaten immediately) and *biroldo* (spiced blood sausage made in Garfagnana from pig's head and blood).

Sampling any of these Tuscan items guarantees an authentic tasting experience.

Meat & Game

The icon of Tuscan cuisine is Florence's *bistecca alla fiorentina,* a chargrilled T-bone steak rubbed with olive oil, seared on the chargrill, seasoned and served *al sangue* (blue and bloody). A born-and-bred rebel, this feisty cut of meat is weighed before it's cooked and priced on menus per *l'etto* or 100g. Traditionally it is butchered from creamy Chianina cows, one of the oldest breeds of cattle, originating from the wide green Val de Chiana in eastern Tuscany.

Tuscan markets conjure up animal parts many wouldn't dream of eating. In the past, prime beef cuts were the domain of the wealthy and offal was the staple peasant fare: tripe was simmered for hours with onions, carrots and herbs to make *lampredotto* or with tomatoes and herbs to make *trippa alla fiorentina* – two classics still going strong.

Pasto, an ancient mix of *picchiante* (cow's lungs) and chopped potatoes, is not even a gastronomic curiosity these days – due to lack of demand it has died a quiet death and is no longer possible to find on restaurant menus. You'll still find equally ancient *cibrèo* (chicken's kidney, liver, heart and cockscomb stew) and *colle ripieno* (stuffed chicken's neck). Another golden oldie featured on many a medieval fresco is *pollo al mattone* – boned chicken splattered beneath a brick, rubbed with herbs and baked beneath the brick. The end result is handsomely crispy.

Cinghiale (wild boar), hunted in autumn, is turned into *salsicce di cinghiale* (wild-boar sausages) or simmered with tomatoes, pepper and herbs to create a rich stew.

In Tuscany the family pig invariably ends up on the plate as a salty slice of *soprassata* (head, skin and tongue boiled, chopped and flavoured with garlic, rosemary and other herbs and spices), *finocchiona* (fennel-spiced sausage), prosciutto, nearly black *mallegato* (blood sausage spiked with nutmeg, cinnamon, raisins and pine kernels from San Miniato) or *mortadella* (a smooth-textured pork sausage speckled with cubes of white fat). *Lardo di colonnata* (thin slices of local pork fat aged in a mix of herbs and oils for at least six months) is a treat hard to find outside Tuscany.

Fish

The old Medici port of Livorno leads the region in seafood: *cacciucco* (one 'c' for each type of fish thrown into it) is the signature dish. Deriving its name from the Turkish *kukut,* meaning 'small fry', *cacciucco* is a stew of five fish simmered with tomatoes and red peppers, served atop stale bread. *Triglie alla livornese* is red or white mullet cooked in tomatoes, and *baccalà alla livornese,* also with tomatoes, features cod, traditionally salted aboard the ships en route to the port. *Baccalà* (salted cod), not to be confused with *stoccofisso* (unsalted air-dried stockfish), is a trattoria mainstay, served on Fridays as tradition and old-style Catholicism demands.

Pulses, Grains & Vegetables

Pulses were poor man's meat to Tuscans centuries ago. Jam-packed with protein, cheap and available year-round (eaten fresh in summer, dried in winter), pulses go into traditional dishes like *minestra di fagioli* (bean soup), *minestra di pane* (bread and bean soup) and *ribollita* (a 'reboiled' bean, vegetable and bread soup with black cabbage that is left to sit for a day before being served).

Of the dozens of bean varieties, *cannellini* and dappled *borlotti* are the most common; both are delicious drizzled with olive oil to accompany meat. The round, yellow *zolfino* from Pratomagno and the silky-smooth *sorano* bean from Pescia are prized. Of huge local pride to farmers in the Garfagnana is *farro della garfagnana* (spelt), an ancient grain grown in Europe as early as 2500 BC.

Best T-Bone Steak

Trattoria Mario (Florence, p118)

Osteria La Taverna di San Giuseppe (Siena, p153)

Officina della Bistecca (Chianti, p165)

Sergio Falaschi (San Miniato, p278)

Ristorante Da Muzzicone (Val de Chiana, p312)

Pasta is as Tuscan as it is Italian, and no Tuscan banquet would be complete without a *primo* (first course) of homemade *maccheroni* (wide, flat ribbon pasta), *pappardelle* (wider flat ribbon pasta) or Sienese *pici* (a thick, hand-rolled version of spaghetti) served with a duck, hare, rabbit or boar sauce.

Tuscany's lush vegetable patch sees medieval vegetables grow alongside tomatoes. Wild fennel, black celery (braised as a side dish), sweet red onions (delicious when oven-roasted), artichokes and zucchini flowers (stuffed and oven-baked), black cabbage, broad beans, chicory, chard, thistle-like cardoons and green tomatoes are among the ones to look out for.

Prized as one of the most expensive spices, saffron is all the rage around San Gimignano, where it was enthusiastically traded in medieval times. Fiery red and as fine as dust by the time it reaches the kitchen, saffron in its rawest state is the dried stigma of the saffron crocus.

Bread

One bite and the difference is striking: Tuscan *pane* (bread) is unsalted, creating a disconcertingly bland taste many a bread lover might never learn to enjoy.

Yet it is this centuries-old staple – deliberately unsalted to ensure it lasted for a good week and to complement the region's salty cured meats – that forms the backbone of Tuscany's most famous dishes: *pappa al pomodoro* (bread and tomato soup), *panzanella* (tomato and basil salad mixed with a mush of bread soaked in cold water) and *ribollita* (a thick vegetable, bread and bean soup). None sounds or looks particularly appetising, but the depth of flavour is extraordinary.

Thick-crusted *pane toscana* is the basis of two antipasti delights: *crostini* (lightly toasted slices of bread topped with liver pâté) and *fettunta* (a kind of Tuscan bruschetta that's also called *crogiantina*; toast fingers doused in garlic, salt and olive oil).

Best Traditional Tuscan

Il Teatro del Sale (Florence, p120)

Trattoria Mario (Florence, p118)

Il Leccio (Val d'Orcia, p184)

L'Osteria di Casa Chianti (Val di Pesa, p163)

Ristorante La Nena (Anghiari, p302)

Il Cedro (Casentino, p308)

THE TUSCAN TABLE A COUNTRY KITCHEN

DINING ETIQUETTE

Dining in Tuscany has its own set of unspoken rules – heed them to make your dining experience a whole lot smoother.

Eating outside Pretty much guaranteed from anytime in May through to early October. In towns and cities, think twice before you plop yourself down on church steps or in the middle of a historic piazza to grab a quick *oanino* (sandwich) or other takeaway lunch – it is forbidden. Look for the nearest bench or city park.

Dress Smart casual is best, particularly in Florence and other cities and large towns, where working urbanites go home to freshen up between *aperitivo* and dinner.

Courses Don't feel obliged to order the Tuscan full monty; it's quite acceptable to order just one or two courses such as an *antipasto* (starter) and a *primo* (pasta course), or even just a *secondo* (main course).

Bread This is plentiful, unsalted and served without either butter or a side plate (put it on the table).

Spaghetti Twirl it around your fork as if you were born twirling – no spoons, please.

Young children It is perfectly acceptable to ask for a plate of plain pasta with butter and Parmesan.

Coffee Never order a cappuccino after 11am, and certainly not after a meal, when an espresso is the only respectable choice (with, perhaps, a digestif of grappa or another fiery spirit).

Il conto (the bill) Whoever invites pays.

Splitting the bill Common enough.

Tipping If there is no *servizio* (service charge), leave a 10% to 15% tip.

Cheese

So important was cheesemaking in the past that it was a dowry skill. Still respected, the sheep's-milk *pecorino* crafted in Pienza ranks among Italy's greatest *pecorini:* taste it young and mild with broad beans, fresh pear or chestnuts and honey, or try it mature and tangy, spiked with *toscanello* (black peppercorns) or as *pecorino di tartufo* (infused with black-truffle shavings). *Pecorino* massaged with olive oil during the ageing process turns red and is called *rossellino*.

Organic Food

Cibo biologico (organic food) is increasingly popular in farm-rich Tuscany, where some outstanding dining choices are built around organic farm produce; *agriturismo* Fattoria San Martino in Montelpuciano is exclusively vegetarian and vegan.

Sweets & Gelato

Be it the honey, almond and sugar-cane sweets served at the start of 14th-century banquets in Florence or the sugar sculptures made to impress at the flamboyant 16th- and 17th-century feasts of the Medici, *dolci* (sweets) have always been reserved for festive occasions. In more humble circles street vendors sold *bomboloni* (doughnuts) and *pandiramerino* (rosemary-bread buns), while Carnevale in Florence was marked by *stiacchiata* (Florentine flat bread made from eggs, flour, sugar and lard, then dusted with icing sugar).

As early as the 13th century, servants at the Abbazia di Montecelso near Siena paid tax to the nuns in the form of *panpepato* (a pepper and honey flatbread), although legend tells a different tale: following a siege in Siena, Sister Berta baked a revitalising flat cake of honey, dried fruit, almonds and pepper to perk up the city's weakened inhabitants. Subsequently sweetened with spices, sprinkled with sugar and feasted on once a year at Christmas, Siena's *panforte* (literally 'strong bread') – a rich cake with nuts and candied fruit – is now eaten year-round. An adage says it stops couples quarrelling.

Tuscan *biscotti* (biscuits) – once served with candied fruit and sugared almonds at the start of and between courses at Renaissance banquets – are dry, crisp and often double baked. *Cantucci* are hard, sweet biscuits studded with almonds. *Brighidini di lamporecchio* are small, round aniseed-flavoured wafers; *ricciarelli* are almond biscuits, sometimes with candied orange; and *lardpinocchiati* are studded with pine kernels. In Lucca, locals are proud of their *buccellato* (a sweet bread loaf with sultanas and aniseed seeds), a treat given by godparents to their godchild on their first Holy Communion and eaten with alacrity at all other times.

Unsurprisingly, it was at the Florentine court of Catherine de' Medici that Italy's most famous product, gelato, first appeared, thanks to court maestro Bernardo Buontalenti (1536–1608), who engineered a way of freezing sweetened milk and egg yolks. For centuries, ice cream and sherbets – a mix of shaved ice and fruit juice served between courses at Renaissance banquets to aid digestion – only appeared on wealthy tables.

Best Creative Tuscan

Essenziale (Florence, p122)

·········

Filippo (Pietrasanta, p289)

·········

Ristorante Enzo (Siena, p153)

·········

Il Grillo è Buoncantore (Chiusi, p194)

·········

Aliciati (Arezzo, p302)

·········

Ristorante Al Coccio (Sansepolcro, p307)

Celebrations

Be it harvest, wedding, birth or religious holiday, traditional celebrations are intrinsically woven into Tuscan culinary culture. They are not as raucous as festivals of the past, when an animal was sacrificed, but most remain meaty affairs.

Tuscans have baked breads and cakes, such as ring-shaped *berlingozzo* (Tuscan sweet bread) and *schiacciata alla fiorentina* (a flattish, spongy bread-cake best made with old-fashioned lard) for centuries during Carnevale, the period of merrymaking leading up to Ash Wednesday.

Top: *Panforte*

Bottom: *Pecorino* for sale in Pienza (p184)

Fritters are another sweet Carnevale treat: *cenci* are plain twists (literally 'rags') of fried, sweet dough sprinkled with icing sugar, *castagnole* look like puffed-up cushions, and *fritelle di mele* are slices of apple battered, deep fried and eaten warm with sugar.

On Easter Sunday families take baskets of hard-boiled white eggs covered in a white-cloth napkin to church to be blessed, and return home to a luncheon feast of roast lamb gently spiced with garlic and rosemary, preceded by the blessed eggs.

September's grape harvest sees grapes stuck on top of *schiacciata* to make *schiacciata con l'uva* (grape cake), and autumn's chestnut harvest brings a flurry of chestnut festivals and the appearance of *castagnaccio* (chestnut cake baked with chestnut flour, studded with raisins, topped with a rosemary sprig and served with a slice of ricotta) on the Tuscan table.

Come Christmas, *bollito misto* (boiled meat) with all the trimmings is traditional for many families: various animal parts, eg trotters, are thrown into the cooking pot and simmered for hours with a vegetable and herb stock. The meat is later served with mustard, green salsa and other sauces. A whole pig, notably the recently revived ancient white-and-black *cinta senese* indigenous breed, roasted on a spit, is the other option.

On the Wine Trail

There's far more to this vine-rich region than cheap, raffia-wrapped bottled Chianti – *that* was the 1970s, darling! Something of a viticulture powerhouse, Tuscany excites oenophiles with its myriad full-bodied, highly respected reds. Wine tasting is an endless pleasure and the region is peppered with *enoteche* (wine bars) and *cantine* (wine cellars) designed especially for tasting and buying.

Many are planted on Tuscany's *strade del vino* (wine roads): signposted itineraries that lead motorists and cyclists along wonderfully scenic back roads into the heart of Tuscan wine country.

Tuscan white amounts to one label loved by Renaissance popes and artists alike: the aromatic Vernaccia di San Gimignano, best drunk as an aperitif on a terrace in or around San Gimignano.

Brunello di Montalcino

Brunello di Montalcino is one of Italy's most prized wines: count on up to €20 for a glass, €60 to €150 for an average bottle and €5000 for a 1940s collectible. The product of Sangiovese grapes grown south of Siena, it must spend at least two years ageing in oak. It is intense and complex, with an ethereal fragrance, and it's best paired with game, wild boar and roasts. Brunello grape rejects go into Rosso di Montalcino, Brunello's substantially cheaper but wholly drinkable kid sister.

WINE CLASSIFICATIONS

The quality and origin of Tuscan wine is flagged with these official classifications.

DOC (Denominazione d'Origine Controllata; Protected Designation of Origin) Must be produced within a specified region using defined methods to meet a certain quality; the rules spell out production area, grape varietals and viticultural/bottling techniques.

DOCG (Denominazione d'Origine Controllata e Garantita; Protected Designation of Origin and Quality) The most prestigious stamp of quality, DOCG wines are particularly good ones, produced in subterritories of DOC areas. Of Italy's 44 DOCGs, eight are Tuscan – Brunello di Montalcino, Carmignano, Chianti, Chianti Classico, Morellino di Scansano, Vernaccia di San Gimignano, Vino Nobile di Montepulciano and Elba Aleatico Passito.

IGT (Indicazione Geografica Tipica; Protected Geographical Indication) High-quality wines, such as Super Tuscans, that don't meet DOC or DOCG definitions.

Vino Nobile di Montepulciano

Prugnolo Gentile grapes (a clone of Sangiovese) form the backbone of the distinguished Vino Nobile di Montepulciano (2006 was an exceptional year). Its intense but delicate nose and dry, vaguely tannic taste make it the perfect companion to red meat and mature cheese.

Chianti

The cheery, full and dry Chianti is known the world over as being easy to drink, suited to any dish and wholly affordable. It was more famous than good in the 1970s, but contemporary Chianti gets the thumbs up from wine critics today. Produced in seven subzones from Sangiovese and a mix of other grape varieties, Chianti Classico – the traditional heart of this long-standing wine-growing area – is the best known, with a DOCG guarantee of quality and a Gallo Nero (Black Cockerel) emblem that once symbolised the medieval Chianti League. Young, fun Chianti Colli Senesi from the Siena hills is the largest subzone; Chianti delle Colline Pisane is light and soft in style; and Chianti Rùfina comes from the hills east of Florence.

Super Tuscans

One result of Chianti's 'cheap wine for the masses' reputation in the 1970s was the realisation by some Tuscans – including the Antinoris, Tuscany's most famous wine-producing family – that wines with a rich, complex, internationally acceptable taste following the New World tradition of blending mixes could be sold for a lot more than local wines. Thus, innovative, exciting wines were developed and cleverly marketed to appeal to buyers both in New York and in Florence. And when an English-speaking scribe dubbed the end product 'Super Tuscans', the name stuck. (Italian winemakers prefer the term IGT – *indicazione geografica tipica*.) Sassaicaia, Solaia, Bolgheri, Tignanello and Luce are all superhot Super Tuscans.

More and more international wine producers are turning to Tuscan soil to blend Super Tuscans and other modern wines. American-owned Castello Banfi (p181), in the Tuscan biz for over three decades, is one of the most state-of-the-art wineries in Italy and continues to impress the international wine world with its pioneering work, quietly underscoring the demise of winemaking as the exclusive domain of old, blue-blooded Tuscan families. These days, in this ancient land first cultivated by the Etruscans, Tuscany's oldest craft is open to anyone with wine-wizardry nous.

Celebrity Wine

Celebrity-backed wine followed hot on the heels of the Super Tuscans. English pop star Sting owns an organically farmed estate, **Tenuta Il Palagio** (www.palagioproducts.com), near Figline Valdarno in Chianti

Best Wine Bars

Le Volpi e l'Uva (Florence, p129)

Il Santino (Florence, p127)

E Lucevan Le Stelle (Montepulciano, p192)

Enoteca Tognoni (Bolgheri, p228)

Idyllium (Val d'Orcia, p186)

TUSCAN OLIVE OIL

Olive oil heads Tuscany's culinary trinity (bread and wine are the other two members) and epitomises the earthy simplicity of Tuscan cuisine: dipping chunks of bread into pools of this liquid gold or biting into a slice of oil-doused *fettunta* (bruschetta) are sweet pleasures here.

The Etruscans were the first to cultivate olive trees and press the fruit to make oil, a process refined by the Romans. As with wine, strict rules govern when and how olives are harvested (October to December), the varieties used, and so on.

The best Tuscan oils wear a Chianti Classico DOP or Terre di Siena DOP label and an IGP certificate of quality issued by the region's Consortium of Tuscan Olive Oil. In Florence look out for prize-winning oils from local producer Marchesi de' Frescobaldi.

where he produces various wines (as well as olive oil and honey), each named after one of his songs: Message in a Bottle, When We Dance, and so forth.

Super Tuscan reds are produced by the son of Florentine designer Roberto Cavalli at **Tenuta degli Dei** (www.deglidei.com) outside Panzano in Chianti, where top-of-the-range bottles are packaged in a typical Cavalli, flashy leopard-skin box. Wines produced southeast of Pisa on the family estate of opera singer Andrea Bocelli form the irresistible backbone of wine boutique and food court Officine Bocelli (p283), on the family estate in rural La Sterza, northwestern Tuscany.

If celebrity design is more your cup of tea, taste wine at the subterranean, design-driven **Rocca di Frassinello** (www.castellare.it/it/rocca-di-frassinello) winery near Grosseto by Renzo Piano; or the equally breathtaking Petra (p232) winery by Swiss architect Mario Botta in the Etruscan hills near Suvereto.

Then, of course, there is the spectacular Antinori nel Chianti Classico (p162) cellar, groundbreaking in design – quite literally: an entire hillside in the heart of Chianti Classico was dug up, a designer cellar was popped inside and earthed over, and new vines were planted, leaving just two giant slashes (the panoramic terraces of the 26,000-sq-metre building) visible from the opposite Chianti hill.

Tuscany's Wine and Oil Roads

Meander past olive groves, vines and farms plump with local produce with these delightful *strade del vino e dell'olio* (wine and oil roads).

Strada del Vino e dei Sapori Colli di Maremma (www.stradevinoditoscana.it/strade/collimaremma) This route southeast of Grosseto highlights several DOC and DOCG wines, extra-virgin olive-oil Toscano IGP and the Maremmana breed of cattle.

Strada del Vino e dell'Olio Lucca Montecarlo e Versilia (www.stradavinoeolio lucca.it) Seravezza in the Apuane Alps to Lucca, then east to Montecarlo and Pescia. This route features Lucca's famous DOP olive oil and the Colline Lucchesi and Montecarlo di Lucca DOCs.

Strada del Vino e dell'Olio Costa degli Etruschi (www.lastradadelvino.com) A scenic 150km itinerary along the Etruscan Coast from Livorno to Piombino and then over to the Tuscan island of Elba; Super Tuscan Sassicaia is the big tasting highlight.

Wine Tasting in Situ

....

Antinori nel Chianti Classico (Chianti, p162)

....

Petra Wine (Etruscan Coast, p232)

....

Castello di Ama (Chianti, p165)

....

Enoliteca Consortile (Montepulciano, p188)

....

Vernaccia di San Gimignano Wine Experience (San Gimignano, p168)

....

Enoteca La Fortezza (Montalcino, p181)

Tuscany on Page & Screen

Few destinations have such a rich history and landscape to draw on for inspiration as Tuscany – or offer writers, actors and crews such a sybaritic location in which to research, write and shoot their works. The birthplace of Italian literature (courtesy of the great Dante Alighieri) and the setting for the greatest Italian film of recent decades (*Life is Beautiful*), Tuscany offers the visitor plenty of options when it comes to predeparture reading and viewing.

Tuscany in Print

The region's literary heritage is rich and varied, and it nurtures both local and foreign writers to this day.

Local Voices

Prior to the 13th century, Italian literature was written in Latin. But all that changed with Florentine-born Dante Alighieri (c 1265–1321). One of the founders of the Dolce Stil Novo (Sweet New Style) literary movement, whose members wrote lyric poetry in the Tuscan vernacular, Dante went on to use the local language when writing the epic poem that was to become the first, and greatest, literary work published in the Italian language: *La grande commedia* (The Great Comedy), published around 1317 and later renamed *La divina commedia* (The Divine Comedy) by his fellow poet Boccaccio. Divided into three parts – *Inferno, Purgatorio* and *Paradiso* – The Divine Comedy delivered an allegorical vision of the afterlife that made an immediate and profound impression on readers and, through its wide-reaching popularity, established the Tuscan dialect as the new standardised form of written Italian.

Another early adapter to the new language of literature was Giovanni Boccaccio (1303–75), who hailed from Certaldo. His masterpiece, *Decameron,* was written in the years following the plague of 1348. A collection of 100 allegorical tales recounted by 10 characters, it delivered a vast panorama of personalities, events and symbolism to contemporary readers and was nearly as popular and influential as *The Divine Comedy*.

The remaining member of the influential triumvirate that laid down the course for the development of a rich literature in Italian was Petrarch (Francesco Petrarca; 1304–74), born in Arezzo to Florentine parents. Although most of his writings were in Latin, he wrote his most popular works, the poems, in Italian. *Il canzoniere* (Songbook; c 1327–68) is the distilled result of his finest poetry. Although the core subject is his unrequited love for a woman named Laura, the breadth of human grief and joy is treated with a lyrical quality unseen until then. His influence spread far and across time: the Petrarchan sonnet form, rhyme scheme and even subject matter was adopted by English metaphysical poets of 17th-century England such as John Donne.

Brits Abroad

Pictures from Italy (Charles Dickens; 1846)

Along the Road (Aldous Huxley; 1925)

Etruscan Places (DH Lawrence; 1932)

Another outstanding writer of this period was Niccolò Machiavelli (1469–1527), known above all for his work on power and politics, *Il Principe* (The Prince; 1532).

19th Century Onwards

After its stellar start during the Renaissance, Tuscany took a literary break in the 17th and 18th centuries. The scene regained momentum in the 19th century with Giosuè Carducci (1835–1907), a Maremma-born writer who spent the second half of his life in Bologna. The best of his poetry, written in the 1870s, ranged in tone from a pensive evocation of death (such as in 'Pianto antico') or memories of youthful passion ('Idillio Maremmano') to a nostalgia harking back to the glories of ancient Rome.

During the pre-WWI years Florence's Aldo Palazzeschi (1885–1974) was in the vanguard of the futurist movement. In 1911 he published arguably his best work, *Il codice di Perelà* (Perelà's Code), a sometimes bitter allegory that in part becomes a farcical imitation of the life of Christ.

Another Florentine, Vasco Pratolini (1913–91), set four highly regarded neo-realist novels in his birthplace: *Le ragazze di San Frediano* (The Girls of San Frediano; 1949), *Cronaca familiare* (Family Diary; 1947), *Cronache di poveri amanti* (Chronicle of Poor Lovers; 1947) and *Metello* (1955).

Fiesole-born Dacia Maraini (b 1936), for many years the partner of author Alberto Moravia, is one of Italy's most lauded contemporary writers, with novels, plays and poetry to her credit. Her best-known works include *Buio* (1999), which won the Premio Strega, Italy's most prestigious literary award, and *La lunga vita di Marianna Ucrìa* (published in English as *The Silent Duchess*; 1990). Her most recent work, *Writing Like Breathing* (2017), is an anthology spanning her 50-year-long writing career.

Through Foreign Eyes

The trend of setting English-language novels in Tuscany kicked off during the era of the Grand Tour, when wealthy young men from Britain and northern Europe travelled around Europe to view the cultural legacies of antiquity and the Renaissance, completing their liberal educations and being introduced to polite society in the process. The Grand Tour's heyday was from the mid-17th century to the mid-19th century.

With the advent of rail travel in the 1840s, the prospect of a cultural odyssey opened to the middle classes. Wealthy travellers from Britain, America and Australasia flocked to Italy, and some wrote about their experiences. Notable among these were Henry James, who set parts of *The*

Americans Abroad

Italian Hours (Henry James; 1909)

The Stones of Florence (Mary McCarthy; 1956)

The City of Florence (RWB Lewis; 1995)

TUSCAN MEMOIRS

Many people visit Tuscany and dream of purchasing their own piece of paradise. The following writers did just that, some establishing wildly successful literary franchises in the process.

Kinta Beevor (*A Tuscan Childhood*; 1993) Beautiful evocation of life in the Tuscan countryside between the two world wars, by the daughter of an English painter who bought a castle in Tuscany and hobnobbed with the likes of DH Lawrence, Aldous Huxley et al.

Eric Newby (*A Small Place in Italy*; 1994) The original Tuscan memoir; Newby bought a farmhouse in northeastern Tuscany in the 1960s and so came to pen this sensitive portrait of rural Tuscany, its people, seasons and ancient rituals.

Frances Mayes (*Under the Tuscan Sun: At Home in Italy; Bella Tuscany; In Tuscany; Every Day in Tuscany*; 1996–2010) Following the end of her marriage, American writer and poet (and subsequent Tuscan bard) bought a dilapidated house in Cortona, did it up and wrote about it in *Under the Tuscan Sun* – a classic today.

Portrait of a Lady (1881) and *Roderick Hudson* (1875) here; George Eliot, whose *Romola* (1862) was set in 15th-century Florence; and EM Forster, who set *A Room with a View* (1908) in Florence and *Where Angels Fear to Tread* (1905) in San Gimignano (fictionalised as Monteriano).

Things slowed down in the early 20th century, with only a few major novelists choosing to set their work here. These included Somerset Maugham (*Up at the Villa;* 1941) and Aldous Huxley (*Time Must Have a Stop;* 1944).

In recent decades, a number of highly regarded novels have been set in Tuscany. Perhaps the best known of these is the Renaissance fiction by English writer Linda Proud, whose Botticelli trilogy – *A Tabernacle for the Sun* (1997), *Pallas and the Centaur* (2004) and *The Rebirth of Venus* (2008) – is set in Renaissance Florence during the Pazzi conspiracy, the Medici exile and the rise of Savonarola. The historical detail in all three is exemplary, and each is a cracking good read. Her novel about Botticelli's master Fra' Filippo Lippi, *A Gift for the Magus,* was published in 2012.

Other writers who have used Renaissance Florence as a setting include Sarah Dunant (*The Birth of Venus;* 2003), Salman Rushdie (*The Enchantress of Florence;* 2008), Michaela-Marie Roessner-Hermann (*The Stars Dispose;* 1997, and *The Stars Dispel;* 1999) and Jack Dann (*The Memory Cathedral;* 1995). Of these, Dann wins the prize for constructing the most bizarre plot, setting his novel in a version of the Renaissance in which Leonardo da Vinci actually constructs a number of his inventions (eg the flying machine) and uses them during a battle in the Middle East while in the service of a Syrian general.

Also set in Florence are *Innocence* (1986), written by Booker Prize–winning novelist Penelope Fitzgerald and set during the 1950s; *The Sixteen Pleasures* (1994) by Robert Hellenga, set after the devastating flood of 1966; *The English Patient* (1992) by Michael Ondaatje; and *Inferno* (2013) by Dan Brown (author of *The Da Vinci Code).*

In *Across the Big Blue Sea* (2017), Swiss writer Katja Meier shares the lessons she learnt during her time working in a home for refugees in the Tuscan hills; Maremma is the setting.

Tuscany on Film

Cinema heavyweight Franco Zeffirelli (1923–2019) was born in Florence and set many of his films in the region. His career took him from radio and theatre to opera (both stage productions and film versions) and his films included *Romeo and Juliet* (1968), *Brother Sun, Sister Moon* (1972), *Hamlet* (1990) and the semi-autobiographical *Tea with Mussolini* (1999). Learn about his life and works at the Fondazione Zeffirelli in Florence.

Actor, comedian and director Roberto Benigni was born near Castiglion Fiorentino in 1952. He picked up four Oscars and created a genre all of his own – Holocaust comedy – with the extraordinarily powerful *La vita é bella* (Life Is Beautiful; 1998), a film shot in the east Tuscan town of Arezzo that he directed, cowrote and starred in. Often compared with Charlie Chaplin and Buster Keaton, he has directed nine films (two set in Tuscany) and acted in many more, including three directed by American independent film-maker Jim Jarmusch.

Four films based on neo-realist novels by Vasco Pratolini were shot in Florence: *Le ragazze di San Frediano* (The Girls of San Frediano; Valerio Zurlini; 1954), *Cronache di poveri amanti* (Chronicle of Poor Lovers; Carlo Lizzani; 1954), *Cronaca familiare* (Family Diary; Valerio Zurlini; 1962) and *Metello* (Mauro Bolognini; 1970).

Award-winning film-makers Paolo and Vittorio Taviani were born in San Miniato and have set parts of three of their films in Tuscany: *La notte di San Lorenzo* (The Night of the Shooting Stars; 1982), *Le affinità elettive* (Elective Affinities; 1996) and *Good Morning Babylon* (1987).

Art & Architecture

In many respects, the history of Tuscan art is also the history of Western art. Browse through any text on the subject and you'll quickly develop an understanding of how influential the Italian Renaissance, which kicked off and reached its greatest flowering in Florence, has been over the past 500 years. Indeed, it's no exaggeration to say that architecture, painting and sculpture rely on its technical innovations and take inspiration from its major works to this very day.

The Etruscans

Roughly 2800 years before we all started dreaming of a hilltop getaway in Tuscany, the Etruscans had a similar idea: the hill towns that they founded are dotted throughout the countryside.

From the 8th to the 3rd centuries BC, Etruscans held their own against friends, Romans and countrymen, worshipped their own gods and goddesses, and farmed lowlands using sophisticated drainage systems of their own invention. How well they lived between sieges and war is unclear, but they sure knew how to throw a funeral. Etruscan *necropoli* (tombs) are found throughout southern, central and eastern Tuscany. Excavation of these tombs often yields a wealth of jewellery, cinerary urns (used for body ashes) made from terracotta and alabaster, earthenware pottery (particularly the glossy black ceramic known as *bucchero*) and bronze votive offerings.

Of course, the Romans knew a good thing when they plundered it. After conquering swaths of Etruscan territory in Tuscany in the 3rd century BC, they incorporated the Etruscans' highly refined, geometric style into their own art and architecture.

Top Etruscan Museums

Museo Etrusco Guarnacci (Volterra, p176)

Museo dell'Accademia Etrusca (Cortona, p313)

Museo Civico Archeologico 'Isidoro Falchi' (Vetulonia, p203)

Museo Archeologico Nazionale 'Gaio Cilnio Mecenate' (Arezzo, p299)

Enter Christianity

Roman centurions weren't in the area for long before Christianity began to take hold. After abandoning his studies and a promising career in Rome to adopt the contemplative life around AD 500, a young local man named Benedict went on to be credited with a number of miracles, personally establish 12 monasteries and inspire the founding of many more. His story is visually narrated in great detail in the stunning fresco series (1497–1505) by Il Sodoma and Luca Signorelli in the Great Cloister at Abbazia di Monte Oliveto Maggiore, near Siena.

One early Benedictine monastery, San Pietro in Valle, was built in neighbouring Umbria by order of the Lombard duke of Spoleto, Faroaldo II. It kick-started a craze for the blend of Lombard and Roman styles known as Romanesque, and many local ecclesiastical structures were built in this style. The basic template was simple: a stark nave stripped of extra columns ending in a domed apse, surrounded by chapels usually donated by wealthy patrons.

In the 11th century the Romanesque style acquired a distinctly Tuscan twist in Pisa, when the coloured marble banding and veneering of the city's *duomo* (cathedral) set a new gold standard for architectural decoration. This new style (sometimes described as Pisan) was then applied to a swath of churches throughout the region, including the Chiesa di San Miniato al Monte in Florence, and the Chiesa di San Michele in Foro and the Cattedrale di San Martino, both in Lucca.

Siena was not about to be outdone in the architectural stakes by its rivals Florence and Pisa, and so in 1196 its city council approved a no-expenses-spared program to build a new *duomo*. They certainly got their money's worth, ending up with a spectacular Gothic facade by Giovanni Pisano, a pulpit by Nicola Pisano and a rose window designed by Duccio di Buoninsegna.

While Tuscany's churches were becoming increasingly more spectacular, nothing prepared pilgrims for what they would find inside the upper and lower churches of the Basilica di San Francesco in Assisi, Umbria. Not long after St Francis' death in 1226, an all-star team of Tuscan artists was hired to decorate these churches in his honour, kicking off a craze for frescoes that wouldn't abate for centuries. Cimabue, Giotto, Pietro Lorenzetti and Simone Martini captured the life and gentle spirit of St Francis while his memory was still fresh in the minds of the faithful. For medieval pilgrims unaccustomed to multiplexes and special effects, entering a space that had been covered from floor to ceiling with stories told in living colour must have been a dazzling, overwhelming experience.

As madness and profligacy often run in families, so too does artistic genius. Italian artistic dynasties include the della Robbias (Luca, Marco, Andrea, Giovanni and Girolamo), the Lorenzettis (Ambrogio and Pietro) and the Pisanos (Nicola and Giovanni, Andrea and Nino).

The Middle Ages: the Rise of the Comune

While communities sprang up around hermits and holy men in the hinterlands, cities began to take on a life of their own from the 13th and 14th centuries. Roman road networks had been serving as handy trade routes starting in the 11th century, and farming estates and villas began to spring up outside major trading centres as a new middle class of merchants, farmers and skilled craftspeople emerged. Taxes and donations sponsored the building of hospitals such as Ospedale Santa Maria della Scala in Siena. Streets were paved, town walls erected and sewerage systems built to accommodate an increasingly sophisticated urban population not keen on sprawl or squalor.

GIOTTO DI BONDONE

The 14th-century Tuscan poet Giovanni Boccaccio wrote in the *Decameron* that his fellow Tuscan Giotto di Bondone (c 1266–1337) was 'a genius so sublime that there was nothing produced by nature...that he could not depict to the life'.

Boccaccio wasn't the only prominent critic of the time to consider Giotto extraordinary – Giorgio Vasari was also a huge fan, arguing that Giotto initiated the 'rebirth' (*rinascità* or *renaissance*) in art. In his paintings, Giotto abandoned popular conventions such as the three-quarter view of head and body, and presented his figures from behind, from the side or turning around, just as the story demanded. Giotto had no need for lashings of gold paint and elaborate ornamentation to impress the viewer with the significance of the subject. Instead, he enabled the viewer to feel the dramatic tension of a scene through a naturalistic rendition of figures and a radical composition that created the illusion of depth.

Giotto's important works in Tuscany include an altarpiece portraying the Madonna and Child among angels and saints in Florence's Galleria degli Uffizi, a painted wooden crucifix in the Basilica di Santa Maria Novella and frescoes in the Basilica di Santa Croce. His magnificent *Life of St Francis* fresco cycle graces the walls of the upper church of the Basilica di San Francesco in Assisi, Umbria.

Many Renaissance painters included self-portraits in their major works. Giotto didn't, possibly due to the fact that friends such as Boccaccio described him as the ugliest man in Florence. With friends like these...

Once townsfolk came into a bit of money, they weren't necessarily eager to part with it, and didn't always agree on how their tax dollars should be spent. *Comuni* (local governments) were formed to represent the various interests of merchants, guilds and competing noble families, and the first order of business in major medieval cities, such as Siena, Florence and Volterra, was the construction of an impressive town hall to reflect the importance and authority of the *comune*. The greatest example is Siena's Palazzo Comunale.

In addition to being savvy political lobbyists and fans of grand architectural projects that kept their constituents gainfully employed, medieval *comuni* were masters of propaganda, and perfectly understood the influence that art and architecture could wield. A case in point is Ambrogio Lorenzetti's *Allegories of Good and Bad Government* fresco series in Siena's Palazzo Comunale, which is better and bigger than any political billboard could ever be. In the *Allegory of Good Government,* Lorenzetti's grey-bearded figure of Legitimate Authority is surrounded by an entourage that would certainly put White House interns to shame: Peace, Fortitude, Prudence, Magnanimity, Temperance and Justice. Above them flit Faith, Hope and Charity, and to the left Concord sits confidently on her throne while she holds the reins of justice are held taut overhead.

Next to this fresco is another depicting the effects of good government: townsfolk make their way through town in an orderly fashion, pausing to do business, greet one another, join hands and dance a merry jig. But things couldn't be more different in the *Allegory of Bad Government,* where horned and fanged Tyrannia rules over a scene of chaos surrounded by winged vices, and Justice lies unconscious, her scales shattered. Like the best campaign speeches, this cautionary tale was brilliantly rendered but not always heeded.

On the World Stage

When they weren't busy politicking, late-medieval farmers, craftspeople and merchants did quite well for themselves. Elegant, locally made ceramics, tiles and marbles were showcased in churches across Tuscany and became all the rage throughout Europe and the Mediterranean when pilgrims returned home to England and France with examples after following the Via Francigena pilgrimage route from Canterbury to Rome. Artisans were kept busy applying their skills to civic-works projects and churches, which had to be expanded and updated to keep up with the growing numbers and rising expectations of pilgrims in the area.

With outside interest came outside influence, and local styles adapted to international markets. Florence became famous for lustrous, tin-glazed *maiolica* (majolica ware) tiles and plates painted with vibrant metallic pigments that were inspired by the Islamic ceramics of Mallorca (Spain). The prolific della Robbia family started to create richly glazed ceramic reliefs that are now enshrined at the Museo del Bargello in Florence and in churches and museums across the region.

Modest Romanesque cathedrals were given an International Gothic makeover befitting their appeal to pilgrims of all nations, but the Italian take on the French style was more colourful than the grey-stone spires and flying buttresses of Paris. The local version often featured a simple layout and striped stone naves fronted by multilayer birthday-cake facades, which might be frosted with pink paint, glittering mosaics and rows of arches capped with sculptures. The most famous example of this confectionery approach is the *duomo* in Siena.

The evolution from solid Romanesque to airy Gothic to a yin-and-yang balance of the two can be witnessed in buildings throughout the region, many of which blend a relatively austere Romanesque exterior with high

Romanesque Churches

Collegiata (San Gimignano, p167)

Abbazia di Sant'Antimo (near Montalcino, p186)

Cattedrale di San Pietro (Sovana, p207)

Chiesa di Santa Maria della Pieve (Arezzo, p298)

Best Sculpture Parks

Il Giardino di Daniel Spoerri (Seggiano, p202)

Fattoria di Celle (Pistoia, p270)

Giardino dei Tarocchi (southern Tuscany, p213)

Parco Sculture del Chianti (Chianti, p166)

Castello di Ama (Chianti, p166)

Gothic drama indoors. This set a new ecclesiastical architecture standard that was quickly exported into Italy at large and on to the rest of Europe.

Dark Times

By the 14th century the smiling Sienese townsfolk of Ambrogio Lorenzetti's *Allegory of Good Government* must have seemed like the figment of a fertile imagination. After a major famine in 1329 and then a bank collapse, Siena's *comune* went into debt to maintain roads, continue work on the *duomo*, help the needy and jump-start the local economy. But just when the city seemed set for a comeback, the plague brought devastation in 1348. Three-quarters of Siena's population – including Pietro and Ambrogio Lorenzetti – died, and virtually all economic and artistic activity ground to a halt. Another plague hit in 1374, killing 80,000 Sienese, and was swiftly followed by a famine. It was too much – the city never entirely recovered.

Florence was also hit by the plague in 1348, and despite fervent public prayer rituals, 96,000 Florentines died in just seven months. Those who survived experienced a crisis of faith, making Florence fertile territory for humanist ideals – not to mention macabre superstition, attempts to raise the dead, and a fascination with corpses that the likes of Leonardo da Vinci would call science and others morbid curiosity.

At the plague's end, a Florentine building boom ensued when upstart merchants such as Cosimo I de' Medici (Cosimo the Elder) and Palla Strozzi competed to put their stamp on a city that needed to be reimagined after the horrors it had undergone.

The Renaissance

It wasn't only merchants who were jockeying for power at this time. To put an end to the competing claims of the Tuscan Ghibelline faction that was allied with the Holy Roman Empire, the Rome-backed Guelph faction had marked its territory with impressive new landmarks, predominantly in Florence. Giotto – often described as the founding artist of the Renaissance – had been commissioned to design the city's iconic 85m-tall square *campanile* (bell tower) and one-up the 57m-tall tower

Best Gothic Churches

Duomo (Siena, p142)

Abbazia di San Galgano (south of Siena, p178)

Chiesa di Santa Maria della Spina (Pisa, p250)

GIORGIO VASARI'S 'LIVES OF THE ARTISTS'

Painter, architect and writer Giorgio Vasari (1511–74) is rightly described as a 'Renaissance man'. Born in Arezzo, he grew up in what is now the small but fascinating house museum Museo di Casa Vasari. He later trained as a painter in Florence, working with artists such as Andrea del Sarto and Michelangelo (he idolised the latter). As a painter, he is best remembered for his floor-to-ceiling frescoes in the Salone dei Cinquecento in Florence's Palazzo Vecchio. As an architect, his most accomplished work was the elegant loggia of the Galleria degli Uffizi (he also designed the enclosed, elevated corridor that connected the Palazzo Vecchio with the Uffizi and Palazzo Pitti and was dubbed the 'Corridoio Vasariano' in his honour). But posterity remembers him predominantly for his work as an art historian. His *Lives of the Most Excellent Painters, Sculptors and Architects, from Cimabue to Our Time,* an encyclopaedia of artistic biographies published in 1550 and dedicated to Cosimo I de' Medici, is still in print (as *The Lives of the Artists*) and is full of wonderful anecdotes and gossip about his artistic contemporaries in 16th-century Florence.

Memorable passages include his recollection of visiting Donatello's studio one day to find the great sculptor staring at his extremely lifelike statue of the *Prophet Habakkuk* and imploring it to talk (we can only assume that Donatello had been working too hard). Vasari also writes about a young Giotto painting a fly on the surface of a work by Cimabue that the older master then tried to brush away.

1. Di Bondone's *Life of St Francis* 2. Botticelli's *Primavera*
3. Fra' Angelico's *Annunciation* 4. Michelangelo's *David*

Tuscan Artists

Plenty of the big names jostle for precedence in the pantheon of Tuscan artists, so narrowing any list down to a 'Top Five' is a near impossible task. Here's our best attempt.

Michelangelo Buonarroti (1475–1564)

The quintessential Renaissance man: a painter, sculptor and architect with more masterpieces to his credit than any other artist either before or since. In Florence, view his *David* in the Galleria dell'Accademia (p90) and his *Tondo Doni* (Holy Family) in the Uffizi (p70).

Sandro Botticelli (c 1444–1510)

His Renaissance beauties charmed commissions out of the Medicis and continue to exert their siren call on the millions who visit the Uffizi Gallery (p70) each year. Don't miss his *Primavera* and *Birth of Venus*.

Giotto di Bondone (c 1266–1337)

Giotto kick-started the Renaissance with action-packed frescoes in which each character pinpoints emotions with facial expressions and poses that need no translation. Make the pilgrimage to Assisi (p301) to see his *Life of St Francis* fresco cycle.

Fra' Angelico (c 1395–1455)

Few artists are saints – they're far more likely to be sinners. One of the exceptions was Il Beato Angelico, who was canonised in 1982. His best-loved work is the *Annunciation*, versions of which are on display in Florence's Museo di San Marco (p92) and Cortona's Museo Diocesano (p313).

Duccio di Buoninsegna (c 1255–1318)

Head honcho of the Sienese school, he's known for his riveting Madonnas with level gazes and pale-green skin against glowing gold backgrounds. His masterwork is the *Maestà* in the Museo dell'Opera (p143) in Siena.

under construction in Ghibelline Pisa that was already looking a bit off kilter. And this was only one of many such projects.

'Mess with Florence, and you take on Rome' was the not-so-subtle hint delivered by Florentine architects, who made frequent reference to the glories of the ancient power and its classical architecture when designing the new churches, *palazzi* and public buildings that started sprouting across the city during the *Trecento* (14th century) and proliferated in the *Quattrocentro* (15th century). This new Florentine style became known as Renaissance or 'rebirth', and it really started to hit its stride after architect Filippo Brunelleschi won a competition to design the dome of Florence's *duomo*. Brunelleschi was heavily influenced by the achievements of the classical masters, but he was able to do something that they hadn't been able to do themselves – discover and record the mathematical rules by which objects appear to diminish as they recede from us. In so doing, he gave local artists and architects a whole new visual perspective and a means to glorious artistic ends.

To decorate the new buildings, artists enjoyed a bonanza of commissions to paint heroic battle scenes, fresco private chapels and carve busts

RENAISSANCE FRESCOES

They may look like ordinary bible stories now, but in their heyday Renaissance frescoes provided running social commentary as well as religious inspiration. In them, human adversity looked divine, and vice versa.

Fantastic examples are found throughout Tuscany, but to see the very best head to the following churches and museums.

Collegiata, San Gimignano (p167) There are hardly any undecorated surfaces in this cathedral, with every wall sporting huge, comic-strip-like frescoes by Bartolo di Fredi, Lippo Memmi, Domenico Ghirlandaio and Benozzo Gozzoli. The highlight is Taddeo di Bartolo's gleefully grotesque *Final Judgment* (1396).

Libreria Piccolomini, Duomo, Siena (p142) Umbrian artist Bernardino Pinturicchio extols the glory of Siena in 10 vibrant fresco panels (c 1502–07) celebrating Enea Silvio Piccolomini, aka the humanist Pope Pius II. St Catherine of Siena makes a cameo appearance.

Museo di San Marco, Florence (p92) Fra' Angelico's frescoes portray religious figures in all-too-human moments of uncertainty, reflecting the humanist spirit of the Renaissance. The highlight is his *Annunciation* (c 1440).

Museo Civico, Siena (p140) Magnificent is the only word to use when describing Ambrogio Lorenzetti's *Allegories of Good and Bad Government* (1338–40) and Simone Martini's *Maestà* (Virgin Mary in Majesty; 1315).

Cappella Brancacci, Florence (p103) Masaccio's *The Expulsion of Adam and Eve from Paradise* and *The Tribute Money* (c 1427) showcase architectural perspective and sly political satire.

Cappella Bacci, Chiesa di San Francesco, Arezzo (p295) Piero della Francesca's *Legend of the True Cross* (c 1452–66) displays a veritable encyclopaedia of Renaissance painting tricks (directional lighting, steep perspective etc).

Chiesa di Sant'Agostino, San Gimignano (p168) Benozzo Gozzoli's bizarre fresco of San Sebastian (c 1464) shows the fully clothed saint protecting the citizens of San Gimignano, helped by a bare-breasted Virgin Mary and a semirobed Jesus. Wins the prize for the weirdest religious iconography.

Cappella dei Magi, Palazzo Medici-Riccardi, Florence (p94) More Gozzoli, but this time there's nothing strange about his subject matter, which has members of the Medici family making a guest appearance in the *Procession of the Magi to Bethlehem* (c 1459–63).

of the latest power players – works that sometimes outlived their patrons' clout. A good example is the Peruzzi family, whose members had risen to prominence in 14th-century Florence as bankers, with interests reaching from London to the Middle East. They set the trend for art patronage by commissioning Giotto to fresco the family's memorial chapel in Santa Croce, completed in 1320. When Peruzzi client King Edward III of England defaulted on loans the family went bankrupt – but, as patrons of Giotto's precocious experiments in perspective and Renaissance illusionism, their legacy set the tone for the artistic flowering of Florence.

One Florentine family to follow the Peruzzis' lead was the prominent Brancacci, who commissioned Masolino da Panicale and his precocious assistant Masaccio to decorate a chapel in the Basilica di Santa Maria del Carmine in Florence. After Masaccio's premature death aged only 27, the frescoes were completed by Filippino Lippi. In these dramatic frescoes, framed in astonishingly convincing architectural sets, scenes from the life of St Peter allude to pressing Florentine concerns of the day: the new income tax, unfair imprisonment and hoarded wealth. Masaccio's image of the expulsion of Adam and Eve from the Garden of Eden proved especially prophetic: the Brancacci were allied with the Strozzi family, and were exiled from Florence by the Medici before they could see the work completed.

But the patrons with the greatest impact on the course of art history were, of course, the Medicis. Patriarch Cosimo the Elder was exiled in 1433 by a consortium of Florentine families who considered him a triple threat: powerful banker, ambassador of the Church, and consummate politician with the savvy to sway emperors and popes. But the flight of capital from Florence after his departure created such a fiscal panic that the banishment was hastily rescinded, and within a year the Medicis were well and truly back in town. To announce his return in grand style, Cosimo funded the 1437 rebuilding of the Convento di San Marco (now Museo di San Marco) by Michelozzo, and commissioned Fra' Angelico to fresco the monks' quarters with scenes from the life of Christ. Another artist pleased to see Cosimo return was Donatello, who had completed his lithe bronze statue of *David* (now in the city's Museo del Bargello) with his patronage.

Through such commissions, early Renaissance innovations in perspective, closely observed realism and *chiaroscuro* (the play of light and dark) began to catch on throughout the region. In Sansepolcro, a painter named Piero della Francesca earned a reputation for figures who were glowing with otherworldly light, and who were caught in personal predicaments that people could relate to: Roman soldiers snoozing on the job, crowds left goggle-eyed by miracles and bystanders distressed to witness cruel persecution. His fresco series *Legend of the True Cross,* commissioned by the Bacci family for a chapel in Arezzo's Chiesa di San Francesco, was one of the supreme artistic achievements of the time.

The High Renaissance

The decades leading up to and beginning the *Cinquecento* (16th century) are often seen as a kind of university faculty meeting, with genteel, silver-haired sages engaged in a collegial exchange of ideas. A bar brawl might be closer to the metaphorical truth, with artists, scientists, politicians and clergy mixing it up and everyone emerging bruised. The debate was never as simple as Church versus state, science versus art or seeing versus believing; in those days, politicians could be clergy, scientists could be artists, and artists could be clergy.

There were many artistic superstars during this period, and most were locals who ended up honing their skills in Florence and then moving elsewhere in Italy. Their careers were well documented by Giorgio Vasari in his gossipy *Lives of the Artists.*

ART & ARCHITECTURE THE HIGH RENAISSANCE

Masaccio's *Trinity,* a wall painting in the Basilica di Santa Maria Novella in Florence, is often described as one of the founding works of Renaissance painting and the inspiration for Leonardo da Vinci's *Last Supper* fresco.

Tuscan Architecture

Italy has more than its share of great buildings, and a large percentage of these are in Tuscany. Brunelleschi and Michelangelo both designed masterpieces here, and every town and city seems to have at least one notable Romanesque, Gothic or Renaissance structure.

Churches

Tuscany's *chiese* (churches) are headline attractions where worship can take many forms. Every village, town and city has at least one church, and many are repositories of great art. Florence has masterpieces galore (don't miss Santa Maria Novella, Santa Croce and San Lorenzo), but Siena, Pisa and San Gimignano are richly endowed too, with their respective *duomos* (cathedrals) being the best-loved and most distinctive buildings in town.

On the border of Tuscany and Umbria, Orvieto's *duomo* is one of the most beautiful in the country.

Baptistries

Important cathedrals often have a detached *battistero* (baptistry) with a dedicated altar and font. Pisa's cupcake-shaped example in the Piazza dei Miracoli, with its exquisite hexagonal marble pulpit carved by Nicola Pisano, is wonderful, as is Florence's Romanesque version with its famous door panels sculpted by Lorenzo Ghiberti.

Hospitals

Funded by the church, the *comune* (municipality) or wealthy philanthropists, *ospedali* (hospitals) have historically been among the largest and grandest of civic buildings. Siena's Santa Maria della Scala

1. *Duomo* (p142), Siena **2.** Piazza Grande (p298), Arezzo **3.** Collegiata and Palazzo Comunale (p167), San Gimignano

is perhaps the best known, but architecture buffs adore Brunelleschi's Ospedale degli Innocenti in Florence.

Mansions

The Medicis weren't the only dynasty with a penchant for building *palazzi* (palaces). In the medieval and Renaissance periods, wealthy families in every city built houses aimed to impress, as did ambassadors, popes, cardinals and *podestàs* (chief magistrates). Architecturally notable examples include Palazzo Strozzi, Palazzo Pitti and Palazzo Medici-Riccardi in Florence; Palazzo Piccolomini, Palazzo Salimbeni and Palazzo Chigi-Saracini in Siena; and Palazzo Piccolomini in Pienza.

Piazzas

These triumphs of town planning are the lifeblood of every Tuscan community, the places where locals come to connect with their neighbours and where important institutions such as churches and town halls are almost inevitably situated. The two most famous examples, Piazzo Pio II in Pienza and Piazza dei Miracoli in Pisa, feature in Unesco's World Heritage List. Worthy of an honourable mention are Livorno's Piazza dei Domenicani, Arezzo's Piazza Grande and Massa Marittima's Piazza Garibaldi.

Town Halls

Built to showcase wealth and civic pride, the *palazzo comunale* (municipal palace) is often the most impressive secular building in a Tuscan town. Noteworthy examples include those on Siena's Piazza del Campo, Volterra's Piazza dei Priori and Florence's Piazza della Signoria.

Filippo Lippi (1406–69) entered the Carmelite order as a monk aged 14, but renounced his vows after eloping with a novice who was sitting for the figure of the Madonna in a fresco he was painting for Prato's *duomo*. Their son Filippino (1457–1504) became a notable painter too.

Inspired by Masaccio, tutored by Fra' Filippo Lippi and backed by Lorenzo de' Medici, Sandro Botticelli was a rising Florentine art star who was sent to Rome to paint a fresco celebrating papal authority in the Sistine Chapel. The golden boy who'd painted the *Birth of Venus* for Lorenzo de' Medici's private villa in 1485 (now in Florence's Galleria degli Uffizi) could do no wrong until he was accused of sodomy in 1501. The charges didn't stick, but the rumours did, and Botticelli's work was critiqued as too decadently sensual for religious subjects. When religious reformer Savonarola ousted the Medici and began to purge Florence of decadent excess in the face of surely imminent Armageddon, Botticelli paintings went up in flames in the massive 'Bonfire of the Vanities'. Botticelli repudiated mythology and turned his attention to Madonnas, some of whom bear a marked family resemblance to his Venus.

Michelangelo, a Tuscan village lad from Caprese (today Caprese Michelangelo) in the remote Tuscan outback of Casentino in eastern Tuscany, was another of Lorenzo de' Medici's protégés. His classically inspired work was uniformly admired until the Medicis were ousted by Savonarola in 1494. By some accounts, Savonarola tossed rare early paintings by Michelangelo onto his bonfires. Without his Medici protectors, Michelangelo seemed unsure of his next move: he briefly hid in the basement of San Lorenzo and then roamed around Italy. In Rome he carved a *Bacchus* for Cardinal Raffaele Riaro that the patron deemed unsuitable – but this only seemed to spur Michelangelo on to make a bigger and still more sensuous statue of *David* in 1501. It's now exhibited in Florence's Galleria dell'Accademia.

Leonardo, who hailed from Vinci, southwest of Florence, had so many talents that it is hard to isolate only a few for comment. In his painting, he took what some critics have described as the decisive step in the

FILIPPO BRUNELLESCHI

Many Renaissance men left their mark on Florence, but few did so with as much grace and glory as Filippo Brunelleschi (1377–1446). An architect, mathematician, engineer and sculptor, Brunelleschi trained as a master goldsmith and showed early promise as a sculptor – he was an entrant in the 1401 competition to design the doors of the baptistry in Florence (won by fellow goldsmith Lorenzo Ghiberti) and shortly after travelled to Rome with Donatello, another goldsmith by training, to study that city's ancient architecture and art. When he returned to Florence in 1419 he took up an architectural commission from the silk merchant's guild to design a hospital for foundlings on Piazza della Santissima Annunziata in San Marco. Known as the Ospedale degli Innocenti (Hospital of the Innocents – today a stunning museum), his classically proportioned and detailed building featured a distinctive nine-arched loggia and was a radical departure from the High Gothic style that many of his artistic contemporaries were still embracing. Its design was sober, secular and sophisticated, epitomising the new humanist age.

In 1419, after completing his work on the foundling hospital, Brunelleschi moved on to a commission that was to occupy him for the next 42 years – the dome of Florence's *duomo*. His mathematical brain and talent for devising innovative engineering solutions enabled him to do what many Florentines had thought impossible: deliver the largest dome to be built in Italy since antiquity.

Brunelleschi's other works in Florence include the Basilica di San Lorenzo, the Basilica di Santo Spirito and the Cappella de' Pazzi in the Basilica di Santa Croce. Vasari said of him: 'The world having for so long been without artists of lofty soul or inspired talent, heaven ordained that it should receive from the hand of Filippo the greatest, the tallest, and the finest edifice of ancient and modern times, demonstrating that Tuscan genius, although moribund, was not yet dead'. He is buried in the *duomo*, under the dome that was his finest achievement.

history of Western art – namely, abandoning the balance that had previously been maintained between colour and line and choosing to modulate his contours using shading. This technique is called *sfumato* and it is perfectly displayed in his *Mona Lisa* (now in the Louvre in Paris). Few of his works remain in his birthplace; the exceptions are his *Adoration of the Magi* and *Annunciation,* both in the Uffizi.

In 1542 the Inquisition arrived in Italy, marking a definitive end to the Renaissance exploration of humanity in all its glorious imperfections. Tuscan art and architecture would never again lead the world by example.

A Stop on the Grand Tour

A 'Grand Tour' of Italy became an obligatory display of culture and class status by the 18th century, and Tuscany was a key stop on the itinerary. German and English artists enraptured with Michelangelo, Perugino and other early High Renaissance painters took the inspiration home, kick-starting a neoclassicist craze. Conversely, trends from northern Europe (impressionism, plein-air painting and Romanticism) became trendy among Italian artists, as witnessed in the collection at Florence's Galleria d'Arte Moderna in the Palazzo Pitti, which is dominated by late-19th-century works by artists of the Tuscan Macchiaioli school (the local equivalent of impressionism). These include Telemaco Signorini (1835–1901) and Giovanni Fattori (1825–1908).

In architecture, the most fascinating case of artistic import-export is Italian art nouveau, often referred to as Liberty after the London shop that put William Morris' Italian-inspired visual ideals into commercial action.

The 20th Century

After centuries under the thumbs of popes and sundry imperial powers, Tuscany had acquired a certain forced cosmopolitanism, and local artists could identify with Rome, Paris and other big cities in addition to their own *contrada* (neighbourhood). The two biggest stars in the early decades of this century were Livorno-born painter and sculptor Amedeo Modigliani (1884–1920), who lived most of his adult life in Paris, and Greek-born painter Giorgio de Chirico (1888–1978), who studied in Florence and painted the first of his 'Metaphysical Town Square' series there.

Other than Modigliani and di Chirico, no Tuscan painters of note were represented within the major artistic movements of the century: *futurismo* (futurism), *pittura metafisica* (metaphysical painting), Spazialismo (Spatialism) and Arte Povera (conceptual art using materials of little worth). Architecture didn't have many local stars either, with the only exception being Giovanni Michelucci (1891–1990), whose buildings include Santa Maria Novella Railway Station in Florence (1932–34).

In the field of abstract art, installation art and sculpture, it was the small town of Pistoia that made itself heard in the 1950s and 1960s through a trio of artists. Pistoia-born Fernando Melani (1907–85) lived all his life in Pistoia, rarely exhibiting elsewhere. His playful works used an abundance of recycled materials, with thin metal wire being shaped and twisted in all directions to create the most extraordinary forms and models. His contemporary Mario Nigro (1917–92) moved to Livorno when he was 12 and later, once the abstract-art bug bit, to the brighter lights of Milan. In the field of sculpture, Pistoia's Marino Marini (1901–80) drew on Tuscany's Etruscan heritage in his work, developing a strong equestrian theme – nudes and men on horseback are what Marini did best.

In the 1980s there was a return to painting and sculpture in a traditional (primarily figurative) sense. Dubbed 'Transavanguardia', this movement broke with the prevailing international focus on conceptual

---

ART & ARCHITECTURE A STOP ON THE GRAND TOUR

As well as endowing churches, building palaces and funding frescoes, the wealthy merchant families of the Renaissance commissioned plenty of portraits. Cosimo I de' Medici's favourite portrait painter was Agnolo di Cosimo (1503–72), called Bronzino because of his dark complexion. Look for his Medici portraits in the Uffizi, Florence.

Best Best Modern Art Museums

Museo Novecento (Florence, p86)

Galleria Continua (San Gimignano, p168)

Palazzo Fabroni (Pistoia, p271)

Museo Marino Marini (Pistoia, p273)

Lucca Center of Contemporary Art (Lucca, p265)

Palazzo Strozzi (Florence, p69)

art and was thought by some critics to signal the death of avant-garde – view works at Prato's top-billing contemporary-art centre, the Centro per l'Arte Contemporanea Luigi Pecci. Tuscan artists who were part of this movement include Sandro Chia (b 1946).

Contemporary Art

A heritage of rich artistic traditions spanning three millennia means job security for legions of Tuscan art-conservation specialists and art historians, but can also have a stultifying effect on artists attempting to create something wholly new. Fortunately, there's more going on than the daubs by pavement artists outside major museums and tourist attractions would indicate.

One of the most notable visual artists working here is Massimo Bartolini (b 1962), who radically alters the local landscape with just a few deceptively simple (and quintessentially Tuscan) adjustments of light and perspective that fundamentally change our experience: a bedroom where all the furniture appears to be sinking into the floor, Venice style; or a gallery where the viewer wears special shoes that subtly change the gallery's lighting with each step. Bartolini has also changed the local flora of the tiny Tuscan town of Cecina, near Livorno, where he lives and works, attracting colourful flocks of contemporary-art collectors and curators.

The bijou town of Pietrasanta in the hinterland of the Versilian coast in northwestern Tuscany has a vibrant arts community and is home to the much-lauded Colombian-born sculptor Fernando Botero (b 1932). In the Val d'Orcia, Volterra's homegrown sculptor Mauro Staccioli (1937–2018) encourages visitors to admire the landscape from an alternative perspective with his series of monumental geometric installations scattered around town.

Also notable is San Gimignano's Galleria Continua, a world-class commercial gallery whose portfolio of artists includes Tuscans Giovanni Ozzola (b 1982) and Luca Pancrazzi (b 1961). In Prato, the contemporary-art flag is flown by the cutting-edge Centro per l'Arte Contemporanea Luigi Pecci.

The term 'Macchiaioli' (the name given to a 19th-century group of Tuscan plein-air artists) was coined by a journalist in 1862. It mockingly implied that the artists' finished works were no more than sketches, and was drawn from the phrase *darsi alla macchia* (to hide in bushes or scrubland).

Survival Guide

DIRECTORY A–Z 358

Accessible Travel 358
Climate. 358
Customs Regulations . . . 358
Discount Cards. 358
Electricity 359
Food 359
Health. 359
Insurance. 360
Internet Access. 360
Legal Matters 360
LGBTIQ+ Travellers 360
Maps. 360
Money. 360
Post. 361
Public Holidays. 361
Safe Travel 361
Telephone 361
Time 362
Toilets. 362
Tourist Information 362
Visas. 362

TRANSPORT 364

GETTING THERE
& AWAY 364
Entering Tuscany 364
Air. 364
Land 364
Sea 365
GETTING AROUND. 365
Air. 365
Bicycle 365
Boat 366
Bus 366
Car & Motorcycle 366
Local Transport. 367
Train 367

LANGUAGE 369

Directory A–Z

Accessible Travel

Most Tuscan towns and cities are not easy for travellers with disabilities to navigate, and getting around can be a problem for wheelchair users – many streets are cobbled, and narrow pavements in historic centres are not wide enough for a wheelchair.

If you have an obvious disability and/or appropriate ID, many museums and galleries offer free admission for yourself and a companion.

An increasing number of museums, including Flor-ence's **Uffizi** (Uffizi Gallery; Map p82; ☎055 29 48 83; www.uffizi.it; Piazzale degli Uffizi 6; adult/reduced Mar-Oct €20/10, Nov-Feb €12/6; ☺8.15am-6.50pm Tue-Sun) and **Museo dell'Opera del Duomo** (Cathedral Museum; Map p100; ☎055 230 28 85; www.museumflorence.com; Piazza del Duomo 9; adult/reduced incl cathedral bell tower, cupola, baptistry & crypt €15/3; ☺9am-7pm), include tactile models of major artworks for visitors with impaired vision. Some museums, such as the excellent **Museo del Bargello** (Map p100; ☎055 238 86 06; www.bargellomusei.beniculturali.it; Via del Proconsolo 4; adult/reduced €8/4; ☺8.15am-2pm, closed 2nd & 4th Sun, 1st, 3rd & 5th Mon of month) in Florence, run organised tours for the visually impaired; reserve by telephone in advance.

Customs Regulations

Visitors coming into Italy from non-EU countries can import the following items duty free.

➡ 1L spirits (or 2L wine)

➡ 200 cigarettes

➡ up to a total of €430 (€150 for travellers aged under 15) in value for other goods, including perfume and eau de toilette

Anything over these limits must be declared on arrival and the appropriate duty paid. On leaving the EU, non-EU citizens can reclaim any Value Added Tax (VAT) on any purchases over €154.94.

For more information, visit www.italia.it.

Discount Cards

Free admission to many galleries and cultural sites is available to youths under 18 years and seniors over 65. EU citizens aged between 18

Climate

Florence

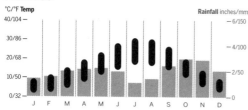

Elba

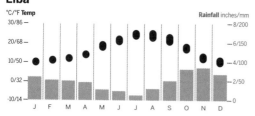

and 25 also often qualify for a 50% discount.

In many towns – Siena and San Gimignano included – you can save money by purchasing a **biglietto cumulativo**: a ticket that allows admission to a number of associated sights for less than the combined cost of separate admission fees.

Youth & Teacher Cards

➡ Student, teacher or youth travel cards (www.isic.org) can save you money on accommodation, travel, food and drink. They're available online and worldwide from student unions, hostelling organisations and youth travel agencies such as STA Travel (www.statravel.com). Options include the International Student Identity Card (ISIC; for full-time students), International Teacher Identity Card (for full-time teachers) and the International Youth Travel Card (for travellers under 31).

➡ Many places in Italy give discounts according to age rather than student status. An ISIC may not always be accepted without proof of age (eg passport).

Firenzecard

When in Florence, consider purchasing a Firenzecard (€85; www.firenzecard.it), valid for 72 hours and covering admission to 70-plus museums, villas and gardens. To add on unlimited public transport, pay an additional €7 for a Firenzecard+. Buy both online (and collect upon arrival in Florence or download the Firenzecard app and store it digitally). If you're an EU citizen, your card also covers family members aged under 18 travelling with you.

Electricity

Type F
230V/50Hz

Type L
220V/50Hz

Food

The following price ranges refer to a meal consisting of two courses and a *bicchiere di vino della casa* (glass of house wine), and include a *coperto* (cover charge).

€ less than €25
€€ €25–45
€€€ more than €45

Health
Before You Go
HEALTH INSURANCE

➡ The free European Health Insurance Card (EHIC) covers EU citizens and those from Switzerland, Norway and Iceland for most medical care in public hospitals free of charge.

➡ The EHIC does not cover emergency repatriation home or nonemergencies. It is available from health centres and, in the UK, online (www.ehic.org.uk) and from post offices.

➡ Citizens from other countries should check whether there's a reciprocal arrangement for free medical care between their country and Italy – Australia, for instance, has such an agreement; carry your Medicare card.

➡ Additional health insurance should cover the worst possible scenario, such as an accident requiring an emergency flight home.

➡ Check in advance whether your insurance plan will make payments directly to providers or reimburse you later for overseas health expenditures.

RECOMMENDED VACCINATIONS

No jabs are required to travel to Italy. However, the World Health Organization (WHO) recommends that all travellers should be covered for diphtheria, tetanus, measles, mumps, rubella and polio, as well as hepatitis B.

In Tuscany
HEALTHCARE

Pharmacists can give you valuable advice and sell over-the-counter medication for minor illnesses. They can also advise you when more

BOOK YOUR STAY ONLINE

For more accommodation reviews by Lonely Planet authors, check out http://lonelyplanet.com/hotels/. You'll find independent reviews, as well as recommendations on the best places to stay. Best of all, you can book online.

specialised help is required and point you in the right direction.

Pharmacies generally keep the same hours as other shops, closing at night and on Sundays. However, in big cities a handful remain open on a rotation basis *(farmacie di turno)* for emergency purposes. Check the door of any pharmacy closed for business – it will display a list of the nearest emergency pharmacies.

If you need an ambulance, call 118. For emergency treatment, head straight to the *pronto soccorso* (casualty) section of a public hospital, where you can also get emergency dental treatment.

TAP WATER

Despite the Tuscan enthusiasm for consuming bottled mineral water with meals, tap water in the region is perfectly drinkable.

Insurance

A travel insurance policy to cover theft, loss and medical problems is a good idea. Some policies specifically exclude dangerous activities, which can include scuba diving, motorcycling and even hiking – read the fine print.

Worldwide travel insurance is available at www.lonelyplanet.com/travel-insurance. You can buy, extend and claim online any time – even if you're already on the road.

Internet Access

Internet access is widespread. Hotels, *pensione*, B&Bs and most *agriturismi* (farm stays) offer free wi-fi, as do some restaurants, cafes and bars. In older buildings – namely thick stone-walled, 15th-century *palazzo* – the internet connection might not be great in top-floor rooms or corners tucked well away from the router.

Legal Matters

The most likely reason for a brush with the law is to report a theft. If you have something stolen and you want to claim it on insurance, you must make a statement to the police, as insurance companies won't pay up without official proof of a crime.

In Florence, should you have a theft or other unfortunate incident to report, the best time to visit the city's **questura** (☎055 4 97 71, English-language service 055 497 72 68; http://questure.poliziadistato.it/it/Firenze; Via Zara 2; ⏲24hr, English-language service 9.30am-1pm Mon-Fri) (police station) is between 9.30am and 1pm weekdays when the foreign-language service – meaning someone speaks English – kicks in.

In Siena the central **police station** (Questura; ☎0577 20 11 11; http://questure.poliziadistato.it/Siena; Via del Castoro 6; ⏲8am-8pm Mon-Sat) is by the Duomo.

LGBTIQ+ Travellers

Homosexuality is legal in Italy and well accepted in the major cities. On the Tuscan coast, Viareggio and Torre del Lago have lively gay scenes.

Resources include the following:

Arcigay (www.arcigay.it) Bologna-based national organisation for the LGBTIQ+ community.

Azione Gay e Lesbica Firenze (☎371 3761738; www.azionegayelesbica.it; Via Pisana 32-34r) Active Florence-based organisation for gays and lesbians.

GayFriendlyItaly.com (www.gayfriendlyitaly.com) English-language site produced by Gay.it, featuring events and information on homophobia issues and the law.

Gay.it (www.gay.it) Website featuring LGBTIQ+ news, feature articles and gossip.

Pride (www.prideonline.it) National monthly magazine of art, music, politics and gay culture.

Maps

Once you meander off the main road and dip into rural Tuscany, a map definitely comes in handy. Several sheet maps cover the region, including Michelin's *Toscana* (1:200,000), Marco Polo's *Toscana/Tuscany* (1:200,000) and Touring Editore's *Toscana* (1:200,000). Buy them from bookshops and some petrol stations.

If you're relying on digital maps, download offline versions before departure: in rural Tuscany you will frequently find yourself with zero connectivity.

Money

ATMs

Bancomats (ATMs) are widely available throughout Tuscany and are the best way to obtain local currency.

Credit Cards

International credit and debit cards can be used at any *bancomat* displaying the appropriate sign. Cards are also good for payment in most hotels, restaurants, shops, supermarkets and tollbooths.

If your card is lost, stolen or swallowed by an ATM, you can telephone toll-free to have an immediate stop put on its use.

American Express ⏻06 7290 0347

Diners Club ⏻800 393939

MasterCard ⏻800 870866

Visa ⏻800 819014

Currency

The euro is Italy's currency. Notes come in denominations of €500, €200, €100, €50, €20, €10 and €5. Coins are in denominations of €2 and €1, and 50, 20, 10, five, two and one cents.

Moneychangers

You can change money in banks, at the post office or in a *cambio* (exchange office). Post offices and banks tend to offer the best rates; exchange offices keep longer hours, but watch for high commissions and inferior rates.

Tipping

Taxis Round the fare up to the nearest euro.

Restaurants Many locals don't tip waiters, but most visitors leave 10% to 15% if there's no service charge.

Cafes Leave a coin (as little as €0.10 is acceptable) if you drank your coffee at the counter or 10% if you sat at a table.

Hotels Bellhops usually expect €1 to €2 per bag; it's not necessary to tip the concierge, cleaners or front-desk staff.

Post

Le Poste (www.poste.it), Italy's postal system, is reasonably reliable. *Franco-bolli* (stamps) are available at post offices and authorised *tabacchi* (tobacconists; look for the official sign: a big 'T', often white on black). Since letters often need to be weighed, what you get at the tobacconist for international airmail will occasionally be an approximation of the proper rate. If you've any concerns about ensuring an accurate stamp price, use a post office. *Tabacchi* keep regular shop hours.

Public Holidays

Most Italians take their annual holiday in August, with the busiest period occurring around 15 August, known locally as Ferragosto. This means that many businesses and shops close for at least a part of that month. Setti-mana Santa (Easter Week) is another busy holiday period for Italians.

In addition to the following national public holidays, Florence has a public holiday on 24 June to celebrate the Festa di San Giovanni (the feast of its patron saint John). Other towns likewise enjoy a public holiday to celebrate the feasts of their patron saint.

New Year's Day (Capodanno or Anno Nuovo) 1 January

Epiphany (Epifania or Befana) 6 January

Easter Sunday (Domenica di Pasqua) March/April

Easter Monday (Pasquetta or Lunedì dell'Angelo) March/April

Liberation Day (Giorno della Liberazione) 25 April – marks the Allied victory in Italy, and the end of the German presence in 1945

Labour Day (Festa del Lavoro) 1 May

Republic Day (Festa della Repubblica) 2 June

Feast of the Assumption (Assunzione or Ferragosto) 15 August

All Saints' Day (Ognissanti) 1 November

Feast of the Immaculate Conception (Immaculata Concezione) 8 December

Christmas Day (Natale) 25 December

Boxing Day (Festa di Santo Stefano) 26 December

Safe Travel

The region is a safe place generally.

➡ The usual street-smart rules apply in Florence, Siena and other key urban hubs: avoid wandering around town alone late at night; stick to main roads rather than narrow back alleys.

➡ Watch out for pickpockets in heavily touristed zones such as around Florence's Piazza del Duomo and Ponte Vecchio, Piazza dei Miracoli in Pisa and Piazza del Duomo in Siena.

➡ Keep alert on crowded buses to/from Florence and Pisa airports.

➡ Some *autostradas* (motorways) are far from silky-smooth, making them something of a safety hazard. Drive with care on unmaintained roads.

Telephone
Mobile Phones

Local SIM cards can be used in European and Australian phones. Other phones must be set to roaming.

➡ Italy uses GSM 900/1800, which is compatible with the rest of Europe and Australia but not with North American GSM 1900 or the totally different Japanese system.

➡ Many modern smartphones are multiband, meaning they are compatible with a number of international networks – check with your service provider about using your phone in Italy.

➡ Beware of mobile calls being routed internationally; it can be very expensive for a 'local' call.

➡ You can get a temporary or prepaid account from several companies if you already own a GSM, dual- or multiband mobile phone.

➡ Always check with your provider in your home country to see whether

PRACTICALITIES

Newspapers Major dailies include *Corriere della Sera* (www.corriere.it/english) and *La Repubblica* (in Italian; www.firenze.repubblica.it).*The Florentine* (www.theflor entine.net) covers local news, views and classifieds, and is published monthly in English online and in print (free).

Weights and measures Italy uses the metric system.

Smoking Banned in all enclosed public spaces.

your handset allows use of another SIM card. If yours does, it can cost as little as €20 to activate a local prepaid SIM card (sometimes with €10 worth of calls on the card). You'll need to register with a mobile-phone shop, bring your passport and wait for about 24 hours for your account to be activated.

➡ You can easily top up an Italian account with *ricarica* (prepaid minutes) from your selected mobile company at *tabacchi*, supermarkets and banks.

➡ TIM (www.tim.it), Vodafone (www.vodafone.it) and Wind (www.wind.it) have the densest networks of outlets across the country.

➡ If you have an internet-enabled phone, turn off data roaming when you're not using it, otherwise it devours credit.

Pay Phones & Phonecards

➡ Telecom Italia public phones can be found on the streets, in train stations and in Telecom offices.

➡ Most pay phones accept only *carte/schede telefoniche* (phonecards), although some also accept credit cards. Prepaid phonecards (costing €1, €2.50, €3, €5 and €7.50) are sold at post offices, *tabacchi* and newsstands.

➡ Telecom offers a wide range of prepaid cards for both domestic and international use.

Domestic Calls

➡ Italian telephone area codes all begin with 0 and consist of up to four digits. The area code is followed by a number of anything from four to nine digits. The area code is an integral part of the telephone number and must *always* be dialled, even when calling from next door.

➡ Mobile-phone numbers begin with a three-digit prefix such as 330.

➡ Toll-free (free-phone) numbers are known as *numeri verdi* and usually start with 800.

➡ Nongeographical numbers start with 840, 841, 848, 892, 899, 163, 166 or 199.

➡ Some six-digit national rate numbers are also in use (such as those for Alitalia and rail and postal information). As elsewhere in Europe, Italians choose from a host of providers of phone plans and rates, making it difficult to make generalisations about costs.

International Calls

➡ To call another country from Italy, first dial 00, then the relevant country and area codes, followed by the telephone number.

➡ To call Italy from abroad, call the international access number (011 in the USA; 00 from most other countries), Italy's country code (39) and then the area code of the location you want, including the leading 0.

➡ Cut-price call centres can be found in all of the main cities; rates can be considerably lower than from Telecom Italia pay phones for international calls. Place your call from a private booth inside the centre and pay when you've finished.

➡ International calling cards, sold at *tabacchi*, also offer cheaper rates. They can be used at public telephones.

Time

Italy operates on a 24-hour clock. It is one hour ahead of GMT/UTC. Daylight-saving time starts on the last Sunday in March, when clocks are put forward one hour. Clocks are put back an hour on the last Sunday in October. This is especially valuable to know in Italy, as 'summer' and 'winter' hours at museums and other sights are usually based on daylight-saving time.

Toilets

Public toilets are nonexistent. Your best bet is to nip into the closest cafe, order an espresso at the bar and pay the €1 – the price for using their facilities.

Can't turn on the tap to wash your hands? Press the floor pedal beneath the sink with your foot to get the water flowing.

Tourist Information

Visit Tuscany (www.visittusca ny.com) is Tuscany's regional tourist authority website.

Visas

These are not needed for residents of Schengen countries or for many visitors staying for less than 90 days.

➡ European citizens of the 26 countries of the Schengen Area can enter Italy with nothing more than a valid identity card or passport. British nationals only need a passport.

→ Residents of 28 non-EU countries, including Australia, Brazil, Canada, Israel, Japan, New Zealand and the USA, do not require visas for tourist visits of up to 90 days.

→ All non-EU and non-Schengen nationals entering Italy for more than 90 days, or for any reason other than tourism (such as study or work), may need a specific visa. For details, visit www.esteri.it or contact an Italian consulate.

→ EU citizens do not require any permits to live or work in Italy but, after three months' residence, are supposed to register themselves at the municipal registry office where they live and offer proof of work or sufficient funds to support themselves.

→ Non-EU foreign citizens with five years' continuous legal residence may apply for permanent residence.

→ You should have your passport stamped on entry as, without a stamp, you could encounter problems if trying to obtain a residence permit (permesso di soggiorno). If you enter the EU via another member state, get your passport stamped there.

Permesso di Soggiorno

Non-EU citizens planning to stay at the same address for more than one week are supposed to report to the police station to receive a permesso di soggiorno. Tourists staying in hotels are not required to do this.

A permesso di soggiorno only really becomes a necessity if you plan to study, work (legally) or live in Italy. Obtaining one is never a pleasant experience; it often involves long queues and the frustration of arriving at the counter only to find you don't have the necessary documents.

The exact requirements, such as specific documents and marche da bollo (official stamps), can change. In general, you will need a valid passport (if possible contain-ing a stamp with your date of entry into Italy), a special visa issued in your own country if you are planning to study (for non-EU citizens), four passport photos and proof of your ability to support yourself financially. You can apply at the ufficio stranieri (foreigners' bureau) of the police station closest to where you're staying.

EU citizens do not require a permesso di soggiorno.

Study Visas

Non-EU citizens who want to study at a university or language school in Italy must have a study visa. These can be obtained from your nearest Italian embassy or consulate. You will normally require confirmation of your enrolment, proof of payment of fees and adequate funds to support yourself. The visa covers only the period of the enrolment. This type of visa is renewable within Italy but, again, only with confirmation of ongoing enrolment and proof that you are able to support yourself (bank statements are preferred).

Transport

GETTING THERE & AWAY

Flights, cars and tours can be booked online at lonelyplan et.com/bookings.

Entering Tuscany

➡ European citizens of the 26 countries of the Schengen Area can travel to Italy with their national identity card alone. All other nationalities must have a valid passport and may be required to fill out a landing card at airports.

➡ By law you are supposed to have your passport or ID card with you at all times. You'll need one of these documents for police registration every time you check in to a hotel.

➡ In theory, there are no passport checks at land crossings from neighbouring countries, but random customs controls do

occasionally still take place between Italy and Switzerland.

Air

➡ High season for air travel to Italy is mid-April to mid-September.

➡ Shoulder season runs from mid-September to the end of October and from Easter to mid-April.

➡ Low season is November to March.

➡ Tickets around Christmas and Easter often increase in price or sell out in advance.

Airports & Airlines

Domestic flights into and out of the region are offered by the following carriers.

Alitalia (www.alitalia.it) Italy's national carrier. Flies from Pisa International Airport, Florence Airport and Bologna Airport to Rome.

Ryanair (www.ryanair.com) Flies from Pisa International

Airport to Alghero, Bari, Brindisi, Cagliari, Catania, Comiso, Crotone, Lamezia, Palermo and Trapani; from Umbria International Airport to Brindisi, Cagliari and Trapani; from Bologna Airport to Bari, Brindisi, Trapani and Palermo.

Land

Border Crossings

If you are entering Italy from a neighbouring EU country, you do not require a passport check.

Bus

Buses are the cheapest overland option to Italy, but services are less frequent, less comfortable and significantly slower than the train.

Car & Motorcycle

Every vehicle travelling across the border should display a valid national licence plate and an accompanying registration card.

Train

➡ Milan is the major rail hub in northern Italy. Most European services arrive there; onward connections include Florence and Pisa.

➡ **Thello** (www.thello.com) overnight sleeper trains travel from Paris-Gare de Lyon to Venice via Milan.

➡ From France, you can change at Turin for connecting services to Pisa.

TUSCANY AIRPORTS

AIRPORT	ALTERNA-TIVE NAME/S	LOCATION	WEBSITE
Florence Airport (FLR)	Amerigo Vespucci; Peretola	Florence	www.aeroporto.firenze.it
Pisa International Airport (PSA)	Aeroporto Galileo Galilei	Pisa	www.pisa-airport.com

➡ For train times and fares, go to **Rail Europe** (www.raileurope-world.com). For rail passes, see **Eurail** (www.eurail.com).

Sea

Ferries connect Italy with its islands and with countries all across the Mediterranean. However, the only options for reaching Tuscany directly by sea are the ferry crossings to Livorno from Spain, Sardinia and Corsica.

For a comprehensive guide to ferry services into and out of Italy, consult **Traghettionline** (www.traghettionline.com). The website lists every route and includes links to ferry company sites where you can buy tickets or search for deals.

GETTING AROUND

Air

There are no internal flights within Tuscany.

Bicycle

Cycling is a national pastime in Italy and a wonderful way to get around rural Tuscany. Bikes are prohibited on the *autostrada* (expressway), but there are few other special road rules.

Folded bikes or those packed in a bike bag can be taken free of charge on any

EXPRESS TRAINS FROM CONTINENTAL EUROPE

FROM	TO	FREQUENCY	DURATION (HR)	COST (€)
Geneva	Milan	4 daily	4	68
Milan	Ventimiglia	6 daily	3¾-5½	40
Munich	Verona	5 daily	5½	64
Paris	Milan	4 daily	7¼-10¾	115
Vienna	Florence	nightly	11	60-80
Zurich	Milan	7 daily	3¾	61

regional or national train. Trains bearing a bicycle logo accept nonfolded bikes with a separate bicycle ticket – the price of a single second-class ticket for *regionale* (slow local train) services and €12 on international services. Tickets are valid for 24 hours and must be validated before boarding. Ferries allow free bicycle passage.

Rental

There are bike-rental outlets in practically every town and city, and a handful of online companies offering tours and rental with bike delivery directly to your hotel. Expect to pay around €12/25 per day for a regular city/mountain bike, including bike lock and helmet.

Electric bikes are increasingly popular – not to mention a godsend given some of Tuscany's unexpectedly challenging hills. Expect to pay €39 per day at **Florence by Bike** (☎055 48 89 92; www.florencebybike.com;

Via San Zanobi 54r; 1hr/5hr/1 day €3/9/12; ⊗9am-1pm & 3.30-7.30pm Mon-Sat, 10am-7pm Sun). **Urban Bikery** (Map p188; ☎377 5453297; www.urbanbikery.it; Via Ricci 2; per 2hr/half-day/day €40/45/65; ⊗9.30am-7pm Mar-Oct, 11am-6pm Nov-Feb) in Montepulciano and **E-Bikes Florence** (www.e-bikesflorence.com) provide e-cyclists with ingenious GPS maps of some fantastic self-guided itineraries around Florence and Montepulciano wine country.

There are city-funded bike-sharing schemes in Florence, Pisa, Livorno and Siena. Siena's **SiPedela** (www.sienaparcheggi.com/it/1125/bike-sharing.htm) is the region's only electric-bike-sharing scheme, with 18 stations dotted around town and a one-/two-day ticket (€10/15) easily accessible to visitors via the **Bicincittà** website (www.bicincitta.com) or app (iPhone and Android).

CLIMATE CHANGE & TRAVEL

Every form of transport that relies on carbon-based fuel generates CO_2, the main cause of human-induced climate change. Modern travel is dependent on aeroplanes, which might use less fuel per kilometre per person than most cars but travel much greater distances. The altitude at which aircraft emit gases (including CO_2) and particles also contributes to their climate change impact. Many websites offer 'carbon calculators' that allow people to estimate the carbon emissions generated by their journey and, for those who wish to do so, to offset the impact of the greenhouse gases emitted with contributions to portfolios of climate-friendly initiatives throughout the world. Lonely Planet offsets the carbon footprint of all staff and author travel.

Boat

Year-round, regular ferries connect Piombino on the mainland with Portoferraio on Elba, and the smaller ports of Cavo and Rio Marina. From Livorno, ferries run to the island of Capraia, also year-round.

Bus

Although trains are the most convenient and economical way to travel between major towns, a bus is often the best public-transport link between small towns and villages. For a few intercity routes, such as the one between Florence and Siena, the bus is your best bet.

➡ Dozens of regional companies are loosely affiliated under the **Tiemme** (tiemmespa.it) network.

➡ Most reduce or even drop services on holidays and at weekends, especially on Sunday.

➡ Local tourist offices often carry bus timetables.

➡ Buy tickets at ticket booths and dispensing machines at bus stations, or from *tabacchi* (tobacconists) and newsstands. Tickets can usually also be bought on board at a slightly higher cost.

➡ Validate tickets in the machine on board.

➡ In larger cities, ticket companies often have offices at the bus terminal; some offer good-value daily tourist tickets.

➡ Turn up on time: in defiance of deep-seated Italian tradition, buses are almost always punctual.

Car & Motorcycle

The **Automobile Club d'Italia** (ACI; www.aci.it) is a driver's best resource in Italy. For 24-hour roadside emergency service, dial 803 116. Foreigners do not have to join, but instead pay a per-incident fee.

Car Hire

To rent a car you must be at least 25 years old and have a credit card. Car-rental agencies expect you to bring the car back with a full tank of petrol and will charge astronomically if you don't. You should also make sure that the office where you are returning your car will be open when you arrive – if not you will face fines.

Make sure you understand what is included in the price (unlimited kilometres, tax, insurance, collision damage waiver and so on). Also consider vehicle size carefully: high fuel prices, extremely narrow streets and tight parking conditions mean that smaller is always better.

Motorcycle & Scooter Hire

Agencies throughout Tuscany rent out everything from small Vespas to larger touring bikes.

Helmets are compulsory. Most firms won't hire motorcycles to under 18s. Many require a sizeable deposit, and you could be responsible for reimbursing the company for part of the cost of the bike if it is stolen.

You don't need a licence to ride a scooter under 50cc. The speed limit is 45km/h, you must be 14 or over and you can't carry passengers. To ride a motorcycle or scooter between 50cc and 125cc, you must be aged 16 or over and have a licence (a car licence will do). For motorcycles over 125cc you will need a motorcycle licence.

Mopeds below 150cc can't be ridden on motorways. Motorcycles can access some Zona a Traffico Limitato (ZTLs; Limited Traffic Zones).

Driving Licences

All EU member states' driving licences are fully recognised throughout Europe. Drivers with a non-EU licence are supposed to obtain an International Driving Permit (IDP) to accompany their national licence, though anecdotal testimonies indicate that this rule is rarely enforced.

Fuel & Spare Parts

Italy's petrol (gas) prices are among the highest in Europe and vary from one service station (*benzinaio, stazione di servizio*) to another. Lead-free gasoline (*senza piombo*; 95 octane) typically costs €1.60 per litre, with diesel (*gasolio*) averaging €1.50 per litre. Many petrol stations are unattended at lunchtime, at night and at weekends; at

BUS COMPANIES IN TUSCANY

REGIONAL BUS COMPANY	WEBSITE (MOST IN ITALIAN ONLY)	SERVICES
ATL	www.atl.livorno.it	Livorno
CPT	www.cpt.pisa.it	Pisa & Volterra
Etruria Mobilità	www.etruriamobilita.it	Eastern Tuscany
Siena Mobilità	www.sienamobilita.it	Siena & around
SITA	www.sitabus.it	Florence & Chianti
Vaibus	www.vaibus.it	Lucca, Garfagnana & Versilia

these times credit cards can often be used for payment (note, though, that not all foreign cards are accepted).

Spare parts are available at many garages or via the 24-hour ACI motorist-assistance number (☑803 116).

Insurance

Always carry proof of vehicle ownership and evidence of third-party insurance. If driving an EU-registered vehicle, your home-country insurance is sufficient. Ask your insurer for a European Accident Statement (EAS) form, which can simplify matters in the event of an accident.

Parking

Parking spaces outlined in blue are designated for paid parking (look for a nearby ticket machine and display the ticket on your dashboard). White outlines indicate free parking; yellow outlines indicate that residential permits are needed. Traffic police generally turn a blind eye to motorcycles or scooters parked on footpaths.

Road Network

Tuscany has an excellent road network, including autostradas, *superstradas* (dual carriageways) and major highways. Most of these are untolled, with the main exceptions being the A11 and A12 (FI-PI-LI) autostrada connecting Florence, Pisa and Livorno and the A1 autostrada linking Milan and Rome via Florence and Arezzo. For information about driving times and toll charges on these, check www.autostrada.it/en.

There are several minor road categories, listed here in descending order of importance.

Strade statali (state highways) Represented on maps by 'S' or 'SS', they vary from toll-free, four-lane highways to two-lane main roads. The latter can be extremely slow, especially in mountainous regions.

Strade regionali (regional highways connecting small villages) Coded SR or R.

Strade provinciali (provincial highways) Coded SP or P.

Strade locali Often not even paved or mapped.

Rules of the Road

➡ Cars drive on the right and overtake on the left.

➡ Unless otherwise indicated, always give way to cars entering an intersection from a road on your right.

➡ Seat belts (front and rear) are required by law; violators are subject to an on-the-spot fine.

➡ Children under 12 years must travel in the back seat, those under four must use child seats, and those under 1.5m must be in an approved restraint system or a suitable seat.

➡ Cars must carry a warning triangle and a reflective vest; they must be used in rural areas in the event of a breakdown or accident.

➡ Italy's blood-alcohol limit is 0.05% and random breath tests take place. Penalties can be severe.

➡ Speeding fines follow EU standards and are proportionate to the number of kilometres per hour over the speed limit you are travelling. The maximum penalty is a fine of €2000 and the suspension of your driving licence.

➡ Headlights are compulsory day and night for all vehicles on autostradas, and they are

advisable for motorcycles even on smaller roads. Many Tuscan towns and cities have a Limited Traffic Zone (ZTL) in their historic centre. This means only local vehicles with parking permits can enter – all other vehicles must stay outside the ZTL or face fines. Hire cars are not exempt – travellers who unknowingly breach ZTLs can end up with hefty charges (fine plus administrative fee) on their credit cards.

Local Transport
Taxi

You can usually find taxi ranks at train and bus stations, or you can telephone for taxis. It's best to go to a designated taxi stand, as it's illegal for taxis to stop in the street if hailed. If you phone a taxi, bear in mind that the meter starts running from the moment of your call rather than when the taxi picks you up.

Tram

Florence is the only city where you might possibly use a tram, including to/from Florence airport.

Train

➡ **Trenitalia** (☑from abroad 06 6847 5475, within Italy 89 20 21; www.trenitalia.com; ⊙call centre 7am-11.59pm) runs most of the services in Italy.

➡ The train network throughout Tuscany is limited.

Train Routes

Ⓝ 0 ⟼ 100 km
0 ⟼ 50 miles

→ Tickets can be purchased from the ticket office, automated ticket machines at stations or via the Trenitalia app on your smartphone.

→ Validate printed tickets before boarding by using the yellow *convalida* machines installed at the entrance to train platforms.

→ Travelling without a validated ticket risks a fine of at least €50. It's paid on the spot to an inspector who will escort you to an ATM if you don't have the cash on you.

→ Train timetables at stations generally display *arrivi* (arrivals) on a white background and *partenze* (departures) on a yellow one.

Italy has several types of trains:

Regionale (R) Slow and cheap, they stop at nearly all stations; *regionale veloce* (fast regional) trains stop at fewer stations.

InterCity (IC) Faster, more expensive services operating between major cities.

Alta Velocità (AV) State-of-the-art high-speed services travelling up to 350km/h. More expensive than InterCities, but journey times can be cut by half. The AV *Frecciarossa* stops at Florence, en route between Turin, Milan, Bologna, Rome and Salerno. Reservations are required.

Classes & Costs

There are 1st and 2nd classes on most Italian trains; a 1st-class ticket costs just under double the price of a 2nd-class one. There's not a huge amount of difference between the two – just a bit more space in 1st class, along with complimentary tea and coffee.

If you are taking a short trip, check the difference between the *regionale* and IC/AV ticket prices, as *regionale* tickets are always considerably cheaper – you might arrive 10 minutes earlier on an IC or AV service, but you'll also pay at least €5 more. Check up-to-date prices on www.trenitalia.com.

Train Passes

Trenitalia offers various discount passes, including the Carta Verde (€40) for those aged 12 to 26 years and the Carta d'Argento (€30) for seniors (60-plus years). The passes give 10% to 15% off basic fares and 25% off international connections. See www.trenitalia.com for details.

LEFT LUGGAGE

Most sizeable train stations have either a guarded left-luggage office or self-service lockers. The guarded offices are usually open 24 hours or 6am to midnight and charge around €5 per 12 hours for each piece of luggage.

Language

Modern standard Italian began to develop in the 13th and 14th centuries, predominantly through the works of Dante, Petrarch and Boccaccio – all Tuscans – who wrote chiefly in the Florentine dialect. The language drew on its Latin heritage and many dialects to develop into the standard Italian of today. Although many dialects are spoken in everyday conversation in Italy, standard Italian is understood throughout the country. Despite the Florentine roots of standard Italian – and the fact that standard Italian is widely used in Florence and Tuscany – anyone who has learned some Italian will notice the peculiarity of the local accent. In Florence, as in other parts of Tuscany, you are bound to hear the hard 'c' pronounced as a heavy 'h'. For example, *Voglio una cannuccia per la Coca Cola* (I want a straw for my Coca Cola) sounds more like *Voglio una hannuccia per la Hoha Hola*.

Italian pronunciation is relatively easy as the sounds used in spoken Italian can all be found in English. If you read our coloured pronunciation guides as if they were English, you'll be understood. The stressed syllables are indicated with italics. Note that ai is pronounced as in 'aisle', ay as in 'say', ow as in 'how', dz as the 'ds' in 'lids', and that r is a strong and rolled sound. Keep in mind that Italian consonants can have a stronger, emphatic pronunciation – if the consonant is written as a double letter, it should be pronounced a little stronger, eg *sonno son*·no (sleep) versus *sono so*·no (I am).

WANT MORE?

For in-depth language information and handy phrases, check out Lonely Planet's *Italian Phrasebook*. You'll find it at **shop.lonelyplanet.com**, or you can buy Lonely Planet's iPhone phrasebooks at the Apple App Store.

BASICS

Italian has two words for 'you' – use the polite form *Lei* lay if you're talking to strangers, officials or people older than you. With people familiar to you or younger than you, you can use the informal form *tu* too.

Hello.	*Buongiorno.*	bwon·*jor*·no
Goodbye.	*Arrivederci.*	a·ree·ve·*der*·chee
Yes./No.	*Sì./No.*	see/no
Excuse me.	*Mi scusi.* (pol)	mee *skoo*·zee
	Scusami. (inf)	*skoo*·za·mee
Sorry.	*Mi dispiace.*	mee dees·*pya*·che
Please.	*Per favore.*	per fa·*vo*·re
Thank you.	*Grazie.*	*gra*·tsye
You're welcome.	*Prego.*	*pre*·go

How are you?
Come sta/stai? (pol/inf)   *ko*·me sta/stai

Fine. And you?
Bene. E Lei/tu? (pol/inf)   *be*·ne e lay/too

What's your name?
Come si chiama?   *ko*·me see *kya*·ma

My name is ...
Mi chiamo ...   mee *kya*·mo ...

Do you speak English?
Parla/Parli   *par*·la/*par*·lee
inglese? (pol/inf)   een·*gle*·ze

I don't understand.
Non capisco.   non ka·*pee*·sko

ACCOMMODATION

Do you have a ... room?	*Avete una camera ...?*	a·*ve*·te oo·na *ka*·me·ra ...
double	*doppia con letto matrimoniale*	*do*·pya kon *le*·to ma·tree·mo·*nya*·le
single	*singola*	*seen*·go·la

KEY PATTERNS

To get by in Italian, mix and match these simple patterns with words of your choice:

When's (the next flight)?
A che ora è   a ke o·ra e
(il prossimo volo)?   (eel pro·see·mo vo·lo)

Where's (the station)?
Dov'è (la stazione)?   do·ve (la sta·tsyo·ne)

I'm looking for (a hotel).
Sto cercando   sto cher·kan·do
(un albergo).   (oon al·ber·go)

Do you have (a map)?
Ha (una pianta)?   a (oo·na pyan·ta)

Is there (a toilet)?
C'è (un gabinetto)?   che (oon ga·bee·ne·to)

I'd like (a coffee).
Vorrei (un caffè).   vo·ray (oon ka·fe)

I'd like to (hire a car).
Vorrei (noleggiare   vo·ray (no·le·ja·re
una macchina).   oo·na ma·kee·na)

Can I (enter)?
Posso (entrare)?   po·so (en·tra·re)

Could you please (help me)?
Può (aiutarmi),   pwo (a·yoo·tar·mee)
per favore?   per fa·vo·re

How much is it per ...?	*Quanto costa per ...?*	kwan·to kos·ta per ...
night	*una notte*	oo·na no·te
person	*persona*	per·so·na

Is breakfast included?
La colazione è   la ko·la·tsyo·ne e
compresa?   kom·pre·sa

air-con	*aria condizionata*	a·rya kon·dee·tsyo·na·ta
bathroom	*bagno*	ba·nyo
campsite	*campeggio*	kam·pe·jo
guesthouse	*pensione*	pen·syo·ne
hotel	*albergo*	al·ber·go
youth hostel	*ostello della gioventù*	os·te·lo de·la jo·ven·too
window	*finestra*	fee·nes·tra

DIRECTIONS

Where's ...?
Dov'è ...?   do·ve ...

What's the address?
Qual è l'indirizzo?   kwa·le leen·dee·ree·tso

Could you please write it down?
Può scriverlo,   pwo skree·ver·lo
per favore?   per fa·vo·re

Can you show me (on the map)?
Può mostrarmi   pwo mos·trar·mee
(sulla pianta)?   (soo·la pyan·ta)

at the corner	*all'angolo*	a·lan·go·lo
at the traffic lights	*al semaforo*	al se·ma·fo·ro
behind	*dietro*	dye·tro
far	*lontano*	lon·ta·no
in front of	*davanti a*	da·van·tee a
left	*a sinistra*	a see·nee·stra
near	*vicino*	vee·chee·no
next to	*accanto a*	a·kan·to a
opposite	*di fronte a*	dee fron·te a
right	*a destra*	a de·stra
straight ahead	*sempre diritto*	sem·pre dee·ree·to

EATING & DRINKING

What would you recommend?
Cosa mi consiglia?   ko·za mee kon·see·lya

What's in that dish?
Quali ingredienti   kwa·li een·gre·dyen·tee
ci sono in   chee so·no een
questo piatto?   kwe·sto pya·to

That was delicious!
Era squisito!   e·ra skwee·zee·to

Cheers!
Salute!   sa·loo·te

Please bring the bill.
Mi porta il conto,   mee por·ta eel kon·to
per favore?   per fa·vo·re

I'd like to reserve a table for ...	*Vorrei prenotare un tavolo per ...*	vo·ray pre·no·ta·re oon ta·vo·lo per ...
(two) people	*(due) persone*	(doo·e) per·so·ne
(eight) o'clock	*le (otto)*	le (o·to)

I don't eat ...	*Non mangio ...*	non man·jo ...
eggs	*uova*	wo·va
fish	*pesce*	pe·she
nuts	*noci*	no·chee
(red) meat	*carne (rossa)*	kar·ne (ro·sa)

Key Words

bar	*locale*	lo·ka·le
bottle	*bottiglia*	bo·tee·lya
breakfast	*prima colazione*	pree·ma ko·la·tsyo·ne
cafe	*bar*	bar

cold	freddo	fre·do
dinner	cena	che·na
drink list	lista delle bevande	lee·sta de·le be·van·de
fork	forchetta	for·ke·ta
glass	bicchiere	bee·kye·re
grocery store	alimentari	a·lee·men·ta·ree
hot	caldo	kal·do
knife	coltello	kol·te·lo
lunch	pranzo	pran·dzo
market	mercato	mer·ka·to
menu	menù	me·noo
plate	piatto	pya·to
restaurant	ristorante	ree·sto·ran·te
spicy	piccante	pee·kan·te
spoon	cucchiaio	koo·kya·yo
vegetarian (food)	vegetariano	ve·je·ta·rya·no
with	con	kon
without	senza	sen·tsa

Meat & Fish

beef	manzo	man·dzo
chicken	pollo	po·lo
(dried) cod	baccalà	ba·ka·la
crab	granchio	gran·kyo
duck	anatra	a·na·tra
fish	pesce	pe·she
(cured) ham	prosciutto	pro·shoo·to
herring	aringa	a·reen·ga
lamb	agnello	a·nye·lo
lobster	aragosta	a·ra·gos·ta
meat	carne	kar·ne
mussels	cozze	ko·tse
octopus	polpi	pol·pee
oysters	ostriche	o·stree·ke
pork	maiale	ma·ya·le
prawn	gambero	gam·be·ro
rabbit	coniglio	ko·nee·lyo
salmon	salmone	sal·mo·ne
sausage	salsiccia	sal·see·cha
scallops	capasante	ka·pa·san·te
seafood	frutti di mare	froo·tee dee ma·re
shrimp	gambero	gam·be·ro
squid	calamari	ka·la·ma·ree
thinly sliced raw meat	carpaccio	kar·pa·cho
tripe	trippa	tree·pa
trout	trota	tro·ta

tuna	tonno	to·no
turkey	tacchino	ta·kee·no
veal	vitello	vee·te·lo

Vegetables

artichokes	carciofi	kar·cho·fee
asparagus	asparagi	as·pa·ra·jee
aubergine/ eggplant	melanzane	me·lan·dza·ne
beans	fagioli	fa·jo·lee
black cabbage	cavolo nero	ka·vo·lo ne·ro
cabbage	cavolo	ka·vo·lo
capsicum	peperone	pe·pe·ro·ne
carrot	carota	ka·ro·ta
cauliflower	cavolfiore	ka·vol·fyo·re
cucumber	cetriolo	che·tree·o·lo
fennel	finocchio	fee·no·kyo
lentils	lenticchie	len·tee·kye
lettuce	lattuga	la·too·ga
mushroom	funghi	foon·gee
nuts	noci	no·chee
olive	oliva	o·lee·va
onions	cipolle	chee·po·le
peas	piselli	pee·ze·lee
potatoes	patate	pa·ta·te
rocket	rucola	roo·ko·la
salad	insalata	een·sa·la·ta
spinach	spinaci	spee·na·chee
tomatoes	pomodori	po·mo·do·ree
vegetables	verdura	ver·doo·ra

Fruit & Gelato Flavours

apple	mela	me·la
cherry	ciliegia	chee·lee·e·ja
chocolate	cioccolata	cho·ko·la·ta
chocolate and hazelnuts	bacio	ba·cho
forest fruits (wild berries)	frutta di bosco	froo·ta dee bos·ko

Question Words		
How?	Come?	ko·me
What?	Che cosa?	ke ko·za
When?	Quando?	kwan·do
Where?	Dove?	do·ve
Who?	Chi?	kee
Why?	Perché?	per·ke

fruit	frutta	froo·ta
grapes	uva	oo·va
hazelnut	nocciola	no·cho·la
lemon	limone	lee·mo·ne
melon	melone	me·lo·ne
orange	arancia	a·ran·cha
peach	pesca	pe·ska
pear	pere	pe·re
pineapple	ananas	a·na·nas
plum	prugna	proo·nya
strawberry	fragola	fra·go·la
trifle	zuppa inglese	tsoo·pa een·gle·ze
vanilla	vaniglia	va·nee·ya
wild/sour cherry	amarena	a·ma·re·na

Other

bread	pane	pa·ne
butter	burro	boo·ro
cheese	formaggio	for·ma·jo
cream	panna	pa·na
cone	cono	ko·no
cup	coppa	ko·pa
eggs	uova	wo·va
honey	miele	mye·le
ice	ghiaccio	gya·cho
jam	marmellata	mar·me·la·ta
noodles	pasta	pas·ta
oil	olio	o·lyo
pepper	pepe	pe·pe
rice	riso	ree·zo
salt	sale	sa·le
soup	minestra	mee·nes·tra
soy sauce	salsa di soia	sal·sa dee so·ya
sugar	zucchero	tsoo·ke·ro
truffle	tartufo	tar·too·fo
vinegar	aceto	a·che·to

Drinks

beer	birra	bee·ra
coffee	caffè	ka·fe
(orange) juice	succo (d'arancia)	soo·ko (da·ran·cha)
milk	latte	la·te
red wine	vino rosso	vee·no ro·so
soft drink	bibita	bee·bee·ta

tea	tè	te
(mineral) water	acqua (minerale)	a·kwa (mee·ne·ra·le)
white wine	vino bianco	vee·no byan·ko

EMERGENCIES

Help!
Aiuto! — a·yoo·to

Leave me alone!
Lasciami in pace! — la·sha·mee een pa·che

I'm lost.
Mi sono perso/a. (m/f) — mee so·no per·so/a

There's been an accident.
C'è stato un incidente. — che sta·to oon een·chee·den·te

Call the police!
Chiami la polizia! — kya·mee la po·lee·tsee·a

Call a doctor!
Chiami un medico! — kya·mee oon me·dee·ko

Where are the toilets?
Dove sono i gabinetti? — do·ve so·no ee ga·bee·ne·tee

I'm sick.
Mi sento male. — mee sen·to ma·le

It hurts here.
Mi fa male qui. — mee fa ma·le kwee

I'm allergic to ...
Sono allergico/a a ... (m/f) — so·no a·ler·jee·ko/a a ...

SHOPPING & SERVICES

I'd like to buy ...
Vorrei comprare ... — vo·ray kom·pra·re ...

I'm just looking.
Sto solo guardando. — sto so·lo gwar·dan·do

Can I look at it?
Posso dare un'occhiata? — po·so da·re oo·no·kya·ta

How much is this?
Quanto costa questo? — kwan·to kos·ta kwe·sto

It's too expensive.
È troppo caro/a. (m/f) — e tro·po ka·ro/a

Signs

Entrata/Ingresso	Entrance
Uscita	Exit
Aperto	Open
Chiuso	Closed
Informazioni	Information
Proibito/Vietato	Prohibited
Gabinetti/Servizi	Toilets
Uomini	Men
Donne	Women

Can you lower the price?
Può farmi lo sconto?   pwo *far*·mee lo *skon*·to

There's a mistake in the bill.
C'è un errore nel conto.   che oo·ne·*ro*·re nel *kon*·to

ATM	*Bancomat*	*ban*·ko·mat
post office	*ufficio postale*	oo·*fee*·cho pos·*ta*·le
tourist office	*ufficio del turismo*	oo·*fee*·cho del too·*reez*·mo

TIME & DATES

What time is it?	*Che ora è?*	ke o·ra e
It's one o'clock.	*È l'una.*	e *loo*·na
It's (two) o'clock.	*Sono le (due).*	so·no le (*doo*·e)
Half past (one).	*(L'una) e mezza.*	(*loo*·na) e *me*·dza

in the morning	*di mattina*	dee ma·*tee*·na
in the afternoon	*di pomeriggio*	dee po·me·*ree*·jo
in the evening	*di sera*	dee *se*·ra

yesterday	*ieri*	*ye*·ree
today	*oggi*	*o*·jee
tomorrow	*domani*	do·*ma*·nee

Monday	*lunedì*	loo·ne·*dee*
Tuesday	*martedì*	mar·te·*dee*
Wednesday	*mercoledì*	mer·ko·le·*dee*
Thursday	*giovedì*	jo·ve·*dee*
Friday	*venerdì*	ve·ner·*dee*
Saturday	*sabato*	*sa*·ba·to
Sunday	*domenica*	do·*me*·nee·ka

January	*gennaio*	je·*na*·yo
February	*febbraio*	fe·*bra*·yo
March	*marzo*	*mar*·tso
April	*aprile*	a·*pree*·le
May	*maggio*	*ma*·jo
June	*giugno*	*joo*·nyo
July	*luglio*	*loo*·lyo
August	*agosto*	a·*gos*·to
September	*settembre*	se·*tem*·bre
October	*ottobre*	o·*to*·bre
November	*novembre*	no·*vem*·bre
December	*dicembre*	dee·*chem*·bre

Numbers

1	*uno*	*oo*·no
2	*due*	*doo*·e
3	*tre*	tre
4	*quattro*	*kwa*·tro
5	*cinque*	*cheen*·kwe
6	*sei*	say
7	*sette*	*se*·te
8	*otto*	*o*·to
9	*nove*	*no*·ve
10	*dieci*	*dye*·chee
20	*venti*	*ven*·tee
30	*trenta*	*tren*·ta
40	*quaranta*	kwa·*ran*·ta
50	*cinquanta*	cheen·*kwan*·ta
60	*sessanta*	se·*san*·ta
70	*settanta*	se·*tan*·ta
80	*ottanta*	o·*tan*·ta
90	*novanta*	no·*van*·ta
100	*cento*	*chen*·to
1000	*mille*	*mee*·lel

TRANSPORT

Public Transport

At what time does the ... leave/arrive?	*A che ora parte/ arriva ...?*	a ke o·ra *par*·te/ a·*ree*·va ...
boat	*la nave*	la *na*·ve
bus	*l'autobus*	*low*·to·boos
ferry	*il traghetto*	eel tra·*ge*·to
metro	*la metro-politana*	la me·tro-po·lee·*ta*·na
plane	*l'aereo*	la·*e*·re·o
train	*il treno*	eel *tre*·no

... ticket	*un biglietto ...*	oon bee·*lye*·to
one-way	*di sola andata*	dee *so*·la an·*da*·ta
return	*di andata e ritorno*	dee an·*da*·ta e ree·*tor*·no

bus stop	*fermata dell'autobus*	fer·*ma*·ta del ow·to·boos
platform	*binario*	bee·*na*·ryo
ticket office	*biglietteria*	bee·lye·te·*ree*·a
timetable	*orario*	o·*ra*·ryo
train station	*stazione ferroviaria*	sta·*tsyo*·ne fe·ro·*vyar*·ya

Does it stop at ...?
Si ferma a ...?   see *fer*·ma a ...

Please tell me when we get to ...
Mi dica per favore   mee *dee*·ka per fa·*vo*·re
quando arriviamo a ...   *kwan*·do a·ree·*vya*·mo a ...

I want to get off here.
Voglio scendere qui.   *vo*·lyo *shen*·de·re kwee

Driving & Cycling

I'd like   *Vorrei*   vo·*ray*
to hire   *noleggiare*   no·le·*ja*·re
a/an ...   *un/una ... (m/f)*   oon/*oo*·na ...

  bicycle   *bicicletta (f)*   bee·chee·*kle*·ta
  car   *macchina (f)*   *ma*·kee·na
  motorbike   *moto (f)*   *mo*·to

bicycle   *pompa della*   *pom*·pa de·la
  pump   *bicicletta*   bee·chee·*kle*·ta
child seat   *seggiolino*   se·jo·*lee*·no
helmet   *casco*   *kas*·ko

mechanic   *meccanico*   me·*ka*·nee·ko
petrol/gas   *benzina*   ben·*dzee*·na
puncture   *gomma bucata*   *go*·ma boo·*ka*·ta
service   *stazione di*   sta·*tsyo*·ne dee
  station   *servizio*   ser·*vee*·tsyo

Is this the road to ...?
Questa strada porta a ...?   *kwe*·sta *stra*·da *por*·ta a ...

(How long) Can I park here?
(Per quanto tempo)   (per *kwan*·to *tem*·po)
Posso parcheggiare qui?   *po*·so par·ke·*ja*·re kwee

The car/motorbike has broken down (at ...).
La macchina/moto si è   la *ma*·kee·na/*mo*·to see e
guastata (a ...).   gwas·*ta*·ta (a ...)

I have a flat tyre.
Ho una gomma bucata.   o *oo*·na *go*·ma boo·*ka*·ta

I've run out of petrol.
Ho esaurito la   o e·zow·*ree*·to la
benzina.   ben·*dzee*·na

I've lost my car keys.
Ho perso le chiavi della   o *per*·so le *kya*·vee de·la
macchina.   *ma*·kee·na

Behind the Scenes

SEND US YOUR FEEDBACK

We love to hear from travellers – your comments keep us on our toes and help make our books better. Our well-travelled team reads every word on what you loved or loathed about this book. Although we cannot reply individually to your submissions, we always guarantee that your feedback goes straight to the appropriate authors, in time for the next edition. Each person who sends us information is thanked in the next edition – the most useful submissions are rewarded with a selection of digital PDF chapters.

Visit **lonelyplanet.com/contact** to submit your updates and suggestions or to ask for help. Our award-winning website also features inspirational travel stories, news and discussions.

Note: We may edit, reproduce and incorporate your comments in Lonely Planet products such as guidebooks, websites and digital products, so let us know if you don't want your comments reproduced or your name acknowledged. For a copy of our privacy policy visit lonelyplanet.com/privacy.

WRITER THANKS

Nicola Williams

Heartfelt thanks to those who shared their love and insider knowledge with me: family tour guide & art historian extraordinaire Molly McIlwrath, Ambra Nepi & Avila Fernandez (Duomo), Doreen & Carmello (Hotel Scoti), Betti Soldi, Coral Sisk (@curiousappetite), Nardia Plumridge (@lostinflorence), Katja Meier, Ilaria & Stella (Mus.e), Mary Gray, Anne Davis, Georgette Jupe (@girlinflorence) and Paolo Bresci (Pistoia tourist office). Finally, kudos to my very own expert, trilingual, family-travel research team: Niko, Mischa & Kaya.

Virginia Maxwell

As always, many locals assisted me in my research for this project. Many thanks to Ilaria Crescioli, Elisa Grisolaghi, Serena Nocciolini, Sean Lawson, Valentina de Pamphilis, Rodolfo Ademollo, Sonia Corsi, Elena Giovenco, Eleonora Sandrelli, Valentina Pierguidi, Maria Guarriello and the staff at Strada Vino Nobile Montepulciano e Sapori Valdichiana Senese, Maja Malbasa, Lucrezia Lorini, Vanessa Brezzi, Roberta Benini, Gerardo Giorgi, Caterina Mori and Silvia Fiorentini. Thanks to Anna Tyler for giving me this and many past Italy gigs, and thanks and much love to my favourite travelling companion, Peter Handsaker, who loves Italy as much as I do.

ACKNOWLEDGEMENTS

Cover photograph: The *duomo* (cathedral) in Florence, Maurizio Rellini, 4Corners Images ©

Illustrations p74–5 by Javier Zarracina.

Climate map data adapted from Peel MC, Finlayson BL & McMahon TA (2007) 'Updated World Map of the Köppen-Geiger Climate Classification', *Hydrology and Earth System Sciences*, 11, 1633–44.

THIS BOOK

This 11th edition of Lonely Planet's *Florence & Tuscany* guidebook was curated by Nicola Williams and re-searched and written by Nicola Williams and Virginia Maxwell. The previous edition was also written by Nicola and Virginia. This guidebook was produced by the following:

Destination Editor Anna Tyler
Senior Product Editor Elizabeth Jones
Regional Senior Cartographer Anthony Phelan
Product Editor Barbara Delissen
Book Designer Clara Monitto
Assisting Editors Kellie Langdon, Kate Morgan, Lauren O'Connell, Fionnuala Twomey, Simon Williamson
Cartographers David Connolly, Rachel Imeson
Cover Researcher Naomi Parker
Thanks to Imogen Bannister, Bailey Freeman, Edwin & Wendy Gieling, Laura Mazzullo, Jenna Myers

Index

A

abbeys 305
Abbazia di Monte Oliveto Maggiore 192, 305, **304**
Abbazia di San Galgano 178
Abbazia di Sant'Antimo 171, 182-3, 186, **171**
accessible travel 358
accommodation 36-7, 115, 162, 360, **37**, see also individual locations
language 369-70
activities 48-55, see also individual activities, agriturismo
agriturismo 13, 36, 47, 58, **13**
air travel 364, 365
airports 364
albergo 36
Alighieri, Dante 117, 321
Alta Maremma 198-204
Anghiari 302
aperitivo 15, **15**
Apuane Alps 15, 50, 279, **280-1**, **15**
aquariums 220-1
aqua-trekking 286
archaeological sites
Chiusi 193
Cortona 313
Golfo di Baratti 233-4
Grosseto 212
Pitigliano 205
Portoferraio 237
San Vincenzo 229
Sorano 208
Sovana 207
Vetulonia 203
Volterra 177
architecture 171, 344-56, 352-3

Map Pages **000**
Photo Pages **000**

Arezzo 14, 295-303, **298**, **14**, **332**, **353**
accommodation 300-1
drinking 302
festivals & events 300
food 301
shopping 302
sights 295-300
tourist information 302-3
travel to/from 303
art 22-3, 24
art galleries, see museums & galleries
art restoration 300
artists 349, see also Michelangelo
Abraham, Clet 111
Botticelli, Sandro 71-2, 349, **348**
Caravaggio, Michelangelo 73, 216
da Vinci, Leonardo 72-3, 304-5
de Saint Phalle, Niki 213
della Francesca, Piero 306
di Bondone, Giotto 345, 349, **348**
di Buoninsegna, Duccio 170, 349
Fra' Angelico 349, **348**
Fra' Filippo Lippi 71, 354
Machiavelli, Niccolò 323
Uccello, Paolo 71
Vasari, Giorgio 80, 81, 299-300, 347
arts 344-56, see also literature
Assisi 301, **304**
ATMs 360
Aulla 291

B

Badia a Passignano 158-62
Bagni di Lucca 283-4, **15**
Bagni San Filippo 190
Bagnone 291
ballooning 53, 162, **54**

bank scandal 327-8
baptistries 352
Battistero di Pietrasanta 287
Battistero di San Giovanni (Florence) 78
Battistero di San Giovanni (Pisa) 253, **252**, **255**
Battistero di San Giovanni (Pistoia) 271
Battistero di San Giovanni (Siena) 143
Barga 281-3
Basilica di San Francesco 305, **304**
Basilica di Santa Maria Novella 88-9, 351, **3**, **88**, **89**, **97**
Bassa Maremma 209-16
bathrooms 362
B&Bs 36
beaches **49**, **243**
Capraia 246
Elba 240, 241, 242, 244, **49**, **243**
Florence 108
Livorno 223
Marciana Marina 240
beekeeping 51
beer 21, 185, 288
Belvedere 233
bicycle travel, see cycling
birdwatching 214
Black Death 321, 323
boat tours 349
boat travel 365, 366
Boboli Garden 106, **112**
Bocelli, Andrea 283
Bolgheri 228-9, 230-1
Bonaparte, Napoleon 324
booking services 37
books, see literature
border crossings 364
Borgo 303-7
Botticelli, Sandro 71-2, 349, **348**
boutique hotels 36

breweries 21
Brigate Rosse 327
Brunelleschi, Filippo 77, 354
Brunello di Montalcino 338, **45**
budget 17
Buffalmacco, Buonamico 21
bus travel 39, 364, 366
bushwalking, see hiking

C

cable cars 240
canoeing 55, 214, 241
canyoning 286
Capoliveri 244-5
cappuccino 331
Capraia 246
Caprese Michelangelo 316
car travel 38-9, 364, 366-7, see also road distance charts, road trips
car hire 38
language 374
road rules 39
safety 361
Caravaggio, Michelangelo 73, 216
Carnevale 292
Carrara 284-6, **274-5**
Casentino Valley 307-13
Castagneto Carducci 231
Castellina in Chianti 163-4
castello 36
Castello di Verrazzano 160
Castelnuovo di Garfagnana 279-81, **274**
Castiglion Fiorentino 312
Castiglioncello 227-8
castles
Bolgheri 228
Castello dei Conti Guidi 311
Castello di Brolio 166
Castello di Romena 310-11
Castello di Verrazzano 160
Fortezza Medicea 154

castles *continued*
   Monteriggioni 174
   Rocca Aldobrandesca 232
   Rocca Ariostesca 279-80
cathedrals, *see* churches & cathedrals
Cattedrale di San Cerbone 198, **211**
Cattedrale di Santa Maria del Fiore 76-9
Cecchini, Dario 165
cell phones 361-2
central coast 60, 217-46, **218-19**
   accommodation 217
   children, travel with 57-8
   food 43-4, 217
   highlights 218-19
   itineraries 221
   road distances 217
central Tuscany 59, 137-94
   accommodation 137
   children, travel with 57
   food 44, 137
   highlights 138-9, **138-9**
   itineraries 141
   road distances 137
cheese 336, **337**
Chianti 10, 156-67, **158**, **11, 23**
   accommodation 162
   driving tour 160
   festivals & events 168
   food 164, 165
   hiking 51
   shopping 163
children, travel with 36, 56-8, 154
Chiusi 193-4, **2**
churches & cathedrals 352
   Basilica di San Francesco 305, **304**
   Basilica di Santa Croce 98-101
   Basilica di Santa Maria Novella 88-9, 351, **3**, **88, 89, 97**
   Cappella Bacci 295-8
   Cattedrale di San Cerbone 198, **211**
   Cattedrale di San Martino 261
   Cattedrale di San Zeno 270
   Cattedrale di Santa Maria del Fiore 76-9

Chiesa di San Nicola 255, **255**
Collegiata 167, 171, **170, 353**
duomo (Florence) 9, 76-9, **8, 76**
duomo (Pienza) 185
duomo (Pisa) 252-3, **252**
duomo (Siena) 142-3, **142, 352**
Pieve di Romena 311
Pieve di Soprano 290
Santuario della Madonna di Montenero 220
Santuario di Santa Maria delle Grazie 311
Città del Tufo 204-9
city wall (Lucca) 261
city wall (Pisa) 251
climate 16, 358
climate change 365
coffee 112, 331
Colle d'Orano 241
Collegiata 167, 171, **170, 353**
Colline Metallifere 202
cooking courses
   Barga 283
   Be Tuscan for a Day 156
   Lucca 266
   Montepulciano 190
   Siena 149
Corridoio Vasariano 20, 86, **70**
Cortona 313-16, **314, 304**
Costa degli Etruschi 227-34
credit cards 360-1
culture 329-32
currency 361
customs regulations 358
cycling 39, 48, 51-3, 365
   Arezzo 14
   bike hire 52
   Capraia 246
   Carrara 284
   Chianti 157
   e-bike rental 39, 157, 190, 214, 365
   e-bikes 20, 52
   Elba 245, 246
   events 26, 28, 168
   language 374
   Parco Regionale della Maremma 214
   Pisa 260
cycling tours 53
   Chianti 157
   Florence 110
   Garfagnana 286

Lucca 265
Montepulciano 190
Cypress Alley 230

D
da Vinci, Leonardo 72-3, 354-5
dangers 361
Dante Alighieri 117, 321
David 90, 99, **90, 349**
debit cards 360-1
design 332
di Bondone, Giotto 345, 349, **348**
disabilities, travellers with 358
discount cards & tickets 358-9
   Chiusi 193
   Florence 69
   Lucca 261
   Pistoia 271
   Portoferraio 237
   San Gimignano 174
   Sansepolcro 303
   Siena 148
   Volterra 176
diving 54, 241, 246
driving licences 366
driving tours, *see* road trips
duomo (Florence) 9, 76-9, **8, 76**
duomo (Pisa) 252-3, **252**
duomo (Siena) 142-3, **142, 352**

E
eastern Tuscany 60, 294-316, **296-7**
   accommodation 294
   children, travel with 58
   food 294
   highlights 296-7
   itineraries 295
   road distances 294
e-bike rental 39, 157, 190, 214, 365
e-bikes 20, 52
Elba 60, 217, 234-45, **236, 242, 243**
   beaches 240, 242, 243, 244, **49**
   children, travel with 58
   food 44, 242
   hiking 51
   history 234
   travel to/from 235
   travel within 235

electricity 359
emergencies 17
   language 372
Enfola 241
enoteche 47
Eremo Francescano Le Celle 305, 313-14, **304**
etiquette 19, 335
Etruscan Coast 227-34
Etruscans 318-19, 344
Etruscan Wine & Oil Road 230-1
events, *see* festivals & events
exchange rates 17

F
family travel, *see* children, travel with
farming 329
fashion 332
ferries 365, 366
festivals & events 12, 25-8, **12**
   Chianti 168
   food 25, 28
   Palio 27
   White Carrara Downtown 21
   wine 156
Fetovaia 241
Fiat 500 110
Fiesole 134
Filetto 291
film 343
Flagellants 320
Florence 59, 62-136, **82-3, 92, 100-1, 104, 106-7, 8, 11, 41, 70, 73, 76, 79, 80, 88, 89, 90, 112, 96**
   accommodation 62, 111-17
   activities 108
   Boboli 67, 104-8, 116-17, 122-3, 129, 133
   children, travel with 57
   discount cards 69
   drinking 123-9
   duomo area 66, 68-86, 111-14, 117-18, 123-4, 130
   entertainment 129
   festivals & events 110-11
   food 43, 62, 112, 117-23, 124, 126, 127, 130
   highlights 64-5, **64-5**
   history 63
   itineraries 68, 93
   medical services 135

museum tickets 95
neighbourhoods 66-7, **66-7**
nightlife 123-9
Oltrarno 67, 103-4, 115-16, 121-2, 127-8, 132-3
Piazza della Signoria area 66, 68-86, 111-14, 117-18, 123-4, 130
police 135
San Lorenzo 66, 87-98, 114-15, 118-19, 125-6, 132
San Marco 66, 87-98, 114-15, 118-19, 125-6, 132
San Miniato al Monte 67, 104-8, 116-17, 122-3, 129, 133
Santa Croce 67, 98-103, 115, 119-21, 126-7, 132
Santa Maria Novella 66, 86-7, 114, 118, 124-5, 131
shopping 129-32
sights 68-108
tourist information 135
tours 108-10
travel to/from 135
travel within 135
walking tours 109, **109**
food 22, 41-7, 333-40, 359, **43, 58, 96, 337**, see also individual locations
books 332
festivals 25, 28
highlights 335, 336
language 47, 370-4
literature 45
meal types 45
tours 46, 286, **46**
truffles 13, 47
Fra' Angelico 349, **348**
Fra' Filippo Lippi 71, 354
frescoes 350

G
Gaiole in Chianti 165-7
Galileo Galilei 85, 322-3
Galleria degli Uffizi 9, 20, 70-5, 327, **74-5, 70, 73, 74, 75, 113**
Galleria dell'Accademia 90-1, **9, 90, 91**
galleries, see museums & galleries
gardens 24
Florence 102, 106, 112, **112**
Giardino dei Tarocchi 213

La Foce 191
Lucca 265
Monte Amiata 202
Pian della Fioba 282
Pisa 259
Pistoia 270
Siena 145
Garfagnana 279, **280-1, 274**
gay travellers 360
gelateria 47, 122, **44**
Giardino di Boboli 106, **112**
Giglio 246
Golfo di Baratti 233-4
Gorgona 246
government 327
Grand Tour 355
Greve in Chianti 156-7, 161
Grosseto 212-13
Gucci 85, 327

H
Habsburgs 323, 324, 325
health 359-60
hiking 50-1
Capraia 246
Elba 241, 245
Giglio 246
highlights 48, 49
Monte Argentario 216
northwestern Tuscany 286
Parco Regionale della Maremma 214
history 318-28
books 326, 328
Elba 234
Florence 63
Livorno 220
Pisa 250
Siena 140
Volterra 175-6
holidays 361
horse riding 54, 156, 214, 232
hot springs, see spas & hot springs

I
ice cream 47, **58**
Il Mugello 51
immigration 364
Innamorata 241
insurance
car 367
health 359
travel 360
internet resources 17, 21, 37, 38, 49-50, 360

Italian language 369-74
itineraries 29-35, **29, 30, 32, 33, 34-5**, see also road trips
central coast 221, 230-1
central Tuscany 141
eastern Tuscany 295
Fiesole 134
Florence 68
northwestern Tuscany 251
Pisa 250
southern Tuscany 199

K
kayaking 55, 241, 286

L
La Biodola 241
Lajatico 283
language 19, 47, 369-74
Lari 278
Leaning Tower 252, 253, 254-5, **23, 254**
legal matters 119, 360
LGBTIQ+ travellers 360
literature 341-3
food 45, 332
history 326, 328
memoirs 342
Tuscan life 329, 330
Livorno 220-7, **222, 224**
accommodation 223-7
activities 223
drinking 226-7
entertainment 227
food 224-6
history 220
nightlife 226-7
sights 220-3
tourist information 227
tours 223
travel to/from 227
locanda 36
Lucca 14, 261-70, **262, 14, 274**
accommodation 265-7
discount tickets 261
drinking 268-9
food 267-8
nightlife 268-9
shopping 269
sights 261-5
tourist information 269
tours 265
travel to/from 269
travel within 269-70
Lunigiana 292-3

M
Machiavelli, Niccolò 323
Magazzini 239-40
Magliano in Toscana 215
maps 39, 360
marble 285, **274**
marble mountain 285
Marciana 240-4
Marciana Marina 240-4
Marina di Campo 244
markets **11**
Arezzo 302
Florence 129-30, 132, **41, 43, 96**
Livorno 226
Pisa 251
Pistoia 270, 276, **275**
San Gimignano 172
Siena 155
Marozia 319
Massaciuccoli 53
Massa Marittima 198-202, **200, 12, 211**
Matilda of Tuscany 319
measures 362
Medici family 71, 86, 220, 321-2, 323, 351
Anna Maria 25, 110
Cosimo I 80, 81, 220, 234, 321-2
Eleonora 81
events 25
Giovanni 80
history 63
Lorenzo 322, 354
portraits 72, 86
Medici sights
Basilica di San Lorenzo 94-5
Biblioteca Medicea Laurenziana 94
Fortezza del Girifalco 314
Galleria degli Uffizi 70-5
Museo delle Cappelle Medicee 87-92
Palazzo Medici-Riccardi 94
meditation 51, 203
Michelangelo 349, 354
birthplace 316
David 90, 99, **90, 349**
Fondazione Casa Buonarroti 102
Galleria degli Uffizi 72
Galleria dell'Accademia 90-1
Museo del Bargello 98
Museo delle Cappelle Medicee 87-92
Pietà 79

Michelangelo continued
   tomb 98
   Tribuna di
      Michelangelo 79
Middle Ages 319, 320,
   345-6
mobile phones 361-2
Mocrone 291
monasteries 305
   Basilica di Santa Maria
      Novella 88-9, 351, **88**,
      89, **97**
   Eremo Francescano Le
      Celle 305, 313-14, **304**
   Sacro Eremo e Monas-
      tero di Camaldoli 305,
      312-13, **31**
   Santuario della Verna
      305, 309-12, **305**
money 17, 360-1, see also
   discounts cards &
   tickets
moneychangers 361
Montalcino 180-4
Monte Amiata 202-3
Monte Calamita 246
Montecatini Terme 264
Montefioralle 159
Montepulciano 183, 187-93,
   188
   accommodation 190-1
   drinking 192-3
   festivals & events 190
   food 191-2
   nightlife 192-3
   sights 187-8
   tourist information 193
   tours 190
   travel to/from 193
Monteriggioni 174-5
Morcone 241
motorcycle hire 366
motorcycle travel 364,
   366-7
Mura di Pisa 21, 251
Museo dell'Opera del
   Duomo 79, **79**
museums & galleries
   Antico Palazzo dei
      Vescovi 270
   Complesso Museale
      di Santa Maria della
      Scala 144
   Galleria degli Uffizi 9, 20,
      70-5, 327, **9**, **70**, **73**,
      74, **75**, **113**

Map Pages **000**
Photo Pages **000**

Galleria dell'Accademia
   90-1, **90**, **91**
Museo Archeologico e
   d'Arte della Maremma
   212
Museo Archeologico
   Etrusco di Chiusi 193
Museo Civico 140-1, 303
Museo del Bargello 98
Museo delle Cappelle
   Medicee 87-92
Museo delle Sinopie 253
Museo dell'Opera 143, **170**
Museo dell'Opera del
   Duomo 79, **79**
Museo Diocesano d'Arte
   Sacra Volterra 21,
   176-7
Museo Diocesano di Arte
   Sacra 313
Museo di Palazzo
   Davanzati 68-9
Museo di San Marco
   92-3
Museo Etrusco
   Guarnacci 176
Museo Novecento 86
Museo Villa Napoleonica
   di San Martino 237
Palazzo Comunale 167-8,
   353
Vernaccia di San Gimig-
   nano Wine Experience
   168
music festivals
   Cortona 314
   Florence 120
   Lucca 264
   Massa Marittima 199
   Pistoia 273
   San Gimignano 169
   Siena 149
Mussolini, Benito 327, 325-6

N
national parks & reserves
   23-4, 52-3
Oasi WWF Laguna di
   Orbetello 215
Parco delle Biancane
   202
Parco Nazionale dell'Arc-
   ipelago Toscano
   52, 235
Parco Nazionale delle
   Foreste Casentinesi
   52, 309-13
Parco Regionale della
   Maremma 53
Parco Regionale delle
   Alpi Apuane 52, 279
nature 23-4

newspapers 362
northwestern Tuscany 60,
   247-93
   accommodation 247
   children, travel with 58
   food 43, 247
   highlights 248-9, **248-9**
   itineraries 251
   road distances 247

O
olive oil 230-1, 339
opera 283
Orbetello 215
Origo, Iris 191
ostello 36
osteria 45
Otone 239-40

P
palaces 353
Palazzo Borgia 185
Palazzo Comunale 167-8,
   353
Palazzo degli Uffizi, see
   Galleria degli Uffizi
palazzo hotel 36
Palazzo Medici-Riccardi 94
Palazzo Pfanner 263
Palazzo Piccolomini 185
Palazzo Pitti 105, **112**
Palazzo Pubblico 145,
   171, **170**
Palazzo Vecchio 80-1, **80**,
   96, **113**
Palio 27, 144
Panzano in Chianti 161, 165
Parco Nazionale dell'Arci-
   pelago Toscano 52, 235
Parco Nazionale delle
   Foreste Casentinesi 52,
   309-13
Parco Regionale della
   Maremma 53
Parco Regionale delle Alpi
   Apuane 52, 279
Parco Regionale
   Migliarino 53
Pareti 241
parks, see gardens
passports 364
pasta 278, 334
pensione 36
phonecards 362
Pian della Fioba 282
Pianosa 246
piazzas 353
   Piazza dei Miracoli 15,
      252-3, **15**, **252**

Piazza del Campo 10,
   141-4, **10**, **31**, **170**
Piazza della Passera 121
Piazza della Sala 276,
   275
Piazza della Signoria 85
Piazza Grande 298,
   14, **353**
Piazza Matteotti 244
pickpocketing 361
picnic 268, 276
Pienza 183, 184-7
Pietrasanta 287-9
Pisa 250-60, **256**, **15**, **23**,
   252, **254**, **255**
   accommodation 257
   drinking 258-9
   festivals & events 256-7
   food 258
   history 250
   itineraries 250
   nightlife 258-9
   sights 250-1, 259
   tourist information 260
   travel to/from 260
   travel within 260
Pistoia 270-7, **272**, **275**
Pitigliano 204-7, **2**, **210**
pizza 126
pizzerias 45
plague 321, 323
planning 48, see also
   individual regions
   accommodation 36-7
   budgeting 17, 36
   calendar of events 25-8
   children, travel with 56-8
   first-time visitors 18-19
   food 41-7, 42
   internet resources 17
   itineraries 29-35
   repeat visitors 20-1
   travel seasons 16
   Tuscany basics 16-17
   Tuscany regions 59-60
Poggio 240-4
Ponte Vecchio 103, **96**
Pontremoli 292-3
Poppi 307-9, 311
Porto Azzurro 245, **242**
Portoferraio 235-9
postal services 361
Prato 288
Pratovecchio 309
Procchio 241
public holidays 361
Puccini, Giacomo 27, 264

R

Radda in Chianti 164-5
rafting 55, 108, 286
Red Brigades 327
Renaissance 321
reserves, *see* national parks & reserves
rifugio 36
ristorante 45
road distances charts 7, *see also* individual locations
road rules 367
road trips 23, 40, 46, **40**, **46**
  Casentino Valley 310-11, **310-11**
  Chianti 160-1, **160**
  Etruscan Wine & Oil Road 230-1, **230**
  northwestern Tuscany 282
  Val d'Orcia 182-3, **182**
  Via Francigena 50, 175, 290-1, **290**
  wine & oil roads 340
Rocca d'Orcia 183
Romans 318, 319
rooftop bars 128
running 50, 149

S

Sacro Eremo e Monastero di Camaldoli 305, 312-13, **31**
safety 361
sailing 55
San Casciano in Val di Pesa 162-3
San Galgano 178
San Gimignano 12, 167-74, **172**, **5**, **12**, **44**, **170**, **353**
San Miniato 277-9
San Pellegrino in Alpe 282
San Quirico d'Orcia 183
San Rossore 53
San Vincenzo 229-32
Sansepolcro 303-7
Sansone 241
Santuario della Verna 305, 309-12, **305**
Savonarola 322
Schioppparello 239-40
scooter hire 366
sculpture parks 346
self-flagellation 320
shopping 163

Siena 59, 140-56, **146-7**, **150**, **10**, **31**, **142**, **170**, **352**
  accommodation 149-52
  activities 149
  children, travel with 57, 154
  courses 149
  drinking 153
  festivals & events 144, 149
  food 44, 152-3
  history 140
  museum discount tickets 148
  nightlife 153
  shopping 153-5
  sights 140-9
  tourist information 155
  tours 149
  travel to/from 155
  travel within 155-6
slavery 220
Slow Food 333
smoking 362
snorkelling 54, 241, 246
Sorano 208-9
Sorgente 241
southern Tuscany 59, 195-216
  accommodation 195
  children, travel with 57
  food 44-5, 195
  highlights 196-7, **196-7**
  itineraries 199
  road distances 195
Sovana 207-8
spas & hot springs 55
  Bagni di Lucca 284
  Bagni San Filippo 190
  Montecatini Terme 264
  San Vincenzo 229
  Sassetta 234
  Saturnia 206, **210-11**
Stia 311
Strada del Vino e dell'Olio Costa degli Etruschi 230-1, **230**
summer solstice 51
sunsets 242
surfing 55
Suvereto 231, 232-3
swimming 223

T

taxes 37
taxis 367
T-bone steak 334
Teatro del Silenzio 283

telephone services 361-2
Tenuta Argentiera 231
time 362
  language 373
tipping 19, 361
toilets 362
tourist information 362
tours
  boat 223
  cycling 53, 110, 157, 190, 265, 286
  Fiat 500 110
  food 286
  nature 286
  photography 51
  Siena 149
  Vespa 51, 260
  walking 109, 110, 212
towers 24, 57
  Campanile della Cattedrale 270
  Leaning Tower 252, 253, 254-5, **23**, **254**
  Torre di Frederico II 278
  Torre Guinigi 263
train travel 39, 364-5, 367-8, **368**
trams 367
transport 38-40
trattoria 45
travel to/from Tuscany 364-5
travel within Tuscany 365-8
  language 373-4
trekking, *see* hiking
tripe 120
truffles 13, 47, 279, **13**
Tuscan Archipelago 234-46

U

Uffizi Gallery 9, 20, 70-5, 327, **74-5**, **9**, **70**, **73**, **74**, **75**, **113**
Unesco World Heritage Sites 140, 179, 185, 331, 353

V

vacations 361
vaccinations 359
Val di Chiana 313-16
Val d'Orcia 10, 179-87, **182**, **10**
  food 184
  road trip 182-3
Vasari Corridor 20, 86, **70**
Vasari, Giorgio 80, 81, 299-300, 347
Versilian Coast 286-92

Vespa 51, 260, 332, **332**
Vetulonia 203-4
via cava 205, **210**
Via Francigena 50, 175, 290-1
Viareggio 264, 289-92
Villafranca di Lunigiana 291
villas 266
Vino Nobile di Montepulciano 339
visas 362-3
Volpaia 166
Volterra 175-9, **176**

W

walking, *see* hiking
walking tours
  Florence 109, 110, **109**
  Grosseto 212
water 360
water sports 48, 54, 55, 246
weather 16, 358
websites, *see* internet resources
weights 362
white-water rafting, *see* rafting
wine 22, 338-40
  Brunello di Montalcino 181, **45**
  Chianti 160-1, 167, 339, **160**
  classifications 338
  festivals & events 28, 156, 190
  Vernaccia di San Gimignano Wine Experience 168
wineries 20
  Brunello 181
  Castello di Ama 161
  Castiglioncello 227-8
  Chianti 167
  Gaiole in Chianti 165-6
  La Regola 229
  Montepulciano 188-9
  Petra Wine 231, 232
  San Casciano in Val di Pesa 162
  Scansano 209
  Sovana 207
  Tenuta Argentiera 229
  Tenuta La Chiusa 239
World War I 325
World War II 326-7

Y

yoga 51, 108, 203

LONELY PLANET IN THE WILD

Send your 'Lonely Planet in the Wild' photos to social@lonelyplanet.com
We share the best on our Facebook page every week!

Map Legend

Sights

- Beach
- Bird Sanctuary
- Buddhist
- Castle/Palace
- Christian
- Confucian
- Hindu
- Islamic
- Jain
- Jewish
- Monument
- Museum/Gallery/Historic Building
- Ruin
- Shinto
- Sikh
- Taoist
- Winery/Vineyard
- Zoo/Wildlife Sanctuary
- Other Sight

Activities, Courses & Tours

- Bodysurfing
- Diving
- Canoeing/Kayaking
- Course/Tour
- Sento Hot Baths/Onsen
- Skiing
- Snorkelling
- Surfing
- Swimming/Pool
- Walking
- Windsurfing
- Other Activity

Sleeping

- Sleeping
- Camping
- Hut/Shelter

Eating

- Eating

Drinking & Nightlife

- Drinking & Nightlife
- Cafe

Entertainment

- Entertainment

Shopping

- Shopping

Information

- Bank
- Embassy/Consulate
- Hospital/Medical
- Internet
- Police
- Post Office
- Telephone
- Toilet
- Tourist Information
- Other Information

Geographic

- Beach
- Gate
- Hut/Shelter
- Lighthouse
- Lookout
- Mountain/Volcano
- Oasis
- Park
- Pass
- Picnic Area
- Waterfall

Population

- Capital (National)
- Capital (State/Province)
- City/Large Town
- Town/Village

Transport

- Airport
- Border crossing
- Bus
- Cable car/Funicular
- Cycling
- Ferry
- Metro station
- Monorail
- Parking
- Petrol station
- S-Bahn/Subway station
- Taxi
- T-bane/Tunnelbana station
- Train station/Railway
- Tram
- U-Bahn/Underground station
- Other Transport

Routes

- Tollway
- Freeway
- Primary
- Secondary
- Tertiary
- Lane
- Unsealed road
- Road under construction
- Plaza/Mall
- Steps
- Tunnel
- Pedestrian overpass
- Walking Tour
- Walking Tour detour
- Path/Walking Trail

Boundaries

- International
- State/Province
- Disputed
- Regional/Suburb
- Marine Park
- Cliff
- Wall

Hydrography

- River, Creek
- Intermittent River
- Canal
- Water
- Dry/Salt/Intermittent Lake
- Reef

Areas

- Airport/Runway
- Beach/Desert
- Cemetery (Christian)
- Cemetery (Other)
- Glacier
- Mudflat
- Park/Forest
- Sight (Building)
- Sportsground
- Swamp/Mangrove

Note: Not all symbols displayed above appear on the maps in this book

OUR STORY

A beat-up old car, a few dollars in the pocket and a sense of adventure. In 1972 that's all Tony and Maureen Wheeler needed for the trip of a lifetime – across Europe and Asia overland to Australia. It took several months, and at the end – broke but inspired – they sat at their kitchen table writing and stapling together their first travel guide, *Across Asia on the Cheap*. Within a week they'd sold 1500 copies. Lonely Planet was born.

Today, Lonely Planet has offices in Franklin, London, Melbourne, Oakland, Dublin, Beijing and Delhi, with more than 600 staff and writers. We share Tony's belief that 'a great guidebook should do three things: inform, educate and amuse'.

OUR WRITERS

Nicola Williams

Florence, Central Coast & Elba, Northwestern Tuscany Border-hopping is a way of life for British writer, runner, foodie, art aficionado and mum-of-three Nicola Williams, who has lived in a French village on the southern side of Lake Geneva for more than a decade. Nicola has authored more than 50 guidebooks on Paris, Provence, Rome, Tuscany, France, Italy and Switzerland for Lonely Planet and covers France as a destination expert for the Telegraph. She also writes for the Independent, Guardian, lonelyplanet.com, Lonely Planet Magazine, French Magazine, Cool Camping France and others. Catch her on the road on Twitter and Instagram at @tripalong. Nicola also wrote the Plan, Understand and Survival Guide sections.

Virginia Maxwell

Siena & Central Tuscany, Eastern Tuscany, Southern Tuscany Although based in Australia, Virginia spends at least half of her year updating Lonely Planet destination coverage across the globe. The Mediterranean is her major area of interest – she has covered Spain, Italy, Turkey, Syria, Lebanon, Israel, Egypt, Morocco and Tunisia for Lonely Planet – but she also covers Finland, Bali, Armenia, the Netherlands, the US and Australia for Lonely Planet products. Follow her on Instagram and Twitter at @maxwellvirginia.

Published by Lonely Planet Global Limited
CRN 554153
11th edition – February 2020
ISBN 978 1 78701 415 2
© Lonely Planet 2020   Photographs © as indicated 2020
10 9 8 7 6 5 4 3 2 1
Printed in China